Graph–Based Methods in Computer Vision:

Developments and Applications

Xiao Bai
Beihang University, China

Jian Cheng
Chinese Academy of Sciences, China

Edwin Hancock
University of York, UK

Information Science
REFERENCE

Managing Director:	Lindsay Johnston
Senior Editorial Director:	Heather A. Probst
Book Production Manager:	Sean Woznicki
Development Manager:	Joel Gamon
Development Editor:	Hannah Abelbeck
Assistant Acquisitions Editor:	Kayla Wolfe
Typesetter:	Alyson Zerbe
Cover Design:	Nick Newcomer

Published in the United States of America by
  Information Science Reference (an imprint of IGI Global)
  701 E. Chocolate Avenue
  Hershey PA 17033
  Tel: 717-533-8845
  Fax: 717-533-8661
  E-mail: cust@igi-global.com
  Web site: http://www.igi-global.com

Library of Congress Cataloging-in-Publication Data

Graph-based methods in computer vision: developments and applications / Xiao Bai, Jian Cheng, and Edwin Hancock, editors.
  p. cm.
 Includes bibliographical references and index.
  ISBN 978-1-4666-1891-6 (hardcover) -- ISBN 978-1-4666-1892-3 (ebook) -- ISBN 978-1-4666-1893-0 (print & perpetual access) 1. Computer vision. 2. Computer vision--Mathematical models. 3. Graph theory. I. Xiao, Bai. II. Cheng, Jian, 1977- III. Hancock, Edwin R.
 TA1634.G763 2012
 006.3'7--dc23
       2012004763

British Cataloguing in Publication Data
A Cataloguing in Publication record for this book is available from the British Library.

All work contributed to this book is new, previously-unpublished material. The views expressed in this book are those of the authors, but not necessarily of the publisher.

Editorial Advisory Board

Table of Contents

Preface...xiv

Acknowledgment...xviii

Section 1
Graph-Based Methods for Image Matching

Chapter 1
Graph Matching Techniques for Computer Vision 1
Mario Vento, Università di Salerno, Italy
Pasquale Foggia, Università di Salerno, Italy

Chapter 2
Geometric-Edge Random Graph Model for Image Representation 42
Bo Jiang, Anhui University, China
Jing Tang, Anhui University, China
Bin Luo, Anhui University, China

Chapter 3
The Node-to-Node Graph Matching Algorithm Schema 58
Guoxing Zhao, Beijing Normal University, China
Jixin Ma, University of Greenwich, UK

Section 2
Graph-Based Methods for Image Segmentation

Chapter 4
Unsupervised and Supervised Image Segmentation Using Graph Partitioning 72
Charles-Edmond Bichot, Université de Lyon, France

Chapter 5
Motion Segmentation and Matting by Graph Cut.. 95
Jiangjian Xiao, Ningbo Industrial Technology Research Institute, P.R. China

Chapter 6

Hypergraph Based Visual Segmentation and Retrieval 118

    Yuchi Huang, General Electric Global Research, USA

Chapter 7

Recent Advances on Graph-Based Image Segmentation Techniques 140

    Chao Zeng, University of Technology-Sydney, Australia

    Wenjing Jia, University of Technology-Sydney, Australia

    Xiangjian He, University of Technology-Sydney, Australia

    Min Xu, University of Technology-Sydney, Australia

Section 3
Graph-Based Methods for Image and Video Analysis

Chapter 8

Graph Embedding Using Dissimilarities with Applications in Classification 156

    Horst Bunke, University of Bern, Switzerland

    Kaspar Riesen, University of Bern, Switzerland

Chapter 9

Generative Group Activity Analysis with Quaternion Descriptor 174

    Guangyu Zhu, National University of Singapore, Singapore

    Shuicheng Yan, National University of Singapore, Singapore

    Tony X. Han, University of Missouri, USA

    Changsheng Xu, Chinese Academy of Sciences, China

Chapter 10

Shape Retrieval and Classification Based on Geodesic Paths in Skeleton Graphs........................... 190

    Xiang Bai, Huazhong University of Science and Technology, P.R. China

    Chunyuan Li, Huazhong University of Science and Technology, P.R. China

    Xingwei Yang, Temple University, USA

    Longin Jan Latecki, Temple University, USA

Chapter 11

Discriminative Feature Selection in Image Classification and Retrieval... 216

    Shang Liu, Beihang University, China

    Xiao Bai, Beihang University, China

Chapter 12

Normalized Projection and Graph Embedding via Angular Decomposition 231

    Dengdi Sun, Anhui University, China

    Chris Ding, Anhui University, China & University of Texas at Arlington, USA

    Jin Tang, Anhui University, China

    Bin Luo, Anhui University, China

Chapter 13
Region-Based Graph Learning Towards Large Scale Image Annotation 244
 Bao Bing-Kun, Institute of Automation, Chinese Academy of Sciences, China
 Yan Shuicheng, National University of Singapore, Singapore

Chapter 14
Copy Detection Using Graphical Model: HMM for Frame Fusion 261
 Wei Shikui, Beijing Jiaotong University, China
 Zhao Yao, Beijing Jiaotong University, China
 Zhu Zhenfeng, Beijing Jiaotong University, China

Section 4
Graph-Based Methods for Image Processing

Chapter 15
Multi-Scale Exemplary Based Image Super-Resolution with Graph Generalization 281
 Wang Jinjun, Epson Research and Development, Inc. USA

Chapter 16
Graph Heat Kernel Based Image Smoothing 302
 Zhang Fan, University of York, UK
 Edwin R. Hancock, University of York, UK
 Liu Shang, Beihang University, China

Compilation of References 331

About the Contributors 364

Index 372

Detailed Table of Contents

Preface... xiv

Acknowledgment... xviii

Section 1
Graph-Based Methods for Image Matching

Chapter 1

Graph Matching Techniques for Computer Vision 1
Mario Vento, Università di Salerno, Italy
Pasquale Foggia, Università di Salerno, Italy

Many computer vision applications require a comparison between two objects, or between an object and a reference model. When the objects or the scenes are represented by graphs, this comparison can be performed using some form of graph matching. The aim of this chapter is to introduce the main graph matching techniques that have been used for computer vision, and to relate each application with the techniques that are most suited to it.

Chapter 2

Geometric-Edge Random Graph Model for Image Representation 42
Bo Jiang, Anhui University, China
Jing Tang, Anhui University, China
Bin Luo, Anhui University, China

This chapter presents a random graph model for image representation. The first contribution the authors propose is a Geometric-Edge (G-E) Random Graph Model for image representation. The second contribution is that of casting image matching into G-E Random Graph matching by using the random dot product graph based matching algorithm. Experimental results show that the proposed G-E Random Graph model and matching algorithm are effective and robust to structural variations.

Chapter 3

The Node-to-Node Graph Matching Algorithm Schema 58
Guoxing Zhao, Beijing Normal University, China
Jixin Ma, University of Greenwich, UK

Many graph matching algorithms follow the approach of node-similarity measurement, that is, matching graphs by means of comparing the corresponding pairs of nodes of the graphs. Based on this idea, the authors propose a high-level schema for node-to-node graph matching, namely N2N graph matching algorithm schema. The chapter shows that such a N2N graph matching algorithm schema is versatile enough to subsume most of the representative node-to-node based graph matching algorithms. It is also shown that improved algorithms can be derived from this N2N graph matching schema, compared with various corresponding algorithms. In addition, the authors point out the limitation and constraints of the propose algorithm schema and suggest some possible treatments.

Section 2
Graph-Based Methods for Image Segmentation

Chapter 4

Unsupervised and Supervised Image Segmentation Using Graph Partitioning 72
    Charles-Edmond Bichot, Université de Lyon, France

Image segmentation is an important research area in computer vision and its applications in different disciplines, such as medicine, are of great importance. It is often one of the very first steps of computer vision or pattern recognition methods. This is because segmentation helps to locate objects and boundaries into images. The objective of segmenting an image is to partition it into disjoint and homogeneous sets of pixels. When segmenting an image it is natural to try to use graph partitioning, because segmentation and partitioning share the same high-level objective, to partition a set into disjoints subsets. However, when using graph partitioning for segmenting an image, several big questions remain: What is the best way to convert an image into a graph? Or to convert image segmentation objectives into graph partitioning objectives (not to mention what are image segmentation objectives)? What are the best graph partitioning methods and algorithms for segmenting an image? In this chapter, the author tries to answer these questions, both for unsupervised and supervised image segmentation approach, by presenting methods and algorithms and by comparing them.

Chapter 5

Motion Segmentation and Matting by Graph Cut.. 95
    Jiangjian Xiao, Ningbo Industrial Technology Research Institute, P.R. China

Given a video sequence, obtaining accurate layer segmentation and alpha matting is very important for video representation, analysis, compression, and synthesis. By assuming that a scene can be approximately described by multiple planar or surface regions, this chapter describes a robust approach to automatically detect the region clusters and perform accurate layer segmentation for the scene. The approach starts from optical flow field or small corresponding seed regions and applies a clustering approach to estimate the layer number and support regions. Then, it uses graph cut algorithm combined with a general occlusion constraint over multiple frames to solve pixel assignment over multiple frames to obtain more accurate segmentation boundary and identify the occluded pixels. For the non-textured ambiguous regions, an alpha matting technique is further used to refine the segmentation and resolve the ambiguities by determining proper alpha values for the foreground and background, respectively. Based on the alpha mattes, the foreground object can be transferred into the other video sequence to generate a virtual video. The author's experiments show that the proposed approach is effective and robust for both the challenging real and synthetic sequences.

Chapter 6

Hypergraph Based Visual Segmentation and Retrieval 118

Yuchi Huang, General Electric Global Research, USA

This chapter explores original techniques for the construction of hypergraph models for computer vision applications. A hypergraph is a generalization of a pairwise simple graph, where an edge can connect any number of vertices. The expressive power of the hypergraph models places a special emphasis on the relationship among three or more objects, which has made hypergraphs better models of choice in a lot of problems. This is in sharp contrast with the more conventional graph representation of visual patterns where only pairwise connectivity between objects is described. This chapter draws up from three aspects to carry the discussion of hypergraph based methods in computer vision: (i) The advantage of the hypergraph neighborhood structure is analyzed. The author argues that the summarized local grouping information contained in hypergraphs causes an 'averaging' effect which is beneficial to the clustering problems. (ii)The chapter discusses how to build hypergraph incidence structures and how to solve the related unsupervised and semi-supervised problems for two different computer vision scenarios: video object segmentation and image retrieval. (iii) For the application of image retrieval, the chapter introduces a novel hypergraph model — probabilistic hypergraph to exploit the structure of the data manifold by considering not only the local grouping information, but also the similarities between vertices in hyperedges.

Chapter 7

Recent Advances on Graph-Based Image Segmentation Techniques 140

Chao Zeng, University of Technology-Sydney, Australia
Wenjing Jia, University of Technology-Sydney, Australia
Xiangjian He, University of Technology-Sydney, Australia
Min Xu, University of Technology-Sydney, Australia

Image segmentation techniques using graph theory has become a thriving research area in computer vision community in recent years. This chapter mainly focuses on the most up-to-date research achievements in graph-based image segmentation published in top journals and conferences in computer vision community. The representative graph-based image segmentation methods included in this chapter are classified into six categories: minimum-cut/maximum-flow model (called graph-cut in some literatures), random walk model, minimum spanning tree model, normalized cut model and isoperimetric graph partitioning. The basic rationales of these models are presented, and the image segmentation methods based on these graph-based models are discussed as the main concern of this chapter. Several performance evaluation methods for image segmentation are given. Some public databases for testing image segmentation algorithms are introduced and the future work on graph-based image segmentation is discussed at the end of this chapter.

Section 3
Graph-Based Methods for Image and Video Analysis

Chapter 8

Graph Embedding Using Dissimilarities with Applications in Classification 156
Horst Bunke, University of Bern, Switzerland
Kaspar Riesen, University of Bern, Switzerland

The domain of graphs contains only little mathematical structure. That is, most of the basic mathematical operations, actually required by many standard computer vision and pattern recognition algorithms, are not available for graphs. One of the few mathematical concepts which has been successfully transferred from the vector space to the graph domain is distance computation between graphs, commonly referred to as graph matching. Yet, distance based pattern recognition is basically limited to nearest-neighbor classification. The present chapter reviews a novel approach for graph embedding in vector spaces built upon the concept of graph matching. The key-idea of the proposed embedding method is to use the distances of an input graph to a number of training graphs, termed prototypes, as vectorial description of the graph. That is, all graph matching procedures proposed in the literature during the last decades can be employed in this embedding framework. The rationale for such a graph embedding is to bridge the gap between the high representational power and flexibility of graphs and the large amount of algorithms available for object representations in terms of feature vectors. Hence, the proposed framework can be considered a contribution towards unifying the domains of structural and statistical pattern recognition.

Chapter 9

Generative Group Activity Analysis with Quaternion Descriptor 174
Guangyu Zhu, National University of Singapore, Singapore
Shuicheng Yan, National University of Singapore, Singapore
Tony X. Han, University of Missouri, USA
Changsheng Xu, Chinese Academy of Sciences, China

Activity understanding plays an essential role in video content analysis and remains a challenging open problem. Most of previous research is limited due to the use of excessively localized features without sufficiently encapsulating the interaction context or focus on simply discriminative models but totally ignoring the interaction patterns. In this chapter, a new approach is proposed to recognize human group activities. Firstly, the authors designed a new quaternion descriptor to describe the interactive insight of activities regarding the appearance, dynamic, causality, and feedback, respectively. The designed descriptor along with the conventional velocity and position are capable of delineating the individual and pairwise interactions in the activities. Secondly, considering both activity category and interaction variety, the authors propose an extended pLSA (probabilistic Latent Semantic Analysis) model with two hidden variables. This extended probabilistic graphic paradigm constructed on the quaternion descriptors facilitates the effective inference of activity categories as well as the exploration of activity interaction patterns. The extensive experiments on realistic movie and human group activity datasets validate that the multilevel features are effective for activity interaction representation and demonstrate that the graphic model is a promising paradigm for activity recognition.

Chapter 10

Shape Retrieval and Classification Based on Geodesic Paths in Skeleton Graphs............................ 190

Xiang Bai, Huazhong University of Science and Technology, P.R. China

Chunyuan Li, Huazhong University of Science and Technology, P.R. China

Xingwei Yang, Temple University, USA

Longin Jan Latecki, Temple University, USA

Skeleton is well-known to be superior to contour based representation when shapes have large nonlinear variability, especially articulation. However, approaches to shape similarity based on skeletons suffer from the instability of skeletons, and matching of skeleton graphs is still an open problem. To deal with this problem for shape retrieval, the authors first propose to match skeleton graphs by comparing the geodesic paths between skeleton endpoints. In contrast to typical tree or graph matching methods, they do not explicitly consider the topological graph structure. Their approach is motivated by the fact that visually similar skeleton graphs may have completely different topological structures, while the paths between their end nodes still remain similar. The proposed comparison of geodesic paths between endpoints of skeleton graphs yields correct matching results in such cases. The experimental results demonstrate that the method is able to produce correct results in the presence of articulations, stretching, and contour deformations. The authors also utilize the geodesic skeleton paths for shape classification. Similar to shape retrieval, direct graph matching algorithms like graph edit distance have great difficulties with the instability of the skeleton graph structure. In contrast, the representation based on skeleton paths remains stable. Therefore, a simple Bayesian classifier is able to obtain excellent shape classification results.

Chapter 11

Discriminative Feature Selection in Image Classification and Retrieval... 216

Shang Liu, Beihang University, China

Xiao Bai, Beihang University, China

In this chapter, the authors present a new method to improve the performance of current bag-of-word based image classification process. After feature extraction, they introduce a pairwise image matching scheme to select the discriminative features. Only the label information from the training-sets is used to update the feature weights via an iterative matching processing. The selected features correspond to the foreground content of the images, and thus highlight the high level category knowledge of images. Visual words are constructed on these selected features. This novel method could be used as a refinement step for current image classification and retrieval process. The authors prove the efficiency of their method in three tasks: supervised image classification, semi-supervised image classification, and image retrieval.

Chapter 12

Normalized Projection and Graph Embedding via Angular Decomposition 231

Dengdi Sun, Anhui University, China

Chris Ding, Anhui University, China & University of Texas at Arlington, USA

Jin Tang, Anhui University, China

Bin Luo, Anhui University, China

Dimensionality reduction plays a vital role in pattern recognition. However, for normalized vector data, existing methods do not utilize the fact that the data is normalized. In this chapter, the authors propose to employ an Angular Decomposition of the normalized vector data which corresponds to embedding them on a unit surface. On graph data for similarity/kernel matrices with constant diagonal elements, the authors propose the Angular Decomposition of the similarity matrices which corresponds to embedding objects on a unit sphere. In these angular embeddings, the Euclidean distance is equivalent to the cosine similarity. Thus data structures best described in the cosine similarity and data structures best captured by the Euclidean distance can both be effectively detected in our angular embedding. The authors provide the theoretical analysis, derive the computational algorithm, and evaluate the angular embedding on several datasets. Experiments on data clustering demonstrate that the method can provide a more discriminative subspace.

Chapter 13

Region-Based Graph Learning Towards Large Scale Image Annotation 244

Bao Bing-Kun, Institute of Automation, Chinese Academy of Sciences, China
Yan Shuicheng, National University of Singapore, Singapore

Graph-based learning provides a useful approach for modeling data in image annotation problems. In this chapter, the authors introduce how to construct a region-based graph to annotate large scale multi-label images. It has been well recognized that analysis in semantic region level may greatly improve image annotation performance compared to that in whole image level. However, region level approach increases the data scale to several orders of magnitude and lays down new challenges to most existing algorithms. To this end, each image is firstly encoded as a Bag-of-Regions based on multiple image segmentations. And then, all image regions are constructed into a large k-nearest-neighbor graph with efficient Locality Sensitive Hashing (LSH) method. At last, a sparse and region-aware image-based graph is fed into the multi-label extension of the Entropic graph regularized semi-supervised learning algorithm. In combination they naturally yield the capability in handling large-scale dataset. Extensive experiments on NUS-WIDE (260k images) and COREL-5k datasets well validate the effectiveness and efficiency of the framework for region-aware and scalable multi-label propagation.

Chapter 14

Copy Detection Using Graphical Model: HMM for Frame Fusion.. 261

Shikui Wei, Beijing Jiaotong University, China
Yao Zhao, Beijing Jiaotong University, China
Zhenfeng Zhu, Beijing Jiaotong University, China

With the growing popularity of video sharing websites and editing tools, it is easy for people to involve the video content from different sources into their own work, which raises the copyright problem. Content-based video copy detection attempts to track the usage of the copyright-protected video content by using video analysis techniques, which deals with not only whether a copy occurs in a query video stream but also where the copy is located and where the copy is originated from. While a lot of work has addressed the problem with good performance, less effort has been made to consider the copy detection problem in the case of a continuous query stream, for which precise temporal localization and some complex video transformations like frame insertion and video editing need to be handled. In this chapter, the authors attack the problem by employing the graphical model to facilitate the frame fusion based video copy detection approach. The key idea is to convert frame fusion problem into graph model decoding problem with the temporal consistency constraint and three relaxed constraints. This work employs the HMM model to perform frame fusion and propose a Viterbi-like algorithm to speedup frame fusion process.

Section 4
Graph-Based Methods for Image Processing

Chapter 15

Multi-Scale Exemplary Based Image Super-Resolution with Graph Generalization 281
Wang Jinjun, Epson Research and Development, Inc. USA

Exemplary based image super-resolution (SR) approaches decompose low-resolution (LR) images into multiple overlapped local image patches, and find the best high-resolution (HR) pair for each LR patch to generate processed HR images. The super-resolving process models these multiple HR/LR patches in a Markov Network where there exists both confidence constraint between the LR patch and the selected HR patch from database, and the harmonic constraint between neighboring HR patches. Such a graphical structure, however, makes the optimization process extremely slow, and therefore extensive research efforts on improving the efficiency of exemplary based SR methods have been reported. In this chapter, the focus is on those methods that aim at generating high quality HR patches from the database, while ignoring the harmonic constraint to speed up processing, such as those that model the problem as an embedding process, or as a feature selection process. As shown in this chapter, these approaches can all be regarded as a coding system. The contributions of the paper are two-fold: First, the chapter introduces a coding system with resolution-invariance property, such that it is able to handle continues-scale image resizing as compared to traditional methods that only support single integer-scale upsizing; second, the author generalizes the graphical model where the typical non-linear coding process is approximated by an easier-to-compute function. In this way, the SR process can be highly parallelized by modern computer hardware. As demonstrated by the chapter, the proposed system gives very promising image SR results in various aspects.

Chapter 16

Graph Heat Kernel Based Image Smoothing 302
Zhang Fan, University of York, UK
Edwin R. Hancock, University of York, UK
Liu Shang, Beihang University, China

This chapter presents a new method for smoothing both gray-scale and color images, which relies on the heat diffusion equation on a graph. The image pixel lattice using a weighted undirected graph is presented. The edge weights of the graph are determined by the Gaussian weighted distances between local neighboring windows. The associated Laplacian matrix (the degree matrix minus the adjacency matrix) is computed then. The authors capture anisotropic diffusion across this weighted graph-structure with time by the heat equation, and find the solution, i.e. the heat kernel, by exponentiating the Laplacian eigen-system with time. Image smoothing is accomplished by convolving the heat kernel with the image, and its numerical implementation is realized by using the Krylov subspace technique. The method has the effect of smoothing within regions, but does not blur region boundaries. The relationship is also demonstrated between the authors' method, standard diffusion-based PDEs, Fourier domain signal processing, and spectral clustering. The effectiveness of the method is illustrated by experiments and comparisons on standard images.

Compilation of References 331

About the Contributors 364

Index 372

Preface

Computer vision has been a rapidly developing research area since the mid of 1970s. It is the science and technology of machines that see, and focuses on the understanding of digital input images, in many forms including videos and 3D range data. Although it is a diverse and relatively new field of study, it has achieved many scientific breakthroughs and has been successfully applied to a variety of challenging real-world applications. These include automatic face recognition, medical image analysis, and car registration plate recognition.

The process of computer vision can be divided into the stages of a) low-level processing, b) image feature extraction, and c) high-level visual understanding. At low-level, the focus is on how to extract geometrically invariant features in a robust manner so as to characterize the structures present in the visual data. Early contributions include the Harris corner detector and the Canny edge detector, which have both proved effective and have been used as the basis of higher level shape and object recognition. More recently, more robust feature extraction approaches have been proposed and these include SIFT (scale-invariant feature transform), Shape Contexts, and LSS (local self-similarity). These methods can be used to extract translation, scale, and rotation invariant features from local image patches. After low-level processing and feature extraction have been performed, high-level vision processing borrows ideas from both statistical and structure based machine learning to make final decisions concerning object classification or recognition and parameter estimation.

In computer vision, information concerning scene and object structure plays an important role. For example, after extracting SIFT features, it is not only the extracted feature vectors, but also the relative positions of these feature points that are crucial in the subsequent recognition stage. Structural pattern recognition has been a mature field of research for over three decades, and has played a pivotal role in computer vision. Importing ideas from the mathematics of graph theory is an effective and natural way to represent the structural information residing in a scene. There are also many well-developed algorithms for the analysis of graphs. Hence, graph based methods have found widespread use to solve problems in computer vision. Although there is an active and vibrant literature in the area, the use of graph-based methods for computer vision applications is a niche topic. This book aims to address problems related to applying graph-based methods in computer vision. The book includes accounts of the latest developments in graph-based methodology and its application to a variety of problems in computer vision. The list includes successful examples in the areas of image segmentation, image matching, and classification, where graph-based methods play a vital role. The remainder of the book is organized as follows:

Section 1 focuses on graph-based image matching. Image matching is a fundamental issue in computer vision. It is a vital step in object detection, stereovision, and image recognition. The basic idea is to find the correspondence parts between two images. Early attempts try to extract feature points i.e. using the

Harris or SIFT methods, in given images and then find the most similar pairs by computing the feature vector difference. Sophisticated statistical methods have been proposed recently i.e. RANSAC, to improve the consistency of the matching stage. However, the process of image matching should rely not only on the value of the extracted feature vectors, but also upon the positions of these feature points. The positions of the feature points can be used to construct a graph structure representing the arrangement of points, and then graph based methods can be used for image matching. In the graph-based literature, the methods for finding correspondences between nodes in different graphs are referred to as "graph matching." However, graph matching is normally an NP hard problem. However, this problem is alleviated using optimization techniques such as mathematical relaxation. Many statistical methods have also been used to solve relaxated graph matching problems and these include the EM (Expectation and Maximization) algorithm and RANSAC. These methods normally iterate to the optimal solution. The iteration time depends on the specific algorithms used and the initial parameters chosen. One interesting research topic is how to combine probabilistic relaxation methods with machine learning. Image matching with learning can increase the performance, especially in situations where prior knowledge is available.

This section contains three chapters. The chapter "Graph Matching Techniques for Computer Vision" introduces and reviews the many different graph matching techniques that have been used for computer vision, and relates each application with the techniques that are most suited to it. The second chapter, "Geometric-Edge Random Graph Model for Image Representation," casts image matching into a G-E random graph matching problem by using the random dot product algorithm. The third chapter, "The Node-to-Node Graph Matching Algorithm Schema" proposes a new graph matching algorithm which can be used for directed attributed graph matching and has been applied to the problem of scenario matching.

Section 2 discusses graph-based methods for image segmentation. Image segmentation is a mid-level process in vision processing. The basic idea is to segment the image into meaningful subparts. As mentioned earlier, in graphs can represent the structural information present in an image. The region adjacency graph produced by image segmentation provides a simple and effective representation of scene structure. Graph cut methods are used in graph theory to recursively bipartition a graph. The bipartition is effects by identifying edges which, when removed, give edge isolated cliques. Well known examples of graph cut algorithms include the normalized cuts method of Shi and Malik. This is a graph spectral method which uses both the total dissimilarity between the different subgraphs together with the total similarity within them. Subsequently, many improvements have been proposed to normalized cuts. Recent examples include, hierarchical segmentation, which can better reflect perceptual models of image segmentation. Graph methods play a critical role in hierarchical image segmentation, where they capture not only structural relationships at the same level of representation but also in the relationships between different levels. Prior knowledge can also be used within the segmentation stage, especially to capture object-part sub-structure. The required prior knowledge can be extracted from training samples using machine learning techniques. By representing object-part relationships using a graph, the image segmentation process can incorporate semantic knowledge. These methods can additionally be used in object detection.

In Section 2 of the book, the editors and authors present four chapters concerning graph-based methods for image segmentation. The chapter "Unsupervised and Supervised Image Segmentation Using Graph Partitioning" presents a method for image segmentation using an improved graph partition algorithm. The integrated probabilistic models in this paper increase the segmentation performance compared with that obtained using traditional graph partition segmentation algorithms. The chapter "Motion Segmentation and Matting by Graph Cut" uses graph cuts to implement motion segmentation, and is then applied graph to motion analysis. The chapter "Hypergraph Based Visual Segmentation and Retrieval" imports ideas from hyepergraph analysis for segmentation. "Recent Advances on Graph-Based Image Segmentation Techniques" gives a review of the available graph-based methods for image segmentation.

Section 3 concerns image or video classification based on graph-methods. Image recognition is one of the most important tasks in computer vision, pattern recognition, and machine learning. Since the inception of the field, considerable attention has been devoted to image and object recognition. Early attempts focused on simple objects occurring in face images, fingerprint images, and iris images. The images studied were normally devoid of complex background structure. Traditional methods such as histogram-based classification cannot incorporate the spatial arrangement of the objects. For example, in face recognition, graph structure can be used to represent the arrangement of facial features. The use of spatial arrangement information can increase the recognition performance. Moreover, when used in conjunction with problems such as face detection and face recognition, spatial arrangement information leads to algorithms that can function effectively even when there is a complex background. Pictorial structure is another example where such benefits can be reaped using graph structure. For instance deformable structure model can be used for object detection. Here the deformable model can capture high-level knowledge that can be used for scene understanding based on the arrangement of objects.

Graph representations are an effective way to represent pictorial structure and one particularly effective class of methods are based on spectral graph theory. When an object is represented by a graph structure, graph spectral methods can be used to extract a fixed length feature vector to characterize the structure of the object. Then tradition pattern classification techniques can be used for recognition. Central to the successful use of graph spectral methods in image recognition is the issue of how to efficiently extract stable and invariant features from the eigenvalues and eigenvectors of a suitable matrix representation of the graph. Many algorithms have been proposed and an evaluation of the different alternatives is therefore necessary. For complex images with background, more complex algorithms are needed. Image segmentation can be combined with graph-based methods for recognition. Another application for graph-based methods is shape analysis. In shape analysis, shapes can be represented by graph structures. The analysis on shapes then transferred to graph structure analysis.

Section 3 includes seven chapters on image and video recognition or classification. "Graph Embedding Using Dissimilarities with Applications in Classification" uses graph embedding to find a similarity measure in the embedded space and then uses this to classify graphs. The chapter "Generative Group Activity Analysis with a Quaternion Descriptor" uses graphical models to analyse group activities. "Shape Retrieval and Classification Based on Geodesic Paths in Skeleton Graphs" extends traditional shock graph methods to better characterize shapes for classification and retrieval. The chapter "Discriminative Feature Selection in Image Classification and Retrieval" describes a new method for discriminative feature selection which can be used to improve the performance of image classification and retrieval. "Normalized Projection and Graph Embedding via Angular Decomposition" introduces graph embedding for image analysis. "Region-based Graph Learning towards Large Scale Image Annotation" concerns image annotation using graph-based methods. Finally, in "Copy Detection Using Graphical Model: HMM for Frame Fusion," the authors use graphical model for video analysis for copy detection.

Finally, in Section 4, there are two chapters that use graph based methods to solve image-processing problems. The chapter "Multi-Scale Exemplary Based Super-Resolution with Graph Generalization" introduces a coding system with a resolution-invariance property, such that it is able to handle continuous-scale image resizing. This is to be compared with traditional methods that only support single integer-scale upsizing. This chapter generalizes the graphical model to the case where the typical non-linear coding process is approximated by an easier-to-compute function. Thus, the SR process can be highly parallelized by modern computer hardware. As demonstrated by the chapter, the proposed system gives very promising image SR results in various aspects. In the chapter "Graph Heat Kernel Based Image Smoothing," heat kernel diffusion process is used to smooth the images. Heat kernel relates to graph spectral theory and contains structural information of the graphs. Image smoothing is accomplished by convolving the heat kernel with the image, and its numerical implementation is realized by using the Krylov subspace technique. The method has the effect of smoothing within regions, but does not blur region boundaries.

To conclude, although they have found a useful niche, the widespread use of graph-based methods to solve traditional computer vision problems has yet to take place. This is a disappointing and represents a missed opportunity. Almost all problems in computer vision are formulated over arrangements of objects. Although techniques such as projective geometry capture the details of projection from scene to camera plane, they do not furnish a natural way of representing the types of relational or semantic detail necessary for scene or image understanding. Moreover, even at low level, graph representations are a more natural way to capture image models expressed over discrete pixel lattice, and avoid problems involved in discretising intrinsically continuous models such as those furnished by partial differential equations. This said, there is also a research imperative to explore further and more demanding computer vision application areas to understand how to apply graph-based algorithms to a greater variety of problems. After decades of development, a rich literature exists in this area. In this book, the contributors present a flavour of the research issues related to applying graph-based methods in computer vision. This book will be both timely and of value to the research community. It not only provides a snapshot of current activity in the field, but also provides a reference work that, it is hoped, will attract others to this fascinating topic, and hopefully inspire them to develop both novel graph-based method in more challenging application area, which in turn will lead to vision systems with better performance.

Acknowledgment

The editors of this book sincerely thank Prof. Horst Bunke, Prof. Richard Wilson, Dr. Andrea Torsello, Prof. Marcello Pellilo, Prof. Ali Shokoufandeh, Prof. Steven Zucker, Prof. Xiaoyi Jiang, Prof. Francesco Escolano, Prof. Mario Vento, and Prof. Alberto Sanfeliu, for serving as members of the Editorial Advisory Board. They all contributed valuable ideas and suggestions which contributed to the book in its current form.

Thanks are also due to Hannah Abelbeck, the Editorial Assistant from IGI Global, for providing templates throughout every major step in the editing process, helping compile and correct each chapter to ensure the high quality of the book. We sincerely thank the Development Division at IGI Global for publishing this book.

Section 1
Graph-Based Methods for Image Matching

Chapter 1
Graph Matching Techniques for Computer Vision

Mario Vento
Università di Salerno, Italy

Pasquale Foggia
Università di Salerno, Italy

ABSTRACT

Many computer vision applications require a comparison between two objects, or between an object and a reference model. When the objects or the scenes are represented by graphs, this comparison can be performed using some form of graph matching. The aim of this chapter is to introduce the main graph matching techniques that have been used for computer vision, and to relate each application with the techniques that are most suited to it.

INTRODUCTION

A crucial step in many Computer Vision applications is the comparison between two objects, or between an object and a reference model. For instance, in Object Recognition it is necessary to compare a description of a given object with a description of a larger scene in order to find whether, and where, the object occurs within the scene. In Object Classification, an object needs to be compared with the descriptions of a set of classes that are significant for the particular appli-cations, in order to ascribe the object to one of these classes. In Object Tracking, an object detected in a frame acquired by a camera has to be compared with all the objects present in the previous frame, for reconstructing the trajectories of the objects. Many more examples could be found in virtually all Computer Vision applications.

How the comparison is performed is obvi-ously dependent on the representation adopted for describing the objects of interest, or the scene containing them. In statistical approaches, objects are represented by a vector of global, numerical

DOI: 10.4018/978-1-4666-1891-6.ch001

features, and comparison is based typically on a vector norm or distance measure, possibly taking into account probabilistic considerations. Different approaches, the so-called structural ones, represent the objects using simpler primitives (e.g. regions, lines and so on) and their spatial relations, in order to capture and to exploit the information conveyed by the very structure of the objects. In these approaches, object representations are typically given in terms of strings or graphs; in both cases it is not possible to use the well-known vector operations to compare the objects, but a more complex algorithm is needed. In particular, if a Graph-based representation is adopted for the object/scene descriptions, the comparison entails some form of Graph Matching, the determination of a mapping between the nodes/edges of a graph and the nodes/edges of a second, possibly larger, graph. In the literature there are literally hundreds of Graph Matching algorithms, differing with respect to the properties of the desired mapping, the methodology used to find it, the kind of graphs supported, the techniques adopted for keeping the problem solvable in a reasonable time. For instance, there are exact matching algorithms, where the desired mapping must strictly preserve the node adjacency relationships, and inexact matching algorithms, where the structure of the two graphs being compared can be more or less different, and a strict correspondence is not required. In optimal matching algorithms, the goal is to find the global optimum of a measure characterizing the quality of the found mapping, while in approximate matching algorithms global optimality is sacrificed in name of speed. General matching algorithms support all kinds of graphs; specialized algorithms, instead, can be used only with particular classes of graphs (for instance, trees or planar graphs).

Given this large number of algorithms, it is not easy to choose the right one for a particular Computer Vision problem. The aim of this chapter is to provide some guidance for this purpose,

introducing the matching techniques that have been most commonly used in Computer Vision, discussing the peculiarities of each problem that make it particularly suitable (or particularly unsuitable) for a specific technique, and finally presenting the recent trends in the literature, such as the growing interest in techniques based on graph kernels.

GRAPH MATCHING ALGORITHMS

In this section we will present a short introduction to the most commonly used graph matching techniques. The techniques are grouped on the basis of how the matching problem is formulated, giving rise to the following categories:

- **Exact Graph Matching Algorithms:** Have strict requirements on the preservation of the structure of the graphs across the mapping
- **Inexact Graph Matching Algorithms:** Tolerant about structure differences in the parts of the graphs being matched
- **Graph Embeddings and Graph Kernels:** Techniques to apply algorithms developed for vectorial representations to the graph domain; such techniques are gaining a growing interest in the recent literature
- **Other Matching Techniques:** The structure of the graphs plays only a minor role

Exact Graph Matching

Exact graph matching is characterized by the fact that the mapping between the nodes of the two graphs must be edge-preserving in the sense that if two nodes in the first graph are linked by an edge, they are mapped to two nodes in the second graph that are linked by an edge as well.

Conceptually, the simplest form of graph matching is graph isomorphism, where an exact structural correspondence is sought: there must be a bijective mapping between the nodes of the two graphs that preserves the edges of both graphs.

A slightly weaker form of matching is subgraph isomorphism, which requires the existence of an isomorphism between one of the graphs and a subgraph of the other. In other words, one of the graphs may have extra nodes and extra edges linking these new nodes to the rest. Subgraph isomorphism is often confused with monomorphism, which is a little more relaxed matching: in monomorphism, extra edges in the larger graph are allowed also between nodes that do have a correspondent in the smaller graph. In subgraph isomorphism, instead, one of the ends of the extra edges must be an extra node. In other words, while isomorphism and subgraph isomorphism impose a two-way constraint on the edges of the graphs, monomorphism imposes a one-way constraint.

A more robust form of graph matching is based on the computation of the Maximum Common Subgraph (MCS), which is the largest subgraph of one of the two graphs that is isomorphic to a subgraph of the other. This kind of matching allows both graphs to have extra nodes and edges, but is also significantly more expensive from a computational viewpoint.

It has been demonstrated that the MCS problem is equivalent to the determination of the maximum clique (i.e. fully connected subgraph) in a so-called association graph, encoding the possible mappings between the nodes of the two graphs being matched; hence, many authors formulate the graph matching algorithm in terms of clique detection. A generalization of MCS is Weighted Graph Matching (WGM), where the edges of the graphs have a weight, and the goal is to find the common subgraph with the largest total weight.

Because of its strict requirements, isomorphism is not very used in Computer Vision applications, where it happens very frequently that the graphs representing different instances of a same object have some structural differences due to noise or occlusions or to other causes. On the other hand,

subgraph isomorphism, monomorphism, and MCS are generally used for finding an object, represented by a graph, as a part of a larger model graph (prototype), or for detecting the parts shared by two objects, structurally represented by graphs.

Exact graph matching has an exponential time complexity in the worst case. However, in many PR applications the actual computation time can be still acceptable, because of two factors: first, the kinds of graphs encountered in practice are usually different from the worst cases for the algorithms. Second, node and edge attributes can be used very often to reduce dramatically the search time.

The first attempts for reducing the computational complexity of graph matching were aimed to define algorithms devised for special kinds of graphs. Among them, we find algorithms for some common graph topologies, as trees (special cases of graphs), proposed by Aho et al. in 1974 (Aho, 1974), planar graphs by Hopcroft and Wong in 1974 (Hopcroft, 1974), and bounded valence graphs by Luks in 1982 (Luks, 1982). Despite the historical relevance, this family of graph matching algorithms can be used only in specific applicative areas, where the graphs being matched always have a same predefined structure.

Most of the algorithms for exact graph matching are based on some form of tree search with backtracking. The basic idea is that a partial match (initially empty) is iteratively expanded by adding to it new pairs of matched nodes; the pair is chosen using some necessary conditions that ensure its compatibility with the constraints imposed by the matching type with respect to the nodes mapped so far, and usually using also some heuristic condition to prune as early as possible unfruitful search paths. Eventually, either the algorithm finds a complete matching, or it reaches a point where the current partial mapping cannot be further expanded because of the matching constraints. In this latter case the algorithm backtracks, i.e. undoes the last additions until it finds a partial matching for which an alternative extension is possible. If all the possible mappings that satisfy the constraints have already been tried, the algorithm halts. Several different implementation strategies of this kind of algorithm have been employed; differing in the order the partial matches are visited. Probably the simplest is depth-first search that requires less memory than others and lends itself very well to a recursive formulation; it is also known as branch and bound. A nice property of such algorithms is that they can be very easily adapted to take into account the attributes of nodes and edges in constraining the desired matching, with no limitations on the kind of attributes that can be used. This is very important for PR applications where often attributes play a key role in reducing the computational time of the matching.

The first important algorithm of this family is due to Ullmann, in 1976 (Ullman, 1976), still widely used today. Also the approach proposed by Schmidt and Druffel in 1976 (Schmidt, 1976) adopts the same strategy, with the addition of a preprocessing that creates an initial partition of the graph nodes on the basis of the distance matrix, to reduce the search space. Another interesting monomorphism algorithm based on backtracking has been proposed by Ghahraman et al. in 1980 (Ghahraman, 1980); it prunes the search space, using a so-called netgraph obtained from the Cartesian product of the nodes of two graphs being matched. Monomorphisms between these two graphs correspond to particular subgraphs of the netgraph. A major drawback of the algorithm is that the netgraph is represented using a matrix of size N^2xN^2, where N is the number of nodes of the largest graph. Consequently, only small graphs can be reasonably dealt with.

A more recent algorithm for both isomorphism and subgraph isomorphism is the VF algorithm (Cordella, 1998) (Cordella, 2000). The authors define a heuristic that is based on the analysis of the sets of nodes adjacent to the ones already considered in the partial mapping. This heuristic is fast to compute leading in many cases to a significant improvement over Ullmann's and other

algorithms, as shown in (Cordella, 1999) (De Santo, 2003). Successively, the authors propose a modification of the algorithm (Cordella, 2001) (Cordella, 2004), called VF2, that reduces the memory requirement from $O(N^2)$ (that compares favorably with other algorithms) to $O(N)$ with respect to the number of nodes in the graphs, thus making the algorithm particularly interesting for working with large graphs.

One of the most recent tree search methods for isomorphism has been proposed by Larrosa and Valiente in 2002 (Larrosa, 2002); the authors reformulate graph isomorphism as a Constraint Satisfaction Problem (CSP), a problem that has been studied very deeply in the framework of discrete optimization and operational research. Thus the authors apply to graph matching some heuristics derived from the CSP literature.

The backtracking approach has been applied also to problems different from graph isomorphism and subgraph isomorphism. For instance, Durand et al. (Durand, 1999) have used this approach to solve the maximal clique detection problem.

Probably the most interesting matching algorithm that is not based on tree search is Nauty, developed by McKay in 1981 (McKay, 1981). The algorithm deals only with the isomorphism problem, and is regarded by many authors as the fastest isomorphism algorithm available today. It uses some results coming from group theory for constructing the automorphism group of each of the input graphs. From them, a canonical labeling is derived, so that two graphs can be checked for isomorphism by simply verifying the equality of their canonical forms. The equality verification can be done in $O(N^2)$ time, but the construction of the canonical labeling can require an exponential time in the worst case. In the average case this algorithm has quite impressive performance, although in (Foggia, 2001) (De Santo, 2003) it has been verified that under some conditions it can be outperformed by other algorithms like the above mentioned VF2. Furthermore, it does not lend itself very well to exploit node and edge attributes of the graphs, that in many PR applications can provide an invaluable contribution to reduce the matching time.

Some matching algorithms are specifically aimed at reducing the cost of matching one input graph against a large library of graphs, suitably preprocessed. Messmer and Bunke proposed a very impressive algorithm in 1997 (Bunke, 1997) (Messmer, 1999). The algorithm that deals with isomorphism and subgraph isomorphism, in a preprocessing phase builds a decision tree from the graph library. Using this decision tree, an input graph can be matched against the whole library in a time that is $O(N^2)$ with respect to the input graph size. An extension to MCS is presented in a paper by Shearer et al. in 1997 (Shearer, 1997), further improved in (Shearer, 2001).

Other two recent papers, by Lazarescu et al. in 2000 (Lazarescu, 2000) and by Irniger and Bunke in 2001 (Irniger, 2001), proposed the use of decision trees for speeding up the matching against a large library of graphs. In these cases, the decision tree is not used to perform the matching process, but only for quickly filtering out as many library graphs as possible, applying then a complete matching algorithm only to the remaining ones.

Inexact Graph Matching

The stringent constraints imposed by exact matching are in some circumstances too rigid for the comparison of two graphs. In many applications, the observed graphs are subject to deformations due to several causes: intrinsic variability of the patterns, noise in the acquisition process, presence of non-deterministic elements in the processing steps leading to the graph representation, are among the possible reasons for having actual graphs that differ somewhat from their ideal models.

So the matching process must accommodate the differences by relaxing, to some extent, the constraints that define the matching type. Usually, in these algorithms the matching between two

nodes that do not satisfy the edge-preservation requirements of the matching type is not forbidden. Instead, it is penalized by assigning to it a cost that may take into account other differences (e.g. among the corresponding node/edge attributes). So the algorithm must find a mapping that minimizes the matching cost.

Optimal inexact matching algorithms always find a solution that is the global minimum of the matching cost so implying that if an exact solution exists, it will be found. Hence they can be seen as a generalization of exact matching algorithms. Optimal algorithms face the problem of graph variability, and they do not necessarily provide an improvement of the computation time, usually resulting fairly more expensive than their exact counterparts.

Approximate or suboptimal matching algorithms, instead, only ensure to find a local minimum of the matching cost, generally not very far from the global one. Even if an exact solution exists, they may not be able to find it and for some applications this may not be acceptable, but the suboptimality of the solution is abundantly repaid by a shorter, usually polynomial, matching time.

A significant number of inexact graph matching algorithms base the definition of the matching cost on an explicit model of the errors (deformations) that may occur (i.e. missing nodes etc.), assigning a possibly different cost to each kind of error. These algorithms are often denoted as error-correcting or error-tolerant. Another way of defining a matching cost is to introduce a set of graph edit operations (e.g. node insertion, node deletion etc.), each assigned a cost; the cheapest sequence of operations needed to transform one of the two graphs into the other is computed, and called graph edit cost.

Some of the inexact matching methods also propose the use of the matching cost as a measure of dissimilarity of the graphs, e.g. for selecting the most similar in a set of graphs, or for clustering. In some cases, the cost formulation verifies the mathematical properties of a distance function (e.g. the triangular inequality); then we have a graph distance that can be used to extend to graphs some of the algorithms defined in metric spaces. Of particular interest is the graph edit distance, obtained if the graph edit costs satisfy some constraints (e.g. the cost of node insertion must be equal to the cost of node deletion).

Some papers demonstrate equivalences holding between the graph edit distance and relevant graph matching problems, as the graph isomorphism and subgraph isomorphism and MCS (Bunke, 1999) (Bunke, 1997) (Bunke, 1998) (Fernàndez, 2001) (Wallis, 2001).

Tree search with backtracking can also be used for inexact matching. In this case the search is usually directed by the cost of the partial matching obtained so far, and by a heuristic estimate of the matching cost for the remaining nodes. This information can be used either to prune unfruitful paths in a branch and bound algorithm, or also to determine the order in which the search tree must be traversed, as in the A* algorithm. In this latter case, if the heuristic provides a close estimate of the future matching cost, the algorithm finds the solution quite rapidly; but if this is not the case, the memory requirement is considerably larger than for the branch and bound algorithm.

The first tree based inexact algorithm is due to Tsai and Fu, in 1979 (Tsai, 1979), and in an extended version in 1983 (Tsai, 1983). The paper introduces a formal definition of error-correcting graph matching of Attributed Relational Graphs (ARG), based on the introduction of a graph edit cost, and defines a search method ensuring to find the optimal solution. A more recent paper by Wong et al. in 1990 (Wong, 1990) proposes an improvement of the heuristic of Tsai and Fu for error-correcting monomorphism, taking into account also the future cost of edge matching.

A similar approach is used in a paper by Sanfeliu and Fu in (Sanfeliu, 1983) (Eshera, 1984a) (Eshera, 1984b), where the definition of a true graph edit distance is attempted, and a suboptimal method, working in a polynomial time, for the

distance computation is introduced. In a paper of 1980, Gharaman et al. (Ghahraman, 1980), propose an optimal inexact graph monomorphism algorithm that is based on the use of branch and bound together with a heuristic derived from the netgraph.

Interesting early papers are due to Shapiro and Haralick in 1981 (Shapiro, 1981) and later in 1985 (Shapiro, 1985), with algorithms for finding the optimal error-correcting homomorphism and for evaluating the distance between two hypergraphs.

Among the more recent proposals based on tree search we can cite the algorithm proposed by Dumay et al. in 1992 (Dumay, 1992), using A* for evaluating a graph distance; A* search appears also in a recent paper by Gregory and Kittler in 2002 (Gregory, 2002), where a fast, simple heuristic is used that takes into account only the future cost of unmatched nodes. The authors assume that at least for small graphs the less accurate estimate of the future cost is abundantly repaid by the time savings obtained in computing a less complicated heuristic.

Another recent inexact algorithm has been proposed by Cordella et al. in two papers of 1996 and 1997 (Cordella, 1996) (Cordella, 1997). This algorithm deals with deformations by defining a transformation model in which under appropriate conditions a subgraph can be collapsed into a single node. The transformation model is contextual, in the sense that a given transformation may be selectively allowed depending on the attributes of neighboring nodes and edges. Along the same lines, Serratosa et al. in 1999 (Serratosa, 2000) (Serratosa, 1999) present an inexact matching method that also exploits some form of contextual information. The authors define a distance between Function Described Graphs (FDG) that are ARG's enriched with additional information relative to the joint probability of the nodes in order to model with one FDG a set of observed ARG's.

As in the case of exact approach, efficient inexact matching algorithms have been proposed for dealing with special, restricted classes of graphs, as planar graphs and Region Adjacency Graphs (RAGs). For planar graphs, Rocha and Pavlidis (Rocha, 1994) present an optimal algorithm for error-correcting homomorphism, while in a paper by Wang and Abe (1995) (Wang, 1995), a distance between RAG's is proposed, and is computed using a suboptimal algorithm. More recently, Llados et al. in a 2001 paper (Llados, 2001) define a graph edit distance for RAGs using edit operations that are devised to model common distortions in image segmentation; the distance is computed using an optimal algorithm based on branch and bound.

The matching methods examined so far rely on a formulation of the matching problems directly in terms of graphs. A radically different approach is to cast graph matching, that is inherently a discrete optimization problem, so as to use one of the many continuous, non-linear optimization algorithms. The found solution needs to be converted back from the continuous domain into the initial discrete problem by a process that may introduce an additional level of approximation. Nevertheless, in many application contexts this approach is very appealing because of its extremely reduced computational cost that is usually polynomially dependent (and with a low exponent) on the size of the graphs.

The first family of methods based on this approach uses relaxation labeling. One of the pioneering works is due to Fischler and Elschlager in 1973 (Fischler, 1973). The basic idea is that each node of one of the graphs can be assigned one label out of a discrete set of possible labels that determines which node of the other graph it corresponds to. During the matching process, for each node there is a vector of the probabilities of each candidate label, dynamically re-evaluated until the process converges to a stable solution. At this point, for each node the label having the maximum probability is chosen. In 1989 Kittler and Hancock (Kittler, 1989) provide a probabilistic framework for relaxation labeling, in which the update rules previously used for the probabilities are given a theoretical motivation. In 1995, Christ-mas et al. (Christmas, 1995) propose a method, based on the theoretical framework of Kittler and Hancock, that is able to take into account during the iteration process both node and edge attributes. Wilson and Hancock, in 1997 (Wilson, 1997), extended the probabilistic framework by introducing a Bayesian consistency measure, that can be used as a graph distance. An extension of this method has been proposed by Huet and Hancock in 1999 (Huet, 1999). This method also takes into account edge attributes in the evaluation of the consistency measure.

Myers et al. (Myers, 2000) in 2000 propose a new matching algorithm that introduces the definition of a Bayesian graph edit distance, approximated by considering independently the supercliques of the graphs, so as to perform the computation in polynomial time. Finally, in a recent paper (2001), Torsello and Hancock (Torsello, 2001) propose the use of relaxation labeling also for computing an edit distance between trees.

A recent method by Luo and Hancock (Luo, 2001) is based on a probabilistic model of matching: the nodes of the input graph play the role of observed data while the nodes of the model graph act as hidden random variables; the matching is then found by using the Expectation-Maximization (EM) algorithm (Dempster, 1977).

A different family of methods is based on a formulation of the problem as a Weighted Graph Matching Problem (WGM) that permits the enforcement of two-way constraints on the correspondence. It consists in finding a matching, usually expressed by means of a matching matrix M, between a subset of the nodes of the first graph and a subset of the nodes of the second graph. The edges of the graphs are labeled with weights that are real numbers, usually between 0 and 1. The desired matching must optimize a suitably defined goal function. Usually the problem is transformed into a continuous one by allowing M elements to have continuous values so making the WGM problem a quadratic optimization problem. An important limitation of this approach, from the perspective of PR applications, is that nodes cannot have attributes and edges cannot have other attributes than their weight. This restriction imposes a severe limit on the use of the semantic information often available in real applications.

Among the first papers based on this formulation is the work by Almohamad and Duffuaa in 1993 (Almohamad, 1993). In this paper the quadratic problem is linearized and solved using the simplex algorithm (Lawler, 2001). The approximate, continuous solution found this way is then converted back into discrete form using the so-called Hungarian method (Lawler, 2001) for the assignment problem. Rangarajan and Mjolsness (Rangarajan, 1996), in 1996, proposed a method based on Lagrangian relaxation networks in which the constraints on the rows and on the columns of the matching matrix are satisfied separately and then equated through a Lagrange multiplier. Also in a 1996 paper, Gold and Rangarajan (Gold, 1996) present the Graduated Assignment Graph Matching (GAGM) algorithm. In this algorithm a technique known as graduated nonconvexity is employed to avoid poor local optima.

Another approach is based on a theorem by Motzkin and Straus that establishes a close relation between the clique problem and continuous optimization. Namely, they prove that all the maximum cliques of a graph correspond to maxima of a well-defined quadratic functional. In 1997, Bomze (Bomze, 1997) proposed a modified functional for which the correspondence holds in both senses.

The papers by Pelillo and Jagota in 1995 (Pelillo, 1995a) (Pelillo, 1995b) propose a matching method based on the above cited theorem and an implementation where the quadratic problem is solved by means of relaxation networks (Rosenfeld, 1976). In (Pelillo, 1998) (Luo, 2001), a unified framework for relational matching based on the Bomze functional is presented. In 1999, Pelillo et al. (Pelillo, 1999) (Luo, 2003) introduced a technique to reduce the MCS problem between trees to a clique problem and then solved it using replicator equations. Branca et al. (Branca, 1999)

proposed in 1999 an extension of the framework defined by Pelillo (Pelillo, 1998) that is able to deal with a weighted version of the clique problem.

Several other inexact matching methods based on continuous optimization have been proposed in the recent years, as the Fuzzy Graph Matching (FGM) by Medasani et al. (Medasani, 2001) (Medasani, 1999), that is a simplified version of WGM based on fuzzy logic. Another recent approach, proposed by van Wyk et al. in 2002 (van Wyk, 2002a) (van Wyk, 2002b) is based on the theory of the so-called Reproducing Kernel Hilbert Spaces (RHKS) for casting the matching problem into a system identification problem; this latter is then solved by constructing a RKHS interpolator to approximate the unknown mapping function.

Spectral methods are based on the following observation: the eigenvalues and the eigenvectors of the adjacency matrix of a graph are invariant with respect to node permutations. Hence, if two graphs are isomorphic, their adjacency matrices will have the same eigenvalues and eigenvectors. Unfortunately, the converse is not true: we cannot deduce from the equality of eigenvalues/eigenvectors that two graphs are isomorphic. However, since the computation of eigenvalues/eigenvectors is a well studied problem that can be solved in polynomial time, there is a great interest in their use for graph matching. An important limitation of these methods is that they are purely structural, in the sense that they are not able to exploit node or edge attributes that often, in PR applications, convey information very relevant for the matching process. Further, some of the spectral methods are actually able to deal only with real weights assigned to edges by using an adjacency matrix with real valued elements.

The pioneering work on spectral methods is the paper by Umeyama, in 1988 (Umeyama, 1988), proposing an algorithm for the weighted isomorphism between two graphs. It uses the eigendecomposition of adjacency matrices of the graphs to derive a simple expression of the orthogonal matrix that optimizes the objective function, under the assumption that the graphs are isomorphic. From this expression he derives a method for computing the optimal permutation matrix when the two graphs are isomorphic, and a suboptimal permutation matrix if the graphs are nearly isomporphic. In 2001, Xu and King (Xu, 2001), propose a solution to the weighted isomorphism problem, by approximating the permutation matrix with a generic orthogonal matrix. An objective function is defined using Principal Component Analysis and then gradient descent is used to find the optimum of this function.

In 2001 Carcassoni and Hancock (Carcassoni, 2001) propose a spectral method that is based on the use of spectral features to define clusters of nodes that are likely to be matched together in the optimal correspondence; the method uses hierarchical matching by first finding a correspondence between clusters and then between the nodes in the clusters. Another method that combines a spectral approach with the idea of clustering has been presented by Kosinov and Caelli in 2002 (Kosinov, 2002): a vector space, called the graph eigenspace, is defined using the eigenvectors of the adjacency matrices, and the nodes are projected onto points in this space and a clustering algorithm is used to find nodes of the two graphs that are to be put in correspondence.

A method that is partly related to spectral techniques has been proposed in 2001 by Shoko-ufandeh and Dickinson (Shokoufandeh, 2001). The authors use the eigenvalues to associate to each node of a Directed Acyclic Graph a "Topological Signature Vector" (TSV) that is related to the structure of the subgraph made of the descendants of the node. These TSV are used both for a quick indexing in a graph database and for the actual graph matching algorithm. This latter is based on the combination of a greedy search procedure and of bipartite graph matching.

Finally, we must say that other heuristic approaches to inexact graph matching have been proposed: at least in principle, any of the heuristic techniques that have been used for combinatorial

problems or for continuous global optimization problems can be adapted to some approximate form of graph matching. With no presumption of completeness, we can cite here, as examples, simulated annealing (Jagota et al., 2000 (Jagota, 2000)) and tabu search (Gendreau et al., 1993 (Gendreau, 1993); Williams et al., 1999 (Williams, 1999)).

Other Matching Techniques

In both exact and inexact graph matching problems, the correspondence between the nodes of the two graphs must take into account, in some way, the edges connecting the nodes. In several computer vision applications, however, often the comparison between two object representations given in terms of graphs are performed considering mostly, or sometime exclusively, the information associated to the nodes of the graphs. In this way, the matching problem is simplified and can be solved with a considerably reduced computational effort.

The most commonly used formulation of the problem, in such cases, is Bipartite Graph Matching (BGM). In the classical definition of the problem, a correspondence has to be found between two sets of nodes; the nodes in the first set are linked by edges to the nodes in the second set that are compatible, and the goal is to find a mapping between the two sets that uses the maximum number of nodes, with the constraints that each node can be used at most once and corresponding nodes must be compatible. A more sophisticated formulation is the Weighted Bipartite Graph Matching problem (WBGM), also known as the assignment problem, in which the edges connecting the two sets of nodes have a real-valued weight, and the goal is to find the mapping that maximizes the sum of the weights for the corresponding nodes. The most popular algorithm for solving the WBGM problem is the so-called Hungarian method by Kuhn (Lawler, 2001), which has a worst-case time complexity that is $O(n^3)$ with respect to the number of nodes. Other algorithms for the WBGM have been proposed in the Computer Vision literature, with the aim of reducing the complexity in the average case, usually at the price of a greater complexity in the worst case. An example is the algorithm proposed by Berretti et al. in their 2000 and 2001 papers (Berretti, 2000a) (Berretti, 2000b) (Berretti, 2001), which is based on the A* search.

Another matching problem commonly found in Computer Vision is Elastic Graph Matching (EGM). Despite its name, it is not really a graph matching problem but, rather, an image matching problem that is based on a graph structure. More precisely, a regular or irregular grid is superimposed on the model image; some image features are computed at the intersections of the grid lines and are used as attributes. Successively, an isomorphic grid is superimposed on the sample image, and is then deformed in order to have the best matching between the features computed at the sample grid points and the ones recorded previously for the model. This deformation process uses the graph structure of the two grids to define a deformation cost that constrains the entity of the permissible deformations. The best placement of the grid on the sample is usually looked for using simulated annealing (but genetic algorithms also have been used).

Probably the first paper proposing EGM is the work by Lades et al. in 1993 (Lades, 1993), where the problem is formulated in a neural framework. A 1997 paper by Wiskott et al. (Wiskott, 1997) extends the method by introducing a bunch graph for the model, that is a graph in which multiple alternative feature vectors are assigned to each node. In 1999 Duc et al. (Duc, 1999) improve the matching error definition by allowing nodes with different weights.

Recent Trends: Graph Embeddings and Graph Kernels

Matching methods examined so far treat the comparison problem directly in the domain of graphs, and thus cannot exploit the large number of theoretical results and techniques developed in statistics and in Pattern Recognition. In the recent years, however, a growing number of research efforts have attempted to extend to graphs the methodologies developed for vectorial representations.

A possible solution to this issue is the use of Graph Embedding, which is a methodology aimed at representing a whole graph (possibly with attributes attached to its nodes and edges) as a point in a suitable vectorial space. Of course there are countless ways for mapping a graph to a vector; but interesting embeddings are characterized by the fact that they preserve the similarity of the graphs: the more two graphs are similar, the closer the corresponding points are in the target vector space.

Graph embedding, in this sense, is a real bridge joining the two worlds: once the object at hand has been described in terms of graphs, and the latter represented in the vectorial space, all the problems of matching, learning and clustering can be performed using classical Statistical Pattern Recognition algorithms.

Possible approaches proposed for performing the graph embedding include spectral methods (Luo, 2003) (Wilson, 2005), based on the eigen-decomposition of the adjacency matrix or of some matrix related to it. In (Bai, 2004), a statistical technique known as Multi-Dimensional Scaling (MDS) is used to embed a graph, characterized by the matrix of the geodesic distances between nodes, into a manifold. In (Torsello, 2007), an embedding algorithm for the special case of trees is proposed. The algorithm is based on the computation of the minimum common super-tree of a set of trees; then each tree is represented as a vector whose elements encode the nodes of the super-tree which are present in the tree. In (Emms,

2007) random walks are used to derive a graph embedding; in particular the embedding encodes the expected time needed for a random walk to travel between two nodes. In (Riesen, 2007) the embedding is built by choosing at random a small set of graphs as prototypes, and representing a graph with the vector of the graph-edit distances from each prototype. Since graph-edit distance calculation is an NP-complete problem, an approximation of this measure is actually used.

A different way to extend vector-based algorithms to graph is through the introduction of Graph Kernels. A Graph Kernel is a function K, defined in the graph space that shares the properties of the dot-product operator in a vector space:

The function has as its domain a couple of graphs, and as its range the real numbers:

$K: G{\times}G{\rightarrow}\mathbb{R}$

- The function is symmetric: $K(g_1, g_2) = K(g_2, g_1)$
- The function is *positive semi-definite*, in the sense that for all n-tuples of graphs $g_1,..., g_n$ and for all n-tuples of real values $c_1,...,c_n$, then

$$\sum_{i,j=1}^{n} K\left(g_i, g_j\right) c_i c_j \geq 0$$

Given a suitable kernel function, all the algorithms based on vector dot product can be easily reformulated in terms of graphs; among the algorithms that have been used with kernels we can cite several types of Artificial Neural Networks, the Support Vector Machines, and the Principal Component Analysis.

Many Graph Kernels proposed in the literature have been built on the notion of "bag of patterns" which considers each graph as composed by an unordered collection of simpler substructures. For instance, Graphlets Kernels (Shervashidze, 2009) are based on the number of common sub-graphs of two graphs. Vert (Mah, 2008) and Borgwardt (Shervashidze, 2009) proposed to compare the set of sub-trees of two graphs. Furthermore, many graph kernels are based on simpler patterns such as walks (Kashima, 2003), trails (Dupé, 2009) or paths. A different approach is to define a kernel on the basis of graph edit distance. Kernels based on this approach do not rely on the (often simplistic) assumption that a bag of patterns preserves most of the information of its associated graph. The main difficulty in the design of such Graph Kernels is that the edit distance does not usually correspond to a metric. Trivial kernels based on edit distances are thus usually non definite positive. Neuhaus and Bunke (Neuhaus, 2007) proposed several kernels based on edit distances. These kernels are either based on a combination of graph edit distances (trivial kernel, zeros graph kernel), use the convolution framework introduced by Haussler (Haussler, 1999) (convolution kernel, local matching kernel), or incorporate within the kernel construction schemes several features deduced from the computation of the edit distance (maximum similarity edit path kernel, random walk edit kernel). A noticeable exception to this classification is the diffusion kernel introduced by the same authors (Neuhaus, 2007), which defines the Gram matrix associated to the kernel as the exponential of a similarity matrix deduced from the edit distance.

COMPUTER VISION APPLICATIONS USING GRAPH MATCHING

In this section we will present the most important Computer Vision applications for which methods have been proposed that make use of Graph Matching techniques. In particular, after a short description of each problem, we will describe the most important contributions in the literature, highlighting which kind of matching algorithm has been adopted.

Object/Shape Recognition and Visual Inspection

In object recognition the goal is to find all the occurrences, within an image, of a distinguished set of objects. Usually objects of interest belong to different classes (having different shapes) and neither their number nor their positions within the image are known; the image often contains also background elements (possibly complex) that should not be detected by the system. In some cases, the objects of interest may be partially occluded by other objects or by background elements. The basic idea of graph-based object recognition is to decompose the whole image into smaller parts, obtaining a graph representation describing those parts and their relations, and then to look for subgraphs of this large graph that correspond to the shapes of the objects of interest, by means of some kind of inexact matching algorithm. The above mentioned papers differ in the adopted representations, ranging from low-level (Meth, 1996) to middle level representations (Li, 2000) (Belongie, 2000), and also in matching techniques (error-correcting subgraph isomorphism with a similarity measure (Meth, 1996), inexact matching with a neural approach (Li, 2000), weighted bipartite matching (Belongie, 2000)). The 3D object recognition problem is quite similar to the 2D version; the main differences are the need to take into account the changes in the object appearance due to a different point of view, and the increased importance of the occlusion phenomenon. These differences lead to the use of graph matching algorithms more tolerant to structural changes.

Shape recognition is very similar to object recognition, differing for the fact that only shape information is available (and not, say, color or texture information), and usually the image is not cluttered with background elements. If the shapes are simply connected (i.e., they not contain holes), they can be represented using a tree instead of a fully general graph, and the matching can be performed using error correcting tree isomorphism (Sebastian, 2005).

Visual inspection is also similar to the object recognition problem, with the important difference that a model of which objects are expected to be in the image and which should be their positions is known; indeed, the purpose of visual inspection is actually to spot any difference with respect to the expected situation. For this reason, exact matching methods can be more appropriate for this problem (Koo, 1998).

Entering into details, in the field of 2D object recognition, Meth and Chellappa in (Meth, 1996) work on SAR images. They use a low-level representation: a node of the graph is associated to each pixel of the image. The node labels depend on the so-called TPS (topographical primal sketch). A TPS assigns to each pixel a label that is invariant under monotonic transformations of the grey levels. This is obtained by fitting a local two-dimensional cubic surface on the image for estimating the intensity surface around each pixel. On the basis of the derivatives of this surface, one of the following six labels is given to the pixel: peak, pit, ravine, ridge, saddle, "no zero crossing". Two graph matching techniques are proposed, the first one is based on a distance measure between node labels, while the second one is based on a similarity measure between features associated to node labels. In both cases, the test and the model image are first registered with respect to the node labels position. The first matching technique calculates a cost based on the relative distance between nodes with the same label in the test and in the model image. The second one associates a feature vector (by calculating the 2nd derivative extrema, the directions of the 2nd derivative extrema and the gradient) to nodes that have a certain label; on the basis of these feature vectors a similarity measure is computed. Results are reported on 81 images belonging to three different categories.

In (Belongie, 2000) Belongie and Malik define a new middle-level shape descriptor that they call shape context, for measuring shape similarity. Given an image, the edges are extracted and a certain number of uniformly spaced points, say N, on these edges are selected. A compact descriptor for each sample point is obtained by computing a coarse histogram of the relative coordinates of the remaining points, in a log-polar coordinate system. All the N histograms are flattened and concatenated so as to obtain the so-called shape context of the image. In addition to this representation, another one based on the local appearance, in particular on the tangent angle calculated for each of the N points, is also used. So, if a node of a graph is associated to each of these points, the cost of matching two nodes relative to points on two images can be expressed by taking into account two contributions, one relative to the difference between histograms and the other one relative to the tangent angles dissimilarity. The object recognition problem is then viewed as a Weighted Bipartite Graph matching problem that can be solved with the Hungarian method. Results on the same database used in (Sharvit, 1998) are presented and also on other silhouette image databases. Furthermore, the authors suggest that their method can be also used for the retrieval from an image database, as it provides a similarity measure between 2D objects.

As regards 3D object recognition, Bauckhage et al. present in (Bauckhage, 2001) a system that uses graphs to recognize mechanical assemblies in a dynamic construction environment. In particular, the main objective of their project is to develop a robot that assembles parts from a wooden construction-kit for children, made up of bolts, rings, bars and cubes. So, given an assembly described by a graph, they use a graph matching technique for recognizing if that assembly is already present in the knowledge base of the robot. In the negative case it will be added to the database. They introduce the mating feature graph for representation. The nodes of this graph represent mating features or subparts of an assembly and are labeled with the type of the subpart.

Nodes connected with a pair of edges represent subparts that belong to the same object, while single directed edges between nodes represent the fact that the corresponding subparts are attached to the same bolt. If an object is connected to several bolts, the nodes that correspond to these bolts are linked by a bi-directional edge; this edge is labeled with a value that indicates the angle between the bolts. For matching two mating feature graphs, they use the error-correcting matching procedure presented in (Messmer, 1998). They also propose an application of the mating feature graph to the 3D reconstruction of assembled objects.

Another approach is proposed in Olatunbosun et al. (Olatunbosun, 1996), where a special kind of Region Adjacency Graphs, called CRAG (color region adjacency graph), is used for representing 3D objects. Graph nodes are the segmented regions, using the coordinates of their centroids as node attributes, and edges represent connections between regions. By using the line length ratio, i.e. the ratio of the distance between a pair of nodes into the model image and a pair of nodes in a test image, and the line angles, i.e. angles between three nodes into the model and the test image, an association graph where the nodes are provisionally matched is built. Then the Bron-Kerbosh (Bron, 1973) algorithm is used to find the maximal clique on this association graph: a high clique value imply high similarity between the model image and a test image. The authors also propose to reduce the computational complexity of the maximal clique search method, by adopting a model-based approach. In order to recognize an object, a test images is first filtered, by eliminating from it all the color regions that do not belong to the model CRAG. So, the maximal clique search is performed on a smaller association graph.

Now let us turn our attention to shape recognition. In the paper by Li and Lee (Li, 2000), a graph represents a 2D scene that is described by using a polygonal approximation. The nodes of the graph are the vertices of the polygon and the edges represent the sides. The angle subtended by each vertex is the node attribute, while the distance between two nodes is used as edge attribute. Given such a graph (called scene graph), in order to cope with distortions and occlusions, the authors propose to divide it into smaller pieces, called sub-scene graphs. Then, an inexact sub-scene graph matching is performed between each sub-scene graph and a model graph by using a Hopfield neural net. The correct match for the complete scene graph can be obtained from the statistics of the matching results between each sub-scene graph and the model graph. In the paper, tests are made on images representing 2D hand tools.

Sebastian et al. (Sebastian, 2005) propose a system to recognize object shapes on the basis of their silhouette. They represent each object using a shock tree, which is derived from a thinning of the shape. For the matching, they propose the definition of a tree edit distance, in which the edit costs are not fixed arbitrarily but are derived analytically from a small set of hypotheses related to the cost of deforming a silhouette. This distance is computed by means of an error correcting tree isomorphism algorithm based on dynamic programming.

Finally, Koo and Yoo (Koo, 1998) address the problem of visual inspection by using a high-level representation scheme. They consider Printed Circuit Board images that are represented by means of a tree. Images are first binarized, then the binarized image is partitioned into non-overlapping regions (blobs) each one made up of adjacent pixels having the same value. A node is associated to each blob; a tree is constructed by adding an edge between two nodes if the blobs they represent are spatially included into each other and have different pixel values. The root of the tree is the blob that contains the outer boundary pixels of the image. The tree obtained from a test image is compared with the tree derived from a defect-free image by means of the tree isomorphism algorithm proposed in (Aho, 1974). If the two trees are not isomorphic a defect is detected and the inspection process stops. Otherwise, additional polygonal-boundary

information is extracted and a second matching step is performed. In particular, a tolerance zone is defined and the proposed algorithm through a polygonal-boundary matching function checks if such tolerance is respected between pairs of matched nodes.

Classification and Identity Verification

Among the Computer Vision problems involving some sort of classification, OCR, handwritten recognition, string recognition, symbol and graphic recognition have been often addressed in the literature by using graph matching techniques.

These problems are relatively similar to each other, entailing the recognition of small elements having a definite meaning within an image. The number of different categories (classes) to be considered varies from ten to several hundred, and also the shape variability of the elements belonging to a same class can range from reasonably small (e.g. for high resolution printed characters) to very high (for handwritten characters or symbols). As regards the strategy adopted to face the problem, entities to be recognized (characters, symbols or graphics) are usually decomposed into geometric primitives, which are in most cases approximated as thin lines (also called strokes), since in hand writing and in printed scripts, thickness does not convey useful information. This decomposition is then represented as a graph, and the recognition process is performed as a graph matching with model graphs corresponding to the different classes of characters, symbols or graphics to be recognized. The proposed approaches differ in complexity of the geometric primitives, in the way the decomposition is translated into a graph, and in the kind of graph matching performed. A problem that is strongly related is the construction of such model graphs from a set of examples, which is usually performed by means of algorithms that involve a graph matching as one of their steps.

Graph Based Techniques have been widely used within the context of identification problems, where the task is to determine the identity of a person from some biometric features. Among all the biometric identification problems, a key role is played by face authentication, face recognition and fingerprint recognition. Moreover, there are other applications based on facial images, as facial expression recognition and face pose estimation, as well as other probably less known applications, as hand posture recognition and ear recognition. In all these problems, the goal is to compare a graph representation obtained from a sample image of some biometric trait of an individual with a model graph. This comparison has to take into account the possibility of severe distortion of the sample graph with respect to the model, due to the extreme variability in the appearance of biometric traits. In the case of authentication, there is only one model graph, and the problem is to decide whether the model and the sample correspond to the same person. In biometric recognition problems, instead, there are several models (corresponding to different persons, but also possibly to different gestures of a single person) and the system has to identify the person (or the gesture) shown in the sample. A characteristic that is common to many applications of this category is that the reliability of the identification is extremely important, since the cost of errors is significantly larger than, for example, the one incurred in document processing applications.

Now let us turn our attention to classification problems. Since OCR and handwritten recognition are among the most classical pattern recognition problems, and many of large datasets are available, they are often used as test cases in technique-driven papers. This is the case of the papers by Sanfeliu and Fu (Sanfeliu, 1983), Foggia et al. (Cordella, 1996) (Foggia, 2001) (Foggia, 1999), Chan (Chan, 1996) and Rangarajan and Mjolness (Rangarajan, 1996). But also several application-driven papers have been written on the handwritten recognition problem (both off-line and on-line) or on the optical character recognition problem: this is the case of the papers by Lee and Liu (Lee, 1999) and Suganthan and Yan (Suganthan, 1998), and Liu et al. (Liu, 2000), Lu et al. (Lu, 1991), Chen and Lieu (Chen, 1990) and Rocha and Pavlidis (Rocha, 1994).

Independently on the main focus of the considered papers, both printed and handwritten characters are typically described by ARGs (Cordella, 1996) (Foggia, 2001) (Foggia, 1999) (Lu, 1991) (Chen, 1990) (Rocha, 1994) (Sanfeliu, 1983) (Suganthan, 1998). Two description schemes have been used: i) the nodes of the graph represent the structural primitives in which a character can be decomposed after a thinning process and the edges represent the relations between them these primitives, or ii) the nodes are the junctions between strokes (singular points) and edges represent the primitives into which characters are decomposed. Authors dealing with Latin characters and Arabic digits (Cordella, 1996) (Foggia, 2001) Foggia, P., Sansone, C., Tortorella, F., & Vento, M. (1999) (Rocha, 1994) (Sanfeliu, 1983) use circular arcs and segments as primitives, while straight line segments or strokes are typically used in case of Chinese characters (Liu, 2000) (Lu, 1991) (Chen, 1990) (Suganthan, 1998). As regards the representation, a quite different approach is proposed in (Lee, 1999), where the authors propose an architecture for the recognition of handwritten Chinese character that integrates the feature extraction, the segmentation and the recognition phase. The feature extraction phase is performed by means of Gabor filters; such features are used to segment characters using an optimization module based on a genetic algorithm. Finally, elastic graph matching is used in the recognition phase. Besides this paper, other authors mainly use error-correcting graph matching for dealing with the high variability of handwritten characters. Another feature that is peculiar to this kind of applications is the graph size: graphs describing characters are typically made up of few nodes.

As regards technique-driven papers on handwritten recognition, in (Sanfeliu, 1983) and (Foggia, 1999) the authors use respectively handwritten characters and handwritten digits to validate a distance measure between ARGs in the framework of error-correcting graph matching. In the same framework, a matching algorithm using subgraph transformations is applied to handwritten characters (Cordella, 1996). Chinese characters are used in (Chan, 1996) as test case for a learning algorithm that build templates starting from fuzzy-attribute graphs; while in (Rangarajan, 1996) the authors present a sub-optimal method for exact graph matching, based on a lagrangian relaxation network, using handwritten digits for testing. Finally, handprinted digits are used as application of a graph learning algorithm (Foggia, 2001).

As regards the recognition of Chinese characters, both offline and on-line approaches are present in the literature. In (Suganthan, 1998) the matching between input graph and model graph for offline Chinese character recognition is performed by means of an Hopfield network (presented in (Suganthan, 1995)) that is specifically devised to allow the segments of a broken stroke of an input character to be matched to a stroke of the model graph.

The recognition of on-line handwritten Chinese character addressed by graph matching has the additional problem of a significant computational cost due to the large number of categories. Therefore for developing an on-line recognition system it is mandatory to find an adequate structural representation together with matching algorithms that can efficiently address this recognition problem. To this aim, some authors (Lu, 1991) (Chen, 1990) used a sort of hierarchical graphs to represent a character. Such graphs have two layers: nodes and edges in the first layer represent high level components and relations between them; while in the second layer each component is described by a graph in which nodes and edges represent the strokes of that component and their relations.

In (Liu, 2000) a Chinese character is described with a complete relational graph (CRG), where each node describe one of the segments in which a stroke obtained from a pen down-pen up movement on a digitizer can be decomposed. In order to reduce matching time, a suboptimal solution is proposed. The problem of matching CRGs is transformed into a two-layer assignment problem and solved with the Hungarian method.

Within the OCR field, in (Rocha, 1994) an error-correcting subgraph matching algorithm is used. It allows a multiple-to-one matching from a set of feature (a path) of an input graph to a feature of a model graph (prototype), on the basis of a set of predefined transformations. These graph transformations regard straightening of strokes, rewriting of strokes into arcs, insertion and deletion of features and attribute transformations. Having associated a cost to each transformation, the matching procedure for each input graph selects the prototype that gives rise to the matching with the minimum cost. It is worth noting that prototypes are manually defined, without using a specific learning procedure.

A quite peculiar approach is proposed in (Pavlidis, 1995), where the OCR problem is addressed with an ad-hoc matching defined between the so-called graph embeddings. A graph embedding, used in this paper for representing characters, is a labeled graph where each node is labeled with its coordinates in the x-y plane.

The handwritten digit string recognition problem has been addressed by (Filatov, 1995). Starting from an input image and after a thinning process, the authors construct a graph whose nodes are the branches or the ending points of the thinned image and whose edges represent lines of the thinned image. The input graph is then submitted to a segmentation process by using a set of heuristic rules. It gives rise to a number of separate symbols, called blocks. The recognition procedure consists in matching the input blocks with the prototype graphs of the digits, by applying a set of transformations to each input block. The matching is therefore an error-correcting graph-subgraph isomorphism. As transformations, the combination of two nodes into one, the transformation of a loop to an edge, and the deletion of edges or nodes are considered.

Finally, in the field of symbol and graphics recognition fall the paper of Lladòs et al. (Llados, 1996) (Llados, 2001), Changhua et al. (Changhua, 2000), Cordella et al. (Cordella, 2000) and Jiang et al. (Jiang, 1999)

While the last two papers are devoted to exploit the performance of an exact subgraph matching algorithm in detecting component parts within technical drawings (Cordella, 2000) and of a graph clustering algorithm (Jiang, 1999) respectively, the others have their main focus on the application domain.

As in case of character recognition, almost all the approaches use ARGs for representing symbols or graphical drawings; as already said, in (Cordella, 2000) an exact subgraph matching algorithm is used, while other authors employs different kinds of error-correcting subgraph matching algorithms for recognition. The main difference with respect to the case of character recognition is in the number of the nodes of graphs representing maps, diagrams or technical drawings that can be up to some hundreds or even thousands.

In (Llados, 2001) the problem of finding a model graph, that represents a prototype symbol, as a subgraph of an input graph, that represents a drawing, is addressed. To do this, a two-level graph representation for graphical symbols is used. In the first level, a vectorized document is approximated by graphs whose nodes represent characteristic points (i.e. junctions, end or corner points and so on) and whose edges approximate the segments between them. In the second level, data is organized in terms of Region Adjacency Graphs (RAG). The RAG nodes represent the regions, i.e., minimal closed loops of the first level graphs, and the edges are the neighboring relations between regions. Symbols are then recognized by means of an inexact subgraph

matching procedure that computes the minimum distance from a model RAG to an input RAG. This distance is considered to be the weighted sum of the costs of edit operations to transform one RAG into another one.

In (Llados, 1996) the authors try to identify building blocks in a hand-drawn floor plan. After a scanning and a vectorization process, drawings are described by means of ARGs. An inexact subgraph isomorphism algorithm based on discrete relaxation is used for matching the obtained ARG against model graphs representing the building elements. In order to speed up the process, a straight line Hough transform is also used. It allows the detections of regions filled with parallel straight lines, such as walls that are typically characterized by hatching patterns.

Finally in (Changhua, 2000) graphical hand-sketched symbols are represented through ARGs and a similarity measure calculated using the A* algorithm is used for recognition.

As regards identification problems, in the areas of face authentication and face recognition graph matching has been used in the systems proposed by Van Der Malsburg, Wiskott et al. (Lades, 1993) (Wiskott, 1997a) (Wiskott, 1997b), by Lim and Reinders (Lim, 2001), by Kotropoulos, Pitas and Tefas (Kotropoulos, 2000) (Tefas, 2001), by Duc et al. (Duc, 1999) and by Lyons et al. (Lyons, 1999). All these approaches use a graph, in particular a labeled rectangular grid, as an intermediate representation level for representing a face. In this grid, each node of the graph is associated to a specific facial landmark, called fiducial point. The labels associated to the nodes are of two different types: those based on Gabor coefficients (Duc, 1999) (Lades, 1993) (Lim, 2001) (Lyons, 1999) (Wiskott, 1997a) (Wiskott, 1997b), the so-called jets, and those made up of a vector of features evaluated on small areas of interest in the input image by means of multiscale dilation-erosion techniques (Kotropoulos, 2000) (Tefas, 2001). The face identification process is carried out by standard elastic graph matching algorithms. The grid representing the input face is compared with the ones representing face models. During the matching process the feature vectors associated to matched nodes are used to calculate a distance, so as to evaluate an overall distance between the two compared input graphs. The matching procedure is elastic in the sense that it copes with deformations, rotations or scale variations in the areas of interest of the input image.

In more details, one of the simplest description schemes is the one proposed in (Lim, 2001), where the authors describe a face image by a graph made of four nodes representing prefixed landmark points of the face as eyes, the nose and the mouth. Each node is labeled with a jet, while an edge of the graph is associated an attribute representing the distance existing between the points of the images relative to the nodes it connects. In this paper the elastic graph matching procedure is specifically tailored for dealing with affine transformations on the considered images in the neighbors of the landmark points, and the authors denote their matching algorithm as affine graph matching. The algorithm is used for localizing a face within an image, and this task is accomplished by maximizing the similarity measure proposed in (Wiskott, 1997); they take into account only the magnitude value of the jets, and use a genetic algorithm for exploring the search space more efficiently.

In the papers by Van der Malsburg, Wiskott et al. Lades, (1993) (Wiskott, 1997a) (Wiskott, 1997b) faces are described by a larger graph, in particular a rectangular graph (a grid graph) where each node label is associated to a vector of Gabor wavelet complex coefficients. In (Lades, 1993) only the magnitude of these coefficients is used in the recognition process; while in (Wiskott, 1997) the addition of the phase of the coefficients allowed to achieve a more accurate location of the landmark points within the considered image. Moreover, in the latter paper, a new data structure, called bunch graph, is introduced for dealing with generalized representations of faces. A face

bunch graph (FBG) is a sort of prototype of a set of images. As the previous graphs, it has a grid structure, and each node is devoted to represent the homologous nodes (fiducial points) of the represented graphs. The term bunch is used to denote the set of jets referring to the same fiducial point, and associated to a node of a FBG. The FBGs used to represent the images are obtained by an elastic graph matching procedure, described in more details in (Wiskott, 1997). The latter paper also explores the possibility of determining facial attributes, as sex, presence or absence of glasses or beard by using FBGs.

The magnitude of Gabor coefficients as features associated to grid nodes have been also used by Duc et al. (Duc, 1999) and Lyons et al. (Lyons, 1999) in combination with techniques based on discriminant analysis. In particular in (Duc, 1999), after the elastic graph matching phase, the authors use a local discriminant analysis on the feature vectors associated to grid node to verify the correct identity of the input face. In (Lyons, 1999), instead, the authors use discriminant analysis before the matching. In particular, they submit the feature vectors to a principal component analysis so as to reduce the dimensionality of the feature space. They also present results on sex, race and expression recognition.

Instead of using Gabor coefficients, Pitas and al. in (Kotropoulos, 2000) associate to each node of the grid a feature vector obtained by applying a multiscale dilation-erosion operator to the input image; they also propose a variant of the elastic graph matching, called MEGM (morphological elastic graph matching), that uses in the elastic graph matching procedure the feature vectors obtained by morphological operators. The use of such operators is justified by considering that the computation of Gabor coefficients is time consuming while dilation and erosions can be computed in a very fast way. Moreover, dilations and erosions deal with local minima or maxima in an image and revealed to provide an effective characterization of facial features. In a more recent paper (Tefas, 2001) the same authors describe a method to improve the recognition performance of MEGM. In particular they propose to estimate the best coefficients for weighting the similarity values associated to the grid nodes by means of discriminant analysis techniques and support vector machines.

Among the other applications dealing with face images, papers by Wang et al. (Wang, 1998) and Hong et al. (Hong, 2000) make use of graph matching techniques in the context of facial expression recognition while Elagin et al. (Elagin, 1998) use graph matching for pose estimation.

In particular, as usual in this application area, Hong et al. (Hong, 2000) use grid graphs, labeled with jets, for representing faces and rather standard elastic graph matching algorithm for recognizing seven face expressions: neutrality (that means no expression), happiness, sadness, anger, disgust, fear, and surprise.

Only three expressions are instead considered by Wang et al. in (Wang, 1998): happiness, surprise and anger. Indeed, their main goal is rather different and is aimed to estimate the changes of face expression from sequences of facial images. To this concern, the correspondence between images relative to successive frames is viewed as an elastic matching, even if the authors call it "labeled graph matching problem". In details, nineteen nodes are used to represent a face image. Each node is labeled using a template matrix of the 17x17 pixels (in gray levels) around each node, while to each edge is associated a measure of the distance between the nodes it links. The graph matching is carried out by minimizing a cost function that takes into account both the template similarity and the topological information.

In the framework of the pose estimation problem, Elagin et al. (Elagin, 1998) use graphs with 16 nodes to represent a face. Each node is associated to a facial landmark, as the pupils, the tip of the nose, the mouth angles and so on. Also in this case, the nodes are labeled with Gabor coefficients, while the labels of the edges represent the distances between the points of the image associated to the nodes. Five different orientations are considered for the pose. As in (Wiskott, 1997) a bunch graph is used to represent set of faces, and so a bunch graph matching procedure is used in order to perform the estimation.

The use of graph matching in the context of hand posture recognition is described in the paper by Triesch and von der Malsburg (Triesch, 2001). The authors employ a description and recognition scheme similar to those typically utilized in the field of face recognition. In fact, Gabor coefficient as graph labels and elastic graph matching for recognition are used. In addition to conventional Gabor jets, a colorGabor jet is introduced. It measures the similarity of each pixel to the skin color and together with the Gabor jet constitutes the so-called compound jet. The elastic graph matching procedure is also modified in order to cope with this compound jet. After describing each hand by graphs made up of fifteen nodes manually placed at anatomically significant points, twelve different hand postures are recognized.

Another biometric system is the one proposed by Burge and Burger (Burge, 2000), that makes use of features extracted by ear images for subject identification. They consider 300x500 pixels images, acquired using a CCD camera. Also in this case a middle level representation is used; after the localization of the ear within the images, an edge extraction based on the Canny operator is performed, followed by a curve extraction. On the basis of the regions delimited by the obtained curves, a Voronoi neighborhood graph is constructed. The identification process is accomplished by a subgraph error-correcting graph matching between the model graph and the input graph. To this aim, the authors propose a matching procedure that specifically takes into account the possibility of broken curves into the input graph. This procedure tries to merge neighboring curves if their Voronoi regions indicate that they are part of the same underlying feature.

Finally, fingerprint recognition by means of graph matching has been addressed in the papers by Maio and Maltoni (Maio, 1996) by Fan et al. (Fan, 1998) and by Neuhaus and Bunke (Neuhaus, 2003). This latter is a technique driven paper, while the other two are application-driven. They use different approaches both for representing fingerprint and for recognizing them.

The first paper (Maio, 1996) uses attributed relational graphs for describing fingerprints. The original fingerprint image is first processed in order to calculate a directional image. Then the directional image is segmented into regions, and each region is represented by a node of the graph. Each node has an attribute that measures the area of the region it represents, while each edge has three attributes: the phase difference between the average directions, the distance between the centroids, the length of the boundary between the regions represented by the two nodes it links. For the recognition phase an inexact graph matching is proposed, based on a branch and bound search within the space state.

On the other hand, Fan et al. (Fan, 1998) use bipartite graphs for representing the sample fingerprint image and template fingerprints. A fingerprint image is preprocessed in order to extract clusters of feature points (minutiae). A set of 24 attributes is then calculated for each feature point cluster and is associated to a node of the graph. The feature point clusters of a test image are the set of the left nodes of a fuzzy bipartite weighted graph while the feature point clusters of the template fingerprint are the right nodes. Fingerprint verification is then treated as a fuzzy bipartite graph matching problem.

A biological application is the identification of diatoms described by Fischer et. al (Fischer, 2002) and Ambauen et al. (Ambauen, 2003). Diatoms are unicellular algae found in water and in other places where there is sufficient humidity and light for allowing photosynthesis. The technique used for describing diatom images is the same used in the face recognition field. A middle level representation based on labeled grid graphs is used. On each image a rectangular 16x8 grid is superimposed and each node of the graph is associated to a rectangle of the image. Each node is labeled with thirteen features derived from the gray-level co-occurrence matrices and from the Gabor coefficients. In (Fischer, 2002) the matching procedure can be seen as a simple form of error-correcting graph matching. A dissimilarity measure is evaluated between two grid graphs as the sum of the distance between the features vectors associated to the nodes. Moreover, in order to cope with geometric distortions, also translations of the nodes are allowed and a specific cost is introduced into the dissimilarity measure in order to weigh such translations. In (Ambauen, 2003) a more complex matching algorithm is proposed, based on the addition of new edit operations to the classical set of deletion, insertion and mutation.

Stereo Reconstruction and Robot Navigation

Robot Navigation, also called Autonomous Navigation, consists in the detection of still or moving objects (such as obstacles a vehicle has to avoid) in a 3D scene, usually represented by means of a pair of stereo images. The problem is different from object recognition since the shape of the objects is not known a priori. However it turns out that this problem can be faced with techniques very similar to the ones used for 3D object recognition. In fact, by finding for each part of one of the two images the corresponding part in the other (which is similar to what an object recognizer does), the distance of each part from the camera can be estimated.

The Stereo Reconstruction, also called 3D Object Reconstruction, is aimed at deriving the three-dimensional structure of a scene from 2D images. Under some constraints on the objects being reconstructed, it can be faced with an approach that reduces this problem to object recognition, by defining a set of 3D structural primitives whose occurrence can be recognized in the image.

With more detail, Branca et. al (Branca, 1999) presents an application of graph matching to autonomous navigation. In particular, the detection of ground floor obstacles and of moving objects are considered. Relational graphs are used for object representation, where the object features extracted by means of the Moravec interest operator are the nodes and the edge linking them are weighted by projective invariant values. Given two graphs obtained from two different images acquired by a TV camera mounted on a mobile vehicle, the goal is to determine, into the association graph, the maximal clique of nodes that are mutually compatible according to the similarity imposed by the invariant relations encoded into the edges. The nodes of this clique will belong to the same object and this permit to detect into a given image the features that belong to an obstacle, or to individuate the feature pertaining to a moving object. In the paper an algorithm for finding the maximum edge-weighted clique in an high-order association graph is presented, based on an optimization procedure that use the Motzkin-Straus theorem.

As regards stereo reconstruction, Fuchs and Le Men in (Fuchs, 2000) and (Fuchs, 1999) use graph matching in the field of 3-D building reconstruction from aerial stereo-pairs. In particular, in (Fuchs, 1999) the 3-D object extraction problem is addressed, while in (Fuchs, 2000) the goal is the reconstruction of the structure of the roofs. They use a model driven strategy: the models used are ARGs, where each nodes represent a 3-D feature (a 3-D line segment, or a 3-D planar region, or a facade of a building), while each edge encodes a geometric property (such as parallelism, orthogonality, etc) between nodes. The building reconstruction is based on the computation of a subgraph isomorphism between a model and a graph built on a set of 3-D features derived from the images. As regards the matching procedure, in (Fuchs, 1999) they use the error-correcting

subgraph isomorphism detection presented in (Messmer, 1998), with an estimation of the subgraph distance based on a stochastic heuristic, while in (Fuchs, 2000) propose a modification of the algorithm proposed in (Messmer, 1998) in order to take benefit of an external information (e.g. an user input or a pre-computed information). If the correspondence between some nodes of the model and some nodes of the input data is already known before the matching, the search space of the matching problem can be pruned by integrating the external information in the error-correcting subgraph isomorphism algorithm.

Motion Estimation and Object Tracking

The Motion Estimation and Object Tracking problems are peculiar of intelligent video analytics. In particular, their common aspect is that they are focused on extracting some kind of information from the sequence of the frames composing a video. This implies a comparison between successive frames, and the need to establish a correspondence between regions of two frames representing the same object or the same part of it. In motion estimation, the goal is to measure the velocity of moving elements of the scene. In object tracking, which can be considered as an evolution of motion estimation, where the application should be able to follow the motion of an object and compute its trajectory, distinguishing the different objects presents in the scene.

The papers by Chen et. al (Chen, 2001), Gomila and Mayer (Gomila, 2001) and Conte et al. (Conte, 2004) (Conte, 2006) exploit the use of graph matching for object tracking in video sequences. They use different middle level representations and also different matching techniques.

In Conte et al. (Conte, 2004) the definition and the performance assessment of a tracking method devised for video-surveillance applications are presented. The tracking problem is factorized into two sub-problems: the first is the definition of a suitable measure of similarity between regions in adjacent frames. Provided with this measure, the second sub-problem is the search for an optimal matching between the regions appearing in the frames. As regards the first sub-problem (the definition of a similarity measure), several different metrics are proposed, jointly used during the detection phase, according to a sort of signal fusion approach. The sub-problem of the optimal matching has been instead formulated in a graph-theoretic framework, and then reduced to a weighted bipartite graph matching, for which a standard algorithm has been used.

Chen et al. (Chen, 2001) apply a shape contour extraction and a shadow deletion to each frame. Therefore they obtain the silhouette of each object within the scene. To each object a probability distribution is associated, that takes into account the intensity values of the area within the object contour. To model the multi-object tracking problem a bipartite graph is used. Each node represents an object and has as attributes its position, its intensity distribution and the dimension of its enclosing bounding box. The two classes of nodes in the bipartite graph are the so-called profile nodes and object nodes that correspond to the objects in the past and the present frame respectively. A bipartite matching algorithm is used to find the best match among nodes of the two successive frames in order to resolve the identities of the objects. If there are unmatched nodes, it implies that new objects have been detected and so new profiles will be created for tracking them within the successive frames.

On the other hand, Gomila and Mayer (Gomila, 2001) segment the image of each frame on the basis of the color information and represents the segmented image with a multivalued neighborhood graph. Node attributes measure the intrinsic features of the region they represent, while edge attributes represent relational constraints between nodes. Matching graphs relative to two successive frames permits to follow the objects along the video sequence. In order to cope with different

segmentation of the same object in two successive frames, split and merge operation are performed on the images before the matching. The proposed matching algorithm is an error-correcting one using the relaxation labeling.

Conte et al. (Conte, 2006) use a multi-resolution graph pyramid for representing objects at different levels of detail. They use a hierarchical graph matching procedure to deal with partial occlusions of the objects being tracked. The advantage of their approach is that it uses a fast, coarse grained, weighted bipartite graph matching as long as there are no occlusions in the scene. When two tracked objects come to overlap, a more refined subgraph isomorphism procedure is used to distinguish the parts of the occluding objects, possibly recurring to a finer level or detail until a reasonable solution is found.

Finally, Salotti and Laachfoubi in (Salotti, 2001) present an application of motion estimation in aerial videos. Given an aerial video, their aim is to estimate the shift of the part of the image that represents the smoke, in order to collect information for preventing fires. They use topographic graphs (that are similar to medial graphs) for describing aerial images. Each frame of the video is segmented on the basis of the color information and the smoke area is described by means of a topographic graph. The shift estimation is performed by means of an inexact matching procedure that defines a cost function for matching nodes of two topographic graphs relative to successive images. These cost function examines only shifts in a small square window centered on each node, since it is reasonable that the move of the smoke is not too fast.

Database Indexing, Retrieval, and Automatic Annotation

Among the problems to which Graph Based techniques have been applied, there are the indexing and the retrieval from image or video databases.

The indexing and retrieval problems are very similar from a conceptual point of view, but their different requirements in terms of performance and accuracy have brought to the use of different techniques and algorithms. In both cases, the goal is to find the images (or videos) in the database that are similar to a given query image (or video). While this can bear some resemblance to a recognition problem, there is an important conceptual difference: the images in the database are not partitioned in a set of fixed, non-overlapping classes, to which the unknown class of the query image belongs. Instead, the images have to be considered relevant to the query only on the basis of a vaguely defined perceptual similarity; there is no clear-cut, exact desired response for the system. Furthermore, the number of items in the database can be really large, imposing strong constraints on the performance of the algorithm. In the retrieval problem it is usually desired that the result images are provided in an order that reflects a similarity scoring, to allow the user to choose interactively the one that fits his needs. This mandates for a matching technique that yields some sort of cost or distance, such as error-correcting graph matching techniques. Retrieval from video databases is similar to retrieval from static image databases from a conceptual point of view; the main differences are the considerably larger size of the databases and the possibility to exploit information about the motion of parts of the scene to improve the retrieval performance.

As regards the indexing problem, the focus is to obtain a fast screening of the images before performing a retrieval operation, to reduce the search time. So it is not required to provide a distance measure, and it is acceptable if some images that are not relevant to the query are returned in the result set (the converse is not true, i.e. it is not acceptable if indexing excludes strongly relevant images). The main concerns for indexing are how fast it performs, and how many non-relevant images it is able to filter out.

A further vision-based problem that is of interest for applications working with video databases is the recognition, on the basis of the object trajectories, of events that bear a specific meaning within the context of the application: this gives rise to the possibility of Automatic Annotation of the video sequence, allowing a user to perform retrieval with classic, keyword-based search.

Among the papers that address both the indexing and the retrieval problem, Berretti et al. in (Berretti, 2001) propose the use of a metric indexing scheme for managing the organization of large archives of ARGs with a common size. In particular, the indexing is performed using m-trees. They also propose a new algorithm for retrieval, combining the A* search with an original look-ahead estimate. The estimate is derived as the optimal solution of a weighted assignment, which relaxes the optimal look-ahead problem so as to remove its basic factor of exponential complexity. This sort of minimal simplification results in an extremely well-informed estimate which can still be computed in polynomial time. The database used for testing the approach is composed of about 1000 images, coming from paintings of the library of a web-museum. For each image of the database 10 further images are generated, synthetically changing color and color positions. In the system they proposed, for querying the database, an user can both select an example image or submit a query by sketch by drawing a set of colored regions and by arranging them in order to represent the expected appearance of the searched images. All the images are modeled with ARGs having a fixed number of nodes, namely eight. Each node comes from the clustering of the color histogram in the $L^*u^*v^*$ color space and the node attributes encode the triple of normalized coordinates of the average color of the cluster. For any two objects corresponding to different regions in the user sketch, the edge attribute encodes the relationship between the regions themselves.

In the paper by Petrakis and Faloutsos (Petrakis, 1997) ARGs that model medical images are reduced to a vectorial representation, so enabling R-tree indexing, under the assumption that all the graphs contain a set of anchor entities with predefined labels. Non-anchor entities are also allowed, but their number determines a linear degradation in the efficiency of the index. In addition to this indexing technique, the authors propose a subgraph isomorphism algorithm with a distance measure for retrieval. In particular, given an iconic query, all the images under a suitably chosen threshold are selected. As regards the representation, each image is segmented into regions, each one represented by a node. Size, roundness and orientation of each region have been chosen as node attributes.

Among the papers that mainly address the retrieval problem, Cho and Yoo in (Cho, 1998) use graphs whose nodes represent objects of the image, while the edges encode spatial relations between objects. An object is characterized by its color, the ratio between its area and the whole image area, the ratios between the x-coordinate and the width and the ratio between the y-coordinate and the height of the image. The attribute edge can assume one of the eight possible spatial relations between two objects (N,NE,E,SE,S,SW,W,NW). They also define the prime edge graph, obtainable from a graph by deleting edges that are unnecessary for representing the structure of the image. The matching is realized with a subgraph isomorphism algorithm that makes use of a similarity measure.

In (Folkers, 2000) Folkers et al. propose an exact subgraph isomorphism with a bottom-up strategy. They also define a similarity measure for pruning some isomorphism checks. The proposed measure takes into account both the contextual and the spatial similarity between ARGs. In their description scheme, once again nodes represent the symbols of the image and the edge the relationships between them.

In the papers by Hancock and Huet (Huet, 1998) (Huet, 1999) (Huet, 2001), the aim is to retrieve 2D images from large databases. In their description scheme, a set of line-patterns are represented by means of a special type of ARG, i.e., a N-nearest-neighbor graph. In a N-nearest-neighbor graph, each node represent a line structure segmented from a 2D image. For each node n of the graph exactly N edges are created, the ones that link n to the nodes representing the N line segments having the closest distances from the line represented by n itself. Distances between lines are computed by considering distances between their centers.

In (Huet, 1998) the authors use 6 nearest-neighbor graphs. The line orientation and the line length constitute the attributes of the nodes, while the measure of the relative position and of the relative orientation of two lines whose representing nodes are linked by an edge are the attribute of that edge. The proposed matching is of inexact type; in particular a fuzzy variant of the Hausdorff distance that uses only the values of the edge attributes is proposed for comparing graphs. For each image graphs of 3-400 nodes are considered. A first screening of a possible query result is made by considering only the histograms of the edge attributes that are compared using the Bhattacharyya distance. Then, the fuzzy version of the Hausdorff distance is employed on the N nearest images that are found, for refining the search.

In (Huet, 1999) the node attributes are two normalized histograms, the one of the relative angles and the one of the relative lengths with respect to the remaining line segments in the pattern. The matching process is realized by means of a Bayesian graph-matching algorithm that utilizes a two step process. Firstly, a correspondence matches between the nodes in the query pattern and each of the patterns in the database is established. This is made by maximizing an a posteriori measurement probability. In particular, the authors use an extension of the graph-matching technique reported by Wilson and Hancock in (Wilson, 1997); in order to minimize the computational overheads associated with establishing correspondence matches only edge information is used.

Once the maximum a posteriori probability correspondence matches have been established for each pattern in the database, the pattern which has maximum matching probability is selected. This is made by using the Bhattacharyya distance for comparing the histogram attributes of the matched nodes.

In (Huet, 2001) Huet et al. present an application of the image retrieval for verifying similarities among different technical drawings representing patents. They use ARGs obtained as 6-nearest-neighbour graph from the line drawings, using the same description model of (Huet, 1998). The matching is of inexact type, and is realized by means of the fuzzy variant of the Hausdorff distance presented in (Huet, 1998).

Among the other representation schemes employed in the literature, in (Gregory, 2002) Gregory and Kittler utilizes Region Adjacency Graphs. Images are segmented so that a RAG can be built. Each pixel in the image is represented as a 5D vector, where the first three dimensions are the RGB color values for the pixel and the last two dimensions are the pixel coordinates. This feature space is then clustered and to every pixel a label corresponding to the cluster which it has been classified to is given. The region labels correspond to homogeneous color regions within the image. A connected component analysis stage ensures that only to connected pixels may be assigned the same label. At this point each obtained region is represented by a node, whose attributes are the number of pixels and the average values of the red, green and blue pixels within the region it represent. The segmentation is further improved by merging adjacent nodes which have a small number of pixels, or 'similar' feature space representation. The database used for the testing phase is made up of flag images, that give rise to graphs of about fifteen nodes. The matching is performed by using an error correcting subgraph isomorphism with edit operations and the A* procedure.

On the other hand, in (Sharvit, 1998) Sharvit et al. use shock graphs for representing images. The shock graph is directly extracted from the image on the basis of the symmetries exhibited by the image itself. As regards the matching procedure, they use a weighted graph matching that is a variant of the method presented in (Gold, 1996). For testing, they employ a database consisting of binary shapes, and match greyscale images of isolated objects and user-drawn sketches against this database. The resulting shock graphs are made up of few nodes.

Finally, in (Park, 1997) Park et al. propose the use of dual graphs for representing images. In particular, an ARG called MCAG (modified color adjacency graph) is used for indexing and a spatial variance graph (SVG) is used to disambiguate different images having equal MCAG representations. In a MCAG each node represents a bin of the quantized RGB color histogram. Node attributes are then the pixel count of each RGB chromatic component, while the edge attributes encodes spatial adjacency (based on 8-connectivity) between two color regions. The average number of nodes of a MCAG is about 100. On the other hand, each node of the SVG graph has as attribute the within-class variance relative to the pixels of the node it represents, while each edge attribute encodes the between-class variance. Graph matching is performed by defining a similarity measure directly obtainable by the adjacency matrices of the graphs.

Finally, in (De Mauro, 2003) a learning technique for facing the retrieval problem is proposed by De Mauro et al. Database images are described by means of RAG that are successively transformed into DOAG (directed ordered acyclic graphs). This transformation becomes necessary because it is more difficult to process undirected graphs than directed ones. The task of learning the search criteria for visual retrieval is accomplished by means of a Recursive Neural Network that maps DOAGs into vectors. This net learns to map DOAG representing similar images into near vectors. Then, the retrieval problem is reformulated as the one of finding the N-nearest neighbors of the vector into which the net transform the DOAG of the query image.

In the framework of the retrieval from video databases, Shearer et al. (Shearer, 2001a) (Shearer, 2001b) proposed two different approaches that do not make particular hypotheses on the nature of the video at hand, where Doulamis et al. (Doulamis, 1999) propose a system specifically tailored for the retrieval of people images in a video database. Furthermore, in the first two papers ARGs are used for representing video frames, while the last one propose the use of pyramidal graphs.

Entering into details, in (Shearer, 2001) Shearer et al. describe a new algorithm to solve the largest common subgraph problem. Such algorithm significantly reduces the computational complexity of detection of the largest common subgraph between a known database of models, and a query given on-line. This approach can be fruitfully applied to video databases. In fact, when searching a video database, we are typically interested in the largest subpicture match that can be found. So, the largest common subgraph method will find the largest subpicture in common between a query image and a database of video frames. As regard the representation, ARGs are used. The authors consider each frame of the video and decompose it into objects. Then, graph nodes represent objects, while the edges are labeled with one of five categories (Disjoint, Meets, Contains, Belongs to, Overlaps) that represent the relationships between two objects. The proposed retrieval procedure is realized by using a decision tree algorithm based on a decision tree constructed using the adjacency matrix representation for the model graphs.

A different approach is presented in (Shearer, 2001), where a modified version of an algorithm presented by Bunke and Messmer in (Bunke, 1997) is proposed. It is able to cope with dynamically changing graphs. Such graphs can be employed for representing videos: the sequence of images that make a video can be represented by means of an initial graphs that represent the initial image and a sequence of graph edit operation that represent

the successive images. As in the previous paper, for each image the nodes of the graph represent objects, while the edges encode the spatial relations between objects. An experimental evaluation of the algorithm is also presented, by using query graphs with 9 nodes against models having 4-10 nodes. In particular, the application of this algorithm consists in querying a video database with a sequence of frames. Each query frame is built starting from a number of object labels that can be spatially arranged by the user. The system transforms these query frames into a graph representing the initial frame and into a set of edit operations. Then, it uses the proposed matching algorithm in order to find the video sequence that match the sequence of selected frames.

In (Doulamis, 1999) Doulamis et al. propose a system for extracting people images from MPEG-coded videos. After a segmentation phase in which objects such as the face, the human body and the background are extracted from each frame, graphs are used for representing these objects and their spatial relationships. As attribute of the nodes, the average color and the texture of an object, as well as its size and location within the scene are considered. The authors make use of two different types of graphs, one with edge attributes, that encode the direction and the orientation between two objects, and another one without edge attributes. Moreover, in order to enhance the querying flexibility of their system, they also propose a further decomposition of each node into other graphs, so giving rise to a pyramidal graph representation of the visual content. As an example, the human face can be considered as an object containing the regions of eyes, mouth and lips, each having their own properties. As regards the problem of retrieval from a video database, they do not clarify in the paper what type of graph matching technique they use.

A quite peculiar approach to the problem of retrieval from databases is the one presented by Ozer et al. in (Ozer, 1999). The aim of this work is to annotate images and/or videos where a particular object of interest (OOI) is present. So, a simple textual query can be performed to extract images of OOI from a preprocessed database. As an example, they consider cars in video and image libraries, that they describe using ARGs. In case of video sequences, the feature points of an object are tracked and then grouped together according to their moving directions and distances. The object extraction is performed by means of a color image segmentation technique combined with an edge detector algorithm. Since an object usually contains several sub-objects (in this case wheels, windows, lights, etc. of a car) a hierarchical segmentation scheme is also proposed. Three different views of a car are considered - front view, rear view and side view. The three subgraphs relative to these views are joined together to form a unique graph representing all the possible views of the object. As attributes of the nodes, Hu moments and the compactness of the segmented regions are considered. Given two adjacent regions represented by two nodes, the ratio of the areas, the ratio of the perimeters, the relative position and orientation, and the overlapping area between two adjacent regions are the attribute of the edge that links those nodes. As regards the graph matching procedure, they propose an inexact subgraph matching with a matching cost based on the attribute values, using a depth-first search with a brute force approach.

Model-Based Segmentation

In Model-Based Segmentation, the application must compare a given image with a reference model, and partition the image into regions labeled according to the corresponding regions in the model. This task is complicated by the fact that the comparison must take into account possibly severe spatial deformations of the image with respect to the model, and that the pixels belonging to adjacent regions may be not so easy to differentiate on the basis of intensity, color or texture. An application field in which this problem recurs frequently is the analysis of biomedical images,

both in 2D (for example, radiographic images) and in 3D (e.g. Computer Aided Tomography, CAT). In this field, often an image must be confronted with an atlas representing the anatomical district in order to correctly separate the different tissues.

In the paper by Dumay et al. (Dumay, 1992), the authors start from an arteriogram image and project a geometric model of the artery against the image. From this projected model, an ARG made up of about ten nodes is constructed: the nodes of the graph represents arterial segments and have as attributes the position, the mean diameter and the orientation of the segments, while edges represent the parental relationship (parent-child and grandparent-child) between segments. Starting from the anatomy of a left coronary tree of normal functioning hearts, an inexact graph matching procedure is used in order to assign anatomic labels to the node of an input image. Since missing branch and/or false structures can corrupt the input image, a cost function is defined in order to cope with transformations (substitution, insertion and deletion of a node and/or an edge) of the input graph. An A* algorithm is used to perform the state space search.

Also the paper by Charnoz et al. (Charnoz, 2005) faces a somewhat analogous problem: the matching of several CAT-images of the intra-hepatic vascular system of a same patient, acquired at different times. The authors propose an error-correcting tree matching algorithm that is robust with respect to topological modifications.

In the paper by Haris et al. (Haris, 1999), the authors use ARGs to represent the CAT. Starting from the input image, the CAT is detected by constructing an approximation of its centerline and borders. This results in a directed acyclic graph representing the CAT. The attribute of each node of this graph are the position of the artery element it represents, the direction of the artery and its approximate width.

Given the input graph and a 3-D CAT model which encapsulates the expected anatomic and geometric structure of a normal human CAT, a graph matching algorithm assigns the appropriate labels to the input CAT using weighted maximal cliques on the association graph corresponding to the two given graphs. So the labeling problem is reformulated as one of finding the best maximal clique of the association graph.

CONCLUSION

In this chapter we have presented an overview of the Graph Matching techniques that in the last years have been used for Computer Vision applications. Also, we have examined application fields such as Object/Shape Recognition, Classification and Identify Verification, Stereo Reconstruction and Autonomous Navigation, Motion Estimation and Object Tracking, Indexing, Retrieval and Automatic Annotation of Image/Video Databases, Model-based Segmentation, and for each field we have discussed the most important works that have applied the aforementioned Graph Matching techniques, in order to understand which technique is most suited for each application domain.

REFERENCES

Aho, A. V., Hopcroft, J. E., & Ullman, J. D. (1974). *The design and analysis of computer algorithms.* Addison Wesley.

Allen, R., Cinque, L., Tanimoto, S., Shapiro, L. G., & Yasuda, D. (1997). A parallel algorithm for graph matching and its MasPar implementation. *IEEE Transactions on Parallel and Distributed Systems, 8*(5), 490–501. doi:10.1109/71.598276

Almohamad, H. A., & Duffuaa, S. O. (1993). A linear programming approach for the weighted graph matching problem. *IEEE Transactions on Pattern Analysis and Machine Intelligence, 15*(5), 522–525. doi:10.1109/34.211474

Ambauen, R., Fischer, S., & Bunke, H. (2003). Graph edit distance with node splitting and merging, and its application to diatom identification. *Lecture Notes in Computer Science, 2726.* doi:10.1007/3-540-45028-9_9

Ambler, A. P., Barrow, H. G., Brown, C. M., Burstall, R. M., & Popplestone, R. J. (1973). A versatile computer-controlled assembly system. *Proceedings of the 3rd International Joint Conference on Artificial Intelligence,* (pp. 298-307).

Baeza-Yates, R., & Valiente, G. (2000). An image similarity measure based on graph matching. *Proceeding of the Seventh International Symposium on String Processing and Information Retrieval,* (pp. 28 – 38).

Bai, X., & Hancock, E. R. (2004). Graph matching using spectral embedding and alignment. *Proceedings of the 17th International Conference on Pattern Recognition,* (pp. 398–401).

Balas, E., & Yu, C. S. (1986). Finding a maximum clique in an arbitrary graph. *SIAM Journal on Computing, 15*(4), 1054–1068. doi:10.1137/0215075

Bauckhage, C., Wachsmuth, S., & Sagerer, G. (2001). 3D assembly recognition by matching functional subparts. *Proceedings of the 3rd IAPR-TC15 Workshop on Graph-based Representations in Pattern Recognition,* (pp. 95 – 104).

Belongie, S., & Malik, J. (2000). Matching with shape contexts. *Proceedings of IEEE Workshop on Content-based Access of Image and Video Libraries,* (pp. 20 – 26).

Berretti, S., Del Bimbo, A., & Vicario, E. (2000a). A look-ahead strategy for graph matching in retrieval by spatial arrangement. *International Conference on Multimedia and Expo,* (pp. 1721 – 1724).

Berretti, S., Del Bimbo, A., & Vicario, E. (2000b). The computational aspect of retrieval by spatial arrangement. *Proceedings of 15th International Conference on Pattern Recognition*, pp. 1047 - 1051.

Berretti, S., Del Bimbo, A., & Vicario, E. (2001). Efficient matching and indexing of graph models in content-based retrieval. *IEEE Transactions on Pattern Analysis and Machine Intelligence, 23*(10), 1089–1105. doi:10.1109/34.954600

Boeres, M. C., Ribeiro, C. C., & Bloch, I. (2004). A randomized heuristic for scene recognition by graph matching. In C. C. Ribeiro & S. L. Martins (Eds.), *Lecture Notes in Computer Science, Vol. 3059, Experimental and Efficient Algorithms: Third International Workshop*, (WEA 2004), (pp. 100 – 113).

Bomze, I. M. (1997). Evolution towards the maximum clique. *Journal of Global Optimization, 10*, 143–164. doi:10.1023/A:1008230200610

Branca, A., Stella, E., & Distante, A. (1999). Feature matching by searching maximum clique on high order association graph. *Proceedings of the 10th International Conference on Image Analysis and Processing*, (pp. 642 – 658).

Bron, C., & Kerbosch, J. (1973). Finding all cliques of an undirected graph. *Communications of the ACM, 16*(9), 575–577. doi:10.1145/362342.362367

Bunke, H. (1997). On a relation between graph edit distance and maximum common subgraph. *Pattern Recognition Letters, 18*(8), 689–694. doi:10.1016/S0167-8655(97)00060-3

Bunke, H. (1999). Error correcting graph matching: On the influence of the underlying cost function. *IEEE Transactions on PAMI, 21*(9), 917–922. doi:10.1109/34.790431

Bunke, H., Foggia, P., Guidobaldi, C., & Vento, M. (2003). Graph clustering using the weighted minimum common supergraph. In Hancock, E., & Vento, M. (Eds.), *Graph Based Representations in Pattern Recognition* (*Vol. 2726*, pp. 235–246). Lecture Notes in Computer Science Berlin, Germany: Springer. doi:10.1007/3-540-45028-9_21

Bunke, H., Foggia, P., Vento, M., Sansone, C., & Guidobaldi, C. (2002). A comparison of algorithms for maximum common subgraph on randomly connected graphs. *Proceeding of the Joint IAPR International Workshops SSPR and SPR*, (pp. 123 – 132).

Bunke, H., & Messmer, B. T. (1997). Recent advances in graph matching. *International Journal of Pattern Recognition and Artificial Intelligence, 11*(1), 169–203. doi:10.1142/S0218001497000081

Bunke, H., & Shearer, K. (1998). A graph distance metric based on the maximal common subgraph. *Pattern Recognition Letters, 19*(3), 255–259. doi:10.1016/S0167-8655(97)00179-7

Bunke, H., & Vento, M. (1999). Benchmarking of graph matching algorithms. *Proceedings of the 2nd IAPR TC-15 GbR Workshop*, Haindorf, (pp. 109-114).

Burge, M., & Burger, W. (2000). Ear biometrics in computer vision. *Proceedings of 15th International Conference on Pattern Recognition*, (pp. 822 – 826).

Carcassoni, M., & Hancock, E. R. (2001). Weighted graph-matching using modal clusters. *Proceedings of the 3rd IAPR-TC15 Workshop on Graph-based Representations in Pattern Recognition*, (pp. 260 – 269).

Chan, K. P. (1996). Learning templates from fuzzy examples in structural pattern recognition. *IEEE Transactions on Systems, Man and Cybernetics. Part B, 26*(1), 118–123.

Changhua, L., Bing, Y., & Weixin, X. (2000). On-line hand-sketched graphics recognition based on attributed relational graph matching. *Proceedings of the 3rd World Congress on Intelligent Control and Automation,* (pp. 2549 – 2553).

Charnoz, A., Agnus, V., Malandain, G., Soler, L., & Tajine, M. (2005). Tree matching applied to vascular system. In L. Brun & M. Vento (Eds.), *Proceedings of 5th IAPR-TC-15 Workshop on Graph-based Representations in Pattern Recognition (GbRPR 2005), Lecture Notes in Computer Science, Vol. 3434,* (pp. 183-192).

Chen, H. T., Lin, H., & Liu, T. L. (2001). Multi-object tracking using dynamical graph matching. *Proceedings of the 2001 IEEE Computer Society Conference on Computer Vision and Pattern Recognition,* (pp. 210 – 217).

Chen, L. H., & Lieh, J. R. (1990). Handwritten character recognition using a 2-layer random graph model by relaxation matching. *Pattern Recognition, 23,* 1189–1205. doi:10.1016/0031-3203(90)90115-2

Cho, S. J., & Yoo, S. I. (1998). Image retrieval using topological structure of user sketch. *IEEE International Conference on Systems, Man, and Cybernetics,* (pp. 4584 – 4588).

Christmas, W. J., Kittler, J., & Petrou, M. (1995). Structural matching in computer vision using probabilistic relaxation. *IEEE Transactions on Pattern Analysis and Machine Intelligence, 17*(8), 749–764. doi:10.1109/34.400565

Conte, D., Foggia, P., Guidobaldi, C., Limongiello, A., & Vento, M. (2004). An object tracking algorithm combining different cost functions. In Campilho, A., & Kamel, M. (Eds.), *ICIAR 2004 (Vol. 3212,* pp. 614–622). Lecture Notes in Computer Science Berlin, Germany: Springer. doi:10.1007/978-3-540-30126-4_75

Conte, D., Foggia, P., Jolion, J. M., & Vento, M. (2006). A graph-based, multi-resolution algorithm for tracking objects in presence of occlusions. *Pattern Recognition, 39*(4), 562–572. doi:10.1016/j.patcog.2005.10.012

Conte, D., Foggia, P., Sansone, C., & Vento, M. (2004). Thirty years of graph matching in pattern recognition. *International Journal of Pattern Recognition and Artificial Intelligence, 18*(3), 265–298. doi:10.1142/S0218001404003228

Conte, D., Guidobaldi, C., & Sansone, C. (2003). A comparison of three maximum common subgraph algorithms on a large database of labeled graphs. In Hancock, E., & Vento, M. (Eds.), *Graph Based Representations in Pattern Recognition (Vol. 2726,* pp. 130–141). Lecture Notes in Computer Science Berlin, Germany: Springer. doi:10.1007/3-540-45028-9_12

Cordella, L. P., Foggia, P., Sansone, C., Tortorella, F., & Vento, M. (1998). Graph matching: A fast algorithm and its evaluation. *Proceedings of 14th International Conference on Pattern Recognition,* (pp. 1582 - 1584).

Cordella, L. P., Foggia, P., Sansone, C., & Vento, M. (1996). An efficient algorithm for the inexact matching of ARG graphs using a contextual transformational model. *Proceedings of the 13th International Conference on Pattern Recognition,* (pp. 180 – 184).

Cordella, L. P., Foggia, P., Sansone, C., & Vento, M. (1997). Subgraph transformations for inexact matching of attributed relational graphs. *Computing, 12,* 43–52.

Cordella, L. P., Foggia, P., Sansone, C., & Vento, M. (1999). Performance evaluation of the VF graph matching algorithm. *Proceedings of the International Conference on Image Analysis and Processing,* (pp. 1172 – 1177).

Cordella, L. P., Foggia, P., Sansone, C., & Vento, M. (2000). Fast graph matching for detecting CAD image components. *Proceedings of 15th International Conference on Pattern Recognition*, (pp. 1034 – 1037).

Cordella, L. P., Foggia, P., Sansone, C., & Vento, M. (2001). An improved algorithm for matching large graphs. *Proceedings of the 3rd IAPR-TC15 Workshop on Graph-based Representations in Pattern Recognition*, (pp. 149 – 159).

Cordella, L. P., Foggia, P., Sansone, C., & Vento, M. (2002). Learning structural shape descriptions from examples. *Pattern Recognition Letters*, *23*(12), 1427–1437. doi:10.1016/S0167-8655(02)00103-4

Cordella, L. P., Foggia, P., Sansone, C., & Vento, M. (2004). A (sub)graph isomorphism algorithm for matching large graphs. *IEEE Transactions on Pattern Analysis and Machine Intelligence*, *26*(10), 1367–1372. doi:10.1109/TPAMI.2004.75

De Mauro, C., Diligenti, M., Gori, M., & Maggini, M. (2003). Similarity learning for graph-based image representations. *Pattern Recognition Letters*, *24*(8), 1115–1122. doi:10.1016/S0167-8655(02)00258-1

De Santo, M., Foggia, P., Sansone, C., & Vento, M. (2003). A large database of graphs and its use for benchmarking graph isomorphism algorithms. *Pattern Recognition Letters*, *24*(8), 1067–1079. doi:10.1016/S0167-8655(02)00253-2

Demko, C. (1997). Generalization of two hypergraphs: Algorithm of calculation of the greatest sub-hypergraph common to two hypergraphs annotated by semantic information. *Computing*, *12*, 1–9.

Dempster, A. P., Laird, N. M., & Rubin, D. B. (1977). Maximum-likelihood from incomplete data via the EM algorithm. *Journal of the Royal Statistical Society. Series B. Methodological*, *39*, 1–38.

Depiero, F., Trivedi, M., & Serbin, S. (1996). Graph matching using a direct classification of node attendance. *Pattern Recognition*, *29*(6), 1031–1048. doi:10.1016/0031-3203(95)00140-9

Doulamis, N., Doulamis, A., & Kollias, S. (1999). Efficient content-based retrieval of humans from video databases. *Proceedings of the International Workshop on Recognition, Analysis, and Tracking of Faces and Gestures in Real-Time Systems*, (pp. 89 – 95).

Duc, B., Fischer, S., & Bigun, J. (1999). Face authentication with Gabor information on deformable graphs. *IEEE Transactions on Image Processing*, *8*(4), 504–516. doi:10.1109/83.753738

Dumay, A. C. M., van der Geest, R. J., Gerbrands, J. J., Jansen, E., & Reiber, J. H. C. (1992). Consistent inexact graph matching applied to labelling coronary segments in arteriograms. *Proceedings of the International Conference on Pattern Recognition, Conference C*, (pp. 439 – 442).

Dupé, F. X., & Brun, L. (2009). Tree covering within a graph kernel framework for shape classification. In *Proceedings of the Fifteenth Int. Conference on Image Analysis and Processing*.

Durand, P. J., Pasari, R., Baker, J. W., & Tsai, C.-C. (1999). An efficient algorithm for similarity analysis of molecules. *Internet Journal of Chemistry, 2*.

El-Sonbaty, Y., & Ismail, M. A. (1998). A new algorithm for subgraph optimal isomorphism. *Pattern Recognition*, *31*(2), 205–218. doi:10.1016/S0031-3203(97)00041-1

Elagin, E., Steffens, J., & Neven, H. (1998). Automatic pose estimation system for human faces based on bunch graph matching technology. *Proceedings of the Third IEEE International Conference on Automatic Face and Gesture Recognition*, (pp. 136 – 141).

Emms, D., Wilson, R., & Hancock, E. R. (2007). Graph embedding using quantum commute times. In *Graph-Based Representations in Pattern Recognition* (*Vol. 4538*, pp. 371–382). LNCS. doi:10.1007/978-3-540-72903-7_34

Englert, R., Cremers, A. B., & Seelmann-Eggebert, J. (1997). Recognition of polymorphic pattern in parameterized graphs for 3D building reconstruction. *Computing, 12*, 11–20.

Eshera, M. A., & Fu, K. S. (1984a). A similarity measure between attributed relational graphs for image analysis. *Proceedings of the 7th International Conference on Pattern Recognition*, (pp. 75 – 77).

Eshera, M. A., & Fu, K. S. (1984b). A graph distance measure for image analysis. *IEEE Transactions on Systems, Man, and Cybernetics, 14*(3), 398–408.

Eshera, M. A., & Fu, K. S. (1986). An image understanding system using attributed symbolic representation and inexact graph-matching. *IEEE Transactions on Pattern Analysis and Machine Intelligence, 8*(5), 604–618. doi:10.1109/TPAMI.1986.4767835

Fan, K. C., Liu, C. W., & Wang, Y. K. (1998). A fuzzy bipartite weighted graph matching approach to fingerprint verification. *Proceedings of the IEEE International Conference on Systems, Man, and Cybernetics*, (pp. 4363 – 4368).

Feder, J. (1971). Plex languages. *Information Sciences, 3*, 225–241. doi:10.1016/S0020-0255(71)80008-7

Fernàndez, M. L., & Valiente, G. (2001). A graph distance metric combining maximum common subgraph and minimum common supergraph. *Pattern Recognition Letters, 22*(6), 753–758. doi:10.1016/S0167-8655(01)00017-4

Filatov, A., Gitis, A., & Kil, I. (1995). Graph-based handwritten digit string recognition. *Proceedings of the 3rd International Conference on Document Analysis and Recognition*, (pp. 845 – 848).

Fischer, S., Gilomen, K., & Bunke, H. (2002). Identification of diatoms by grid graph matching. *Proceeding of the Joint IAPR International Workshops SSPR and SPR*, (pp. 94 – 103).

Fischler, M., & Elschlager, R. (1973). The representation and matching of pictorial structures. *IEEE Transactions on Computers, 22*, 67–92. doi:10.1109/T-C.1973.223602

Foggia, P., Genna, R., & Vento, M. (2001). Symbolic vs. connectionist learning: an experimental comparison in a structured domain. *IEEE Transactions on Knowledge and Data Engineering, 13*(2), 176–195. doi:10.1109/69.917559

Foggia, P., Sansone, C., Tortorella, F., & Vento, M. (1999). Definition and validation of a distance measure between structural primitives. *Pattern Analysis & Applications, 2*, 215–227. doi:10.1007/s100440050030

Foggia, P., Sansone, C., & Vento, M. (2001). A database of graphs for isomorphism and subgraph isomorphism benchmarking. *Proceedings of the 3rd IAPR TC-15 Workshop on Graph-based Representations in Pattern Recognition*, Ischia, May 23-25, (pp. 176-187).

Foggia, P., Sansone, C., & Vento, M. (2001). A performance comparison of five algorithms for graph isomorphism. *Proceedings of the 3rd IAPR-TC15 Workshop on Graph-based Representations in Pattern Recognition*, (pp. 188 – 199).

Folkers, A., Samet, H., & Soffer, A. (2000). Processing pictorial queries with multiple instances using isomorphic subgraphs. *Proceedings of the 15th International Conference on Pattern Recognition*, (pp. 51 – 54).

Fuchs, F., & Le Men, H. (1999). Building reconstruction on aerial images through multi-primitive graph matching. *Proceedings of the 2nd IAPR-TC15 Workshop on Graph-based Representations in Pattern Recognition,* (pp. 21 – 30).

Fuchs, F., & Le Men, H. (2000). Efficient subgraph isomorphism with 'a priori' knowledge. *Proceeding of the Joint IAPR International Workshops SSPR and SPR,* (pp. 427 – 436).

Gendreau, M., Salvail, L., & Soriano, P. (1993). Solving the maximum clique problem using a Tabu search approach. *Annals of Operations Research, 41,* 385–403. doi:10.1007/BF02023002

Ghahraman, D. E., Wong, A. K. C., & Au, T. (1980). Graph optimal monomorphism algorithms. *IEEE Transactions on Systems, Man, and Cybernetics, 10*(4), 181–188. doi:10.1109/TSMC.1980.4308468

Ghahraman, D. E., Wong, A. K. C., & Au, T. (1980). Graph monomorphism algorithms. *IEEE Transactions on Systems, Man, and Cybernetics, 10*(4), 189–197. doi:10.1109/TSMC.1980.4308468

Gold, S., & Rangarajan, A. (1996). A graduated assignment algorithm for graph matching. *IEEE Transactions on Pattern Analysis and Machine Intelligence, 18*(4), 377–388. doi:10.1109/34.491619

Gomila, C., & Meyer, F. (2001). Tracking objects by graph matching of image partition sequences. *Proceedings of the 3rd IAPR-TC15 Workshop on Graph-based Representations in Pattern Recognition,* (pp. 1 – 11).

Gregory, L., & Kittler, J. (2002). Using graph search techniques for contextual colour retrieval. *Proceeding of the Joint IAPR International Workshops SSPR and SPR,* (pp. 186 – 194).

Grimson, W. E. (1991). *Object recognition by computer: The role of geometric constraints.* MIT Press.

Hagenbuchner, M., Gori, M., Bunke, H., Tsoi, A. C., & Irniger, C. (2003). Using attributed plex grammars for the generation of image and graph databases. *Pattern Recognition Letters, 24*(8), 1081–1087. doi:10.1016/S0167-8655(02)00254-4

Haris, K., Efstradiatis, S. N., Maglaveras, N., Pappas, C., Gourassas, J., & Louridas, G. (1999). Model-based morphological segmentation and labeling of coronary angiograms. *IEEE Transactions on Medical Imaging, 18*(10), 1003–1015. doi:10.1109/42.811312

Haussler, D. (1999). *Convolution kernels on discrete structures. Technical report.* Department of Computer Science, University of California at Santa Cruz.

Hlaoui, A., & Wang, S. (2002). A new algorithm for graph matching with application to content-based image retrieval. *Proceeding of the Joint IAPR International Workshops SSPR and SPR,* (pp. 291 – 300).

Hong, P., Wang, R., & Huang, T. (2000). Learning patterns from images by combining soft decisions and hard decisions. *Proceedings of the 2000 IEEE Computer Society Conference on Computer Vision and Pattern Recognition,* (pp. 79 – 83).

Hopcroft, J. E., & Wong, J. (1974). Linear time algorithm for isomorphism of planar graphs. *Proceedings of the 6th Annual ACM Symposium on Theory of Computing,* (pp. 172-184).

Hsieh, A. J., Fan, K. C., & Fan, T. I. (1995). Bipartite weighted matching for on-line handwritten Chinese character recognition. *Pattern Recognition, 28,* 143–151. doi:10.1016/0031-3203(94)00090-9

Huet, B., & Hancock, E. R. (1998). Fuzzy relational distance for large-scale object recognition. *Proceedings of IEEE Conference on Computer Vision and Pattern Recognition,* (pp. 138-143).

Huet, B., & Hancock, E. R. (1999). Shape recognition from large image libraries by inexact graph matching. *Pattern Recognition Letters, 20*, 1259–1269. doi:10.1016/S0167-8655(99)00093-8

Huet, B., Kern, N. J., Guarascio, G., & Merialdo, B. (2001). Relational skeletons for retrieval in patent drawings. *Proceedings of the International Conference on Image Processing*, (pp. 737–740).

Irniger, C., & Bunke, H. (2001). Graph matching: Filtering large databases of graphs using decision trees. *Proceedings of the 3rd IAPR-TC15 Workshop on Graph-based Representations in Pattern Recognition*, (pp. 239–249).

Irniger, C., & Bunke, H. (2003). Theoretical analysis and experimental comparison of graph matching algorithms for database filtering. In Hancock, E., & Vento, M. (Eds.), *Graph Based Representations in Pattern Recognition (Vol. 2726*, pp. 118–129). Lecture Notes in Computer Science Berlin, Germany: Springer. doi:10.1007/3-540-45028-9_11

Jagota, A., Pelillo, M., & Rangarajan, A. (2000). A new deterministic annealing algorithm for maximum clique. *Proceedings of the International Joint Conference on Neural Networks*, (Vol. 6, pp. 505–508).

Jia, J., & Abe, K. (1998). Automatic generation of prototypes in 3D structural object recognition. *Proceedings of the Fourteenth International Conference on Pattern Recognition*, (pp. 697–700).

Jiang, X., & Bunke, H. (1998). Marked subgraph isomorphism of ordered graphs. *Proceeding of the Joint IAPR International Workshops SSPR and SPR*, (pp. 122–131).

Jiang, X., Munger, A., & Bunke, H. (1999). Synthesis of representative symbols by computing generalized median graphs. *Proceedings of the International Workshop on Graphics Recognition GREC ' 99*, (pp. 187–194).

Kälviäinen, H., & Oja, E. (1990). Comparisons of attributed graph matching algorithms for computer vision. In *Proceedings of STEP-90, Finnish Artificial Intelligence Symposium*, (pp. 354-368). Oulu, Finland, June.

Kashima, H., Tsuda, K., & Inokuchi, A. (2003). Marginalized kernel between labeled graphs. In *Proceedings of the Twentieth International Conference on Machine Learning*.

Khoo, K. G., & Suganthan, P. N. (2001). Multiple relational graphs mapping using genetic algorithms. *Proceedings of the 2001 Congress on Evolutionary Computation*, (pp. 727–733).

Kitchen, L., & Rosenfeld, A. (1979). Discrete relaxation for matching relational structures. *IEEE Transactions on Systems, Man, and Cybernetics, 9*, 869–874. doi:10.1109/TSMC.1979.4310140

Kittler, J., & Hancock, E. R. (1989). Combining evidence in probabilistic relaxation. *International Journal of Pattern Recognition and Artificial Intelligence, 3*, 29–51. doi:10.1142/S021800148900005X

Koch, I. (2001). Enumerating all connected maximal common subgraphs in two graphs. *Theoretical Computer Science, 250*(1), 1–30. doi:10.1016/S0304-3975(00)00286-3

Koo, J. H., & Yoo, S. I. (1998). A structural matching for two-dimensional visual pattern inspection. *Proceedings of the IEEE International Conference on Systems, Man, and Cybernetics*, (pp. 4429–4434).

Kosinov, S., & Caelli, T. (2002). Inexact multisubgraph matching using graph Eigenspace and clustering models. *Proceeding of the Joint IAPR International Workshops SSPR and SPR*, (pp. 133–142).

Kotropoulos, C., Tefas, A., & Pitas, I. (2000). Frontal face authentication using morphological elastic graph matching. *IEEE Transactions on Image Processing, 9*(4), 555–560. doi:10.1109/83.841933

Kropatsch, W. (2001). Benchmarking graph matching algorithms – A complementary view. *Proceedings of the 3rd IAPR – TC15 Workshop on Graph-based Representations*, Italy, (pp. 170-175).

Lades, M., Vorbruggen, J. C., Buhmann, J., Lange, J., von der Malsburg, C., Wurz, R. P., & Konen, W. (1993). Distortion invariant object recognition in the dynamic link architecture. *IEEE Transactions on Computers, 42*(2-3), 300–311. doi:10.1109/12.210173

Larrosa, J., & Valiente, G. (2002). Constraint satisfaction algorithms for graph pattern matching. *Mathematical Structures in Computer Science, 12*, 403–422. doi:10.1017/S0960129501003577

Lawler, E. S. (2001). *Combinatorial optimization: Networks and matroids* (p. 374). Dover Books.

Lazarescu, M., Bunke, H., & Venkatesh, S. (2000). Graph matching: Fast candidate elimination using machine learning techniques. *Proceeding of the Joint IAPR International Workshops SSPR and SPR*, (pp. 236 – 245).

Lee, R. S. T. Liu, & J. N. K. (1999). An oscillatory elastic graph matching model for recognition of offline handwritten Chinese characters. *Third International Conference on Knowledge-Based Intelligent Information Engineering Systems*, (pp. 284 – 287).

Li, W. J., & Lee, T. (2000). Object recognition by sub-scene graph matching. *IEEE International Conference on Robotics and Automation*, (pp. 1459 – 1464).

Lim, R., & Reinders, M. J. T. (2001). Facial landmarks localization based on fuzzy and gabor wavelet graph matching. *The 10th IEEE International Conference on Fuzzy Systems*, (pp. 683 – 686).

Liu, C. W., Fan, K. C., Horng, J. T., & Wang, Y. K. (1995). Solving weighted graph matching problem by modified microgenetic algorithm. *IEEE International Conference on Systems, Man and Cybernetics*, (pp. 638 – 643).

Liu, J. Z., Ma, K., Cham, W. K., & Chang, M. M. Y. (2000). Two-layer assignment method for online Chinese character recognition. *IEEE Proceedings Vision. Image and Signal Processing, 147*(1), 47–54. doi:10.1049/ip-vis:20000103

Llados, J., Lopez-Krahe, J., & Marti, E. (1996). Hand drawn document understanding using the straight line Hough transform and graph matching. *Proceedings of the 13th International Conference on Pattern Recognition*, (pp. 497 – 501).

Llados, J., Marti, E., & Villanueva, J. J. (2001). Symbol recognition by error-tolerant subgraph matching between region adjacency graphs. *IEEE Transactions on Pattern Analysis and Machine Intelligence, 23*(10), 1137–1143. doi:10.1109/34.954603

Lu, S. W., Ren, Y., & Suen, C. Y. (1991). Hierarchical attributed graph representation and recognition of handwritten Chinese characters. *Pattern Recognition, 24*, 617–632. doi:10.1016/0031-3203(91)90029-5

Luks, E. M. (1982). Isomorphism of graphs of bounded valence can be tested in polynomial time. *Journal of Computer and System Sciences, 25*, 42–65. doi:10.1016/0022-0000(82)90009-5

Luo, B., & Hancock, E. R. (2001). Structural graph matching using the EM algorithm and singular value decomposition. *IEEE Transactions on Pattern Analysis and Machine Intelligence, 23*(10), 1120–1136. doi:10.1109/34.954602

Luo, B., Robles-Kelly, A., Torsello, A., Wilson, R. C., & Hancock, E. R. (2001). Clustering shock trees. *Proceedings of the 3rd IAPR-TC15 Workshop on Graph-based Representations in Pattern Recognition,* (pp. 217 – 228).

Luo, B., Wilson, R. C., & Hancock, E. R. (2003). Spectral embedding of graphs. *Pattern Recognition, 36,* 2213–2230. doi:10.1016/S0031-3203(03)00084-0

Lyons, M. J., Budynek, J., & Akamatsu, S. (1999). Automatic classification of single facial images. *IEEE Transactions on Pattern Analysis and Machine Intelligence, 21*(12), 1357–1362. doi:10.1109/34.817413

Mah, P., & Vert, J. P. (2008). Graph kernels based on tree patterns for molecules. *Machine Learning, 75*(1), 3–35. doi:10.1007/s10994-008-5086-2

Maio, D., & Maltoni, D. (1996). A structural approach to fingerprint classification. *Proceedings of the 13th International Conference on Pattern Recognition,* (pp. 578 – 585).

McGregor, J. J. (1982). Backtrack search algorithm and the maximal common subgraph problem. *Software, Practice & Experience, 12*(1), 23–34. doi:10.1002/spe.4380120103

McKay, B. D. (1981). Practical graph isomorphism. *Congressus Numerantium, 30,* 45–87.

Medasani, S., & Krishnapuram, R. (1999). A fuzzy approach to content-based image retrieval. *Proceedings of the IEEE International Conference on Fuzzy Systems,* (pp. 1251 – 1260).

Medasani, S., Krishnapuram, R., & Choi, Y. S. (2001). Graph matching by relaxation of fuzzy assignments. *IEEE Transactions on Fuzzy Systems, 9*(1), 173–182. doi:10.1109/91.917123

Messmer, B. (1995). *Efficient graph matching algorithm for preprocessed model graphs.* PhD Thesis, Institut fur Informatik und Angewandte Mathematik, Univ. of Bern.

Messmer, B. T., & Bunke, H. (1998). A new algorithm for error-tolerant subgraph isomorphism detection. *IEEE Transactions on Pattern Analysis and Machine Intelligence, 20*(5), 493–504. doi:10.1109/34.682179

Messmer, B. T., & Bunke, H. (1999). A decision tree approach to graph and subgraph isomorphism detection. *Pattern Recognition, 32*(12), 1979–1998. doi:10.1016/S0031-3203(98)90142-X

Messmer, B. T., & Bunke, H. (2000). Efficient subgraph isomorphism detection: A decomposition approach. *IEEE Transactions on Knowledge and Data Engineering, 12*(2), 307–323. doi:10.1109/69.842269

Meth, R., & Chellappa, R. (1996). Target indexing in synthetic aperture radar imagery using topographic features. *Proceedings of the IEEE International Conference on Acoustics, Speech, and Signal Processing,* (pp. 2152 – 2155).

Miyazaki, T. (1997). The complexity of McKay's canonical labeling algorithm. *Groups and Computation II. DIMACS Series Discrete Mathematics Theoretical Computer Science, 28,* 239–256.

Myers, R., Wilson, R. C., & Hancock, E. R. (2000). Bayesian graph edit distance. *IEEE Transactions on Pattern Analysis and Machine Intelligence, 22*(6), 628–635. doi:10.1109/34.862201

Neuhaus, M., & Bunke, H. (2003). An error-tolerant approximate matching algorithm for attributed planar graphs and its application to fingerprint classification. In Fred, A., Caelli, T., & Camphilho, A. (Eds.), *SSPR 2004 (Vol. 3138,* p. 180). Lecture Notes in Computer Science. doi:10.1007/978-3-540-27868-9_18

Neuhaus, M., & Bunke, H. (2007). *Bridging the gap between graph edit distance and kernel machines.* River Edge, NJ: World Scientific Publishing.

Oflazer, K. (1997). Error-tolerant retrieval of trees. *IEEE Transactions on Pattern Analysis and Machine Intelligence*, *19*(12), 1376–1380. doi:10.1109/34.643897

Olatunbosun, S., Dowling, G. R., & Ellis, T. J. (1996). Topological representation for matching coloured surfaces. *Proceedings of the International Conference on Image Processing*, (pp. 1019 – 1022).

Ozer, B., Wolf, W., & Akansu, A. N. (1999). A graph based object description for information retrieval in digital image and video libraries. *Proceedings of the IEEE Workshop on Content-Based Access of Image and Video Libraries*, (pp. 79 – 83).

Pardalos, P., Rappe, J., & Resende, M. G. C. (1998). *An exact parallel algorithm for the maximum clique problem: High performance algorithms and software in nonlinear optimization*. Kluwer Academic Publishers.

Park, I. K., Yun, I. D., & Lee, S. U. (1997). Models and algorithms for efficient color image indexing. *Proceedings of the IEEE Workshop on Content-Based Access of Image and Video Libraries*, (pp. 36 – 41).

Pavlidis, T., Sakoda, W. J., & Shi, H. (1995). Matching graph embeddings for shape analysis. *Proceedings of the Third International Conference on Document Analysis and Recognition*, (pp. 729 – 733).

Pelillo, M. (1995a). Relaxation labeling networks for the maximum clique problem. *Journal of Artificial Neural Networks*, *2*, 313–328.

Pelillo, M. (1998). A unifying framework for relational structure matching. *Proceedings of Fourteenth International Conference on Pattern Recognition*, (pp. 1316 – 1319).

Pelillo, M. (1999). Replicator equations, maximal cliques, and graph isomorphism. *Neural Computation*, *11*(8), 1933–1955. doi:10.1162/089976699300016034

Pelillo, M. (2002). Matching free trees, maximal cliques and monotone game dynamics. *IEEE Transactions on Pattern Analysis and Machine Intelligence*, *24*(11), 1535–1541. doi:10.1109/TPAMI.2002.1046176

Pelillo, M., & Jagota, A. (1995b). Feasible and infeasible maxima in a quadratic program for maximum clique. *Journal of Artificial Neural Networks*, *2*, 411–420.

Pelillo, M., Siddiqi, K., & Zucker, S. W. (1999). Matching hierarchical structures using association graphs. *IEEE Transactions on Pattern Analysis and Machine Intelligence*, *21*(11), 1105–1120. doi:10.1109/34.809105

Perchant, A., Boeres, C., Bloch, I., Roux, M., & Ribeiro, C. (1999). Model-based scene recognition using graph fuzzy homomorphism solved by genetic algorithm. *Proceedings of the 2nd IAPR-TC15 Workshop on Graph-based Representations in Pattern Recognition*, (pp. 61 – 70).

Petrakis, G. M., & Faloutsos, C. (1997). Similarity searching in medical image databases. *IEEE Transactions on Knowledge and Data Engineering*, *9*(3), 435–447. doi:10.1109/69.599932

Rangarajan, A., & Mjolsness, E. D. (1996). A Lagrangian relaxation network for graph matching. *IEEE Transactions on Neural Networks*, *7*(6), 1365–1381. doi:10.1109/72.548165

Riesen, K., Neuhaus, M., & Bunke, H. (2007). Graph embedding in vector spaces by means of prototype selection. *Graph-Based Representations in Pattern Recognition, LNCS*, *4538*, 383–39. doi:10.1007/978-3-540-72903-7_35

Robles-Kelly, A., & Hancock, E. R. (2005). Graph edit distance from spectral seriation. *IEEE Transactions on Pattern Analysis and Machine Intelligence, 27*(3), 365–378. doi:10.1109/TPAMI.2005.56

Rocha, J., & Pavlidis, T. (1994). A shape analysis model with applications to a character recognition system. *IEEE Transactions on Pattern Analysis and Machine Intelligence, 16*(4), 393–404. doi:10.1109/34.277592

Rosenfeld, A., Hummel, R. A., & Zucker, S. W. (1976). Scene labelling by relaxation operations. *IEEE Transactions on Systems, Man, and Cybernetics, 6*(6), 420–433. doi:10.1109/TSMC.1976.4309519

Russel, S. J., & Norvig, P. (1995). *Artificial intelligence: A modern approach*. Prentice Hall Series in Artificial Intelligence.

Salotti, M., & Laachfoubi, N. (2001). Topographic graph matching for shift estimation. *Proceedings of the 3rd IAPR-TC15 Workshop on Graph-based Representations in Pattern Recognition*, (pp. 54 – 63).

Sanfeliu, A., & Fu, K. S. (1983). A distance measure between attributed relational graphs for pattern recognition. *IEEE Transactions on Systems, Man, and Cybernetics, 13*(3), 353–363.

Sanfeliu, A., Serratosa, F., & Alquezar, R. (2004). Second-order random graphs for modeling sets of attributed graphs and their application to object learning and recognition. *International Journal of Pattern Recognition and Artificial Intelligence, 18*(3), 375–396. doi:10.1142/S0218001404003253

Schmidt, D. C., & Druffel, L. E. (1976). A fast back-tracking algorithm to test directed graphs for isomorphism using distance matrices. *Journal of the ACM, 23*, 433–445. doi:10.1145/321958.321963

Sebastian, T. B., Klein, P. N., & Kimia, B. B. (2005). Recognition of shapes by editing their shock graphs. *IEEE Transactions on Pattern Analysis and Machine Intelligence, 26*(5), 550–571. doi:10.1109/TPAMI.2004.1273924

Seong, D., Kim, H. S., & Park, K. H. (1993). Incremental clustering of attributed graphs. *IEEE Transactions on Systems, Man, and Cybernetics, 23*(5), 1399–1411. doi:10.1109/21.260671

Serratosa, F., Alquezar, R., & Sanfeliu, A. (1999). Function-described graphs: A fast algorithm to compute a sub-optimal matching measure. *Proceedings of the 2nd IAPR-TC15 Workshop on Graph-based Representations in Pattern Recognition*, (pp. 71 – 77).

Serratosa, F., Alquezar, R., & Sanfeliu, A. (2000). Efficient algorithms for matching attributed graphs and function-described graphs. *Proceedings of 15th International Conference on Pattern Recognition*, (pp. 867 – 872).

Shapiro, L. G., & Haralick, R. M. (1981). Structural descriptions and inexact matching. *IEEE Transactions on Pattern Analysis and Machine Intelligence, 3*(5), 504–519. doi:10.1109/TPAMI.1981.4767144

Shapiro, L. G., & Haralick, R. M. (1985). A metric for comparing relational descriptions. *IEEE Transactions on Pattern Analysis and Machine Intelligence, 7*(1), 90–94. doi:10.1109/TPAMI.1985.4767621

Sharvit, D., Chan, J., Tek, H., & Kimia, B. B. (1998). Symmetry-based indexing of image databases. *Proceedings of the IEEE Workshop on Content-Based Access of Image and Video Libraries*, (pp. 56 – 62).

Shasha, D., Wang, J. T. L., Zhang, K., & Shih, F. Y. (1994). Exact and approximate algorithms for unordered tree matching. *IEEE Transactions on Systems, Man, and Cybernetics, 24*(4), 668–678. doi:10.1109/21.286387

Shearer, K., Bunke, H., & Venkatesh, S. (2001a). Video indexing and similarity retrieval by largest common subgraph detection using decision trees. *Pattern Recognition, 34*(5), 1075–1091. doi:10.1016/S0031-3203(00)00048-0

Shearer, K., Bunke, H., Venkatesh, S., & Kieronska, S. (1997). Efficient graph matching for video indexing. *Computing, 12*, 53–62.

Shearer, K., Venkatesh, S., & Bunke, H. (2001b). Video sequence matching via decision tree path following. *Pattern Recognition Letters, 22*(5), 479–492. doi:10.1016/S0167-8655(00)00121-5

Shervashidze, N., & Borgwardt, K. M. (2009). Fast subtree kernels on graphs. *Advances in Neural Information Processing Systems, 22*.

Shervashidze, N., Vishwanathan, S. V., Petri, T. H., Mehlhorn, K., & Borgwardt, K. M. (2009). *Efficient graphlet kernels for large graph comparison*. In Twelfth International Conference on Artificial Intelligence and Statistics.

Shinano, Y., Fujie, T., Ikebe, Y., & Hirabayashi, R. (1998). Solving the maximum clique problem using PUBB. *Proceedings of the First Merged International Parallel Processing Symposium*, (pp. 326 – 332).

Shokoufandeh, A., & Dickinson, S. (2001). A unified framework for indexing and matching hierarchical shape structures. In C. Arcelli, L. P. Cordella, & G. Sanniti di Baja (Eds.), *Workshop on Visual Form, Lecture Notes in Computer Science, Vol. 2059,* (pp. 67-84).

Shoukry, A., & Aboutabl, M. (1996). Neural network approach for solving the maximal common subgraph problem. *IEEE Transactions on Systems, Man and Cybernetics. Part B, 26*(5), 785–790.

Suganthan, P. N. (2000) Attributed relational graph matching by neural-gas networks. *Proceedings of the 2000 IEEE Signal Processing Society Workshop on Neural Networks for Signal Processing X, 2000,* (pp. 366 – 374).

Suganthan, P. N., Teoh, E. K., & Mital, D. (1995). Pattern recognition by graph matching using the potts MFT neural networks. *Pattern Recognition, 28*(7), 997–1009. doi:10.1016/0031-3203(94)00166-J

Suganthan, P. N., Teoh, E. K., & Mital, D. (1995). A self organizing Hopfield network for attributed relational graph matching. *Image and Vision Computing, 13*(1), 61–73. doi:10.1016/0262-8856(95)91468-S

Suganthan, P. N., & Yan, H. (1998). Recognition of handprinted Chinese characters by constrained graph matching. *Image and Vision Computing, 16*(3), 191–201. doi:10.1016/S0262-8856(97)00066-8

Tefas, A., Kotropoulos, C., & Pitas, I. (2001). Using support vector machines to enhance the performance of elastic graph matching for frontal face authentication. *IEEE Transactions on Pattern Analysis and Machine Intelligence, 23*(7), 735–746. doi:10.1109/34.935847

Torsello, A., & Hancock, E. R. (2001). Computing approximate tree edit-distance using relaxation labeling. *Proceedings of the 3rd IAPR-TC15 Workshop on Graph-based Representations in Pattern Recognition,* (pp. 125 – 136).

Torsello, A., & Hancock, E. R. (2002). Learning structural variations in shock trees. *Proceeding of the Joint IAPR International Workshops SSPR and SPR,* (pp. 113 – 122).

Torsello, A., & Hancock, E. R. (2007). Graph embedding using tree edit-union. *Pattern Recognition, 40*, 1393–1405. doi:10.1016/j.patcog.2006.09.006

Triesch, J., & von der Malsburg, C. (2001). A system for person-independent hand posture recognition against complex backgrounds. *IEEE Transactions on Pattern Analysis and Machine Intelligence*, *23*(12), 1449–1453. doi:10.1109/34.977568

Tsai, W. H., & Fu, K. S. (1979). Error-correcting isomorphisms of attributed relational graphs for pattern analysis. *IEEE Transactions on Systems, Man, and Cybernetics*, *9*(12), 757–768. doi:10.1109/TSMC.1979.4310127

Tsai, W. H., & Fu, K. S. (1983). Subgraph error-correcting isomorphisms for syntactic pattern recognition. *IEEE Transactions on Systems, Man, and Cybernetics*, *13*(1), 48–61.

Ullman, J. R. (1976). An algorithm for subgraph isomorphism. *Journal of the Association for Computer Machinery*, *23*, 31–42. doi:10.1145/321921.321925

Umeyama, S. (1988). An Eigendecomposition approach to weighted graph matching problems. *IEEE Transactions on Pattern Analysis and Machine Intelligence*, *10*(5), 695–703. doi:10.1109/34.6778

Valiente, G. (2001). An efficient bottom-up distance between trees. *Proceedings of the Eighth International Symposium on String Processing and Information Retrieval*, (pp. 212 – 219).

van Wyk, B. J., & van Wyk, M. A. (2002a). Non-Bayesian graph matching without explicit compatibility calculations. *Proceeding of the Joint IAPR International Workshops SSPR and SPR*, (pp. 74 – 82).

van Wyk, B. J., van Wyk, M. A., & Hanrahan, H. E. (2002b). Successive projection graph matching. *Proceeding of the Joint IAPR International Workshops SSPR and SPR*, (pp. 263 – 271).

van Wyk, M. A., Durrani, T. S., & van Wyk, B. J. (2002). A RKHS interpolator-based graph matching algorithm. *IEEE Transactions on Pattern Analysis and Machine Intelligence*, *24*(7), 988–995. doi:10.1109/TPAMI.2002.1017624

Wallis, W. D., Shoubridge, P., Kraetz, M., & Ray, D. (2001). Graph distances using graph union. *Pattern Recognition Letters*, *22*(6), 701–704. doi:10.1016/S0167-8655(01)00022-8

Wang, C., & Abe, K. (1995). Region correspondence by inexact attributed planar graph matching. *Proceedings of the Fifth International Conference on Computer Vision*, (pp. 440 – 447).

Wang, J. T. L., Zhang, K., & Chirn, G. W. (1994). The approximate graph matching problem. *Proceedings of the 12th IAPR International Conference on Pattern Recognition - Conference B*, (pp. 284 – 288).

Wang, M., Iwai, Y., & Yachida, M. (1998). Expression recognition from time-sequential facial images by use of expression change model. *Proceedings of the Third IEEE International Conference on Automatic Face and Gesture Recognition*, (pp. 354 – 359).

Wang, Y. K., Fan, K. C., & Horng, J. T. (1997). Genetic-based search for error-correcting graph isomorphism. *IEEE Transactions on Systems, Man and Cybernetics. Part B*, *27*(4), 589–597.

Williams, M. L., Wilson, R. C., & Hancock, E. R. (1999). Deterministic search for relational graph matching. *Pattern Recognition*, *32*(7), 1255–1271. doi:10.1016/S0031-3203(98)00152-6

Wilson, R. C., & Hancock, E. R. (1997). Structural matching by discrete relaxation. *IEEE Transactions on Pattern Analysis and Machine Intelligence*, *19*(6), 634–648. doi:10.1109/34.601251

Wilson, R. C., & Hancock, E. R. (1999). Graph matching with hierarchical discrete relaxation. *Pattern Recognition Letters, 20*(10), 1041–1052. doi:10.1016/S0167-8655(99)00071-9

Wilson, R. C., & Hancock, E. R. (2005). Pattern vectors from algebraic graph theory. *IEEE Transactions on Pattern Analysis and Machine Intelligence, 27*(7), 1112–1124. doi:10.1109/TPAMI.2005.145

Wiskott, L. (1997b). Phantom faces for face analysis. *Proceedings of the International Conference on Image Processing,* (pp. 308 – 311).

Wiskott, L., Fellous, J. M., Kruger, N., & von der Malsburg, C. (1997a). Face recognition by elastic bunch graph matching. *IEEE Transactions on Pattern Analysis and Machine Intelligence, 19*(7), 775–779. doi:10.1109/34.598235

Wong, A. K. C., You, M., & Chan, S. C. (1990). An algorithm for graph optimal monomorphism. *IEEE Transactions on Systems, Man, and Cybernetics, 20*(3), 628–638. doi:10.1109/21.57275

Xu, L., & King, I. (2001). A PCA approach for fast retrieval of structural patterns in attributed graphs. *IEEE Transactions on Systems, Man and Cybernetics. Part B, 31*(5), 812–817.

Zhang, H., & Yan, H. (1999). Graphic matching based on constrained Voronoi diagrams. *Proceedings of the Fifth International Symposium on Signal Processing and its Applications,* (pp. 431 – 434).

Chapter 2
Geometric–Edge Random Graph Model for Image Representation

Bo Jiang
Anhui University, China

Jing Tang
Anhui University, China

Bin Luo
Anhui University, China

ABSTRACT

This chapter presents a random graph model for image representation. The first contribution the authors propose is a Geometric-Edge (G-E) Random Graph Model for image representation. The second contribution is that of casting image matching into G-E Random Graph matching by using the random dot product graph based matching algorithm. Experimental results show that the proposed G-E Random Graph model and matching algorithm are effective and robust to structural variations.

INTRODUCTION

Image modeling methods can be divided into two categories, one is spatial domain methods, and the other is transformation domain methods. In this chapter, we focus on spatial domain. In spatial domain, the traditional image models include polygon, skeleton, chain code, run length code, pyramid, and graphs. Recently, more research interests are focused on high level methods, such as graphs. The advantages of the graph model include its capable of describing structural relationships between image units and there exists solid problem solving schemes from mathematics.

BACKGROUND

When images are modeled by graphs, image matching and recognition can be converted to graph matching and recognition (Antonio, 2005) (Antonio, 2003) (Bai, 2004) (Christmas, 1995)

DOI: 10.4018/978-1-4666-1891-6.ch002

(Eshera, 1984) (Gao, 2008) (Llados, 2001) (Luo, 2001) (Luo, 2003). There exist many graph models to represent images and object shapes. The widely used models include region adjacency graph, MST, Delaunary graph, K-NN graph, Geometric graph, Shock graph and so on. When images are segmented into different regions, adjacency graphs can be used to represent images by assigning each separate region to a graph node. A graph edge is added when the two regions are connected. Image key points from Harris or SIFT like algorithms can be used to generate geometric graphs such as Delaunay graph, K-NN graph, et. al.

However, due to the imperfect image segmentation step or key point extraction step, the graphs generated usually have additional and missing nodes, and the edge structure may not be stable. In order to capture the structural variations more effectively, we explore random graph model (Bagdanov, 2003) (Erdös, 1960) (Wong, 1985) instead of traditional graph methods.

As a kind of random graph model, complex networking has been explored in image and object representation successfully (Antiqueira, 2005) (Backes, 2010) (Backes, 2009) (Chalumeau, 2006) (Costa, 2005) (Costa, 2004) (Erdös, 1961) (Watts, 1998). The main idea is that we represent images and objects by complex network, then describe the generated complex network by analyzing their topological and dynamic characteristics.

In this chapter, we propose a generalized edge random graph model (Elizabeth, 2010) which is induced by the random geometric graph. We denote this kind of random graph model by Geometric-Edge Random Graph, or G-E Random Graph. The main idea for the G-E Random Graph is that the probability of an edge connecting nodes i and j is determined by random geometric graph model (Penrose, 2003).

To verify the effectiveness of the proposed random graph model, we pursue graph matching based on the G-E Random Graph model. In real world problem domain, since the process of graph generation from raw image data is a task of some

fragility due to noise and non-rigid deformation, graph matching is inevitably inexact in nature. There is a considerable literature on the problem of inexact graph matching (Bai, 2004) (Christmas, 1995) (Gold, 1996) (Huet, 1999) (Luo, 2001) (Myers, 2000) (Scott, 1991) (Shapiro, 1992) (Tang, 2011) (Umeyama, 1988). Broadly speaking, the first category is based on tree search techniques. The second one is based on relaxation and optimization techniques. More recently, spectral methods (Bai, 2004) (Caelli, 2004) (Luo, 2001) (Tang, 2011) are shown effective for graph matching.

Although many inexact graph matching and similarity measurement methods such as spectral method, probability method for graphs with structural variation have been successfully developed, they will usually collapse when the structural variation extends to some level. Contrast to the traditional graph matching algorithms, the proposed G-E Random Graph model has shown its robustness to structural variations and hence achieved higher correct matching rates.

GEOMETRIC-EDGE (GE) RANDOM GRAPH MODEL

In this section, we develop the G-E Random Graph model starting from the general geometric graph. As a traditional graph model, geometric graph can be used to extract structure information of an image.

Geometric Graph

Definite 1: Let $\|.\|$ be some norm (such as Euclidean norm) on R^d, and let r be some positive parameters. Given finite sets $X, Y \in R^d$, A geometric graph $G(X; r)$ is an undirected graph with vertex set X and with undirected edges connecting all pairs $\{X, Y\}$ if they satisfy $\|Y-X\| \leq r$.

If $\|Y-X\| \leq r$, then X and Y are called mutual neighbor. There is an edge connecting X and Y. In image matching and recognition, we can use geometric graph G(X; *r*) to organize image key points and to extract structural information of the image. One feature of G(*X*; *r*) is that the edge between two nodes is dependent on the end nodes. So it has the ability to handle with some missing or additional nodes. However, the mutual neighbor relation is sensitive to the non-rigid transformation because the ‖Y-X‖ value is changeable due to the transformation.

As shown in Figure 1, the structure of the geometric graph is changeable (notice the red lines) due to the variation of point position. This makes the geometric graph model not robust in image structural information extraction.

On the other hand, it is necessary to develop more robust inexact graph matching and recognition algorithms to handle with graphs with structural variation (Belongie, 2002) (Bunke, 1998) (Caelli, 2004) (Gao, 2008) (Gao, 2010) (Gold, 1996) (Huet, 1999) (Jiang, 1999) (Luo, 2003) (Wilson, 1997). Although, many inexact graph matching and similarity measurement methods such as spectral method and probability method

for graphs with structural variation have been successfully developed, they will usually collapse when the structural variation extends to some level.

In order to capture the structural variations more effectively, we explore random graph modeling instead of the traditional graph method. As shown in Figure1, what we concern is the edge probability between two nodes due to the position variation by exploiting random geometric graph and edge random graph.

In the following, the concept of random geometric graph and generalized edge random graph are first introduced, and then the proposed G-E Random Model is described.

Random Geometric Graph

In this section, we introduce the idea of random geometric graph (RGG) (Elizabeth, 2010) (Penrose, 2003). Let *f* be some specified probability density function on R^d, and let X_1, X_2... X_n be independent and identically distributed d-dimen-

Figure 1. Two geometric graphs are generated based on two point-sets (the right image is obtained by adding Gaussian noise to the point positions of the points in the left image). The lighter edges denote the structure variation between two graphs.

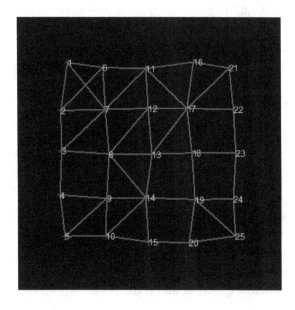
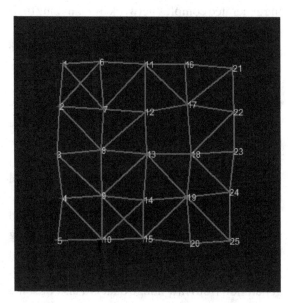

sional variables with common density f and $\mathbf{X} = (X_1, X_2 \ldots X_n)$. A random geometric graph $G(\mathbf{X}; r)$ is an ensemble of geometric graphs with the random variables X_i ($i = 1, 2 \ldots n$) taking different values on R^d.

The random geometric graph is actually a vertex random graph (VRG) (Elizabeth, 2010). For VRG, the randomness lies in the structures attached to the vertices. Once the random variables have been assigned to the vertices, the edges are determined.

Generalized Edge Random Graph

Let n be a positive integer and let $\mathbf{p}$: $[n] \times [n] \rightarrow [0,1]$ be a symmetric probability matrix, a graph $G = (V, E)$ is generated at random. The vertex set V of graph G is $\{v_1, v_2 \ldots v_i \ldots v_n\}$. For $i \neq j$, the probability of the edge connecting nodes i and j is set to $p_{ij} = \mathbf{p}(i, j)$. Let G_n denotes the set of all simple graphs with vertex set $\{v_1, v_2 \ldots v_n\}$, then the probability measure $P_\mathbf{p}(G)$ on G_n is defined as follows:

$$P_\mathbf{p}\left(G\right) = \left(\prod_{i<j, ij \in E} \mathbf{p}(i, j)\right) \times \left(\prod_{i<j, ij \notin E} \left(1 - \mathbf{p}(i, j)\right)\right)$$

(1)

It is worth mention that the Edge Random (E-R) graph is the special case when $\mathbf{p}$ is a constant. It should be also noted that, the above G-E Random Graph is only determined by the symmetric probability matrix $\mathbf{p}$.

G-E Random Graph

In this section we describe the proposed G-E random graph model, and followed by summarizing several measurements on the G-E random graphs.

G-E Random Graph Model

The G-E random graph is denoted as $\mathbf{G}$ ($\mathbf{p}_{G\text{-}E}$, r). Let $V = \{v_1, v_2 \ldots v_n\}$ be node set of a graph. For $i \neq j$, the probability of the edge connecting nodes i and j is set to $p_{ij} = \mathbf{p}_{G\text{-}E}(i, j; r)$, where r is a parameter. Then, the symmetric function $\mathbf{p}_{G\text{-}E}$ can be determined as the following:

For each node in G-E random graph, we allocate random variables $X_i \in R^d$. Let $\mathbf{X} = (X_1, X_2 \ldots X_n)$, and u_{ij} be the distance between node i and node j in the random geometric graph, i.e., $u_{ij} = \|X_i - X_j\|$. Let f_{ij} be probability density function of random variable u_{ij}. Then the probability of edge connecting nodes i and j in G-E Random Graph (symmetric function $\mathbf{p}_{G\text{-}E}$) can be calculated as follows:

$$\mathbf{p}_{E\text{-}G}\left(r; i, j\right) = \int_0^r f_{ij}(u_{ij}) \, d_{u_{ij}}$$

(2)

where the parameter r is determined in RGG ($G(\mathbf{X}; r)$).

It should be noted that, in order to obtain the edge probability of G-E random graph, we utilize the random variables $\mathbf{X}$ which are usually used in random geometric graph. What we concern here is the edge probability i.e., the function $\mathbf{p}_{G\text{-}E}$. Therefore, the G-E random graph is edge random graph in itself.

Measurements on G-E Random Graph

Random graphs can be characterized by some well defined measurements. Some of the measurements used in this paper are presented as the following (Costa, 2005):

1. **Expected Average Degree and Maximum Degree:** The expected degree $E(k_i)$ of a node i is the expected number of edges directly connected to that node, and it is defined in

terms of the adjacency probability matrix **p** as

$$E(k_i) = \sum_{j=1}^{n} \mathbf{p}(i,j) \qquad (3)$$

The expected degree is an important characteristic of a vertex. Based on the degree of the vertices, measurements can be extracted from random graph to express its properties. Two of the simplest measures are the expected average degree,

$$E(k_a) = \frac{1}{n} \sum_{i=1}^{n} E(k_i) \qquad (4)$$

and the expected maximum degree,

$$E(k_m) = \max_i E(k_i) \qquad (5)$$

2. **Expected Number of Edges:** The expected number of edges can be calculated as follows:

$$E(n_e) = \sum_{i=1}^{n} \sum_{j=1}^{n} \mathbf{p}(i,j) \qquad (6)$$

MODELING IMAGE USING G-E RANDOM GRAPH

In this section, we focus on representing images using the G-E random graph model. Our main idea is to represent key points of images using G-E random graph model. We first introduce the basic probability and statistics theory that used in this chapter.

Noncentral Chi-Square $\left(\chi^2\right)$ Distribution

In probability theory and statistics, the noncentral chi-square distribution is a generalization of the chi-square distribution. Let Y_i ($i = 1...k$) be k independent, normal distribution random variables with means μ_i and variances σ_i^2. Then the random variable $\sum_{i=1}^{k} (\frac{Y_i}{\sigma_i})^2$ is noncentral chi-square distributed. It has two parameters: degrees of freedom k which specifies the number of Y_i, and noncentrality parameter λ which is related to the mean of the random variables Y_i by

$$\lambda = \sum_{i=1}^{k} (\frac{\mu_i}{\sigma_i})^2 \qquad (7)$$

The probability density function of chi-square distribution is

$$f_Y(x;k,\lambda) = \frac{1}{2} e^{-(x+\lambda)/2} \left(\frac{x}{\lambda}\right)^{k/4-1/2} I_{k/2-1}(\sqrt{\lambda x}) \qquad (8)$$

where $I_v(z)$ is a modified Bessel function of the first kind given by

$$I_a(y) = (y/2)^a \sum_{j=0}^{\infty} \frac{(y^2/4)^j}{j!\,\Gamma(a+j+1)} \qquad (9)$$

The cumulative distribution function can be written as

$$P(x;k,\lambda) = e^{-\lambda/2} \sum_{j=0}^{\infty} \frac{(\lambda/2)^j}{j!} Q(x;k+2j) \qquad (10)$$

where $Q(x; k)$ is the cumulative distribution function of the central chi-square distribution which is given by

$$Q(x;k) = \frac{\gamma(k/2, x/2)}{\Gamma(k/2)} \qquad (11)$$

and where $\gamma(k, z)$ is the lower incomplete Gamma function.

Image Representation Using the G-E Random Graph Model

Given an image, we first extract the key points using tradition key point detection algorithm such as Harris, SIFT and so on. Let $\mathbf{x} = (\mathbf{x}_1, \mathbf{x}_2 \dots \mathbf{x}_n)$ be the key point set where $\mathbf{x}_i = (x_{i1}, x_{i2})$ is the coordinate of the key point i. Our G-E random graph model for image representation can be described as follows.

Each vertex in the G-E graph corresponds to a key point in the image. For node i, a random attribute vector $\mathbf{y}_i = (\mathbf{y}_{i1}, \mathbf{y}_{i2})$ is allocated. We assume that each $y_{ij} \sim N\left(x_{ij}, \delta^2\right)$ for $j = 1, 2$. Let $\mathbf{y} = (\mathbf{y}_1, \mathbf{y}_2 \dots \mathbf{y}_n)$, then our G-E random graph model can be constructed based on random variables $\mathbf{y}$. The probability of the edge connecting node k and node l for the G-E model can be calculated as the following,

$$\mathbf{p}_{E\text{-}G}(r; k, l) = P(r^2; 2, \lambda) \qquad (12)$$

where $P(x; k, \lambda)$ is defined in Equation 10 and

$$\lambda = \frac{1}{2}\left[\left(\frac{x_{k1} - x_{l1}}{\delta}\right)^2 + \left(\frac{x_{k2} - x_{l2}}{\delta}\right)^2\right].$$

In the above model, we can calculate the edge probability $\mathbf{p}$ using the cumulative distribution function described in Equation 10. This is because the distance $d^2 \sim \chi_k^2\left(\lambda\right)$ when $y_{ij} \sim N\left(x_{ij}, \delta^2\right)$.

G-E RANDOM GRAPH MATCHING BASED ON RANDOM DOT PRODUCT GRAPH

In this section, we aim to show the structural description ability of the proposed model by testing it on graph matching. One of the most popular approaches to the traditional graph matching problem is to use embedding method. By embedding the nodes of a graph in a space (such as eigenspace) the matching process can be achieved by aligning the embedding points. In this section, we aim to match generalized edge random graph using embedding method by exploring random dot product graph model.

We start G-E random graph matching based on the random dot product graph (RDPG) model. We first introduce the basic concepts of random dot product graph (David, 2008) (Scheinerman, 2010) (Tang, 2011) (Young, 2007) (Zhang, 2010). Then, we extend RDPG model to represent G-E random graph, and complete matching based on this model.

Random Dot Product Graph

Given a set of vectors $\{\mathbf{x}_i\}_{i=1}^n$ where $\mathbf{x}_i \in R^d$ is a d-dimensional vector. For $i \neq j$, we assume that $\mathbf{x}_i \cdot \mathbf{x}_j \in [0, 1]$ (we can normalize $\mathbf{x}_i$, $\mathbf{x}_j$ to make $\mathbf{x}_i \cdot \mathbf{x}_j \in [0, 1]$), then a graph $G = (V, E)$ is generated at random. The vertex set V of this graph is $\{v_1, v_2, \dots v_n\}$. For $i \neq j$, the probability of the edge connecting nodes v_i and v_j is set to $\mathbf{x}_i \cdot \mathbf{x}_j$. Let G_n denotes the set of all simple graphs with vertex set $\{v_1, v_2, \dots v_n\}$, the probability measure $P_X(G)$ on G_n is defined as follows:

$$P_X\left(G\right) = \left(\prod_{i<j, ij \in E} \mathbf{x}_i \cdot \mathbf{x}_j\right) \times \left(\prod_{i<j, ij \notin E} \left(1 - \mathbf{x}_i \cdot \mathbf{x}_j\right)\right) \qquad (13)$$

Semi-RDPG

The above random dot product graph (RDPG) is a vertex-edge random graph (David, 2008) (Elizabeth, 2010) (Scheinerman, 2010) (Young, 2007). For these random graphs, all the randomness lies in the structures attached to both the vertices and edges at the same time. In RDPG, the vectors $\{\mathbf{x}_i\}_{i=1}^n$ are all random variables and the edge probability is set to $\mathbf{x}_i \cdot \mathbf{x}_j$. In this chapter, we want to restrict the vectors $\{\mathbf{x}_i\}_{i=1}^n$ to given vectors in d-dimensional space and generate the edge probability with $\mathbf{x}_i \cdot \mathbf{x}_j$. We call this random graph model as Semi-RDPG. The main feature for the Semi-RDPG is that all the randomness lies in the structures attached to the edges, and it is actually an edge random graph.

Rather than generating graphs at random from a set of fixed vectors, we focus on the issue of finding vectors that "best" model a given Generalized Edge Random Graph. The optimal solution of the vectors X is the one which minimizes the approximation error.

Let $\mathbf{p}$ be the adjacency probability matrix where $\mathbf{p}\,(i, j)$ is the edge probability between nodes v_i and v_j. Then, the vectors X is sought to satisfy $\mathbf{x}_i \cdot \mathbf{x}_j \approx \mathbf{p}(i, j)$ where $i \neq j$, i.e.

$$\min_X f_A(X) = \left\| X^T X - \mathbf{p} - \mathrm{I} \circ (X^T X) \right\|^2 \quad (14)$$

where I is the $n \times n$ identity matrix, $\circ$ is the Hadamard product and $\|\cdot\|$ is the Frobenius norm. An iteration algorithm (David, 2008) (Erdös, 1960) is designed to find the "best" vectors X.

G-E Random Graph Matching

Using Equation 14, we embed the nodes of the G-E Random Graph to low dimensional Euclidean space (eigenspace). Then we can complete G-E Random Graph matching by aligning the points using some conventional graph matching algorithms such as Hungarian, SVD and so on. We utilize this method as the initialization for our G-E Random Graph matching algorithm.

This embedding based matching method may be robust to graph distortion in the sense that corresponding nodes are always not very far in the graph eigenspace. However, this method cannot guarantee that the converse hold, since complete unrelated nodes can have very close embeddings. This may lead to some erroneous correspondences. In order to overcome this problem, we first introduce a consistency check process which is designed to remove these erroneous correspondences by enforcing coherent spatial relationships of corresponding nodes between graphs. Then, we propose a new embedding method (called co-embedding) in which we use the positive correspondences obtained from consistency check process and integrate the embedding processes for G_1 and G_2 at the same time.

Consistency Check Process

As discussed above, embedding based graph matching always leads to some erroneous correspondences. The main purpose for consistency check process is to remove these erroneous correspondences and obtain positive correspondences from initial matching result. Its principle is to enforce coherent spatial relationships of corresponding nodes between graphs. There are some methods that can be extent to solve this problem (Leordeanu, 2009) (Tang, 2011). In the following, we propose a new consistency check algorithm.

To do so, a compatibility matrix $C = (c_{ij})_{n \times n}$ is computed for each graph first. The element c_{ij} can simply be obtained from adjacency probability matrix $\mathbf{p}$, i.e. $c_{ij} = \mathbf{p}\,(i, j)$. Also, we can compute c_{ij} as Euclidean distance between two nodes of the graph in some special cases.

Algorithm 1: Consistency check algorithm

- **Input:**
  - The initial correspondences I_{map}, Graph G_1 and G_2
  - The number of positive correspondence nodes to be selected P_{num}
- **Output:**
  - Positive correspondence nodes set P_{set}, Positive correspondence mapping P_{map}
- **Step 1:** Compute the compatibility matrices C_1, C_2 of graph G_1 and G_2 determined by correspondences I_{map}.
- **Step 2:** Initialization of P_{set} and P_{map}.
  - Calculate the residual compatibility matrix $R=|C_1 - C_2|$.
  - Calculate the fitness of node i in G_1 as
    $$f(i) = \frac{1}{d(i)}\sum_{j=1}^{|G_2|} R(i,j), \text{ where } d(i) \text{ is}$$
    the degree of node i in G_1.
  - Select the top P_{num} least fitness nodes as the initial positive correspondences P_{set} and hence the P_{map}.
- **Step 3:** Determine P_{set} and P_{map} iteratively.
  - Re-calculate the fitness index of node i in G_1 as $f(i) = \frac{1}{d(i)}\sum_{j\in P_{set}} R(i,j)$,

where P_{set} is the current positive correspondence node set.
  - Select the top P_{num} least fitness nodes as the positive correspondences (P_{set}) and hence the P_{map} to update the ones in the last iteration.
  - Go to 1, if P_{set} changed in the current iteration, Step 4 otherwise.
- **Step 4:** Output P_{set} and P_{map}.

Association Graph and Co-Embedding

In order to obtain more robust embedding vectors to achieve graph matching, we propose a new embedding method in which we use the positive correspondences obtained from the above consistency check process and integrate the embedding processes for G_1 and G_2 at the same time. We call this embedding as co-embedding. In order to do so, we first turn our attention to build an association graph between the graphs to be matched as shown in Figure 2. Let $P_{map}: I_1 \rightarrow I_2$ where I_1, I_2 are the label subsets of graph G_1 and G_2 respectively. Then the adjacency probability matrices are rearranged to form block matrices

$$P_{G_1} = \begin{bmatrix} P_{I_1} & B_1 \\ B_1^T & C_1 \end{bmatrix} \text{ and } P_{G_2} = \begin{bmatrix} P_{I_2} & B_2 \\ B_2^T & C_2 \end{bmatrix} \quad (15)$$

Figure 2. Flow chart of the association construction

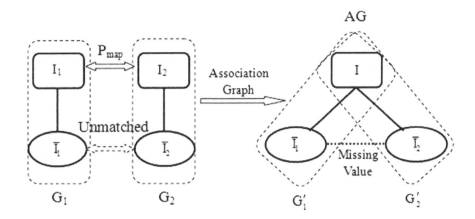

where :

$$\mathbf{P}_{I_1}(i,j) = \mathbf{P}_1(I_1(i), I_1(j)),$$
$$\mathbf{B}_1(i,j) = \mathbf{P}_1(I_1(i), \overline{I}_1(j))$$

and

$\mathbf{C}_1(i,j) = \mathbf{P}_1(\overline{I}_1(i), \overline{I}_1(j)),$ and $\mathbf{P}_{I_2}, \mathbf{B}_2, \mathbf{C}_2$ are similarly obtained. The adjacency probability matrix of the association graph (AG) is then taken the form

$$\mathbf{P}_{AG} = \begin{bmatrix} \mathbf{P}_I & \mathbf{B}_1 & \mathbf{B}_2 \\ \mathbf{B}_1^T & \mathbf{C}_1 & \mathbf{O} \\ \mathbf{B}_2^T & \mathbf{O} & \mathbf{C}_2 \end{bmatrix} \qquad (16)$$

where $\mathbf{O}$ is a zero matrix and $\mathbf{P}_I = (\mathbf{P}_{I_1} + \mathbf{P}_{I_2})/2$.

Let $X_{G_1} = [X_{I_1}, X_{\overline{I}_1}]$ and $X_{G_2} = [X_{I_2}, X_{\overline{I}_2}]$ be the embedding vector set for G_1 and G_2 respectively. The main idea for our co-embedding is that we want to enforce $X_{I_1} = X_{I_2}$ in our embedding process, i.e., the embedding vector for node i in G_1 should be the same with node j in G_2 if they have been matched already. Using association graph, we can achieve our co-embedding by solving the following problem

$$\min_X f_{\mathbf{P}_{AG},\mathbf{M}}(X) = \left\| X^T X - \mathbf{P}_{AG} - \mathbf{M} \circ (X^T X) \right\|^2$$
$$(17)$$

where $X = [X_{I_1}, X_{\overline{I}_1}, X_{\overline{I}_2}]$ and $\mathbf{M}$ is the Missing Data Label Matrix (MDLM) which is defined as follows:

$$\mathbf{M} = \begin{bmatrix} \mathbf{O} & \mathbf{O} & \mathbf{O} \\ \mathbf{O} & \mathbf{O} & \mathbf{I} \\ \mathbf{O} & \mathbf{I} & \mathbf{O} \end{bmatrix} \qquad (18)$$

where $\mathbf{I}$ is an identity matrix.

As pointed by Scheinerman (Scheinerman, 2010), the iterative algorithm can be used for the above problem by gradually eliminating the effect of the unknown or missing entries. Based on association graph we integrate G_1 and G_2 and embed them at the same time.

On the other hand, the above association graph is a missing value graph model (David, 2008) (Scheinerman, 2010) in which we treat the relationship between unmatched nodes as the missing value (as shown in Figure 1). These missing values can be recovered by the solution of Equation 17. Let $X=[\mathbf{x}_1, \mathbf{x}_2, \ldots, \mathbf{x}_n]$ be the final solution of the above problem, the missing value for edge kl can be directly obtained from the dot product of embedding vectors $\mathbf{x}_k$ and $\mathbf{x}_l$.

Graph Matching Based on Semi-DPRG

Using the embedding vectors, we can obtain the correspondences between nodes of graph by aligning the points using some matching algorithms such as Hungarian, SVD and so on. The basic idea behind these matching methods is to determine the correspondence cost for node k and l by calculating the similarity between their corresponding embedding vectors.

Moreover, if we use dot product of $\mathbf{x}_k$ and $\mathbf{y}_l$ as the similarity between them, then we can determine the correspondences cost between node k and l by using missing value of edge kl directly. So, our embedding based graph matching algorithm can also be seen as the missing value recovery process by using Semi-DPRG model.

However, in our matching process, we don't determine the correspondences for all the unmatched nodes at the same time, because the unmatched nodes that have strong connections with nodes in I (I_1) (nodes which are matched already) are most possibly determined robustly. So, we cast the recovery of correspondence matches for unmatched nodes in an iterative framework. For node i_0 in $\overline{I}_1$ we define the correlation strength RS between i_0 and I (I_1) as

$$RS(i_0) = \mathrm{E}(|E_0|)/\mathrm{E}(d(i_0))$$

where $E_0 = \{e_{i_0,j} \mid \mathbf{P}_{G_1}(i_0, j) \neq 0, j \in I_1\}$ and $\mathrm{E}(|E_0|)$, $\mathrm{E}(d(i_0))$ are the expected size of set E_0 and the expected degree of node i_0 in graph G_1 respectively. In our iterative matching process, we only determine the correspondences for the nodes in $\overline{I}_1$ and $\overline{I}_2$ that have high correlation strength value every time. Let P_{map} denote the mapping that is relevant to the node set I, then our Semi-DPRG based graph matching can be described as follow.

Algorithm 2: Graph matching based on semi-DPRG
- **Input:**
  - The initial correspondence I_{map}, Graph G_1 and G_2, threshold T
  - The number of positive correspondence nodes to be selected P_{num}
- **Output:**
  - The correspondences E_{map} between graph G_1 and G_2
- **Step 1:** Initialization. Calculate P_{map} using Algorithm 1.
- **Step 2:** Build an association graph (AG) model based on P_{map} and use co-embedding to obtain the embedding vectors for two graphs by solving Equation 17.
- **Step 3:** Determine the correspondences for the nodes in the E_{set} that have high RS value using the missing data and Hungarian algorithm.
- **Step 4:** If the all nodes have their correspondences, go to step 6, otherwise update P_{map}, E_{set} and go to Step 2.

- **Step 5:** Calculate fitness $f(i) = \frac{1}{d(i)} \sum_{j \in G_2} R(i, j)$ for every node in G_1. If $f(i) < T$ treat the node i as outlier node and delete it from E_{map}.

The last step guaranties that the algorithm can deal with graphs with some outliers and make the algorithm have the ability to handle with graphs with different sizes.

EXPERIMENT

In this section, we use the proposed G-E Random Graph to describe images and then the above developed algorithm is introduced to match the G-E Random Graph. Two house image sequences, one from CMU image database, the other from York house image sequence (Luo, 2011) are selected to test the proposed algorithm. The experiment starts from corner point extraction by Harris corner detector. The detected corner points and their positions are fed to model generating step. The matching is found by the random dot product graph based matching algorithm. Some matching results are shown in Figure 3 and Figure 4. The first line of the figures is the matching of the two images with 5 degree relative rotation. The second line is that of 10 degree relative rotation, and so on. Error correspondences are shown in red line segments. We can see from the figures that, generally speaking, when the relative rotation between the two images increases, the correct matching rate decreases.

To analyse the performance of the proposed algorithm quantitatively, we compare it with the EM (Luo, 2011) and the DPRG (Tang, 2011) graph matching algorithms. From Table 1 and Figure 5, we can see that although the performance of all the methods degenerates significantly after the

Figure 3. Some matching results for CMU images

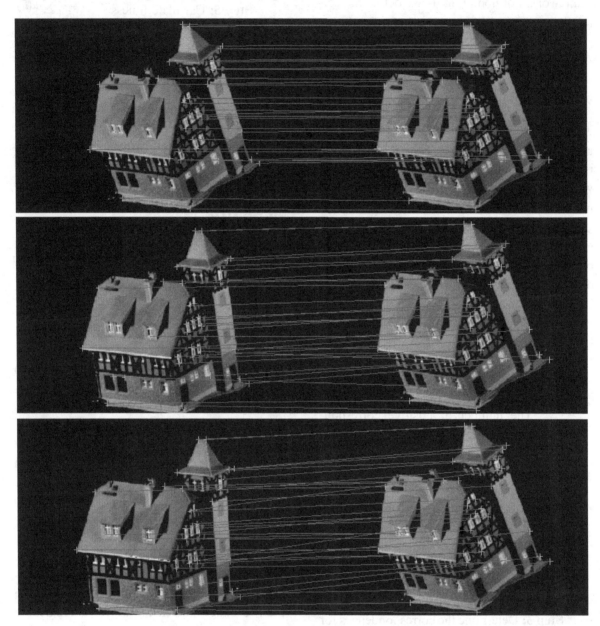

Figure 4. Some matching results for Swiss chalet sequence

Table 1. Summary of three matching algorithms for the CMU House Sequence Images

Images	Points	Methods	Correct Correspondences	False Correspondences	No Correspondences
House 1	30	EM			
		DPRG			
		Our method			
House 2	32	EM	29	0	1
		DPRG	28	1	1
		Our method	28	1	1
House 3	32	EM	28	1	1
		DPRG	28	1	1
		Our method	28	2	0
House 4	31	EM	23	5	2
		DPRG	25	3	2
		Our method	27	2	1
House 5	30	EM	11	10	9
		DPRG	22	4	4
		Our method	28	2	0
House 6	30	EM	5	16	9
		DPRG	19	7	4
		Our method	25	4	1

Figure 5. Summary of experimental result for York house sequence images

relative rotation is greater than 30 degrees, the proposed method outperforms the others in most cases. Especially when the difference is greater than 20 degrees, the performance of the proposed method is clearly better than that of the EM and is significantly better than that of the DPRG.

CONCLUSION

The main contributions of this paper are twofold: First, image structural information is modeled using the apparatus of the random geometric graph and generalized edge random model (G-E random graph model). Second, an algorithm to achieve matching between two G-E random graphs is developed. Therefore, image matching is cast into G-E random graph matching.

Compared to traditional graph-based image representation methods, the proposed one is more robust to graph node position disturbance. When used for graph matching, it has been shown the advantages of correct matching rate.

ACKNOWLEDGEMENT

This research is supported by the National Natural Science Foundation of China (No. 61073116), and "211 Project" in Anhui University.

REFERENCES

Antiqueira, L., Nunes, M. G. V., Oliveira, O. N., et al. (2005). *Strong correlations between text quality and complex networks features*. Retrieved from http://arxiv.org/abs/physics/0504033

Antonio, R. K., & Hancock, E. R. (2003). Edit distance from graph spectra. In *IEEE International Conference on Computer Vision, Vol. 1,* (pp. 234-241).

Antonio, R. K., & Hancock, E. R. (2005). Graph edit distance from spectral seriation. *IEEE Transactions on Pattern Analysis and Machine Intelligence*, *27*(3), 365–377. doi:10.1109/TPAMI.2005.56

Backes, A. R., & Bruno, O. M. (2010). Shape classification using complex network and multi-scale fractal dimension. *Pattern Recognition Letters*, *31*(1), 44–51. doi:10.1016/j.patrec.2009.08.007

Backes, A. R., Casanova, D., & Bruno, O. M. (2009). A complex network-based approach for boundary shape analysis. *Pattern Recognition*, *42*(1), 54–67. doi:10.1016/j.patcog.2008.07.006

Bagdanov, A. D., & Worring, M. (2003). First order Gaussian graphs for efficient structure classification. *Pattern Recognition*, *36*(6), 1311–1324. doi:10.1016/S0031-3203(02)00227-3

Bai, X., Yu, H., & Hancock, E. R. (2004). Graph matching using spectral embedding and alignment. In *International Conference on Pattern Recognition, Vol. 3,* (pp. 23-26).

Beer, E., Fill, J. A., Janson, S., & Scheinerman, E. R. (2010). *On vertex, edge, and vertex-edge random graphs*. Retrieved from http://arxiv.org/abs/0812.1410v2

Belongie, S., Puzhicha, J., & Malik, J. (2002). Shape matching and object recognition using shape contexts. *IEEE Transactions on Pattern Analysis and Machine Intelligence*, *24*(4), 509–522. doi:10.1109/34.993558

Bunke, H., & Shearer, K. (1998). A graph distance metric based on the maximal common subgraph. *Pattern Recognition Letters*, *19*(3-4), 255–259. doi:10.1016/S0167-8655(97)00179-7

Caelli, T., & Kosinov, S. (2004). An Eigenspace projection clustering method for inexact graph matching. *IEEE Transactions on Pattern Analysis and Machine Intelligence*, *26*(4), 515–519. doi:10.1109/TPAMI.2004.1265866

Chalumeau, T. da F.Costa, L., & Laligant, O., et al. (2006). Meriaudeau, texture discrimination using hierarchical complex networks. In *International Conference on Signal–Image Technology and Internet-Based Systems,* (pp. 543–550)

Christmas, W. J., Kittler, J., & Petrou, M. (1995). Structural matching in computer vision using probabilistic relaxation. *IEEE Transactions on Pattern Analysis and Machine Intelligence, 17*(8), 749–764. doi:10.1109/34.400565

Costa, L. D. F., Rodrigues, F. A., Travieso, G., & Villas Boas, P. R. (2005). Characterization of complex networks: A survey of measurements. *Advances in Physics, 56*(1), 167–242. doi:10.1080/00018730601170527

Costa, L. da F. (2004). *Complex networks, simple vision.* Retrieved from http://arxiv.org/abs/cond-mat/0403346

David, J. M., & Carey, E. P. (2008). Predicting unobserved links in incompletely observed networks. *Computational Statistics & Data Analysis, 52*(3), 1373–1386. doi:10.1016/j.csda.2007.03.016

Erdös, P., & Rényi, A. (1960). On the evolution of random graphs. *Publication of the Mathematical Institute of the Hungarian Academy of Sciences, 5*(1), 17–61.

Erdös, P., & Rényi, A. (1961). On the strength of connectedness of a random graph. *Acta Mathematica Academiae Scientiarum Hungaricae, 12*(1-2), 261–267. doi:10.1007/BF02066689

Eshera, M. A., & Fu, K. S. (1984). A similarity measure between attributed relational graphs for image analysis. In *International Conference on Pattern Recognition* (pp. 75-77).

Gao, X. B., Xiao, B., & Tao, D. C. (2008). Image categorization: Graph edit distance + edge direction histogram. *Pattern Recognition, 41*(10), 3179–3191. doi:10.1016/j.patcog.2008.03.025

Gao, X. B., Xiao, B., & Tao, D. C. (2010). A survey of graph edit distance. *Pattern Analysis & Applications, 13*(1), 113–129. doi:10.1007/s10044-008-0141-y

Gold, S., & Rangarajan, A. (1996). A graduated assignment algorithm for graph matching. *IEEE Transactions on Pattern Analysis and Machine Intelligence, 18*(4), 377–388. doi:10.1109/34.491619

Huet, B., & Hancock, E. R. (1999). Shape recognition from large image libraries by inexact graph matching. *Pattern Recognition Letters, 20*(11-13), 1259–1269. doi:10.1016/S0167-8655(99)00093-8

Jiang, X. Y., & Bunke, H. (1999). Optimal vertex ordering of graphs. *Information Processing Letters, 72*(5-6), 149–154. doi:10.1016/S0020-0190(99)00148-9

Leordeanu, M., & Hebert, M. (2009). A spectral technique for correspondence problem using pairwise constraints. In *IEEE International Conference on Computer Vision, Vol.2* (pp. 1482-1489)

Llados, J., Marti, E., & Villanueva, J. J. (2001). Symbol recognition by error-tolerant sub-graph matching between region adjacency graphs. *IEEE Transactions on Pattern Analysis and Machine Intelligence, 23*(10), 1137–1143. doi:10.1109/34.954603

Luo, B., & Hancock, E. R. (2001). Structural graph matching using the EM algorithm and singular value decomposition. *IEEE Transactions on Pattern Analysis and Machine Intelligence, 23*(10), 1120–1136.

Luo, B., Wilson, R. C., & Hancock, E. R. (2003). Spectral embedding of graphs. *Pattern Recognition, 36*(10), 2213–2230. doi:10.1016/S0031-3203(03)00084-0

Myers, R., Wilson, R. C., & Hancock, E. R. (2000). Bayesian graph edit distance. *IEEE Transactions on Pattern Analysis and Machine Intelligence, 22*(6), 628–635. doi:10.1109/34.862201

Penrose, M. (Ed.). (2003). *Random geometric graphs*. Oxford, UK: Oxford University Press. doi:10.1093/acprof:o so/9780198506263.001.0001

Scheinerman, E. R., & Kimberly, T. (2010). Modeling graphs using dot product representations. *Computational Statistics, 25*(1), 1–16. doi:10.1007/s00180-009-0158-8

Scott, G. L., & Longuett-Higgins, H. C. (1991). An algorithm for associating the features of two images. *Proceedings. Biological Sciences, 244*, 21–26. doi:10.1098/rspb.1991.0045

Shapiro, L. S., & Brady, J. M. (1992). Feature-based correspondence: an eigenvector approach. *Image and Vision Computing, 10*(5), 283–288. doi:10.1016/0262-8856(92)90043-3

Tang, J., Jiang, B., & Luo, B. (2011). Graph matching based on dot product representation of graphs. In *Graph-Based Representations in Pattern Recognition* (*Vol. 6658*, pp. 175–184). LNCS. doi:10.1007/978-3-642-20844-7_18

Umeyama, S. (1988). An Eigendecomposition approach to weighted graph matching problems. *IEEE Transactions on Pattern Analysis and Machine Intelligence, 10*(5), 695–703. doi:10.1109/34.6778

Watts, D. J., & Strogatz, S. H. (1998). Collective dynamics of 'small-world' networks. *Nature, 393*, 440–442. doi:10.1038/30918

Wilson, R. C., & Hancock, E. R. (1997). Structural matching by discrete relaxation. *IEEE Transactions on Pattern Analysis and Machine Intelligence, 19*(6), 634–648. doi:10.1109/34.601251

Wong, A. K. C., & You, M. (1985). Entropy and distance of random graphs with application to structure pattern recognition. *IEEE Transactions on Pattern Analysis and Machine Intelligence, 7*(5), 599–609. doi:10.1109/TPAMI.1985.4767707

Young, S. J., & Scheinerman, E. R. (2007). Random dot product graph models for social networks. In Milios, E. (Ed.), *Algorithms and Models for the Web-Graph* (*Vol. 4936*, pp. 138–149). LNCS. doi:10.1007/978-3-540-77004-6_11

Zhang, D. M., Sun, D. D., Fu, M. S., & Luo, B. (2010). Extended dot product representations of graphs with application to radar image segmentation. *Optical Engineering (Redondo Beach, Calif.), 49*(11), 17201. doi:10.1117/1.3505865

Chapter 3
The Node–to–Node Graph Matching Algorithm Schema

Guoxing Zhao
Beijing Normal University, China

Jixin Ma
University of Greenwich, UK

ABSTRACT

Many graph matching algorithms follow the approach of node-similarity measurement, that is, matching graphs by means of comparing the corresponding pairs of nodes of the graphs. Based on this idea, the authors propose a high-level schema for node-to-node graph matching, namely N2N graph matching algorithm schema. The chapter shows that such a N2N graph matching algorithm schema is versatile enough to subsume most of the representative node-to-node based graph matching algorithms. It is also shown that improved algorithms can be derived from this N2N graph matching schema, compared with various corresponding algorithms. In addition, the authors point out the limitation and constraints of the propose algorithm schema and suggest some possible treatments.

INTRODUCTION

Graphs are a powerful and versatile tool used for the description of structural objects which has been widely used in mathematics, computer science, artificial intelligence, biology, geography, or even politics, for representing structural objects and concepts. By graph representation, the task of calculating the similarity degree between two objects can be simply transferred into the problem of matching the corresponding pair of graphs.

Various algorithms for graph matching problems have been developed, which, according to Gold and Rangarajan (1996), can be classified into two categories: (1) search-based methods which rely on possible and impossible pairings between vertices; and (2) optimization-based methods which formulate the graph matching

DOI: 10.4018/978-1-4666-1891-6.ch003

problem as an optimization problem. Generally speaking, explicit search methods directly search the optimal match among permutation space (or permutation matrices space). Since the size of the search spaces increase exponentially according to the graph size, different kinds of heuristic techniques are developed to reduce the search space to a smaller acceptable size. Implicit search methods do not search for the optimal match in permutation space; instead, the permutation space is transferred into some other continuous real number space or mixed 0-1 and real number space and meanwhile the graph matching problems is also represented as an optimization among the continuous or mixed space.

Actually, there are other kinds of graph matching algorithms which do not use any search; instead, they simply explore some kind of node similarity between nodes of graph pairs, and get the optimal solutions by matching those similar nodes. In this paper, those matching algorithms shall be unified as the N2N graph matching algorithm schema, and detailed studied including the formulism of N2N graph matching algorithm schema, the examples of such schema, comparisons of some N2N graph matching algorithms, the limitation of such the N2N graph matching algorithm schema, and possible ways to improve it.

BACKGROUND

In 1987, Umeyama proposed an eigen-decomposition based graph matching algorithm (EDGM) for matching both undirected and directed weighted graphs. The EDGM algorithm is critical examined in (Zhao et al., 2007) that EDGM algorithm only works for graphs with single eigenvalues, and improved as meta-basis based graph matching algorithm MBGM, which can be applied for more general cases.

In 1991, Almohamod presented a symmetric polynomial transform based graph matching algorithm (SPGM), where the node similarity of

two graphs is constructed by the coefficient of the polynomial transform of the weights of the edges.

In 1999, Kleinberg proposed a hubs and authorities graph matching algorithm (HAGM) for internet searching, where the node similarity is based on the idea that two nodes are similarity if their adjacent nodes are similar. An iterative algorithm is provided to calculate such node similarity. This algorithm has been revised in (Zager & Verghese, 2008).

In 2003, van Wyk & van Wyk presented several Kronecker product successive projection based graph matching algorithms. The graph matching problem is transferred into the Kronecker Product Graph Matching formulation, based on which several approaches are derived, such as the least squares Kronecker product graph matching (LSKPGM) algorithm, the interpolator-based Kronecker product graph matching (IBKPGM) algorithm, the gradient-based Kronecker product graph matching (GBKPGM) algorithm and the orthonormal kernel Kronecker product graph matching (OKKPGM) algorithm.

Although these methods are derived from different theories, they are using the same idea to matching graphs by node similarity. These methods are mostly only applicable for certain kinds of graphs, but they can be easily implemented, analyzed and improved. In addition, most of the node similarity based graph matching algorithms have low computational complexities and are consequently applicable to large size graphs.

MAIN FOCUS OF THE CHAPTER

Some basic notions have to be defined before the discussion.

- **Definition 1:** A permutation p is an one-to-one function from {1, 2,..., n} to itself. The set of all permutations of n elements is denoted as SG(n).
- **Definition 2:** A permutation matrix P is a n-by-n matrix such that

$$\sum_{i=1}^{n} P(i,j) = 1 \text{ for all } j=1, 2, \ldots, n$$

$$\sum_{j=1}^{n} P(i,j) = 1 \text{ for all } i=1, 2, \ldots, n$$

$P(i,j) \in \{0, 1\}$ for all $i,j=1,2,\ldots,n$

and the set of all n-by-n matrices are denoted as Perm(n)

- **Proposition 1:** There is a natural one-to-one correspondence between the permutation set SG(n) and the permutation matrices set Perm(n) defined as:

s2p: SG(n)→Perm(n) such that
s2p(p)=I_n(p,:)

p2s: Perm(n) →SG(n) such that
p2s(P)=P×$(1,2,\ldots,n)^T$

for every permutation p∈SG(n) and permutation matrix P∈Perm(n).

The weighted graph matching problem is defined as

$$\arg s \min_{P \in Perm(n)} \left\| G - PHP^T \right\|_F \qquad (1)$$

where G, H∈$R^{n \times n}$ are the adjacency weighted matrices of weighted graphs G and H
The N2N graph matching algorithm schema is a general and abstract method for solving graph matching Equation 1.

- **Definition 3:** Given two graphs G and H, the N2N graph matching algorithm has the following two significant steps:
  ○ Constructing node-similarity matrix S(G, H).

The entry S(G, H)(i,j) denotes the similarity of i-th node of G and j-th node of H. In some cases, if a node-distance matrix D is provided instead of node similarity matrix, then similarity matrix S can be simply set as –D or m-D, where m is the maximum element of D.
  ○ Calculating the maximum similarity match.

$$\arg s \max_{P \in Perm(n)} \sum_{i,j=1}^{n} S(i,j) \times P(i,j) \qquad (2)$$

Requirement

One may ask whether the selection of node similarity matrix S(G, H) is arbitrary or not. The answer is negative. Since the entry of S(G, H) denotes the similarity between the nodes of graph G and H, the similarity must be independent on the order of the nodes. So the node similarity matrix S must satisfy the following important constraint:

- **Independence of Order I:**

$$S(PGP^T, QHQ^T) = P \times S(G,H) \times Q^T, \\ \text{for all } P,Q \in Perm(n) \qquad (3)$$

The independence of order I constraint is the most important and basic principal for the N2N graph matching algorithm schema and directly determine the applying scope of this algorithm schema.

- **Definition 4:** A function from $R^{n \times n} \times R^{n \times n}$ to $R^{n \times n}$ is said to be a node similarity function if it satisfies the independence of order I.

Examples of Node Similarity Based Graph Matching Algorithm

In this section, we shall introduce some examples of N2N graph matching algorithm schema.

- **Theorem 1:** The following functions are all node similarity functions:

$$S_1(G,H)(i,j) = -\left|G(i,i) - H(j,j)\right|$$

$$S_2(G,H)(i,j) = \sum_{k=1}^{n}\sum_{l=1}^{n} G(k,i) \times H(l,j)$$

$$S_3(G,H) =$$
$$unvec((H \otimes G + H^T \otimes G^T)^{\infty} \times vec(1_{n \times n}))$$

where n can be any natural number and $1_{n \times n}$ is a n-by-n matrix with all entries 1, $\otimes$ denotes the Kronecker product operator and vec() and unvec() denote the vectorization operator and its reverse.

The following proposition is important to prove the above theorem:

- **Proposition 2:** Let G be an n-by-n matrix, P and Q be two permutation matrices with p, q as their corresponding permutation vectors, then

$$PGQ(i, j)=G(p(i), q(j)) \tag{4}$$

where PQG(i, j) stands for the (i, j)-th entry of the matrix M=PQG.

- **Proof (to Theorem 1):**

$$S_1(PGP^T, QHQ^T)(i,j)$$
$$= -\left|PGP^T(i,i) - QHQ^T(j,j)\right|$$
$$= -\left|G(p(i), p(i)) - H(q(j), q(j))\right|$$

1.
$$= S_1(G,H)(p(i), q(j))$$

$$= PS_1(G,H)Q(i,j)$$

$$S_2(PGP^T, QHQ^T)(i,j)$$
$$= \sum_{k=1}^{n}\sum_{l=1}^{n} PGP^T(k,i) \times QHQ^T(l,j)$$
$$= \sum_{k=1}^{n}\sum_{l=1}^{n} G(p(k), p(i)) \times H(q(l), q(j))$$

2. $= \sum_{k=1}^{n}\sum_{l=1}^{n} G(k, p(i)) \times H(l, q(j))$

$$= S_2(G,H)(p(i), q(j))$$

$$= PS_2(G,H)Q^T(i,j)$$

It is well known that

3. $vec(AXB) = B^T \otimes A vec(X)$

Let $X_m(G,H) = unvec((H \otimes G + H^T \otimes G^T)^m \times vec(1_{n \times n}))$, then $X_0(G,H) = 1_{n \times n}$, $X_{m+1}(G,H) = GX_m(G,H)$ H+$G^T X_m(G,H)H^T$ and $S_3(G,H) = \lim_{m \to \infty} X_m$

We prove that

$$X_m(PGP^T, QHQ^T)=PX_m(G, H)Q^T \tag{5}$$

by induction on m.

Obviously, Equation 5 holds for m=0. Assume Equation 5 is true for m=k, then

$$X_{m+1}(PGP^T, QHQ^T)$$

$$= PGP^T X_m(PGP^T, QHQ^T) QHQ^T +$$
$$PG^T P^T X_m(PGP^T, QHQ^T) QH^T Q^T$$
$$= PGP^T P X_m(G, H) Q^T QHQ^T +$$
$$PG^T P^T P X_m(G, H) Q^T QH^T Q^T$$

$$= PGX_m(G, H)HQ^T + PG^T X_m(G, H)H^T Q^T$$

$$= P\left(GX_m(G, H)H + G^T X_m(G, H)H^T \right) Q^T$$

$$= PX_{m+1}(G, H)Q^T$$

which means Equation 5 is true for m=k+1. Equation 5 holds for all integer m.

$$S_3(PGP^T, QHQ^T) =$$
$$\lim_{m \to \infty} X_m(PGP^T, QHQ^T) = \lim_{m \to \infty} PX_m(G, H)Q^T =$$
$$P \lim_{m \to \infty} X_m(G, H)Q^T = PS_3(G, H)Q^T$$

The function S_1, S_2 and S_3 have been proved to be node similarity functions, so we can get three corresponding N2N graph matching algorithms. It is easily can be seen that the S_3 node similarity function based matching algorithm is exactly the hubs and authorities graph matching algorithm proposed by Kleinberg (1999). We also get the following theorems showing that the S_2 node similarity function based graph matching algorithm is exactly the least square Kronecker product-successive projection graph matching algorithm proposed in (van Wyk & van Wyk, 2003).

- **Theorem 2:** The S_2 node similarity function based graph matching algorithm is the least square Kronecker product-successive projection graph matching algorithm.
- **Proof:** For the LSKPGM algorithm, the node similarity S(i, j) is calculated by

$$S(i, j) = \frac{\sum_{k=(i-1)n+1}^{i*n} \sum_{l=(j-1)n+1}^{j*n} \Phi_{k,l}}{n}$$

where $\Phi^T = \Theta^+ \Pi$, $\Theta = \begin{bmatrix} vec(H_1)^T \\ \vdots \\ vec(H_m)^T \end{bmatrix}$ and

$$\Pi = \begin{bmatrix} vec(G_1)^T \\ \vdots \\ vec(G_m)^T \end{bmatrix}.$$

For the weighted graphs, where m=1, above formulae degrade to

$$\Phi = \Pi^T (\Theta^+)^T = \frac{vec(G)vec(H)^T}{\left\| vec(H) \right\|_2^2}$$

so the node similarity

$$S\left(i, j\right) = \frac{\sum_{k=(i-1)n+1}^{i*n} \sum_{l=(j-1)n+1}^{j*n} \Phi_{k,l}}{n}$$
$$= \frac{\sum_{k=1}^{n} \sum_{l=1}^{n} G(k, i) \times H(l, j)}{n \left\| vec(H) \right\|_2^2}$$

Since the solution of maximum linear assignment doesn't effect by a positive scalar, so the LSKPGM algorithm coincide with the S_2-N2N graph matching algorithm.

Node Attribute Functions

Obviously, to define node similarity S(G,H), one has to consider both graphs G and H at the same time. It will be much easier if one can define this similarity by dealing with two graphs separately. So a new important notion node attribute function will be introduced.

- **Definition 3**: A node-attribute function is a function $f : R^{n \times n} \to R^{n \times m}$ which satisfies the following:
- **Independence of Order II:**

$$f(PGP^T) = Pf(G),$$
$$\text{for all } G \in R^{n \times n} \text{ and } P \in perm(n) \quad (6)$$

Intuitively, the weight matrix of a graph G describes the edge attributes and the node attribute function f maps these edge-attributes to node attributes of graph G.

The independence of order II constraint has to be satisfied to make sure the node attributes of a graph are independent on the order of its nodes.

- **Theorem 3**: The following functions are all node-attribute functions
    - $f_4(G)(k,:) = [sum(G(k,:)), sum(G(:,k))]$
    - $f_5(G)(k,:) = [poly(G(k,:)), poly(G(:,k))]$
    - $f_6(G)(k,:) = [sort(G(k,:)), sort(G(:,k))]$
    - $$f_7(G)(:,k) = diag\left(\frac{G^k}{n^k}\right),$$
      k=1,2,...,n.
- **Proof:**

$$f_4(PGP^T)(k,:)$$
$$= [sum(PGP^T(k,:)), sum(PGP^T(k,:))]$$
4. $= [sum(G(p(k),p)), sum(G(p(k),p))]$
$$= [sum(G(p(k),:)), sum(G(p(k),:))]$$
$$= f_4(G)(p(k),:)$$
$$= Pf_4(G)(k,:)$$

(Proof of items 5 and 6 is the same as 4.)

7.
$$f_7(PGP^T)(:,k) = diag\left(\frac{(PGP^T)^k}{n^k}\right)$$
$$= diag\left(\frac{PG^kP^T}{n^k}\right)$$
$$= Pdiag\left(\frac{G^k}{n^k}\right)$$
$$= Pf_7(G)(:,k)$$

The next example is more difficult.

- **Theorem 4:** Let f_8 be a function calculated by the following three steps, then f_8 is a node attributed function satisfying Independence of Order II.
    - Calculating the Hermitian matrix
      $$Ht(G) := \frac{G + G^T}{2} + \frac{G - G^T}{2}\sqrt{-1}$$
    - Calculating eigen-decomposition of the matrix Ht(G)=VDV*, where D is the diagonal matrix of eigenvalues in descending order.
      Suppose that Ht(G) has k distinct eigenvalue $\lambda_1 \le \lambda_2 \le \cdots \le \lambda_k$ with repeat times $n_1, n_2, ..., n_k$ and eigenspace $V_1, V_2, ..., V_k$.
    - Let $f_8(G) = [V_1', V_2', \cdots, V_k']$, where V_i' is the meta-basis of eigenspace V_i. (Zhao et al., 2007)
- **Proof:** We calculate $f_8(PGP^T)$ step by step. Obviously, $Ht(PGP^T) = PHt(G)P^T$. Since $Ht(G) = UDU^*$,

$$Ht(PGP^T) =$$
$$[PV_1U_1, \cdots, PV_kU_k]D([PV_1U_1, \cdots, PV_kU_k])^T$$

where $U_i \in U(n_i)$
Calculate meta-basis. The meta-basis of PV_1U_1 is defined by the unitary invariant

vector $V_i V_i^* \vec{1}_n$ of eigenspace V_i. The unitary invariant vector of eigenspace $PV_i U_i$ is

$$(PV_i U_i)(PV_i U_i)^* \vec{1}_n =$$
$$PV_i U_i U_i^* V_i^* P^T \vec{1}_n = PV_i V_i^* \vec{1}_n$$

so $f_8(PGP^T) = Pf_8(G)$.

- **Theorem 5:** Let f_9 be a function calculated by the following three steps:
  - Calculating Hermitian matrix
    $$Ht(G) := \frac{G + G^T}{2} + \frac{G - G^T}{2}\sqrt{-1}$$
  - Calculating eigen-decomposition of the matrix $Ht(G)=VDV^*$, where D is the diagonal matrix of eigenvalues in descending order.
  - Let $f_8(G) = |V|$

If all the eigenvalues of $Ht(G)$ are single, then f_9 is a node attributed function satisfying independence of order II.

- **Proof:** The same as theorem 4, We calculate $f_9(PGP^T)$ step by step.

$Ht(PGP^T) = PHt(G)P^T$

$Ht(G) = UDU^*$, since all the eigenvalues of $Ht(G)$ is single, then

$$Ht(PGP^T) =$$
$$[PV_1 x_1, \cdots, PV_k x_k]D([PV_1 x_1, \cdots, PV_k x_k])^T$$

where $x_i \in U(1)$
Calculate:

$$f_9\left(PGP^T\right) = \left| [PV_1 x_1, \cdots, PV_k x_k] \right| =$$
$$\left| [PV_1, \cdots, PV_k] \right| = P|V| = Pf_9(G)$$

Using the node-attribute function, one can easily construct the corresponding node-similarity function by the following theorem.

- **Theorem 6:** Let f be a node-attribute function, and S_f is defined as:

$$S_f(G, H) = f(G) \times f(H)^T \qquad (7)$$

Then S_f is a node-similarity function.
The Proof is trivial.

Therefore, each node-attribute function in Theorem 3, Theorem 4 and Theorem 5 defines a corresponding node-similarity function denoted as S_4, to S_9. The matching algorithms by node-similarity functions S_5 and S_6 are exactly the symmetric polynomials transformation graph matching algorithm SPGM and the sort based graph matching algorithm STGM; The matching algorithms by node-similarity functions S_9 and S_8 are exactly the eigen-decomposition graph matching algorithm EDGM and the improved meta-basis based graph matching algorithm MBGM.

The node similarity graph matching algorithm based on the similarity function S_1 and S_4 and S_7 is simply named as S_1-N2N, S_4-N2N and S_7-N2N.

Comparisons

In this section, these node similarity based graph matching algorithms associated with node-similarity function S_1 to S_9 are numerically compared.

Figure 1, Figure 2, and Figure 3 is the average error of 9 matching algorithms applied for isomorphic sparse graphs, sparse graph pairs with perturbation $\varepsilon=0.10$, and dense graph pairs with perturbation $\varepsilon=0.10$. Figure 4 shows the CPU time of the 9 matching algorithms.

Figure 1. Matching isomorphic sparse graph pairs

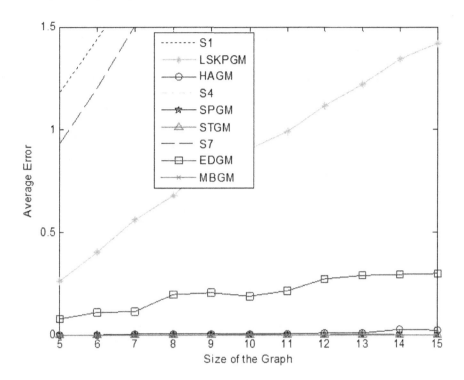

Figure 2. Matching dense graph pairs with perturbation coefficient ε=0.10

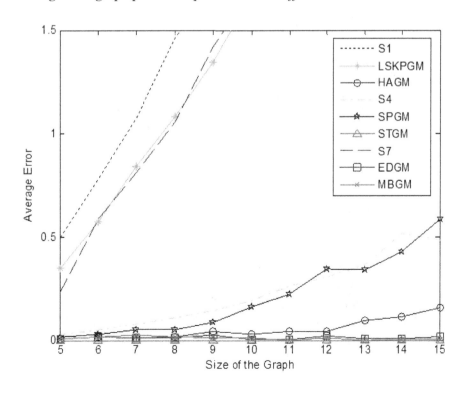

Figure 3. Matching sparse graph pairs with perturbation coefficient ε=0.10

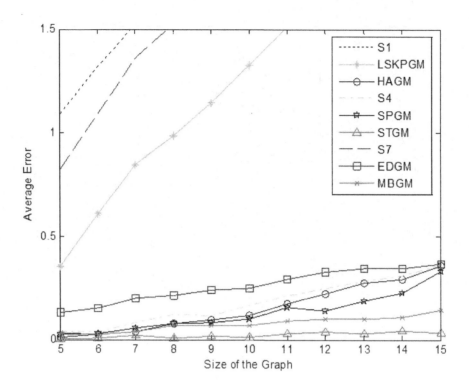

Computational Complexity

All the N2N graph matching algorithms have two main steps, the calculation of node-similarity and the calculation of maximum similarity match. The computational complexity of the N2N algorithm based on S_1 to S_9 is list as Table 1

Obviously, all these algorithm works efficiently with complexity $O(n^3)$ or $O(n^4)$.

Extensions

Weighted Average Node Similarity

In last section, nine different node similarity functions are constructed, where each of them expresses certain kind of node similarity of graphs. And these similarities can be combined into some more complicated similarity functions.

• **Theorem 7:** Given m similarity functions $S_1, \ldots, S_m$, the weighted average function

$$S = \sum_{i=1}^{m} w_i S_i \qquad (8)$$

Then S is also a node similarity function. Based on this weighted average node similarity function, a new matching algorithm can be developed.

Matching Attributed Graphs

In the above discussion, only matching weighted graphs is considered. However, the node similarity based graph matching algorithm can be easily extended to match attribute graphs.

Given two attributed graphs $G=\{G_k\}$, $H=\{H_k\}$, $1 \leq k \leq m$, and Let S be a node similarity function,

Figure 4. CPU time consuming of the nine algorithms

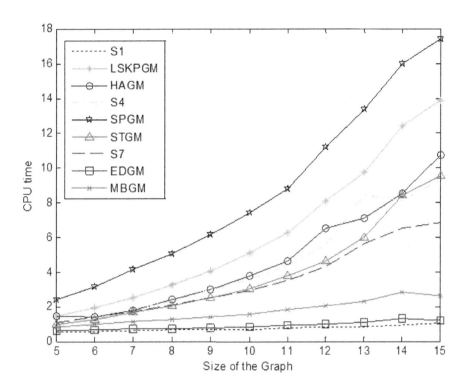

then the node similarity of G and H can be defined by:

$$S\left(G,H\right) = \sum_{k=1}^{m} w_k S(G_k, H_k) \qquad (9)$$

where w_k is the importance coefficient of k-th attribute.

Again, we transfer the attribute graph matching Equation 1 to maximum linear assignment Equation 2.

LIMITATIONS

In this section, we shall show that all the N2N graph matching algorithms fail to work for circles.

- **Theorem 8:** All node similarity graph matching algorithms fail to work for circles.
- **Proof:** Let G and H be two circles as show in Figure 5, then the adjacency matrices are

Table 1. Computational complexity of N2N graph matching algorithms

	S1	**LKPGM**	**HAGM**	**S4**	**SPGM**	**STGM**	**S7**	**MBGM**	**EDGM**
Step1	$O(n^2)$	$O(n^4)$	$O(n^3)$	$O(n^3)$	$O(n^3)$	$O(n^2 \log n)$	$O(n^3)$	$O(n^4)$	$O(n^3)$
Step2	$O(n^3)$								
In all	$O(n^3)$	$O(n^4)$	$O(n^3)$	$O(n^3)$	$O(n^3)$	$O(n^3)$	$O(n^3)$	$O(n^4)$	$O(n^3)$

$$G = \begin{bmatrix} 0 & 1 & 0 & 0 & 0 & 0 \\ 0 & 0 & 1 & 0 & 0 & 0 \\ 0 & 0 & 0 & 1 & 0 & 0 \\ \vdots & \vdots & \vdots & \ddots & \vdots & \vdots \\ 0 & 0 & 0 & 0 & 0 & 1 \\ 1 & 0 & 0 & 0 & 0 & 0 \end{bmatrix}$$

$$H = \begin{bmatrix} 0 & 1 & 0 & 0 & 0 & 0 \\ 0 & 0 & 0 & 1 & 0 & 0 \\ 0 & 0 & 1 & 0 & 0 & 0 \\ \vdots & \vdots & \vdots & \ddots & \vdots & \vdots \\ 0 & 0 & 0 & 0 & 0 & 1 \\ 1 & 0 & 0 & 0 & 0 & 0 \end{bmatrix}$$

Let S be any node similarity function, then S satisfies Independence of Order I, so

$$S(PGP^T, H) = P \times S(G, H),$$
for all $P \in Perm(n)$ \hfill (9)

Specially, let

$$P_0 = \begin{bmatrix} 0 & 1 & 0 & 0 & 0 & 0 \\ 0 & 0 & 1 & 0 & 0 & 0 \\ 0 & 0 & 0 & 1 & 0 & 0 \\ \vdots & \vdots & \vdots & \ddots & \vdots & \vdots \\ 0 & 0 & 0 & 0 & 0 & 1 \\ 1 & 0 & 0 & 0 & 0 & 0 \end{bmatrix}$$

Then it can be easily verified that $P_0 G P_0^T = G$ so

$$S(G, H) = S(P_0 G P_0^T, H) = P_0 \times S(G, H)$$

Figure 5. Two circles

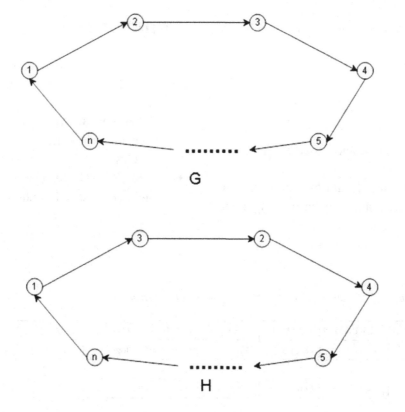

which means all rows of S(G, H) are equal

$$S(G,H) = \begin{bmatrix} a_{1,1} & a_{1,2} & \cdots & a_{1,n} \\ a_{1,1} & a_{1,2} & \cdots & a_{1,n} \\ \vdots & \vdots & \ddots & \vdots \\ a_{1,1} & a_{1,2} & \cdots & a_{1,n} \end{bmatrix}$$

Then any permutation $P \in Perm(n)$ is the solution of maximum linear assignment problem:

$$\underset{P \in Perm(n)}{\arg s \ \max} \sum_{i,j=1}^{n} S(i,j) \times P(i,j)$$

Specially, the identity matrix I is a optimal solution for the above formula, where

$$\left\| G - IHI^{T} \right\|_{F} = \left\| G - H \right\|_{F} = 2$$

but in fact graph G and H are isomorphic by the permutation

$$\overline{P} = \begin{bmatrix} 1 & 0 & 0 & 0 & 0 & 0 \\ 0 & 0 & 1 & 0 & 0 & 0 \\ 0 & 1 & 0 & & 0 & 0 \\ \vdots & \vdots & \vdots & \ddots & \vdots & \vdots \\ 0 & 0 & 0 & 0 & 1 & 0 \\ 0 & 0 & 0 & 0 & 0 & 1 \end{bmatrix}$$

so the node similarity based graph matching algorithm fails to find the best match.

Theorem 8 only claims that all the node similarity based algorithms are not applicable for circles, how about others? In fact, the essence of this failure is that if graph G is self-similar, which means there is a non-trivial automorphism of graph G, the node similarity based graph matching algorithm will fail to distinguish those similar nodes of G. Figure 6 is a simple example which has non-trivial automorphism, such that nodes 1, 2 and 3 are not distinguishable and nodes 4, 5 and 6 are not distinguishable.

Figure 6. Self-similar graph

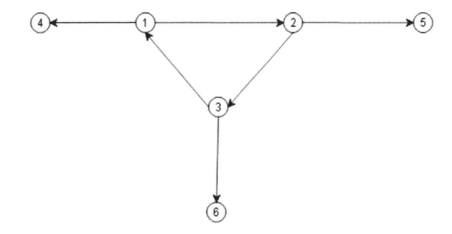

FUTURE RESEARCH DIRECTIONS

In the last section, we showed that the N2N graph matching schema doesn't work for self-similar graphs. There is a simple way to overcome such merit, named k-enumeration improvement, Which is enumerating all the possibility of mapping the nodes $\{1,...,k\}$ of G to the nodes $\{i_1,...,i_k\}$ of graph H to find the best match. This strategy will improve that matching result for self-similar graphs to a certain extent by using $O(C_n^k)$ times CPU time.

CONCLUSION

In this paper the high-level schema N2N graph matching algorithm schema is proposed to unify all the graph matching algorithms based on the similarity of nodes of two graphs. With such algorithm schema, all these algorithms can be expressed, analyzed and improved together. Although it has been pointed out that such algorithm schema has limitations for matching self-similar graphs, there are also possible ways to overcome such defeat by expending more CPU time.

REFERENCES

Almohamad, H. A. (1991). Polynomial transform for matching pairs of weighted graphs. *Applied Mathematical Modelling, 15*, 216–222. doi:10.1016/0307-904X(91)90011-D

Gold, S., & Rangarajan, A. (1996). Graduated assignment algorithm for graph matching. *IEEE Transactions on Pattern Analysis and Machine Intelligence, 18*, 377–388. doi:10.1109/34.491619

Kleinberg, J. M. (1999). Authoritative sources in a hyperlinked environment. *Journal of the ACM, 46*, 604–632. doi:10.1145/324133.324140

Umeyama, S. (1987). Weighted graph matching algorithms using Eigen-decomposition Approach. *Transactions of the Institute of Electronics, Information and Communication Engineers, Section E., 70*, 809–816.

van Wyk, B. J., & van Wyk, M. A. (2003). Kronecker product graph matching. *Pattern Recognition, 36*, 2019–2030. doi:10.1016/S0031-3203(03)00009-8

Zager, L. A., & Verghese, G. C. (2008). Graph similarity scoring and matching. *Applied Mathematics Letters, 21*, 86–94. doi:10.1016/j.aml.2007.01.006

Zhao, G., et al. (2007). Using eigen-decomposition method for weighted graph matching. In *3rd International Conference on Intelligent Computing, ICIC 2007*, (pp. 1283-1294).

Section 2
Graph–Based Methods for Image Segmentation

Chapter 4
Unsupervised and Supervised Image Segmentation Using Graph Partitioning

Charles-Edmond Bichot
Université de Lyon, France

ABSTRACT

Image segmentation is an important research area in computer vision and its applications in different disciplines, such as medicine, are of great importance. It is often one of the very first steps of computer vision or pattern recognition methods. This is because segmentation helps to locate objects and boundaries into images. The objective of segmenting an image is to partition it into disjoint and homogeneous sets of pixels. When segmenting an image it is natural to try to use graph partitioning, because segmentation and partitioning share the same high-level objective, to partition a set into disjoints subsets. However, when using graph partitioning for segmenting an image, several big questions remain: What is the best way to convert an image into a graph? Or to convert image segmentation objectives into graph partitioning objectives (not to mention what are image segmentation objectives)? What are the best graph partitioning methods and algorithms for segmenting an image? In this chapter, the author tries to answer these questions, both for unsupervised and supervised image segmentation approach, by presenting methods and algorithms and by comparing them.

1. INTRODUCTION

Image segmentation aims to partition an image into a set of regions which should be at the same time visually distinct and uniform regarding some properties such as gray level, color, shape or texture. Segmentation is the very first step and a key issue in many computer vision domains such as object recognition, event detection, video tracking, image restoration or scene reconstruction. Image segmentation is used in many applications such as medicine, robotic, industry, etc, where the quality of the final result greatly depends on the quality of the first step: image segmentation.

Image segmentation problems can be modeled by graphs and then, graph partitioning algorithms

DOI: 10.4018/978-1-4666-1891-6.ch004

may be used to find the desired image regions. This modeling can be made either trough an unsupervised approach or trough a supervised one. In the latter, the user has to seed the parts of the image to be segmented, on the other the user had at most to know the number of parts in which the image should be segmented. The graph partitioning image segmentation process is divided into three main steps:

1. Image into graph conversion
2. Graph partitioning optimization
3. Partition projection to the image

The first step converts an image, which is either in color or black and weight, textured or not, small or huge, into a graph. The objectives of this first step are to translate both local and global image information into the graph, like grayscale differences, texture information, patterns, etc. The second steps partitions the resulted graph by optimizing an objective function. The third and last step projects the partition of the graph directly onto the original image. Of course, the partitioning step is very sensitive to the image into graph conversion. A poor graph weighting and structure results to a poor segmentation even if the partition is optimal regarding the objective function. Moreover, it should be noticed that the objective function can not reflect perfectly the image segmentation problem.

What constitutes a good image segmentation? Haralick and Shapiro propose four criteria which have become a classical standard for image segmentation evaluation (Haralick & Shapiro, 1985):

1. **Intra-Region Uniformity:** Regions should be uniform and homogeneous with respect to some characteristic(s).
2. **Inter-Region Disparity**: Adjacent regions should have significant differences with respect to the characteristic on which they are uniform.

3. Region interiors should be simple and without holes.
4. Boundaries should be simple, not ragged, and be spatially accurate.

Criteria 3 and 4 measure semantic cues of objects, such as shape.

Image segmentation objective functions often refer to one or more of these criteria. Those objective functions combined in some arrangement intra-region uniformity and inter-region disparity either by making a weighted sum of them or by dividing them.

This chapter is composed of four sections: This first introductive section; the second section, which explains how to convert an image into a graph. It also presents the classical methods for doing this conversion, and what can be done to improve them. The third section details the unsupervised image segmentation approach based on graph partitioning. It details two main graph partitioning methods: spectral and multilevel methods. The fourth section presents the supervised image segmentation approach based on graph partitioning and shows several methods to solve it. The last section provides discussions, perspectives and concluding remarks.

2. IMAGE INTO GRAPH CONVERSION

The very first step of image segmentation based on graph partitioning is to convert images into graphs.

In this chapter, we formally define a graph G as a pair (V, E), where V is a finite set of elements called vertices, and $E = \{(v, v')|v \in V, v' \in V\}$ is a set of pairs of vertices called edges. Two vertices v and v' are said to be adjacent if their pair is an edge, i.e. there exist an edge $e = (v, v') \in E$. We also say that the vertices v and v' are incident to the edge e. The degree of a vertex is the number of edges incident to the vertex. Assuming any ranking sorting function, a vertex v can be referred by its ranked number I in V, and an edge (v,v') by its vertices ranked numbers, (i,j).

A graph is called regular when each vertex has the same number of neighbors, i.e. when every vertex has the same degree.

2.1 Pixel Adjacency Graph

The simplest way to convert an image into a graph is to associate to each pixel of the image a vertex. These vertices form a graph which represents the image. Then, the image into graph conversion process consists in constructing a pixel adjacency graph. We will see below how to connect vertices together in order to construct graph's edges. The size of the graph is directly related to the resolution of the image; its number of vertices is the number of pixels of the image.

2.1.1 Structure of the Pixel Adjacency Graph

There are several ways to construct the edges of the graph of an image, but commonly vertices of the pixel adjacency graph are connected together regarding their neighborhood in a 2-dimentional (2D) representation: a 4-neighborhood consists to connect a center pixel to its North, South, East and West neighboring pixels; an 8-neighborhood is a 4-neighborhood with four more connections to North-East, South-East, South-West and South-West pixels. Of course, other combinations are possible; we may cite two other configurations: 12-neighborhood (2 square distances to the pixel center), and 28-neighborhood (3 square distances to the pixel center). This graph structure can be extended in 3 dimensions where a 12-neighborhood is often used.

Figure 1 illustrates the general image into pixel adjacency graph conversion process. Two successive zooms into the original image (Figure 1a) show pixels of the image. These pixels are associated in Figure 1c to the corresponding adjacency graph with neighborhood of 4. It means that each pixel is connected to its 4 nearest neighbors, except on the image borders of course.

4-neighborhood and 8-neighborhood pixel adjacency graphs are practically regular graphs. It is easy to understand that by considering images as (practically) regular graphs, patterns of the image are not represented in the topology of the graph. In other words, the graph models only very local patterns of the image – only pixels relations – instead of representing global patterns of the image. Thus, in this case, the graph is a relatively poor representation of the image because it does not take into account global information. To overcome this problem, there are two main approaches: to connect vertices together not only by considering direct neighbors; to consider vertices of the graph as set of pixels (region graph, see below).

2.1.2 Weighting of the Pixel Adjacency Graph

Because the structure of the pixel adjacency graph is very simple, like 4-neighborhood or 8-neighborhood pixel adjacency graphs, it is necessary to define precisely edge weights in order to have a good segmentation of the graph. Edge weights should be defined such that when optimally minimizing the objective function the segmentation results is optimal. However, because what is an optimal segmentation is an open question, it is actually not possible to achieve a perfect weighting. Thus, let just say that edge weights should be defined such that, when minimizing the objective function, the segmentation results are good enough.

Edge weights are all based on the same principle: they measure the proximity and the dissimilarity between the two edges' vertices in order to represent locally the gradient of the image. To do so, edge weights can combine difference of intensity, color, texture, shape, and of course spatial distance.

Figure 1. Adjacency graph of pixels

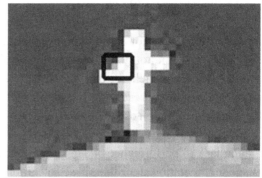

a) Original image

b) Zoom of the box selected in a)

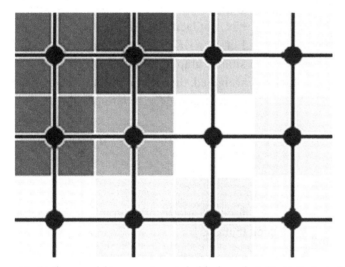

c) In this figure each big square is a pixel of the box selected in b). Each pixel corresponds to a vertex of the graph; edges are constructed by a 4-neighborhood.

The generic edge weighting function can be formulated as:

$$w\left(i, j\right) = \exp\left(-\frac{h\left(i, j\right)}{\sigma}\right)$$

where $h(i,j)$ is a distance between vertices number i and j. This distance can be a difference of intensity, color, texture, shape, spatial distance, or a combination of some or all of them. The distance chosen is mostly the Euclidian distance, even if others may be used.

A very common dissimilarity weighting function is:

$$w_F\left(i, j\right) = \exp\left(-\frac{\left|F\left(i\right) - F\left(j\right)\right|_2^2}{\sigma_F}\right)$$

where $F(i)$ is a feature vector based on intensity, color or texture information at vertex number i. σ_F is a scale parameter to tune.

The dissimilarity weighting function $F()$ can be every descriptor vector, or combination of them. However, $F(i)$ is commonly the brightness value at pixel i (the pixel which corresponds to vertex number i), albeit its represents only a small part of the image information especially for color images or textured images. Here, we want to stress a particular lack of performance of a great number of image segmentation algorithms based on graph partitioning mainly due to the fact that they only use brightness color values and a small neighborhood for constructing the pixel adjacency graph.

The spatial proximity between two vertices is measured by:

$$w_X(i,j) =$$
$$\begin{cases} \exp\left(\dfrac{-\left\|X(i) - X(j)\right\|_2^2}{\tilde{A}_X}\right) & \text{if } \|X(i) - X(j)\|_2 < r \\ 0 & \text{otherwise} \end{cases}$$

where $X(i)$ is the spatial location of vertex i and r the maximal distance allowed between two pixels. σ_X is a scale parameter to tune. Due to the maximal distance r this weighting function is compatible with the pixel adjacency graph neighborhood representation.

Finally, the edge weighting function is a combination of a proximity measure and one or more dissimilarity weighting functions:

$$w(i,j) =$$
$$\exp\left(-\frac{\left\|X(i) - X(j)\right\|_2^2}{\sigma_X} - \sum_{l=1}^{nb_F} \frac{\left\|F_l(i) - F_l(j)\right\|_2^2}{\sigma_{F_l}}\right)$$

where $F_1()$ is the 1st weighting feature vector and σ_{F_l} its corresponding scale parameter.

Another sometimes-used weighting function is simply the Euclidian norm of the difference between weighting features.

2.1.3 Mathematical Representation of the Pixel Adjacency Graph

Because images are 2D representations, it is natural to store graph edges weights into a matrix. This matrix is called the adjacency matrix of the graph.

- **Definition:** Adjacency matrix, degree matrix, Laplacian matrix
  Let $G=(V,E)$ be an undirected weighted simple graph (weighted by w, if it is not weighted, then $w=1$). The adjacency matrix of the graph, M_{Adj}, is defined such that $\forall i, j$

$$\left(M_{Adj}\right)_{ij} \equiv \begin{cases} 0 & \text{if } i = j \\ w(i,j) & \text{else} \end{cases}$$

The degree matrix of the graph, M_{Deg}, is defined such that $\forall i, j$:

$$\left(M_{Deg}\right)_{ij} \equiv$$
$$\begin{cases} deg(i) \equiv \sum_{k=1}^{|V|} w(i,k) & \text{if } i = j \\ 0 & \text{else} \end{cases}$$

The Laplacian matrix of the graph, M_{Lap}, is defined such that $M_{Lap} \equiv M_{Deg} - M_{Adj}$.

These mathematical representations of a graph are commonly used to represent both the pixel adjacency graph and the region adjacency graph. The region adjacency graph, or region graph, is a graph where each vertex corresponds to an image region. This modeling of an image is often used by supervised image segmentation methods based on graphs. Region graphs are obtained using a low level segmentation method (over-segmentation) such as watershed cut (Cousty, Bertrand, Najman, & Couprie, 2009).

2.2 Graph Partitioning Definitions and Objective Functions

- **Definition:** Partition of a graph
  Let $G=(V,E)$ be an undirected simple graph. A partition of G into k parts is a set P_k of k subset of V, noted as $\{V_1,...,V_k\}$, such that: each element of P_k is non-empty; the elements of P_k are pairwise disjoints; the union of all elements of P_k forms V.

- **Definition:** Cut of a partition
  Let $G=(V,E)$ be a weighted undirected simple graph on its edges by w (if it is not, then $w=1$) and $P_k=\{V_1,...V_k\}$ a partition of G into k parts.
  The cut value of a bisection P_2 (when $k=2$) is defined as:

$$cut\left(V_1,V_2\right) = \sum_{u\in V_1}\sum_{v\in V_2}w(u,v)$$

The cut value of a k-partition P_k is defined as:

$$cut\left(P_k\right) = \sum_{i<j}cut(V_i,V_j) = \frac{1}{2}\sum_{i=1}^{k}cut(V_i,V-V_i)$$

The cut value can be viewed as an objective function depending on G and k.
The objective function that aims to minimize, for each part, the ratio between its cut and its weight is called ratio cut.

- **Definition:** Ratio cut of a partition
  Let $G=(V,E)$ be a weighted undirected simple graph on both its vertices and edges by w (if it is not, then $w=1$) and $P_k=\{V_1,...V_k\}$ a partition of G into k parts. The ratio cut value of the partition P_k is defined as:

$$RCut(P_k) = \sum_{i=1}^{k}\frac{cut(V_i,V-V_i)}{w(V_i)}$$

The objective function that aims to minimize, for each part, the ratio between its cut and the sum of the weight of the edges adjacent to at least one of its vertices is called the normalized cut. In other words, the normalized cut objective function aims to minimize, for each part, the ratio between the sum of the weight of the edges adjacent to exactly one of its vertices and the sum of the weight of the edges adjacent to at least one of its vertices.

- **Definition:** Normalized cut of a partition
  The normalized cut value of a partition P_k is defined as:

$$NCut(P_k) = \sum_{i=1}^{k}\frac{cut(V_i,V-V_i)}{cut(V_i,V)}$$

The normalized cut is a very popular objective function for unsupervised segmentation approach using graph partitioning.

3. UNSUPERVISED IMAGE SEGMENTATION USING GRAPH PARTITIONING

Unsupervised graph partitioning methods for image segmentation are less popular than supervised ones. This is probably because of the quality of their results and because, in a past not so old, they hardly dealt with images larger than 300x200. Unlike most supervised graph partitioning methods (see section 4), unsupervised methods deal with graphs of pixels and not graphs of regions. However, thanks to the research done in graph partitioning for numerical analysis these last years(Bichot & Siarry, 2011), these methods can deal with very big graphs – counting million of vertices – and thus big images, in a few seconds.

Unsupervised graph partitioning methods for image segmentation are mainly divided into two categories: spectral graph partitioning methods and multilevel graph partitioning methods. The former are the oldest, but so far the most used. These spectral methods are described in section 3.1. Despite multilevel methods are used since more than ten years in the research field of graph partitioning for numerical analysis, they are not well used for image segmentation. Section 3.2 presents them. Finally, section 3.3 compares both of these methods on several examples.

3.1 Spectral Graph Partitioning Methods for Image Segmentation

Using the spectral method to solve graph partitioning problems is old. The first article offering such an approach is due to W. Donath and A. Hoffman (Donath & Hoffman, Algorithms for partitioning graphs and computer logic based on eigenvectors of connection matrices, 1972). The spectral method was widely used to solve graph partitioning problems before the multilevel method appears. Since then, the multilevel method is more often used than the spectral method for solving graph partitioning problems in the case of numerical analysis.

The theoretical results linked to the spectral graph partitioning method are also numerous. A lower bound of the cut of a partition can be calculated thanks to them (Donath & Hoffman, 1973; Elsässer, Lücking, & Monien, 2003). They can estimate the quality of a graph separator (Guattery & Miller, 1998). It can be proved that obtaining a cut from the spectral method has, at worst, a cut quadratic of the cut of the optimal partition (Alon & Milman, 1985).

The spectral graph partitioning method has been named after the spectral theorem of linear algebra. This theorem can maintain the diagonalization of real symmetric matrices. It also justifies the decomposition of real symmetric matrices in eigenvalues within an orthonormal basis of eigenvectors. And yet, the graph partitioning problem can, at the cost of two approximations explained below, be reduced to the resolution of a numerical system $Mx = \lambda x$. Solving this numerical system consists in finding an orthogonal basis of eigenvectors of the matrix M.

3.1.1 Spectral Formulation of the Graph Partitioning Problem

This section details how a graph partitioning problem can be formulated as a spectral problem. At first, consider that we attempt to find a bisection $P_2 = \{V_1, V_2\}$ of G which minimized the *cut* objective function presented upper. Let x be a vector of size $|V|$ such that for all $v_1 \in V$, if $x_1 \in V_1$ then $x_1 = 1$ else $x_1 = -1$. We have for each i:

$$\left(x^T M_{Lap}\right)_i = x_i \sum_{j=1}^{|V|} w\left(i,j\right) - \sum_{j=1}^{|V|} x_j w\left(i,j\right) = \sum_{j=1}^{|V|} (x_i - x_j) w\left(i,j\right)$$

Then,

$$x^T M_{Lap} x = \sum_{i=1}^{|V|} \sum_{j=1}^{|V|} (x_i^2 - x_i x_j) w\left(i,j\right)$$

and, because the graph is undirected, i.e. $\forall i, j, w\left(i,j\right) = w\left(j,i\right)$ we have:

$$x^T M_{Lap} x = \sum_{(v_i, v_j) \in E} (x_i - x_j)^2 w\left(i,j\right)$$

Regarding the definition of the cut, it can be observed that:

$$x^T M_{Lap} x = 2cut(P_2)$$

Thus, minimizing the cut of a bisection aims at finding a vector x that minimizes $x^T M_{Lap} x$. In other words the minimization of the cut of a bisection of a graph G consists in solving the linear system:

$$M_{Lap} x = \lambda x$$

by finding the smallest real number λ. Doing this aims at finding the minimal eigenvalue of the Laplacian matrix of the graph, as well as its corresponding eigenvector.

Several methods can be used to find the eigenvectors of a matrix, among them: the Lanczos iterative algorithm; the Rayleigh quotient iteration method; the QR decomposition algorithm; or the Jacobi iterative algorithm (Golub & Loan, 1996). However, classical mathematical tools such as Matlab usually provide tools for finding eigenvectors.

It can be proved that the Laplacian matrix of an undirected graph is positive semidefinite. So all its eigenvalues are positive and they can be sorted by ascending order: $0 \leq \lambda_1 \leq \lambda_2 \leq ... \leq \lambda_n$. These vectors are called Fiedler vectors in memory of the first person who study them. There is a trivial eigenvector of the Laplacian matrix of a graph: the unit vector. Its eigenvalue is $\lambda = 0$; thus the first Fiedler vector is the unit vector and its eigenvalue is $\lambda_1 = 0$. In a graph partitioning point of view, it means that a "partition" of the graph into two sets: V and $\varnothing$ (the empty set) minimize the cut. Indeed, because there is no edge between these two sets, $cut = 0$. Obviously, this is of no interest in our case.

The second Fiedler vector is the vector corresponding to the smallest non-zero eigenvalue of this eigenvalues family. It is this second Fiedler vector that will allow finding a bisection of the graph. Indeed, if the values of this vector are real, their discretization to $\{-1; 1\}$ can distribute the vertices of the graph into two sets V_1 and V_2. The discretization scheme can be of great importance in some case. Indeed, the balance of the partition depends on it. If the balance of the partition is of no interest (which means that parts of the partition can be of any size), then the simplest scheme is to discretize positives values as 1 and negatives as -1. On the other hand, different schemes can be proposed to balance the partition.

Consider now that we try to find a 2^i-partition of a graph. The result found in the case of graph bisection can be easily generalized. Indeed, the $i+1$ first Fiedler eigenvectors allow finding a 2^i-partition of the graph. To do so, it only requires to discretize each Fiedler vector to $\{-1; 1\}$, then create the corresponding bisections. However, because of the partitioning balance problem, this method is not often used. A usual way for partitioning a graph into k parts using a bisection algorithm is to recursively bisection the graph and then each part of the bisection, etc (Bichot & Siarry, Graph partitioning, 2011).

3.1.2. Spectral Formulation of the Image Segmentation Graph Partitioning Problem

In the last section, the graph partitioning problem which consists in minimizing the cut objective function as been transformed into a spectral problem. However, the image segmentation problem is almost never formulated as such a problem. Indeed, minimizing cut tends to create very unbalanced partitions resulting in image regions containing very few pixels or too much. To overcome this problem, a constraint on the balance of the partition may be imposed. Adding this constraint results in image regions with similar sizes. Obviously, this is not appropriate for most of the images to segment.

To solve this problem of similarities in image regions sizes, another objective functions are used. There are mainly two objective functions used: the ratio cut and the normalized cut objective functions. Both of these objective functions aim to combine intra-region uniformity and inter-region disparity to produce an effective measure (see section 1). Obviously, the cut objective function only focuses on inter-region disparity; this is why it is not effective enough.

As presented in section 2.2, the objective function that aims to minimize, for each part, the ratio between its cut and its weight is called ratio cut. The objective function that aims to minimize, for each part, the ratio between the sum of the weight of the edges adjacent to exactly one of its vertices and the sum of the weight of the edges adjacent to at least one of its vertices, is called normalized cut.

It can be observed that both ratio cut and normalized cut combine intra-region uniformity and inter-region disparity to produce a more effective measure than the cut. If they used the same value for calculating inter-region disparity – $cut (V_i, V-V_i)$ – they differ on the intra-region uniformity calculation. The ratio cut uses vertices weight as intra-region uniformity, but the normalized cut only consider edges weighting. It can be noticed that the graph has not to be weighted when using the normalized cut.

The minimization of the ratio cut by spectral methods consists in solving the following linear system:

$$M_{Lap}x = \lambda M_{Adj}x$$

The minimization of the normalized cut by spectral methods consists in solving the following linear system:

$$M_{Lap}x = \lambda M_{Deg}x$$

3.2 Multilevel Graph Partitioning Methods for Image Segmentation

Initially, the multilevel method was created to accelerate a spectral graph partitioning algorithm minimizing the cut objective function (Barnard & Simon, 1994). However, it has been soon recog-

nized as a highly effective method that brought a more comprehensive vision of the graph than classic partitioning methods then in use, such as region growing or partition refinement algorithms (Karypis & Kumar, 1998). However, these classical methods are used by the multilevel method as local partitioning heuristics. Thus, the multilevel graph partitioning method became established as a "global" strategy using local graph partitioning algorithms.

If the multilevel method is used since a long time by graph partitioning software for numerical analysis (Bichot & Siarry, Graph partitioning, 2011), it is only recently that it has been successfully applied to image segmentation (Dhillon, Guan, & Kulis, 2007). The multilevel method has been used instead of the spectral method in image segmentation to overcome two problems: an expensive calculation time of spectral methods; and a problem of convergence in the Lanczos iterative algorithm which may occurred (see section 3.1.1). Indeed, the multilevel method is very fast and experimentally as least as efficient as the spectral method.

3.2.1 The Multilevel Method

The multilevel method aims to answer a simple question: how to rapidly create a partition into k parts of a large graph G, knowing that it is very costly to deal with each of the vertices one by one? The natural answer to this question is to group together vertices in order to deal with groups of vertices, rather than independent vertices. This is the idea that originated the multilevel method.

As shown in Figure 2, the multilevel method is divided into three successive levels:

- **Coarsening:** The coarsening level is an iterative process which coarsens vertices of the original graphs in the aim of reducing its size. At each iteration, the vertices of the graph resulting from the previous iteration are grouped together to form a similar

Figure 2. The three levels of the multilevel scheme

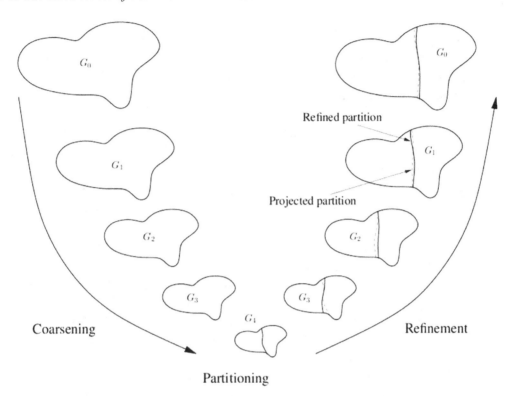

graph, but whose number of vertices is lower than the previous one. Thus, a family of graphs, $\{G_1,...,G_n\}$, with $G_1=G$, is created such that, for each graph G_{i+1}, each of its vertices represents a group of vertices (coarsened vertices) from the previous graph G_i. The process ends when the graph is sufficiently small, or when the new graph generated has a size too close to the previous graph.

- **Partitioning:** This level creates a partition $P_{k,n}$ of the graph G_n into k parts. To do so, the graph G_n, resulting from the coarsening phase, is partitioned using a partitioning heuristic (as for example, a region growing method).

- **Uncoarsening and Refinement:** The uncoarsening level consists in progressively projecting the parts of the partition $P_{k,n}$ of G_n onto the initial graph G. However, projecting directly $P_{k,n}$ onto G often creates a partition of mediocre quality, because this partition will be far from being locally optimal. Thus, the partition $P_{k,n}$ of the graph G_n is first projected onto G_{n-1}, then refined and becomes the partition $P_{k,n}-1$ of the graph G_{n-1}. This process is repeated for all the graphs G_i, $i = n-1$ to 1. The final partition obtained is the partition $P_{k,1}$ of the graph $G_1=G$. Thus, during this level, a family of partitions $\{P_{k,n}, ...,P_{k,1}\}$ is created, where each element $P_{k,i}$ is the refined projection of the partition P_k of G_{i+1} onto the graph G_i. Then, the final partition $P_{k,1}=P_k$, combines the properties of being good globally and locally.

3.2.2 The Coarsening Level

One of the most widely used coarsening algorithm is the Heavy edge matching algorithm (Karypis & Kumar, A Fast and High Quality Multilevel Scheme for Partitioning Irregular Graphs, 1998). The aim of the heavy edge matching algorithm (HEM) is to find a maximal matching[1] of the graph that contributes to minimize the cut objective function. Based on this matching and on the graph G_i, the HEM algorithm creates a coarsened graph G_{i+1}. For creating a matching of a graph G_i, the HEM algorithm proceed iteratively by removing vertices from G_i. Let M_i be the matching of the graph G_i that creates the coarsened graph G_{i+1}. At each iteration, the HEM algorithm randomly selects a vertex v_i among the remaining vertices of the graph G_i, that is to say the vertices that are not already in the matching M_i. Then, it chooses the edge of maximal weight adjacent to the selected vertex v_i. This edge is added to the matching M_i and its two vertices are merged to form a new vertex in G_{i+1}. Then, it must add the edges adjacent to these two vertices in E_{i+1}. The complexity of this algorithm is $O\left(\|E_i\|\right)$

It is because the HEM algorithm chooses, at each iteration, the edge of maximal weight that it contributes to minimize the cut objective function. Indeed, the sum of the weights of the edges of the coarsened graph G_{i+1} returned by HEM will be equal to the sum of the weights of the edges of G_i, minus the sum of the weights of the edges of M_i:

$$w\left(E_{i+1}\right) = w\left(E_i\right) - w(M_i)$$

Thus, maximizing $w(M_i)$ will minimize $w(E_{i+1})$.

As discussed in section 3.1.2, the cut objective function is rarely used for image segmentation application. Instead, it is the normalized cut objective function which is mainly used. It is easy to adapt the HEM algorithm to minimize the normalized cut objective function instead of the cut one.

Once the vertex v_i is selected, instead of choosing the edge of maximal weight, the algorithm must choose the edge (v_i, v_j) which maximizes:

$$\frac{w(v_i, v_j)}{cut(\{v_i\}, V)} + \frac{w(v_i, v_j)}{cut(\{v_j\}, V)}$$

The remaining of this algorithm is the same. For minimizing the ratio cut, ones only have to replace cut({v_i},V) by w(v_i) and cut({v_j},V) by w(v_j) in the previous formula.

3.2.3 The Partitioning Level

The partitioning phase of the multilevel method aims to find a partition $P_{k,n}$ of the coarsened graph G_n into k parts, which will be used as the initial partition of the un-coarsening level. The partitioning algorithm used at this level can be either a direct *k*-partitioning algorithm or a recursive bisection algorithm. But the choice of one of these two approaches determines the approach used at the un-coarsening level. Recursive bisection divides a graph using a bisection algorithm that will be repeated until *k* parts are obtained. Conversely, a direct *k*-partitioning algorithm only applies once on the graph to produce a partition into *k* parts.

The easiest solution to create an initial partition of the coarsened graph is to coarsen the graph until its number of vertices is equal to *k*. Then, the coarsened graph becomes the initial partition. This approach is not often used in the case of numerical analysis because it had a main drawback; it produces a very unbalanced partition (Walshaw & Cross, 2000). However, in the case of image segmentation the balance of the partition is not really important.

Instead of coarsening the graph until its number of vertices is equal to *k*, most multilevel algorithms utilize a state of the art graph partitioning algorithm to create the initial partition. These algorithms can be roughly sorted into two main categories:

1. **Spectral Graph Partitioning Algorithms:** These algorithms are presented in section 3.1. Because the size of the coarsened graph G_n is small (few thousand of vertices), these algorithms are fast and their efficiency make them well fitted for such uses;

2. **Region Growing Algorithms:** These algorithms are fairly intuitive and produce good partitions on small graphs. A variation of the well-known Greedy graph growing partitioning algorithm is proposed below.

The greedy graph growing partitioning algorithm (GGGP) is a region growing graph bisection algorithm introduced in (Karypis & Kumar, A Fast and High Quality Multilevel Scheme for Partitioning Irregular Graphs, 1998). The GGGP algorithm iteratively bisection a graph $G=(V,E)$ into two sets V_1 and V_2 and by moving at each iteration one vertex from V_1 to V_2. It starts by randomly selecting a vertex $u \in V$. It sets $V_1=V - \{u\}$ and $V_2=\{u\}$. At each iteration, the vertices in the border of V_2 – that is to say the vertices in V_1 (thus not in V_2) adjacent to at least one vertex of V_2 – are sorted by their gain value[2]. The vertex v with the maximal gain value is moved from V_1 to V_2. At the end of the iteration, V_2 contains one more vertex, v. The algorithm ends when half of the vertices are in V_2.

It can be noticed that this bisection algorithm is designed for the numerical analysis application, i.e. it minimized the cut objective function while creating a well balanced bisection. However, this algorithm can be adapted to the image segmentation application and more precisely the normalized cut objective function. Instead of sorting border vertices by their gain value, gain referring to the cut, these vertices can be sorted by their gain value, gain referring to the normalized cut. More formally, let $v \in V_1$ in the border of V_2, its gain value referring to the normalized cut is:

$$gain_{NCut}(v) = NCut(V_1 - \{v\}, V_2 \bigcup \{v\}) - NCut(V_1, V_2)$$

Unfortunately, because of the denominator of NCut, this formula cannot be simplified and is more time consuming to calculate than the gain value referring to the cut. Considering the normalized cut objective function, the original GGGP stop condition can be changed. Indeed, the image segmentation application does not required image regions to be of the same size, and thus partitions can be of different sizes. What is important is to minimized the NCut objective function. Then, two stop conditions can be used: the algorithm ends when after a few iterations the NCut value does not decrease; or the loop end when half of the vertices are in V_2, and the partition with the lowest NCut value found during the iterations is returned by the algorithm. This revised GGGP algorithm with both of these stop criterion allows to find a bisection with a low normalized cut value, lower than with the original GGGP algorithm.

3.2.4 The Uncoarsening Level and Refinement Methods

The uncoarsening level of the multilevel method consists in progressively projecting onto the initial graph the partition of the coarsened graph found during the partitioning phase. This level would be very simple if a direct projection of the coarsened graph partition onto the initial graph led to a locally optimal partition. However a locally good partition of a coarsened graph G_{i+1} from G_i is often of lower quality for the graph G_i (Karypis & Kumar, 1995). A refinement algorithm is therefore used to locally improve the quality of the partition after each projection. Because of refinement, the uncoarsening level is the longest step of the multilevel algorithm. Indeed, the two other levels almost always used linear or quasilinear time algorithms. Thus, in order not to increase to much the calculation time of the multilevel algorithm, the refinement algorithm had to be fast.

During the coarsening level a family of coarsened graphs has been constructed, $\{G_1, ..., G_n\}$. The uncoarsening level consists in recursively projecting the partition $P_{k,i+1}$ of a coarsened graph G_{i+1} (starting by the partition $P_{k,n}$ of G_n) onto its parent G_i and then applying to the new partition $P_{k,i}$ a refinement algorithm. At the end of the coarsened level, the final partition $P_{k,1}$, therefore associates a globally good "structure," due to the multilevel method, with a locally efficient division due to the refinement algorithm.

Numerous refinement algorithms exist. However, all refinement algorithms have two characteristics in common: they have to start from an existing partition and their optimization has to be local. Many of these algorithms are based on the Kernighan-Lin notion of gain (Kernighan & Lin, 1970) and used the Fiduccia-Mattheyses data structure (Fiduccia & Mattheyses, 1982). However, other refinement techniques are used, like the weighted kernel k-means algorithm (Dhillon, Guan, & Kulis, 2007).

The Kernighan-Lin algorithm aims to minimize the cut objective function while maintaining the balance of the partition to refine. Indeed, this algorithm is based on the notion of gain. Considering a bisection $P_2=(V_1, V_2)$ of a graph G, the gain value of a vertex $v \in V_1$ is the reduction of the cut value that would result from the move of the vertex v from part V_1 to part V_2:

$$gain_{Cut}(v) = Cut\left(V_1 - \{v\}, V_2 \bigcup \{v\}\right) - $$
$$Cut\left(V_1, V_2\right) = \sum_{v' \in V_2} w\left(v, v'\right) - \sum_{v' \in V_1} w(v, v')$$

The Kernighan-Lin algorithm iteratively exchange pair of vertices (one in V_1, the other in V_2) by selecting the pair of vertices which results in the greatest reduction of cut. If the Kernighan-Lin algorithm is very efficient in terms of partition

refinement, its time complexity is high: $O\left(|E|^2 \log\left(|E|\right)\right)$.

The Fiduccia-Mattheyses data structure allows drastically decreasing the time complexity of the Kernighan-Lin algorithm. This data structure, shown in Figure 3, maintains the gain of the vertices updated during the refinement loop. This data structure consists in maintaining, for each part of the bisection, a sorted table of the vertices gains. A doubly linked list is associated to each cell of the gains table. This doubly linked list contains the vertices whose gain corresponds to the rank of the list in this gains table. Finally, each cell of the vertices table points at the corresponding vertex in one of the doubly linked lists. Thus, accessing a vertex runs in constant time and the change in a vertex gain value also runs in constant time. Finally, the Kernighan-Lin algorithm complexity is linear in the number of edges, $O\left(|E|\right)$, if it uses the Fiduccia-Mattheyses data structure.

The Fiduccia-Mattheyses data structure is well designed for Kernighan-Lin gain values (i.e. referring to the cut) because these values are discrete and thus, the array of gains of vertices has a limited size. However, the gain values referring to the normalized cut are not discrete; these values are real numbers. Then, in order to use the Fiduccia-Mattheyses data structure, these gain values haves to be discretized. This quantization can be easily done during the data structure initialization. Classically, this initialization consists in calculating for each vertex of the graph its gain value and to store it directly in the array of gains of vertices in which the vertex belongs to. These gain values can be temporary stored. When they are all computed, a scalar quantization of these values can be make (i.e. these values are mapped onto a fixed number of discrete values). As an example, if we have ten normalized cut values: 0.1, 0.11, 0.34, 0.42, 0.67, 0.94, 1.23, 1.33, 1.57, 2.2; and we restrict the size of the array of gains of vertices to 5 cells, then we can group the normalized cut

Figure 3. Fiduccia-Mattheyses data structure

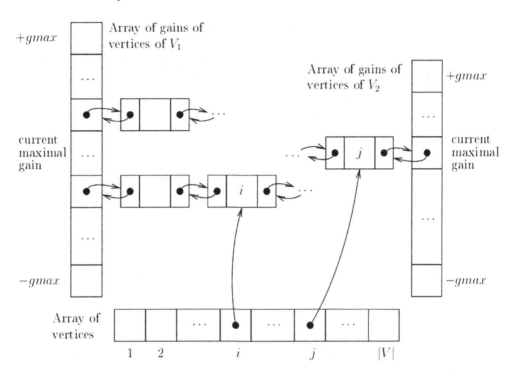

values into 5 clusters of size $\frac{22}{5} = 0.44$: [0, 0.44]; [0.44, 0.88]; [0.88, 1.32]; [1.32, 1.76]; $[1.76 + \infty]$. Of course, other quantization techniques may be used.

Thus, in the case of image segmentation application, a linear time Kernighan-Lin type of refinement algorithm can be made, which minimized the normalized cut objective function, and which uses a quantized Fiduccia-Mattheyses data structure.

The refinement algorithms presented above in this section only concerns bisections. However, there exist direct *k*-partitioning refinement algorithms based on the Kernighan-Lin notion of gain using the Fiduccia-Mattheyses data structure. We may cite the Hendrickson-Leland refinement algorithm (Hendrickson & Leland, 1995), or the Global Kernighan-Lin refinement algorithm (Karypis & Kumar, 1998). Another very efficient refinement algorithm which incorporates a load distribution method is presented in (Walshaw &

Cross, 2000). All these algorithms can be adapted to the normalized cut objective function by using the technique presented above.

3.3 Comparisons

Figures 4, 5, 6, and 7 present several images segmented by using spectral and multilevel algorithms. These images are taken from the Berkley segmentation dataset (Martin, Fowlkes, Tal, & Malik, 2001). The spectral algorithm used is the state-of-the-art normalized cut segmentation code of Timothee Cour, Stella Yu and Jianbo Shi Internet[3] (Shi & Malik, 2000; Cour, Benezit, & JianboShi, 2005). More precisely, we use the Ncut_9 version of the code. The multilevel algorithm used is the Graclus software of Inderjit S. Dhillon, Yuqiang Guan, and Brian Kulis (Dhillon, Guan, & Kulis, 2007). We use the version 1.2 of this software which can be requested to the authors or trough this Web

Figure 4. Image of an airplane segmented with Graclus and Ncut softwares for different number of parts

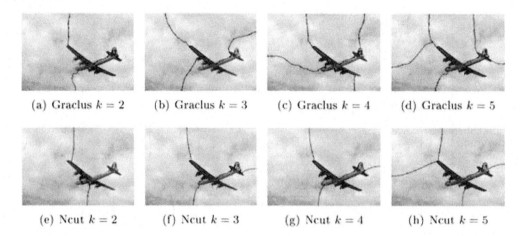

  (a) Graclus $k = 2$ (b) Graclus $k = 3$ (c) Graclus $k = 4$ (d) Graclus $k = 5$

  (e) Ncut $k = 2$ (f) Ncut $k = 3$ (g) Ncut $k = 4$ (h) Ncut $k = 5$

Figure 5. Image of a bird segmented with Graclus and Ncut softwares for different number of parts

  (a) Graclus $k = 2$ (b) Graclus $k = 3$ (c) Graclus $k = 4$ (d) Graclus $k = 5$

  (e) Ncut $k = 2$ (f) Ncut $k = 3$ (g) Ncut $k = 4$ (h) Ncut $k = 5$

Figure 6. Image of a forest surrounded by a field segmented with Graclus and Ncut softwares for different number of parts

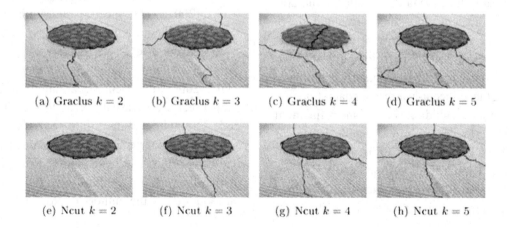

  (a) Graclus $k = 2$ (b) Graclus $k = 3$ (c) Graclus $k = 4$ (d) Graclus $k = 5$

  (e) Ncut $k = 2$ (f) Ncut $k = 3$ (g) Ncut $k = 4$ (h) Ncut $k = 5$

Figure 7. Image of a castle segmented with Graclus and Ncut softwares for different number of parts

(a) Graclus $k = 2$ (b) Graclus $k = 4$ (c) Ncut $k = 2$ (d) Ncut $k = 4$

page[4]. Graclus use the image-to-graph code of Ncut. However, to be sure that, when segmenting an image, the underlying graph used by both of these algorithms is the same, we use the same code for the image-to-graph step.

The first remark about these segmented images is that the segmentation is not really good for both of these methods. There is still lot of improvements to be done to make these algorithms more accurate. Regarding rapidly the segmented image, it is difficult to sort these two approaches. The airplane in Figure 4 is equivalently segmented by the two algorithms. If, when k=2, the Graclus software finds more borders of the airplane than Ncut, when k=4, the segmentation proposed by Ncut seems more accurate. In Figure 5, the bird is maybe better segmented by Ncut because, from k=3, Graclus splits the background in two while Ncut found more borders surrounding the bird and the branches. The image of the forest in Figure 6 is segmented in a very good way by Ncut with k=2. On the other hand, Graclus finds zigzag borders for all number of parts. Finally, for a very difficult image, the castle presented in Figure 7,

the Ncut software finds really tiny segments while Graclus finds more structured object borders.

If it is difficult to decide which of Ncut or Graclus software have better quality results, it should be noticed that the Graclus software is – at least – 3 to 4 times faster than the Ncut code in all our experiments.

Even if the normalized cut objective function is better designed than the cut objective function for the image segmentation application, it is certainly not a perfect objective function. In another subject, document classification, where it is easier to have a ground true experimental evaluation than in the case of image segmentation which remains subjective, it has been proved that the normalized cut was not a perfectly suited objective function for this application (Bichot, 2009). I am truly convinced that in the case of image segmentation, this drawback remains. However, finding a better graph-based objective function is a challenging problem, even if some inspiration may come from other sources like image segmentation evaluation as an example (Zhang, Fritts, & Goldman, 2008).

4. SUPERVISED IMAGE SEGMENTATION BASED ON GRAPH PARTITIONING

Graph partitioning methods are more commonly used for supervised image segmentation applications than for unsupervised ones. Indeed, if unsupervised image segmentation problem modeled by graph partitioning are mainly NP-difficult problems, in the supervised case they often are not. Since the beginning of 2000, there has been an explosion of interest in using combinatorial methods for energy minimization within computer vision. The techniques used are mostly based on solving the minimum cut problem, which is a polynomial time problem. Thus, the user can find rapidly a high quality solution.

In the supervised image segmentation application, the user seeds the parts of the image to be segmented. Then, the graph of the image is segmented by a graph partitioning algorithm by taking into account these marks (seeds). The pixels seeded are fixed into different parts of the partition.

4.1 Energy Minimization Using Graph Cuts

Two popular seeded segmentation methods based on graph partitioning minimizing energy functions are the Graph cuts (Boykov & Jolly, 2001) and Random walks (Grady, 2006) algorithms. Since their energy function are convex, these approaches allow to find the global optimum.

Energy minimization using graph cuts aims at segmenting an image by finding the minimum cut between the foreground and background seeds (marks) via a maximum flow computation. This technique has been used for interactive image segmentation at first in (Boykov & Jolly, 2001). Then, numerous works have extended this approach like (Blake, Rother, Brown, Perez, & Torr, 2004) and (Rother, Kolmogorov, & Blake, 2004) with the "Grabcut" algorithm. In these methods, the foreground and background seeds are respectively treated as source and sink vertices for a max-flow min-cut operation.

- **Definitions:** Let $G=(V,E)$ be a weighted graph with s and t being the source and the sink of G respectively.

  An **s-t cut** $P=(S,T)$ is a partition of V such that $s \in S$ and $t \in T$

  The value of an s-t cut is its cut value.

  An **s-t flow** is a mapping f of E to the real numbers subject to two constraints:

$$\forall (u,v) \in E, f(u,v) \leq w(u,v) \text{ and}$$
$$\forall v, \Sigma_u f(u,v) = \Sigma_u f(v,u)$$

- **Theorem of the Max-Flow Min-Cut:** The maximum value of an s-t flow is equal to the minimum value of an s-t cut.

  Using a max-flow min-cut algorithm, a set of edges minimizing the cut (an edge separator) is found. This edge separator forms the boundary of the segmented object in the image. A common problem with the graph cut method is the over segmentation behavior (as seen in the unsupervised approach in section 3). Since the graph cut method tries to minimize the cut, it may return small segmented regions as a result of a small number of seeds, low contrast, protruded objects or noise.

  Thanks to their efficiency and rapidity, graph cuts methods have gained lot of interest in image analysis. However, these methods are not able to deal with every kind of energy function to minimize. It has been proved that only some kind of function dependent on two or more binary variables can be minimized via graph cut techniques (Freedman & Drineas, 2005):

- **Theorem:** Let $a_{i,j}$, b_i, and c be real numbers. A function of $n \geq 2$ binary variables $x_i \in \{0,1\}$,

$$E\left(x_1, \ldots, x_n\right) = \Sigma_{i,j} a_{ij} x_i x_j + \Sigma_i b_i x_i + c$$

can be minimized via graph cut techniques if and only if $\forall i, j, a_{ij} \leq 0$.

4.2 Geodesic Active Contours

Geodesic active contours is a well-known method of image segmentation. This method aims to find object boundaries (its contours). Computing a geodesic curve means computing the shortest curve between two points. The geodesic active contour approach is based on active contours evolving in time according to intrinsic geometric measures of the image: the computation of geodesics or minimal distance curves.

Geodesic active contours expressed the image segmentation problem as an optimization problem and more precisely an energy minimization problem (Caselles, Kimmel, & Sapiro, 1997):

$$E\left(\mathcal{C}\right) = \int_0^1 g\left(\nabla I\left(\mathcal{C}\left(s\right)\right)\right) ds$$

where I is the image to segment, $C(s)$ is a closed and parameterized planar curve with s its curvilinear abscissa, and g is a positive and strictly decreasing function. $\left\|\nabla I\left(\mathcal{C}\left(s\right)\right)\right\|$ is the gradient module of the image on the curve. Geodesic active contours aim to find a curve such that the gradient module (i.e. the contrast) on the curve is maximal. Euclidian or Riemannian metrics can be used for modeling the curves. However, the Riemannian space has been proved to be more relevant. Thus, the minimal distance curve expressed above lays in a Riemannian space whose metric is defined by the image content.

In (Boykov & Kolmogorov, 2003), Boykov and Kolmogorov have connected graph cuts and level sets. Their idea is to compute geodesics and minimal surfaces via graph cuts. Given the geometric function $E(C)$ expressed above, a graph is constructed such that $E\left(C\right) \approx \left\|C\right\| \equiv \sum_{e \in \mathcal{C}} w(e)$. A graph cut value can be interpreted as a geometric length (or area in 3D) of the corresponding contour (surface). A graph cut metric approximates the Riemannian metric thanks to the Cauchy-Crofton formula from integral geometry. Given an image, it had to be marked by object markers and background markers. The graph is constructed such that the source vertices are connected to the object markers and the sink vertices to the background markers. A graph-cut algorithm (Boykov & Jolly, 2001) finds the partition of the graph and thus the segmentation of the image. This technique is known as geo-cut.

4.3 Watershed Cuts and Power Watersheds

The intuitive idea underlying the notion of a watershed comes from the field of topography. A drop of water falling on a topographic surface follows a descending path and reaches a minimum (local or global). The watershed can be viewed as the separating lines of the domain of attraction of drops of water. The watershed computation of an image has been extensively studied in image segmentation application. However, a recent work, (Cousty, Bertrand, Najman, & Couprie, 2009), proposed a fast and efficient modeling of the image segmentation problem by watershed and graph cuts, named watershed cut. The gradient of the image to segment is considered as a relief map where marks specify the segmentation of the image into desired regions. A quasi-linear time algorithm computes the optimal (maximum or minimum) spanning forest by computing trees spanning all the vertices of the graph, each tree being connected to exactly one connected mark, and the weight of the set of trees being maximum (or minimum).

Recently, the power watershed method (Couprie, Grady, Najman, & Talbot, 2009) unified several image segmentation models: graph cuts/random walker (Sinop & Grady, 2007), geodesics-based algorithm (Bai & Sapiro, 2007), and wa-

tershed cuts (Cousty, Bertrand, Najman, & Couprie, 2009). The power watershed model is a
generalized model for image segmentation which
includes graph cuts, random walker, geodesics
and watershed cuts. Given an image I and its
graph $G = (V, E)$, a foreground F and a background B seeds, two parameters, p and q, the
generalized model for producing segmentation s
is given by:

$$min\left(\sum_{e_{ij} \in E} w_{ij}^p \left|x_i - x_j\right|^q + \sum_{v_i} w_{Fi}^p x_i^q + \sum_{v_i} w_{Bi}^p \left|x_i - 1\right|^q\right)$$

such that $x(F){=}1$, $x(B){=}0$, and $s_i{=}1$ if $x_i \geq \dfrac{1}{2}$, 0
else. w_{Fi} and w_{Bi} are unary weights penalizing
foreground and background affinity at node v_i.
When p is a small finite value, then the various
values of q may be interpreted respectively as the
graph cuts ($q{=}1$), and random walker ($q{=}2$) algorithms. When q and p converge toward infinity
together with the same speed, then the solution

to this equation can be computed by the geodesics
algorithm. The power watersheds family of segmentation models is obtained by raising $p \rightarrow \infty$
and varying the power q. It had been proved that
there exists a value of p beyond which any
power watersheds algorithms can be calculated
using an optimal spanning forest algorithm, which
is extremely efficient.

4.4 Results

Figures 8, 9, and 10 presented in this section
are from the Grabcut database images (Rother,
Kolmogorov, & Blake, 2004). These images
comport seeds. Figures 8 and 9 presents the results
returned by five supervised image segmentation
approaches based on graph partitioning (Couprie,
Grady, Najman, & Talbot, 2009), namely: graph
cuts, random walker, geodesic algorithm, wateshed
cuts and power watersheds. The segmented images
shows that power watersheds and watershed cuts

*Figure 8. Examples of image segmentations using eroded seeds on the Grabcut database images (Cou-
prie, Grady, Najman, & Talbot, 2009)*

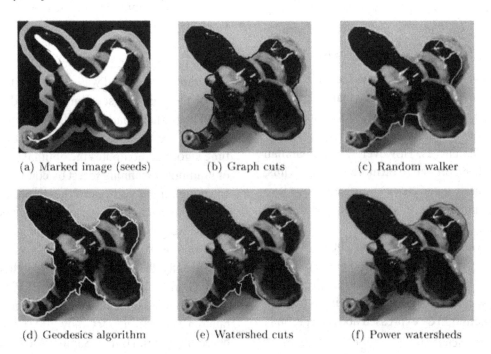

(a) Marked image (seeds)   (b) Graph cuts   (c) Random walker

(d) Geodesics algorithm   (e) Watershed cuts   (f) Power watersheds

Figure 9. Examples of image segmentations using eroded seeds on the Grabcut database images (Couprie, Grady, Najman, & Talbot, 2009)

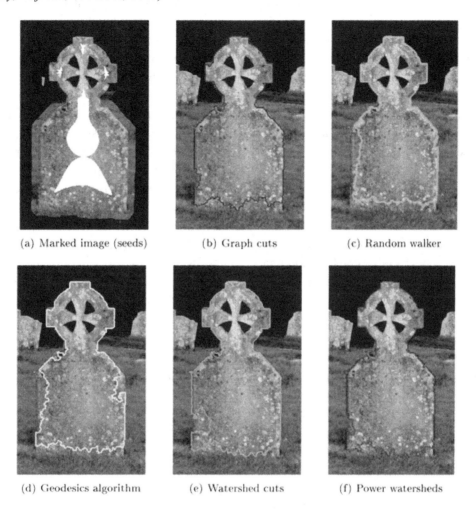

(a) Marked image (seeds)   (b) Graph cuts   (c) Random walker

(d) Geodesics algorithm   (e) Watershed cuts   (f) Power watersheds

Figure 10. Segmented images of the grave (Figure 9) found by the Graclus and Ncut softwares

(a) Graclus $k = 2$ (b) Ncut $k = 2$

perform better than the other approaches. These methods are (respectively) followed by graph cuts, and then, random walkers and geodesics. More precision about these results may be found in (Couprie, Grady, Najman, & Talbot, 2009).

In order to illustrate the differences between the unsupervised and the supervised approach, Figure 10 presents the segmented images of the grave (Figure 9) found by the Ncut and Graclus softwares (see section 3).

5. CONCLUSION

This chapter presents the two main image segmentation approaches based on graph partitioning: unsupervised and supervised approaches. Both of these approaches share the same initial step, a modeling of the image by a graph. This image to graph conversion step is a very sensitive step because the final segmented image greatly depends on the quality of this step. Thus, in practical applications, this step should be carefully handled. However, this step is often the least well described step in the literature, probably because it does not concern the methodological and algorithmic parts of the papers.

After this image into graph conversion step, the unsupervised approach consists in partitioning the graph by using either a spectral or a multilevel algorithm. If spectral algorithms are mainly used, multilevel algorithms are very promising and demonstrate good performances. In this chapter, two main new improvements are presented to make them even more efficient: an adaptation of the Greedy graph growing partitioning algorithm to the normalized cut objective function; and an adaptation of the Fiduccia-Mattheyses data structure in order to manage the Kernighan-Lin notion of gain improved for normalized cut.

The supervised image segmentation approach based on graph partitioning has been extensively studied these last years. In the supervised image

segmentation application, the user seeds the parts of the image to be segmented. Then, the graph of the image is segmented by a graph partitioning method: graph cuts, random walker, geodesics algorithm, watershed cut or power watershed. There is actually a trend to unify graph partitioning approach for supervised image segmentation, as demonstrated by the power watershed method. These methods are fast and efficient and their results always better. However, their supervised nature makes them dependent on seeds qualities.

In the literature, these two image segmentation approach based on graph are almost never presented together. However, they can be mixed in different ways to improve image segmentation results. As an example, supervised methods can be used in the partitioning level of the multilevel method. They can also be very efficient as partition refinement algorithms.

REFERENCES

Alon, N., & Milman, V. (1985). $\lambda 1$, isoperimetric inequalities for graphs, and superconcentrators. *Journal of Combinatorial Theory Series B, 38*, 73–88. doi:10.1016/0095-8956(85)90092-9

Bai, X., & Sapiro, G. (2007). *A geodesic framework for fast interactive image and video segmentation and matting* (pp. 1–8). IEEE Computer Society.

Barnard, S. T., & Simon, H. D. (1994). A fast multilevel implementation of recursive spectral bisection for partitioning unstructured problems. *Concurrency (Chichester, England), 6*, 101–107. doi:10.1002/cpe.4330060203

Bichot, C.-E. (2009). Co-clustering documents and words by minimizing the normalized cut objective function. *Journal of Mathematical Modelling and Algorithms, 9*, 131–147. doi:10.1007/s10852-010-9126-0

Bichot, C.-E., & Siarry, P. (Éds.). (2011). *Graph partitioning*. ISTE - Wiley.

Blake, A., Rother, C., Brown, M., Perez, P., & Torr, P. (2004). Interactive image segmentation using an adaptive GMMRF model. In T. Pajdla, & J. Matas (Eds.), *Proceedings of the European Conference on Computer Vision (ECCV)* (Vol. 3021, pp. 428-441). Berlin, Germany Springer.

Boykov, Y., & Kolmogorov, V. (2003). Computing geodesics and minimal surfaces via graph cuts. *Proceedings of the Ninth IEEE International Conference on Computer Vision*, Vol. 2, (pp. 26-33). IEEE Computer Society.

Boykov, Y. Y., & Jolly, M.-P. (2001). Interactive graph cuts for optimal boundary & region segmentation of objects in N-D images. *Proceedings of the Eighth IEEE International Conference on Computer Vision*, Vol. 1, (pp. 105-112).

Caselles, V., Kimmel, R., & Sapiro, G. (1997). Geodesic active contours. *International Journal of Computer Vision*, *22*(1), 61–79. doi:10.1023/A:1007979827043

Couprie, C., Grady, L., Najman, L., & Talbot, H. (2009). Power watersheds: A new image segmentation framework extending graph cuts, random walker and optimal spanning forest, (pp. 731-738).

Cour, T., Benezit, F., & Shi, J. (2005). Spectral segmentation with multiscale graph decomposition. *Proceedings of the 2005 IEEE Computer Society Conference on Computer Vision and Pattern Recognition* (pp. 1124-1131).

Cousty, J., Bertrand, G., Najman, L., & Couprie, M. (2009). Watershed cuts: Minimum spanning forests and the drop of water principle. *IEEE Transactions on Pattern Analysis and Machine Intelligence*, *31*(8), 1362–1374. doi:10.1109/TPAMI.2008.173

Dhillon, I. S., Guan, Y., & Kulis, B. (2007). Weighted graph cuts without Eigenvectors: A multilevel approach. *IEEE Transactions on Pattern Analysis and Machine Intelligence*, *29*, 1944–1957. doi:10.1109/TPAMI.2007.1115

Donath, W., & Hoffman, A. (1972). Algorithms for partitioning graphs and computer logic based on eigenvectors of connection matrices. *IBM Technical Disclosure Bulletin*, *15*, 938–944.

Donath, W., & Hoffman, A. (1973). Lower bounds for the partitioning of graphs. *IBM Journal of Research and Development*, 420–425. doi:10.1147/rd.175.0420

Elsässer, R., Lücking, T., & Monien, B. (2003). On spectral bounds for the k-partitioning of graphs. *Theory of Computing Systems*, *36*, 461–478. doi:10.1007/s00224-003-1083-9

Fiduccia, C. M., & Mattheyses, R. M. (1982). A linear-time heuristic for improving network partitions. *Proceedings of the 19th Design Automation Conference*, (pp. 175-181).

Freedman, D., & Drineas, P. (2005). Energy minimization via graph cuts: Settling what is possible. *Proceedings of the 2005 IEEE Computer Society Conference on Computer Vision and Pattern Recognition*, (pp. 939-946).

Golub, G., & Loan, C. V. (1996). *Matrix computations* (3rd ed.). Baltimore, MD: Johns Hopkins University Press.

Grady, L. (2006). Random walks for image segmentation. *IEEE Transactions on Pattern Analysis and Machine Intelligence*, *28*, 1768–1783. doi:10.1109/TPAMI.2006.233

Guattery, S., & Miller, G. L. (1998). On the quality of spectral separators. *SIAM Journal on Matrix Analysis and Applications*, *19*, 701–719. doi:10.1137/S0895479896312262

Haralick, R. M., & Shapiro, L. G. (1985). Image segmentation techniques. *Computer Vision Graphics and Image Processing, 29,* 100–132. doi:10.1016/S0734-189X(85)90153-7

Hendrickson, B., & Leland, R. W. (1995). A multilevel algorithm for partitioning graphs. *Proceedings of Supercomputing.*

Karypis, G., & Kumar, V. (1995). Analysis of multilevel graph partitioning. *Proceedings of Supercomputing.*

Karypis, G., & Kumar, V. (1998a). A fast and high quality multilevel scheme for partitioning irregular graphs. *SIAM Journal on Scientific Computing, 20,* 359–392. doi:10.1137/S1064827595287997

Karypis, G., & Kumar, V. (1998b). Multilevel k-way partitioning scheme for irregular graphs. *Journal of Parallel and Distributed Computing, 48,* 96–129. doi:10.1006/jpdc.1997.1404

Kernighan, B. W., & Lin, S. (1970). an efficient heuristic procedure for partitioning graphs. *The Bell System Technical Journal, 49,* 291–307.

Martin, D. R., Fowlkes, C., Tal, D., & Malik, J. (2001). *A database of human segmented natural images and its application to evaluating segmentation algorithms and measuring ecological statistics. Technical report* (pp. 416–425). University of Caloifornia at Berkeley.

Rother, C., Kolmogorov, V., & Blake, A. (2004). "GrabCut": Interactive foreground extraction using iterated graph cuts. *ACM Transactions on Graphics, 23*(3), 309–314. doi:10.1145/1015706.1015720

Shi, J., & Malik, J. (2000). Normalized cuts and image segmentation. *IEEE Transactions on Pattern Analysis and Machine Intelligence, 22,* 888–905. doi:10.1109/34.868688

Sinop, A. K., & Grady, L. (2007). A seeded image segmentation framework unifying graph cuts and random walker which yields a new algorithm. *Proceedings of the 2007 International Conference on Computer Vision,* (pp. 1-8).

Walshaw, C., & Cross, M. (2000). Mesh partitioning: A multilevel balancing and refinement algorithm. *SIAM Journal on Scientific Computing, 22,* 63–80. doi:10.1137/S1064827598337373

Zhang, H., Fritts, J. E., & Goldman, S. A. (2008). Image segmentation evaluation: A survey of unsupervised methods. *Computer Vision and Image Understanding, 110,* 260–280. doi:10.1016/j.cviu.2007.08.003

ENDNOTES

[1] A graph matching is a set of edges that have no vertex in common. It is said to be maximal when each edge of the graph has one vertex in common with at least one edge of the matching.

[2] The gain value associated to a vertex $v \in V_1$ is the reduction of the cut that would result from the move of v from V_1 to V_2. This notion is more precisely explained in section 3.2.4

[3] http://www.seas.upenn.edu/~timothee/software/ncut/ncut.html

[4] http://www.cs.utexas.edu/users/dml/Software/graclus.html

Chapter 5
Motion Segmentation and Matting by Graph Cut

Jiangjian Xiao
Ningbo Industrial Technology Research Institute, P.R. China

ABSTRACT

Given a video sequence, obtaining accurate layer segmentation and alpha matting is very important for video representation, analysis, compression, and synthesis. By assuming that a scene can be approximately described by multiple planar or surface regions, this chapter describes a robust approach to automatically detect the region clusters and perform accurate layer segmentation for the scene. The approach starts from optical flow field or small corresponding seed regions and applies a clustering approach to estimate the layer number and support regions. Then, it uses graph cut algorithm combined with a general occlusion constraint over multiple frames to solve pixel assignment over multiple frames to obtain more accurate segmentation boundary and identify the occluded pixels. For the non-textured ambiguous regions, an alpha matting technique is further used to refine the segmentation and resolve the ambiguities by determining proper alpha values for the foreground and background, respectively. Based on the alpha mattes, the foreground object can be transferred into the other video sequence to generate a virtual video. The author's experiments show that the proposed approach is effective and robust for both the challenging real and synthetic sequences.

INTRODUCTION

Layer-based motion segmentation has been investigated by computer vision researchers for a long time (Adiv 1985, Wang 1994, Ayer 1995, Patras 2001, Ke 2004, Xiao 2004). Once motion segmentation is achieved, a video sequence can be efficiently represented by different layers. Given a video sequence, motion segmentation consists of two major steps: (1) layer clustering, which is to determine the number of layers in the scene and the associated motion parameters for each layer; (2) dense layer segmentation, which is to assign each pixel in the image sequence to the corresponding layer and identify the occluded pixels. Currently, a number of approaches have been proposed for

DOI: 10.4018/978-1-4666-1891-6.ch005

layer clustering problem, which have achieved good results, such as linear subspace (Ke 2001, Ke 2002, Ke 2004), GPCA (Vidal 2004), K-means (Wang 1994), and hierarchical merging (Wills 2003,Xiao 2004).

However, once the initial layer clustering is achieved, how to correctly assign the pixels to different layers is a difficult problem (Ayer 1995, Ke 2004, Khan 2001, Xiao 2004) as shown in Figure 1. Particularly, if the images contain some non-textured regions such as the blue or white regions corresponding to the sky in Figure 1a, the pixels in these regions may satisfy different layer motion parameters. Hence, the segmentation only using the motion cue may not provide an accurate layer boundary for those regions due to the motion ambiguities.

In digital matting, the observed color of the pixels around layer boundaries can be considered as a mixture of foreground and background colors, which is formulated as $C = \alpha F + (1 - \alpha)B$, where C, F, and B are the observed, foreground, and background colors, and α is the pixel's opacity channel. For single image matting, once a trimap (unknown, definitely foreground, and definitely background regions) is manually specified, the alpha values, foreground, and background colors of the unknown regions can be estimated under certain constraints (Rother 2004, Sun 2004, Ruzon 2000, Chuang 2001). Typically,

the alpha matting techniques are more suitable for smooth regions since they strongly rely on an assumption that the color of the estimated background and foreground should smoothly change in the unknown areas. Given a cluttered background, the performance of the existing alpha matting approaches tends to deteriorate. Compared to the traditional motion segmentation problem, pulling alpha mattes between two overlapping layers can be considered as a refinement step of the segmentation particularly for those ambiguous, smooth regions.

In this chapter, we introduce a novel approach, which combines the merits of motion segmentation and alpha matting technique together, to extract accurate layer boundaries and alpha mattes simultaneously from a video sequence. Our algorithm is implemented in two stages. The first stage is layer clustering and the second stage is accurate layer segmentation and matting.

In the first stage, we determine seed correspondences over a short video clip (3-5 frames). Then, we gradually expand each seed region from an initial square patch into an enlarged support region of an arbitrary shape to eliminate the over-fitting problem and detect the outliers. This is achieved using a graph cuts approach integrated with the level set representation. After that, we employ a two-step merging process to obtain a layer description of the video clip.

Figure 1. Previous results for flower-garden sequence. (a) One frame from the original sequence. (b) Result of Ayer and Sawhney (Ayer 1995). (c) Result of Ke and Kanade (Ke 2004). (c) Result of (Xiao 2004), where the red pixels are occluded between the neighboring frames.

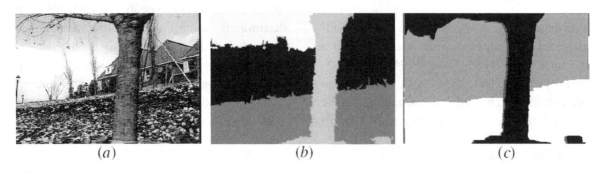

At the second stage, another graph cuts framework is presented to successfully solve the motion segmentation problem for the rich textured regions using multiple frames. In this framework, a novel three-node pixel graph is designed to perform multi-frame segmentation, which correctly maintain the interactions between neighboring frame pairs and handle the general occlusion relationship among these frames. Based on the initial layer segmentation, we automatically estimate the trimap and the corresponding colors for the foreground and background. Then, after obtaining an initial alpha matte from this trimap, we enhance the mattes by employing the poisson editing technique (Perez 2003). Further, a temporal constraint is applied to ensure the temporal consistency over the estimated alpha mattes. Finally, applying the accurate alpha mattes as a priori on multi-frame segmentation framework, more precise layer segmentation is achieved and the occluded pixels between overlapping layers are also correctly identified.

BACKGROUND

In motion segmentation area, Expectation-Maximization (EM) and Maximum-Likelihood Estimation (MLE) frameworks are the most popular approaches to estimate the number of layers and perform pixel assignment (Ayer 1995). Based on this framework, several other approaches use Maximum A-Posteriori (MAP) or MLE for estimation of model parameters assuming different constraints and motion models (Tao 2002, Zhou 2003, Weiss 1997, Khan 2001, Patras 2001). For instance, (Khan and Shah 2001) employ MAP framework combining multiple cues, like spatial location, color, and motion, for segmentation. Another class of motion segmentation approaches groups pixels in a region by using linear subspace constraints (Ke 2004,Zelnik 1999} or factorization of the motion parameter space (Vidal 2004}. In

(Ke 2004), Ke and Kanade expand the seed regions into the initial layers by using k-connected components. After enforcing a low dimensional linear affine subspace constraint on multiple frames, they cluster these initial layers into several groups and assign the image pixels to these layers. For the layer clustering step, most of the existing approaches have achieved reasonable results when the motion parameters are distinct. However, the results for the dense pixel assignment are not good in most cases due to an improper energy formulation or minimization as shown in Figure 1.

Recently, graph cut approaches (Kolmogorov 2002, Kolmogorov 2001, Boykov 2001, Birchfield 1999) are proposed to successfully minimize energy functions for various computer vision problems, such as stereo, image segmentation, image restoration, and texture synthesis. After formulating these different energy minimization problems into a graph cuts framework, an approximate global optimized solution can be obtained in a polynomial time. In stereo area, in order to handle occlusion problem, (Kolmogorov and Zabih 2001) introduce occlusion cost into graph cuts framework to solve stereo problem. In (Kolmogorov 2002), they extend this framework to multiple frames where another term is introduced to enforce the visibility constraint among the frames. In motion segmentation area, (Shi and Malik 1998) use the normalized graph cut to extract layers from a video sequence. However, since they group pixels based on the affinity of motion profile, a local measurement, their method ignores the global constraints and appears unstable for noisy image sequences. Birchfield and Tomasi propose an approach to use a graph cuts framework to combine layer segmentation and stereo for the scene with slant surfaces, where the stereo disparities and discontinuities are improved by the explicit layer segmentation (Birchfield 1999). Wills et al. propose the use of graph cuts to extract layers between two wide baseline images (Wills 2003). After employing the RANSAC technique, they cluster the correspondences into several initial layers, then perform the dense pixel assignment via graph cuts.

Xiao and Shah start from a set of seed correspondences to estimate layer description (Xiao 2003), and then assign pixels into different layers using a graph cuts framework (Xiao 2004). Similar to Kolmogorov's occlusion model in the stereo problem, this approach also integrate occlusion penalties into the graph cuts framework for motion segmentation problem (Xiao 2004). Beyond that, an occlusion order constraint is explored and applied on the graph cuts framework, which has achieved good results for small motion video sequences. In this occlusion order constraint, an assumption is made based on an observation that occlusion has a temporal order for a linearly moving object. Nevertheless, if the object is thin and moving fast, or even moving back and forth, the occluded pixels may re-appear in certain frames and this constraint will be violated. Another limitation of this framework is that it can only use the first frame as the reference image due to the temporal order assumption. In this chapter, we present a novel framework to use a three-node pixel graph to construct a graph for multi-frame segmentation, which correctly maintain the interactions between the neighboring frame pairs and satisfy the general occlusion observation.

Using the motion information available in video sequence, several approaches have been proposed to reduce the manual work for trimap generation and have achieved good matting results for two-layer scenes (Chuang 2002, Apostoloff 2004, Hasinoff 2004, Wexler 2002).

In such scenes, there are only two layers corresponding to the background and foreground. After manually specifying the trimaps for a set of key-frames, Chuang et al. use the estimated 2D optical flow to interpolate the trimaps at the remaining frames. If the matte is not satisfactory,

an additional manual process is needed to refine the interpolated trimaps. Recently, Apostoloff and Fitzgibbon present a Bayesian background substraction approach to automatically obtain the trimaps and recover the background (Apostolof 2004). In their approach, a priori knowledge is required to train the foreground model from a selected image set. None of the existing approaches have demonstrated results containing multiple layers.

GRAPH CUTS NOTATION

In this chapter, we use the terminology and notations similar to (Boykov 2001). For example, Figure 2 shows a typical weighted graph with four nodes. This graph $G = (V, E)$ is defined by a set of nodes V (image pixels) and a set of directed edges E which connect these nodes as shown in Figure 2. In this graph, there are two distinct nodes (or terminals) s and t, called the source and sink respectively. The edges connected to the source or sink are called t-links, such as (s,p) and (p,t). The edges connected to two neighboring pixel nodes are called n-links, which are bi-directional, such as (p,q) and (q,p). The weights of these n-links in both directions may not be equal. A cut C is a subset of edges which separates the nodes into two parts; one part belongs to the source and the other belongs to the sink. The cost of a cut is the summation of the weights of its edges. Using a standard max-flow algorithm, the cost of the cut is globally minimized, and such a cut is called a minimum cut. Given a labeling system f, each pixel in image will be assigned one label. In this chapter, we use f_p to represent the label of pixel p. $D(p,f_p)$ is the data penalty of pixel p when it is assigned a label f_p. $V(p,q)$ is a smoothness penalty function between two neighboring pixels p and q.

Figure 2. An example of a graph G for a 1D image. Nodes p, q, r, and o correspond to the pixels in the image. After computing a minimum cut C, the nodes are partitioned into supporting pixels p, q (source) and unsupporting pixels r, o (sink). The weights of the links are listed in the table on the right.

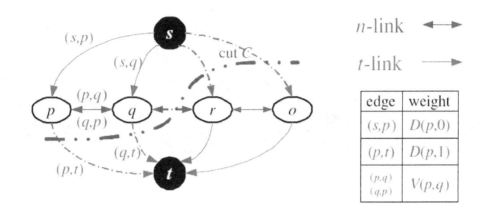

edge	weight
(s,p)	$D(p,0)$
(p,t)	$D(p,1)$
(p,q) (q,p)	$V(p,q)$

EXTRACTING THE LAYER DESCRIPTIONS

In our approach, the first stage is to extract the layer descriptions from the video sequence, which includes the number of layers and the motion parameters for each layer. In this stage, we first detect the robust seed correspondences over a short video clip. Then, using the shape prior of the previous seed region, the region's front is gradually propagated along the normal direction using a bi-partitioning graph-cuts algorithm integrated with the level set representation. Third, we design a two-step merging process to merge the seed regions into several groups, such that each group has an independent motion field.

In order to correctly extract the layer descriptions, we consider a short video clip instead of only two consecutive frames. The reason is that if the motion between two consecutive frames is too small, the motion parameters between different layers are not distinct. In our approach, we detect the Harris corners in the first frame, then we use the KLT tracking algorithm (Shi 1994) or our algorithm (Xiao 2003) to track the corners over this short period using a 17×17 pixel window. Compared to the KLT algorithm, our wide baseline matching approach can efficiently compensate for the rotation component between two corners by breaking the affine transformation into different parts. Figure 3 shows the tracking results for frames 1 to 5 of the mobile-calendar sequence using (Xiao 2003), where the corresponding corners on the ball are accurate even with a large rotation.

Once the seed correspondences are determined between frames I_1 and I_n, we consider a patch around each seed corner as an initial layer, which corresponds to a planar patch in the scene. This way, we get a number of initial layers, and each layer is supported by a small patch with a corresponding affine transformation. Nevertheless, the affine motion parameters estimated using the small patches may over-fit the pixels inside the region, and may not correctly represent the global motion of a larger region. Particularly, when the corner is located at the boundary between two true layers, the estimated affine transformation may over-fit the pixels of one layer and may cause a serious distortion on the patch after warping.

One straightforward solution is to simply extend the region by including neighboring pixels which are consistent with the affine transformation. Such pixels can be determined by applying

Figure 3. The corner tracking results for frames 1 and 5 of the mobile-calendar sequence

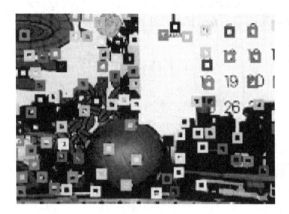 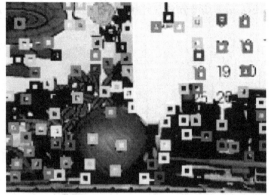

a threshold to the difference map (Figure 4d) computed between the patch in the first image (Figure 4a and the corresponding patch warped from the second image (Figure 4b-4c). However, this scheme has two problems: First, the resulting expanded region may not be compact and smooth. Second, the new patch may include pixels from multiple layers, and may not be consistent with a single planar patch in the scene. Figure 4e shows one sample result obtained by using this simple scheme. The seed region is originated from the seed on the rotating ball (Figure 4a). After expanding the boundary and bi-partitioning by applying a threshold, the region is not smooth, and it also includes pixels from the other layers.

In order to deal with these problems, we propose a novel approach to gradually expand the seed region by identifying the correct supporting pixels by using the bi-partitioning graph cuts method integrated with the level set representation. We introduce a smoothness energy term, which can maintain the partitions piecewisely smooth and naturally solve the first problem. Then, using the level set representation, the contour of the seed region is gradually evolved by propagating the region's front along its normal direction, which effectively block the pixels from the other layer and eliminates the second problem.

The process of expanding the seed region can be easily formulated into the graph cuts framework as a bi-partitioning problem of a node set. In this framework, we seek the labeling function f by minimizing the energy

$$E = E_{smooth}(f) + E_{data}(f) = \sum_{(p,q) \in N} V(p,q) \cdot T(f_p \neq f_q) + \sum_{p \in P} D(p, f_p)$$

where E_{smooth} is a piecewise smoothness term, E_{data} is a data error term, P is the set of pixels in the image, $V(p,q)$ is a smoothness penalty function, $D(p, f_p)$ is a data penalty function, N is a 4-neighbor system, f_p is the label of a pixel p, and $T(.)$ is 1 if its argument is true and 0 otherwise. In this bi-partitioning problem, the label f_p is either 0 or 1. If $f_p = 1$, the pixel p is supporting the seed region, otherwise this pixel is not supporting the region.

However, the partitioning using graph cuts cannot guarantee the gradual expansion or shrinking of a region along the normal direction as shown in Figure 4f, where some pixels not belonging to this region are also included. As a result, the computed transformation may not be representative of the real layer. Since the contour information of the initial seed region is not integrated in the energy function, the graph cuts algorithm cannot

Figure 4. A procedure for expansion of an initial 17×17 seed region to a large support region. (a) An initial seed region in the first frame. (b) The corresponding seed region in the second frame. (c) The warped version of the second frame using the estimated affine parameters. (d) The difference map between (a) and (c). (e) The result after simple expansion and partitioning. (f) The result after bi-partitioning without the level set representation. (g)-(j) are the intermediate steps of bi-partitioning with the level set representation. (g) and (i) respectively are the expansions of the seed region during the first and fourth iterations using the level set representation. (h) and (j) are the results obtained after the graph cuts partitioning, where the new region can have an arbitrary compact contour. (k) and (l) are 3D visualization of the level sets of (g) and (i). Note: The red box is the initial seed region. The green contours are obtained after using bi-partitioning algorithm.

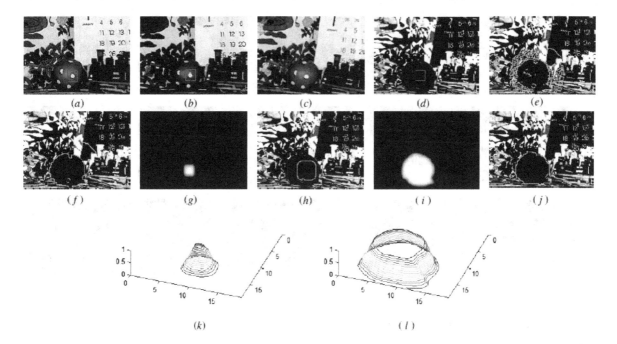

correctly evolve the region contour along the normal direction. In order to solve this problem, we use the contour of the seed region as a prior to compute the level set, v, of this region. Then, we apply v on the t-links at the sink side and adjust the weights of the t-links for pixels outside of the region in graph G. Therefore, we effectively restrict the graph cuts algorithm to gradually expand the seed region.

Figure 4 and Figure 5 show the detailed process for seed region expansion started from different seeds. Figure 4g shows the level set representation obtained from the initial seed region (Figure 4a).

Figure 4h and 4j are the partitioning results after the first and fourth iterations. In Figure 5c, we show some good results for seed region expansion of the mobile-calendar and flower-garden sequences. Figure 5d shows that we can identify the poor seed regions using the coverage threshold. Most of these poor seed regions are located at the boundary of multiple layers.

After the region expansion, each good seed region becomes an initial layer. Most of these layers may share the same affine transformation. Therefore, we use a two-step merging algorithm

Figure 5. Region expansion process. (a) Seed region expansion started from a seed on the train in the mobile-calendar sequence, which is similar to the process in Figure 4.d-g. (b) Seed region expansion started from a seed on the background in the mobile-calendar sequence. (c) Some results of the good regions (inliers) after expansion. (d) Some results of the poor regions (outliers) after expansion, where the new region cannot cover the most of the area of the original seed.

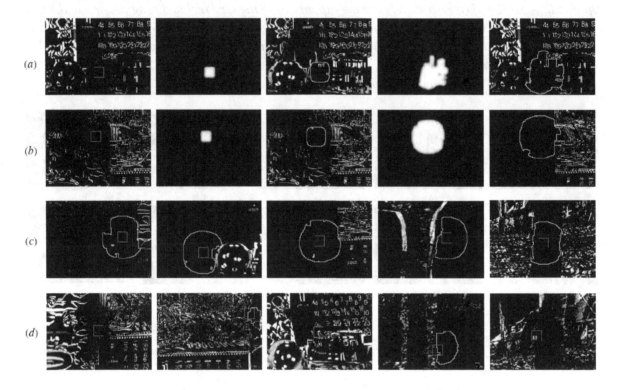

to merge these layers to obtain the layer descriptions.

In the first step, we only merge the overlapping layers. Given two regions, we test whether the number of overlapping pixels is more than half of the pixels in the smaller region. If this is true, we compute the SSD after warping the first region to the second region. Using this SSD as the measure and employing the graph cuts algorithm, we can detect how many pixels support this warping transformation. If the majority (say 80%) pixels of the first region support the second region, we merge these two regions and recompute the motion parameters using the merged pixels.

After that, we use the bi-partitioning graph cuts algorithm again to prune the unsupporting pixels from the new region. In order to achieve large merged regions, we iterate the whole process a few times (typically 3 to 4) to make sure that the merging process converges.

After the first step of merging, only a few large regions may survive. Some of the non-overlapping regions may still share a single motion transformation. During the second step, we also merge these non-overlapping regions. Figure 6 shows the results for the mobile-calendar and flower-garden sequences.

Figure 6. Extracting layer descriptions. Top: Four layers of the mobile-calendar sequence, which correspond to the calendar, train, ball, and wall respectively. Bottom: Three layers of the flower-garden sequence, which correspond to the tree, house, and flower-garden respectively. The green contour is the region boundary, and non-supporting pixels are marked by red.

MULTI-FRAME LAYER SEGMENTATION

However, these extracted layer clusters only provide rough layer representations and layer boundaries may be incorrect. In this section, we will address this problem as: Given an initial layer clustering, how to assign labels to pixels in a multiple labeling system in order to achieve a robust layer segmentation. Before starting the discussion on the multi-frame layer segmentation issue, we first go through multi-way cuts framework. Then, we indicate the limitations of the existing graph model for multi-frame segmentation. Finally, a graph model is presented to remove these limitations.

We formulate the multi-labeling problem into a multi-way graph cuts framework. In this framework, there is a label set $L=\{l_1, l_2, ..., l_k\}$ as shown in Figure 7a, and each node in the graph will be assigned one of these labels according to its data penalties (*t*-links) and smoothness penalties (*n*-links). In (Dahlhaus 1992), it has been proved by Dahlhaus et al. that finding a minimal cost

for this multiway cuts problem is NP-complete. Instead of searching for a global minimum, one feasible solution for this multi-labeling problem is to use *a*-expansion (Boykov 2001) to achieve an approximate optimal solution. In *a*-expansion algorithm, a set of two-terminal subgraphs are used as shown in Figure 7a and 7b. In each step, we randomly or sequentially pickup a label as the source terminal which is named as l_a (such as l_1 in Figure 7a), and merge the other labels as one sink terminal. Then, the maximum flow algorithm is used to compute an optimal solution for this bi-partitioning problem at a linear computational time. This process is repeated until no further energy reduction. The final energy of the graph corresponds to one approximate optimal solution for this problem.

Traditionally, each node in the graph is only associated with one image pixel such as shown in Figure 7. Thus, each pixel has one individual two-state pixel graph as shown in Figure 8a. In this case, during each step of *a*-expansion, each pixel is either assigned a new label l_a or it keeps its original label l_o, which can be naturally repre-

Figure 7. A typical multiway cuts problem. $\{l_1, l_2, ..., l_k\}$ is the label set. p,q,r,...,x,y,z are the nodes (or two-state pixel graphs) associated with the pixels in an image. (a) l_1 is selected as the l_a label (or source terminal s) and the other label terminals are grouped as one sink terminal t, a bi-partitioning can be achieved, where red nodes are assigned label l_a and the blue nodes will keep their original label l_o. (b) An example for another step of α-expansion.

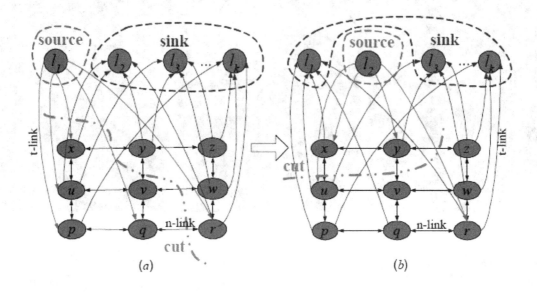

sented by state [0] or state [1] of each node respectively. For example, the node is assigned state [0] or source when a minimal cut pass the sink side *t*-link as the cut 2 shown in Figure 8a.

However, in motion segmentation application, a pixel can be assigned one of three labels during one step of α-expansion. These three labels are the new label l_a, original label l_o, and occlusion label l_z, where the label set L will be the union of occlusion label and other layer labels:

$$L = \{l_1, l_2, \cdots, l_k\} \cup \{l_z\}.$$

Therefore, we need to introduce two nodes into one pixel graph such that it provides four states for a single pixel. After setting the weight of link $(p_{1,1}, p_{1,0}) = \infty$ as shown in Figure 8b, only three possible combination ([0,0], [1,1], [0,1]) of these two nodes are vailable for this pixel, which correspond to three states after one step

of α-expansion. Here state [0,0] corresponds the cut 2 in Figure 8b and the pixel keeps original label after cut, state [1,1] corresponds the cut 1 in Figure 8b and the pixel changes its label to new label l_a after cut, state [0,1] corresponds the cut 3 in Figure 8b and the pixel is assigned occlusion label change label l_z after cut.

In order to overcome the limitation of the occlusion order constraint (Xiao 2004), we need to revisit the occlusion problem in multiple frames. In general case, if the object is moving back and forth or the object is thin and moving fast, the occlusion area may not keep increasing and the occluded pixels may also re-appear in certain frames. For example, in Figure 9 we show a synthetic image sequence in the top row, where several black lines, two ellipses, and one triangle are moving from the top-right to the bottom-left on a background with random colors. After setting the first frame as the reference image, we can see that the pixels occluded between frame

Figure 8. Pixel graphs. (a) A one-node pixel graph has two states which correspond to cut 1 (l_d) and 2 (l_s) respectively. (b) A two-node pixel graph has three states which correspond to cut 1 (l_d), 2 (l_d), and 3 (l_z) respectively. (c) A three-node pixel graph designed for general occlusion constraint of multi-frame problem. It has four states which are corresponding to cut 1 (l_d), 2 (l_d), 3, and 4 respectively. In both states 3 and 4, the pixel will be assigned occlusion label (l_z). Note: the minimal cut will not pass through the links with weight ∞.

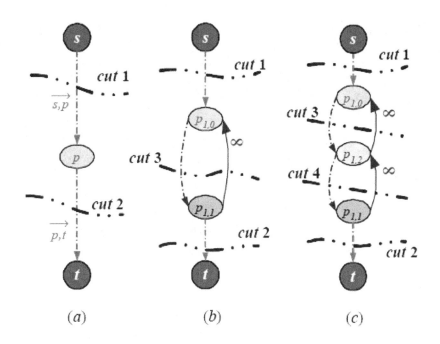

pair (1,2) may re-appear and be assigned a layer label $l_x{\neq}l_z$ in the other frame pair (1,j). If we use the occlusion order constraint to perform the segmentation, the incorrect results are obtained as shown in Figure 9a. Figure 9b shows that the occluded pixels are correctly detected by using our novel general occlusion constraint even for the lines with single pixel width.

Now we summarize the general occlusion constraint as follows: If a pixel p is assigned a layer label $l_x{\neq}l_z$ between frames i and j, then pixel p should either keep the same label l_x or be assigned the occlusion label l_z between frames i and k, where k $\neq$j.}

According to this constraint, the reference image is not necessary is set to frame 1. We can set any frame as the reference frame as shown in

Figure 9c, where frame 3 is the reference frame. It is clear to see that the occlusion areas are located at the upper-right side of the foreground layer for k<3, while the occlusion areas are located at the bottom-left side of the foreground layer when k>3.

Based on the general occlusion constraint, we design a multi-frame graph to solve the occlusion problem as shown in Figure 10, where a new three-node pixel graph (Figure 8c) is employed. Compared to the two-node pixel graph (Figure 8b), an additional node, $p_{1,2}$, is introduced to make the interactions between the pixels from the consecutive frame pairs, such as (1,2) and (1,3). In a single three-node pixel graph, there are four possible cuts, and two of them correspond to the occlusion case as shown in Figure 8c. In this way, we introduce a new concept for the pixel graph

Figure 9. Multi-frame segmentation for a two-layer synthetic image sequence. Top: several black lines, two ellipses, and one triangle is moving form top-right to bottom-left on a random fixed background. (a) The results obtained using the occlusion order constraint (Xiao 2004), where the pixels occluded between frame 1 and 2 will be always occluded between frame 1 and j (j>2). (b) The correct results by our approach using frame 1 as the reference image. (c) The correct results by our approach using frame 3 as the reference image. The corresponding frame pair numbers are indicated below the segmented images, and the occluded pixels are marked by red.

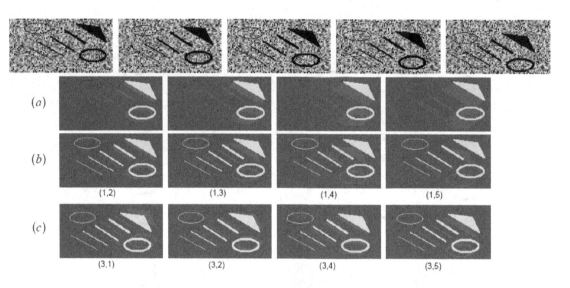

design. It effectively breaks the mapping from traditional one-to-one (one pixel graph to one node) to one-to-multiple and provides flexibility to the more complex state transformation. Therefore, we can design more flexible graph primitives to implement a sophisticated algorithm for different labeling problems.

In Figure 10, each image pair is separated by the dotted lines. In each image pair (1,j+1), j>1, only the pixels in the reference image (e.g. frame 1) are assigned pixel graphs. Here we use p_j to refer the pixel in the reference frame of frame pair (1,j+1). All p_js have the same location p in the reference frame (frame 1). For each pixel p_j, a pixel graph is created with three nodes $p_{j,0}$, $p_{j,1}$, and $p_{j,2}$. In each image pair (1,j+1), p_j belongs to a pixel set, P_j, where P_j is the set of pixels in the reference image for the image pair (1,j+1).

After assigning the link weights, the total energy of this multi-frame graph can be minimized by seeking a labeling system such that

$$E = \sum_{j=1}^{n-1} E_{smooth_j}(l) + E_{d_j}(l) + E_{oc_j}(l) + \sum_{j=1}^{n-2} E_{g_j}(l)$$

where $E_{smooth_j}(l)$ is smoothness energy, $E_{d_j}(l)$ is data energy, $E_{oc_j}(l)$ is occlusion energy in each frame pair, and $E_{g_j}(l)$ is the occlusion energy between frame pairs. $E_{smooth_j}(l)$ is defined as

$$E_{smooth_j}(l) = \sum_{i=0}^{1} \left(\sum_{(p_j,q_j)\in N} V(p_j,q_j) \cdot T(f_{p_j} \neq f_{q_j}) \right)$$

Figure 10. This graph is constructed using five consecutive frames, which have four image pairs related to the reference image. The red lines separate each pair of images into one block. The blue dotted n-links are introduced to connect $p_{j,2}s$ to maintain the general occlusion constraint. Note: Only some of the nodes and links are shown here.

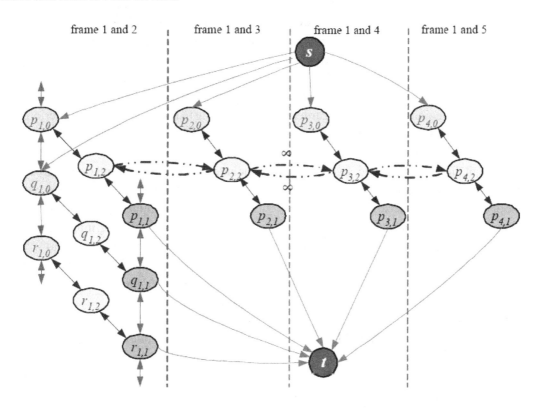

where $V(p_j, q_j)$ is designed to more likely maintain the same label for $p_{j,i}$ and $q_{j,i}$ if they have similar intensities. $E_{d_j}(l)$ is defined as

$$E_{d_j}(l) = \sum_{p_j \in P_j} \left(D(p_j, l_{p_j}) \cdot T(l_{p_j} \neq l_z) \right)$$

where $D(p_j, l_{p_j})$ depends on the difference between images I_l and I_{j+1}. The occlusion energy

$$E_{oc_j}(l) = \sum_{p_j \in P_j} \left(D_z \cdot T(l_{p_j} = l_z) \right)$$

where the occlusion penalty, D_z is an empirical constant. The last term $E_{g_j}(l)$ is used to maintain the general occlusion constraint between frame pairs, which can be defined as

$$\sum_{j=1}^{n-2} E_{g_j}(l) =$$
$$\sum_{(p_j, p_k) \in P} \infty \cdot T(l_{p_j} \neq l_z \wedge l_{p_k} \neq l_z \wedge l_{p_j} \neq l_{p_k} \wedge j \neq k)$$

After adding ∞ n-links to connect the corresponding $p_{j,2}s$ between the neighboring frame pairs, some cuts are disabled. Therefore, for the pixels at the same location in different frame pairs, such as $p_1, p_2,..., p_{n-1}$, no more than one kind of layer label will be assigned to them. For example, if pixel p_1 in frame pair (1,2) is assigned a layer label l_x, then pixel p_j in frame pair (1,j+1) will be assigned either the same label l_x or the occlusion label l_z.

Using our graph cuts framework, we achieve good segmentation results for the synthetic image sequences without non-textured motion ambiguities as shown in Figure 9. However, in the real video, the images may have some non-textured areas such as the sky regions in the flower-garden sequence. Figure 11 shows the segmentation results by using the proposed framework, where some of tree branches are segmented. Even compared to Figure 1, our results are indeed better than those obtained by the other approaches, there are still a number of artifacts in the segmentation results, particularly in the non-textured region due to the motion ambiguities.

VIDEO MATTING AND SEGMENTATION REFINEMENT

With the aim of eliminating the segmentation artifacts, in this section we combine the merits of motion cue with the alpha matting techniques to automatically extract accurate matting and refine the layer segmentation.

Once the initial segmentation of the reference image is obtained, we first apply layer order analysis to determine foreground and background layers by testing the occlusion areas. If the occlusion areas are visible in the other frames in some layer l_x, l_x should be a background layer since the foreground layer should never be occluded. According to this layer ordering criterion, we can identify that in the flower-garden sequence the foreground is the tree layer and the background includes both sky-house and flower layers. Then, an initial trimap is directly obtained, where the tree layer is the definite foreground, F, sky-house and flower layers are the definite background, B, and the occlusion areas are the unknown regions, U, as shown in Figure 12c. It is obvious that this trimap is not good due to the imprecise motion segmentation.

Therefore, we have to refine F and B using their color distributions. To estimate the color distribution, we associate a 4-neighborhood system to each pixel and then form one data vector for this pixel, where the dimension of this data vector is 5×3 (RGB). Instead of using one pixel, five neighboring pixels will provide more robust

Figure 11. Segmentation results of flower-garden sequence. Here frame 3 is used as the reference image, two segmented images of frame pairs (3,2) and (3,4) are shown, where part of branches are extracted.

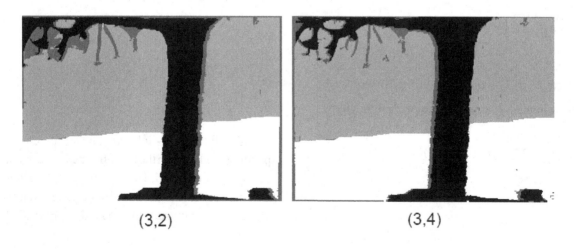

(3,2)   (3,4)

Figure 12. Alpha matting process. (a) and (b) are PDFs of F and B respectively after PCA. (c) and (d) are trimaps before and after using PDF estimation. (e) and (f) are the color estimations of foreground, U_F, and background, U_B, for the whole image (not restricted on U only). (g) and (h) are alpha mattes before and after poisson editing enhancement.

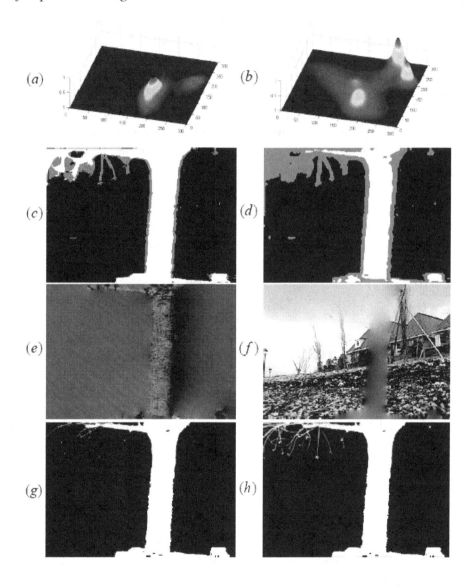

results typically for the noisy motion imagery. Next, we apply Principal Component Analysis (PCA) to all the data points and only the first few significant components are retained. After projecting the data on the new coordinates, a probability density function (PDF) can be obtained for F and B respectively by applying a proper Gaussian convolution. Figure 12a-12b show the PDFs using the first two components of PCA. Based on the PDFs, we can detect the pixels with low probability in both regions and mark them with the unknown label. Then, a shrinking process is applied to both F and B to further enlarge the unknown regions. As a result, we obtain a good trimap (Figure 12d) for the next step of the matting process.

After determining the trimap, we need to estimate foreground color, U_F, and background color, U_B, for each pixel in the unknown region, U. For U_F, there is no way to find the pixels from any frames since they do not exist in this region. In this case, an inpainting technique is a good choice to propagate the color information from the definite foreground, F, to the unknown region. Figure 12e shows using this approach we even can fill the whole image and not only restrict to U. To estimate U_B, we first apply motion compensation (mosaic) approach to fill some parts of U using the pixels from its neighboring frames. Then for the remaining uncovered holes, similarly we apply the inpainting approach to fill them as shown in Figure 12f. After that, an initial alpha value, a_0, in U can be computed by

$$a_0 = \frac{(U_C - U_B) \cdot (U_F - U_B)}{\| U_F - U_B \|^2}$$

where U_C is the observed color of the pixel in U. Figure 12g shows the initial alpha matting results. However, this matting equation does not enforce the boundary condition where the alpha values at the boundary of F are 1 and those at the boundary of B are 0. To enforce this boundary condition, we employ the ∇a_0 as a guidance field and apply poisson editing approach (Perez 2003} to re-estimate the alpha value. Figure 12h shows the final alpha matting results where the details of the branches are clearer than before.

Once the alpha mattes are computed for each frame, a Gaussian kernel is further applied in the temporal domain to ensure that the alpha mattes are consistent along the time dimension. After the temporal filtering, some boundary noise is removed particularly for the irregular boundaries, such as tree branch or hair.

EXPERIMENTS

In the experiments, we tested our approach on both synthetic and real data. For the synthetic data, we achieved perfect segmentation even for the thin objects with one pixel width as shown in Figure 9. We also provide one multi-layer synthetic sequence in our supplementary results. For the real data, we demonstrate our results on both standard motion sequences and some additional sequences.

Figure 13 shows that after alpha matting step, we can further refine the segmentation by integrating the matting information. In our implementation, we keep the mattes of foreground as much as possible during the new segmentation since the foreground is not occluded by any other layers. Figure 13 shows the segmentation and matting (or called soft segmentation) results from "flower-garden" sequence. At the bottom of Figure 13, we show one promising application of video composition, where the tree layer of "flower-garden" is transferred to another video sequence. Figure 14 shows one real sequence, "doll", taken by a hand-held moving video camera. In this static scene, a doll is located in front of a chaotic background. Due to the depth variations, the motion parameters of the doll are different from the background. For this sequence, our approach not only obtains the correct layer segmentation but also pulls accurate mattes for the doll even for her hair.

We have also extended our approach to background substraction where the non-rigid foreground is considered as the occluded region of the background. Figure 15 shows the results for another standard sequence, "mom-daughter". After obtaining the initial segmentation for each frame, we can generate a background mosaic using all background layers from the video sequence (Figure 15f). For the remaining unfilled background, we still use the inpainting technique to estimate the color of U_B (Figure 15g). Then, the proposed matting process is further used to estimate alpha channel for each frame (Figure 15h),

Figure 13. Left: segmentation results of three layers where the occluded pixels are marked by red. Middle: alpha mattes of the foreground layer. Right: new composited frames after superimposing the foreground of flower-garden in another video sequence.

Figure 14. Results of the "doll" sequence. (a): Several original frames. (b): Alpha mattes of the doll. (c) Segmentation results. (d) Video composition on a still background.

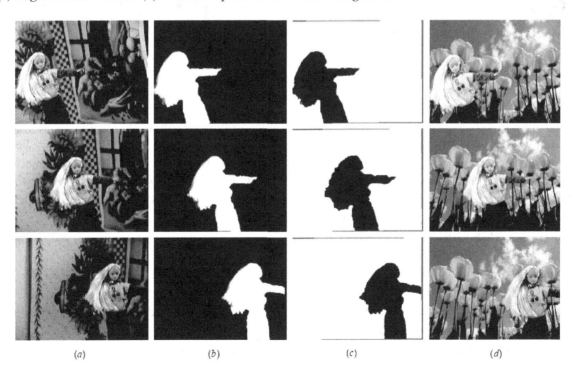

Figure 15. (a) One original frame from the "mom-daughter" sequence. (b) Mean image of the sequence. (c) Initial segmentation of (a). (d) Refined segmentation after PCA and PDF classification. (e) Background region using mosaicing technique. (f) Estimated background color. (g) Trimap of (a). (h) Alpha mattes of the non-rigid foreground. (i) Video composition on a still background.

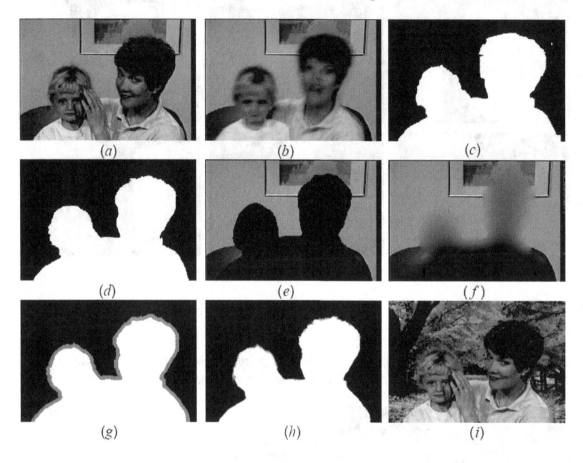

and we also transfer the foreground to other background as shown in Figure 15i.

In order to assess our algorithm for the general occlusion case, we selected three frames from a video sequence, then reordered them as if they were taken by a back-and-forth camera as shown in Figure 16. From the three input images, we can see that relative to the background layers the scissor layer first moves to the right and then moves to the left. Using our algorithm, the detected occlusion areas are consistent with this back-and-forth motion. For the evaluation purpose, we compare our results to other approaches for another standard sequence "mobile-calendar" in

Figure 17, where we obtain precise layer boundaries. Compared to the results obtained from (Xiao 2004), the new results (Figure 17d) have not been improved quite much since the objects' motion in this sequence follows the occlusion order constraint very well (slow moving and no back-and-forth motion).

FUTURE RESEARCH DIRECTIONS

One of future research directions is extending the segmentation from 2D scenario into 3D case, where the objects may not be modeled by a planar

Figure 16. Top: Three frames selected from a "scissor" video sequence to form a back-and-forth sequence. Middle: segmentation results of three layers with occluded pixels, which are consistent with the back-and-forth motion. Bottom: segmentation results obtained by using the occlusion order constraint (Xiao 2004).

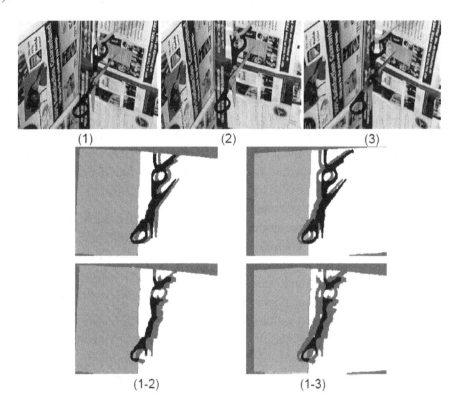

Figure 17. Results comparison. (a) One frame of the "mobile-calendar" sequence. (b) Result of Ayer and Sawhney 1995. (c) Result of Ke and Kanade 2004. (d) Our result with occluded pixels.

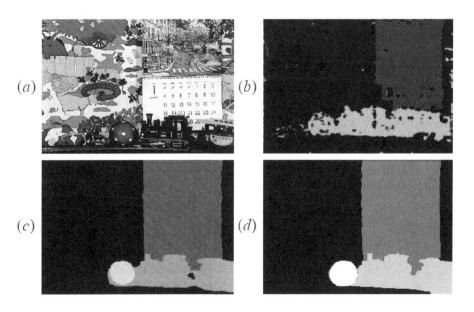

surface. The other direction is to unify the matting process with segmentation to ensure matting is more consistent over time.

CONCLUSION

In this chapter, we presented an effective approach to correctly segment the layers and pull accurate alpha mattes for the video sequences containing 2-D motion. Our contributions consist of: (1) Initial layer descriptions by integrating the level set representation into the graph cuts method to obtain gradually expanding seed regions. (2) The formulation of a general occlusion constraint among multiple frames. (3) A novel three-node pixel graph is designed to break the mapping relationship between the pixel-graph and nodes from one-to-one to one-to-multiple, which successfully solves the layer-based motion segmentation problem for textured regions. (4) An alpha matting technique to improve the segmentation around the non-textured ambiguous regions. After applying our approach to several challenging real and synthetic sequences, we achieved much better results compared to the other state-of-art approaches.

REFERENCES

Adiv, G. (1985). Determining three-dimensional motion and structure from optical flow generated by several moving objects. *IEEE Transactions on Pattern Analysis and Machine Intelligence*, 7(4), 384–401. doi:10.1109/TPAMI.1985.4767678

Apostoloff, N., & Fitzgibbon, A. (2004). Bayesian video matting using learnt image priors. *Proceedings of the IEEE Conference on Computer Vision and Pattern Recognition*.

Ayer, S., & Sawhney, H. (1995). *Layered representation of motion video using robust maximum-likelihood estimation of mixture models and MDL encoding*. International Conference on Computer Vision.

Birchfield, S., & Tomasi, C. (1999). *Multiway cut for stereo and motion with slanted surfaces.* International Conference on Computer Vision.

Boykov, Y., Veksler, O., & Zabih, R. (2001). Fast approximate energy minimization via graph cuts. *IEEE Transactions on Pattern Analysis and Machine Intelligence*, 23(11), 1222–1239. doi:10.1109/34.969114

Chuang, Y., Agarwala, A., Curless, B., Salesin, D., & Szeliski, R. (2002). Video matting of complex scenes. *Proceedings of Association of Computing Machinery's Special Interest Group on Computer Graphics and Interactive Techniques.*

Dahlhaus, E., Johnson, D., Papadimitriou, C., Seymour, P., & Yannakakis, M. (1992). *The complexity of multiway cuts. ACM Symposium on Theory of Computing*, (pp. 241-251).

Hasinoff, S., Kang, S., & Szeliski, R. (2004). *Boundary matting for view synthesis.* IEEE Workshop on Image and Video Registration.

Ke, Q., & Kanade, T. (2001). *A subspace approach to layer extraction.* IEEE Conference on Computer Vision and Pattern Recognition.

Ke, Q., & Kanade, T. (2002). *A robust subspace approach to layer extraction.* IEEE Workshop on Motion and Video Computing.

Ke, Q., & Kanade, T. (2004). *Robust subspace clustering by combined use of kNND metric and SVD algorithm.* IEEE Conference on Computer Vision and Pattern Recognition.

Khan, S., & Shah, M. (2001). *Object based segmentation of video using color, motion and spatial information.* IEEE Conference on Computer Vision and Pattern Recognition.

Kolmogorov, V., & Zabih, R. (2001). *Visual correspondence with occlusions using graph cuts*. International Conference on Computer Vision.

Kolmogorov, V., & Zabih, R. (2002). *Multi-camera scene reconstruction via graph cut*. European Conference on Computer Vision.

Patras, I., Hendirks, E., & Lagendijk, R. (2001). Video segmentation by MAP labeling of watershed segments. *IEEE Transactions on Pattern Analysis and Machine Intelligence*, *23*(3), 326–332. doi:10.1109/34.910886

Perez, P., Gangnet, M., & Blake, A. (2003). Poisson image editing. *Proceedings of Association of Computing Machinery's Special Interest Group on Computer Graphics and Interactive Techniques.*

Rother, C., Kolmogorov, V., & Blake, A. (2004). GrabCut? Interactive foreground extraction using iterated graph cuts. *Proceedings of the Association of Computing Machinery's Special Interest Group on Computer Graphics and Interactive Techniques.*

Ruzon, M., & Tomasi, C. (2000). *Alpha estimation in natural images*. IEEE Conference on Computer Vision and Pattern Recognition.

Shi, J., & Malik, J. (1998). *Motion segmentation and tracking using normalized cuts*. International Confeerence on Computer Vision.

Shi, J., & Tomasi, C. (1994). *Good features to track*. IEEE Conference on Computer Vision and Pattern Recognition.

Sun, J., Jia, J., Tang, C., & Shum, H. (2004). *Poisson matting*. ACM SIGGRAPH, 2004.

Tao, H., Sawhney, H., & Kumar, R. (2002). Object tracking with Bayesian estimation of dynamic layer representations. *IEEE Transactions on Pattern Analysis and Machine Intelligence*, *24*(1), 75–89. doi:10.1109/34.982885

Vidal, R., & Ma, Y. (2004). *A unified algebraic approach to 2-D and 3-D motion segmentation*. European Conference on Computer Vision.

Wang, J., & Adelson, E. (1994). Representing moving images with layers. *IEEE Transactions on Image Processing*, *3*(5), 625–638. doi:10.1109/83.334981

Wexler, Y., Fitzgibbon, A., & Zisserman, A. (2002). *Bayesian estimation of layers from multiple images*. European Conference on Computer Vision.

Wills, J., Agarwal, S., & Belongie, S. (2003). *What went where*. IEEE Conference on Computer Vision and Pattern Recognition.

Xiao, J., & Shah, M. (2003). *Two-frame wide baseline matching*. International Conference on Computer Vision.

Xiao, J., & Shah, M. (2004). *Motion layer extraction in the presence of occlusion using graph cut*. IEEE Conference on Computer Vision and Pattern Recognition.

Zelnik-Manor, L., & Irani, M. (1999). *Multi view subspace constraints on homographies*. International Conference on Computer Vision.

Zhou, Y., & Tao, H. (2003). *A background layer model for object tracking through occlusion*. International Conference on Computer Vision.

ADDITIONAL READING

Appleton, B., & Talbot, H. (2006). Globally minimal surfaces by continuous maximal flows. *IEEE Transactions on Pattern Analysis and Machine Intelligence*, 106–118. doi:10.1109/TPAMI.2006.12

Bergen, L., & Meyer, F. (2000). *A novel approach to depth ordering in monocular image sequences.* IEEE Conference on Computer Vision and Pattern Recognition.

Besag, J. E. (1986). On the statistical analysis of dirty pictures (with discussion). *Journal of the Royal Statistical Society. Series B. Methodological, 48,* 259–302.

Boykov, Y., & Kolmogorov, V. (2003). *Computing geodesics and minimal surfaces via graph cuts.* International Conference on Computer Vision.

Boykov, Y., & Kolmogorov, V. (2004). An experimental comparison of min-cut/max-flow algorithms for energy minimization in vision. *IEEE Transactions on Pattern Analysis and Machine Intelligence, 26*(9), 1124–1137. doi:10.1109/TPAMI.2004.60

Boykov, Y., Veksler, O., & Zabih, R. (1998). *Markov random fields with efficient approximations.* International Conference on Computer Vision and Pattern Recognition.

Funka-Lea, G., Boykov, Y., Florin, C., Jolly, M., Moreau-Gobard, R., Ramaraj, R., & Rinck, D. (2006). Automatic heart isolation for CT coronary visualization using graph cuts. IEEE International Symposium on Biomedical Imaging, (pp. 614–617).

Geman, D., & Geman, S. (1984). Stochastic relaxation, Gibbs distributions and the Bayesian restoration of images. *IEEE Transactions on Pattern Analysis and Machine Intelligence, 6,* 721–741. doi:10.1109/TPAMI.1984.4767596

Giaccone, P., & Jones, G. (1998). *Segmentation of global motion using temporal probabilistic classification.* British Machine Vision Conference.

Grady, L., & Alvino, C. (2009). The piecewise smooth Mumford-Shah functional on an arbitrary graph. *IEEE Transactions on Image Processing,* 2547–2561. doi:10.1109/TIP.2009.2028258

Greig, D. M., Porteous, B. T., & Seheult, A. H. (1989). Exact maximum a posteriori estimation for binary images. *Journal of the Royal Statistical Society. Series B. Methodological, 51,* 271–279.

Ishikawa, H., & Geiger, D. (1998). *Occlusions, discontinuities, and epipolar lines in stereo.* European Conference on Computer Vision.

Joshi, N., Matusik, W., & Avidan, S. (2006). Natural video matting using camera arrays. In *Proceedings of the Association of Computing Machinery's Special Interest Group on Computer Graphics and Interactive Technology,* (pp. 779–786).

Kang, S., Szeliski, R., & Chai, J. (2001). *Handing occlusions in dense multi-view stereo.* IEEE Conferencew on Computer Vision and Pattern Recognition.

Kolmogorov, V., & Boykov, Y. (2005). What metrics can be approximated by geo-cuts, or global optimization of length/area and flux. *International Conference on Computer Vision* (pp. 564-571).

Kwatra, V., Essa, I., Schl, A., Turk, G., & Bobick, A. (2003). Graphcut textures: Image and video synthesis using graph cuts. *Proceedings of the Association of Computing Machinery's Special Interest Group on Computer Graphics and Interactive Technology.*

Osher, S., & Fedkiw, R. (2003). *Level set methods and dynamic implicit surfaces.* Springer-Verlag.

Rhemann, C., Rother, C., Rav-Acha, A., & Sharp, T. (2008). High resolution matting via interactive trimap segmentation. In *Proceedings of IEEE Conference on Computer Vision and Pattern Recognition.*

Sethian, J. (1999). *Level set methods and fast marching methods.* Cambridge University Press.

Sinop, A., & Grady, L. (2007). *A seeded image segmentation framework unifying graph cuts and random walker which yields a new algorithm.* International Conference on Computer Vision.

Smith, P., Drummond, T., & Cipolla, R. (2004). Layered motion segmentation and depth ordering by tracking edges. *IEEE Transactions on Pattern Analysis and Machine Intelligence, 26*(4), 479–494. doi:10.1109/TPAMI.2004.1265863

Szeliski, R. (1996). Video mosaics for virtual environments. *IEEE Computer Graphics and Applications, 16*(2), 22–30. doi:10.1109/38.486677

Torr, P., & Murray, D. (1993). Outlier detection and motion segmentation. *SPIE Sensor Fusion Conference VI*, (pp. 432-443).

Wang, J., Agrawala, M., & Cohen, M. (2007). Soft scissors: An interactive tool for realtime high quality matting. In *Proceedings of ACM SIGGRAPH*, 2007.

Weiss, Y. (1997). *Smoothness in layers: Motion segmentation using nonparametric on homographics*. IEEE Conference on Computer Vision and Pattern Recognition.

Xu, N., Bansal, R., & Ahuja, N. (2003). *Object segmentation using graph cuts based active contours*. IEEE Conference on Computer Vision and Pattern Recognition.

Chapter 6
Hypergraph Based Visual Segmentation and Retrieval

Yuchi Huang
General Electric Global Research, USA

ABSTRACT

This chapter explores original techniques for the construction of hypergraph models for computer vision applications. A hypergraph is a generalization of a pairwise simple graph, where an edge can connect any number of vertices. The expressive power of the hypergraph models places a special emphasis on the relationship among three or more objects, which has made hypergraphs better models of choice in a lot of problems. This is in sharp contrast with the more conventional graph representation of visual patterns where only pairwise connectivity between objects is described. This chapter draws up from three aspects to carry the discussion of hypergraph based methods in computer vision: (i) The advantage of the hypergraph neighborhood structure is analyzed. The author argues that the summarized local grouping information contained in hypergraphs causes an 'averaging' effect which is beneficial to the clustering problems; (ii)The chapter discusses how to build hypergraph incidence structures and how to solve the related unsupervised and semi-supervised problems for two different computer vision scenarios: video object segmentation and image retrieval; (iii) For the application of image retrieval, the chapter introduces a novel hypergraph model — probabilistic hypergraph to exploit the structure of the data manifold by considering not only the local grouping information, but also the similarities between vertices in hyperedges.

1. INTRODUCTION

In computer vision and other applied machine learning problems, a fundamental task is to cluster a set of data in a manner such that elements of the same cluster are more similar to each other than elements in different clusters. In these prob-lems, we generally assume pairwise relationships among the objects of our interest. For example, a common distance measure for data points lying in a vector space is the Euclidean distance, which is used in a lot of unsupervised central clustering methods such as k-means (Macqueen, 1967), k-centers clustering (Macqueen, 1967)

DOI: 10.4018/978-1-4666-1891-6.ch006

and affinity propagation (Frey, 2007). Actually, a data set endowed with pairwise relationships can be naturally organized as a pairwise graph (for simplicity, we denote the pairwise graph as simple graph in the following). The simple graph partitioning problem in mathematics consists of dividing a graph G into k pieces, such that the pieces are of about the same size and there are few connections between the pieces. With a few notable exceptions, the similarities between objects in a simple graph are utilized to present the pairwise relationships. The simple graph can be undirected or directed, depending on whether the relationships among objects are symmetric or not. Usually a computed kernel matrix is associated to a directed or undirected graph, a lot of methods for unsupervised and semi-supervised learning can then be formulated in terms of operations on this simple graph and achieve better clustering results compared to central clustering methods (Shi, 2000) (Ng, 2001) (Luxburg,2008).

However, in many real world problems, it is not complete to represent the relations among a set of objects as simple graphs. This point of view is illustrated in a good example used in (Zhou, 2006). In this example, a collection of articles need to be grouped into different clusters by topics. The only information that we have is the authors of all the articles. One way to solve this problem is to construct an undirected graph in which two vertices are connected by an edge if they have at least one common author (Table 1 and Figure 1), and then spectral graph clustering can be applied (Fieldler, 1973) (Chan, 1993) (Shi, 2000). Each edge weight of this undirected graph may be assigned as the number of authors in common between two articles. It is an easy, nevertheless, not natural way to represent the relations between the articles because this graph construction loses the information whether the same person is the author of three or more articles or not. Such information loss is unexpected because the articles by the same person likely belong to the same topic and hence

Table 1. An author set $E = \{e_1, e_2, e_3\}$ and an article set $V = \{v_1, v_2, v_3, v_4, v_5, v_6, v_7\}$. The entry (v_i, e_j) is set to 1 if e_j is an author of article v_i and 0 otherwise.

	e_1	e_2	e_3
v_1	1	0	0
v_2	1	0	1
v_3	0	0	1
v_4	0	0	1
v_5	0	1	0
v_6	0	1	1
v_7	0	1	0

the information is useful for our grouping task. A more natural way to remedy the information is to represent the data points as a hypergraph. An edge in a hypergraph is called a hyperedge, which can connect more than two vertices; that is, a hyperedge is a subset of vertices. For this article clustering problem, it is quite straightforward to construct a hypergraph with the vertices representing the articles, and the hyperedges the authors (Figure 1). Each hyperedge contains all articles by its corresponding author. Furthermore, positive weights may be put on hyperedges to emphasize or weaken specific authors' work. For those authors working on a smaller range of fields, we may assign a larger weight to the corresponding hyperedge. Compared to a simple pairwise graph, in this example hypergraph structure more completely illustrates the complex relationships among authors and articles.

Figure 1. The hypergraph and corresponding simple graph, constructed from the incidence matrix in Table 1. Left: an undirected graph in which two articles are joined together by an edge if there is at least one author in common. Right: a corresponding hypergraph.

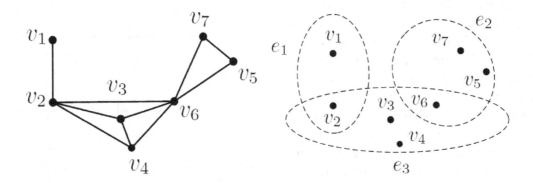

Another reason to adopt hypergraphs is that sometimes there is not a simple similarity measure for pairwise data points. Sometimes one may consider the relationship among three or more data points to determine if they belong to the same cluster. For example, in a k-lines clustering problem, we need to cluster data points in a d-dimensional vector space into k clusters where elements in each cluster are well approximated by a line (Agarwal, 2005). In this problem, there is not a useful measure of similarity only using pairs of points, because we cannot define a line only by a pair of data points. However, it is possible to define measures of similarity over three or more points that indicate how close they are to being collinear. This kind of similarity/dissimilarity measured over triples or more than three points can be referred as higher order relations, which is useful in a lot of model based clustering task where the fitting error of a group of data points to a model can be considered a measure of the dissimilarity among them (Agarwal, 2005).

A powerful technique for partitioning simple graphs is spectral clustering. While the understanding of hypergraph spectral methods relative that of simple graphs is very limited, a number of authors have considered extensions of spectral graph theoretic methods to hypergraphs (Rodrequez,2003) (Bolla,1993) (Zhou, 2006). In this chapter, we

focus on Zhou's normalized hypergraph Laplacian because of its efficiency and simplicity of implementation. In Zhou's work, spectral clustering techniques are generalized to hypergraphs; more specifically, the normalized cut approach of (Shi, 2000). As in the case of simple graphs, a real-valued relaxation of the hypergraph normalized cut criterion leads to the eigen-decomposition of a positive semidefinite matrix called hypergraph Laplacian, which can be regarded as an analogue of the Laplacian for simple graphs (Chung, 1997). Based on the concept of hypergraph Laplacian, algorithms can be developed for unsupervised data partition, hypergraph embedding and transductive inference.

The rest of this chapter is organized as follows. In Section 2, we survey the related theoretic work on unsupervised and semi-supervised hypergraph learning. We lay stress on the normalized hypergraph Laplacian and spectral hypergraph partitioning algorithms. In Section 3 and Section 4, we will discuss how to build hypergraph incidence structures and how to solve the related unsupervised and semi-supervised problems for two different computer vision scenarios: video object segmentation and relevance feedback image retrieval. Two hypergraph based algorithms, hypergraph cut and hypergraph ranking are adopted to solve optimization problems under unsupervised and semi-supervised learning settings. Finally, Section 5 summarizes the contributions of this work, along with a discussion of future work possibilities.

2. BACKGROUND

The study of measurement defined over triples or point sets of size greater than two is not new. The primary focus of this literature is the study of topological and geometrical properties of these generalized measures (Deza, 2000) (Hayashi, 1973). Some researchers have developed generalizations of Multidimensional Scaling (MDS) (Borg, 2005) to the case of triadic data or higher order data (Carroll, 1970) (Cox, 1993) (Heiser, 1997) (Joly, 1995).

The initial practical application of hypergraph partitioning algorithms occurs in the field of VLSI design and synthesis (Agarwal, 2005). In this application, the circuit elements are the vertices of the hypergraph and the nets that connect these circuit elements are the hyperedges (Alpert, 1995). The development of the tools for partitioning these hypergraphs is almost entirely heuristic and very little theoretical work exists that analyzes their performance beyond empirical benchmarks (Karypis, 1999) (Fiduccia, 1982) (Kernighan, 1970).

The previously proposed algorithms for partitioning a hypergraph can be divided into two categories. The first category aims at constructing a simple graph from the original hypergraph, and then partitioning the vertices by spectral clustering techniques. These methods include clique expansion (Zien, 1996), star expansion (Hu, 1985), Rodriquez's Laplacian (Rodrequez, 2003) and clique averaging (Agarwal, 2005) etc. Clique Expansion and Star Expansion are two most commonly used graph approximations. Clique Expansion, as the name suggests, expands each hyperedge into a clique. Star expansion introduces a dummy vertex for each hyperedge and connects

each vertex in the hyperedge to it (Hu, 1985). As can be expected, the weights on the edges of the clique and the star determine the cut properties of the approximating graph (Ihler, 1993). Another method to approximate the hypergraph using a weighted graph is clique averaging, which is closely related to clique expansion but is able to preserve more information contained in original hypergraphs. The second category of approaches define a hypergraph 'Laplacian' using analogies from the simple graph Laplacian. Representative methods in this category include Bolla's Laplacian (Bolla, 1993), Zhou's normalized Laplacian (Zhou, 2006), etc. In (Agarwal, 2005), the above algorithms are analyzed and verified that they are equivalent to each other under specific conditions. Another possible representation of higher order relations is a tensor (Chen, 2009), which is a generalization of matrices to higher dimensional arrays.

3. UNSUPERVISED AND SEMI-SUPERVISED LEARNING WITH HYPERGRAPHS

Notation and Terminology

The key difference between the hypergraph and the simple graph lies in that the former uses a subset of the vertices as an edge, i.e., a hyperedge connecting more than two vertices. Let V represent a finite set of vertices and E a family of subsets of V such that $\bigcup_{e \in E} = V$, $G = (V, E, w)$ is called a hypergraph with the vertex set V and the hyperedge set E, and each hyperedge e is assigned a positive weight $w(e)$. For a vertex $v \in V$, its degree is defined to be $d(v) = \sum_{\{e \in E | v \in e\}} w(e)$. For a hyperedge $e \in E$, its degree is defined by $\delta(e) = |e|$. Let us use D_v, D_e and W to denote the diagonal matrices of the vetex degrees, the hyperedge degrees, and the hyperedge weights respectively. The hypergraph

G can be represented by a $|V| \times |E|$ matrix H which $h(v,e) = 1$ if $v_H \in e_H$ and 0 otherwise. According to the definition of H, $d(v) = \sum_{e \in E} w(e)h(v,e)$ and $\delta(e) = \sum_{v \in V} h(v,e)$

For a vertex subset $S \subset V$, let S^c denote the compliment of S. A cut of a hypergraph $G = (V, E, w)$ is a partition of V into two parts S and S^c. We say that a hyperedge e is cut if it is incident with the vertices in S and S^c simultaneously.

Given a vertex subset $S \subset V$ define the hyperedge boundary ∂S of S to be a hyperedge set which consists of hyperedges which are cut:

$$\partial S := \{e \in E \mid e \cap S \neq \emptyset, e \cap S^c \neq \emptyset\}. \tag{1}$$

Define the volume $volS$ of S to be the sum of the degrees of the vertices in S, that is, $volS := \sum v \in Sd(v)$. Moreover, define the volume of ∂S by

$$vol\partial S := \sum_{e \in \partial S} w(e) \frac{|e \cap S||e \cap S^c|}{|\delta(e)|}. \tag{2}$$

According to Equation 2, we have $vol\partial S = vol\partial S^c$. The definition given by above equations can be understood as follows: if we treat the defined volume of the hyperedge boundary across S and S^s as the connection between two clusters and the volume of S or S^c as the connection inside S or S^c, we try to obtain a partition in which the connection among the vertices in the same cluster is dense while the connection between two clusters is sparse. Then a natural partition can be formalized as follows:

$$\arg \min_{\emptyset \neq S \subset V} c(S) := vol(S, S^c)\left(\frac{1}{vol(S)} + \frac{1}{vol(S^c)}\right) \tag{3}$$

For a simple graph, $|e \cap S| = |e \cap S^c| = 1$, and $\delta(e) = 2$. According to the derivation in (Chen, 2009), the right-hand side of above equation reduces to the simple graph normalized cut (Shi, 2000) up to a factor $\frac{1}{2}$

Normalized Hypergraph Laplacian

Recall the cost function in Equation 3. This objective function characterizes how an optimal partitioning of a given hypergraph should look like: the volume of the boundary $vol(\partial S)$ is minimized, while the 'size' of S and Sc are balanced; otherwise, a small $vol(S)$ or $vol(Sc)$ will make the objective value prohibitively large. According the derivation in (Chen, 2009), the objective value $c(S)$ coincides with a Rayleigh quotient. Let a column vector q have elements

$$q(v) := \begin{cases} +\sqrt{\eta_2 / \eta_1}, & if \ v \in S \\ -\sqrt{\eta_1 / \eta_2}, & if \ v \in S^c. \end{cases} \tag{4}$$

where $\eta_1 = vol(S)$ and $\eta_2 = vol(S^c)$, then

$$c(S) = \frac{q^T L q}{q^T \Lambda q}, \tag{5}$$

where $L = D_v - HWD_e^{-1}H^T$ is called the Laplacian of the hypergraph and Λ is the diagonal matrix with diagonal elements equal to $vol(v)$. We call q the partition vector. The claim implies that the problem of finding an optimal hypergraph cut can be reduced to computing a vector q in the form 4 which minimizes the quotient 5. However, this is a combinatorial optimization problem that is NP-complete (Garey, 1990). From standard results in linear algebra, minimizing the above quotient over real vectors q, is equivalent to finding the bottom eigenvector of the matrix pencil (L, Λ). According to (Shi, 2000), this problem can be further reduced to solve the second smallest eigenvector of the following matrix:

$$\Delta = I - D_v^{-1/2}HWD_e^{-1}H^TD_v^{-1/2}, \tag{6}$$

where Δ is called the normalized hypergraph Laplacian. Actually, this result can be reached from another direction. For a hypergraph partition problem, the normalized cost function (Zhou, 2006) $\Omega(f)$ could be defined as

$$\frac{1}{2}\sum_{e \in E}\sum_{u,v \in e}\frac{w(e)h(u,e)h(v,e)}{\delta(e)}\left(\frac{f(u)}{\sqrt{d(u)}} - \frac{f(v)}{\sqrt{d(v)}}\right)^2, \tag{7}$$

where the vector f is the image labels to be learned. By minimizing this cost function, vertices sharing many incidental hyperedges are guaranteed to obtain similar labels. Defining $\Theta = D_v^{-\frac{1}{2}}HWD_e^{-1}H^TD_v^{-\frac{1}{2}}$, we can derive Equation 7 as follows:

$$-0.2cm\Omega(f) =$$

$$\sum_{e \in E}\sum_{u,v \in e}\frac{w(e)h(u,e)h(v,e)}{\delta(e)}\left(\frac{f^2(u)}{d(u)} - \frac{f(u)f(v)}{\sqrt{d(u)d(v)}}\right)$$

$$= \sum_{u \in V}f^2(u)\sum_{e \in E}\frac{w(e)h(u,e)}{d(u)}\sum_{v \in V}\frac{h(v,e)}{\delta(e)}$$

$$-\sum_{e \in E}\sum_{u,v \in e}\frac{f(u)h(u,e)w(e)h(v,e)f(v)}{\sqrt{d(u)d(v)}\delta(e)}$$

$$= f^T(I - \Theta)f, \tag{8}$$

where I is the identity matrix. Above derivation shows that (i) $\Omega(f,w) = f^T(I-\Theta)f$ if and only if $\sum_{v \in V}\frac{h(v,e)}{\delta(e)} = 1$ and $\sum_{e \in E}\frac{w(e)h(u,e)}{d(u)} = 1$, which

is true because of the definition of $\delta(e)$ and $d(u)$; (ii) $\Delta = I - \Theta$ is a positive semi-definite matrix introduced above -- the normalized hypergraph Laplacian and $\Omega(f) = f^T\Delta f$. The above cost function has the similar formulation to the normalized cost function of a simple graph $G_s = (V_s, E_s)$:

$$\Omega_s(f) = \frac{1}{2}\sum_{v_i,v_j \in V_s}A_s(i,j)\left(\frac{f(i)}{\sqrt{D_{ii}}} - \frac{f(j)}{\sqrt{D_{jj}}}\right)^2$$

$$= f^T(I - D^{-\frac{1}{2}}A_sD^{-\frac{1}{2}})f = f^T\Delta_s f, \tag{9}$$

where D is a diagonal matrix with its (i,i)-element equal to the sum of the ith row of the affinity matrix A_s; $\Delta_s = I - \Theta_s = I - D^{-\frac{1}{2}}A_sD^{-\frac{1}{2}}$ is called the normalized simple graph Laplacian.

In an unsupervised framework, Equation 7 and Equation 9 can be optimized by the eigenvector related to the smallest nonzero eigenvalue of Δ and Δ_s (Zhou, 2006), respectively.

In the transductive learning setting (Zhou, 2006), we define a vector y to introduce the labeling information and to assign their initial labels to the corresponding elements of y: $y(v) = 1$ if a vertex v is in the positive set Pos, $y(v) = -1$, if it is in the negative set Neg. If v is unlabeled, $y(v) = 0$. To force the assigned labels to approach the initial labeling y, a regularization term is defined as follows:

$$\|f - y\|^2 = \sum_{u \in V}(f(u) - y(u))^2. \tag{10}$$

After the feedback information is introduced, the learning task is to minimize the sum of two cost terms with respect to f (Zhou, 2003) (Zhou, 2006), which is

$$\Phi(f) = f^T\Delta f + \mu\|f - y\|^2, \tag{11}$$

where $\mu > 0$ is the regularization parameter. Differentiating $\Phi(f)$ with respect to f, we have

$$f = (1-\gamma)(I - \gamma\Theta)^{-1}y, \qquad (12)$$

where $\gamma = \dfrac{1}{1+\mu}$. This is equivalent to solving the linear system $\big((1+\mu)I - \Theta\big)f = \mu y$.

For the simple graph, we can simply replace Θ with Θ_s to fulfill the transductive learning.

The Connections between Hypergraph Learning Algorithms

In (Agarwal, 2005), different hypergraph learning algorithms are analyzed and proved to be equivalent to each other. At first, (Agarwal, 2005) verifies that for a k-uniform hypergraph (each hyperedge contains a fixed number of k vertices), the eigenvectors of the normalized Laplacian for the bipartite graph G_c^* (obtained from Star Expansion) are exactly the eigenvectors of the normalized Laplacian for the standard clique expansion graph G^x. This is a surprising result since the two graphs are completely different in the number of vertices and the connectivity between these vertices. Even for non-uniform hypergraphs, the difference between two formulations are not large and may obtain similar decomposed eigenvectors. (Agarwal, 2005) also proved that all different hypergraph Laplacians correspond to either clique or star expansion of the original hypergraph under specific conditions.

To analyze the advantage of hypergraphs over simple graphs, let's consider that we take the sum of the pairwise similarities inside a hyperedge as the hyperedge weight (similar configurations are used in the following chapters). We transfer this hypergraph into a simple graph by Clique Expansion. In the obtained simple graph, the edge weight between two vertices v_i and v_j is not decided by the pairwise affinity $A_{i,j}$ between two vertices, but the averaged neighboring affinities close to them; furthermore, this edge weight is influenced more by those pairwise affinities whose two incident vertices share more hyperedges with v_i and v_j. Through the hyergraph, the `higher order' or `local grouping' information is used for the construction of graph neighborhood. We argue that such an `averaging' effect may be beneficial to the image clustering task, just as local image smoothing may be beneficial to the image segmentation task.

4. HYPERGRAPH BASED VIDEO OBJECT SEGMENTATION

Video object segmentation is a hot topic in the communities of computer vision and pattern recognition. Compared to the object segmentation in static images, temporal correlation between consecutive frames, i.e., motion cues, will alleviate the difficulties in video object segmentation. Prior works can be divided into two categories. A large category of approaches attempts to segment video objects with spatio-temporal information, such as (DeMenthon, 2002), (Wills, 2003), (Fischler, 1987), (Chung, 2004), and (Stein, 2007). Different from these methods, Shi and Malik (Shi, 1998) have proposed a pairwise graph based model to describe the spatio-temporal relations in the 3D video data and have employed the spectral clustering analysis to solve the video segmentation problem, which is beautiful and has achieved promising results.

In this section, we introduce a novel framework of video object segmentation based on hypergraph (Huang, 2009), as shown in Figure 2. Inspired by (Stein, 2007), we initially over-segment the sequential images into small patches with consistent local appearance and motion information, as shown in Figure 3. Using the pixel values in the

LUV color space, we get a 3-D features (l, u, v) for each pixel in the image sequence. With this feature, we adopt a multi-scale graph decomposition method (Cour, 2005) to do over-segmentation, for its ability to capture both the local and middle range relationship of image intensities, and its linear time complexity. This over-segmentation provides a good preparation for high-level reasoning of spatial-temporal relationship among the patches. We take these over-segmented patches as the vertices of the graph.

Hyperedge Computation

The computation of the hyperedges is actually equivalent to generating some attributes of the image patches. We treat the task of attribute assignment as a problem of binary classification according to different criteria. We first perform the spectral analysis in the spatio-temporal domain on two different motion cues, i.e., the optical flow and the appearance based motion profile, respectively. Then we cluster the data into two classes (2-way cut) on each spectral eigenvector respectively. Some representative 2-way cut results are finally selected to indicate the attributes of the patches. By analyzing the 2-way cut results, we assign different weights to different hyperedges. As mentioned above, the hyperedge is used to connect the vertices with same attribute value, so the task of hyperedges computation is actually to assign attributes for each image patch in spatio-temporal domain.

Computing Motion Cues

We use the optical flow and the appearance based motion profile to describe the over-segmented patches in the spatio-temporal domain. The Lucas-Kanade optical flow method (Lucas, 1981) is adopted to obtain the translations (x, y) of each pixel, and we indicate each pixel with the motion

Figure 2. Illustration of the framework

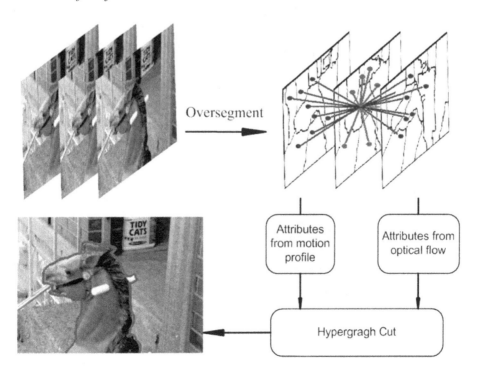

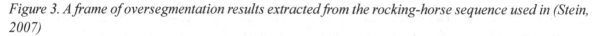

Figure 3. A frame of oversegmentation results extracted from the rocking-horse sequence used in (Stein, 2007)

intensity $z = \sqrt{x^2 + y^2}$ and the motion direction $o = arctan(\frac{x}{y})$. We assume that pixels in the same patch have a similar motion, and then the motion of a patch can be estimated, $f^o = (u, d)$, by computing the weighted average of all the pixel motions in a patch:

$$u = \frac{1}{N}\sum_i \omega_i z_i, d = \frac{1}{N}\sum_i \omega_i o_i, \qquad (13)$$

where N is the total number of pixels in a region, and w_i is the weight generated from a low-pass 2-D Gaussian centered on the centroid of the patch. u, d are the motion intensity and the motion angle of the patch, respectively.

Besides the optical flow, we also apply the appearance based motion profile to describe the over-segmented patches, inspired by the idea in (Shi, 1998). Based on a reasonable assumption that the pixels in one patch have the same move-ment and color components and remain stable between consecutive frames too, the motion profile is defined as a measure of the probability distribution of image velocity to every patch based on appearance information. Let $I^t(X_i)$ denote the vector containing all the (l, u, v) pixel values of patch i centered at X and denote $P_i(dx)$ as the probability of the image patch i at time t corresponding to another image patch $I^{t+1}(X_i + dx)$ at $t+1$:

$$P_i(dx) = \frac{S_i(dx)}{\sum_{dx} S_i(dx)} \qquad (14)$$

where $S_i(dx)$ denotes the similarity between $I^t(X_i)$ and $I^{t+1}(X_i + dx)$ which is based on the SSD difference between $I^t(X_i)$ and $I^{t+1}(X_i + dx)$:

$$S_i(dx) = exp(-SSD(I^t(X_i), I^{t+1}(X_i + dx))). \qquad (15)$$

Spectral Analysis for Hyperedge Computation

The idea of spectral analysis is based on an affinity matrix A where $A(i,j)$ is the similarity between sample i and j (Shi, 2000) (Ng, 2001) (Weiss, 1999). Based on the affinity matrix, the Laplacian matrix can be defined as $L = D^{-\frac{1}{2}}(D-A)D^{-\frac{1}{2}}$ where D is the diagonal matrix $D(i,i) = \sum_j A(i,j)$. Then unsupervised data clustering can be achieved by doing eigenvalue decomposition of the Laplacian matrix. The popular way is to use the k-means method on the first several eigenvectors associated with the smallest non-zero eigenvalues (Ng, 2001) to get the final clustering result.

To set up the hyperedges, we perform the spectral analysis on the optical flow and the appearance based motion profile respectively. As in (Shi, 2000) (Ng, 2001) (Weiss, 1999), only local neighbors are taken into account for the similarity computation. We defined two patches to be spatial-temporal neighbors if 1) in the same frame they are 8-connected or both their centroids fall into a ball of radius R, or 2) in the adjacent frames (± 1 frame in the work) their regions are overlapped or 8-connected, as illustrated in Figure 2.

Denote the affinity matrices of the optical flow as A^o and the motion profile as A^p respectively. For the motion profile, we define the similarity between two neighbor patches i and j is defined as:

$$A^p(i,j) = e^{-\frac{dis(i,j)}{\sigma^p}}, dis(i,j) = 1 - \sum_{dx}P_i(dx)P_j(dx), \tag{16}$$

where $dis(i,j)$ is defined as the distance between two patches i and j, and σ^p is constant computed as the standard deviation of $dis(i,j)$

Based on the optical flow, the similarity metric between two neighbor patches i and j is defined as:

$$A^o(i,j) = e^{-\frac{P f_i^m - f_j^m P_2}{\sigma^o}}, \tag{17}$$

where σ^o is a constant computed as the standard deviation of $\left\| f_i^o - f_j^o \right\|_2$

Based on A^o and A^p, we can compute the corresponding Laplacian matrix of L^o and L^p and their eigenvectors associated with the first k smallest non-zero eigenvalues respectively. Each of these eigenvectors may lead to a meaningful but not optimal 2-way cut result. Figure 4 shows some examples, where the patches without the gray mask are regarded as the vertices having the *attribute* value 1 and the patches with the gray mask having the *attribute* 0. A hyperedge can be formed by those vertices with same attribute values. With all the hyperedges, the complex relationship between the image patches can be represented by the hypergraph completely.

Hyperedge Weights

According to (Shi, 2000), the eigenvectors of the smallest k non-zero eigenvalues can be used for clustering. Then a nature idea is to choose the first k eigenvectors to compute the hyperedges, and weight those heyperedges with their corresponding reciprocals of the eigenvalues. In our experiments, we find that the eigenvalues of the first k eigenvectors are very close and may not absolutely reflect the importance of the corresponding eigenvectors. In order to emphasize more important hyperedges which contain moving objects, larger weights should be assigned to them.

We impose the weights to the hyperedges from two different cues, w_H^o and w_H^p, by the following equations:

Figure 4. Four binary partition results got by the first 4 eigenvectors computed from motion profile (for one frame of the sequence WalkByShop1cor.mpg, CAVIAR database)

(1) (2)

(3) (4)

$$w_H^o = c^o \left\| f_1^o - f_0^o \right\|_2 \qquad (18)$$

$$w_H^p = c^p dis(1,0) \qquad (19)$$

where c^o and c^p are constant, and $dis(1,0)$ means the dissimilarity between two regions in the binary image with value 1 and 0, based on the first motion feature; f_1^o and f_0^o means the weighted motion intensity and direction of two regions in the binary image with value 1 and 0. Based on above definition, a larger weight is assigned to the binary frame whose two segmented regions have distinct appearance (motion) distributions.

In practice, we select the first 5 hyperedges with larger weights computed from appearance and motion respectively; and then proper c^p and c^o are chosen to let $\sum_{i=1}^{5} w_H^p(i) = 1$ and $\sum_{i=1}^{5} w_H^o(i) = 1$. In Figure 5, we show the corresponding weight values under the binary attribute images. It is obvious that more meaningful attributes are assigned larger weights in our algorithm.

After the construction of hypergraphs for video object segmentation, the theoretical solution of this real value problem is the eigenvector associated with the smallest non-zeros eigenvector of the hypergraph Laplacian matrix $\Delta = I - D_v^{-\frac{1}{2}} HWD_e^{-1} H^T D_v^{-\frac{1}{2}}$. As in (Ng, 2001), to make a multi-way classification of vertices in a hypergraph, we take the first several eigenvec-

Figure 5. 4 binary partition results with largest hyperedge weights (for one frame of WalkByShop1cor. mpg). Obviously, how the heperedge got from the 1st and 4th frames is a good description of how objects should be segmented according to their importance. The computed hyperedge weights are shown below those binary images.

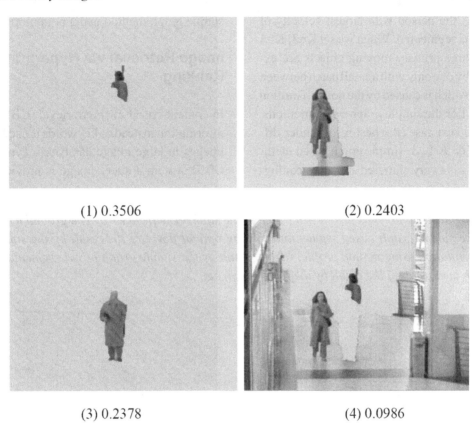

(1) 0.3506   (2) 0.2403

(3) 0.2378   (4) 0.0986

tors with non-zeros eigenvalues of Δ as the indicators (we take 3 in this work), and then use a k-means clustering algorithms on the formed eigenspace to get final clustering results.

Results

To evaluate the performance of our segmentation method based on the hypergraph cut, we compare it with three clustering approaches based on the simple graph, i.e., the conventional simple graph with pairwise relationship. In these three approaches, we measure the similarity between two over-segmented patches using (1) the optical flow, (2) the motion profile, and (3) both the motion

cues. Then corresponding Laplacian matrix of these three approaches can be computed accordingly and the k-means algorithm can be performed on the first n eigenvectors with nonzero eigenvalues. In our experiment, we choose $n = 10$ for all these three simple graph based methods. See more details in (Huang, 2009).

In (Huang, 2009), we report our experiments on 5 video sequences. Here we list two of them to demonstrate the advantage of hypergraph based method, as shown in Figure 6 and Figure 7. In Figure 6 for the squirrel sequence, we show the ground truth frames, the results of three simple graph based methods, and the results of hypergraph cut for these two sequences. In Figure 7 (*Walk-*

ByShop1front.mpg, from CAVIAR database), a couple walk along the corridor, and another person moves to the door of the shop hastily and is occluded by the couple during his moving. When we set K=2, the person with largest velocity of movement is segmented. When we set K=3, K=4 and K=5, three primary moving objects are extracted one by one only with a small patch between the couple, which is caused by the noise of motion estimation. For the simple graph based methods, we give the best case (the best result under different K). For $K > 3$, simple graph based methods usually give very cluttered and not meaningful results. For the simple graph based methods using the motion profile or the optical flow, K=2 can give the most meaningful results, and K=3 can give a good extraction of the couple for the simple graph method using both motion cues.

Image Retrieval via Hypergraph Ranking

In content-based image retrieval (CBIR), visual information instead of keywords is used to search images in large image databases. Typically in a CBIR system a query image is provided by the

Figure 6. Segmentation results for the 4th frame of the squirrel sequence. (a) The ground truth, (b) the result by the simple graph based segmentation using optical flow, (c) the result by the simple graph based segmentation using motion profile, (d) the result by the simple graph based segmentation using both motion cues, and (e) the result by the hypergraph cut.

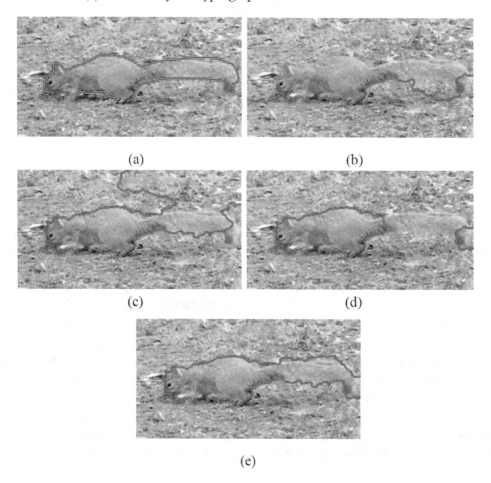

(a)   (b)

(c)   (d)

(e)

Figure 7. Segmentation results for one frame of the WalkByShop1front.mpg, different colors denote different clusters in each sub-figure. (a) The ground truth, (b) the result by the simple graph based segmentation using optical flow (K=2), (c) the result by the simple graph based segmentation using motion profile (K=2), (d) the result by the simple graph based segmentation using both motion cues (K=3), (e) the result by the hypergraph cut (K=2), (f) the result by the hypergraph cut (K=3), (g) the result by the hypergraph cut (K=4), and (h) the result by the hypergraph cut (K=5).

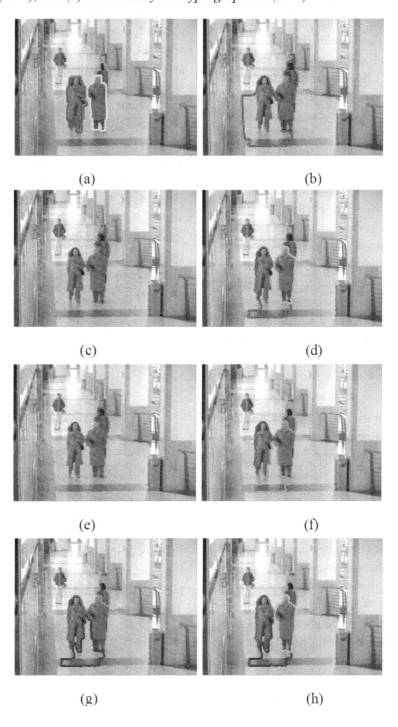

user and the closest images are returned according to a decision rule. In order to learn a better representation of the query concept, a lot of CBIR frameworks make use of an online learning technique called relevance feedback (RF) (Rui, 1999) (He, 2002). Previous work on relevance feedback often aims at learning discriminative models to classify the relevant and irrelevant images, such as, RF methods based on support vector machines (SVM) (Tong, 2001), decision trees (MacArthur, 2000), boosting (Tieu, 2000), Bayesian classifiers (Cox, 2000), and graph-cut (Sahbi, 2007). In (He, 2004) and (He, 2006), a pairwise graph based manifold ranking algorithm (Zhou, 2003) is adopted to build an image retrieval system.

In this section, we introduce a new transductive learning framework for image retrieval (Huang, 2010), in which images are taken as vertices in a weighted hypergraph and the task of image search is formulated as the problem of hypergraph ranking. Based on the similarity matrix computed from various feature descriptors, we take each image as a 'centroid' vertex and form a hyperedge by a centroid and its k-nearest neighbors. To further exploit the correlation information among images, we propose a probabilistic hypergraph, which assigns each vertex v_i to a hyperedge e_j in a probabilistic way. In the incidence structure of a probabilistic hypergraph, we describe both the local grouping information and the affinity relationship between vertices within each hyperedge. After feedback images are provided, our retrieval system ranks image labels by a transductive inference approach, which tends to assign the same label to vertices that share many incidental hyperedges, with the constraints that predicted labels of feedback images should be similar to their initial labels. We compare the proposed method to several other methods and its effectiveness is demonstrated by extensive experiments on Corel5K, the Scene dataset and Caltech 101.

Probabilistic Hypergraph Model

As introduced in Section 2.2, the traditional hypergraph structure assigns a vertex v_i to a hyperedge e_j with a binary decision, i.e., $h_t(v_i, e_j)$ equals 1 or 0. In this model, all the vertices in a hyperedge are treated equally; relative affinity between vertices is discarded. This 'truncation' processing leads to the loss of some information, which may be harmful to the hypergraph based applications.

In this work, we propose a probabilistic hypergraph model to overcome this limitation. Assume that a $|V| \times |V|$ affinity matrix A over V is computed based on some measurement and $A(i, j) \in [0, 1]$. We take each vertex as a 'centroid' vertex and form a hyperedge by a centroid and its k-nearest neighbors. That is, the size of a hyperedge in our framework is $k + 1$. The incidence matrix H of a probabilistic hypergraph is defined as follows:

$$h(v_i, e_j) = \begin{cases} A(j, i), & if \ v_i \in e_j \\ 0, & otherwise. \end{cases} \qquad (20)$$

According to this formulation, a vertex v_i is 'softly' assigned to e_j based on the similarity $A(i, j)$ between v_i and v_j, where v_j is the centroid of e_j. A probabilistic hypergraph presents not only the local grouping information, but also the probability that a vertex belongs to a hyperedge. In this way, the correlation information among vertices is more accurately described. Actually, the representation in original hypergraph can be taken as the discretized version of Equation 20. The hyperedge weight $w(e_i)$ is computed as follows:

$$w(e_i) = \sum_{v_j \in e_i} A(i, j). \qquad (21)$$

Based on this definition, the 'compact' hyperedge (local group) with higher inner group similarities is assigned a higher weight. For a vertex $v \in V$, its degree is defined to be $d(v) = \sum_{e \in E} w(e)h(v,e)$. For a hyperedge $e \in E$, its degree is defined as $\delta(e) = \sum_{v \in e} h(v,e)$. Notice that these definitions are relaxed from those definition in ordinary hypergraphs. Let us use D_v, D_e and W to denote the diagonal matrices of the vertex degrees, the hyperedge degrees and the hyperedge weights respectively. Figure 8 shows an example to explain how to construct a probabilistic hypergraph. The procedure of the probabilistic hypergraph ranking algorithm is listed in Algorithm 1.

Algorithm 1: Probabilistic Hypergraph Ranking

1. Compute similarity matrix A based on various features using Equation ??, where $A(i,j)$ denotes the similarity between the ith and the jth vertices.
2. Construct the probabilistic hypergraph G. For each vertex, based on the similarity matrix A, collect its k-nearest neighbors to form a hyperedge.
3. Compute the hypergraph incidence matrix H where $h(v_i, e_j) = A(j,i)$ if $v_i \in e_j$ and $h(v_i, e_j) = 0$ otherwise. The hyperedge weight matrix is computed using Equation 21.
4. Compute the hypergraph Laplacian $\Delta = I - \Theta = I - D_v^{-\frac{1}{2}} HWD_e^{-1} H^T D_v^{-\frac{1}{2}}$
5. Given a query vertex and the initial labeling vector y, solve the linear system $\left((1+\mu)I - \Theta\right)f = \mu y$. Rank all the vertices according to their ranking scores in descending order.

To define the similarity measurement between two images, we utilize 13 descriptors in total (Huang, 2010); for each descriptor, we follow the method in (Gemert, 2008) to obtain histograms by soft feature quantization. See more details in (Huang, 2010) about feature descriptors and similarity measurements.

Figure 8. Left: A simple graph of six points in 2-D space. Pairwise distances ($Dis(i,j)$) between v_i and its 2 nearest neighbors are marked on the corresponding edges. Middle: A hypergraph is built, in which each vertex and its 2 nearest neighbors form a hyperedge. Right: The H matrix of the probability hypergraph shown above. The entry (v_i, e_j) is set to the affinity $A(j,i)$ if a hyperedge e_j contains v_i or 0 otherwise. Here $A(i,j) = \exp(-\dfrac{Dis(i,j)}{\bar{D}})$ where $\bar{D}$ is the average distance.

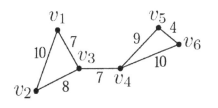

	e_1	e_2	e_3	e_4	e_5	e_6
v_1	1.0	0.28	0.41	0	0	0
v_2	0.28	1.0	0	0	0	0
v_3	0.41	0.36	1.0	0.41	0	0
v_4	0	0	0.41	1.0	0.32	0.28
v_5	0	0	0	0.32	1.0	0.60
v_6	0	0	0	0	0.60	1.0

Experiments

In the experiment, we used SVM and similarity based ranking as the baselines. The similarity based ranking method sorts retrieved image i according to the formula $\frac{1}{|Pos|}\sum_{j \in Pos} A(i,j) - \frac{1}{|Neg|}\sum_{k \in Neg} A(i,k),$ where Pos and Neg denote positive/negative sets of feedback images respectively. We compare the proposed hypergraph ranking frameworks to the simple graph based manifold ranking algorithm (He,

Figure 9. Precision vs. scope curves for Corel5K (when full Δ matrices images are used), under the passive learning setting

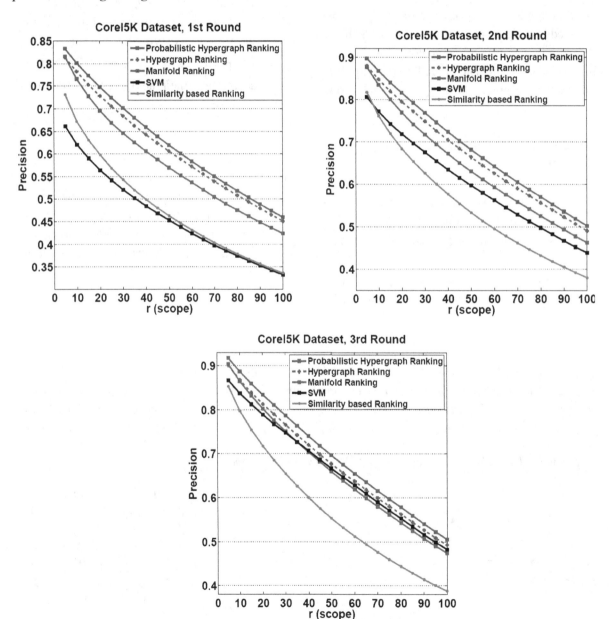

2004) (He, 2006), and we also evaluate the performances of the probabilistic hypergraph ranking against the hypergraph based ranking. Two measures are employed to evaluate the performance of above five ranking methods: (1) the precision vs. scope curve, (2) the precision vs. recall curve. We use each image in a database as a query ex-

ample and both measures are averaged over all the queries in this database. We choose best K parameters of both graph and hypergraph based algorithms for a fair comparison. based See more details of experiment setting in (Huang, 2010). Figure 9 shows results on Corel5K dataset. Figure

Figure 10. The precision-recall curves for Caltech-101 (when full Δ matrices images are used)

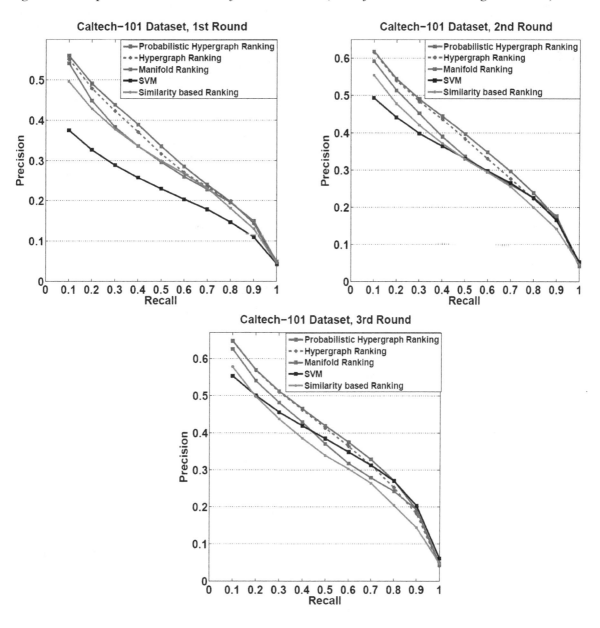

10 shows results on Caltech 101 dataset. More results could be found in (Huang, 2010).

Above analysis and experimental results confirm the hypergraph method from two aspects: (1) by considering the local grouping information, both hypergraph models can better approximate relevance between the labeled data and unlabeled images than the simple graph based model; (2) probabilistic incidence matrix H is more suitable for defining the relationship between vertices in a hyperedge.

5. CONCLUSION

In this section, at first we summarized the basic concept of hypergraphs and relative learning algorithms. Then we construct hypergraph models for two scenarios: (1) video object segmentations, (2) content based image retrieval. In the first application the unsupervised hypergraph cut algorithm are used for clustering, which involves eigen-decomposition of the hypergraph Laplacian matrix. The second application utilized the hypergraph based transductive learning or semi-supervised learning algorithm, which involves the solving of a linear system.

Since hypergraph based algorithm is a open system, in the future work, we may add more feature descriptors (such as texture information) into our frameworks to construct more hyperedges to further improve the expressive power of hypergraph based models. Prior information could also be introduced into the hypergraph framework for video object segmentation and solve this problem under the semi-supervised setting. Hopefully this will largely enhance the accuracy of segmentation results.

REFERENCES

Agarwal, S., Branson, K., & Belongie, S. (2005). Higher order learning with graphs. In the *Proceedings of the 22nd International Conference on Machine Learning*.

Agarwal, S., Lim, J., Zelnik-Manor, L., Perona, P., Kriegman, D., & Belongie, S. (2005). Beyond pairwise clustering. In *Proceedings of the 2005 IEEE Computer Society Conference on Computer Vision and Pattern Recognition (CVPR'05) - Vol. 2*, (pp. 838–845). Washington, DC, USA, 2005.

Alpert, C. J., & Kahng, A. B. (1995). Recent directions in netlist partitioning: A survey. *Integration: The VLSI Journal, 19*, 1–81. doi:10.1016/0167-9260(95)00008-4

Bolla, M. (1993). Spectra, Euclidean representations and clusterings of hypergraphs. *Discrete Mathematics, 117*(1-3), 19–39. doi:10.1016/0012-365X(93)90322-K

Borg, I., & Groenen, P. (2005). *Modern multidimensional scaling: Theory and applications*. Springer.

Carroll, J., & Chang, J. (1970). Analysis of individual differences in multidimensional scaling via an n-way generalization of Eckart-Young decomposition. *Psychometrika, 35*(3), 283–319. doi:10.1007/BF02310791

Chan, P. K., Schlag, M. D. F., & Zien, J. Y. (1993). Spectral k-way ratio-cut partitioning and clustering. In *DAC '93: Proceedings of the 30th International Design Automation Conference*, (pp. 749–754). New York, NY: ACM.

Chen, J., & Saad, Y. (2009). *Co-clustering of high order relational data using spectral hypergraph partitioning. Technical Report UMSI 2009/xx*. University of Minnesota Supercomputing Institute.

Chung, D., MacLean, W. J., & Dickinson, S. (2004). Integrating region and boundary information for improved spatial coherence in object tracking. In *CVPRW '04: Proceedings of the 2004 Conference on Computer Vision and Pattern Recognition Workshop (CVPRW '04)*, Vol. 1.

Chung, F. (1997). *Spectral graph theory.* American Mathematical Society.

Cour, T., Benezit, F., & Shi, J. (2005). Spectral segmentation with multiscale graph decomposition. In *CVPR '05: Proceedings of the 2005 IEEE Computer Society Conference on Computer Vision and Pattern Recognition (CVPR '05)*, (pp. 1124–1131).

Cox, I. J., Miller, M. L., Minka, T. P., Papathomas, T. V., & Yianilos, P. N. (2000). The Bayesian image retrieval system – Pichunter: Theory, implementation and psychophysical experiments. *IEEE Transactions on Image Processing, 9*, 20–37. doi:10.1109/83.817596

Cox, T., Cox, M., & Branco, J. (1991). Multidimensional scaling for n-tuples. *The British Journal of Mathematical and Statistical Psychology, 44*.

DeMenthon, D., & Megret, R. (2002). Spatiotemporal segmentation of video by hierarchical mean shift analysis. In *CVPR '02: Proceedings of the 2002 IEEE Computer Society Conference on Computer Vision and Pattern Recognition (CVPR '02)*.

Deza, M. M., & Rosenberg, I. (2000). n-Semimetrics. *European Journal of Combinatorics, 21*, 797–806. doi:10.1006/eujc.1999.0384

Fiduccia, C. M., & Mattheyses, R. M. (1982). A linear-time heuristic for improving network partitions. In *DAC '82: Proceedings of the 19th Design Automation Conference*, (pp. 175–181). Piscataway, NJ: IEEE Press.

Fieldler, M. (1973). Algebraic connectivity of graphs. *Czechoslovak Mathematical Journal, 23*(98), 298–305.

Fischler, M. A., & Bolles, R. C. (1987). Random sample consensus: a paradigm for model fitting with applications to image analysis and automated cartography. In *Readings in computer vision: Issues, problems, principles, and paradigms* (pp. 726–740). San Francisco, CA: Morgan Kaufmann Publishers Inc. doi:10.1145/358669.358692

Frey, B. J. J., & Dueck, D. (2007). Clustering by passing messages between data points. *Science, 315*.

Garey, M. R., & Johnson, D. S. (1990). *Computers and intractability; A guide to the theory of NP-completeness.* New York, NY: W. H. Freeman & Co.

Hadley, S. W. (1995). Approximation techniques for hypergraph partitioning problems. *Discrete Applied Mathematics, 59*(2), 115–127. doi:10.1016/0166-218X(93)E0166-V

Hayashi, C. (1972). Two dimensional quantification based on the measure of dissimilarity among three elements. *Annals of the Institute of Statistical Mathematics, 24*(1), 251–257. doi:10.1007/BF02479755

He, J., Li, M., Zhang, H., Tong, H., & Zhang, C. (2006). Generalized manifold ranking-based image retrieval. *IEEE Transactions on Image Processing, 15*(10), 3170–3177. doi:10.1109/TIP.2006.877491

He, J., Li, M., Zhang, H.-J., Tong, H., & Zhang, C. (2004). *Manifold-ranking based image retrieval.* In ACM MULTIMEDIA '04.

He, X., Ma, W.-Y., King, O., Li, M., & Zhang, H. (2002). *Learning and inferring a semantic space from user's relevance feedback for image retrieval.* In ACM MULTIMEDIA '02.

Heiser, W. J., & Bennani, M. (1997). Triadic distance models: Axiomatization and least squares representation. *Journal of Mathematical Psychology*, *41*(2), 189–206. doi:10.1006/jmps.1997.1166

Hu, T., & Moerder, K. (1985). Multiterimnal flows in hypergraphs. In Hu, T. C., & Kuh, E. S. (Eds.), *VLSI circuit layout* (pp. 81–86). IEEE Press.

Huang, Y., Liu, Q., & Metaxas, D. (2009). Video object segmentation by hypergraph cut. *IEEE Computer Society Conference on Computer Vision and Pattern Recognition,* (pp. 1738–1745).

Huang, Y., Liu, Q., Zhang, S., & Metaxas, D. N. (2010). *Image retrieval via probabilistic hypergraph ranking*. IEEE Computer Society Conference on Computer Vision and Pattern Recognition.

Ihler, E., Wagner, D., & Wagner, F. (1993). Modeling hypergraphs by graphs with the same mincut properties. *Information Processing Letters*, *45*(4), 171–175. doi:10.1016/0020-0190(93)90115-P

Joly, S., & Calv, G. (1995). Three-way distances. *Journal of Classification*, *12*(2), 191–205. doi:10.1007/BF03040855

Karypis, G., & Kumar, V. (1999). Multilevel k-way hypergraph partitioning. In *DAC '99: Proceedings of the 36th Annual ACM/IEEE Design Automation Conference*, (pp. 343–348). New York, NY: ACM.

Kernighan, B. W., & Lin, S. (1970). An efficient heuristic procedure for partitioning graphs. *The Bell System Technical Journal*, *49*(1), 291–307.

Lucas, B. D., & Kanade, T. (1981). An iterative image registration technique with an application to stereo vision. In *Proceedings of the 7th International Joint Conference on Artificial Intelligence (IJCAI '81)*, (pp. 674–679).

MacArthur, S., Brodley, C., & Shyu, C. (2000). Relevance feedback decision trees in content-based image retrieval. In *CBAIVL '00: Proceedings of the IEEE Workshop on Content-based Access of Image and Video Libraries*, (p. 68).

Macqueen, J. B. (1967). Some methods of classification and analysis of multivariate observations. In *Proceedings of the Fifth Berkeley Symposium on Mathematical Statistics and Probability*, (pp. 281–297).

Ng, A., Jordan, M., & Weiss, Y. (2001). On spectral clustering: Analysis and an algorithm. In *Advances in Neural Information Processing Systems*. NIPS.

Rodriquez, J. (2003). On the Laplacian spectrum and walk-regular hypergraphs. In *Linear and Multilinear Algebra, 51*(3), 285-297.

Rui, Y., Huang, T. S., & Chang, S.-F. (1999). Image retrieval: Current techniques, promising directions, and open issues. *Journal of Visual Communication and Image Representation*, *10*(1), 39–62. doi:10.1006/jvci.1999.0413

Sahbi, H., Audibert, J., & Keriven, R. (2007). *Graph-cut transducers for relevance feedback in content based image retrieval*. In ICCV'07: IEEE International Conference on Computer Vision.

Shi, J., & Malik, J. (1998). Motion segmentation and tracking using normalized cuts. In *IEEE International Conference on Computer Vision (ICCV)*, (pp. 1154–1160).

Shi, J., & Malik, J. (2000). Normalized cuts and image segmentation. *IEEE Transactions on Pattern Analysis and Machine Intelligence*, *22*(8), 888–905. doi:10.1109/34.868688

Stein, A., Hoiem, D., & Hebert, M. (2007). *Learning to find object boundaries using motion cues*. In IEEE International Conference on Computer Vision (ICCV), October 2007.

Tieu, K., & Viola, P. (2000). Boosting image retrieval. *International Journal of Computer Vision, 56*(1-2), 228–235.

Tong, S., & Chang, E. (2001). *Support vector machine active learning for image retrieval.* In ACM MULTIMEDIA '01. Gemert, J. van, Geusebroek, J., Veenman, C., & Smeulders, A. (2008). *Kernel codebooks for scene categorization.* In ECCV'08: European Conference on Computer Vision 2008.

von Luxburg, U. (2007). A tutorial on spectral clustering. *Statistics and Computing, 17*(4), 395–416. doi:10.1007/s11222-007-9033-z

Weiss, Y. (1999). Segmentation using eigenvectors: A unifying view. In *IEEE International Conference on Computer Vision (ICCV)*, (pp. 975–982).

Wills, J., Agarwal, S., & Belongie, S. (2003). What went where. In *CVPR '03: Proceedings of the 2003 IEEE Computer Society Conference on Computer Vision and Pattern Recognition (CVPR'03)*, (pp. 37–44).

Zhou, D., Bousquet, O., Lal, T. N., Weston, J., & Schokopf, B. (2003). *Learning with local and global consistency.* In NIPS'03: Advances in Neural Information Processing Systems (NIPS) 2003.

Zhou, D., Huang, J., & Schokopf, B. (2006). *Learning with hypergraphs: Clustering, classification, and embedding.* In Advances in Neural Information Processing Systems, 2006.

Zien, J. Y., Schlag, M. D. F., & Chan, P. K. (1996). Multi-level spectral hypergraph partitioning with arbitrary vertex sizes. In *Proceedings of the International Conference on Computer-Aided Design*, (pp. 201–204). IEEE Press.

Chapter 7
Recent Advances on Graph–Based Image Segmentation Techniques

Chao Zeng
University of Technology-Sydney, Australia

Wenjing Jia
University of Technology-Sydney, Australia

Xiangjian He
University of Technology-Sydney, Australia

Min Xu
University of Technology-Sydney, Australia

ABSTRACT

Image segmentation techniques using graph theory has become a thriving research area in computer vision community in recent years. This chapter mainly focuses on the most up-to-date research achievements in graph-based image segmentation published in top journals and conferences in computer vision community. The representative graph-based image segmentation methods included in this chapter are classified into six categories: minimum-cut/maximum-flow model (called graph-cut in some literatures), random walk model, minimum spanning tree model, normalized cut model and isoperimetric graph partitioning. The basic rationales of these models are presented, and the image segmentation methods based on these graph-based models are discussed as the main concern of this chapter. Several performance evaluation methods for image segmentation are given. Some public databases for testing image segmentation algorithms are introduced and the future work on graph-based image segmentation is discussed at the end of this chapter.

DOI: 10.4018/978-1-4666-1891-6.ch007

INTRODUCTION

In computer vision applications, image segmentation is to separate an image into several regions, of which each has certain properties in terms of predefined rules. These regions can represent objects, parts of an object, or background. The aim of image segmentation is to find the regions of interest (ROI) in an image according to a particular application.

As a very important technique in computer vision, image segmentation has been found in a wide variety of practical applications, such as medical image processing, satellite image analysis, biometric recognition (e.g. human face recognition, fingerprint recognition and palm recognition), traffic control systems (e.g. vehicle number plate recognition, vehicle counting), digital photo editing, robotic vision and so on. Image segmentation approaches include clustering methods (Mignotte, 2008), compression-based methods (Rao, 2009), histogram-based methods (Otsu, 1979), edge detection methods (Senthilkumaran, 2009), region growing methods (Fan, 2005), partial differential equation-based methods (Zhang, 2010), graph-based methods (Boykov, 2001), watershed transformation methods (Grau, 2004) and so on. Among these image segmentation methods, the graph-based approach has attracted many attentions and become one of the most thriving research areas in computer vision in recent years. Meanwhile, many high quality papers on graph-based image segmentation techniques have been published in top journals and conferences in the field of image processing and computer vision. Therefore, this chapter is to gather the information on the most up-to-date graph-based image segmentation research together and give a clear overview of research work on this topic.

The remaining parts of this chapter are arranged as follows. Firstly, the background mathematical knowledge of graph theory is given. We then present the five most representative graph-based models used for image segmentation and classify them into two major groups based on whether interactions of users are involved. The summary of the reviewed methods are illustrated in Table 1. Then, methods used for evaluating segmentation performance are discussed. Some benchmark image segmentation datasets are introduced. Conclusions are given in the end.

BACKGROUND

Mathematically, a graph $G=(V,E)$ is composed of a set of nodes (or vertices) $v \in V$ and a set of edges $e \in E \subseteq V \times V$ connecting two nodes $v_i \in V$ and $v_j \in V$. There are two types of edges: undirected edge and directed edge. An undirected edge is an unordered pair of nodes $e_{\{v_i,v_j\}}$. A directed edge is an ordered pair of nodes $e_{(v_i,v_j)}$, in which v_i is called the starting node and v_j is called the ending node. The weight of an edge is a value assigned to the edge, which describes the relationship between the two nodes.

In graph-based image segmentation models, a node can be a pixel, a set of pixels with common characteristics, a super pixel, or a feature vector of the pixel. The edge weight w is defined to describe the similarity or dissimilarity of two nodes connected by it according to the specific application.

The categorization of graph-based image segmentation techniques can be seen from Figure 1. Following this structure, the image segmentation techniques based on the five models will be discussed one by one. The relative graph theory knowledge will be presented at first. Then, the detailed content of different techniques will be shown. Meanwhile, the above mathematical notations of graph, node and edge will be used in the following content.

Table 1. Summary of the five reviewed graph-based image segmentation methods

	Min-Cut/Max-Flow	Random Walker	MST-Based	Normalized Cut	Isoperimetric Graph Partitioning
Applications	Psychological vision, Photo/video editing and medical image segmentation	Medical image segmentation and object/background segmentation	Object segmentation and image segmentation	Natural scene image segmentation	Natural scene image segmentation, medical image and psychological vision
Testing Dataset	Gestalt example, medical image and video sequence	2D/3D medical image and Berkeley dataset	Natural scene image, Columbia COIL image database	Natural scene image, weather radar image	Gestalt example, natural scene image
Performance	Less than a second for most 2D images (up to 512*512)	Around 3 seconds on a 256*256 image for an Intel Xeon 2.40GHz with 3GB RAM	None	2 mins on Intel Pentium 200MHz machines for 100*120 test image	0.5863 seconds are required on a 1.4GHz AMD Athlon with 512k RAM
Time Complexity	$O(mn^2)$ in worst case, n is the number of nodes and m is the number of edges	$O(n)$, n is the number of nodes in the graph	$O(m \log m)$ for m graph edges	$O(mn)$, n is the number of pixels and m is the number of steps for convergence	$O(m + n \log n)$, n is the number of nodes and m is the number of edges

Figure 1. The categorization of graph-based image segmentation techniques

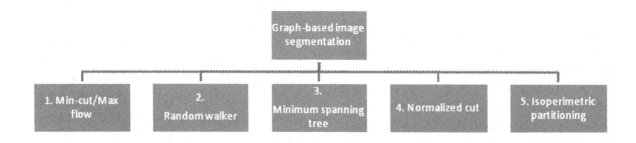

SUPERVISED IMAGE SEGMENTATION METHODS

Supervised segmentation methods involve the interactions of users, such as marking some pixels for object and background or drawing a rectangle which embracing the whole object to be segmented. This kind of segmentation methods can obtain the desired foreground and background.

Among the five reviewed models, the minimum-cut/maximum flow model and the random walk model are used for supervised image segmentation.

Minimum Cut/Maximum-Flow Models

In minimum-cut/maximum flow (also called graph cut) image segmentation model, an image is represented by an undirected graph *G=(V,E)*.

Two special additional terminals are included in the graph, and they are usually called the source (object terminal), denoted by s, and the sink (background terminal), denoted by t, as shown in Figure 1. Let P and N denote a set of pixels in an image and a set of all unordered pairs $\{v_1, v_2\}$ of neighboring pixels in P respectively. Let $A = (A_1, ..., A_p, ..., A_{|P|})$ denote a binary vector of which each component is a label A_p assigned to a pixel p representing either object ("obj" in abbreviation) or background ("bkg" in abbreviation). So the binary vector A is the segmentation result. Among all of the possible segmentations, the optimal segmentation is found by incorporating the soft constraints and the hard constraints. The soft constraints are the boundary and regional properties of segmentation A described by the cost function which is defined as:

$$E(A) = \lambda \cdot R(A) + B(A) \tag{1}$$

where

$$R(A) = \sum_{p \in P} R_p(A_p) \tag{2}$$

$$B(A) = \sum_{\{p,q\} \in N} B_{\{p,q\}} \cdot \delta(A_p, A_q) \tag{3}$$

and

$$\delta(A_p, A_q) = \begin{cases} 1 & \text{if } A_p \neq A_q \\ 0 & \text{otherwise.} \end{cases} \tag{4}$$

In Equation 1, $R(A)$ and $B(A)$ are usually called the regional term (or data term) and the boundary term (or smoothness term) respectively. λ is a non-negative scalar to adjust the trade-off of importance between the regional and boundary terms. In Equation 2, $R_p(A_p)$ denotes the penalty for assigning A_p to pixel p. In Equation 3, $B_{\{p,q\}}$ denotes the penalty for discontinuity between p

and q. The hard constraints are some restrictions imposed by user interaction. In interactive segmentation method, one popular kind of hard constraints are some pixels are marked as "obj" and some pixels are marked as "bkg" by a user:

$$\begin{aligned} \forall p \in O, \qquad A_p &= \text{"obj"} \\ \forall p \in B, \qquad A_p &= \text{"bkg"}. \end{aligned} \tag{5}$$

where O and B represent the set of pixels marked as "obj" and "bkg" respectively. At the meantime, $O \subset P$ and $B \subset P$ such that $O \cap B = \varnothing$

Obeying the hard constraints, the remaining unmarked pixels are assigned to "obj" or "bkg" in the optimal segmentation $A_{optimal}$. $A_{optimal}$ globally minimizes the cost function in Equation 1 among all of the possible "obj/bkg" segmentations of the given image. The minimum cut $C_{optimal}$ is a subset of E which bi-partitions the graph corresponding to $A_{optimal}$. As a theoretical support, the existence of the optimal segmentation defined by the minimum cut minimizing the cost function (1) among all segmentations satisfying the hard constraints in Equation 5 has been proven in (Boykov, 2001). A concise presentation of the min-cut/max-flow model is shown in Figure 2. Figure 3 gives a segmentation example based on the graph model constructed in Figure 2.

Based on the original min-cut/max-flow algorithm, some researches focus on modification for the purpose of obtaining improved algorithms with better segmentation performances. In (Boykov, 2004), a new min-cut/max-flow algorithm was developed and its efficiency was compared with three standard algorithms belonging to Goldbery-Tarjan style 'push-relabel" methods and Ford-Fulkerson style "augmenting paths". Based on augmenting paths, the new algorithm builds two search trees starting from the source and the sink. The algorithm iteratively repeats the "growth" stage, the "augmentation" stage and the "adoption" stage, and it terminates when the two

Figure 2. (a) The illustration of constructed min-cut/max-flow model; (b) A cut on the constructed graph (courtesy of Boykov, 2004)

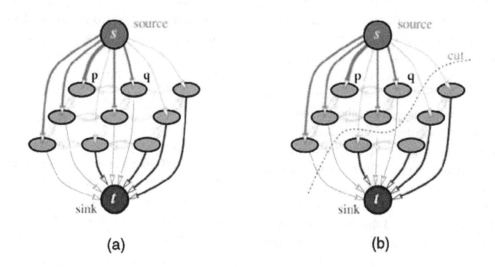

(a)   (b)

search trees can no longer grow and the trees are separated by saturated edges. The termination condition represents that a maximum flow is found which means the minimum cut is achieved. Although the complexity could be worse than the standard algorithms in theory, the proposed algorithm greatly outperforms standard algorithms on typical problem instances in vision (including interactive image segmentation) in terms of running time based on the experimental comparison.

Yuan (2010) presented a study on the max-flow models in terms of the continuous case instead of the discrete situation. The proposed continuous max-flow model corresponds to the continuous min-cut formulation as in the case of normal discrete situation. New explanations

Figure 3. (a) Original image; (b) The segmentation result of minimum cut (courtesy of Boykov, 2004)

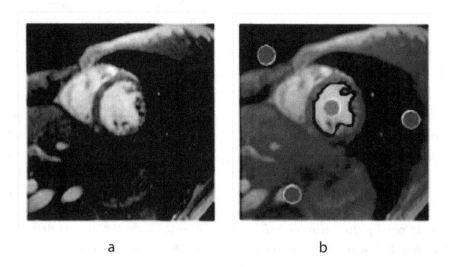

a   b

of the basic conceptions were given to describe graph cuts in continuous model. Based on the continuous max-flow formulation, new interactive (stated as supervised) graph-cut algorithms were developed and the complexities are the same as the unsupervised ones.

The selection of the parameter λ in the cost function is not trivial, because different choice of λ could highly affect the segmentation result. Efforts have been made to get the optimal λ value. Peng et al. (2008) observed that different values of parameter λ may result in over-segmentations, good segmentations and under-segmentations, a supervised algorithm for automatic parameter selection was proposed to obtain the best segmentation for each image. A measure of segmentation quality was developed based on intensity, gradient, contour continuity and texture features which are normalized by a novel way. After performing graph cut segmentation for each λ the segmentation with the highest segmentation quality was chosen according to the measurement learnt by the AdaBoost algorithm. In (Candemir, 2010), according to the observation that a same parameter λ in the cost function would not be a good choice for the whole image, a method adaptively changing λ for different regions of the image was proposed to overcome over-segmentation and under-segmentation. Canny edge detection algorithm was performed on the given image at different hysteresis threshold. Then, the edge probability of each pixel $\overline{I}_i$ was calculated based on the generated edge maps. By changing λ into $\left(1 - \overline{I}_i\right)\lambda$, the effect of the regional term and the boundary term became adaptive for different regions of the image.

Combining two approaches to exert the advantages of each other to generate a more effective method is a common idea in practical issues. Working together with other models, the min-cut/max-flow model could produce better segmentation results. Borrowing the ideas of the topology

preserving level set method in (Han, 2003), a novel min-cut/max-flow algorithm embedding geometric prior knowledge constraints was developed for image segmentation in (Zeng, 2008). Five elements (a foreground/background label attribute, a level set style initialization, inter-label and intra-label stages of max-flow computation, a distance map and bucket priority queue data structure) were considered to implement the discrete graph-based algorithm. Topology was preserved by checking the simple point (Bertrand, 1994) condition. The experimental results showed that the proposed algorithm could get the better medical image segmentation results than the graph cut method (as shown in Figure 4) and was faster than the level set method.

In Price (2010), both the geodesic approach and the graph cut approach were revisited. Moreover, the causes of their segmentation errors were analysed. The geodesic segmentation approach and the graph cut method were combined for interactive image segmentation task. The cost function is the min-cut/max-flow graph cut framework was modified by adding geodesic distance information into the regional term. Furthermore, the boundary term was adjusted to incorporate geodesic confidence. The proposed method was superior at two aspects: less sensitive to shortcutting than standard graph cut methods; less prone to seed placement and better at edge localization than pure geodesic methods.

Tensor voting framework was embedded into graph cuts to use principles of perceptual grouping (Koo, 2009). The tensor map was generated by adding the votes at each receiving site. Then, a local Riemannian metrics was designed to encode tensor voting framework into the weight of edge in the graph construction. Compared with isotropic metrics, better results were obtained by the proposed framework as both the edge strength and the edge orientation were taken into account. While, compared with the flux-based approach, the proposed framework did not need shape priors.

Figure 4. (a) Initialization; (b) Segmentation result of minimum cut; (c) Segmentation result of topology cut (courtesy of Zeng, 2008)

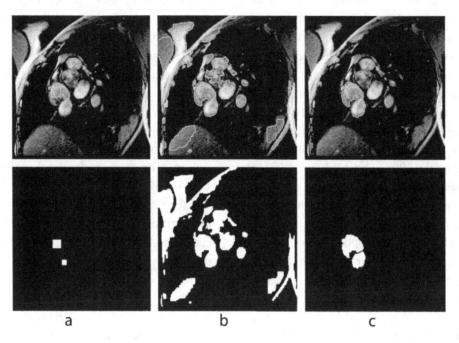

a   b   c

In some applications, the user's interaction is infeasible for segmentation task. So the full automation of image segmentation with graph cut model has become a common concern. Usually, an automatic pre-processing functioning as the user interference is indispensible. Due to the observations that user interactions could lead to wrong segmentation or be not feasible in some cases, Fu et al. (2008) presented an automatic object segmentation method called saliency cuts. The saliency detection was performed first. Then, the "Professional Labels" were generated automatically by the multi-resolution framework as the imposed seeds for the object and the background. Finally, the graph cuts algorithm was implemented for the segmentation. The experimental results showed the advantages of automation and accuracy of the proposed method. Jung et al. (2010) proposed a novel fully automatic scheme for segmenting objects from images. A saliency detection method was used as the automatic generation of object seeds and background seeds. As the generated object seeds may position at the parts belonging to background or vice versa, an iterative self-adaptive graph cut method was developed to reduce the wrongly positioned seeds.

Random Walk Models

The random walker algorithm for multilabel, interactive image segmentation was firstly described in (Grady, 2004; Grady, 2006). Based on its theory, the definition of a "walk" is a sequence of nodes and edges, both starting and ending with a node and there is no restriction on the number of times a node can be visited. An edge weight of the graph is treated as a probability in the random walker algorithm. The probability of an unlabeled pixel reaches one of seeds with a pre-marked label by a random walk is calculated. If an unlabeled pixel has a higher probability to reach one seed with a label L than to reach other seeds with other labels, this pixel is assigned to a label L. In this way, the segmentation is accomplished by assigning all of the unlabeled pixels to one of the pre-marked labels. An illustration of the random walker algorithm is shown in Figure 5. The random walker algorithm presented in (Grady, 2006) is of the following qualities: fast computation, fast editing, an ability to produce an arbitrary segmentation with enough interaction and intuitive segmentations.

In (Sinop, 2007), a general framework of interactive image segmentation was presented. The min-cut/max-flow algorithm and the random walker algorithm corresponded to the cases of ℓ_1 norm and ℓ_2 norm of energy minimization respectively. A new segmentation algorithm based

Figure 5. Illustration of the random walker algorithm: (a) Initialization of seed points L_1, L_2, and L_3; (b) Probability of a random walker starting from each node first reaches L_1; (c) Probability of a random walker starting from each node first reaches L_2; (d) Probability of a random walker starting from each node first reaches L_3 (courtesy of Grady, 2006)

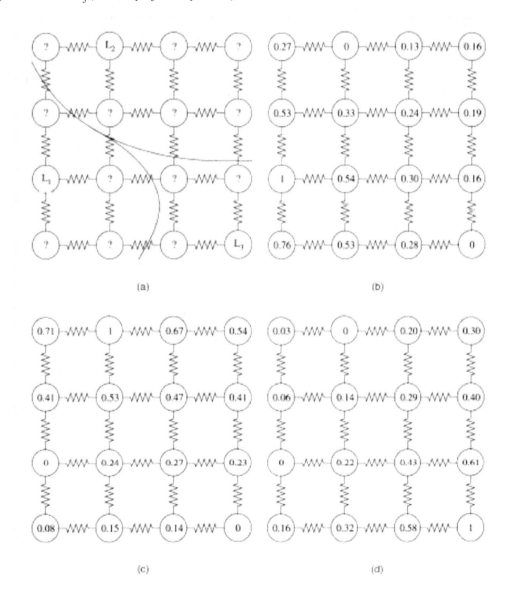

on ℓ_∞ norm was proposed which is more stable in terms of the seed number.

How to increase the processing speed of image segmentation algorithms is always the pursuit of researchers. In order to speed up the image segmentation, an offline precomputation of the segmentation was performed before marking the seeds for object and background by a user (Grady, 2008). A linear-time approximation of the random walker algorithm was developed by using several eigenvectors of the weighted Laplacian matrix of a graph. The proposed algorithm could converge to the random walker segmentation with the usage of more eigenvectors. With the offline precomputation of the segmentation, the final segmentation could be generated around 14 times faster than the original random walker algorithm (Grady, 2006) in MATLAB. Although the prior knowledge can make the segmentation more accurate (Grady, 2005), not all the prior knowledge is available before the user interaction. Similar to (Grady, 2008), a method for speeding up the medical image segmentation was proposed in (Andrews, 2010). An algorithm combining the random walker with priors and additional offline precomputation was derived to increase the speed of segmentation process.

For the purpose of making interactive image segmentation algorithms understand more intelligently the seeds provided by users, Yang (2010) created a random walk-based algorithm which can make use of three types of seeds: the seeds for object and background, the seeds indicating the region that the object boundary should pass through, and the seeds specifying the pixels that the boundary must align with. The last two kinds of seeds, which are different from the normal object or background seeds, require local editing to refine the segmentation.

UNSUPERVISED IMAGE SEGMENTATION METHODS

Unsupervised segmentation methods divide an image into several regions based on some predefined metrics without the interference of users. The minimum spanning tree-based method, the normalized cut method and the isoperimetric method are classified into unsupervised image segmentation.

Minimum Spanning Tree Model (Local Variation)

In Felzenszwalb (2004), a segmentation of an image was defined as a partition of all nodes into components such that each component belonging to the segmentation corresponds to a connected component. A predicate D was defined to describe the existence of a boundary between two components. The internal difference of a component was defined as the largest weight in the minimum spanning tree of the component. The difference between two components was defined as the minimum weight of the edges connecting the two components. If the difference between two components is greater than the minimum internal difference of the two components, it was judged that there is a boundary between these two components. Otherwise, there is no boundary between these two components. As this algorithm considered local properties, it is also called local variation-based image segmentation in some literatures. An intuitive example of minimum spanning tree-based method is presented in Figure 6. Following the predicate D, the proposed image segmentation was neither "too coarse" nor "too fine" and this property was proved.

Figure 6. Results of minimum spanning tree-based image segmentation (courtesy of Felzenszwalb, 2004)

Normalized Cut (Spectral Graph Theory-Based)

In Shi (2001), the image segmentation problem was transferred to a graph partitioning problem. To avoid cutting small sets of nodes as what the minimum cuts do (Wu, 1993), the normalized cut, denoted as N_{CUT}, was proposed as a global criterion to evaluate the disparity between different groups and the homogeneity inside the groups. The normalized cut of two disjoint set A and B in a graph $G=(V,E)$ is defined as below:

$$Ncut\left(A,B\right) = \frac{cut\left(A,B\right)}{assoc\left(A,V\right)} + \frac{cut\left(A,B\right)}{assoc\left(B,V\right)}$$

(6)

where $cut(A,B)$, $assoc(A,V)$ and $assoc(B,V)$ are defined in Equations 2, 3, and 4.

$$cut\left(A,B\right) = \sum_{u\in A, v\in B} w\left(u,v\right)$$

(7)

$$assoc\left(A,V\right) = \sum_{u\in A, t\in V} w\left(u,t\right)$$

(8)

$$assoc\left(B,V\right) = \sum_{s\in B, t\in V} w\left(s,t\right)$$

(9)

The minimization of the normalized cut was transferred into solving an eigenvalue system. The eigenvector with the second smallest eigenvalue of the eigenvalue system was used to bipartition the graph. The final segmentation was obtained by recursive repartition of the segmented parts.

In Xu (2009), the normalized cut algorithm and prior knowledge constraints were combined together to enhance the performance of image segmentation. At this point, the proposed method is analogical to interactive min-cut/max-flow method. As the constraints could not be incorporated with the original normalized cut method, an iterative approach was used and its convergence was guaranteed. The proposed algorithm could also be a solution to other graph cut methods.

Turbo pixels were used as the nodes in a graph and the normalized cut algorithm was performed on the graph to get the final image segmentation in Cigla (2010). The original input image was over-segmented into turbo pixels which were enforced to be convex. In this way, the image segmentation process consumed less time, while good segmentation results were still available.

In Hochbaum (2010), the first polynomial time algorithms were developed to solve the ratio region problem and the variant of normalized cut problem. The normalized cut variant problem belongs to the optimization of the ratio of the similarity within each group over the dissimilarity between groups, which is the target of image segmentation.

Isoperimetric Graph Partitioning

Following the classic isoperimetric problem in geometry (for a fixed area, find the region with minimum perimeter), (Grady, 2006) proposed an isoperimetric algorithm for image segmentation by dividing the image into regions with large areas and small perimeters. For a graph $G=(V,E)$, the isoperimetric ratio of an isoperimetric set $S \subset G$ is defined as

$$h(S) = \min_{S} \frac{|\partial S|}{\text{Vol}_S} \qquad (10)$$

In Equation 10, the boundary of S is defined as $\partial S = \left\{ e_{\{v_i,v_j\}} \mid v_i \in S, v_j \in \bar{S} \right\}$ and $\bar{S}$ is the complementary set of S. $|\partial S| = \sum_{e_{ij} \in \partial S} w\left(e_{ij}\right)$ and $\text{Vol}_S = \sum_i d_i \ \forall v_i \in S$. The target of the isoperimetric algorithm is to maximize Vol_S and minimize $|\partial S|$. In contrast with the normalized cut algorithm, isoperimetric graph partitioning is faster and more stable.

OTHER CONCERNS AND FUTURE RESEARCH DIRECTIONS

Being a specific group of image segmentation algorithms, graph-based segmentation methods can be evaluated by general image segmentation evaluation methods. In this part, we deal with the methods for assessing the performances of image segmentation algorithms. Also, three public datasets for testing image segmentation methods are listed in Table 1 as the experimental resources for other researchers working in image segmentation area.

Segmentation Evaluation Methods

Image segmentation is an ill-defined problem as there is often no sole ground-truth segmentation result for a specific image. The segmentation of an image by different algorithms can be totally different. When the ground truth segmentation of each image is available, this can be done accurately in a supervised way. For instance, in (Ge, 2006), a supervised image segmentation evaluation method was used, where a measure was defined as the ratio between the area of the intersection of the ground-truth foreground and the segmented foreground and the area of the union of the ground-truth foreground and the segmented foreground. Image segmentation methods such as normalized-cut based method, efficient graph-based method, mean-shift based method, level-set method and ratio-contour method were evaluated. By using this evaluation method, the experimental comparison showed that the normalized cut method and the minimum spanning tree-based method outperformed others as a whole.

However, as the ground-truth is often not available in many applications, objective evaluation methods are necessary to assess the quality of segmentation. Many unsupervised evaluation methods have been proposed and used to compare different image segmentation methods. Different from subjective evaluation and supervised evaluation methods, unsupervised evaluation methods do not need the involvement of user and a manually pre-segmented image as reference. Unsupervised evaluation can automatically judge the quality of segmentation results, so it is suitable for real-time applications. A comprehensive literature review of the proposed evaluation methods for unsupervised image segmentation can be found in (Zhang, 2008).

According to the criteria proposed by Haralick and Shapiro (Haralick, 1985), the metrics used in the reviewed evaluation methods were classified into five categories: intra-region uniformity metrics, inter-region disparity metrics, shape measures, composite metrics and edge-based metrics.

Cardoso (2005) presented a partition distance-based evaluation method for image segmentation algorithms. The proposed measure framework was related to symmetric distance d_{sym}, asymmetric discrepancy d_{asy} and mutual refinement d_{mut}. The experiment showed that this evaluation criterion is capable to judge the quality of image segmentation like a human.

In (Unnikrishnan, 2007), the Probabilistic Rand (PR) index (Unnikrishnan, 2005) was normalized to prevent from impractical assumptions. The Normalized Probabilistic Rand (NPR) index was used to evaluate the performance of segmentation algorithms. The mean-shift algorithm, an efficient graph-based algorithm, a hybrid algorithm and expectation maximization algorithm were chosen and performed on the images from Berkeley dataset (http://www.eecs.berkeley.edu/Research/Projects/CS/vision/bsds/) for comparison

Public Database for Image Segmentation

Several public image databases are widely used for testing image segmentation algorithms. The most common ones used include Berkeley dataset, MSR Cambridge dataset and ICDAR 2003 dataset. We briefly introduce them:

- **Berkeley Segmentation Dataset and Benchmark** (http://www.eecs.berkeley.edu/Research/Projects/CS/vision/bsds/): This database includes 300 images with natural sight, animals, human and object.
- **MSR Cambridge Dataset** (http://research.microsoft.com/en-us/um/cambridge/projects/visionimagevideoediting/segmentation/grabcut.htm): this dataset includes 30 images and ground truth images for evaluation.
- **ICDAR2003 Text Dataset** (http://algoval.essex.ac.uk/icdar/Datasets.html): This dataset includes more than 2000 text images and more than 11000 single character images manually cropped from text images. This dataset has been used for testing text segmentation algorithms in publications list in Table 2.

CONCLUSION

In this chapter, some state-of-the-art graph-based image segmentation techniques have been reviewed. Those techniques are classified into five models (min-cut/max-flow model, random walk model, minimum spanning tree model, normalized cut model and isoperimetric graph partitioning model) according to the specific graph models in the algorithms. Those techniques are published in quality international conferences and international journals in computer vision research area and

Table 2. Dataset usage in literatures

Datasets:	Berkeley Dataset	MSR Cambridge Dataset	ICDAR2003 Text Dataset
Literature using the relevant datasets	(Martin, 2001), (Cigla, 2010), (Jung, 2010), (Xu, 2009), (Unnikrishnan, 2007), (Zhang, 2008), (Yang, 2010), (Candemir, 2010)	(Yuan, 2010), (Peng, 2009), (Rother, 2004)	(Yokobayashi, 2006), (Thillou, 2007), (Yokobayashi, 2005), (Thillou, 2006)

can be regarded as a trend of research in image segmentation.

Due to the fact that the assessment of the performance of image segmentation methods is still an open question, many researchers are making efforts in providing supervised and unsupervised evaluation methods. As unsupervised evaluation methods can be included into the framework of image segmentation, they are more suitable to real applications than the supervised methods.

Some public image segmentation dataset are provided for the readers' reference. The Berkeley segmentation dataset is the most common one used in image segmentation experiments. The ICDAR2003 text dataset can be used for text image segmentation, which is a sub-area of the whole family of image segmentation.

REFERENCES

Andrews, S., Hamarneh, G., & Saad, A. (2010). Fast random walker with priors using precomputation for interactive medical image segmentation. *Lecture Notes in Computer Science, 6363*, 9–16. doi:10.1007/978-3-642-15711-0_2

Bertrand, G. (1994). Simple points, topological numbers and geodesic neighborhoods in cubic grids. *Pattern Recognition Letters, 15*(10), 1003–1011. doi:10.1016/0167-8655(94)90032-9

Boykov, Y., & Jolly, M. P. (2001). Interactive graph cuts for optimal boundary & region segmentation of objects in N-D images. *Proceedings of International Conference on Computer Vision*, Vol. 1. (pp. 105-112).

Boykov, Y., & Kolmogorov, V. (2004). An experimental comparison of min-cut/max-flow algorithms for energy minimization in vision. *IEEE Transactions on Pattern Analysis and Machine Intelligence, 26*(9), 1124–1137. doi:10.1109/TPAMI.2004.60

Boykov, Y., Veksler, O., & Zabih, R. (2001). Fast approximate energy minimization via graph cuts. *IEEE Transactions on Pattern Analysis and Machine Intelligence, 23*(11), 1222–1239. doi:10.1109/34.969114

Candemir, S., & Akgul, Y. S. (2010). Adaptive regularization parameter for graph cut segmentation. *Lecture Notes in Computer Science, 6111*, 117–126. doi:10.1007/978-3-642-13772-3_13

Cardoso, J. S., & Real, L. C. (2005). Toward a generic evaluation of image segmentation. *IEEE Transactions on Image Processing, 14*(11), 1773–1782. doi:10.1109/TIP.2005.854491

Çigla, C., & Alatan, A. A. (2010). Efficient graph-based image segmentation via speeded-up turbo pixels. *17th IEEE International Conference on Image Processing* (pp. 3013-3016).

Correia, P. L., & Pereira, F. (2003). Objective evaluation of video segmentation quality. *IEEE Transactions on Image Processing, 12*(2), 186–200. doi:10.1109/TIP.2002.807355

Fan, J., Zeng, G., Body, M., & Hacid, M. S. (2005). Seeded region growing: An extensive and comparative study. *Pattern Recognition Letters, 26*(8), 1139–1156. doi:10.1016/j.patrec.2004.10.010

Felzenszwalb, P. F., & Huttenlocher, D. P. (2004). Efficient graph-based image segmentation. *International Journal of Computer Vision, 59*(2), 167–181. doi:10.1023/B:VISI.0000022288.19776.77

Fu, Y., Cheng, J., Li, Z., & Lu, H. (2008). Saliency cuts: An automatic approach to object segmentation. *19th International Conference on Pattern Recognition* (pp. 1-4).

Ge, F., Wang, S., & Liu, T. (2006). Image-segmentation evaluation from the perspective of salient object extraction. *IEEE Conference on Computer Vision and Pattern Recognition* (pp. 1146-1153).

Grady, L. (2005). Multilabel random walker image segmentation using prior models. *IEEE Conference on Computer Vision and Pattern Recognition* (Vol. 1, pp. 763-770).

Grady, L. (2006). Random walks for image segmentation. *IEEE Transactions on Pattern Analysis and Machine Intelligence, 28*(11), 1768–1783. doi:10.1109/TPAMI.2006.233

Grady, L., & Funka-Lea, G. (2004). Multi-label image segmentation for medical applications based on graph-theoretic electrical potentials. *Proceedings of the 8th ECCV Workshop on Computer Vision Approaches to Medical Image Analysis and Mathematical Methods in Biomedical Image Analysis* (pp. 230-245).

Grady, L., & Schwartz, E. L. (2006). Isoperimetric graph partitioning for image segmentation. *IEEE Transactions on Pattern Analysis and Machine Intelligence, 28*(3), 469–475. doi:10.1109/TPAMI.2006.57

Grady, L., & Sinop, A. K. (2008). Fast approximate random walker segmentation using eigenvector precomputation. *IEEE Conference on Computer Vision and Pattern Recognition* (pp. 1-8).

Grau, V., Mewes, A. U. J., Alcaniz, M., Kikinis, R., & Warfield, S. K. (2004). Improved watershed transform for medical image segmentation using prior information. *IEEE Transactions on Medical Imaging, 23*(4), 447–458. doi:10.1109/TMI.2004.824224

Han, X., Xu, C., & Prince, J. L. (2003). A topology preserving level set method for geometric deformable model. *IEEE Transactions on Pattern Analysis and Machine Intelligence, 25*(6), 755–768. doi:10.1109/TPAMI.2003.1201824

Haralick, R., & Shapiro, L. (1985). Survey: image segmentation techniques. *Computer Vision Graphics and Image Processing, 29*(1), 100–132. doi:10.1016/S0734-189X(85)90153-7

Hochbaum, D. S. (2010). Polynomial time algorithms for ratio regions and a variant of normalized cut. *IEEE Transactions on Pattern Analysis and Machine Intelligence, 32*(5), 889–898. doi:10.1109/TPAMI.2009.80

Jung, C., Kim, B., & Kim, C. (2010). Automatic segmentation of salient objects using iterative reversible graph cut. *International Conference on Multimedia and Expo* (pp. 590-595).

Koo, H. I., & Cho, N. I. (2009). Graph cuts using a riemannian metric induced by tensor voting. *IEEE 12th International Conference on Computer Vision* (pp. 514-520).

Martin, D., Fowlkes, C., Tal, D., & Malik, J. (2001). *IEEE 8th International Conference on Computer Vision* (Vol. 2, pp. 416-423).

Mignotte, M. (2008). Segmentation by fusion of histogram-based K-means clusters in different color spaces. *IEEE Transactions on Image Processing, 17*(5), 780–787. doi:10.1109/TIP.2008.920761

Otsu, N. (1979). A threshold selection method from gray-level histograms. *IEEE Transactions on Systems, Man, and Cybernetics, 9*(1), 62–66. doi:10.1109/TSMC.1979.4310076

Peng, B., & Veksler, O. (2008). *Parameter selection for graph cut based image segmentation.* British Machine Vision Conference.

Peng, B., Zhang, L., & Yang, J. (2009). *Iterated graph cuts for image segmentation.* 9th Asian Conference on Computer Vision.

Price, B. L., Morse, B., & Cohen, S. (2010). Geodesic graph cut for interactive image segmentation. *IEEE Conference on Computer Vision and Pattern Recognition* (pp. 3161-3168).

Rao, S. R., Mobahi, H., Yang, A. Y., Sastry, S. S., & Ma, Y. (2009). *Natural image segmentation with adaptive texture and boundary encoding.* 9th Asian Conference on Computer Vision.

Rother, C., Kolmogorove, V., & Blake, A. (2004). Grabcut-interactive foreground extraction using iterated graph cuts. *ACM Transactions on Graphics, 23*(3), 309–314. doi:10.1145/1015706.1015720

Senthilkumaran, N., & Rajesh, R. (2009). Edge detection techniques for image segmentation-a survey of soft computing approaches. *International Journal of Recent Trends in Engineering, 1*(2), 250–254.

Shi, J., & Malik, J. (2001). Normalized cuts and image segmentation. *IEEE Transactions on Pattern Analysis and Machine Intelligence, 22*(8), 888–905.

Sinop, A. K., & Grady, L. (2007). A seeded image segmentation framework unifying graph cuts and random walker which yields a new algorithm. *Proceedings of International Conference on Computer Vision* (pp. 1-8).

Thillou, C., & Gosselin, B. (2007). Color text extraction with selective metric-based clustering. *Computer Vision and Image Understanding, 107*(1-2), 97–107. doi:10.1016/j.cviu.2006.11.010

Thillou, C. M., & Gosselin, B. (2006). Spatial and color spaces combination for natural scene text extraction. *International Conference on Image Processing* (pp. 985-988).

Unnikrishnan, R., & Hebert, M. (2005). Measures of similarity. *IEEE Workshop on Applications of Computer Vision* (pp. 394-400).

Unnikrishnan, R., Pantofaru, C., & Hebert, M. (2007)... *IEEE Transactions on Pattern Analysis and Machine Intelligence, 29*(6), 929–944. doi:10.1109/TPAMI.2007.1046

Wu, Z., & Leahy, R. (1993). An optimal graph theoretic approach to data clustering: Theory and its application to image segmentation. *IEEE Transactions on Pattern Analysis and Machine Intelligence, 15*(11), 1101–1113. doi:10.1109/34.244673

Xu, L., Li, W., & Schuurmans, D. (2009). Fast normalized cut with linear constraints. *IEEE Conference on Computer Vision and Pattern Recognition* (pp. 2866-2873).

Yang, W., Cai, J., Zheng, J., & Luo, J. (2010). User-friendly interactive image segmentation through unified combinatorial user inputs. *IEEE Transactions on Image Processing, 19*(9), 2470–2479. doi:10.1109/TIP.2010.2048611

Yokobayashi, M., & Wakahara, T. (2005). Segmentation and recognition of characters in scene images using selective binarization in color space and GAT correlation. *8th International Conference on Document Analysis and Recognition* (Vol. 1, pp. 167-171).

Yokobayashi, M., & Wakahara, T. (2006). Binarization and recognition of degraded characters using a maximum separability axis in color space and GAT correlation. *18th International Conference on Pattern Recognition* (Vol. 2, pp. 885-888).

Yuan, J., Bae, E., & Tai, X. C. (2010). A study on continuous max-flow and min-cut approaches. *IEEE Conference on Computer Vision and Pattern Recognition* (pp. 2217-2224).

Zeng, Y., Samaras, D., Chen, W., & Peng, Q. (2008). Topology cuts: a novel min-cut/max-flow algorithm for topology preserving segmentation in N-D images. *Computer Vision and Image Understanding, 112*(1), 81–90. doi:10.1016/j.cviu.2008.07.008

Zhang, H., Fritts, J. E., & Goldman, S. A. (2008). Image segmentation evaluation: A survey of unsupervised methods. *Computer Vision and Image Understanding, 110*(2), 260–280. doi:10.1016/j.cviu.2007.08.003

Zhang, J., Zheng, J., & Cai, J. (2010). A diffusion approach to seeded image segmentation. *IEEE Conference on Computer Vision and Pattern Recognition* (pp. 2125-2132).

Section 3
Graph–Based Methods for Image and Video Analysis

Chapter 8
Graph Embedding Using Dissimilarities with Applications in Classification

Horst Bunke
University of Bern, Switzerland

Kaspar Riesen
University of Bern, Switzerland

ABSTRACT

The domain of graphs contains only little mathematical structure. That is, most of the basic mathematical operations, actually required by many standard computer vision and pattern recognition algorithms, are not available for graphs. One of the few mathematical concepts that has been successfully transferred from the vector space to the graph domain is distance computation between graphs, commonly referred to as graph matching. Yet, distance-based pattern recognition is basically limited to nearest-neighbor classification. The present chapter reviews a novel approach for graph embedding in vector spaces built upon the concept of graph matching. The key-idea of the proposed embedding method is to use the distances of an input graph to a number of training graphs, termed prototypes, as vectorial description of the graph. That is, all graph matching procedures proposed in the literature during the last decades can be employed in this embedding framework. The rationale for such a graph embedding is to bridge the gap between the high representational power and flexibility of graphs and the large amount of algorithms available for object representations in terms of feature vectors. Hence, the proposed framework can be considered a contribution towards unifying the domains of structural and statistical pattern recognition.

DOI: 10.4018/978-1-4666-1891-6.ch008

INTRODUCTION

The question how to represent objects in a formal way is a key issue in the whole discipline of computer vision and pattern recognition. There are two major ways to tackle this crucial problem, viz. the statistical and the structural approach. In the statistical approach, objects are represented by feature vectors. That is, an object is formally represented as a vector $x=(x_1,..., x_n) \in R^n$ of n measurements. Representing objects or patterns by feature vectors $x \in R^n$ offers a number of useful properties, in particular, the mathematical wealth of operations available in a vector space. That is, computing the sum, the product, the mean, or the distance of two entities is well defined in vector spaces, and moreover, can be efficiently accomplished. The convenience and low computational complexity of algorithms that use feature vectors as their input have eventually resulted in a rich repository of algorithmic tools for computer vision, pattern recognition, and related fields (Duda, 2000).

However, the use of feature vectors implicates two limitations. First, as vectors always represent a predefined set of features, all vectors in a given application have to preserve the same length regardless of the size or complexity of the corresponding objects. Second, there is no direct possibility to describe binary relationships that might exist among different parts of an object. These two drawbacks are severe, particularly when the patterns under consideration are characterized by complex structural relationships rather than the statistical distribution of a fixed set of pattern features (Bunke, 1990).

The structural approach is based on symbolic data structures, such as strings, trees, or graphs, out of which graphs are the most general one. In fact, from an algorithmic perspective both strings and trees are simple instances of graphs. A string is a graph in which each node represents one symbol, and two consecutive symbols are connected by an edge. A tree is a graph in which

any two nodes are connected by exactly one path. Although we focus on graphs in this chapter, the reader should keep in mind that strings and trees are always included as special cases.

The above-mentioned drawbacks of feature vectors, namely the size constraint and the lacking ability of representing relationships, can be overcome by graph based representations (Conte, 2004). In fact, graphs are not only able to describe properties of an object, but also binary relationships among different parts of the underlying object by means of edges. Note that these relationships can be of various nature (spatial, temporal, conceptual, etc.). Moreover, graphs are not constrained to a fixed size, i.e. the number of nodes and edges is not limited a priori and can be adapted to the size and the complexity of each individual object under consideration.

Yet, one drawback of graphs, when compared to feature vectors, is the significantly increased complexity of many algorithms. Nevertheless, new computer generations, which are now able to more efficiently handle complex data structures, as well as the development of fast approximate algorithms for graph comparison definitively empower researchers to use graphs in their respective problem domains (Conte, 2004). Yet, another serious limitation in the use of graphs for object classification arises from the fact that there is little mathematical structure in the domain of graphs. For example, computing the (weighted) sum or the product of a pair of entities, which are elementary operations needed in many standard algorithms in pattern recognition, is not possible in the domain of graphs, or is at least not defined in general for graph structures.

A promising approach to overcoming the lack of algorithmic tools without losing the power of graphs is offered through graph embedding in vector spaces. Basically, such an embedding of graphs establishes access to the rich repository of algorithmic tools for pattern recognition originally reserved for vectorial data. That is, graph embedding addresses the question of how to combine the complementary properties of feature vectors and graphs.

The objective of the present chapter is to review recent work in graph based pattern recognition and computer vision, including graph kernels and a novel graph embedding framework proposed by the the authors recently (Riesen, 2008b; Riesen, 2008c; Riesen, 2009b; Riesen, 2009c; Riesen, 2010). This recent approach to graph embedding is primarily based on the idea proposed in (Pekalska, 2005) where the dissimilarity representation for pattern recognition in conjunction with feature vectors was first introduced. The key idea is to use the dissimilarities of an input graph g to a number of training graphs, termed prototypes, as a vectorial description of g. In other words, the dissimilarity representation rather than the original graph representation is used for pattern recognition.

RECENT DEVELOPMENTS IN GRAPH BASED PATTERN RECOGNITION

The intensive study of problems where the objects under consideration consist of interrelated entities has emerged rapidly in the last decade (Cook, 2007; Bunke, 2007; Neuhaus, 2007). The reason for this emerging trend can be found in recent developments in graph based pattern recognition such as graph kernels and graph embeddings.

Graph Kernels

During the past decade kernel methods have become one of the most rapidly emerging sub-fields in intelligent information processing. The reason for this development is twofold. First, kernel methods allow one to extend basic linear algorithms to complex non-linear ones in a unified and elegant manner. Hence, by means of kernel methods the issue of non-linear regularities in the data is inherently coped with. There is theoretical evidence

that under some conditions kernel methods are more appropriate for difficult pattern recognition tasks than traditional methods (Vapnik, 1998). Second, kernel theory makes standard algorithms (originally developed for vectorial representation) applicable to more complex data structures such as strings, trees, or graphs. That is, the concept of kernel machines can be extended from the domain of vectors to structural domains.

Let G be a (finite or infinite) set of graphs. Function $\kappa: G \times G \to R$ is called a graph kernel if there exists a possibly infinite-dimensional Hilbert space F and a mapping $\Phi: G \to F$ such that

$$\kappa(g,g')=\{\surd(g), \Phi(g')\}$$

for all $g,g' \in G$ where $\{.,.\}$ denotes a dot product in F.

According to this definition, every graph kernel κ can be thought of as a dot product $\{.,.\}$ in some (implicitly existing) feature space F. In other words, instead of mapping graphs from G to the feature space F and computing their dot product there, one can simply evaluate the value of the kernel function in G (Neuhaus, 2007).

Consider now an algorithm formulated entirely in terms of dot products. Such algorithms are commonly referred to as kernel machines. Prominent examples of kernel machines are support vector machine, principal component analysis, and k-means clustering. Clearly, any kernel machine can be turned into an alternative algorithm by merely replacing the dot product $\{.,.\}$ by a valid kernel $|(.,.)$. This procedure is commonly referred to as the kernel trick (Shawe, 2004; Schölkopf, 2002). It allows one to cope with non-linear problems in an elegant and efficient manner.

The kernel trick has a huge impact in practice and allows us to compute geometrical properties of graphs $g,g' \in G$. From a higher level perspective, the kernel trick allows one to run algorithms (kernel machines) in implicitly existing feature spaces F without computing the mapping $\Phi: G \to F$ and even without knowing F. Consequently, kernels provide us with an implicit embedding of the symbolic data space - e.g. the graph domain - into an inner product space. In other words, graph kernels offer an elegant way to overcome the problems arising from the lack of mathematical structure in the domain of graphs.

While it might be cumbersome to define mathematical operations in some graph domain G, a kernel $\kappa: G \times G \rightarrow R$ might be much easier to obtain. Clearly, by means of graph kernels one can benefit from both the high representational power of graphs and the large repository of algorithmic tools available for feature vector representations. A number of graph kernels have been proposed in the literature (Neuhaus, 2007; Gärtner, 2008; Gärtner, 2003a). In the present section three classes of graph kernels are briefly discussed.

Diffusion Kernels

A first class of graph kernels is given by diffusion kernels. The kernels of this class are defined with respect to a base similarity measure which is used to construct a kernel matrix $\mathbf{K} = (\kappa_{ij})_{N \times N}$ (Kondor, 2002; Kandola, 2002; Smola, 2003; Lafferty, 2003; Lafferty, 2005). This base similarity measure only needs to satisfy the condition of symmetry to guarantee that the resulting kernel matrix is positive definite. Obviously, the diffusion kernel can be defined for any kind of objects and particularly for graphs. Assume that a graph set $\{g_1,..., g_N\} \subseteq G$, a decay factor $0 < \lambda < 1$, and a similarity measure $s: G \times G \rightarrow R$ are given. The N × N matrix $\mathbf{S} = (s_{ij})_{N \times N}$ of pairwise similarities s_{ij} can be turned into a positive definite kernel matrix $\mathbf{K} = (\kappa_{ij})_{N \times N}$ through the exponential diffusion kernel (Kondor, 2002) defined by

$$K = \sum_{k=0}^{\infty} \frac{1}{k!} \lambda^k S^k = \exp(\lambda S)$$

or the von Neumann diffusion kernel (Kandola, 2002) defined by

$$K = \sum_{k=0}^{\infty} \lambda^k S^k$$

The decay factor λ assures that the weighting factor λ^k will be negligibly small for sufficiently large k. Therefore, only the first t addends in the diffusion kernel sums have to be evaluated in practice. Of course, any graph (dis)similarity measure can be used to build a diffusion kernel for graphs.

Convolution Kernel

A seminal contribution to the field of graph kernel is the work on convolution kernels, which provides a general framework for dealing with complex objects (Haussler, 1999; Watkins, 2000). Convolution kernels infer the similarity of composite objects from the similarity of their parts. The rationale behind this approach is that a similarity function might more easily be defined or more efficiently be computed for smaller parts rather than for the whole composite object. Given the similarities between the simpler parts of the underlying objects, a convolution operation is eventually applied in order to turn them into a kernel function.

Clearly, graphs are complex composite objects as they consist of nodes and edges. The concept of decomposing a graph g into its parts is mathematically denoted by a relation R, where $R(g_1,..., g_d, g)$ represents the decomposition of g into parts $(g_1,..., g_d)$. By $R^{-1}(g) = \{(g_1,..., g_d): R(g_1,..., g_d, g)\}$ we denote the set of decompositions of graph g. For a simple example, assume that the set of all decompositions of a graph $g \in G$ is defined by $R^{-1}(g) = V$, where V denotes the set of nodes of g. Hence, all of g's nodes are a valid decomposition of g. For the definition of the convolution kernel, a kernel function κ_i is required for each part of a decomposition $\{g_i\}_{1 \leq i \leq d}$. For instance, if $R^{-1}(g) = V$, a kernel function measuring the similarity of the involved nodes could be employed for κ_i. The convolution kernel function for graphs $g, g' \in G$ can then be written as

$$\kappa(g, g') = \sum_{\substack{(g_1, \ldots, g_d) \in R^{-1}(g) \\ (g'_1, \ldots, g'_d) \in R^{-1}(g')}} \prod_{i=1}^{d} \kappa_i(g_i, g'_i)$$

Hence, this graph kernel derives the similarity between two graphs g and g' from the sum, over all decompositions, of the similarity product of the parts of g and g' (Neuhaus, 2007). The ANOVA kernel (Watkins, 1999), for instance, is a particular convolution kernel, which uses a subset of the components of a composite object for comparison.

Walk Kernel

A third class of graph kernels is based on the analysis of random walks in graphs. These kernels measure the similarity of two graphs by the number of random walks in both graphs that have all or some labels in common (Borgwardt, 2005a; Borgwardt, 2005b; Gärtner, 2003a; Kashima, 2002; Kashima, 2003). In (Gärtner. 2003a) an important result is reported. It is shown that the number of matching walks in two graphs g and g' can be computed by means of the direct product graph $g \times g'$, without the need to explicitly enumerate the walks. This allows us to consider random walks of arbitrary length.

The direct product graph, by definition, identifies the compatible nodes and edges in the two graphs. Given a weighting parameter $\lambda \geq 0$, one can derive a kernel function for graphs $g, g' \in G$ from the adjacency matrix $\mathbf{A}$ of their product graph $g \times g'$ by defining

$$\kappa(g, g') = \sum_{i,j=1}^{|V_X|} \left[\sum_{n=1}^{\infty} \lambda^n A_X^n \right]$$

with a weighting factor $\lambda < 1$ it is assured that the contribution of $\lambda^n \mathbf{A}^n$ to the overall sum will be negligibly small for sufficiently large n. Therefore, only the first t terms in the random walk kernel sums have to be evaluated.

In order to handle continuous labels, the random walk kernel has been extended in (Borgwardt, 2005b). This extension allows one to also take non-identically labeled walks into account. In (Borgwardt, 2005a) two kernels, the so-called all-path and the shortest-path kernel, are introduced. These kernels consider paths between two pairs of nodes in a graph and use the similarity of two pairs of paths in order to derive the final kernel value. Another kernel that considers paths and label sequences encountered along the paths in two graphs is described in (Ralaivola, 2005). The problem of tottering is addressed in (Mahe, 2005). Tottering is the phenomenon that, in a walk, a node may be revisited immediately after it has been left. In order to prevent tottering, the random walk transition probability model is appropriately modified in (Mahe, 2005).

Graph Embedding

Another approach to overcoming the lack of algorithmic tools for graphs is graph embedding in vector spaces. The objective of graph embedding is similar to that of graph kernels, i.e. we want to benefit from both the universality of graphs for pattern representation and the computational convenience of vectors for pattern recognition. In contrast to graph kernels, however, graph embedding procedures result in an explicit embedding of graphs from some graph domain G in a real vector space $\mathbb{R}^n$. Formally, a graph embedding is a function $\Phi: G \rightarrow \mathbb{R}^n$ mapping graphs from arbitrary graph domains to a vector space. Based on the resulting graph maps, the considered pattern recognition task is eventually carried out. Hence, the whole arsenal of algorithmic tools readily available for vectorial data can be applied to graphs (more exactly to graph maps $\Phi(g) \in \mathbb{R}^n$).

A prominent class of graph embedding is based on spectral methods (Chung, 1997; Luo, 2003; Caelli, 2004; Wilson, 2005; Kelly, 2007;

Luo, 2001). Spectral graph theory is concerned with understanding how the structural properties of graphs can be characterized using eigenvectors of the adjacency or Laplacian matrix (Wilson, 2005). Although graph spectralization exhibits interesting properties which can be used for vector space embedding of graphs, this approach remains somewhat limited. For instance, spectral methods are not fully able to cope with larger amounts of noise. This stems from the fact that the eigendecomposition is very sensitive towards structural errors, such as missing or spurious nodes. Moreover, spectral methods are applicable to unlabeled graphs or labeled graphs with severely constrained label alphabets only, making this approach only to a limited extent applicable to graphs extracted from real-world data. Only recently, first attempts to overcome these limitations have been reported (Lee, 2009).

Graph Embedding Procedure Using Dissimilarities

Recently, a new class of graph embedding procedures has been proposed which can be applied to both directed and undirected graphs, as well as to graphs with arbitrary labels on their nodes and/or edges (Riesen, 2010). Furthermore, this graph embedding framework is distinguished by its ability to handle structural errors.

The idea of this approach to graph embedding stems from the seminal work done by Duin and Pekalska (2005) where dissimilarities for pattern representation were proposed for the first time. Later this method was extended so as to map string representations into vector spaces (Spillmann, 2006). Recently, the methods described in (Pekalska, 2005; Spillmann, 2006) were generalized and substantially extended to the domain of graphs (Riesen, 2010). The key idea of this approach is to use the distances of an input graph g to a number of training graphs, termed prototype graphs, as a vectorial description of g.

Assume we have a set of sample graphs, T $=\{g,..., g_N\}$ from some graph domain G and an arbitrary graph dissimilarity measure d: $G \times G \to$ R. Note that T can be any kind of graph set. However, for the sake of convenience we assume in the following that T is a given training set of graphs. After selecting a set of prototypical graphs P$\subseteq$T, we compute the dissimilarity of a given input graph g to each prototype graph $p_i \in$ P. Note that g can be an element of T or any other graph set S. Given n prototypes, i.e. P = $\{p_1,...,$ $p_n\}$, this procedure leads to n dissimilarities, $d_1 = d(g,p_1),...,d_n = d(g,p_n)$, which can be arranged in an n-dimensional vector $(d_1,..., d_n)$.

Formally, let us assume a graph domain G is given. If T= $\{g,...,g_N\} \subseteq$ G is a training set with N graphs and P = $\{p_1,..., p_n\} \subseteq$ T is a prototype set with n graphs, the mapping Φ: G $\to$ R^n is defined as the function

$$\Phi(g) = (d(g, p_1),..., d(g,p_n))$$

where $d(g, p_i)$ is any graph dissimilarity measure between graph g and the i-th prototype graph.

Obviously, by means of this definition we obtain a vector space where each axis corresponds to a prototype graph $p_i \in$ P and the coordinate values of an embedded graph g are the distances of g to the elements in P. In this way we can transform any graph g from the training set T as well as any other graph set S (for instance a validation or a test set of a classification problem), into a vector of real numbers.

Graph Matching Using Edit Distance

Originally, the motivation for dissimilarity based embedding is based on the argument that the notion of proximity (similarity or dissimilarity) is more fundamental than that of a feature or a class (Pekalska, 2005). The major motivation for using the dissimilarity representation for graphs stems from to the fact that though there is little mathematical foundation in the graph domain, numerous procedures for computing pairwise similarities or dissimilarities for graphs can be found in the literature (Conte, 2004). The process of evaluating the similarity of two graphs is commonly referred to as graph matching. The overall aim of graph matching is to find a correspondence between the nodes and edges of two graphs that satisfies some, more or less, stringent constraints.

Roughly speaking, there are two categories of algorithms in graph matching, viz. exact graph matching and inexact graph matching. The main restriction of exact graph matching is the requirement that a significant part of the topology together with the corresponding node and edge labels in two graphs are identical for obtaining a high degree of similarity. In fact, this is not realistic for many real world applications. Especially if the nodes and/or the edges are continuously labeled, the exact matching paradigm is too restrictive. In order to make graph matching better applicable to real world problems, several error-tolerant, or inexact, graph matching methods have been proposed. Inexact matching algorithms are endowed with a certain tolerance to errors, enabling them to detect similarities in a more general way than the exact matching approach. For an extensive review of graph matching methods and applications, the reader is referred to (Conte, 2004).

In this chapter we focus on graph edit distance (Bunke, 1983; Sanfeliu, 1983), which is one of the most flexible methods for error-tolerant graph matching. The key idea of graph edit distance is to define the dissimilarity, or distance, of graphs by the minimum amount of distortion that is needed to transform one graph into another. A standard set of distortion operations is given by insertions, deletions, and substitutions of nodes and edges.

Other operations, such as merging and splitting of nodes (Ambauen, 2003), can be useful in certain applications but are not considered in this chapter.

Given two graphs, the source graph g and the target graph g', the main idea underlying graph edit distance computation is to delete some nodes and edges from g, relabel (substitute) some of the remaining nodes and edges, and insert some nodes and edges in g', such that g is finally transformed into g'. A sequence of edit operations $e_1, ..., e_k$ that transform g into g' is called an *edit path* between g and g'. In Figure 1 an example of an edit path between two graphs is given. Obviously, for every pair of graphs (g, g'), there exist a number of different edit paths transforming g into g'. Let $Y(g, g')$ denote the set of all such edit paths. To find the most suitable edit path out of $Y(g, g')$, one introduces a cost for each edit operation, measuring the strength of the corresponding operation. The idea of such cost functions is to define whether or not an edit operation represents a strong modification of the graph. Hence, between two similar graphs, there should exist an inexpensive edit path, representing low cost operations, while for substantially different graphs, an edit path with high costs is needed. Consequently, the edit distance of two graphs is defined by the minimum cost edit path between two graphs.

The computation of the edit distance is usually carried out by means of a tree search algorithm, which explores the space of all possible mappings of the nodes and edges of the first graph to the nodes and edges of the second graph. Due to the fact that the error-tolerant nature of edit distance potentially allows every node of a graph g to be mapped to every node of another graph g', the computational complexity of the edit distance

Figure 1. A possible edit path between graph g_1 and g_2 (node labels are represented by different shades of grey)

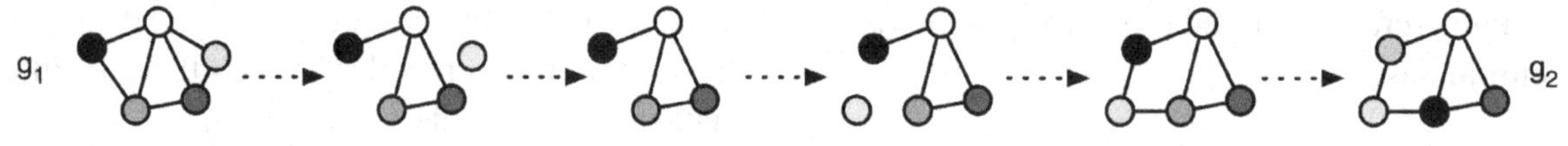

algorithm is exponential in the number of nodes of the involved graphs. This means that the running time and space complexity may be huge even for rather small graphs.

In order to reduce the complexity of graph edit distance computation, approximate, or suboptimal, matching algorithms can be used instead of exact, or optimal, ones. In contrast to optimal error-tolerant graph matching, approximate algorithms do not guarantee to find the global minimum of the matching cost, but only a local one. Usually this approximation is not very far from the global one, but there are no guarantees, of course (Conte, 2004). The approximate nature of such suboptimal algorithms is typically repaid by polynomial matching time.

In some suboptimal approaches, the basic idea is to perform a local search to solve the graph matching problem, that is, to optimize local criteria instead of global, or optimal ones (Sorlin, 2005). In (Justice, 2006), a linear programming method for computing the edit distance of graphs with unlabeled edges is proposed. The method can be used to derive lower and upper edit distance bounds in polynomial time. Two fast but suboptimal algorithms for graph edit distance computation are proposed in Neuhaus (2006). The authors propose simple variants of an optimal edit distance algorithm that make the computation substantially faster. Another approach to efficient graph edit distance computation has been proposed in (Eshera, 1984). The basic idea is to decompose graphs into sets of subgraphs. These subgraphs consist of a node and its adjacent nodes and edges. The graph matching problem is then reduced to the problem of finding an optimal match between the sets of subgraphs by means of dynamic programming. In (Riesen, 2009a) another efficient algorithm for solving the problem of graph edit distance computation is introduced. This approach is somewhat similar to the method described in (Eshera, 1984), i.e. the graph edit distance is approximated by finding an optimal match between nodes of two graphs and their local structure.

However, in order to find the optimal match, a bipartite matching procedure is used rather than dynamic programming.

Relation to Kernel Methods

Dissimilarity embedding is closely related to kernel methods. In the kernel approach the patterns are described by means of pairwise kernel functions, and in the dissimilarity approach they are represented by pairwise dissimilarities. However, there is also one fundamental difference between kernels and dissimilarity embeddings. In the former method, the kernel values are interpreted as dot products in some implicit feature space. By means of kernel machines, the pattern recognition task is eventually carried out in this kernel feature space. In the latter approach, the set of dissimilarities is interpreted as a vectorial description of the pattern under consideration. Hence, no implicit feature space, but an explicit dissimilarity space is obtained.

Although conceptually different, the embedding paradigm established by the mapping Φ: $G \rightarrow R^n$ constitutes a foundation for a novel class of graph kernels. One can define a valid graph kernel κ based on the graph embedding Φ: $G \rightarrow R^n$ by computing the standard dot product of two graph maps in the resulting vector space. Note that is approach is very similar to the empirical kernel map described in (Tsuda, 1999) where general similarity measures are turned into kernel functions.

Of course, not only the standard dot product can be used but any valid kernel function defined for vectors. For instance an RBF kernel function can thus be applied to graph maps. We refer to this procedure as graph embedding kernel using some specific vector kernel function.

In a recent book, graph kernels were proposed that directly use graph edit distances (Neuhaus, 2007). This approach turns an existing dissimilarity measure (e.g. graph edit distance) into a similarity measure by mapping low distance values to high similarity values and vice versa. To this end monotonically decreasing transformations are used. Given the edit distance $d(g,g')$ of two graphs g and g', the similarity kernel is defined, for instance, as $\kappa(g,g') = \exp(-\lambda d(g,g'))$, with $\lambda > 0$. Note that this kernel function is not positive definite in general. However, there is theoretical evidence that using kernel machines in conjunction with indefinite kernels may be reasonable if some conditions are fulfilled (Haasdonk, 2005). We refer to this method as similarity kernel, or sim for short, in the following.

The Problem of Prototype Selection

The selection of the $n\$$ prototypes $P = \{p_1, ..., p_n\}$ is a critical issue in graph embedding since not only the prototypes $p_i \in P$ themselves but also their number affect the resulting graph mapping and thus the performance of the corresponding pattern recognition algorithm. A good selection of prototypes seems to be crucial to succeed with the algorithm in the embedding vector space. A first and very simple solution might be to use all available training graphs from T as prototypes. Yet, two severe shortcomings arise with such a plain approach. First, the dimensionality of the resulting vector space is equal to the size N of the training set T. Consequently, if the training set is large, the mapping results in (possibly too) high dimensional feature vectors disabling efficient computation. Second, the presence of similar prototypes as well as outlier graphs in the training set T is likely. Therefore, redundant and noisy or irrelevant information will be captured in the graph maps which in turn may harm the performance of the algorithms applied subsequently.

The selection of prototypes for graph embedding has been addressed in various papers (Riesen, 2008b; Riesen, 2008c; Riesen, 2009c). In (Riesen, 2009c), for instance, a number of prototype selection methods are discussed. These selection strategies use some heuristics based on the underlying dissimilarities in the original graph domain. The

basic idea of these approaches is to select prototypes from T that best reflect the distribution of the training set T or cover a predefined region of T. The rationale of this procedure is that capturing distances to significant prototypes from T leads to meaningful dissimilarity vectors. All of the proposed prototype selection methods can be applied classwise or classindependent. Classindependent selection means that the selection is executed over the whole training set T to get n prototypes, while in classwise selection the selection is performed individually for each of the classes occurring in T.

The Border prototype selector (bps), for instance, selects prototypes situated at the border of the training set T. In Figure 2 (a) and (b) the classindependent and the classwise bps is illustrated, respectively. The data underlying these illustrative examples are two-dimensional vec-

Figure 2. Illustration of the different prototype selectors applied to the training set $\mathcal{T}$ of the Letter data set. The number of prototypes is defined by n=30. The prototypes selected by the respective algorithms are represented by heavy dots.

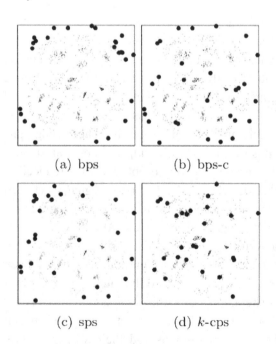

(a) bps   (b) bps-c

(c) sps   (d) k-cps

tors obtained through multidimensional scaling applied to the original graph edit distances from the Letter data set (this data set is used in the experimental evaluation and is described in detail in the next Section).

Another prototype selection strategy is spanning selection (sps). This iterative selection algorithm considers all distances to the prototypes selected before. The first prototype is the set median graph (Jiang, 2001). Each additional prototype is the graph furthest away from the already selected prototype graphs.

The *k*-Centers prototype selector (*k*-cps) is a third strategy for prototype selection which is based on *k*-medians clustering. The prototypes are given by the set medians of the *n* disjoint clusters provided through *k*-medians clustering of the training set T. In contrast to sps, we note that *k*-cps avoids selecting prototypes from the border by focusing on graphs that are in the center of densely populated areas (cf. Figure 2 (c) and (d) for a comparison between sps and *k*-cps).

Another solution to the problem of noisy and redundant embedding vectors with too high dimensionality is offered by the following procedure. Rather than selecting the prototypes beforehand, the embedding is carried out first and then the problem of prototype selection is reduced to a feature subset selection problem. That is, we define P=T and use all available elements from the training set for graph embedding. Next, a large number of different feature selection strategies can be applied to the resulting large scale vectors eliminating redundancies and noise, finding good features, and reducing the dimensionality. In (Riesen, 2008c), for instance, principal component analysis (PCA) and Fisher linear discriminant analysis (LDA) are applied to the vector space embedded graphs. Kernel PCA (Schölkopf, 1998), rather than traditional PCA, is used for feature transformation in (Riesen, 2008b}.

EXPERIMENTAL EVALUATION

In this section we provide the results of an experimental evaluation of the proposed embedding procedure. We aim at empirically confirming that the method of prototype based graph embedding and subsequent classification in real vector spaces is applicable to different graph classification problems and matches, or even surpasses, the performance of traditional techniques. For graph edit distance computation the suboptimal algorithm introduced in (Riesen, 2009a) has been used. This graph edit distance algorithm shows superior performance in time and accuracy compared to other suboptimal algorithms. For prototype selection we focus on three classwise selectors, viz. bps-c, sps-c, and *k*-cps-c. The classifier used in the embedding space is the support vector machine (SVM) (Vapnik, 1998). Of course, any other classifier could be used for this purpose as well. However, we feel that the SVM is particularly suitable because of its theoretical advantages and its superior performance that has been empirically confirmed in many practical classification problems.

Graph Data Sets

For evaluation, eight data sets from the IAM graph database repository (www.iam.unibe.ch/fki/databases/iam-graph-database) for graph based pattern recognition and machine learning are used (Riesen, 2008a).

The first graph data set involves graphs that represent distorted letter drawings (Letter). We consider the 15 capital letters of the Roman alphabet that consist of straight lines only (A, E, F,..., Z). For each class, a prototype line drawing is manually constructed. These prototype drawings are then converted into prototype graphs by representing lines by undirected edges and ending points of lines by nodes. Each node is labeled with a two-dimensional attribute giving its position relative to a reference coordinate system. Edges are unlabeled.

The second graph set (Digit) consists of graphs representing handwritten digits (Alpaydin, 1998). During the recording of the digits, the position of the pen was recorded at constant time intervals. The resulting sequences of (x, y)-coordinates were converted into graphs by inserting nodes in regular intervals between the starting and ending points of a line. Successive nodes are connected by undirected edges. Each node is labeled with a two-dimensional attribute giving its position relative to a reference coordinate system. The edges are attributed with an angle denoting the orientation of the edge with respect to the horizontal direction.

The third graph data set consists of graphs representing fingerprint images out of the four classes arch, left, right, and whorl from the Galton-Henry classification system (Fingerprint). The fingerprint database used in our experiments is based on the NIST reference database of fingerprints. In order to obtain graphs from fingerprint images, the relevant regions are binarized and a noise removal and thinning procedure is applied. This results in a skeletonized representation of the extracted regions. Ending points and bifurcation points of the skeletonized regions are represented by nodes. Additional nodes are inserted in regular intervals between ending points and bifurcation points. Finally, undirected edges are inserted to link nodes that are directly connected through a ridge in the skeleton. Each node is labeled with a two-dimensional attribute giving its position. The edges are attributed with an angle denoting the orientation of the edge with respect to the horizontal direction.

The GREC data set consists of graphs representing symbols from architectural and electronic drawings. The images occur at five different distortion levels. Depending on the distortion level, either erosion, dilation, or other morphological operations are applied. The result is thinned to obtain lines of one pixel width. Finally, graphs are extracted from the resulting denoised images

by tracing the lines from end to end and detecting intersections as well as corners. Ending points, corners, intersections and circles are represented by nodes and labeled with a two-dimensional attribute giving their position. The nodes are connected by undirected edges which are labeled as line or arc. An additional attribute specifies the angle with respect to the horizontal direction or the diameter in case of arcs. From the original GREC database (Dosch, 2006), 22 classes are considered.

The AIDS data set consists of graphs representing molecular compounds. We construct graphs from the AIDS Antiviral Screen Database of Active Compounds. This data set consists of two classes (active, inactive), which represent molecules with activity against HIV or not. The molecules are converted into graphs in a straightforward manner by representing atoms as nodes and the covalent bonds as edges. Nodes are labeled with the number of the corresponding chemical symbol and edges by the valence of the linkage.

In order to convert molecular compounds of the Mutagenicity data set (Kazius, 2004) into attributed graphs the same procedure as for the AIDS data set is applied. The Mutagenicity data set is divided into two classes: mutagen and nonmutagen.

The protein data set consists of graphs representing proteins originally used in (Borgwardt, 2005a). The proteins database consists of six classes (EC 1, EC 2, EC 3, EC 4, EC 5, EC 6), which represent proteins out of the six enzyme commission top level hierarchy (EC classes). The proteins are converted into graphs by representing the secondary structure elements of a protein with nodes and edges of an attributed graph. Nodes are labeled with their type (helix, sheet, or loop) and their amino acid sequence (e.g. TFKEVVRLT). Every node is connected with an edge to its three nearest neighbors in space. Edges are labeled with their type and the distance they represent in angstroms.

In (Schenker, 2005) several methods for creating graphs from web documents are introduced. For the graphs included in this data set (Web), the following method was applied. First, all words occurring in the web document -- except for stop words, which contain only little information -- are converted into nodes in the resulting web graph. We attribute each node with the corresponding word and its frequency. Next, different sections of the web document are investigated individually. If a word w_i immediately precedes word w_{i+1}, a directed edge from the node corresponding to word w_i to the node corresponding to the word w_{i+1} is inserted in our web graph. The resulting edge is attributed with the corresponding section label. In our experiments we make use of a data set with documents from 20 categories (Business, Health, Politics, etc). In Figure 3, a summary of the graph data set characteristics is given.

REFERENCE SYSTEMS AND EXPERIMENTAL SETUP

In contrast with the high representational power of graphs, we observe a lack of general classification algorithms that can be applied in the graph domain. One of the few classifiers directly applicable to arbitrary graphs is the k-nearest-neighbor classifier (k-NN). Given a labeled set of training graphs, an unknown graph is assigned to the class that occurs most frequently among the k nearest graphs (in terms of edit distance) from the training set. The decision boundary of this classifier is a piecewise linear function which makes it very flexible. This classifier in the graph domain will serve us as our first reference system.

The second reference system is the similarity kernel described before (sim) in conjunction with an SVM. Comparing the performance of this similarity kernel function with the performance of the dissimilarity embedding procedure offers us the possibility to understand whether the power

of our system is primarily due to the embedding process or to the strength of the kernel classifier.

In the validation phase, the costs of the edit operations are determined first. For all considered graph data sets but the web data, node and edge labels are integer numbers, real numbers, or real vectors. Here the substitution cost of a pair of labels is given by a distance measure (e.g. Euclidean distance), and only the deletion and insertion costs have to be determined. For the sake of symmetry, we assume in all experiments identical costs for node deletions and insertions, and for edge deletions and insertions. Hence only two parameters, i.e. node deletion/insertion cost, and edge deletion/insertion cost, need to be validated. For the web data set we followed the cost model used in (Schenker, 2005), i.e. node substitutions are not admissible and the costs of all other edit operations are set to an arbitrary constant. Consequently, no edit cost validation is needed for this data set.

For the second reference system (sim) the same edit distances as for the k-NN classifier are used. Hence, the weighting parameter C of the SVM, which controls whether the maximization of the margin or the minimization of the error is more important, and the meta parameter γ in the kernel function $\kappa(g,g')= \exp(-\gamma\, d(g,g'))$ have to be additionally validated.

For the task of graph embedding in real vector spaces one additional meta parameter has to be validated, namely the number of prototypes n, i.e. the dimensionality of the resulting vector space. In order to determine suitable values of n, each graph set is embedded in a vector space with all of the prototype selectors described, varying the dimensionality of the target vector space over a certain interval. With the resulting vector sets, which still consist of a validation, a training, and a test set, an SVM is trained. We make use of an SVM with RBF-kernel where besides the weighting parameter C, the meta parameter γ in the kernel function has to be optimized. In Figure 4(a) such

Figure 3. Summary of graph data set characteristics, viz. the size of the training (tr), the validation (va) and the test set (te), the number of classes (|Ω|), the label alphabet of both nodes and edges, the average and maximum number of nodes and edges (Ø/max nodes/edges)

Database	size (*tr, va, te*)	|Ω|	node labels	edge labels	Ø/max nodes	Ø/max edges
Letter	750, 750, 750	15	x, y coordinates	none	4.7/9	4.5/9
Digit	1,000, 500, 2,000	10	x, y coordinates	Angle	11.8/32	13.1/30
Fingerprint	500, 300, 2,000	4	x, y coordinates	Angle	5.4/26	4.4/24
GREC	836, 836, 1,628	22	Type/x, y coordinates	Type	11.5/25	12.2/30
AIDS	250, 250, 1,500	2	Chemical symbol	Valence	15.7/95	16.2/103
Mutagenicity	1,500, 500, 2,337	2	Chemical symbol	Valence	30.3/417	30.8/112
Protein	200, 200, 200	6	Type/AA-sequence	Type/length	32.6/126	62.1/149
Web	780, 780, 780	20	Word/Frequency	Type	186.1/834	104.6/596

an SVM parameter validation on the Fingerprint data set is illustrated.

The SVM optimization is performed on a validation set for every possible dimension of the target space and every prototype selection method. Thus, for each embedding procedure the classification accuracy can be regarded as a function of the dimensionality and the prototype selector. This final optimization is illustrated on the Fingerprint data set in Figure 4(b) where the ac-

curacies for three classwise prototype selectors (bps-c, sps-c, k-cps-c) and each dimensionality are shown.

By means of this procedure for each prototype selector the number of prototypes n and the SVM parameters (C, γ) can be determined for every data set on the validation set. The parameter combination that results in the lowest classification error is finally applied to the independent test set.

Figure 4. (a) Validation of the meta parameter tuple (C, γ) for a specific prototype selector and a certain number of prototypes (the parameter values are on a logarithmic scale to the basis 2); (b) Validation of three classwise prototype selectors

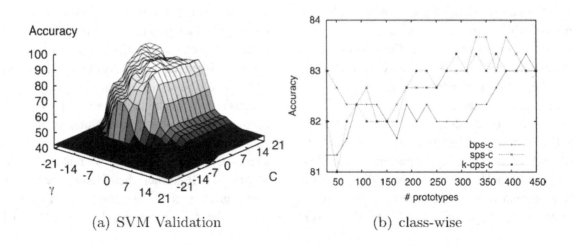

(a) SVM Validation   (b) class-wise

RESULTS AND DISCUSSION

The results obtained on the test set by means of this procedure are reported for three prototype selectors in Figure 5. Let us first compare the classification accuracies achieved by our embedding framework with the first reference system (*k*-NN). It clearly turns out that the novel procedure is much more powerful than the traditional *k*-NN classifier in the graph domain as on all tested applications the embedding based method outperforms the first reference system. Note that 19 out of 23 improvements are statistically significant.

Next we compare the embedding procedure with the similarity kernel (sim). It turns out that the similarity kernel is better on the Letter, Fingerprint, and Web data sets compared to at least one prototype selection method. However, the embedding framework outperforms the similarity kernel 16 times on the Digit, Fingerprint, GREC, AIDS, Mutagenicity and Protein data sets. Note that twelve of the improvements, but only

one of the deteriorations are statistically significant. From these findings we can conclude that the power of our novel approach primarily results from the embedding process itself and not from to the strength of the kernel classifier.

For a more detailed analysis of the proposed approach including a more thorough description of the achieved results we refer to (Riesen, 2010).

CONCLUSION

For objects given in terms of feature vectors a rich repository of algorithmic tools for classification has been developed over the last decades. Graphs are a versatile alternative to feature vectors, and are known to be a powerful and flexible representation formalism. The representational power of graphs is due to their ability to represent not only feature values but also relationships among different parts of an object, and their flexibility comes from the fact there are no size or labeling

Figure 5. Embedding methods vs. reference systems. ①/② Stat. significant improvement over the first/ second reference system (k-NN and sim). ② Stat. significant deterioration compared to the second reference system.

Data Set	ref. systems		embedding methods		
	k-NN	sim	sps-c	bps-c	*k*-cps-c
Letter	89.1	92.9	92.3 ①	92.9 ①	92.0 ①
Digit	97.4	98.1	98.6 ①②	98.7 ①②	98.7 ①②
Fingerprint	79.1	82.0	82.0 ①	83.1 ①②	81.7 ①
GREC	82.2	71.6	92.4 ①②	92.3 ①②	92.4 ①②
AIDS	94.9	97.0	98.1 ①②	98.0 ①②	98.1 ①②
Mutagenicity	66.9	68.6	71.6 ①②	70.7 ①	71.8 ①②
Protein	68.5	68.5	73.0	73.0	73.0
Web	80.6	82.9	82.7 ①	80.4 ❷	82.3

restrictions that constrain the representation of a given object. Due to their power and flexibility graphs have found widespread applications in computer vision and pattern recognition.

One of the major drawbacks of graph based representations is, however, that there is only little mathematical structure in the graph domain. In contrast to vectors, most of the basic mathematical operations required for many standard pattern recognition algorithms do not exist for graphs. Consequently, we observe a severe lack of algorithmic tools in the domain of graphs. Traditionally, tasks such as classification of graphs are solved by defining an appropriate distance measure and then using an algorithm that is based on distances exclusively (e.g. a nearest-neighbor classifier).

In the present chapter some recent approaches to implicit and explicit graph embedding are reviewed. Particularly, this chapter describes a novel approach to graph embedding using dissimilarities. The basic idea of the embedding method is to describe a graph by means of n dissimilarities to a predefined set of graphs termed prototypes. That is, a graph g is mapped explicitly to the n-dimensional real space R^n by arranging the distances of g to all of the n prototypes as a vector. By means of this procedure both statistical classifiers and vector kernels can be applied to the resulting graph maps.

As basic dissimilarity model the concept of graph edit distance is employed. The key advantages of graph edit distance are its high degree of flexibility, which makes it applicable to any type of graph, and the fact that one can integrate domain specific knowledge about object similarity by means of specific edit cost functions. Therefore, in contrast with some other graph embedding methods, there are no restrictions on the type of graphs the proposed embedding framework can deal with. Moreover, the dissimilarity embedding for graphs is particularly able to cope with noisy data.

The task of prototype selection is an issue in the proposed graph embedding framework. Several possible solutions have been proposed in the literature. Three algorithms from the category of heuristic prototype selection are described in detail in the present chapter. Note that none of them performs generally the best. That is, the quality of a particular selection strategy depends on the underlying data set.

In the experimental evaluation, the proposed graph embedding framework is compared to a nearest-neighbor classifier and another kernel-based classifier. In several experiments a high degree of robustness and flexibility of the proposed approach has been empirically verified in this chapter.

REFERENCES

Alpaydinm, E., & Alimoglu, F. (1998). *Pen-based recognition of handwritten digits*. Dept. of Computer Engineering, Bogazici University.

Ambauen, R., Fischer, S., & Bunke, H. (2003). Graph edit distance with node splitting and merging and its application to diatom identification. In E. Hancock & M. Vento (Eds.), *Proceedings of the 4th International Workshop on Graph Based Representations in Pattern Recognition, LNCS 2726*, (pp. 95-106). Springer.

Borgwardt, K., & Kriegel, H.-P. (2005a). Shortest-path kernels on graphs. In *Proceedings of the 5th International Conference on Data Mining*, (pp. 74-81).

Borgwardt, K., Ong, C., Schönauer, S., Vishwanathan, S., Smola, A., & Kriegel, H.-P. (2005b). Protein function prediction via graph kernels. *Bioinformatics (Oxford, England), 21*(1), 47–56. doi:10.1093/bioinformatics/bti1007

Bunke, H., & Allermann, G. (1983). Inexact graph matching for structural pattern recognition. *Pattern Recognition Letters, 1*, 245–253. doi:10.1016/0167-8655(83)90033-8

Bunke, H., Dickinson, P. J., Kraetzl, M., & Wallis, W. D. (2007). A graph-theoretic approach to enterprise network dynamics. *Progress in Computer Science and Applied Logic, 24.*

Bunke, H., & Sanfeliu, A. (Eds.). (1990). *Syntactic and structural pattern recognition*. World Scientific.

Caelli, T., & Kosinov, S. (2004). Inexact graph matching using eigen-subspace projection clustering. *International Journal of Pattern Recognition and Artificial Intelligence, 18*(3), 329–355. doi:10.1142/S0218001404003186

Chung-Graham, F. (1997). *Spectral graph theory*. AMS.

Conte, D., Foggia, P., Sansone, C., & Vento, M. (2004). Thirty years of graph matching in pattern recognition. *International Journal of Pattern Recognition and Artificial Intelligence, 18*(3), 265–298. doi:10.1142/S0218001404003228

Cook, D., & Holder, L. (Eds.). (2007). *Mining graph data*. Wiley-Interscience.

Dosch, P., & Valveny, E. (2007). Report on the second symbol recognition contest. In W. Liu & J. Llados (Eds.), *Graphics Recognition: Ten Years Review and Future Perspectives– Proceedings of the 6th International Workshop on Graphics Recognition, LNCS 3926*, (pp. 381-397). Springer.

Duda, R., Hart, P., & Stork, D. (2000). *Pattern classification* (2nd ed.). Wiley-Interscience.

Eshera, M. A., & Fu, K. S. (1984). A similarity measure between attributed relational graphs for image analysis. In *Proceedings of the 7th International Conference on Pattern Recognition*, (pp. 75-77).

Gärtner, T. (2003a). A survey of kernels for structured data. *SIGKDD Explorations, 5*(1), 49–58. doi:10.1145/959242.959248

Gärtner, T. (2008). *Kernels for structured data*. World Scientific.

Gärtner, T., Flach, P., & Wrobel, S. (2003b). On graph kernels: Hardness results and efficient alternatives. In B. Schökopf & M. Warmuth (Eds.), *Proceedings of the 16th Annual Conference on Learning Theory*, (pp. 129-143).

Haasdonk, B. (2005). Feature space interpretation of SVMs with indefinite kernels. *IEEE Transactions on Pattern Analysis and Machine Intelligence, 27*(4), 482–492. doi:10.1109/TPAMI.2005.78

Haussler, D. (1999). *Convolution kernels on discrete structures*. Technical Report UCSC-CRL-99-10, University of California, Santa Cruz.

Jiang, X., Münger, A., & Bunke, H. (2001). On median graphs: Properties, algorithms, and applications. *IEEE Transactions on Pattern Analysis and Machine Intelligence, 23*(10), 1144–1151. doi:10.1109/34.954604

Justice, D., & Hero, A. (2006). A binary linear programming formulation of the graph edit distance. *IEEE Transactions on Pattern Analysis and Machine Intelligence, 28*(8), 1200–1214. doi:10.1109/TPAMI.2006.152

Kandola, J., Shawe-Taylor, J., & Cristianini, N. (2002). Learning semantic similarity. *Neural Information Processing Systems, 15*, 657–664.

Kashima, H., & Inokuchi, A. (2002). Kernels for graph classification. In *Proceedings of the ICDM Workshop on Active Mining*, (pp. 31-36).

Kashima, H., Tsuda, K., & Inokuchi, A. (2003). Marginalized kernels between labeled graphs. In *Proceedings of the 20th International Conference on Machine Learning*, (pp. 321-328).

Kazius, J., McGuire, R., & Bursi, R. (2005). Derivation and validation of toxicophores for mutagenicity prediction. *Journal of Medicinal Chemistry, 48*(1), 312–320. doi:10.1021/jm040835a

Kondor, R., & Lafferty, J. (2002). Diffusion kernels on graphs and other discrete input spaces. In *Proceedings of the 19th International Conference on Machine Learning*, (pp. 315-322).

Lafferty, J., & Lebanon, G. (2003). Information diffusion kernels. *Advances in Neural Information Processing Systems, 15*, 375–382. MIT Press.

Lafferty, J., & Lebanon, G. (2005). Diffusion kernels on statistical manifolds. *Journal of Machine Learning Research, 6*, 129–163.

Lee, W. J., & Duin, R. (2009). A labelled graph based multiple classifier system. In J. A. Benediktsson, J. Kittler, & F. Roli (Eds.), *Proceedings of the 8th International Workshop on Multiple Classifier Systems, LNCS 5519*, (pp. 201-210).

Luo, B., & Hancock, E. (2001). Structural graph matching using the EM algorithm and singular value decomposition. *IEEE Transactions on Pattern Analysis and Machine Intelligence, 23*(10), 1120–1136. doi:10.1109/34.954602

Luo, B., Wilson, R., & Hancock, E. (2003). Spectral embedding of graphs. *Pattern Recognition, 36*(10), 2213–2223. doi:10.1016/S0031-3203(03)00084-0

Mahe, P., Ueda, N., & Akutsu, T. (2005). Graph kernels for molecular structures -- Activity relationship analysis with support vector machines. *Journal of Chemical Information and Modeling, 45*(4), 939–951. doi:10.1021/ci050039t

Neuhaus, M., & Bunke, H. (2007). *Bridging the gap between graph edit distance and kernel machines*. World Scientific.

Neuhaus, M., Riesen, K., & Bunke, H. (2006). Fast suboptimal algorithms for the computation of graph edit distance. In D.-Y. Yeung, J. T. Kwok, A. Fred, F. Roli, & D. de Ridder (Eds.), *Proceedings of the 11th International Workshop on Structural and Syntactic Pattern Recognition, LNCS 4109*, (pp. 163-172). Springer.

Pekalska, E., & Duin, R. (2005). *The dissimilarity representation for pattern recognition: Foundations and applications*. World Scientific, 2005.

Ralaivola, L., Swamidass, S. J., Saigo, H., & Baldi, P. (2005). Graph kernels for chemical informatics. *Neural Networks, 18*(8), 1093–1110. doi:10.1016/j.neunet.2005.07.009

Riesen, K., & Bunke, H. (2008a). IAM graph database repository for graph based pattern recognition and machine learning. In N. da Vitoria Lobo, et al., (Eds.), *Proceedings of the International Workshops on Structural, Syntactic, and Statistical Pattern Recognition, LNCS 5342*, (pp. 287-297).

Riesen, K., & Bunke, H. (2008b). Non-linear transformations of vector space embedded graphs. In Juan-Ciscar, A., & Sanchez-Albaladejo, G. (Eds.), *Pattern recognition in information systems* (pp. 173–186).

Riesen, K., & Bunke, H. (2008c). Reducing the dimensionality of dissimilarity space embedding graph kernels. *Engineering Applications of Artificial Intelligence, 22*(1), 48–56. doi:10.1016/j.engappai.2008.04.006

Riesen, K., & Bunke, H. (2009a). Approximate graph edit distance computation by means of bipartite graph matching. *Image and Vision Computing, 27*(4), 950–959. doi:10.1016/j.imavis.2008.04.004

Riesen, K., & Bunke, H. (2009b). Dissimilarity based vector space embedding of graphs using prototype reduction schemes. In P. Perner (Ed.), *Proceedings of the 6th International Conference on Machine Learning and Data Mining in Pattern, LNCS 5632*, (pp. 617-631).

Riesen, K., & Bunke, H. (2009c). Graph classification based on vector space embedding. *International Journal of Pattern Recognition and Artificial Intelligence, 23*(6), 1053–1081. doi:10.1142/S021800140900748X

Riesen, K., & Bunke, H. (2010). *Classification and clustering of vector space embedded graphs*. World Scientific.

Robles-Kelly, A., & Hancock, E. (2007). A Riemannian approach to graph embedding. *Pattern Recognition, 40*, 1024–1056. doi:10.1016/j.patcog.2006.05.031

Sanfeliu, A., & Fu, K. S. (1983). A distance measure between attributed relational graphs for pattern recognition. *IEEE Transactions on Systems, Man, and Cybernetics (Part B), 13*(3), 353–363.

Schenker, A., Bunke, H., Last, M., & Kandel, A. (2005). *Graph-theoretic techniques for Web content mining*. World Scientific.

Schölkopf, B., & Smola, A. (2002). *Learning with kernels*. MIT Press.

Schölkopf, B., Smola, A., & Müller, K.-R. (1998). Nonlinear component analysis as a kernel eigenvalue problem. *Neural Computation, 10*, 1299–1319. doi:10.1162/089976698300017467

Shawe-Taylor, J., & Cristianini, N. (2004). *Kernel methods for pattern analysis*. Cambridge University Press. doi:10.1017/CBO9780511809682

Smola, A., & Kondor, R. (2003). Kernels and regularization on graphs. In *Proceedings of the 16th International Conference on Comptuational Learning Theory*, (pp. 144-158).

Sorlin, S., & Solnon, C. (2005). Reactive tabu search for measuring graph similarity. In L. Brun & M. Vento (Eds.), *Proceedings of the 5th International Workshop on Graph-based Representations in Pattern Recognition, LNCS 3434*, (pp. 172-182). Springer.

Spillmann, B., Neuhaus, M., Bunke, H., Pekalska, E., & Duin, R. (2006). Transforming strings to vector spaces using prototype selection. In D.-Y. Yeung, J. T. Kwok, A. Fred, F. Roli, & D. de Ridder (Eds.), *Proceedings of the 11th International Workshop on Structural and Syntactic Pattern Recognition, LNCS 4109*, (pp. 287-296). Springer.

Tsuda, K. (1999). Support vector classification with asymmetric kernel function. In M. Verleysen (Ed.), *Proceedings 7th European Symposium on Artificial Neural Networks*, (pp. 183-188).

Vapnik, V. (1998). *Statistical learning theory*. John Wiley.

Watkins, C. (1999). *Kernels from matching operations*. Technical Report CSD-TR-98-07, Royal Holloway College.

Watkins, C. (2000). Dynamic alignment kernels. In Smola, A., Bartlett, P. L., Schölkopf, B., & Schuurmans, D. (Eds.), *Advances in large margin classifiers* (pp. 39–50). MIT Press.

Wilson, R. C., Hancock, E., & Luo, B. (2005). Pattern vectors from algebraic graph theory. *IEEE Transactions on Pattern Analysis and Machine Intelligence, 27*(7), 1112–1124. doi:10.1109/TPAMI.2005.145

Chapter 9
Generative Group Activity Analysis with Quaternion Descriptor

Guangyu Zhu
National University of Singapore, Singapore

Shuicheng Yan
National University of Singapore, Singapore

Tony X. Han
University of Missouri, USA

Changsheng Xu
Chinese Academy of Sciences, China

ABSTRACT

Activity understanding plays an essential role in video content analysis and remains a challenging open problem. Most of previous research is limited due to the use of excessively localized features without sufficiently encapsulating the interaction context or focus on simply discriminative models but totally ignoring the interaction patterns. In this chapter, a new approach is proposed to recognize human group activities. Firstly, the authors designed a new quaternion descriptor to describe the interactive insight of activities regarding the appearance, dynamic, causality, and feedback, respectively. The designed descriptor along with the conventional velocity and position are capable of delineating the individual and pairwise interactions in the activities. Secondly, considering both activity category and interaction variety, the authors propose an extended pLSA (probabilistic Latent Semantic Analysis) model with two hidden variables. This extended probabilistic graphic paradigm constructed on the quaternion descriptors facilitates the effective inference of activity categories as well as the exploration of activity interaction patterns. The extensive experiments on realistic movie and human group activity datasets validate that the multilevel features are effective for activity interaction representation and demonstrate that the graphic model is a promising paradigm for activity recognition.

DOI: 10.4018/978-1-4666-1891-6.ch009

INTRODUCTION

Video-based human activity analysis is one of the most promising applications of computer vision and pattern recognition. Turaga *et al.* (2008) presented a recent survey of the major approaches pursued over the last two decades. Large amount of the existing work on this problem mainly focused on the relatively simple activities of single person (Laptev, 2003; Liu, 2009; Niebles, 2008; Schuldt, 2004; Wang, 2009), e.g., sitting, walking and hand-waving, which has achieved particular success. In recent years, recognition of group activity with multiple participators (e.g., fighting and gathering) is gaining increasing amount of interests (Marszalek, 2009; Ni, 2009; Ryoo, 2007; Zhou, 2008) from both academia and industry.

Upon the definition given by Turaga (2008), where an activity is referred to a complex sequence of actions performed by several objects who could be interacting with each other, the interactions among the participants reflect the elementary characteristics of different activities. The effective interaction descriptor is therefore essential for developing sophisticated approaches of activity recognition. Most previous research stems from the local representation in image processing. As shown in Figure 1(a), the common sense of constructing local representation is to extract the pattern descriptors (*e.g.*, SIFT (Lowe, 2004)) from spatial salient points and generate the feature representation (*e.g.*, bag-of-SIFT accordingly) using bag-of-words strategy. Such successful scenario has been naturally extended to the video processing by extracting the pattern descriptors based on spatio-temporal salient points (Laptev, 2003; Liu, 2009; Marszalek, 2009; Niebles, 2008; Schuldt, 2004). Although the widely used local descriptors are demonstrated to allow for the recognition of activities in the scenes with occlusions and dynamic cluttered backgrounds, they are solely representations of appearance and motion patterns.

Figure 1. Comparison of representation and modeling for image and video analysis: (a) Image representation and modeling; (b) Video representation and modeling

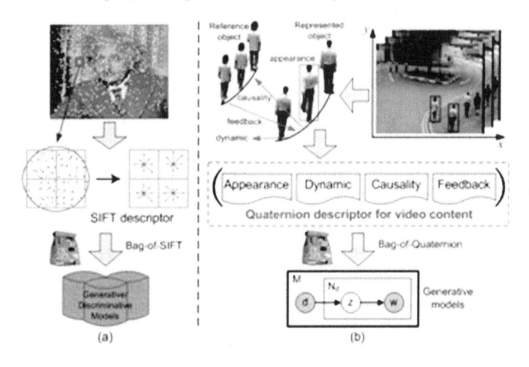

An effective feature descriptor for activity recognition should have the capacity of describing the video in terms of the object appearance, dynamic motion as well as the interactive properties.

With the activity descriptor, how to make the decision for the activity category classification using the feature representation accordingly is another key issue for activity recognition. Two types of approach are widely used: approaches based on generative model (Niebles, 2008; Wang, 2009) and the ones based on discriminative model (Laptev, 2003; Liu, 2009; Marszalek, 2009; Ni, 2009; Ryoo, 2007; Schuldt, 2004: Zhou, 2008). Considering the mechanism of human perception for group activity, the interactions between objects are firstly distinguished and then synthesized as the activity recognition result. Although discriminative models have been extensively employed because they are much easier to build up, the construction of discriminative models essentially focus on the differences among the activity classes yet ignore the interactive properties involved. Therefore, discriminative models cannot facilitate the interaction analysis and discover the insight of the interactive relations in the activities. In this paper, we firstly investigate how to effectively represent video activities in the interaction context.

Figure 1(b) presents a brief illustration of the extraction in video processing for the new feature descriptor, namely the quaternion descriptor. The quaternion descriptor consists of four types' components in terms of appearance, individual dynamic, pairwise causalities and feedbacks of the video active objects, respectively. The components in the descriptor describe the appearance and motion patterns as well as encode the interaction properties in the activities. Resorting to the bag-of-words method, the video is represented as a compact bag-of-quaternion feature vector. To recognize the activity category and facilitate the interaction pattern exploration, we then propose to model and classify the activities in a generative framework which is based on an extended pLSA model. Interactions are modeled in the generative framework, which is able to explicitly infer the activity patterns.

OVERVIEW OF THE PROPOSED FRAMEWORK

In general, the procedure of an activity recognition approach can be divided into three layers: 1) a pre-processing layer in which the elementary processing atoms in the activity video footage are generated; 2) a video representation layer in which the activity footage is described by a compact feature vector extracted from the video atoms; 3) an activity modeling and recognition layer in which the activity category is recognized by classifying the compact feature representation. Following this paradigm, Figure 2 illustrates the framework of our approach.

The proposed approach starts by generating the trajectory atoms since the trajectory encodes the object properties regarding spatial locations for appearance representation and temporal evolutions for interaction representation and causality analysis. For different application requirements, the trajectory atoms can be generated from the salient points using local feature matching (Sun, 2009) or the human blobs using moving object tracking (Ni, 2009).

Interactions are typically demonstrated having considerable variations in both spatial and temporal domains. An effective interaction representation that is invariant or tolerant to both spatial and temporal variations are indispensable for recognizing activities. Our approach strives to capture the characteristics of activities by extracting interaction features from various relations within and among the trajectory atoms. Given a trajectory and the corresponding neighborhood atoms, we extract the quaternion descriptor in terms of its spatial appearance (SIFT descriptor (Lowe, 2004)), individual dynamic transition (Markov stationary distribution (Sun, 2009)),

Figure 2. The proposed activity modeling and recognition framework based on quaternion descriptor and generative model

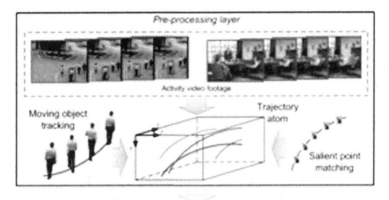

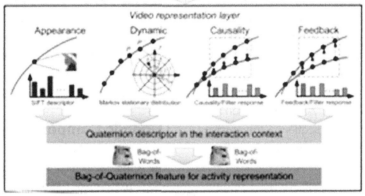

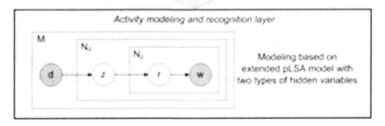

and pairwise influence acting on others (causality (Granger, 1969; Zhou, 2008)) as well as the response getting back (feedback (Granger, 1969; Zhou, 2008)). The bag-of-words (BoW) model is exploited to construct the bag-of-quaternion as the feature representation for the activity footage by measuring the frequencies of extracted quaternion representations with visual vocabulary.

Distinguished from discriminative models, generative models attempt to describe data distributions and infer the dependence among different distributions. Also, as opposed to discriminative methods such as support vector machines, generative methods allow the algorithm to perform meaningful reasoning on the data beyond classification. Probabilistic Latent Semantic Analysis (pLSA) is one of the representative generative modeling methods. In our approach, the activity category is modeled and classified based on a two-hidden-variable pLSA model, which is able to explore the activity interaction patterns. In the proposed modeling scenario, interaction patterns are modeled by one of the hidden variables and reasoned using improved EM algorithm.

QUATERNION DESCRIPTOR FOR ACTIVITY REPRESENTATION

We propose to construct the quaternion descriptor by extracting the trajectory atoms and then modeling the spatio-temporal interaction information within these trajectories.

Appearance Component of Quaternion

The importance of spatial appearance information in activity recognition has been widely discussed in the literature (Liu, 2009; Marszalek, 2009; Niebles, 2008; Sun, 2009; Wang, 2009). It has been demonstrated that the appearance information encoded in the image frames can provide critical implication on the semantic categories (Mortensen, 2005; Torralba, 2003). For video activity recognition over frame sequence, this source of information is also very useful in describing the semantics of activities.

In recent years, the well-known SIFT feature (Lowe, 2004) is acknowledged as one of the most powerful appearance descriptors and has achieved overwhelming success in object categorization and recognition. In our approach, the appearance component of quaternion descriptor is measured as the average of all the SIFT features extracted at the salient points residing on the trajectory. For a motion trajectory with temporal length k, the SIFT average descriptor S is computed from all the SIFT descriptors $\{S_1, S_2, ..., S_k\}$ along the trajectory, namely

$$S = \frac{1}{k} \sum_{i=1}^{k} S_i \qquad (1)$$

The essential idea of the appearance representation is twofold. First, the tracking process ensures that the local image patches on the same trajectory are relatively stable, and therefore the resultant SIFT average descriptor provides a robust representation for certain aspect of visual content in the activity footage. Second, the SIFT average descriptor can also encode partially the temporal context information which will contribute the recognition task (Liu, 2004).

To facilitate efficient processing, we employ the bag-of-words method to describe the appearance representation as a compact feature vector. The bag-of-words method has attracted increasing research attention. We construct a visual vocabulary with 2048 words by K-means algorithm over the sampled SIFT average descriptors. Then, each SIFT average descriptor is assigned to its closest (in the sense of Euclidean distance) visual word. The histogram of visual word occurrences in activity footage forms the final representation at the appearance level for the interaction context of a trajectory.

Dynamic Component of Quaternion

The appearance representation depicts the local image patterns of the objects. The dynamic component however mainly characterizes the transition property of the object motion trajectory, namely how the object affects/interacts with itself over the temporal domain dynamically.

We propose to calculate the Markov stationary distribution (Breiman, 1992) as the dynamic representation in the quaternion. The Markov chain is a powerful tool for modeling the dynamic properties of a system as a compact representation. Its merit mainly lies in its capability of representing directed causal and probabilistic relationships. The Markov stationary distribution related to an ergodic Markov chain provides a compact and effective representation for a dynamic system. We consider each trajectory as a dynamic system and extract such a compact representation to measure the spatio-temporal interactions in the activities. Figure 3 shows the extraction procedure of dynamic component.

The existing work (Sun, 2009) has demonstrated that a trajectory can be encoded by the

Figure 3. The procedure for dynamic component extraction: (a) Displacement vector quantization; (b) State transition diagram; (c) Occurrence matrix; (d) Markov stationary distribution

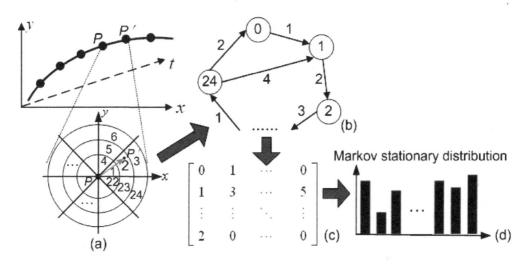

Markov stationary distribution π if it can be converted into an ergodic finite-state Markov chain. To facilitate this conversion, a finite number of states are chosen for quantization. Given points P and P' within two consecutive frames on the same trajectory, $D = PP'$ denotes the displacement vector of two points. To perform a comprehensive quantization on D, both of the magnitude and orientation are considered as shown in Figure 3(a). For magnitude, we can set 3 uniform quantization levels. $|D|$ is firstly normalized by the largest displacement magnitude $|D|_{max}$ residing in the same trajectory, which counters the effect of scale and facilitates the quantization being scale-invariant. For orientation, we can partition the full circle into 8 equal sectors with each subtending 45°. The combination of magnitude and orientation quantization constructs a 24-bin polar coordinate plus an additional bin to collect the zero movement resulting in 25 bins.

We translate the sequential relations between the displacement vectors into a directed graph, which is similar to the state diagram of a Markov chain (Figure 3(b)). In this work, we get a square matrix which is 25 vertices corresponding to the 25 quantization states and weighted edges cor-

responding to the occurrence of each transition among the states. Further, we establish the equivalent matrix presentation of the graph and perform row-normalization on the matrix to obtain a valid transition matrix P for a certain Markov chain (Figure 3(c)). To ensure the transition matrix P associating with an ergodic Markov chain, we initialize the state diagram with some negligible weights (e.g., $w_0 = 0.15$) between any two vertices before calculating the occurrences.

Finally, we use the iterative algorithm in (Sun, 2009) to compute the Markov stationary distribution π (Figure 3(d)), which is

$$A_n = \frac{1}{n}(I + P + \cdots + P^n) \tag{2}$$

where I is an identity matrix and n=100 in the experiments. To further reduce the approximation error from using a finite n, π is calculated as the column average of A_n. More details about the extraction of Markov chain distribution can be found in (Sun, 2009).

We employ the same procedure to transform every trajectory in a video into corresponding stationary vector representation. In order to extract the interaction representation in activity footage, we also utilize the bag-of-words method to build a histogram of the occurrence based on the calculated Markov chain stationary distribution features. The size of the BoW vocabulary is set to be 128 empirically.

Causality and Feedback Components

Motion trajectory has been proved to be effective in single-role activity analysis (Turaga, 2007). The interaction in terms of causality and feedback belongs to a high-level concept and reflects both spatial and temporal information of two active objects. Conventionally, each point on a motion trajectory is characterized by its position, velocity and curvature features. These features are useful for describing the activity of one object but there still exists a large gap between these middle-level information and the high-level concept, which is more complicated than single-trajectory based activity. To describe the causality and feedback properties, we propose a representation scheme based on Granger causality test (GCT) (Granger, 1969) and time-to-frequency transform (Jury, 1958).

Given a concurrent motion trajectory pair of $T_a = [T_a(1),...,T_a(n),...]$ and $T_b = [T_b(1),...,T_b(n),...]$, we assume that the interaction between two trajectories is a stationary process, *i.e.*, the prediction functions $P(T_a(n) \mid T_a(1:n-l), T_b(1:n-l))$ and $P(T_b(n) \mid T_a(1:n-l), T_b(1:n-l))$ do not change within a short time period, where $T_a(1:n-l) = [T_a(1),...,T_a(n-l)]$ and the same to $T_b(1:n-l)$, l is a time lag avoiding the overfitting issue in prediction. To model $P(T_a(n) \mid T_a(1:n-l), T_b(1:n-l))$, we can use k-th order linear predictor which is

$$T_a(n) =$$
$$\sum_{i=1}^{k} \beta(i)T_a(n-i-l) + \gamma(i)T_b(n-i-l) + \varepsilon_a(n)$$

(3)

where $\beta(i)$ and $\gamma(i)$ are the regression coefficients and $\varepsilon_a(n)$ is the Gaussian noise with standard deviation $\sigma(T_a(n) \mid T_a(1:n-l), T_b(1:n-l))$. These model parameters can be derived based on the concurrent motion trajectory segment pair of T_a and T_b. Similarly, we use the linear predictor to model $P(T_a(n) \mid T_a(1:n-l))$ and the standard deviation of the noise signal is denoted as $\sigma(T_a(n) \mid T_a(1:n-l))$. According to the GCT theory, we can calculate two measurements, namely causality ratio r_c as

$$r_c = \frac{\sigma(T_a(n) \mid T_a(1:n-l))}{\sigma(T_a(n) \mid T_a(1:n-l), T_b(1:n-l))}$$

(4)

which measures the relative strength of the causality, and feedback ratio r_f as

$$r_c = \frac{\sigma(T_b(n) \mid T_b(1:n-l))}{\sigma(T_b(n) \mid T_a(1:n-l), T_b(1:n-l))}$$

(5)

which measures the relative strength of the feedback.

The causality ratio and feedback ratio can well characterize how strong one object affects the motion of another one (Ni, 2009; Zhou, 2008), but cannot encode the underlying mechanism that drives the motions of these two objects. The parameters $\beta(i)$ and $\gamma(i)$ however essentially characterize how one object affects another one. If we regard the relationship in Equation 3 as a digital filter with the input signal as $T_b(n)$ and the output signal as $T_a(n)$, we can calculate the z-transforms for both sides and obtain the following equation by ignoring the noise term

$$X_a(z) = \sum_{i=1}^{k} \beta(i)X_a(z)z^{-i-l} + \gamma(i)X_b(z)z^{-i-l} \quad (6)$$

where $X_a(z)$ and $X_b(z)$ are the z-transforms for the output and input signals, respectively. Denoting the impulse response of this digital filter as $H_{ba}(z)$ and based on the relation of $H_{ba} = X_a(z)/X_b(z)$, we can obtain

$$H_{ba}(z) = \frac{\sum_{i=1}^{k} \gamma(i)z^{-i-l}}{1 - \sum_{i=1}^{k} \beta(i)z^{-i-l}} \quad (7)$$

from which we can observe that this digital filter is an infinite impulse response (IIR) digital filter.

Afterwards, the magnitudes and the phases of the z-transform function at a set of evenly sampled frequencies are employed to describe the digital filter for the style of the pairwise causality/feedback. In our approach, we employ the magnitudes of the frequency response at $\{0, \pi/4, \pi/2, 3\pi/4, \pi\}$ and the phases of the frequency response at $\{\pi/4, \pi/2, 3\pi/4\}$ to form the feature vector f_{ba}, namely

$$f_{ba} = [| H_{ba}(e^{j0}) |, | H_{ba}(e^{j\pi/4}) |, \ldots,$$
$$| H_{ba}(e^{j\pi}) |, \angle H_{ba}(e^{j\pi/4}), \ldots, H_{ba}(e^{j3\pi/4})] \quad (8)$$

Similarly, we can define the feature vector f_{ab} by considering T_a as the input and T_b as the output of the digital filter, which characterizes

how the object with the trajectory T_a affects the motion of the object with the trajectory T_b

The causality ratio and feedback ratio characterize the strength of one object affecting another one, while the extracted frequency response f_{ab} and f_{ba} convey how one object affects another one. These mutually complementary features are hence combined to form the causality and feedback components of quaternion descriptor in the pairwise interaction context. Note that an inter-trajectory descriptor named as trajectory proximity was proposed in (Sun, 2009) to describe the pairwise context information. Compared with the trajectory proximity descriptor extracted using global analysis ideology, our causality and feedback descriptors are essentially local description which is able to represent more elegant detail of the pairwise interaction patterns.

Similar to the extraction of appearance level and individual level representation, the bag-of-words histogram feature is calculated as the final interaction level representation of the activity video. The vocabulary size is empirically set to be 256.

GENERATIVE ACTIVITY ANALYSIS

Given a collection of unlabeled video sequences, we would like to discover a set of classes from them. Each of these classes would correspond to an activity category. Additionally, we would like to be able to understand activities that are composed of the mixture of interaction varieties. This resembles the problem of automatic topic discovery which can be figured out by latent topic analysis. In the following, we will introduce a new generative method based on pLSA modeling (Hofmann, 999), which is able to both infer the activity categories and discover the interaction patterns.

Generative Activity Modeling

Figure 4 shows the extended pLSA graphic model which is employed with the consideration of both activity category and interaction variety. Nodes are random variables. Shaded ones are observed and unshaded ones are unobserved (hidden). The plates indicate repetitions. d represents video sequence, z is the activity category, r is the interaction variety and w is the activity representation bag-of-word. The parameters of this model are learnt in an unsupervised manner using an improved EM algorithm.

Compared with the traditional philosophy, the interaction distribution is modeled in our method and integrated into the graphic framework as a new hidden variable. To make the presentation consistently, we adapt the notation and terminology as needed from the ones introduced in (Hofmann, 1999).

In the context of activity recognition, suppose we have a set of M $\left(j = 1, ..., M\right)$ video sequences containing the bag-of-words of interaction representations quantized from the vocabulary of size V $\left(i = 1, ..., V\right)$. The corpus of videos is summarized in a V-by-M co-occurrence table $\bar{M}$ where $m(w_i, d_j)$ is the number of occurrences of a word $w_i \in W = \{w_1, ..., w_V\}$ in video $d_j \in D = \{d_1, ..., d_M\}$. In addition, there are two latent topic variables $z \in Z = \{z_1, ..., z_K\}$ and

$r \in R = \{r_1, ..., r_R\}$ which represent the activity category and interaction variety resided in a certain activity. The variable r_i is sequentially associated with each occurrence of a word w_i in video d_j. Extending from the traditional pLSA model, the joint probability $P(w, d, z, r)$ which translates the inference process in Figure 4 is expressed as follows:

$$P(d, w) = \sum_{z \in Z} \sum_{r \in R} P(d)P(z \mid d)P(r \mid z)P(w \mid r) \qquad (9)$$

To determine $P(d)$, $P(z \mid d)$, $P(r \mid z)$ and $P(w \mid r)$, we can follow the likelihood principle by maximizing the log-likelihood function

$$L = \sum_{d \in D} \sum_{w \in W} m(d, w) \log P(d, w) \qquad (10)$$

It is worth noticing that an equivalent symmetric version of the model can be obtained by inverting the conditional probability $P(z \mid d)$ with the help of Bayes' rule, which results in

$$P(d, w) = \sum_{z \in Z} \sum_{r \in R} P(z)P(d \mid z)P(r \mid z)P(w \mid r) \qquad (11)$$

The standard procedure for maximum likelihood estimation in latent variable models is the

Figure 4. The extended pLSA model with two hidden variables

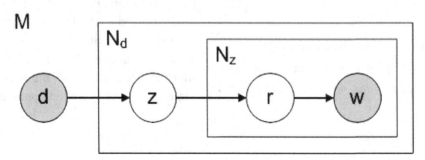

Expectation Maximization (EM). For the proposed pLSA model in the symmetric parameterization, Bayes' rule yields the E-step as

$$P(z, r \mid d, w) =$$
$$\frac{P(z)P(d \mid z)P(r \mid z)P(w \mid r)}{\sum_{z'}\sum_{r'} P(z')P(d \mid z')P(r' \mid z')P(w \mid r')}$$

(12)

$$P(z \mid d, w) = \sum_{r'} P(z, r \mid d, w)$$

(13)

$$P(r \mid d, w) = \sum_{z'} P(z, r \mid d, w)$$

(14)

which is the probability that a word w in a particular video sequence d is explained by the factor corresponding to z and r. By standard calculations, one arrives at the following M-step re-estimation equations:

$$P(d \mid z) = \frac{\sum_{w} m(d, w)P(z \mid d, w)}{\sum_{d', w} m(d', w)P(z \mid d', w)}$$

(15)

$$P(w \mid r) = \frac{\sum_{d} m(d, w)P(z \mid d, w)}{\sum_{d, w'} m(d, w')P(z \mid d, w')}$$

(16)

$$P(z) = \frac{1}{R} \sum_{d, w} m(d, w)P(z \mid d, w)$$

(17)

$$P(z, r) = \frac{1}{R} \sum_{d, w} m(d, w)P(z, r \mid d, w)$$

(18)

$$P(r \mid z) = \frac{P(z, r)}{P(z)}$$

(19)

$$R \equiv \sum_{d, w} m(d, w)$$

(20)

Generative Activity Recognition

Given that our algorithm has learnt the activity category models using extended pLSA, our goal is to categorize new video sequences.

We have obtained the activity-category-specific interaction distribution $P(r \mid z)$ and the interaction-pattern-specific video-word distribution $P(w \mid r)$ from a different set of training sequences at learning stage. When given a new video clip, the unseen video is "projected" on the simplex spanned by the learnt $P(r \mid z)$ and $P(w \mid r)$. We need to find the mixing coefficients $P(z_k \mid d_{test})$ such that the Kullback-Leibler divergence between the measured empirical distribution $\tilde{P}(w \mid d_{test})$ and $P(w \mid d_{test}) = \sum_{k=1}^{K} P(z_k \mid d_{test}) P(r \mid z_k)P(w \mid r)$ is minimized (Hofmann, 1999). Similar to the learning scenario, we apply the EM algorithm to find the solution. The sole difference between recognition and learning is that the learnt $P(r \mid z)$ and $P(w \mid r)$ are never updated during inference. Thus, a categorization decision is made by selecting the activity category that best explains the observation, that is

$$ActivityCategory = \arg\max_{k} P(z_k \mid d_{test})$$

(21)

Interaction Pattern Exploration and Discovery Based on Generative Model

The generative model facilitates the inference of the dependence among the different distributions in the recognition flow. In the extend pLSA paradigm, the distribution of the interaction patterns is modeled as a hidden variable r bridging the category topic z and visual-word observation w explicitly encoded by $P(r \mid z)$ and $P(w \mid r)$, respectively. Two tasks can be achieved by investigating one of the distributions $P(w \mid r)$, namely interaction amount discovery and pattern exploration.

The aim of the discovery is to infer the optimal amount of interaction patterns in the activities. The strategy is to transverse the sampled amounts of interaction patterns and observe the corresponding recognition performance. We define $K = \{1, \ldots, R\}$ as the candidate set of the amount of interaction patterns. Give an interaction pattern amount $k \in K$, the corresponding extended pLSA model is learnt and the recognition performance is denoted as m_k. Therefore, we can obtain the optimal interaction pattern amount *OptInterNo* in the underlying activities as

$$OptInterNo = \arg \max_k \{m_k\} \qquad (22)$$

Given the learnt $P(w \mid r)$ which bears the interaction amount *OptInterNo*, the particular patterns are able to be explored and visualized following three steps. Firstly, we transverse all the interaction patterns to form a set of visual words $WS = \{w_1, \ldots, w_{OptInterNo}\}$ where w_i is the word with the maximum probability $P(w \mid r_i)$ for pattern i, $i = 1, \ldots, OptInterNo$. Then, all the extracted quaternions are calculated with the elements in WS and generate the set $WQ = \{q_1, \ldots, q_{OptInterNo}\}$ where q_i is the quaternion with the minimum Euclidean distance to the

center of pattern i. Finally, we can visualize the trajectory atoms from which q_i is extracted in 3D *xyt*-coordinate space.

EXPERIMENTS

To demonstrate the effectiveness of our approach, we performed thorough experiments on two realistic human activity databases: the HOHA-2 database of movie videos used in (Marszalek, 2009) and the HGA database of surveillance videos used in (Ni, 2009). These two databases are chosen for evaluation because they exhibit the difficulties in recognizing realistic human activities with multiple participants, which is in contrast to the controlled settings in other related databases.

The HOHA-2 database is composed of 8 single activities (*i.e.*, AnswerPhone, DriveCar, Eat, GetOutCar, Run, SitDown, SitUp, and StandUp) and 4 group activities (*i.e.*, FightPerson, HandShake, HugPerson, and Kiss), in which 4 group activities are selected as the evaluation set. The HGA database consists of 6 group activities, in which all the samples are employed for evaluation. A brief summary of these two databases used in the experiments is provided in Table 1. More details about the databases can be found in (Marszalek, 2009; Ni, 2009).

Table 1. A summary of the databases for human group activity recognition

Database:	HOHA-2 group subset (Marszalek, 2009)	HGA (Ni, 2009)
Data source:	Movie clips	Surveillance recorders
# Class category	4	6
# Training samples	823	4 of 5 collected sessions
# Testing samples	884	1 of 5 collected sessions

To facilitate efficient processing, we employ the bag-of-words method to describe the quaternion descriptors in one activity video footage as a compact feature vector, namely bag-of-quaternion. We construct a visual vocabulary with 3000 words by K-means method over the sampled quaternion descriptors. Then, each quaternion is assigned to its closest (in the sense of Euclidean distance) visual word.

Recognition Performance on HOHA Database

In the pre-processing of this evaluation, the trajectory atoms in every shot are firstly generated by salient points matching using SIFT features. It has been demonstrated that this trajectory generation method is effective for the motion capture in movie footage (Sun, 2009).

In the experiment, the appearance and dynamic representations are extracted from every salient point trajectory. The salient points residing in the same region may share the similar appearance and motion patterns. The extraction of causality and feedback descriptors on the raw trajectory atoms is not necessary and computation-intensive. Efficiently, we perform a spectral clustering based on normalized cut algorithm (Shi, 2000) on the set of raw trajectory atoms in one video shot. The average trajectory atom, which is calculated as the representative for the corresponding cluster, is employed as the input of the extraction of causality and feedback descriptors. To construct the graph for clustering, each node represents a trajectory atom and the similarity matrix $W = [e_{i,j}]$ is formed with the similarities defined as

$$e_{i,j} = (P_i^T \cdot P_j) \cdot (S_i^T \cdot S_j) \qquad (23)$$

where i and j represent the indices of trajectory atoms in the video shot, $P = \{(x_1, y_1), (x_2, y_2), ..., (x_n, y_n)\}$

is the set of spatial positions of a trajectory atom and $S = \{s_1, s_2, ..., s_n\}$ is its SIFT descriptor set.

To quantitatively evaluate the performance, we calculate the Average Precision (AP) as the evaluation metric. Note that the AP metric is calculated on the whole database for an equitable comparison with the previous work although we only investigate 4 group activities. Figure 5 shows the recognition results by using different types of interaction features as well as their combination compared with the state-of-the-art performance in (Marszalek, 2009). In (Marszalek, 2009), the SIFT, HoF and HoG descriptors are extracted from the spatio-temporal salient points detected by 2D and 3D Harris detectors. Bag-of-words features are built as the compact representation for the video activities, which are the input of the SVM classifier. From Figure 5, we can conclude that our quaternion descriptor and generative model yields the highest AP performance than the latest report. More specifically, the Mean AP is improved from the latest reported 37.8% in (Marszalek, 2009) to 44.9%.

Another observation from the results is that the pairwise causality and feedback features outperform other components in the quaternion descriptor, which demonstrate that the interaction features are indispensable for the task of group activity recognition.

Recognition Performance on HGA Database

The HGA database is mainly proposed for human trajectory based group activity analysis. The humans in the database are much smaller so that the appearance features do not present any contribution to the recognition task. Consequently, the trajectory atoms of HGA database are generated by blob tracking. Each human in the activity video is considered as a 2D blob, and then the task is to locate the positions in the frame sequence. Our tracking method is based on

Figure 5. Comparison of the authors' approach with the salient point features and discriminative model in (Marszalek, 2009) on HOHA-2 database

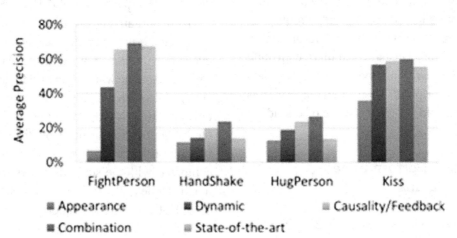

the Condensation algorithm (Isard, 1998) with manual initializations. 100 particles were used in the experiments for the tradeoff of accuracy and computational cost. Accordingly, dynamic and causality/feedback components in the proposed quaternion descriptor are employed to describe the activity video footage.

Figure 6 lists the recognition accuracies in terms of confusion matrices by using different types of interaction descriptors as well as their combination. From Figure 6(a) and Figure 6(b), we can observe that the causality/feedback component outperforms the dynamic component on

HGA database. This is easy to understand that for two different activity categories, e.g., walking-in-group and gathering, the motion trajectory segments of the specific person may be similar while they have different interactive relations, which can be easily differentiated by the pairwise representation. Therefore, when combing two types of interaction descriptors, the recognition performance can be further improved as shown in Figure 6(c). Compared with the results reported in (Ni, 2009), in which the best performance is 74% for average accuracy of all the activities, the proposed work achieves the better result with 87%

Figure 6. The confusion matrices of HGA database recognition results with different interaction representations

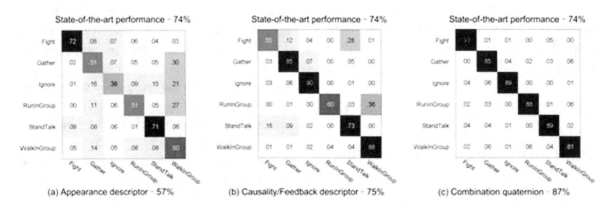

average accuracy. Note that the confusions are reasonable in the sense that most of the misclassification occurs between very similar motions, for instance, there is confusion between run-in-group and walk-in-group.

Interaction Pattern Exploration and Discovery

We further evaluate the capacity of the proposed extended pLSA for exploring and discovering the interaction patterns in HGA database. The reason we select HGA database as the evaluation set is that the trajectory atoms in HGA are the human blob loca in spatio-temporal space which bear the intuitive semantics for visualization.

Taking the pairwise causality and feedback interactions as the example, we explored different numbers of interaction patterns, varying from 8 to 256. The corresponding pLSA model was learnt against each number on the training sessions and then evaluated on the testing session. Figure 7 shows the exploration results of the recognition performance against the variant amount of interaction patterns. From Figure 7, we can observe some

insight between the supposed pattern amount and the recognition performance. The performance is significantly improved by 17.2% for average recognition accuracy when increasing the pattern number from 8 to 32 because more and more interactions can be covered by the learnt model. However, the performance is degenerated and dropped down by 10.5% with the increase of the pattern amount to 256. This is due to the fact that the learnt model with larger pattern amount intends to overfit to the training data, resulting to a less generalizable model.

Therefore, the amount of interaction patterns in HGA database is inferred as 32. Based on the proposed scheme of pattern discovery and visualization, we can illustrate the 32 patterns of the activities out as drawn in Figure 8.

CONCLUSION

In this paper, we propose a novel approach for generative activity analysis based on a quaternion descriptor in the interaction context. Four types of features in terms of appearance, dynamic, causality

Figure 7. The exploration results of the recognition performance against the number of pairwise interaction patterns on HGA database

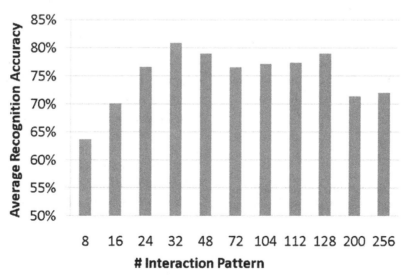

Figure 8. An illustration of the pairwise causality and feedback interaction patterns discovered from the human group activity database. The red segments are the reference object trajectories and the blue ones are the neighbor trajectories of the reference objects.

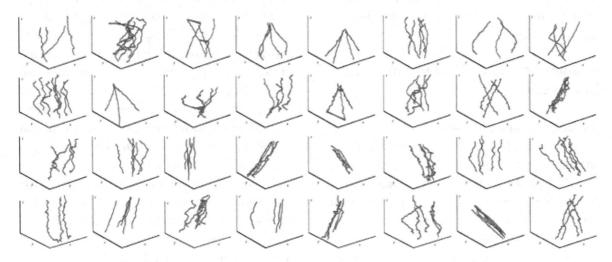

and feedback, characterizing the variant interaction properties within and between trajectory segments, are proposed to obtain the quaternion descriptor for video activity clips. Distinguished from the extensively used discriminative solutions, the activity recognition is performed in a generative manner, which achieves much better performance compared with the state-of-the-art results on two challenging realistic human activity databases.

The future work lies in three directions. Firstly, more elaborate appearance and dynamic features will be investigated to improve the performance. Secondly, label information will be integrated into the learning of pLSA model to enhance the classification power. Thirdly, the semi-supervised learning is also another promising direction.

REFERENCES

Breiman, L. (1992). *Probability*. Society for Industrial Mathematics. doi:10.1137/1.9781611971286

Granger, C. (1969). Investigating causal relations by econometric models and cross-spectral methods. *Econometrica: Journal of the Econometric Society*, *37*(3), 424–438. doi:10.2307/1912791

Hofmann, T. (1998). Probabilistic latent semantic indexing. *In ACM SIGIR International Conference* (pp. 50–57).

Isard, M., & Blake, A. (1998). Condensation - Conditional density propagation for visual tracking. *International Journal of Computer Vision*, *29*(1), 5–28. doi:10.1023/A:1008078328650

Jury, E. (1958). *Sampled-data control systems*. John Wiley & Sons.

Laptev, I., & Lindeberg, T. (2003). Space-time interest points. In *IEEE International Conference on Computer Vision* (pp. 432–439).

Liu, J., Luo, J., & Shah, M. (2009). Recognizing realistic actions from videos in the wild. In *IEEE International Conference on Computer Vision and Pattern Recognition* (pp. 1996–2003).

Liu, Z., & Sarkar, S. (2004). *Simplest representation yet for gait recognition: Averaged silhouette.* In IEEE International Conference on Pattern Recognition.

Lowe, D. (2004). Distinctive image features from scale-invariant keypoints. *International Journal of Computer Vision, 60*(2), 91–110. doi:10.1023/B:VISI.0000029664.99615.94

Marszalek, M., Laptev, I., & Schmid, C. (2009). Actions in context. In *IEEE International Conference on Computer Vision and Pattern Recognition* (pp. 2929–2936).

Mortensen, E., Deng, H., & Shapiro, L. (2005). A SIFT descriptor with global context. In *IEEE International Conference on Computer Vision and Pattern Recognition* (pp. 184–190).

Ni, B., Yan, S., & Kassim, A. (2009). Recognizing human group activities with localized causalities. In *IEEE International Conference on Computer Vision and Pattern Recognition* (pp. 1470–1477).

Niebles, J., Wang, H., & Li, F. (2008). Unsupervised learning of human action categories using spatial-temporal words. *International Journal of Computer Vision, 79*, 299–318. doi:10.1007/s11263-007-0122-4

Ryoo, M., & Aggarwal, J. (2007). Hierarchical recognition of human activities interacting with objects. In *IEEE International Conference on Computer Vision and Pattern Recognition* (pp. 1–8).

Schuldt, C., Laptev, I., & Caputo, B. (2004). Recognizing human actions: A local SVM approach. In *IEEE International Conference on Pattern Recognition* (pp. 32–36).

Shi, J., & Malik, J. (2000). Normalized cuts and image segmentation. *IEEE Transactions on Pattern Analysis and Machine Intelligence, 22*(8), 888–905. doi:10.1109/34.868688

Sun, J., Wu, X., Yan, S., Cheong, L., Chua, T., & Li, J. (2009). Hierarchical spatiotemporal context modeling for action recognition. In *IEEE International Conference on Computer Vision and Pattern Recognition* (pp. 2004–2011).

Torralba, A., Murphy, K., Freeman, W., & Rubin, M. (2003). Context-based vision system for place and object recognition. In *IEEE International Conference on Computer Vision* (pp. 273–280).

Turaga, P., Chellappa, R., Subrahmanian, V., & Udrea, O. (2008). Machine recognition of human activities: A survey. *IEEE Transactions on Circuits and Systems for Video Technology, 18*(11), 1473–1488. doi:10.1109/TCSVT.2008.2005594

Wang, Y., & Mori, G. (2009). Human action recognition by semi-latent topic models. *IEEE Transactions on Pattern Analysis and Machine Intelligence, 31*(10), 1762–1774. doi:10.1109/TPAMI.2009.43

Zhou, Y., Yan, S., & Huang, T. (2008). Pair-activity classification by bi-trajectory analysis. In *IEEE International Conference on Computer Vision and Pattern Recognition* (pp. 1–8).

Chapter 10
Shape Retrieval and Classification Based on Geodesic Paths in Skeleton Graphs

Xiang Bai
Huazhong University of Science and Technology, P.R. China

Chunyuan Li
Huazhong University of Science and Technology, P.R. China

Xingwei Yang
Temple University, USA

Longin Jan Latecki
Temple University, USA

ABSTRACT

Skeleton- is well-known to be superior to contour-based representation when shapes have large non-linear variability, especially articulation. However, approaches to shape similarity based on skeletons suffer from the instability of skeletons, and matching of skeleton graphs is still an open problem. To deal with this problem for shape retrieval, the authors first propose to match skeleton graphs by comparing the geodesic paths between skeleton endpoints. In contrast to typical tree or graph matching methods, they do not explicitly consider the topological graph structure. Their approach is motivated by the fact that visually similar skeleton graphs may have completely different topological structures, while the paths between their end nodes still remain similar. The proposed comparison of geodesic paths between endpoints of skeleton graphs yields correct matching results in such cases. The experimental results demonstrate that the method is able to produce correct results in the presence of articulations, stretching, and contour deformations. The authors also utilize the geodesic skeleton paths for shape classification. Similar to shape retrieval, direct graph matching algorithms like graph edit distance have great difficulties with the instability of the skeleton graph structure. In contrast, the representation based on skeleton paths remains stable. Therefore, a simple Bayesian classifier is able to obtain excellent shape classification results.

DOI: 10.4018/978-1-4666-1891-6.ch010

1. INTRODUCTION

Skeleton (or medial axis), which integrates geometrical and topological features of the object, is an important shape descriptor for object recognition (Blum, 1973). Shape similarity based on skeleton matching usually performs better than contour or other shape descriptors in the presence of partial occlusion and articulation of parts (Sebastian and Kimia, 2005; Basri et al., 1998; Huttenlocher et al., 1993; Belongie et al., 2002). However, it is a challenging task to automatically recognize objects using their skeletons due to skeleton sensitivity to boundary deformation (Shaked and Bruckstein, 1998; August et al., 1999). Usually, the skeleton branches have to be pruned for recognition (Shaked and Bruckstein, 1998; Choi et al., 2003; Bai et al., 2006; Bai et al., 2007; Ogniewicz and Kubler, 1995; Bai et al., 2008). Moreover, another major restriction of recognition methods based on skeleton is a complex structure of obtained tree or graph representations of the skeletons. Graph edit operations are applied to the tree or graph structures, such as merge and cut operations (Zhu and Yuille, 1996; Liu and Gei-

ger, 1999; Geiger et al., 2003; Di Ruberto, 2004; Pelillo et al., 1999), in the course of the matching process. Probably the most important challenge for skeleton similarity is the fact that the topological structure of skeleton trees or graphs of similar objects may be completely different. This fact is illustrated in Figure 1. Although the skeletons of the two horses are similar, their skeleton graphs are very different. This example illustrates the difficulties faced by approaches based on graph edit operations in the context of skeleton matching. To match skeleton graphs or skeleton trees like the ones shown in Figure 1, some nontrivial edit operations (cut, merge, et al.) are inevitable. On the other hand, skeleton graphs of different objects may have the same topology.

This chapter presents a novel scheme for skeleton-based shape similarity measure. The proposed skeleton graph matching is based on similarity of shortest paths between each pair of endpoints of the pruned skeletons, e.g., see the shortest paths (in red) in Figure 2. The shortest paths between every pair of skeleton endpoints are represented as sequences of radii of the maximal disks at corresponding skeleton points.

Figure 1. Visually similar shapes have very different skeleton graphs. The corresponding end nodes between the two skeleton graphs are linked with lines. (The result is accomplished using the method presented in this book chapter, which is also introduced in Bai and Latecki (2008))

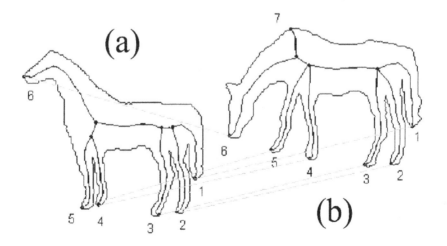

Figure 2. (a) The horse's skeleton; (b) The shortest paths between the pairs of endpoints on the skeleton

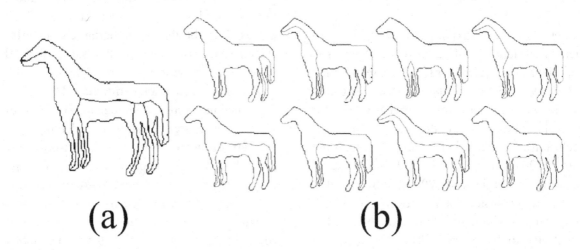

We also benefit from the fact that the skeleton endpoints inherit a cyclic order from the contours. This is possible, since the skeletons are pruned based on contour partitioning with discrete curve evolution (DCE) (Bai et al., 2007), which guarantees that all endpoints of skeleton branches lie on the contour. For example in Figure 3, all the endpoints (denoted by 1, 2, ..., 6) of the horse's skeleton are vertices of the DCE simplified polygon (in red). The DCE was introduced in (Latecki and Lakamper, 1999; Latecki and Lakamper, 2000). An important property of the DCE-based pruning in (Bai et al., 2007) is its stability in that it is able to remove spurious branches while preserving structurally relevant branches. In the case of 3D, we utilize Cornea et al.'s curve skeleton (Cornea et al., 2005). Usually, the final version of the curve skeleton consists of numerous segments, and we illustrate some skeleton segments of a cow shape in different colors in Figure 4(a).

Figure 3. The skeleton pruned with contour partitioning by DCE (Bai et al., 2007)

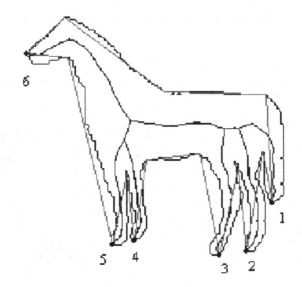

Figure 4. (a) The cow's curve skeleton; (b) The shortest paths between the pairs of endpoints on the skeleton

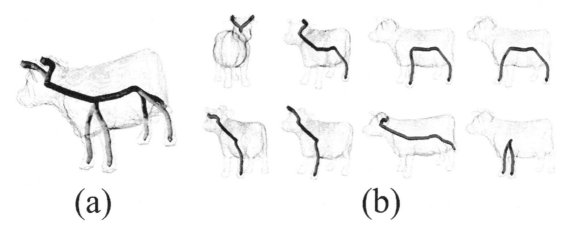

(a) (b)

To construct the geodesic skeleton paths, we first detect the skeleton endpoints in Figure 5. Segment ends that have no neighbor ends within a given threshold distance are detected as skeleton endpoints, and one skeleton path is constructed as the shortest geodesic path between a pair of endpoints on the skeleton. Several 3D shortest skeleton paths are shown in Figure 4(b), and the endpoints are in red.

The proposed skeleton graph matching method is described in Section 4. In contrast to the existing approaches to skeleton similarity, we do not explicitly consider the topological structure of the skeleton trees or graphs. Instead we focus on the similarity of paths connecting the skeleton endpoints. We use the similarity of the shortest paths between each pair of skeleton endpoints to establish a correspondence relation of the endpoints in different graphs. For example, vertex 1 in Figure 1(a) corresponds to vertex 1 in Figure 1(b) since their shortest paths to vertices 2, 3, 4, 5 and 6 are similar. Finally, the dissimilarity value between graphs is easily estimated by the distances between the corresponding endpoints. Thus, the basic idea of our method is to determine the similarity of complex structures (graphs or trees) by examining shortest paths between their endpoints. As we will show in Section 5, the

Figure 5. Illustration of the critical skeleton points using the authors' method on a 3D airplane (left); On the right: (a) endpoint, (b) connected points between two segments, (c) junction points, and (d) connected points in a segment

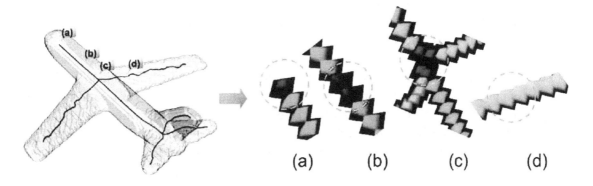

(a)   (b)   (c)   (d)

proposed method yields successful recognition results, and is faster than the existing graph and tree matching methods.

The usage of shortest geodesic paths in skeleton graph and in shape similarity is not new; in particular, many-to-many matching in Demirci et al. (Demirci et al., 2006) and the inner-distance in Ling and Jacobs (Ling and Jacobs, 2007) use shortest paths. However, there are substantial differences in our approach. (Demirci et al., 2006) considers shortest paths between all skeleton nodes and (Ling and Jacobs, 2007) considers shortest paths between all contour points. We only consider shortest skeletal paths between skeleton end nodes, which allows us to avoid the problem of the instability of the skeleton junction points (in comparison to (Demirci et al., 2006)) and makes our approach more robust to contour deformations (in comparison to (Ling and Jacobs, 2007)). Moreover, we use skeletal shortest paths in a different and novel way to define shape similarity. In our approach, we use a two-layer structure. In the first layer, skeletal shortest paths emanating from a given skeleton endpoint form its shape descriptor. In the second layer, we compute the similarity of two shapes by matching the shape descriptors of the skeleton endpoints.

Since similar skeletons may have different number of endpoints, we have to allow for a partial correspondence of the endpoints. This is possible with a recently introduced method for partial similarity of sequences (Latecki et al., 2005), which was extended and used for matching the endpoints of skeletons (Bai and Latecki, 2008). The extended method differs from the other method in (Latecki et al., 2005) in that it allows penalized skipping of outliers in the query sequence in addition to skipping outliers in the target sequence. The method in Latecki et al. (2005) allows only skipping outlier elements in the target sequence. By employing this method, we are able to also match skeletons of object parts to the skeletons of complete objects, and match

parts to parts, which is a necessary requirement for robust object recognition.

The proposed skeleton graph matching is based on the assumption that similar skeletons have similar structure of their end nodes (measured by similarity of shortest paths to other end nodes). This assumption is significantly weaker than a standard assumption that a structure of the whole skeleton graph (based on both end nodes and junction nodes) is similar. Usually, the structure of both end nodes and junction nodes is weighted and edited since, as pointed out above (Figure 1), it is common that skeletons of similar shapes have a different structure of junction nodes. Moreover, as described in Section 2, many approaches to match skeleton graphs require that the graphs are converted to trees prior to finding the correspondence. However, as we will illustrate in Section 5.2, such a conversion may result in lost of important structural information, and consequently negatively influence the object recognition result. The proposed method computes dissimilarity values for graphs that do not have to be trees.

The geodesic skeletal paths are represented as sequences of radii of maximal disks/balls in our approach. Although we do not explicitly consider the topological structure of the skeleton graphs, we do not completely ignore this structure. It is implicitly represented by the fact that overlapping parts of the geodesic skeletal paths are similar, since their overlapping parts have the same subsequences of radii. For our example in Figure 1(a, b), it means that paths from 6 to 1 and from 5 to 2 overlap. The fact that the overlapping segments are slightly different in (a) and (b) does not affect the similarity of corresponding sequences of radii in (a) and (b). Therefore, our approach is flexible enough to perform extremely well on articulated shapes, but it is not too flexible to confuse dissimilar shapes. This fact is also confirmed by our experimental results in Section 5.

Besides skeleton matching, the skeleton paths can also be utilized in a Bayesian framework, where the order information is ignored compared to the skeleton matching. We utilize a three-level statistical framework including distinct models for database, class, and part. Bayesian inference is used to perform classification within this framework. Based on Bayes rule, the posterior probabilities of classes can be computed by the difference between skeletons of query shape and the shape in database. In the proposed framework, it can work well to classify complete shapes. The algorithm is described in Section 7 and the experimental results are shown in Section 8.

2. BACKGROUND

The skeleton-based recognition methods are usually based on the graph or tree representation of the skeletons. Compared with contour matching or other methods, skeleton matching has a lower sensitivity to articulation or rearrangement of parts. However, it involves a higher degree of computational complexity (Sebastian and Kimia, 2005; Sebastian et al., 2004; Sebastian et al., 2003). Since the skeleton or medial axis is always organized into an ARG (Attributed-Relation Graph), the similarity between two objects can be measured by matching their ARGs. Graph matching is an NPC problem, thus, some efforts have been made to obtain approximate solutions. We review now the most influential solutions proposed in the context of shape similarity.

Zhu et al. match the skeleton graphs of objects using a branch-bounding method that is limited to motionless objects (Zhu and Yuille, 1996). Liu et al. match ARGs with the A* algorithm. Before matching the axis trees, the merge or cut operation is essential (Liu and Geiger, 1999; Geiger et al., 2003). In contrast, the proposed approach does not require any editing of the skeleton graph.

Shock graph is a kind of ARG proposed by Siddiqi et al., which is based on Shock Grammar (Siddiqi et al., 1998; Siddiqi et al., 1999a; Siddiqi et al., 1999b; Siddiqi and Kimia, 1995). Later,

Shokoufandeh et al. successfully extend these approaches to structural indexing in a large database (Shokoufandeh et al., 2005). The distance between subgraphs is measured by comparing the eigenvalues of their adjacency matrices. Thus, this method is based on graph topology. It is time consuming because of the complexity of the Shock Grammar and the calculation of eigenvalues. Sebastian et al. have presented a scheme to compute the edit distance between the shock graphs (Sebastian et al., 2001; Sebastian et al., 2004), but because of the expensive computation due to the complex operation on shock graphs, the method may fail to deal with occlusion and scene clutter. Torsello et al. use the length of the corresponding boundary segments to edit the similarity of shock trees (Torsello and Hancock, 2004; Torsello et al., 2005).

A different framework is presented in Pelillo et al. (Pelillo et al., 1999; Pelillo, 2002), where hierarchical trees are matched based on finding maximal cliques of the association graphs. Aslan and Tari posit an unconventional approach to shape recognition using unconnected skeletons in the course level (Aslan and Tari, 2005). Di Di Ruberto uses another kind of ARG, called ASG (Attributed Skeleton Graph) (Di Ruberto, 2004). The ASGs are matched with a graduated assignment algorithm, which converts the match matrix (0-1 matrix) into a continuous matrix. This method can deal well with the occlusion problem, however since the matching matrix is obtained using a heuristic rule, the graduated assignment algorithm can find only a suboptimal matching solution.

In recent work, Demirci et al. transform weighted graphs into metric trees for accurate matching (Demirci et al., 2004; Demirci et al., 2006). However, a heuristic rule is essential to transform graphs to trees (loops need to be removed). An additional problem for this tree matching method is how to select an optimal node as the root, since different root points may have completely different topologies for the same skeleton.

Most of the existing approaches cannot deal with loops. One of few approaches that can deal well with the loop structure is presented in Hilaga et al. (Hilaga et al., 2001). It is a method based on topological matching of Reeb graphs representing 3D models. However, this method distinguishes different shapes only based on topological structure. The proposed method is able to match graphs containing loops, and it yields intuitive results that reflect both geometric and topological shape features.

3. SKELETON GRAPHS

This section describes the initial steps for building the skeleton graphs. The following definitions apply to continuous skeletons as well as to skeletons in digital images (composed of pixels/voxels).

- **Definition 1:** A skeleton point having only one adjacent point is an endpoint (the skeleton endpoint); a skeleton point having three or more adjacent points is a junction point. If a skeleton point is not an endpoint or a junction point, it is called a connection point. (Here we assume the skeleton curve is one pixel/voxel wide.)
- **Definition 2:** The sequence of connection points between two directly connected skeleton points is called a skeleton branch. A standard way to build a skeleton graph is as follows: both the endpoints and junction points are chosen as the nodes for the graph and all the skeleton branches between the nodes are the edges between the nodes.
- **Definition 3:** The endpoint in the skeleton graph is called an end node, and the junction point in the skeleton graph is called a junction node.

4. MATCHING THE SKELETON-GRAPHS

We match skeleton graphs by establishing a correspondence of their end nodes only, since these nodes are the salient points on the contour and all skeleton branches ending on the contour can be seen as visual parts of the original shape. Thus, the proposed representation does not involve any junction nodes.

4.1 The Shape-Path Representation

- **Definition 4:** The shortest path between a pair of end nodes on a skeleton graph is called a skeleton path, e.g., see Figure 2(b). Suppose there are N end nodes in the skeleton graph G to be matched, and let v_i ($i = 1, 2,\ldots, N$) denote the ith end node in the skeleton graph. Let $p(v_m,v_n)$ denote the skeleton path from v_m to v_n. We sample $p(v_m,v_n)$ with M equidistant points, which are all skeleton points. Let $R_{m,n}(t)$ denote the radius of the maximal disk/ball at the skeleton point with index t in $p(v_m,v_n)$. A vector of the radii of the maximal disks/balls centered at the M sample points on $p(v_m,v_n)$ is denoted as

$$R_{m,n} = \left(R_{m,n}\left(t\right)\right)_{t=1,2,\ldots,M} = \left(r_1, r_2, \ldots, r_M\right).$$

$$(1)$$

The radius $R_{m,n}(t)$ is approximated with the values of the distance transform $DT(t)$ at each skeleton point with index t. Suppose there are N_0 pixels/voxels in the original shape S. To make the proposed method invariant to the scale, we normalize $R_{m,n}(t)$ in the following way:

$$R_{m,n}(t) = \frac{DT(t)}{\frac{1}{N_0}\sum_{i=1}^{N_0} DT(s_i)} \qquad (2)$$

where s_i (i=1, 2, ..., N_0) varies over all N_0 pixels/voxels in the shape.

- **Definition 5:** The shape dissimilarity between two skeleton paths is called a path distance. If R and R' denote the vectors of radii of two shape paths $p(u,v)$ and $p(u',v')$ respectively, the path distance is defined as:

$$pd\left(p(u,v), p(u',v')\right) = \sum_{i=1}^{M} \frac{\left(r_i - r_i'\right)^2}{r_i + r_i'} + \alpha \frac{\left(l - l'\right)^2}{l + l'} \qquad (3)$$

where l and l' are the lengths of $p(u,v)$ and $p(u',v')$ respectively, and α is the weight factor. In order to make our representation scale invariant, the path lengths are normalized. We include the path lengths in Equation 3, since the path length is not reflected in the sequences of radii (all paths are sequences of M radii). This way our path representation and the path distance are scale invariant.

In order to deal with the similarity of articulated shapes, the path distance in (3) does not penalize path deformations (e.g., deformations from straight to curved paths) that do not change the vectors of radii and path lengths. This allows us to recognize as similar two deformable objects such as snakes. It may appear that not penalizing path deformations can lead to a danger of recognizing as similar different shapes. However, while it is possible to deform a given shape (e.g., a snake) so that the vectors of radii and path lengths are constant, it is extremely unlikely to have two different shapes with differently deformed skeletal

paths having identical vectors of radii and path lengths. Our excellent experimental results in Section 5 confirm this fact in that we never classified as similar objects of different shapes.

4.2 Matching End Nodes Using Skeleton Paths

In the skeleton graph, each end node has the skeleton paths to all other end nodes in the graph. As we will show the skeleton paths are a useful shape descriptor.

Let G and G' denote two graphs to be matched, and let v_i and v'_j be some end nodes in G and G', respectively. Let the numbers of the end nodes in G and G' be K+1 and N+1, respectively, and $K \leq N$. The matching cost $c(v_i, v'_j)$ between v_i and v'_j is estimated based on the paths to all other vertices in G and G' that emanate from v_i and v'_j, correspondingly. First we order all end nodes. In 2D case, we simply sort all end nodes in G following the clockwise contour with the starting node being v_i which is denoted as v_{i0}. (Here we benefit from the fact that all skeleton endpoints lie on the contour.) In 3D case, no such ordering exists. Therefore, in 3D we base the order of end nodes on the length of paths emanating from them, i.e., sorting endpoints by summing path length. We define the total path length of the end node v_i as

$$T(v_i) = \sum_{j=1}^{N+1} l_{ij}$$

where l_{ij} is the length of the geodesic skeleton path from v_i to v_j. We order all the end nodes in G following these lengths, by ranking an endpoint with a larger length at the top of the list. Therefore, we obtain a sequence of ordered end nodes $v_{i0}, v_{i1}, ..., v_{iK}$ in G, and similarly $v_{j0}, v_{j1}, ..., v_{jN}$ in G'. Then we compute the path distances between the two sequences (They represent the paths emanating from $v_i = v_{i0}$ in G and $v'_j = v'_{j0}$ in G'). We obtain a matrix of the path distances computed with Equation 3:

$$pd(v_i, v'_j) =$$

$$
\begin{pmatrix}
pd(p(v_{i0},v_{i1}),p(v'_{j0},v'_{j1})), & pd(p(v_{i0},v_{i1}),p(v'_{j0},v'_{j2})), \\
pd(p(v_{i0},v_{i2}),p(v'_{j0},v'_{j1})), & pd(p(v_{i0},v_{i2}),p(v'_{j0},v'_{j2})), \\
\vdots & \vdots \\
pd(p(v_{i0},v_{iK}),p(v'_{j0},v'_{j1})), & pd(p(v_{i0},v_{iK}),p(v'_{j0},v'_{j2})), \\
\cdots, & pd(p(v_{i0},v_{i1}),p(v'_{j0},v'_{jN})) \\
\cdots, & pd(p(v_{i0},v_{i2}),p(v'_{j0},v'_{jN})) \\
\vdots & \vdots \\
\cdots, & pd(p(v_{i0},v_{iK}),p(v'_{j0},v'_{jN}))
\end{pmatrix}
$$

$$(4)$$

To compute the dissimilarity value between the two end nodes v_i and v'_j, we utilize a matching method called optimal subsequence bijection (OSB), which is described in (Bai and Latecki, 2008). The main property of OSB is the fact that it can skip outlier elements of matched sequences, which in our case means skipping some of the skeleton endpoints. For example, endpoint 7 in Figure 1 must be skipped in order to establish the correct correspondence of the other skeleton endpoints. By applying OSB to the matrix in (4), we obtain the dissimilarity of two end nodes v_i and v'_j:

$$c\left(v_i, v'_j\right) = OSB\left(pd\left(v_i, v'_j\right)\right) \tag{5}$$

For two graphs G and G', with end nodes v_i ($i = 0, 1, 2, ..., K$) and v'_j ($j = 0, 1, 2, ..., N$), we compute all the dissimilarity costs between their end nodes and obtain a new matrix:

$$C(G,G') =$$
$$
\begin{pmatrix}
c(v_0,v'_0) & c(v_0,v'_2) & \cdots & c(v_0,v'_N) \\
c(v_1,v'_0) & c(v_1,v'_2) & \cdots & c(v_1,v'_N) \\
\vdots & \vdots & \vdots & \vdots \\
c(v_K,v'_0) & c(v_K,v'_2) & \cdots & c(v_K,v'_N)
\end{pmatrix}
$$

$$(6)$$

Finally, we compute the total dissimilarity $c(G, G')$ between G and G' with the Hungarian algorithm on $C(G, G')$. For each end node v_i in G, the Hungarian algorithm can find its corresponding end node v'_j in G'. Since G and G' may have different numbers of end nodes, the total dissimilarity value should include the penalty for end nodes that did not find any partner. To achieve this, we simply add additional rows with a constant value const to (6) so that $C(G, G')$ becomes a square matrix. The constant value const is the average of all the other values in $C(G, G')$. The intuition for using the Hungarian algorithm is that we want to have a globally consistent one-to-one assignment of all end nodes with possibly assigning some end nodes to const, which represents a dummy node. This means that we seek a one-to-one correspondence of the end nodes in the skeleton graphs (with possibly skipping some nodes by assigning them to a dummy node).

Observe that our approach does not require any correspondence of junction nodes. This is extremely important, since as illustrated in Figure 1, in many cases the correspondence of junction nodes is impossible to establish directly, and therefore, graph or tree editing approaches are needed if the correspondence of junction nodes is required. It is also important to observe that it is impossible to change the structure of junction nodes with skeleton pruning without eliminating some important end nodes. On the other hand, skeleton pruning is able to reduce the set of end nodes to structurally relevant nodes by eliminating spurious end nodes, see (Bai et al., 2007). To summarize, the proposed skeleton graph matching is based on the assumption that similar skeletons have a similar structure of their end nodes that is measured by the similarity of shortest paths to other end nodes. This assumption is significantly weaker than the standard assumption that a structure of both end nodes and junction nodes is similar. Usually, the structure of both end nodes and junction nodes is weighted and edited, since as pointed out in Figure 1, it is common that skeletons of similar shapes have a different structure of junction nodes.

The fact that the Hungarian algorithm does not preserve the order of matched sequences does not influence the final score, since we can change the order only for similar end nodes. However, the similarity of end nodes is computed in the context of all other end nodes. Therefore, changing the order is likely due only to symmetry, in which case the final dissimilarity score is unaffected. The Hungarian algorithm has a computational advantage in comparison to order preserving assignment algorithms. When using an order preserving algorithm, we would need to enumerate over different starting nodes, while this is not necessary for the Hungarian algorithm. The Hungarian algorithm is the most popular for finding a maximum matching in a bipartite graph and is a common formulation for globally optimal matching. Examples include Kim and Kak (Kim and Kak, 1991), Siddiqi et al. (Siddiqi et al., 1999b) and, more recently, Belongie et al. (Belongie et al., 2002), to name just a few; these techniques are also unable to enforce global ordering and are confused by object symmetries. A different way to approach the matching problem by allowing many-to-many mapping as proposed in (Demirci et al., 2006) is also possible.

We give now a simple example illustrating our matching approach. Figure 1 shows skeletons of two different horses with the corresponding end nodes linked by lines. We indexed the nodes so that the corresponding nodes have the same index except for node 7 that does not have a partner, and consequently corresponds to a dummy node with the correspondence value of const. The matrix $C(G, G')$ is shown in Table 1. The matching costs between most similar end nodes are marked with red numbers. The last row represents the dummy node.

5. MATCHING EXPERIMENTS

In this section, we evaluate the performance of the proposed method in three parts. In Section 5.1, we illustrate the recognition performance of our method on standard shape databases. We illustrate in Section 5.2, the importance of matching skeleton graph structures as opposed to matching only tree structures. In Section 5.3, we show the result of path similarity based methods on 3D shape retrieval.

5.1 Robustness of Recognition

To evaluate the recognition performance of our method, we tested it on four standard datasets: Aslan and Tari database (Aslan and Tari, 2005), Kimia's two databases (Sebastian et al., 2004) and Rutgers tools database (Siddiqi et al., 1998).

Table 1. The matrix C(G, G') of the dissimilarity values between all end nodes of the two horses in Figure 1. The last row is added to make C(G, G') a square matrix. The bolded values are between the most similar end nodes.

	1	2	3	4	5	6	7
1	**0.912**	4.331	8.805	4.317	7.132	6.165	8.841
2	3.926	**0.628**	2.740	3.603	2.413	5.870	13.36
3	6.110	1.027	**0.512**	4.285	1.994	4.295	11.77
4	4.735	4.050	5.783	**1.264**	3.067	6.592	15.56
5	6.334	2.810	3.407	3.093	**0.952**	4.040	10.53
6	4.308	4.242	3.908	4.514	3.862	**0.605**	5.656
7	*const*	*const*	*const*	*const*	*const*	*const*	*const*

The Aslan and Tari database is used for testing the performance on non-rigid objects. As shown in Figure 6, it includes 14 classes of articulated shapes with 4 shapes in each class. We use each shape in this database as a query. Several representative results are shown in Figure 7, where six most similar shapes are shown for the queries. For each query, a perfect result should have the three most similar shapes in the same class as the query. The red squares mark all the results where this was not the case. Since there are only 5 errors in 168 query results, the recognition rate on this dataset (using the standard percent measure) is 97.0%. Using the bulls-eye test (Latecki et al., 2000), the recognition rate is 99.4%. Moreover, we can easily observe that the wrong results are very similar to the query. For this dataset, we use parameters M=50 and α=40. Although this database was introduced in Aslan and Tari (Aslan and Tari, 2005), their paper does not present results on the whole database, as we do. ((Aslan and Tari, 2005) illustrates only a few example dissimilarities between pairs of shapes). Since no recognition rate on the whole dataset is provided in (Aslan and Tari, 2005), we cannot directly compare the recognition rate of our method to (Aslan and Tari, 2005). We were able to compare our method to the inner distance (Ling and Jacobs, 2007) on this dataset. We compared it to the best performing version in (Ling and Jacobs, 2007), which is the inner distance shape context with dynamic programming, denoted by IDSC + DP. The retrieval results are summarized as the number of correct shapes for all 56 queries among the 1st, 2nd and 3rd closest matches. IDSC + DP obtained 53, 51, 38 while our method achieved 55, 55, 53. The perfect result would be 56, 56, 56. We found that inner distance has problems with non-rigid deformations like bending of an arm. In contrast, the proposed method is designed to perform well in the presence of non-rigid deformations.

Figure 6. Aslan and Tari database (Aslan and Tari, 2005) with 56 shapes

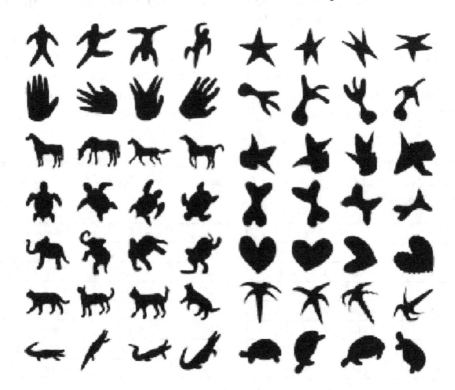

Figure 7. Selected results of the proposed method on Aslan and Tari database (Aslan and Tari, 2005). Since each class is composed of 4 shapes, the query and the first 3 most similar shapes should be in the same class. Outlined boxes mark the results where this is not the case.

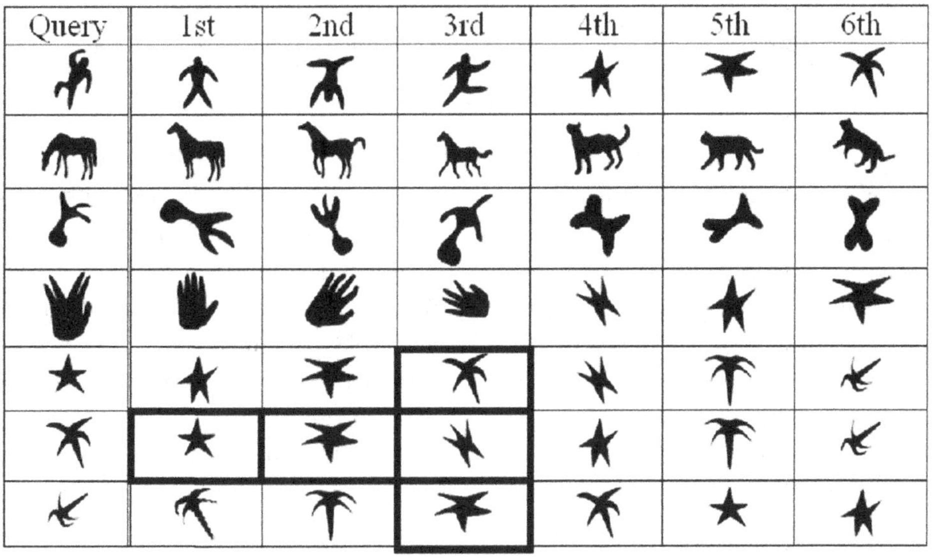

Query	1st	2nd	3rd	4th	5th	6th

We also tested our algorithm on two shape databases provided by Kimia (Sebastian et al., 2004). The first database as shown in Figure 8 contains 216 images from 18 classes, which is a subset of MPEG-7 database (Latecki et al., 2000). For each shape, we check whether the 11 closest matches are in the same class as the query. In Table 2, we compare our result to two typical shape classification methods, and the number of correct matches in each rank is summarized. Our

algorithm performs better than Shock-Edit (Siddiqi et al., 1998) and Shape Context (Belongie et al., 2002). We use parameters M=50 and α=70.

Figure 9 shows another Kimia's dataset with 99 images from 9 classes. In this dataset, some images have protrusions or missing parts. Table 3 compares our results to several other methods in a way similar to Table 2. Our results are acceptable but are not the best, which is due to the presence of protrusions. While small protrusions

Figure 8. Sample shapes from Kimia's 216 shape database (Sebastian et al., 2004). Two shapes are shown for each of the 18 classes.

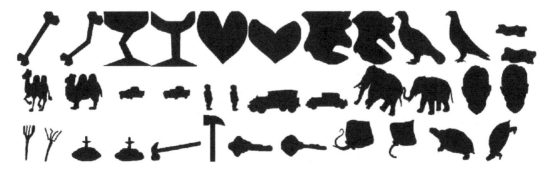

Table 2. Retrieval results on Kimia's 216 shape database

Algorithm	1st	2nd	3rd	4th	5th	6th	7th	8th	9th	10th	11th
SC [5]	214	209	205	197	191	178	161	144	131	101	78
Shock Edit [15]	216	216	216	215	210	210	207	204	200	187	163
Our method	**216**	**216**	**215**	**216**	**213**	**210**	**210**	**207**	**205**	**191**	**177**

do not present any problems, significant ones do. The limitation of our method is that it is able to compute the correct correspondence but the dissimilarity value is relatively large due to the necessity of skipping the skeleton endpoints in the protrusion. We use parameters M=50 and α=30.

To compare our method to other typical skeleton-based approaches, we use the Rutgers Tools Database (Siddiqi et al., 1998), which consists of 25 shapes grouped into 8 classes. Several sample shapes from the Rutgers Tools Database are shown in Figure 10. Here we use parameters M=50 and α=40. The results of the proposed method on the Rutgers Tools Database are shown

in Figure 11. We only have two mismatched entries, which are highlighted with red squares in the class 'Pliers' and the class 'Screwdriver'. Compared with other skeleton based methods, our method outperforms Shock Tree (Pelillo et al., 1999) (5 mismatched entries), Graph-Edit Distance (Sebastian et al., 2004) (5 mismatched entries), and Many-to-Many Matching (Demirci et al., 2006) (3 mismatched entries). It is important to observe that skeleton-based methods significantly outperform contour-based methods on this dataset. As reported in (Sebastian et al., 2004), one of the most popular contour-based methods,

Figure 9. Sample shapes from Kimia's 99 shape database (Sebastian et al., 2004). Two shapes are shown for each of the 9 classes.

Table 3. Retrieval results on Kimia's 99 shape database

Algorithm	1st	2nd	3rd	4th	5th	6th	7th	8th	9th	10th
SC [5]	97	91	88	85	84	77	75	66	56	37
Gen. Model [48]	99	97	99	98	96	96	94	83	75	48
Our method	**99**	**99**	**99**	**99**	**96**	**97**	**95**	**93**	**89**	**73**
Shock Edit [15]	99	99	99	98	98	97	96	95	93	82
IDSC + DP [47]	99	99	99	98	98	97	97	98	94	79

Figure 10. Sample shapes in Rutgers tools database

Shape Contexts (Belongie et al., 2002), misclassified 21 entries on this dataset.

5.2 Matching Skeleton Graphs that Are Not Trees

This section illustrates the advantage of matching directly skeleton graphs as opposed to matching skeleton trees. Many approaches presented in the literature (e.g., Shock Tree (Pelillo et al., 1999), Many-to-Many Matching (Demirci et al., 2006)) are unable to match skeleton graphs. They require first converting skeleton graphs to trees. However, as we illustrate now, this may result in losing important structural information.

For algorithms that are able to match only tree structures, it is necessary to convert graphs to trees by removing some edges in loops of skeleton groups. Therefore, converting graphs to trees may result in the loss of important structural information, and consequently in the inability to correctly differentiate shapes.

To evaluate the performance of our algorithm on distinguishing the topological difference, we use a small database that contains five shapes, in which the skeleton of the broken key in Figure 12 is very similar to the wrenches. The parameters for this database are M=50 and α=30. Since the shortest paths between end nodes change dramatically when a loop is broken, we are able to distinguish the structural difference between a closed loop and a broken loop. Consequently, the broken key (without hole) is more similar to the wrenches than the keys (with holes) as shown in Figure

13(a). It seems to be impossible for tree matching methods to capture this difference since they need to cut the loops on the skeletons before matching (in order to convert a graph to a tree structure). Therefore, we do not see how they could capture the topological difference between the broken key and the two unbroken keys. In analogy, we expect contour-based methods (e.g., (Belongie et al., 2002; Latecki and Lakamper, 2000; Ling and Jacobs, 2007; Tu and Yuille, 2004)) to be unable to capture this difference too. To verify this claim we evaluated one of the best performing contour-based methods on this dataset. The results of IDSC + DP (Ling and Jacobs, 2007) on this database are shown in Figure 13(b). In particular, the last row in Figure 13(b) shows that IDSC + DP cannot properly capture this topological difference.

It is important to mention that the proposed method requires the existence of end branches, which is always the case for polygonal shapes. However, ideal mathematical shapes like a doughnut may not have any end branches in which case the proposed method is not applicable.

Also, we evaluate the performance of proposed method on distinguishing the topological difference for 3D shapes. A small database of four nonrigid 3D shapes (two spectacles and two snakes as shown in Figure 14.) is established. The parameter M for this database was set to M=50. We show the results with α=0 in Figure 15(a) and α=10 in Figure 15(b). By observing the rankings, it is evident that both of them could discriminate the skeleton graphs with different structures. However, considering the path percentage obvi-

Figure 11. The results of the proposed method on Rutgers tools database. There are only two mismatched entries, which are outlined.

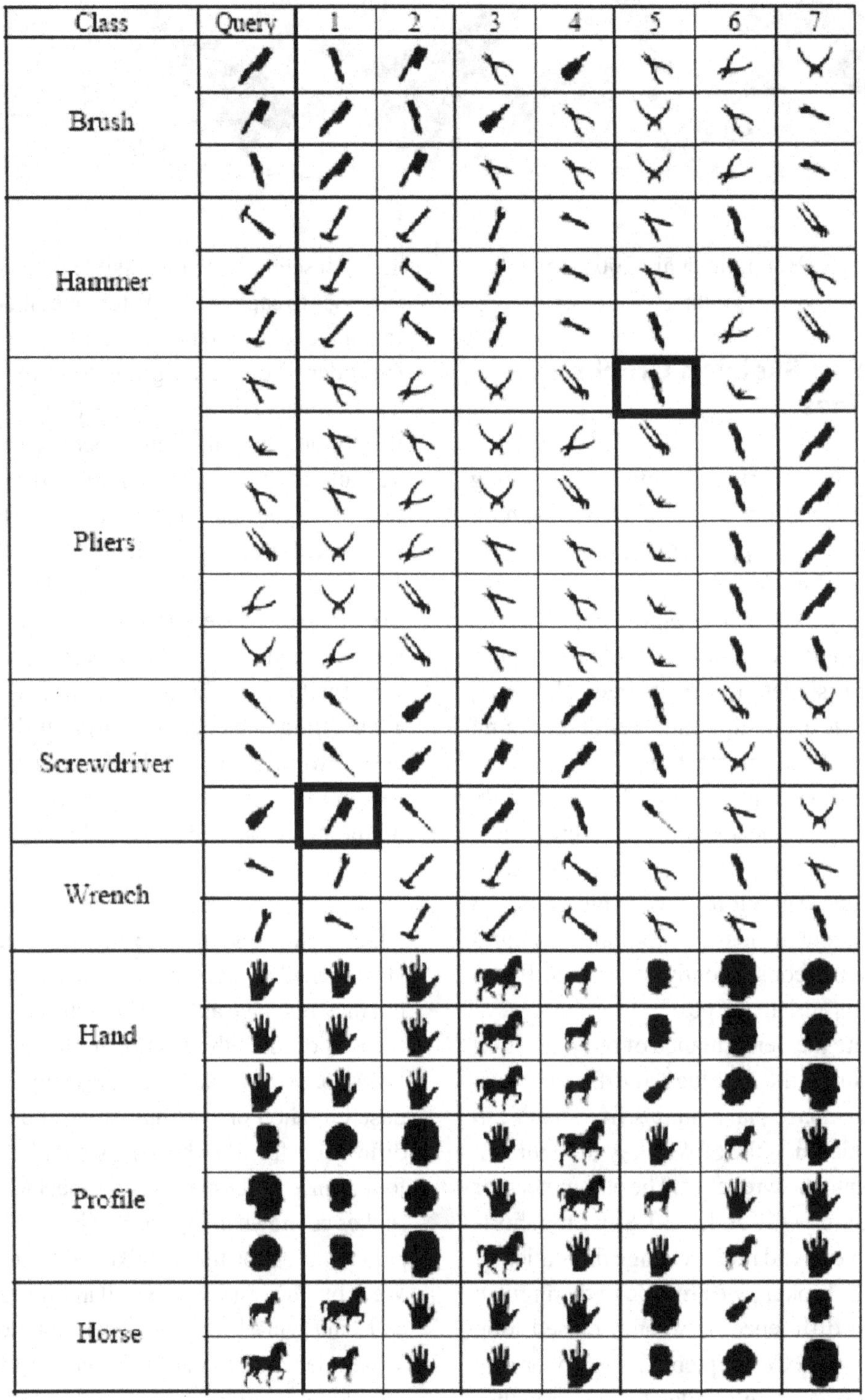

Figure 12. A broken key and its skeleton

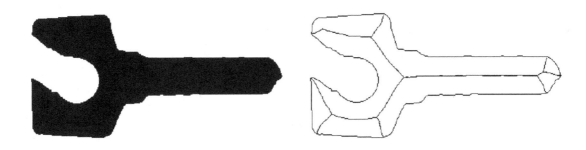

Figure 13. The results of the proposed method on a small database are shown. Since the authors are able to distinguish the structural difference between a closed and open loop, the broken key (without hole) is more similar to the wrenches than the keys (with holes) in (a). Inner-Distance (Ling and Jacobs, 2007) cannot capture this difference as shown in (b).

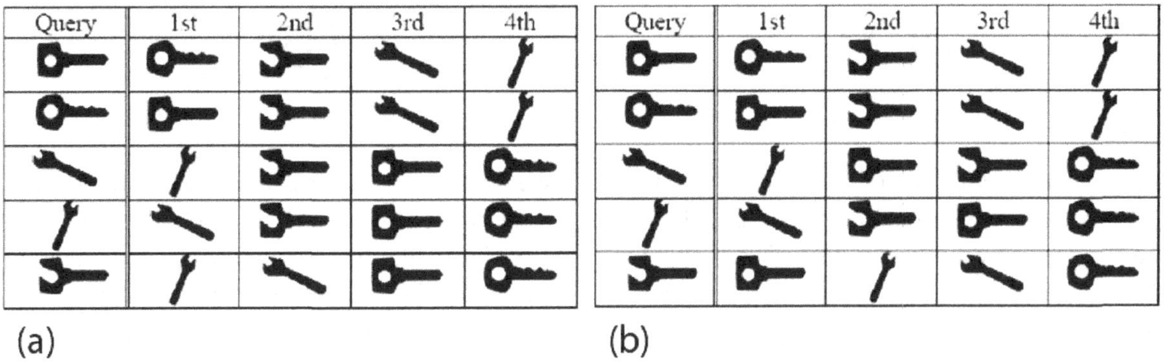

Query	1st	2nd	3rd	4th

(a)

Query	1st	2nd	3rd	4th

(b)

Figure 14. Left: two spectacles and their curve-skeletons; Right: two snakes and their curve-skeletons

Figure 15. Comparison between α=0 in (a) and α=10 in (b) on a small database. The distance between query and the given shape is also displayed.

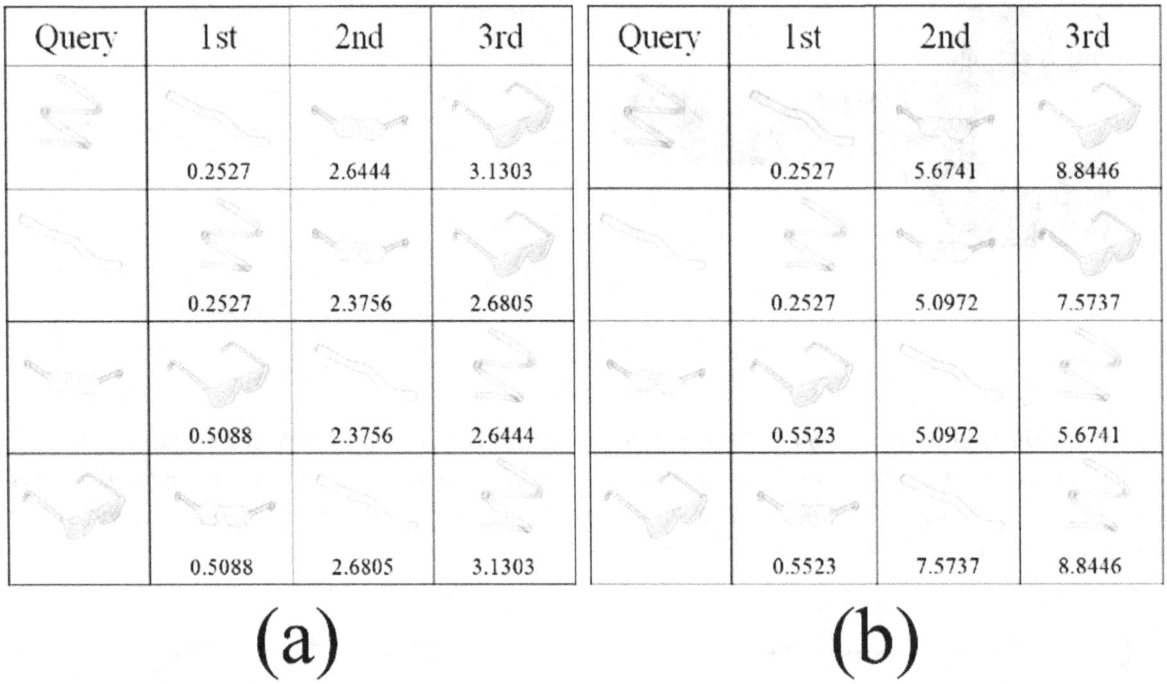

Query	1st	2nd	3rd	Query	1st	2nd	3rd
	0.2527	2.6444	3.1303		0.2527	5.6741	8.8446
	0.2527	2.3756	2.6805		0.2527	5.0972	7.5737
	0.5088	2.3756	2.6444		0.5523	5.0972	5.6741
	0.5088	2.6805	3.1303		0.5523	7.5737	8.8446

(a)　　　　　　　　(b)

ously enhances the discrimination. Although the shortest paths between end nodes of the two classes are similar, the proposed method is still able to distinguish the structural difference between a closed loop and a line better by considering the path length. One reason is that skeleton path is particularly stable in 3D since there's no occlusion, and the path length percentages are almost constant no matter how shapes deform due to articulation. Another reason is that shapes in different classes have different skeleton paths, which lead to more effective discrimination.

5.3 Retrieval on McGill 3D Articulated Shape Database

Based on the above experimental results, our algorithm is validated to be robust to symmetry and discriminative to different graph structures.

We demonstrate it further on the McGill Articulated Shape Database (Siddiqi et al., 2008) with 255 objects divided into ten categories, namely, 'Ants', 'Crabs', 'Spectacles', 'Hands', 'Humans', 'Octopuses', 'Pliers', 'Snakes', 'Spiders', and 'Teddy Bears'. Sample models from this database are shown in Figure 16.

As stated in (Li and Hamza, 2011), retrieving shapes that are similar to a given query shape from a database involves shape matching. However, determining the similarity between two given shapes does not necessarily require finding an exact correspondence between their shape components. In this section, we extend the shape similarity measure discussed in Section 4 to shape retrieval, and we also propose five methods based on the skeleton path. In the sequel, we will use the following abbreviations:

Figure 16. Sample shapes from McGill Articulated Shape Database (only two shapes for each of the 10 classes are shown)

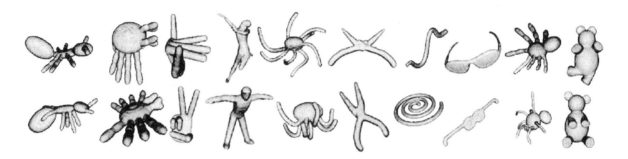

- **SH:** We denote the method in Section 4 as SH, since it uses the square matrix with penalty and Hungarian algorithm.
- **SDP:** We denote the method that uses the square matrix with penalty and dynamic programming algorithm as SDP.
- **NSH:** We denote the method that uses the matrix, which is not square and without penalty, and the Hungarian algorithm as NSH.
- **EMS:** We define the dissimilarity from the query to a shape in the dataset as the sum of minimum endpoint distance of the query to all endpoints of the latter, and denote it as EMS.
- **PMS:** We define the dissimilarity from the query to a shape in the dataset as the sum of minimum skeleton path distance of the query to all skeleton paths of the latter, and denote it as PMS.

Here we use the parameters M=50 and α=50. In our comparative analysis, we have used the precision/recall curve to measure the retrieval performance. Ideally, this curve should be a horizontal line at unit precision. For each query shape, we use the first 77 returned shapes with descending similarity rankings (i.e., ascending Euclidean distance ranking), dividing them into 11 groups accordingly. The retrieval results of

the 5 skeleton path based methods on the whole McGill Articulated Shape Database are shown in Figure 17. Obviously, PMS provides a much better performance that the other methods because it fully exploits the original information that skeleton paths carry. By finding the minimum value of skeleton path distances, we might establish a potential corresponding relationship between paths. However, as a matter of fact, there is no veracious global path correspondence. As for EMS, the second best method, we assume that the endpoints with minimum distance are corresponding to each other, although it may fail to find the global endpoints correspondence. Furthermore, SH and SDP are almost neck-and-neck in terms of retrieval accuracy, and both are superior to NSH, which demonstrate that the penalty plays a key role in shape discrimination.

We choose PMS to represent our skeleton path based methods and compare it with two competitive 3D shape retrieval methods: Light Field Distribution (LFD) method (Chen et al., 2003) and segmentation-based method (Agathos et al., 2009). We chose these two methods because LFD has been reported as one of the best in literature for 3D rigid models (Shilane et al., 2004), and segmentation based method represents a state-of-the-art method for articulated models recently. The evaluation of the retrieval results is based upon the quantification measures in the following:

Figure 17. Precision-recall plot of the proposed skeleton path based methods

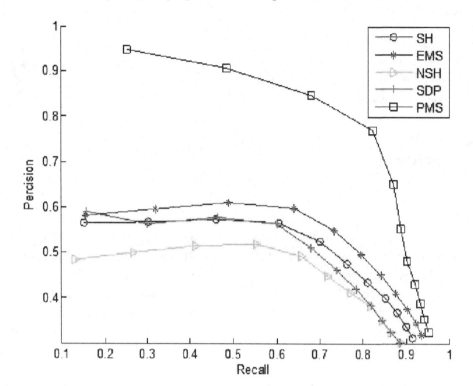

- **Nearest Neighbor (NN):** The percentage of queries where the closest match belongs to the query's class.
- **First Tier (FT):** The recall for the (k-1) closest matches, where k is the cardinality of the query's class.
- **Second Tier (ST):** The recall for the 2(k-1) closest matches, where k is the cardinality of the query's class.
- **Discounted Cumulative Gain (DCG):** A statistic that correct results near the front of the retrieval list are weighted more heavily than correct results near the end under the assumption that a user is most interested in the first results.

The above measures range from 0% to 100% and higher values indicate better performance. We use the code provided by the authors to obtain the result of LFD (Chen et al., 2003) and the result of segmentation-based method is reported in (Agathos et al., 2009). The corresponding scores of each method over the complete database are showed in Table 4. As can be observed, the proposed method performs much better than LFD, which make it valid that the skeleton path based approach has a nature advantage for retrieving articulated shapes. Moreover, compared with the most recent excellent retrieval method for

Table 4. Comparison results on McGill 3D articulated shape database

Algorithm	NN(%)	FT(%)	ST(%)	DCG(%)
LFD [52]	84.6	44.7	59.3	82.7
Segmentation-based [53]	97.6	74.1	91.1	93.3
Our method	96.0	**75.3**	83.8	**95.1**

nonrigid shapes, segmentation-based method, the proposed still outperforms with the First Tier and DCG evaluations.

6. IMPLEMENTATION AND COMPUTATIONAL COMPLEXITY

We briefly describe all the implementation steps: First, we compute skeletons with the algorithm in (Choi et al., 2003). An important next step is proper skeleton pruning. We prune the skeletons with the algorithm in (Bai et al., 2007). Then we find all the shape paths with Dijkstra's shortest path algorithm on the pruned skeleton graph. Finally, the total costs between skeleton graphs are computed with the proposed method.

We now analyze the computational complexity of the proposed graph matching approach. Let n_i be the number of end nodes in the skeleton graphs G_i ($i = 1, 2$), and let mi be the number of all nodes (including junction nodes) in G_i. Observer that $n_i < m_i$, since the number of end nodes is significantly smaller than the number of all nodes in the skeleton graph. Since in our experiment n_i and m_i are usually no more than 20, the time cost for comparing the similarity of two graphs is very small. The average time is approximately 0.015 seconds in our tests.

The time for Dijkstra's algorithm used to find the shortest path between two end modes on G_i is $O(m_i \log m_i)$, thus the time for computing all shape paths on G_i is $O(n_i^2 m_i \log m_i)$, since we have n_i^2 pairs of end nodes. The complexity for computing a shape distance between a pair of shape paths is $O(M)$, so the complexity for computing a path matrix is $O(n_1 n_2 M)$. Since the complexity of OSB is $O(n_1 n_2)$ (Latecki et al., 2005), the time for computing the matrix $C(G_1, G_2)$ is $O(n_1^2 n_2^2)$. Since we assume $n_1 < n_2$, the time cost for the Hungarian algorithm in our method

is $O(n_2^3)$. Thus, the total complexity for our method is

$$O(n_i^2 m_i \log m_i) + O(n_1 n_2 M) + O(n_1^2 n_2^2) + O(n_2^3)$$

Recalling that $n_i < m_i$, for $i = 1, 2$, by substituting the larger number mi for all occurrences of n_i, our time complexity is bounded by $O(m_1^2 m_2^2)$. For example, this is two orders of magnitude smaller than the complexity of the Graph-Edit Distance, which is $O(m_1^3 m_2^3)$ (Sebastian et al., 2004).

7. BAYESIAN CLASSIFICATION

Compared to the method in (Sun and Super, 2005), which uses contour segments and Bayesian classification to perform a recognition task, our method uses paths instead of contour segments. Since paths are normalized, our method does not require any invariant reference frame, and consequently the process of PCA (Sun and Super, 2005) can be removed. For a given query shape and a given shape class, we compute the probability that the shape belongs to the class. This step is repeated for all shape classes, and the query shape is then assigned to the class with the highest probability.

Given a shape ω' that should be classified by Bayesian Classifier, we build the skeleton graph $G(\omega')$ of ω' and input $G(\omega')$ as the query. For a skeleton graph $G(\omega')$, if the number of end nodes is n, the corresponding number of paths is $n(n-1)/2$ compared to the number of parts $n!$ in (Sun and Super, 2005). Then, the Bayesian Classifier computes the posterior probability of all classes for each path $sp' \in G(\omega')$. By accumulating the posterior probability of all of the paths of $G(\omega')$ the system automatically yields the ranking of class hypothesis for the query shape ω'. We use Gaussian distribution to compute the probability p that two skeleton paths are similar:

$$p\left(sp' \mid sp\right) = \cfrac{1}{\sqrt{2\pi\alpha}\,\exp\left[-\cfrac{pd\left(sp',sp\right)^2}{2\alpha}\right]} \tag{7}$$

For example, this probability is high for two different paths with small pd value. For different datasets, α should be different. In our experiments, for the dataset of Aslan and Tari (Aslan and Tari, 2005), $\alpha = 0.15$. The class-conditional probability of observing sp' given that ω' belongs to class c_i is:

$$p\left(sp \mid c_i\right) = \sum_{sp \in G\left(c_i\right)} p\left(sp' \mid sp\right) p\left(sp \mid c_i\right) \tag{8}$$

We assume that all paths within a class path set are equiprobable, therefore, we set

$$p\left(sp \mid c_i\right) = \frac{1}{\left|G\left(c_i\right)\right|} \tag{9}$$

According to the probability that the query shape belongs to a given class, the posterior probability of a class given that path $sp' \in G\left(\omega'\right)$ is determined by Bayes rule:

$$p\left(c_i \mid sp'\right) = \frac{p\left(sp' \mid c_i\right) p\left(c_i\right)}{p\left(sp'\right)} \tag{10}$$

Similar to the above assumption, $p\left(c_i\right) = 1 / M$. The probability of sp' is equal to

$$p\left(sp'\right) = \sum_{i=1}^{M} p\left(sp' \mid c_i\right) p\left(c_i\right) \tag{11}$$

Through the above formulas, we can get the posterior probability of all paths of $G\left(\omega'\right)$. By summing the posterior probabilities of a class over the set of paths in the query shape, we obtain the probability that it belongs to a given class. Obviously, the biggest one, C_m, is the class that input shape belongs to.

$$C_m = \arg\max_{i=1,\dots,M} \sum_{sp' \in G\left(\omega'\right)} p\left(c_i \mid sp'\right) \tag{12}$$

8. CLASSIFICATION EXPERIMENTS

In this section, we evaluate the performance of the proposed method based on the database of Aslan and Tari (Aslan and Tari, 2005). We selected this database due to large variations of shapes in the same classes. As shown in Figure 6, the Aslan and Tari database includes 14 classes of articulated shapes with 4 shapes in each class. We use each shape in this database as a query, and show the classification result of our system in Figure 18(a). We used leave one out classification, i.e., the query shape was excluded from its class. The table in Figure 18(a) is composed of 14 rows and 9 columns. The first column of the table represents the class of each row. For each row, there are four experimental results which belong to the same class. Each experimental result has two elements. The first one is the query shape and the second one is the classification result of our system. If the result is correct, it should be the equal to the first column of the row. The red numbers mark the wrong classes assigned to query objects. Since there is only one error in 56 classification results, the classification accuracy in percentage by this measure is 98.2%. In fact, the only error is reasonable. Even a human could misclassify it. The query shape is very similar to the star, which is the class 8. Therefore, in some sense, we can conclude that all of our results are correct. We compared our method to the method presented by Sun and Super (Sun and Super, 2005), their method uses the same Bayesian classifier but is based on contour parts. As shown in Figure 18(b), their method yields 4 wrong results for 56 query shapes, which yields the classification accuracy of only 92.8%.

The classification time for all 56 shapes with the proposed method takes only 5 minutes on the PC with 1.5 GHZ CPU and 512M RAM. In comparison, Sun and Super's method takes 13 minutes on the same computer.

Figure 18. (a) Results of the authors' method on Aslan and Tari database (Aslan and Tari, 2005); (b) Results of the Sun and Super's method on Aslan and Tari database (Aslan and Tari, 2005). Since each class is composed of 4 shapes, the class of query and the result should be the same. Red numbers mark the results where this is not the case.

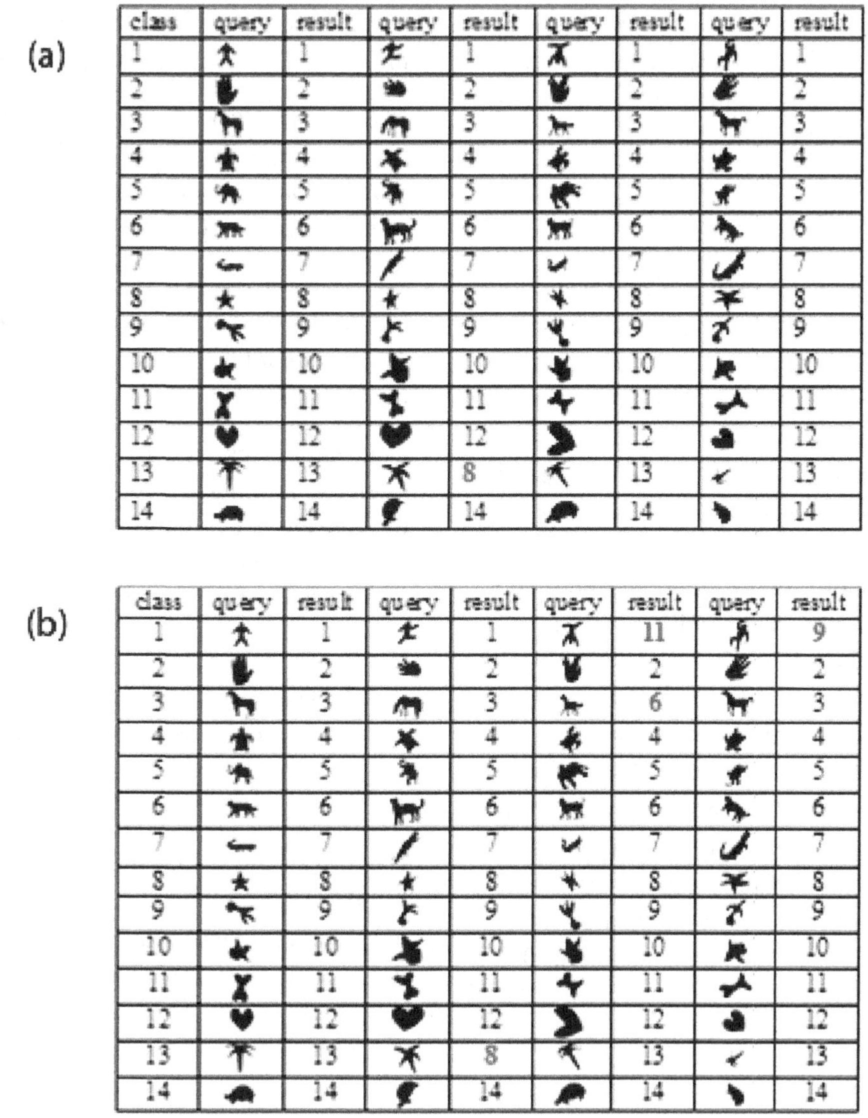

(a)

class	query	result	query	result	query	result	query	result
1		1		1		1		1
2		2		2		2		2
3		3		3		3		3
4		4		4		4		4
5		5		5		5		5
6		6		6		6		6
7		7		7		7		7
8		8		8		8		8
9		9		9		9		9
10		10		10		10		10
11		11		11		11		11
12		12		12		12		12
13		13		8		13		13
14		14		14		14		14

(b)

class	query	result	query	result	query	result	query	result
1		1		1		11		9
2		2		2		2		2
3		3		3		6		3
4		4		4		4		4
5		5		5		5		5
6		6		6		6		6
7		7		7		7		7
8		8		8		8		8
9		9		9		9		9
10		10		10		10		10
11		11		11		11		11
12		12		12		12		12
13		13		8		13		13
14		14		14		14		14

9. CONCLUSION

This book chapter demonstrates the usefulness of geodesic skeleton paths for both matching and classification. We represent a skeleton as a set of geodesic paths between skeleton endpoints. The paths are compared using sequence matching. The proposed approach does not require any complicated strategies for tree/graph matching based on editing of topological structures and complicated weighting of branches/nodes. In addition to superior performance, the proposed method also reduces the time cost. Moreover, the fact that our representation of skeletons is based on their endpoints opens a possibility of new applications. We demonstrated one such application. We are able to compute the main symmetry axes of articulated objects by computing self similarity of skeleton divisions induced by pairs of endpoints.

The performance of our method is limited in the presence of large protrusions, since they require skipping a large number of skeleton endpoints. However, we believe this limitation can be solved with partial matching, e.g., when the dissimilarity is computed only for the pair of subgraphs that are most similar.

Our method is not limited to skeleton graphs. Our future work will also focus on matching any weighted graphs. In the case of planar graphs, we can still benefit from the cyclic order of end nodes. In the case of non-planar graphs, it appears to be possible to replace the cyclic order with the order of end nodes induced by the geodesic distance. We will also work on an efficient indexing scheme that is needed for fast, sub-linear database retrieval. Although our method is significantly faster than other skeleton graph matching approaches in direct comparison of two shapes, some of the existing methods allow for sub-linear database retrieval (Sebastian et al., 2004; Shokoufandeh et al., 2005).

REFERENCES

Agathos, A., Pratikakis, I., Papadakis, P., Perantonis, S., Azariadis, P., & Sapidis, N. (2009). *Retrieval of 3D articulated objects using a graph-based representation*. In Eurographics Workshop on 3D Object Retrieval.

Aslan, C., & Tari, S. (2005). An axis based representation for recognition. *ICCV: IEEE International Conference on Computer Vision*, (pp. 1339-1346).

August, J., Siddiqi, K., & Zucker, S. (1999). Ligature instabilities and the perceptual organization of shape. *Computer Vision and Image Understanding, 76*(3), 231–243. doi:10.1006/cviu.1999.0802

Bai, X., & Latecki, L. J. (2008). Path similarity skeleton graph matching. *IEEE Transactions on Pattern Analysis and Machine Intelligence, 30*(7), 1282–1292. doi:10.1109/TPAMI.2007.70769

Bai, X., Latecki, L. J., & Liu, W.-Y. (2006). Skeleton pruning by contour partitioning. In *International Conference on Discrete Geometry for Computer Imagery*, (pp. 567-579).

Bai, X., Latecki, L. J., & Liu, W.-Y. (2007). Skeleton pruning by contour partitioning with discrete curve evolution. *IEEE Transactions on Pattern Analysis and Machine Intelligence, 29*(3), 449–462. doi:10.1109/TPAMI.2007.59

Bai, X., Yang, X., & Latecki, L. J. (2008). Skeleton-based shape classification using path similarity. *International Journal of Pattern Recognition and Artificial Intelligence, 22*(4), 733–746. doi:10.1142/S0218001408006405

Basri, R., Costa, L., Geiger, D., & Jacobs, D. (1998). Determining the similarity of deformable shapes. *Vision Research, 38*, 2365–2385. doi:10.1016/S0042-6989(98)00043-1

Belongie, S., Puzhicha, J., & Malik, J. (2002). Shape matching and object recognition using shape contexts. *IEEE Transactions on Pattern Analysis and Machine Intelligence*, *24*(4), 509–522. doi:10.1109/34.993558

Blum, H. (1973). Biological shape and visual science. *Journal of Theoretical Biology*, *38*, 205–287. doi:10.1016/0022-5193(73)90175-6

Chen, D., Tian, X., Shen, Y., & Ouhyoung, M. (2003). On visual similarity based 3D model retrieval. *Computer Graphics Forum*, *22*(3), 223–232. doi:10.1111/1467-8659.00669

Choi, W.-P., Lam, K.-M., & Siu, W.-C. (2003). Extraction of the Euclidean skeleton based on a connectivity criterion. *Pattern Recognition*, *36*(3), 721–729. doi:10.1016/S0031-3203(02)00098-5

Cornea, N. D., Silver, D., Yuan, X., & Balasubramanian, R. (2005). Computing hierarchical curve-skeletons of 3D objects. *The Visual Computer*, *21*, 945–955. doi:10.1007/s00371-005-0308-0

Demirci, F., Shokoufandeh, A., Dickinson, S., Keselman, Y., & Bretzner, L. (2004). Many-to-many feature matching using spherical coding of directed graphs. In *ECCV: European Conference on Computer Vision*, (pp. 322-335).

Demirci, F., Shokoufandeh, A., Keselman, Y., Bretzner, L., & Dickinson, S. (2006). Object recognition as many-to-many feature matching. *International Journal of Computer Vision*, *69*(2), 203–222. doi:10.1007/s11263-006-6993-y

Di Ruberto, C. (2004). Recognition of shapes by attributed skeletal graphs. *Pattern Recognition*, *37*(1), 21–31. doi:10.1016/j.patcog.2003.07.004

Geiger, D., Liu, T., & Kohn, R. V. (2003). Representation and self-similarity of shapes. *IEEE Transactions on Pattern Analysis and Machine Intelligence*, *25*(1), 86–99. doi:10.1109/TPAMI.2003.1159948

Hilaga, M., Shinagawa, Y., Kohmura, T., & Kunii, T. L. (2001). Topology matching for fully automatic similarity estimation of 3D shapes. In *ACM SIGGRAPH*, (pp. 203-212).

Huttenlocher, D. P., Klanderman, G. A., & Rucklidge, W. J. (1993). Comparing images using the Hausdorff distance. *IEEE Transactions on Pattern Analysis and Machine Intelligence*, *15*(9), 850–863. doi:10.1109/34.232073

Kim, W. Y., & Kak, A. C. (1991). 3-D object recognition using bipartite matching embedded in discrete relaxation. *IEEE Transactions on Pattern Analysis and Machine Intelligence*, *13*(3), 224–251. doi:10.1109/34.75511

Latecki, L. J., & Lakamper, R. (1999). Convexity rule for shape decomposition based on discrete contour evolution. *Computer Vision and Image Understanding*, *73*(3), 441–454. doi:10.1006/cviu.1998.0738

Latecki, L. J., & Lakamper, R. (2000). Shape similarity measure based on correspondence of visual parts. *IEEE Transactions on Pattern Analysis and Machine Intelligence*, *22*(10), 1185–1190. doi:10.1109/34.879802

Latecki, L. J., Lakamper, R., & Eckhardt, U. (2000). Shape descriptors for non-rigid shapes with a single closed contour. In *CVPR: IEEE International Conference on Computer Vision and Pattern Recognition*, (pp. 424-429).

Latecki, L. J., Megalooikonomou, V., Wang, Q., Lakamper, R., Ratanamahatana, C. A., & Keogh, E. (2005). Partial elastic matching of time series. In *ICDM: IEEE International Conference on Data Mining*, (pp. 701-704).

Li, C., & Hamza, B. A. (2011). Skeleton path based approach for nonrigid 3D shape analysis and retrieval. In *Combinatorial Image Analysis – 14th International Workshop (IWCIA)*, *LNCS 6636/2011*, (pp. 84-95).

Ling, H., & Jacobs, D. W. (2007). Shape classification using inner-distance. *IEEE Transactions on Pattern Analysis and Machine Intelligence, 29*(2), 286–299. doi:10.1109/TPAMI.2007.41

Liu, T., & Geiger, D. (1999). Approximate tree matching and shape similarity. In *ICCV: IEEE International Conference on Computer Vision*, (pp. 456-462).

Ogniewicz, R. L., & Kubler, O. (1995). Hierarchic Voronoi skeletons. *Pattern Recognition, 28*(3), 343–359. doi:10.1016/0031-3203(94)00105-U

Pelillo, M. (2002). Matching free trees, maximal cliques, and monotone game dynamics. *IEEE Transactions on Pattern Analysis and Machine Intelligence, 24*(11), 1535–1541. doi:10.1109/TPAMI.2002.1046176

Pelillo, M., Siddiqi, K., & Zucker, S. W. (1999). Matching hierarchical structures using association graphs. *IEEE Transactions on Pattern Analysis and Machine Intelligence, 21*(11), 1105–1120. doi:10.1109/34.809105

Sebastian, T. B., & Kimia, B. B. (2005). Curves vs skeletons in object recognition. *Signal Processing, 85*(2), 247–263. doi:10.1016/j.sigpro.2004.10.016

Sebastian, T. B., Klein, P. N., & Kimia, B. B. (2001). Recognition of shapes by editing shock graphs. In *ICCV: IEEE International Conference on Computer Vision*, (pp. 755-762).

Sebastian, T. B., Klein, P. N., & Kimia, B. B. (2003). On aligning curves. *IEEE Transactions on Pattern Analysis and Machine Intelligence, 25*(1), 116–125. doi:10.1109/TPAMI.2003.1159951

Sebastian, T. B., Klein, P. N., & Kimia, B. B. (2004). Recognition of shapes by editing their shock graphs. *IEEE Transactions on Pattern Analysis and Machine Intelligence, 26*(5), 550–571. doi:10.1109/TPAMI.2004.1273924

Shaked, D., & Bruckstein, A. M. (1998). Pruning medial axes. *Computer Vision and Image Understanding, 69*(2), 156–169. doi:10.1006/cviu.1997.0598

Shilane, P., Min, P., Kazhdan, M., & Funkhouser, T. (2004). The Princeton shape benchmark. In *Proceedings of Shape Modeling International*, (pp. 167-178).

Shokoufandeh, A., Macrini, D., Dickinson, S., Siddiqi, K., & Zucker, S. W. (2005). Indexing hierarchical structures using graph spectra. *IEEE Transactions on Pattern Analysis and Machine Intelligence, 27*(7), 1125–1140. doi:10.1109/TPAMI.2005.142

Siddiqi, K., & Kimia, B. B. (1995). Parts of visual form: Computational aspects. *IEEE Transactions on Pattern Analysis and Machine Intelligence, 17*(3), 239–251. doi:10.1109/34.368189

Siddiqi, K., Kimia, B. B., Tannenbaum, A., & Zucker, S. (1999). Shocks, shapes, and wiggles. *Image and Vision Computing, 17*(5-6), 365–373. doi:10.1016/S0262-8856(98)00130-9

Siddiqi, K., Shkoufandeh, A., Dickinson, S., & Zucker, S. (1998). Shock graphs and shape matching. In *ICCV: IEEE International Conference on Computer Vision*, (pp. 222-229).

Siddiqi, K., Shokoufandeh, A., Dickinson, S., & Zucker, S. (1999). Shock graphs and shape matching. *International Journal of Computer Vision, 35*(1), 13–32. doi:10.1023/A:1008102926703

Siddiqi, K., Zhang, J., Macrini, D., Shokoufandeh, A., Bouix, S., & Dickinson, S. (2008). Retrieving articulated 3D models using medial surfaces. *Machine Vision and Applications, 19*(4), 261–274. doi:10.1007/s00138-007-0097-8

Sun, K. B., & Super, B. J. (2005). Classification of contour shapes using class segment sets. In *CVPR: IEEE International Conference on Computer Vision and Pattern Recognition*, (pp. 727-733).

Torsello, A., & Hancock, E. R. (2004). A skeletal measure of 2D shape similarity. *Computer Vision and Image Understanding*, *95*(1), 1–29. doi:10.1016/j.cviu.2004.03.006

Torsello, A., Hidovic-Rowe, D., & Pelillo, M. (2005). Polynomial-time metrics for attributed trees. *IEEE Transactions on Pattern Analysis and Machine Intelligence*, *27*(7), 1087–1099. doi:10.1109/TPAMI.2005.146

Tu, Z., & Yuille, A. L. (2004). Shape matching and recognition: using generative models and informative features. In *ECCV: European Conference on Computer Vision*, (Vol. 3, pp. 195-209).

Zhu, S. C., & Yuille, A. L. (1996). FORMS: A flexible object recognition and modeling system. *International Journal of Computer Vision*, *20*(3), 187–212.

Chapter 11
Discriminative Feature Selection in Image Classification and Retrieval

Shang Liu
Beihang University, China

Xiao Bai
Beihang University, China

ABSTRACT

In this chapter, the authors present a new method to improve the performance of current bag-of-words based image classification process. After feature extraction, they introduce a pairwise image matching scheme to select the discriminative features. Only the label information from the training-sets is used to update the feature weights via an iterative matching processing. The selected features correspond to the foreground content of the images, and thus highlight the high level category knowledge of images. Visual words are constructed on these selected features. This novel method could be used as a refinement step for current image classification and retrieval process. The authors prove the efficiency of their method in three tasks: supervised image classification, semi-supervised image classification, and image retrieval.

INTRODUCTION

Image classification and retrieval are important research topics in the areas of computer vision, pattern recognition and machine learning. The earlier attempts can handle images with simple background. However, in modern days, the images on the website or computers normally contain complex background and various depictions. Recent research has made a lot of effort to tackle those complex images. One major attempt is to extract local invariant features from images. Famous contributions include SIFT (Lowe, 2004), PCA-SIFT (Ke, 2004), SURF (Bay, 2008) and more recently,

DOI: 10.4018/978-1-4666-1891-6.ch011

Local Self-Similarity (LSS) (Shechtman, 2007). These descriptors can be used together with Scale-invariant regions (Mikolajczyket, 2005) to extract invariants features within scale-invariant regions. Other attempts mainly focus on building structural or statistical learning framework. Structure-based methods (Bai, 2009) (Bunke, 1998)(Xia, 2009) aim at extracting structure invariant to characterize the objects contained in the images. Statistical learning (Fergus, 2003) (Weber, 2000) (Chum, 2007) on the other hand, tries to characterize the low-level invariant via complex statistical models, which comprised of the positions and the scalar values of the local invariant feature descriptors.

One typical example is bag-of-words approach (Li, 2005), which originates from the area of document analysis. Here in computer vision, the basic bag-of-words approach can be described as following: an image is treated as a special document. Features extracted from the image are considered "visual words." Images can then be analyzed by counting the frequency of the meaningful visual words and represented by a visual words frequency histogram. Traditional pattern analysis methods such as Support Vector Machine (SVM) (Duda, 2002), Gaussian Mixture Model (GMM) (Figueiredo, 2002) or Linear Discrimina-

tive Analysis (Duda, 2002) can then be used for recognition and classification. Although simple and effective, one major problem for bag-of-words approach is that the constructed visual words are general but not discriminative. The reason relies on that any feature extraction method will extract not only the foreground but also background features within an image. An example is given in Figure 1. We can observe that the SIFT features are overlaid on both foreground and background parts of the image. When all the extracted features are used to construct the visual words, many visual words may correspond to the background part of the image. Even for the same category images, the background information varies significantly. The features we expect should be discriminative enough to carry category specific information. However, the background features contain little discriminative information. This influence the visual words construction and classification steps. The classification and recognition process is degraded both in accuracy and efficiency. The existing statistical and structural based methods suffer the same problem. If discriminative features can be extracted, then the high level category information can be better characterized. The classification or retrieval performance can be

Figure 1. Feature extraction example - both foreground and background features are extracted at the same time. The left is the original image, which is a car-tire. The right is processed by SIFT extraction, and the dots represent SIFT features.

improved. In this chapter, we investigate whether discriminative features can be extracted to highlight the category information while diminish the background information.

BACKGROUND

Recent work has considered ways to increase the discriminative information in image analysis. One attempt is to build object category model first. Shape models (Leibeet, 2004)(Zhang, 2007) (McAllester, 2010) have been used to select features overlaid on the objects. A segmentation-and-recognition framework (Fergus, 2006) has been proposed by using object category model. Meanwhile, Quack et al. build object models and find discriminative features from training classes. Another approach (Dork´o, 2003) trains object-part classifiers by labeled positive and negative training samples. Then the classifiers are ranked by their distinctiveness to select features. By removing the background information, the above methods focus on the foreground part of the image. Two difficulties exist in using object category models. The first one is we need extra training samples to build the models for each category. The second problem relies that these models are sensitive to the appearance variation within each object category.

Pairwise matching (Nowak, 2007) (Rother, 2006)(Lee, 2009) is another way to decrease the background influence. By finding common parts between pairs of images, foreground objects can be highlighted. C. Rother et al. introduce "co-segmentation" to find common parts between image pairs via matching. For unsupervised image classification, Lee and Grauman use PKM (Pyramid Match Kernel) (Lee, 2009) to find underlying clusters by iteratively match pairwise images. However, these methods together depend on kernel tricks. No specific discriminative features are explicitly extracted in the whole process.

Little effort has been paid on directly selecting discriminative features for image analysis. In this chapter, we propose a method to find discriminative visual features. The selected discriminative features are object or category-specific and provide more discriminative information. Unlike the previous methods, ours can be used as a further refinement step for the classification process. The inputs of the algorithm are the training-sets of supervised or semi-supervised image classification. We need to emphasis that our work is different from feature selection, which focus on selecting useful attributes to construct a lower dimension feature vectors. The dimension of feature vectors in our work keeps the same. We select the image features which are relevant with the category information.

DISCRIMINATIVE FEATURES SELECTION

Approach Overview

In this subsection, we briefly describe our method and present the motivation of our algorithm. To select the discriminative features, our first observation is that images of the same category shares a set of common features with each other but not those of different categories. These shared features among each category are the discriminative features. Our second observation is that the selected features should improve the category specific information by means of the classification performance. For the first observation, we need to find a pairwise image matching method to incorporate the sets of features into consideration. Many methods are available for this requirement (Torr, 2000; Bai, 2009; Fatih Demirci, 2006; Rubner, 2000). For the second observation, to evaluate the classification performance, the pairwise matching method should be used to compute the metric distance or similarity between pairs of images.

Here in this chapter, we choose EMD (Earth Mover Distance) (Rubner, 2000). The reason to use EMD is two folds. First, EMD can be used as a metric to compute the similarity between images. The second reason is EMD can also find the matching correspondence between features within two images.

The main steps are outlined as following:

1. Feature extraction is performed, i.e. SIFT, on labeled training images. Each feature is assigned an initialized weight 1, which will be iteratively updated to select the discriminative features.
2. The similarities between images are computed based on pairwise image matching via Earth Mover Distance (EMD).
3. With the results of pairwise similarity computation, feature weights are updated in the third step. As describe before, the images of the same category shares a set of common features with each other but not those of different categories. So we analyze the patterns of the correspondences between images and update the feature weights according to this defining significance. The second and the third steps are performed iteratively to highlight the discriminative features. The final stopping criterion for this iterative updating procedure is the separability of the training-sets which can be achieved via step two.
4. From the previous steps, features with high weights are selected as discriminative features. Then we can use these selected features to construct visual words. Three main applications, supervised image classification, semi-supervised image classification and content based image retrieval are proposed to validate our method.

Pairwise Image Matching via EMD

In this part, we describe pairwise image matching by using earth mover distance (EMD). The problem can be formalized as following. Given two images P and Q, let the signature $I_P = \left\{ \left(f_1^P, w_1^P \right), \cdots, \left(f_m^P, w_m^P \right) \right\}$ be the representation of image P where f_i^P corresponds to a feature, i.e. SIFT or LSS, and w_i^P is the weight value of this feature; $I_Q = \left\{ \left(f_1^Q, w_1^Q \right), \cdots, \left(f_n^Q, w_n^Q \right) \right\}$ is the representation of image Q; m and n are the number of features in image P and Q. Initially, all feature weights are assigned as 1. Two matrices are computed, one is the ground distance matrix $\text{Dist}_{PQ} = [d_{ij}]$ where d_{ij} is the ground distance between features f_i^P and f_j^Q. In this chapter, we use normalized Euclidean metric to compute matrix Dist_{PQ}. Another matrix is the flow matrix $\text{Flow}_{P,Q} = [\text{flow}_{ij}]$ with the element flow_{ij} indicating the flow between features f_i^P and f_j^Q. $\text{Flow}_{P,Q}$ matrix is achieved by minimizing the overall cost

$$\text{WORK}\left(I_P, I_Q, \text{Flow}_{P,Q} \right) = \sum_{i=1}^{m} \sum_{j=1}^{n} d_{ij} \text{flow}_{ij} \tag{1}$$

Subject to the following constraints:

$$\text{flow}_{ij} \geq 0 \quad 1 \leq i \leq m, 1 \leq j \leq n \tag{2}$$

$$\sum_{j=1}^{n} \text{flow}_{ij} \leq w_i^P \quad 1 \leq i \leq m \tag{3}$$

$$\sum_{i=1}^{m} \text{flow}_{ij} \leq w_i^Q \quad 1 \leq j \leq n \tag{4}$$

$$\sum_{j=1}^{n}\sum_{i=1}^{m}\text{flow}_{ij} = \min\left(\sum_{j=1}^{n}w_{i}^{Q}, \sum_{i=1}^{m}w_{i}^{P}\right) \qquad (5)$$

To solve the above constraints, we use Dantzig's method (Dantzig, 1951) to find the solution. After solving the $\text{Flow}_{P,Q}$ matrix, we define the Earth Mover's distance between two images P and Q as below:

$$\text{EMD}\left(I_{P}, I_{Q}\right) = \frac{\sum_{i=1}^{m}\sum_{j=1}^{m}d_{ij}\text{flow}_{ij}}{\sum_{i=1}^{m}\sum_{j=1}^{m}\text{flow}_{ij}} \qquad (6)$$

In this chapter, we use $\text{EMD}\left(I_{P}, I_{Q}\right)$ as similarity value between images I_{P} and I_{Q}. We can proceed to construct a similarity matrix Sim for all the training set.

$$\text{Sim} = \left[\text{Sim}_{P,Q} = \exp\left(-\left(\text{EMD}\left(I_{P}, I_{Q}\right)\right)^{2} / 2\tilde{A}^{2}\right)\right] \qquad (7)$$

Although no feature weight is explicitly given in Equation 6, the EMD image matching algorithm has taken them into account as a whole process. In this part, we update the feature weight according to the feature matching contribution. The matching contribution reflect the first observation, discriminative features are shared by the same category images but not those of different categories.

From the previous part, the matrix FlowP,Q reflects the correspondence between features of two images. We define the contribution $c_{P,Q}\left(i\right)$

$$c_{P,Q}\left(i\right) = \sum_{j=1}^{n}\frac{\text{flow}_{ij} \times {'}_{j}^{Q}}{d_{ij}} \qquad (8)$$

where ${'}_{j}^{Q} = \dfrac{n \times w_{j}^{Q}}{\sum_{k=1}^{n}w_{k}^{Q}}$ is used as a normalizing factor. The contribution $c_{P,Q}\left(i\right)$ indicates importance of feature f_{i}^{P} to image I_{Q} in matching. f_{i}^{P} and f_{j}^{Q} are best-matched features if they have the maximum value $\text{flow}_{ij} / d_{ij}$ among all matches between I_{Q} and I_{P}. We use $\text{flow}_{ij} / d_{ij}$ to evaluate the matching strength between features f_{i}^{P} and f_{j}^{Q}. Here, we compute $c_{P,Q}\left(i\right)$ by summing matching strength of the feature f_{i}^{P} from image I_{P} to all other features in the image I_{Q}. A normalizing factor ${'}_{j}^{Q}$ is integrated to represent the significant of feature f_{j}^{Q} within I_{Q}. The mean of all related contributions is used as the new weight of feature f_{i}^{P}:

$$w_{i}^{P'} = \frac{1}{m}\sum_{q=1,\cdots,N}c_{P,Q}\left(i\right) \qquad (9)$$

N is the number of images in one category. By doing so, we highlight the features which have strong matches across all images within the same category. After the iteratively updating, the discriminative features with high weights will be selected.

We use an iterative procedure to update the weights. At initial, all feature weights are assigned the same value 1. EMD based pairwise matching is performed to compute the matrices $\text{Flow}_{P,Q}$ and $\text{Sim}_{P,Q}$. Then each feature weight is updated based on Equations 8 and 9. The updating process is stopped when the whole training data classification performance or separability is no changing. A flow chart is show in Figure 2.

Figure 2. Feature weight update procedure

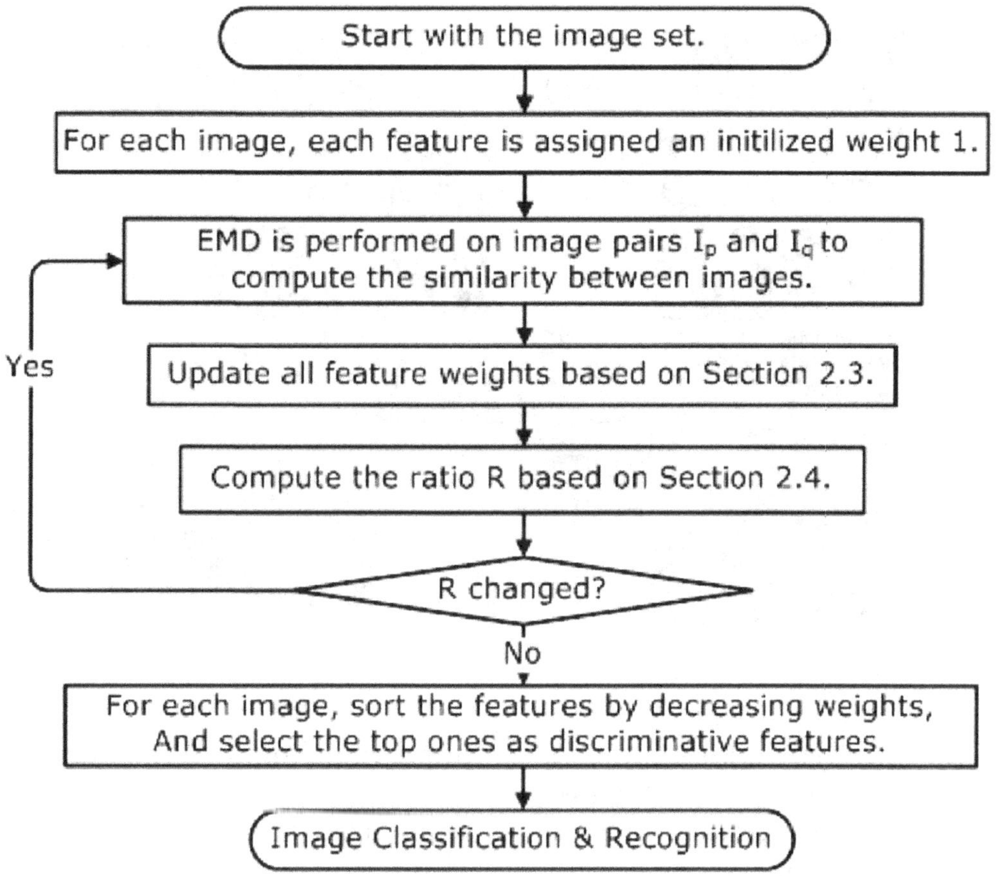

Class Separability Computation

The feature weights update iteration will be stopped when the classification measure R, the training-sets separability, stops changing. The R value can be simply computed by the ratio between the variance for between class variability and within class variability. With the Sim matrix and label information, the R can be computed easily. Finally, we can choose the discriminative features by thresholding the feature weights or choose fixed number of highest weights for each image.

PERFORMANCE EVALUATION

In this section, we presented experimental results to demonstrate the advantages of our method on image classification and retrieval. Two benchmark datasets are used: Caltech 256 and Microsoft Research Cambridge v2 (MSRCv2). Both datasets contain complex background. An example view is given in Figure 3.

Discriminative Feature Selection

We first performed our method to distinguish discriminative features. In this experiment, 20 classes are selected from two datasets with 30 images from each class as training sets. SIFT

Figure 3. Example images from Caltech 256 and MSRC-v2 datasets

descriptors are extracted for each image. We then use the approach described in Section 2 to select the features with high weights. Examples are given in Figure 4. In the third row, we show the SIFT features selected via our approach. While in the second row, the original SIFT features without selection are given. It can be observed that object-specific information has been highlighted and most "background" features have been omitted in the examples of the third row of Figure 4. The selected features correspond to the real content of images.

We also performed quantitative evaluation on our method. In Table 1, we give average percentage between the number of SIFT features overlaid only on foreground object with the number of SIFT features overlaid on the whole image. In Table 1, the left column is the result of SIFT feature extraction without our approach while the right column is the result from our method. It can be seen that SIFT features selected via our method overlaid mainly on the foreground objects.

Supervised Image Classification

In this subsection, we show how our method can be used for supervised image classification. At first, 30 images per class are collected as training-sets. Then we used the cluster label information to update the weights of the features. In this experiment, we selected 50 highest weight features per image. After the discriminative feature selection, K-means are performed on the selected feature sets to build the visual word dictionary with k = 1000. Since the visual words contain mostly object-specific feature groups, the bag-of-words based approach will be more efficient and accuracy. After constructing the histogram representation, we use SVM for classification.

To validate that our method is independent with feature extraction methods, both SIFT and LSS (Local Self-Similarity) are adopted. LSS descriptors are generated by correlating 5×5 image patches with a surrounding region of radius 40 pixels. For comparison, the same procedure is

Figure 4. Examples of discriminative features are shown. The first row contains original images; the second row are SIFT features overlaid on images without selection; and the third row shows the images containing selected features via the authors' approach.

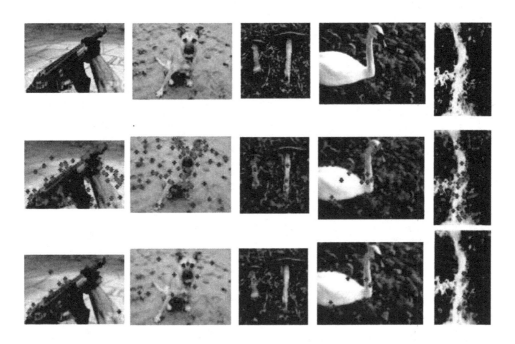

Table 1. Performance of discriminative feature selection. The table shows the percentage between the number of SIFT features overlaid on the foreground with the number of SIFT features overlaid on the whole image. The left column is the results with directly performing SIFT extraction while the right column is the result with our method.

Category	Direct SIFT	Authors' Method
AK47	53%	90%
Bowling pin	38%	93%
Car tire	67%	94%
Dog	61%	88%
Mushroom	40%	86%
People	48%	88%
Sunflower	71%	95%
Swan	53%	87%
Pisa	64%	91%
Face	69%	93%

repeated without using our object specific feature selection process. Figure 5 shows the impact of our feature selection on multi-class classification quality. Each class is trained by 30 images and tested by 50 images, and F-measure evaluation is performed. As shown in Figure 5, two datasets with two different features extractions methods are shown. The left figure of Figure 5 shows the result of MSRC-v2 while the right one is the result of Caltech 256. No matter the features are extracted by SIFT or LSS and no matter the images are from Caltech 256 or MSRC-v2, our approach has increased the accuracy for supervised image classification.

We also selected three classes from the training-sets randomly to show the EMD distance matrices before and after our feature selection scheme. In Figure6, the left distance matrix is the distances computed with all SIFT features while the right one is the distance matrix computed via

Figure 5. Classification with discriminative feature selection method are the red lines. It clearly outperforms the ones without our method. The left figure is based on Caltech 256 dataset while the right one is based on MSRC-v2. For both figures, the solid lines are from the SIF descriptors and the dash-dot line from the LSS decriptors.

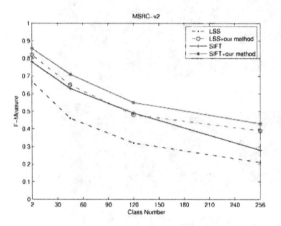
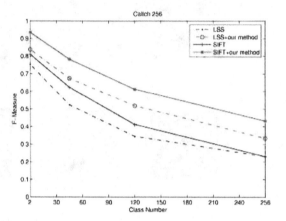

the discriminative SIFT features. The main feature to note from above distance matrices is that our method can increase the separability between different classes and minimize the variance within each class. Hence it can increase the accuracy performance for image classification.

In the third experiment of this subsection, we evaluated the performance of our algorithms on running time consumption. In this experiment, we still used 30 images from each class as train-

ing sets. Then we increase the category number. In Figure 7, we show the number of iteration times till convergence against the category number. From Figure 7, we can see that the iteration times are not increase with the class number as a linear relationship. After the class number exceeds 160, the iteration times keep almost same for around 25. In Figure 8, we also show the running time of our method against the base-line bag-of-words methods. Although our method need pre-process-

Figure 6. The EMD distance matrices for three classes' images. The left one is the distance matrix before the feature selection stage and the right one is the distance matrix after running the authors' method.

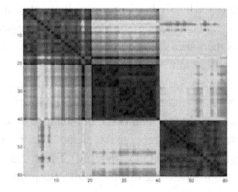
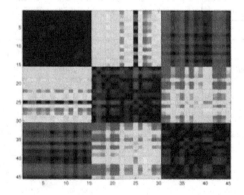

Figure 7. The iteration times of the authors' method against the class number

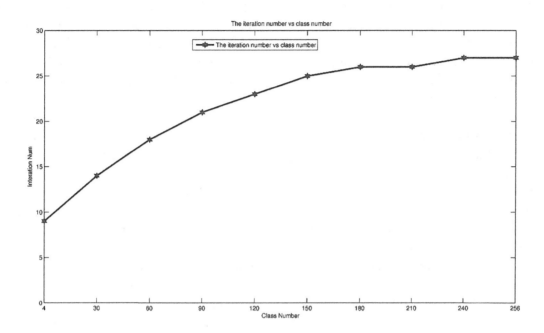

Figure 8. The time cost for the authors' method against baseline methods on Caltech 256 datasets

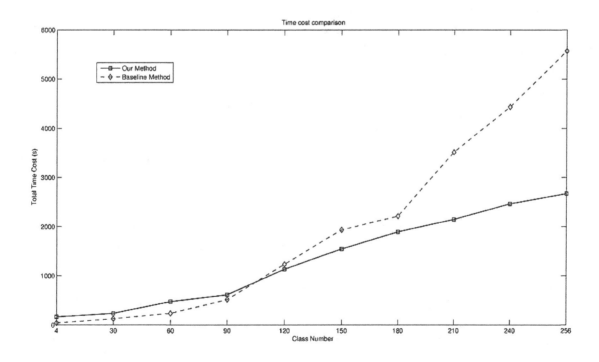

ing the training-sets, the running time can be saved at the later code word building and classification stages. With more categories, the advantages of our method have been emphasized. So far, we have validated that our method can improve the performance of image classification not only in accuracy but also in efficiency.

Semi-Supervised Image Classification

Supervised image analysis uses only labeled data for training, which however are often difficult to obtain. Semi-supervised learning addresses this problem by using large amount of unlabeled data together with the labeled data to build classifiers. There are many available semi-supervised learning methods (Zhu, 2005; Zhu, 2006). In this subsection, we extend our method on semi-supervised image classification.

Here, we adopt graph-based semi-supervised learning algorithms. As pointed out by Zhu, construct a good graph structure for label propagation is a vital step in the whole process. In graph based semi-supervised learning, labeled and unlabeled training sets are used to construct graph structure which is represented by G=(V,E). Each node $v_i \epsilon V$ corresponds to an image while the edge $e_j \epsilon E$ reflects the similarity between image pairs. In this chapter, we use our method to compute the accurate similarities between pairs of images. For the labeled training sets, we first select discriminative features. The bag-of-words method can

then be used to compute the similarities among all the labeled and unlabeled training images. Hence the graph structure for semi-supervised learning can be constructed based on these similarity values. Label propagation is finished and harmonic function is deduced via spectral decomposition.

In this experiment, semi-supervised image classification is performed on both Caltech256 and MSRC-v2 datasets with SIFT and LSS descriptors. Ten classes are randomly chosen with 10 labeled and 50 unlabeled training images per class. Then we used graph based semi-supervised method to compute the harmonic function. From the harmonic function, we classified unlabeled training and testing images. We compared the accuracy of the testing image classification by using and without using our method. The average classification accuracies with the standard deviations for different datasets and detectors are shown in Table 2. Each classification result reported in Table 2 is the average result of 20 independent trails. Table 2 shows that our method has improved the accuracy of graph based semi-supervised image classification. The reason relies that our method can provide more accurate graph structures, which better reflect the similarity between images, for label propagation.

Image Retrieval

Our approach can also be used for image retrieval. Traditionally in CBIR (Content- Based Image Retrieval), when an image is given, the similari-

Table 2. The average accuracies of 20 trails with the standard deviations for 10-classes semi-supervised classification. SIFT and LSS are used on Caltech 256 and MSRC-v2. The first row is the baseline method without discriminative feature selection, while the second row is the authors' method.

Method	SIFT-Caltech236	SIFT-MSRC	LSS-Caltech256	LSS-MSRC
1	47.78 ± 3.67	65.89 ± 7.34	31.37 ± 2.54	54.98 ± 3.21
2	56.62 ± 4.57	78.67 ± 2.15	50.85 ± 4.30	67.73 ± 1.34

ties between the query image and images in the database are computed. The top ranked most similar images are outputs as the searching results.

In this chapter, we introduced a query expansion scheme by using our method. When a query image is given, we first match it with all images in the database. The matching algorithm used in here is described in Section 2. Similarities between images are computed and the n most similar images are selected as the initial searching results. We use these initial searching results to update the feature weights via the iterative feature weight updating process. After this step, we can find the discriminative features. Then, these selected discriminative features are used to construct the visual words. Finally, bag-of-features method is used for refined image retrieval.

In this experiment, we tested our method on the datasets Caltech-256 and MSRC-v2. Given a query, to improve the performance the top n ranked results are used to select the discriminative features. In this experiment, n=10. The refined features are used to re-query the database for better performance. Figure 9 displays the performance of two query schemes which represented by two histograms of average precision (AP) score of 50 queries from two datasets. The left histogram shows the distribution of baseline method results, while the right displays the results of our method. It clearly shows the significant improvement brought by our method, which moves amount of histogram to the high side.

FUTURE RESEARCH DIRECTIONS

In the future, we plan to extend this work in two folds. First, in the matching part, we plan to incorporate structure-based matching or graph matching introduced in (Bai, 2009) to incorporate high-level structure information in the matching process. Secondly, we plan to use complex statistical models such as the PLSA model (Hofmann, 1999) to handle hierarchical image recognition (Deng, 2009).

Figure 9. Histograms of the average precision for 50 queries. The left one displays results without the authors' procedure, while the right one with their method.

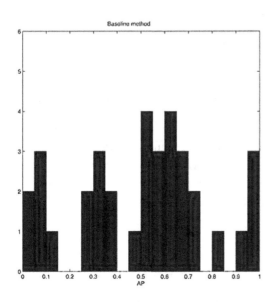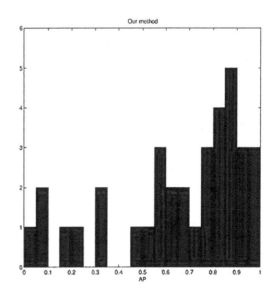

CONCLUSION

In this chapter, we proposed a new approach to find the discriminative features which can be used as a refinement step for image classification and retrieval. The algorithm can decrease the influence from the image background and highlight the object-specific information. Our method can save the running time at word construction and classification stage. Hence the performance of image classification and retrieval can be improved by using our method. In the experiment part, we prove the efficiency and accuracy of the algorithm via three main applications i.e. image classification, semi-supervised image classification and image retrieval. All experiments validate our method on performance improvement.

REFERENCES

Bai, X., Hancock, E. R., & Wilson, R. C. (2009). Graph characteristics from the heat kernel trace. *Pattern Recognition*, *42*(11), 2589–2606. doi:10.1016/j.patcog.2008.12.029

Bai, X., Wilson, R., & Hancock, E. (2009). A generative model for graph matching and embedding. *Computer Vision and Image Understanding*, *113*, 778–789.

Bay, H., Ess, A., Tuytelaars, T., & Gool, L. J. V. (2008). Speeded-up robust features (surf). *Computer Vision and Image Understanding*, *110*(3), 346–359. doi:10.1016/j.cviu.2007.09.014

Bunke, H., & Shearer, K. (1998). A graph distance metric based on the maximal common subgraph. *Pattern Recognition Letters*, *19*(3-4), 255–259. doi:10.1016/S0167-8655(97)00179-7

Chum, O., & Zisserman, A. (2007). *An exemplar model for learning object classes*. In IEEE Conference on Computer Vision and Pattern Recognition.

Dantzig, G. B. (1951). Application of the simplex method to a transportation problem. In Koopmans, T. C. (Ed.), *Activity analysis of production and allocation* (pp. 359–373).

Deng, J., Dong, W., Socher, R., Li, L., Li, K., & Li, F. (2009). ImageNet: A large scale hierarchical image database. In *IEEE Conference on Computer Vision and Pattern Recognition*, (pp. 248–255).

Dorko, G., & Schmid, C. (2003). Selection of scale-invariant parts for object class recognition. In *International Conference on Computer Vision*, (pp. 634–640).

Duda, R. O., Hart, P. E., & Stork, D. G. (2000). *Pattern classification*. Prentice Hall.

Fatih Demirci, M., Shokoufandeh, A., Keselman, Y., Bretzner, L., & Dickinson, S. (2006). Object recognition as many-to-many feature matching. *International Journal of Computer Vision*, *69*(2), 203–222. doi:10.1007/s11263-006-6993-y

Fergus, R., Perona, P., & Zisserman, A. (2003). *Object class recognition by unsupervised scale-invariant learning*. In IEEE Conference on Computer Vision and Pattern Recognition.

Fergus, R., Perona, P., & Zisserman, A. (2006). A sparse object category model for efficient learning and complete recognition. In *Toward Category-Level Object Recognition*, (pp. 443–461).

Figueiredo, M. A. F., & Jain, A. K. (2002). Unsupervised learning of finite mixture models. *IEEE Transactions on Pattern Analysis and Machine Intelligence*, *24*(3), 381–396. doi:10.1109/34.990138

Gehler, P. V., & Nowozin, S. (2009). Let the kernel figure it out; principled learning of pre-processing for kernel classifiers. In *IEEE Conference on Computer Vision and Pattern Recognition*, (pp. 2836–2843).

Hofmann, T. (1999). Probabilistic latent semantic indexing. *Proceedings of the Twenty-Second Annual International SIGIR Conference on Research and Development in Information Retrieval* (SIGIR-99).

Ke, Y., & Sukthankar, R. (2004). PCA-SIFT: A more distinctive representation for local image descriptors. In *IEEE Conference on Computer Vision and Pattern Recognition*, (pp. 506–513).

Lee, Y. J., & Grauman, K. (2009). Foreground focus: Unsupervised learning from partially matching images. *International Journal of Computer Vision*, *85*(2), 143–166. doi:10.1007/s11263-009-0252-y

Leibe, B., Leonardis, A., & Schiele, A. (2004). *Combined object categorization and segmentation with an implicit shape model*. In Workshop on Statistical Learningin Learning in Computer Vision, European Conference on Computer Vision.

Li, F., Fergus, R., & Perona, P. (2006). One-shot learning of object categories. *IEEE Transactions on Pattern Analysis and Machine Intelligence*, *28*(4), 594–611. doi:10.1109/TPAMI.2006.79

Li, F., & Perona, P. (2005). Bayesian hierarchical model for learning natural scene categories. In *IEEE Conference on Computer Vision and Pattern Recognition*, (pp. 524–531).

Lowe, D. (2004). Distinctive image features from scale-invariant keypoints. *InternationalJournal International Journal of Computer Vision*, *1*, 91–110. doi:10.1023/B:VISI.0000029664.99615.94

McAllester, D., Felzenszwalb, P., & Girshick, R. (2010). *Cascade object detection with deformable part models*. In The IEEE Conference on Computer Vision and Pattern Recognition.

Mikolajczyk, K., Tuytelaars, T., Schmid, C., Zisserman, A., Matas, J., & Schaffalitzky, F. (2005). A comparison of affine region detectors. *International Journal of Computer Vision*, *65*(1-2), 43–72. doi:10.1007/s11263-005-3848-x

Nowak, E., & Jurie, F. (2007). *Learning visual similarity measures for comparing neverseen never seen objects*. In IEEE Conference on Computer Vision and Pattern Recognition.

Quack, T., Ferrari, V., Leibe, B., & Gool, L. J. V. (2007). Efficient mining of frequent and distinctive feature configurations. In *International Conference on Computer Vision*, (pp. 1–8).

Rother, C., Minka, T. P., Blake, A., & Kolmogorov, V. (2006). Cosegmentation of image pairs by histogram matching - Incorporating a global constraint into MRFS. In *IEEE Conference on Computer Vision and Pattern Recognition*, (pp. 993–1000).

Rubner, Y., Tomasi, C., & Guibas, L. J. (2000). The earth mover's distance as a metric for image retrieval. *International Journal of Computer Vision*, *40*(2), 99–121. doi:10.1023/A:1026543900054

Shechtman, E., & Irani, M. (2007). *Matching local self-similarities across images and videos*. In IEEE Conference on Computer Vision and Pattern Recognition, June.

Torr, P. H. S., & Zisserman, A. (2000). Mlesac: A new robust estimator with application to estimating image geometry. *Computer Vision and Image Understanding*, *78*(1), 138–156. doi:10.1006/cviu.1999.0832

Weber, M., Welling, M., & Perona, P. (2000). Unsupervised learning of models for recognition. In *European Conference on Computer Vision,* (Vol. 1, pp. 18–32).

Xia, X., & Hancock, E. R. (2009). Graph-based object class discovery. In *International Conference on Computer Analysis of Images and Patterns,* (pp. 385–393).

Zhang, J., Marszalek, M., Lazebnik, S., & Schmid, C. (2007). Local features and kernels for classification of texture and object categories: A comprehensive study. *International Journal of Computer Vision, 73*(2), 213–238. doi:10.1007/s11263-006-9794-4

Zhu, X. (2005). *Semi-supervised learning with graphs*. Unpublished PhD Thesis.

Zhu, X. (2006). *Semi-supervised learning literature survey*.

Chapter 12
Normalized Projection and Graph Embedding via Angular Decomposition

Dengdi Sun
Anhui University, China

Chris Ding
Anhui University, China & University of Texas at Arlington, USA

Jin Tang
Anhui University, China

Bin Luo
Anhui University, China

ABSTRACT

Dimensionality reduction plays a vital role in pattern recognition. However, for normalized vector data, existing methods do not utilize the fact that the data is normalized. In this chapter, the authors propose to employ an Angular Decomposition of the normalized vector data which corresponds to embedding them on a unit surface. On graph data for similarity/kernel matrices with constant diagonal elements, the authors propose the Angular Decomposition of the similarity matrices which corresponds to embedding objects on a unit sphere. In these angular embeddings, the Euclidean distance is equivalent to the cosine similarity. Thus data structures best described in the cosine similarity and data structures best captured by the Euclidean distance can both be effectively detected in our angular embedding. The authors provide the theoretical analysis, derive the computational algorithm, and evaluate the angular embedding on several datasets. Experiments on data clustering demonstrate that the method can provide a more discriminative subspace.

DOI: 10.4018/978-1-4666-1891-6.ch012

INTRODUCTION

Dimensionality reduction is an important problem in pattern recognition, and various methods have been proposed. From the point of view of data embedding, there are two categories of embedding approaches. For vector data embedding, Principal Component Analysis (PCA) for unsupervised data and Linear Discriminate Analysis (LDA) (Duda, Hart & Stork, 2001; Wang Ding, & Huang, 2010) for supervised data are the two most widely used linear algorithms because of their relative simplicity and effectiveness. For graph data embedding, Laplacian Embedding (LE) (Hall, 1971; Belkin & Niyogi, 2003; Luo et al., 2009) is a classical method; in addition, Manifold learning also is one important class of popular approaches such as Isomap (Tenenbaum, de Silva, & Langford, 200), Locally Linear Embedding (LLE) (Roweis & Saul, 2000), Local Tangent Space Alignment (LTSA) (Zhang & Zha, 2004), Locality Preserving Projections (He & Niyogi, 2003), etc.

The most widely used PCA projects data into a subspace using a least square data representation error function. However, in many applications such as information retrieval, image analysis, and genomics, normalized vector data come naturally. PCA does not take advantage of this special nature for the normalized data. Furthermore, in machine learning, many graph data including pairwise similarities are produced by kernel functions (Genton et al., 2001), such as the most widely used RBF kernel, which usually have constant/unit diagonal elements. Most existing embedding methods do not utilize this property.

This motivate us to propose a new embedding method called Angular Decomposition (also called angular embedding) to deal with normalized data or graphs/kernels with constant diagonal elements. The decompositions correspond to embedding data onto a low-dimensional spherical surface. Although Angular Decomposition is best suited to normalized vector data and graph

data with constant diagonal elements, it also applies to un-normalized data or graph data with non-constant diagonal. One important feature of angular embedding is that because the embedded data are on the unit sphere, the cosine similarity is equivalent to the Euclidean distance. Thus data structures best described in the cosine similarity and data structures best captured by the Euclidean distance can both be effectively detected in our angular embedding.

Below, we first introduce Angular Decomposition for vector data and for graph data. We then derive computational algorithms for each decomposition respectively. We evaluate these new data decompositions for unsupervised learning. We perform angular embedding on several common datasets. Experiment results demonstrate the effectiveness of these new decompositions as compared to existing approaches.

ANGULAR DECOMPOSITION

We start with a brief discussion of PCA, which is the most widely used dimensionality reduction method. Let the input data matrix $X = (x_1, \cdots, x_n) \in \Re^{p \times n}$ contains the collection of n data column vectors in p dimension space. In image processing, each column xi is a linearized array of pixels' gray levels; in text processing, x_i is a document. PCA finds the optimal low-dimensional (k-dim) subspace defined (spanned) by the principal directions $U = (u_1, \cdots, u_k) \in \Re^{p \times k}$. The projected data points in the new subspace are $V = (v_1, \cdots, v_n) \in \Re^{k \times n}$. PCA finds U and V by minimizing

$$\min_{U,V} J_{PCA} = \left\| X - UV \right\|_F^2 \qquad (1)$$

The global optimal solution is rank-k singular value decomposition, $X \approx U\Sigma V$. We absorb Σ into V in Equation 1.

Angular Decomposition of Vector Data

Our primary focus is the normalized vector data, i.e., $\left\| x_i \right\|^2 = 1$, $i = 1, \cdots, n$. Here for simplicity, we assume data are normalized into unit length. We note that many data came naturally normalized. Our starting point is that PCA is not specifically designed to work on normalized vector data, i.e., in general, the projection in the PCA subspace $\left\| v_i \right\|^2 \neq 1$. Although we can show

$$1 = \left\| x_i \right\|^2 \approx \left\| U v_i \right\|^2 = v_i^T U^T U v_i = v_i^T v_i = \left\| v_i \right\|^2 \tag{2}$$

This means that for normalized data, the projection (in the PCA subspace) v_i is not normalized, but is approximately normalized if the subspace dimension k is sufficiently large.

To fully take advantage of the special nature of the normalized data, we propose the following Angular Decomposition

$$\min_{U,V} J_1 = \left\| X - UV \right\|^2 \quad s.t. \quad \left\| v_i \right\|^2 = 1, U^T U = I \tag{3}$$

where I is the identical matrix. One improvement can be made. Because the ranks of U, V are low, we introduce an overall scale α to improve the data representation. Furthermore, to distinguish the normalized variable, we use H instead of V as

$$V \to H^T = \left[h_1, \cdots, h_n \right] \in \Re^{k \times n}$$

Please note we use the transposition HT following convention.

Thus the final Angular Decomposition is defined as

$$\min J_2 = \left\| X - \alpha U H^T \right\|^2 \quad s.t. \quad (HH^T)_{ii} = 1, U^T U = I \tag{4}$$

Note that $(HH^T)_{ii} = \left\| h_i \right\|^2$ is the length of embedding vector. The most important advantage of Angular Decomposition is that in the embedding space, the $(k-1)$ dimension sphere, the Euclidean distance is equivalent to the cosine similarity:

- **Theorem 1:** In Angular Decomposition, the Euclidean distance is equivalent to the cosine similarity.
- **Proof:** The cosine similarity for vector h_i and h_j is defined as $\cos\theta(h_i, h_j) = h_i \cdot h_j / \left\| h_i \right\| \left\| h_j \right\|$. The Euclidean distance between vectors h_i and h_j is

$$\left\| h_i - h_j \right\|^2$$
$$= \left\| h_i \right\|^2 + \left\| h_j \right\|^2 - 2 \left\| h_i \right\| \left\| h_j \right\| \cos\theta(h_i, h_j)$$
$$= 2 - 2\cos\theta(h_i, h_j)$$

where $\left\| h_i \right\| = 1$ in our Angular Decomposition. Furthermore, large d_{ij} corresponds to small $\cos\theta(h_i, h_j)$ Thus Euclidean distance is equivalent to cosine similarity. QED

This equivalence is useful because the Euclidean distance captures some intrinsic properties for some datasets while the cosine similarity captures the essential properties for some other datasets. It makes the angular embedding to be a more suitable low-dimensional embedding of vector data. The computational algorithm will be given in Section 3.1. Here we note that the algorithm updates α, U, H one at a time; and each of them is computed from a closed-form optimal solution.

Angular Decomposition for Graph Data

In many applications, the input data are pairwise similarities which are generally viewed as edge weights between nodes of an undirected graph (Yan et al., 2007). We wish to embed the graph data. Most graph data are pairwise similarity matrices Sij that describe similarity between objects i and j.

Consider the linear kernel (the Gram matrix) constructed from the normalized vector data above. The similarity between i, j is

$$S_{ij} = x_i^T x_j \qquad (5)$$

Note that $S_{ii} = 1$ for $i = 1, \cdots, n$

Additionally, many kernel functions such as RBF kernel have unit diagonal elements: $K_{ii} = 1$, $i = 1, \cdots, n$

For any positive semi-definite (p.s.d.) kernel matrix K (rank(K)=r), it can be exactly embedded in full r-dimensional space using the r eigenvectors. Based on spectral expansion, the full space (r-dimensional space) embedding of object i is

$$z_i = \left[\sqrt{\lambda_1} v_1(i), \cdots, \sqrt{\lambda_r} v_r(i) \right]^T \qquad (6)$$

where $v_l(i)$ is the i-th element of eigenvector v_l, $l = 1, \cdots, r$

Define the dissimilarity between i, j as

$$dij = K_{ii} + K_{jj} - 2K_{ij} \qquad (7)$$

We have

- **Theorem 2:** For any p.s.d. kernel matrix K with $K_{ii} = 1$, their dissimilarity can be expressed exactly as

$$dij = \left\| z_i - z_j \right\|^2 \qquad (8)$$

Furthermore, the embedding is unit-normalized: $\left\| z_i \right\|^2 = 1$

- **Proof:** A p.s.d. kernel has a spectral expansion

$$K = \sum_{l=1}^{r} \lambda_l v_l v_l^T, \lambda_l \geq 0 \qquad (9)$$

Thus,

$$\begin{aligned} dij &= K_{ii} + K_{jj} - 2K_{ij} \\ &= \sum_{l=1}^{r} \lambda_l \left[v_l(i)^2 + v_l(j)^2 - 2v_l(i)v_l(j) \right] \\ &= \sum_{l=1}^{r} \left[z_i(l) - z_j(l) \right]^2 = \left\| z_i - z_j \right\|^2 \end{aligned}$$

proving Equation 8. From the definition of z_i, we have

$$\left\| z_i \right\|^2 = \sum_{l=1}^{r} \lambda_l v_l(i) v_l(i) = K_{ii} = 1 \text{ QED}$$

In real application, embedding to low-dimensional space is useful because it reveal the inherent structure of the data. Thus we embed the kernel matrix in a k-dimensional space where k is in general close to the number of distinct clusters, which is much smaller than r. Therefore, for any kernel matrix K, we have

$$\min_Z J_3 = \left\| K - ZZ^T \right\|^2 \quad s.t. \quad (ZZ^T)_{ii} = 1$$

because

$$z_i = (Z_{i1}, \cdots, Z_{ik})^T,$$
$$\left\| z_i \right\|^2 = \sum_{l=1}^{k} Z_{il}^2 = (ZZ^T)_{ii} = 1$$

retains the unit-normalization property. Intuitively, our Angular Decomposition is very natural since both K and ZZ^T have identical diagonal elements.

In this paper, we view graph data, the similarity matrix S, as from a kernel with unit diagonal elements. By introducing α to compensate the fact that the embedding space dimension is k which is far less than rank(S), the final Angular Decomposition is defined as,

$$\min_{\alpha,H} J_3 = \left\| S - \alpha HH^T \right\|^2 \quad s.t. \quad (HH^T)_{ii} = 1 \tag{11}$$

The computational algorithm is given in Section 3.2.

Figure 1 shows the synthetic data points which contain 6 clusters and corresponding Angular Decomposition Embedding result. With Angular Decomposition, the data structures and distributions are generally more apparent. We will show in experiments that our methods also achieve better results.

Brute-Force Angular Embedding (BAE)

We note that for embedding data on spherical surface can be done in a brute-force (naive) way: simply normalize the embedding vectors H. More specifically, this consists of two steps. For vector data, we (1) compute the low-dimensional represents V via $SVD(X) = U\Sigma V^T$, and (2) normalize each column of ΣV^T to unit length as the final embedding vector. For graph data, we also (1) compute eigenvectors of similarity matrix as $S = V\Sigma V^T$ and (2) normalize embedding coordinates rows of $V\Sigma^{1/2}$ to unit length.

The experiments in Section 4 will demonstrate that compared to the brute-force approaches, our more vigorous approaches of Equations 4 and 11 provide embedding coordinates which (a) are better data representation/approximation (in the same sense that PCA is a data representation/approximation method too), (b) provide better machine learning results such as clustering accuracy.

ALGORITHMS AND ANALYSIS

Here we provide algorithms and accompanying analysis for the two Angular Decomposition methods presented above.

Angular Decomposition of Vector Data

We optimize the objective function of Equation 4 via an iterative updating algorithm that alternatively updates α, H, and U one at a time. We give the closed-form solution for each of them explicitly. The algorithm starts with initialization of U, H.

Figure 1. The 3D synthetic data points and two views of the 3D angular decomposition embedding

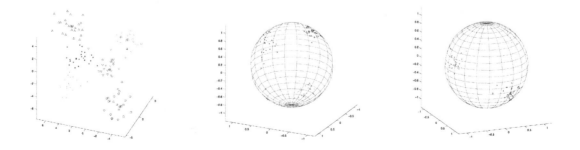

- **Step (V0):** Initialization.

  Compute first k terms of $SVD(X) = U\Sigma V^T$.

  Set $U_0 = U$, $H_0 = V\Sigma$

  We then update α, H, U one at a time in Steps (V1 - V3). They are repeated until convergence.

- **Step (V1):** Compute α while fixing U and H.

  From Equation 4, the optimal solution for α is given by

$$\alpha^* = \frac{1}{n} tr(U^T X H) \qquad (12)$$

- **Proof:** we write the objective function of Equation 4 as

$$\begin{aligned}
J_2 &= tr(\alpha^2 H U^T U H^T - 2\alpha U^T X H + X X^T) \\
&= tr(\alpha^2 H H^T - 2\alpha U^T X H + X X^T) \qquad (13) \\
&= \alpha^2 n - tr(2\alpha U^T X H + X X^T)
\end{aligned}$$

  since $U^T U = I$ and $(HH^T)_{ii} = 1$

  For variable α, the optimization is unrestricted. We set gradient to zero

$$\frac{\partial J_2}{\partial \alpha} = -2tr(U^T X H) + 2n\alpha = 0$$

  and obtain the optimal solution in Equation 12. QED.

- **Step (V2):** Compute H while fixing α and U.

  We update H using the following:

  - **Lemma 1:** Given fixed α and U in Equaton 4, the optimization for H in Equation 4 has close form solution:

$$H_{ij}^* = \frac{(U^T X)}{\sqrt{(X^T U U^T X)_{ii}}} \qquad (14)$$

- **Proof:** This is an optimization with equality constraints. We use Lagrangian multiplier method, where the λ_i is the Lagrangian multiplier to the condition function $(HH^T)_{ii} = 1$. From Equation 13, the Lagrangian function is

$$L(H) = \alpha^2 n - tr(2\alpha U^T X H + X X^T)$$
$$- 2\sum_{i=1}^{n} \lambda_i \left[(HH^T)_{ii} = 1 \right]$$

Setting the derivatives of the Lagrangian function to zero,

$$\frac{\partial L(H)}{\partial H_{ij}} = -2\alpha (U^T X)_{ij} - 2\lambda_i H_{ij} = 0$$

we obtain

$$H_{ij} = \frac{\alpha (U^T X)_{ij}}{\lambda_i} \qquad (15)$$

Now, we need to find the values of the Lagrangian multipliers. Multiply Hij and sum over j for above equation we have:

$$1 = \sum_j H_{ij}^2 =$$
$$\frac{\alpha^2 \sum_j (U^T X)_{ij}^2}{\lambda_i^2} = \frac{\alpha^2 \left[(U^T X)^T (U^T X) \right]_{ii}}{\lambda_i^2}$$

This gives the values of Lagrangian multipliers:

$$\lambda_i = \alpha \sqrt{(X^T U U^T X)_{ii}} \qquad (16)$$

Substituting this into Equation 15, we obtain Equation 14. QED

- **Step (V3):** Update U while fixing α, H.
  We compute U using the following:
  - **Lemma 2:** Given fixed α and H in Equation 4, the optimization for U in Equation 4 has close-form solution:

$$U = AB^T \qquad (17)$$

where A, B are obtained from the singular value decomposition of the p-by-k matrix XH:

$$SVD(XH) = A\Sigma B^T \qquad (18)$$

where $A \in \Re^{p\times k}$ contains the left singular vectors and $B \in \Re^{k\times k}$ contains the right singular vectors. Without loss of generality, we assume $p \geq k$

- **Proof:** From the last equation of Equation 13, the minimization of $J_2(U)$ becomes

$$\max_U J_2(U) = tr(U^T XH) \quad s.t. \quad U^T U = I$$

Substituting $XH = A\Sigma B^T$ from Equation 18, this becomes

$$\max_U J_2(U) = tr(B^T U^T A\Sigma) \quad s.t. \quad U^T U = I$$
$$(19)$$

We now prove that $U^* = AB^T$ is the optimal solution.
The proof is complete if we can prove that $tr(\Sigma)$ is an upper bound of $J_2(U)$: for any feasible solution U, we have

$$tr(B^T U^T A\Sigma) \leq tr(\Sigma) \qquad (20)$$

With this, $U^* = AB^T$ is a global optimal solution because $J_2(U^*) = tr(\Sigma)$ reaches

the upper bound and therefore no other solution has better objective function value.
To prove the upper bound Equation 20, we prove that every element of matrix $(BTUTA)$ is less than 1, i.e.,

$$\left| (B^T U^T A)_{sl} \right| \leq 1 \qquad (21)$$

because if this is the case, we have

$$tr(B^T U^T A\Sigma) =$$
$$\sum_{l=1}^{k} (B^T U^T A)_{ll} \sigma_l \leq \sum_{l=1}^{k} \sigma_l = tr(\Sigma)$$

proving the upper bound Equation 20.
To prove the inequality of Equation 21, we note that there exits the complement space $A^\perp \in \Re^{p\times(p-k)}$ such that matrix $[A, A^\perp]$ forms a complete basis:

$$[A, A^\perp]^T [A, A^\perp] = [A, A^\perp][A, A^\perp]^T = I$$

Thus we have

$$(B^T U^T [A, A^\perp])(B^T U^T [A, A^\perp])^T =$$
$$B^T U^T U B = B^T B = I$$

This implies for any s, $1 \leq s \leq k$ we have

$$1 = \sum_{l=1}^{p} (B^T U^T [A, A^\perp])_{sl}^2$$
$$= \sum_{l=1}^{p} ([B^T U^T A, B^T U^T A^\perp])_{sl}^2$$
$$= \sum_{l=1}^{k} (B^T U^T A)_{sl}^2 + \sum_{l=k+1}^{p} (B^T U^T A^\perp)_{sl}^2$$

implying the inequality of Equation 21 must be true. QED.

Angular Decomposition of Graph Data

We provide the algorithm for computing the Angular Decomposition for an input graph data S (the similarity matrix) using Equation 11. The embedding coordinates on the sphere are computed via an iterative updating algorithm that alternatively updates α, H, λ one at a time, where λ are Lagrangian multipliers for enforcing the constraints when we update H according to Equation 11. Step (G0) is the initialization. Steps (G1 - G3) update α, H, λ and are repeated until convergence.

- **Step (G0):** Initialization.
  Compute first k terms of eigen-decomposition $S = V\Sigma V^T$. Set $H_0 = V\Sigma^{1/2}$
  We update α, H, λ alternately one at a time where λ are Lagrangian multipliers for enforcing the constraints when we update H according to Equation 11 until convergence.

- **Step (G1):** Update α while fix H
  We update parameter α using this formula:

$$\alpha^* = \frac{tr(H^T SH)}{tr(HH^T HH^T)} \quad (22)$$

- **Proof:** Setting the gradient of J4 of Equation 11 to zero,

$$\frac{\partial J_4}{\partial \alpha} = -2tr(SHH^T) + 2\alpha tr(HH^T HH^T) = 0$$

  we obtain optimal $\alpha*$ in Equation 22. QED.

- **Step (G2):** Update Lagrangian multipliers λ while fixing α, H.

When updating H according to Equation 11, we use Lagrangian multipliers $\{\lambda_i\}$ to enforce the constraints, $(HH^T)_{ii} = 1$.
We compute λ_i using the following rule:

$$\lambda_i = \alpha^2(HH^T HH^T)_{ii} - \alpha(SHH^T)_{ii} \quad (23)$$

- **Proof:** This is derived from the KKT condition for constrained optimization. The Lagrangian function of J_4 is

$$L(H) = tr(\alpha^2 HH^T HH^T - 2\alpha H^T SH + S^2) - 2\sum_{i=1}^{n} \lambda_i[(HH^T)_{ii} - 1]$$

Setting the derivatives to zero, we have

$$4\alpha^2(HH^T H)_{ij} - 4\alpha(SH)_{ij} - 4\lambda_i H_{ij} = 0$$

Multiply H_{ij} and sum over j, we obtain

$$\alpha^2(HH^T HH^T)_{ii} - \alpha(SHH^T)_{ii} = \lambda_i(HH^T)_{ii}$$

Using the constraint $(HH^T)_{ii} = 1$, we obtain λ_i as Equation 23.

- **Step (G3):** Update H while fixing α and λ
  We update H using gradient descent method,

$$H_{ij} \leftarrow H_{ij} - \eta \frac{\partial L(H)}{\partial H_{ij}} \quad \text{more specifically}$$

to:

$$H_{ij} = H_{ij} - \eta[\alpha^2(HH^T H)_{ij} - \alpha(SH)_{ij} - \lambda_i H_{ij}] \quad (24)$$

where parameter η adjusts the stepsize the solution goes along the negative gradient direction while the Lagrangian multiplier term enforces the solution on unit sphere. We typically set $\eta = 0.01 \left(\sum_{ij} |H_{ij}| \right) \Big/ \left(\sum_{ij} \left| \frac{\partial L(H)}{\partial H_{ij}} \right| \right)$. The convergence is demonstrated in experiments (see Figure 2).

EXPERIMENTS

We apply Angular Decomposition on six real-world datasets, including vector data and graph data.

Datasets Description

The method is tested on six datasets, involving three available image datasets, one textual dataset, one genomic dataset and one physical dataset.

- **AT&T Faces:** Contains ten different images of each 40 distinct persons and the size of each image is 92×112 pixels, with 256 grey levels per pixel. In our experiment, each face image was resized into 32×32 and reshaped into a vector of 1024 dimension.
- **Binary Alphabet:** Contains 26 handwritten alphabets A:Z. Each sample is a 20×16 binary image. We select 30 images for every alphabet and reshape each image into one vector of 320 dimension.
- **MNIST Hand-Written Digit:** Consists of 8-bit gray-scale images of digits from "0" to "9", about 6000 examples of each class (digit). Each image is centered on a 28 ×28 grid. Here, we randomly choose 100 im-

Figure 2. Algorithm convergence; the object functions decrease with iterations for both vector data and graph algorithms on the six datasets

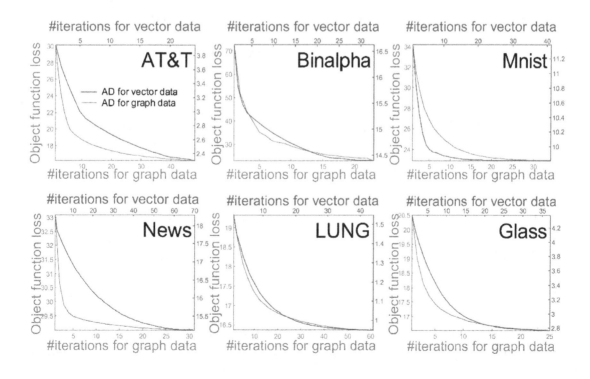

ages from each digit, and convert them to vectors of 784 dimension.

- **Twenty Newsgroups:** A collection of approximately 20,000 message documents, partitioned evenly across 20 different newsgroups. Each message is described by binary data of 100 words. Here, one hundred messages from each of the twenty newsgroups were chosen at random and converted to a binary vector.

- **LUNG:** Contains in total 203 samples in five classes. Each sample has 12600 genes. We removed the genes with standard deviations smaller than 50 expression units, and then obtained a data set with 3312 genes.

- **Glass Identification:** Describes main characteristics of the glass dataset and its attributes. It is consisted of 214 observation containing examples of the chemical analysis of 7 different types of glass. Every sample has 9 features.

The data from above datasets are vector data. To convert them into graph data, the similarity matrix S_{ij}, we choose RBF kernel $S_{ij} = e^{-\gamma \|x_i - x_j\|^2}$ where $\gamma = 0.7/d^2$, $d = \sum_{ij} \|x_i - x_j\|/n(n-1)$

Algorithm Convergence

We first show the convergence of the proposed algorithms on the six datasets. The results are shown in Figure 2. The algorithms converge after around 50 iterations.

Data Reconstruction

We compare the data representation/reconstruction capability of Angular Decomposition (hereinafter AD) with the brute-force angular embedding (BAE, see Section 2). We compute the residual of data representation in Equations 4 and 11 and

the corresponding residual for BAE for the two kinds of data.

For vector data, the residual for BAE is computed by choosing β that minimizes the object function,

$$J_5 = \left\| X - \beta U Q^T \right\|^2 \tag{25}$$

where Q is obtained from the normalized embedding coordinate directly as described in Section 2.3. For graph data, the residual for BAE objective function is computed by optimizing β that minimizes

$$J_6 = \left\| S - \beta Q Q^T \right\|^2 \tag{26}$$

The obtained residual results are shown in Table 1 for six datasets. These results show that AD has consistently lower residual than BAE in all cases. This indicates our vigorous approach is more effective in preserving the structure of data.

Clustering

We evaluate the unsupervised learning on Angular Decomposition. We use Angular Decomposition to embed vector data and graph data on the unit sphere, and then perform the K-means clustering on these embedding coordinates. For comparison purposes, we also show clustering results on the original high-dimensional data X and the PCA projection data. Additionally, we use BAE do subspace embedding for vector data and graph data (with the same parameters as our Angular Decomposition) and run clustering on the embedded data. To get robust statistics, we run K-means 50 times using different random starts and computed the average as the final results.

Clustering accuracy measures the percentage of data points correctly clustered. It is obtained

Table 1. Comparison of object functions between BAE and proposed angular decomposition (AD) on six datasets

	BAE for vector data	AD for vector data	BAE for graph data	AD for graph data
AT&T	3.949	2.302	17.396	16.612
BinAlp	16.579	14.183	24.060	23.026
Mnist	10.328	9.583	24.590	22.869
News	18.664	15.110	34.023	29.012
Lung	1.887	0.956	18.600	16.429
Glass	4.206	2.798	14.210	12.643

by first computing the confusion matrix. The Hungarian algorithm is then used to permutate columns of confusion matrix to maximize the sum of the diagonal elements, which is the clustering accuracy.

Results of clustering on the six datasets are shown in Figure 3. Six different methods are compared and shown in Figure 3. From the experimental results, we observed the following:

- **(F1):** Embedding into low-dimensional subspace improves the performance. On all six datasets, for both vector data and graph data, using either BAE or AD, the K-means clustering results are better than in original high-dimensional data. That

PCA embedding improves K-means clustering is analyzed in (Ding & He, 2004); the improvements for graph embedding can be viewed as kernel PCA improves kernel K-means clustering (Ding & He, 2004).

- **(F2):** Graph data produces better results than the vector data for the same dataset. This is consistent on all six datasets. It is likely due to the flexibility of graph representation, as compared to K-means clustering in vector space with a objective function that favors ball-shaped clusters.
- **(F3):** AD perform consistently better than BAE.

Figure 3. Clustering accuracies for six datasets (six different methods are compared)

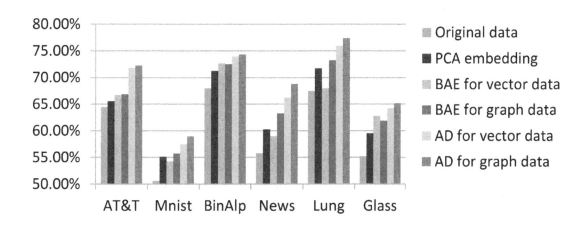

CONCLUSION AND FUTURE WORKS

Angular Decomposition embeds high-dimensional data into a low-dimensional spherical space. This takes advantage of the special nature of the normalized data and integrating the cosine similarity and the Euclidean distance at the same time, and yields a more discriminative subspace for high-dimensional data. Two efficient algorithms are developed to solve the proposed Angular Decomposition problems for vector data and graph data respectively. Extensive experiments on six real datasets show that angular embedding is more effective to exhibit class structures than other related methods. The experiments almost show that (1) clustering in low-dimensional embedding space consistently outperform those in original high dimensional data and (2) Using graph data gives better results than using vector data.

However, we have also considered that there still remain many challenging problems. One area that needs further investigation is the dimensionality reduction and embedding of specific graphs, such as the Geometric and Delaunay graphs, with Angular Decomposition. Another area is to find efficient algorithms for handling vector data and graph data simultaneously, due to the comparability and complementarity between the two kinds of data. Finally, we hope to extend Angular Decomposition to large-scale and complex networks, such as social network. We plan to embed these networks with our methods, investigate the low-dimensional representation of individual and community (Sun et al., 2011).

ACKNOWLEDGMENT

The research is supported by the NSFC 61073116, 61003038, 61003131, NSF-CCF-0830780, NSF-DMS-0915228, NSFCCF-0917274, and 211 Project of Anhui University.

REFERENCES

Belkin, M., & Niyogi, P. (2003). Laplacian eigenmaps for dimensionality reduction and data representation. *Neural Computation*, *15*(6), 1373–1396. doi:10.1162/089976603321780317

Ding, C., & He, X. (2004). *K-means clustering via principal component analysis*. International Conference in Machine Learning (ICML).

Duda, O. R., Hart, E. P., & Stork, G. D. (2001). *Pattern classification* (2nd ed.). New York, NY: Wiley Interscience.

Genton, G. M., Cristianini, N., Taylor, S. J., & Williamson, R. (2001). Classes of kernels for machine learning: a statistics perspective. *Journal of Machine Learning Research*, *2*, 299–312.

Hall, M. K. (1971). R-dimensional quadratic placement algorithm. *Management Science*, *17*, 219–229. doi:10.1287/mnsc.17.3.219

He, X., & Niyogi, P. (2003). *Locality preserving projections*. Seventeenth Annual Conference on Neural Information Processing Systems (NIPS).

Luo, D., Ding, C., Huang, H., & Li, T. (2009). Non-negative Laplacian embedding. *International Conference in Data Mining (ICDM)*, (pp. 337–346).

Roweis, S. T., & Saul, K. L. (2000). Nonlinear dimensionality reduction by locally linear embedding. *Science*, *290*(22), 2323–2326. doi:10.1126/science.290.5500.2323

Sun, D., Ding, C., Luo, B., & Tang, J. (2011). *Angular decomposition*. Twenty-second International Joint Conference on Artificial Intelligence (IJCAI).

Tenenbaum, J. B., de Silva, V., & Langford, C. J. (2000). A global geometric framework for nonlinear dimensionality. *Science*, *290*(22), 2319–2323. doi:10.1126/science.290.5500.2319

Wang, H., Ding, C., & Huang, H. (2010). Multi-label linear discriminant analysis. *11ᵗʰ European Conference on Computer Vision*, (pp. 126–139).

Yan, S., Xu, D., Zhang, B., Zhang, H., Yang, Q., & Lin, S. (2007). Graph embedding and extensions: A general framework for dimensionality reduction. *IEEE Transactions on Pattern Analysis and Machine Intelligence, 29*(1), 40–51. doi:10.1109/TPAMI.2007.250598

Chapter 13
Region–Based Graph Learning towards Large Scale Image Annotation

Bao Bing-Kun
Institute of Automation, Chinese Academy of Sciences, China

Yan Shuicheng
National University of Singapore, Singapore

ABSTRACT

Graph-based learning provides a useful approach for modeling data in image annotation problems. In this chapter, the authors introduce how to construct a region-based graph to annotate large scale multi-label images. It has been well recognized that analysis in semantic region level may greatly improve image annotation performance compared to that in whole image level. However, the region level approach increases the data scale to several orders of magnitude and lays down new challenges to most existing algorithms. To this end, each image is firstly encoded as a Bag-of-Regions based on multiple image segmentations. And then, all image regions are constructed into a large k-nearest-neighbor graph with efficient Locality Sensitive Hashing (LSH) method. At last, a sparse and region-aware image-based graph is fed into the multi-label extension of the Entropic graph regularized semi-supervised learning algorithm (Subramanya & Bilmes, 2009). In combination they naturally yield the capability in handling large-scale dataset. Extensive experiments on NUS-WIDE (260k images) and COREL-5k datasets well validate the effectiveness and efficiency of the framework for region-aware and scalable multi-label propagation.

DOI: 10.4018/978-1-4666-1891-6.ch013

INTRODUCTION

With fast growing number of images on photo-sharing websites such as Flickr and Picasa, it is in urgent need to develop scalable multi-label propagation algorithms for image indexing, management and searching. Given that most of these uploaded images lack for users' annotations, one crucial task is to automatically annotate these images to facilitate subsequent image searching. Automatic annotation of images in large scale dataset at the semantic level is challenging, mainly due to difficulties on: 1) How to explore the relationships between regions and labels. Generally, labels are relative to image local regions instead of whole image. However, most of the existing algorithms associate labels to whole image with assumption that image similarity and label similarity are consistent. Our first task is to associate the labels with specific image regions, which are believed to be more accurate. 2) How to reveal the co-occurrence among labels. Identification of labels with high probability that existing along with each other, e.g. "cloud" and "sky," will improve image annotation performance. This has been discussed in recent years (Qi, 2007; Chen, 2008, Liu, 2006), but not in large scale dataset due to extra computations required. Our second task is to reveal the label co-occurrence in large scale datasets without incurring additional computations. 3) How to explore the relationships among images. To explore such relationships, especially semantic similarity, kernel function is usually used to construct the similarity matrix, which encodes the underlying dependence structure between images. However, it is impractical to calculate the kernel function over a large scale dataset. Our third task is to efficiently explore the image relationships in large scale datasets. 4) How to propagate the labels from labeled images into unlabeled ones. In large scale dataset, it is intractable to obtain full labels for all images. But it is still feasible to label a small subset of images, which are often regarded as "seed images," and propagate the labels from these seed images into unlabeled ones through semi-supervised learning algorithm. Our fourth task is to select an efficient semi-supervised learning algorithm among existing ones for label propagation. To address these four difficulties, we propose a framework of region-aware and scalable multi-label propagation in this chapter.

Most of existing annotation algorithms are based on the assumption that image similarity and label similarity are consistent. This assumption ignores that each label often only characterizes a local semantic region within an image while image similarity is generally calculated based on the whole image, as illustrated in Figure 1. One reasonable solution is to represent the image with semantic region-based features. Xu *et al.* (2004), Chen *et al.* (2006), Zhou *et al.* (2007) proposed to regard each image as a bag consisting of multiple manually segmented regions and predicted the label of each region by a multi-class bag classifier. In practice, the manual segmentation is very time-consuming while without human interaction

Figure 1. Exemplar images with multiple labels: the four images from Corel5k dataset (Yuan, 2007) and their segmented regions with multiple labels

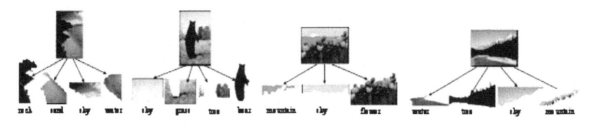

automatic image segmentation algorithms are still far from satisfaction. To address this, Gu *et al.* (2009) proposed to process each image into a robust bag of overlaid regions, which are segmented in different scales, to explore rich cues. The Bag-of-Regions (BOR) representation can not only catch the most semantic regions, but also well suit most existing segmentation algorithms. Therefore, in our framework, we follow Gu's algorithm to represent every image as BOR and extract every region's feature for exploring relationships between semantic regions and labels.

The label co-occurrence is profitable to enhance the accuracy in label propagation. Chen *et al.* constructed graph on label level to reveal the correlations among labels (Chen, 2008). Liu *et al.* introduced a label similarity matrix to provide a semi-supervised learning algorithm (Liu, 2006). Most existing methods are hardly extended to large scale case, especially as the number of labels increases. The Bag-of-Regions representation, which explores the label locality as we mentioned before, also provides us a byproduct to reveal the label co-occurrence. Since the segmented scales are ranged from coarse to fine, the single-label associated regions are generated at the fine segmentation level to explore the label locality, while the multi-label associated regions are generated at the coarse segmentation level to further reveal the label co-occurrence. If the certain multiple labels are frequently segmented into one region, the co-occurrence will be revealed and propagated to unlabeled data.

Image similarity plays an important role in image annotation problems. However, it is hard to calculate all pair-wise similarities in large scale applications due to the storage limitation and the highly computational cost. Sparse k-nearest neighbor (k-NN) graph is a widely used scaling method to explore image similarity. In order to fast search the k-nearest data points to the query one, it is generally a solution to construct a data structure which projects the data points into low-dimensional space, and searches the nearest

neighbors under some (Euclidean) distance function. *kd*-tree is a space partitioning data structure for organizing data points in k-dimensional space A. Moore, (1991). However, it suffers from the query time that is exponential to dimension k. Recent advances in approximate nearest neighbor methods shed some lights on solving this problem. The appeal of this method is that, an approximate nearest neighbor is almost as good as the exact one in many cases, while it improves in computational efficiency. In particular, if the distance measure can accurately capture the underlying data dependence structure between images, then small differences in the distance should not matter. Locality Sensitive Hashing (LSH) scheme (M. Charikar, 2002), a most popular method in approximate search, is explored to separate images by hash key of each one into different buckets to speed up the query rate. The hash key, composed of a b-bit binary code, is generated by several hash functions which provide higher probability of bit collision for the nearby data points. According to this locality-sensitive hash key, the images can be finally separated into different buckets with the different Hamming distance. Therefore, the retrieving process is simplified to search the elements in the bucket which contains the query data point. The experiments show that this data structure achieves large speedup over several tree-based data structures when the data is stored in disk (Indyk, 1998, Gionis, 1999). Jain *et al.* (2008) provided a method to incrementally update locality-sensitive hash keys during the updates of the metric learner, which makes it possible to perform accurate sublinear time nearest neighbor search over the data in an online manner. Adopting the same merit, we utilize LSH to fast search every region's nearest neighbors to construct region-level based k-NN graph. However, it still comes up with a problem that how to convert the region-level based k-NN graph into image-level based k-NN graph. In this chapter, we provide a Region-to-Image (R2I) process to generate the k-NN graph at image-level from the region-level counterpart. More specifically, we first segment every image into regions with different segmentation scales to obtain the BOR and extract the region representation; next utilize LSH to construct the k-NN graph at region level; then, generate the k-NN graph at image level in R2I process; the image similarity provided by image k-NN graph is at last leveraged to propagate the labels from labeled ones into unlabeled ones.

In the phase of label propagation, an appropriate learning algorithm is also a vital factor for effectiveness and efficiency, especially in large scale problem. From a machine learning point of view, our goal of label propagation can be regarded as a special case of semi-supervised learning. With the philosophy that adding quantities of unlabeled data could provide auxiliary information and produce a better classifier, semi-supervised learning algorithms have demonstrated superior performances on many large scale problems. Several efficient algorithms are proposed in recent years. Collobert *et al.* (2006), Sindhwani *et al.* (2006) developed large scale semi-supervised linear SVM. Delalleau *et al.* (2005), proposed an algorithm to improve the induction speed when modeling data with graphs. Karlen *et al.* (2008) solved a large-scale graph transduction problem with up to 650,000 samples. Subramanya *et al.* (2009) performed efficient transduction by optimizing an entropy-regularized objective function. This algorithm is cache-cognizant and obtains linear speedup in parallel computations, which ensures the scalability to large data set. The algorithm proposed in this chapter is primarily adapted from Subramanya's. On the one hand, Subramanya's algorithm is able to process ever largest samples (120 million). On the other hand, this KL-divergence-based algorithm experimentally outperforms other square-loss algorithms such as the harmonic function algorithm. We adapt it according to special requirement underlying the image annotation task.

In this chapter, we introduce a framework of region-aware and scalable multi-label propagation (Bao, 2011), which not only explores the relationships between labels and regions, but also possesses the computational efficiency, especially for large-scale setting. The framework is of the following properties:

1. The relationships between regions and labels are explored by the inter-relationship between the small-regions at the fine segmentation level
2. The label co-occurrence is revealed by large-size regions at the coarse segmentation level
3. The computation for image similarity is accelerated by locality-sensitive hashing. Extensive experiment results on NUS-WIDE and Corel datasets also demonstrate the effectiveness and efficiency of the framework

REGION-AWARE AND SCALABLE MULTI-LABEL PROPAGATION FRAMEWORK

Overview of the Framework

Figure 2 shows the overall flow chart of the framework for region-aware and scalable multi-label propagation. There are four steps, and the first one is region specific representation. In this step, every image is segmented into a Bag-of-Regions with different segmentation scales. Then, we extract every region's Histogram of Oriented Gradient (HOG) features (Dalal, 2005) and color moments (Yu, 2002), to obtain the region specific feature representation. In the second step, the locality-sensitive hashing (LSH) technique is explored to build more than one hash tables using several hash functions on the whole regions. Then we construct the region-level based k-NN graph with the knowledge of each region's nearest neighbors which are retrieved in the hashing tables. In the third step, we exploit a Region-to-Image (R2I) procedure to explore the similarity in the image level. And in the last step, an effective semi-supervised learning algorithm (Subramanya, 2009) is utilized

Figure 2. Overall flow chart of the framework: there are four steps including region specific representation, image region-level based k-NN graph construction, region-to-image process and semi-supervised learning process.

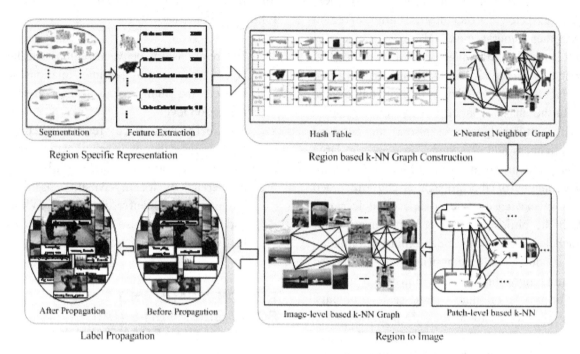

to propagate the labels from the labeled images to the unlabeled images. The details of these four steps are given in the following subsections.

Region Specific Representation

Bag-of-Regions

An image usually contains a set of semantic regions that are merged from the atomic patches. Each homogeneous patch consists of pixels that are spatially coherent and perceptually similar with respect to certain appearance features, such as intensity, color and texture. In order to capture rich cues contained in an image, like in (Gu, 2009), an image is represented by constructing a hierarchical region tree with the atomic regions as the leaf nodes. Each node of the tree represents a localized image region that is either further divided into smaller regions, or merged with other

regions at the same level to form the parent node. By removing the links between nodes, we can obtain an ensemble of image regions at different scales, collectively called the Bag-of-Regions, as illustrated in Figure 3.

In the implementation, we slightly modify the original algorithm (Felzenszwalb, 2004) as follows. First, we resize all the images into a roughly equal resolution and initialize each pixel as one atomic region. Then, we use the color features to describe the appearance of an initial image region and apply the algorithm (Felzenszwalb, 2004) to merge the smaller regions into larger ones. This step iterates until all the image regions are merged into one single region, namely the original image. At each iteration, multiple region pairs are merged and labeled with the same depth in the final hierarchical region tree. On Intel Xeon X5450 workstation with 3.0GHz CPU and 16GB memory, it takes less than 0.2 second

Figure 3. Bag-of-Regions: These two images are from the NUS-WIDE dataset (Chua, 2009). From upper two charts, we can see that these two images are segmented by three scales to get the four-level hierarchical region tree. The leaf nodes are the atomic regions, and the parent nodes are merged by its children nodes. The lower charts illustrate these two images' Bag-of-Regions, obtained by removing the links between nodes in the hierarchical region tree.

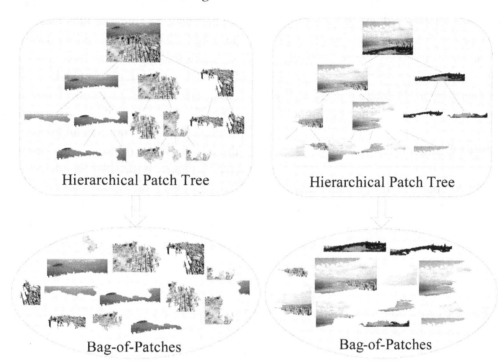

to segment one image. Figure 3 shows an exemplary result of this segmentation step. Note that this solution is general and not tied to any specific image segmentation algorithms. The only assumption of this step is that each atomic region, i.e., the leaf node of the region tree, is entirely within an object/label. This makes our overall algorithm less sensitive to the quality of the image segmentation step.

Feature Extraction

We extract low-level features mainly from two visual properties, *i.e.* texture and color. All low-level features are constructed by dense grid histograms. The detailed descriptions of these used features are listed below:

- **Texture Features:** Describes periodic patterns, and can be considered to be repeating patterns of local variation of pixel intensities. HOG has been widely accepted as one of the best features to capture the texture information. In practice, it is implemented by dividing the image windows into small spatial regions ("cells"), for each cell accumulating a local histogram of gradient direction or edge orientations over the pixels of the cell. In this chapter, the segmented region naturally plays the role of cell, and the gradient direction can be extracted from dense sift features, which results in a 128D histogram vector.
- **Color Features:** Widely used in image representation, and are investigated to

complement the texture features. Here, we adopt three central moments of an image's color distribution, namely Mean, Standard deviation and Skewness. In practice, we operate on RGB color space, therefore, an image is characterized by 9D-color moments vector, 3 moments for mean, standard deviation and skewness respectively.

Finally, every region obtained is represented by a 128(HOG)+9(color)D vector, shown in Figure 4.

k-NN Graph Construction

To efficiently compute the image similarity, we postulate the overall inter-region similarity matrix is sparse, wherein only the matrix entries corresponding to *k*-nearest neighbors are non-zero.

Recently, several approximate similarity search techniques are explored to make the large-scale search practical, where a predictable loss in accuracy is sacrificed in order to allow fast queries even for high-dimensional inputs and massive indexed data. The most popular locality-sensitive hashing (LSH) technique is an effective method to search the approximate nearest neighbors. It first projects each region into a low dimensional binary (Hamming) space with certain bits of hash keys. Then, relying on the fact that highly similar examples are most possible to be assigned with the same hash key (known as the "locality sensitive" property in the LSH literature), we can efficiently obtain the short-listed *k*-NN candidates to an arbitrary query by hashing it to a unique bucket. Given n data points in a Hamming space and a query u_i, LSH scheme guarantees that the

Figure 4. Feature extraction: Illustration of feature extraction for every region. The features are composed by HOG and color moments.

$$\begin{pmatrix}
0.0982 & 0.3497 & \cdots & 0.1076 & \cdots \\
0.1391 & 0.2370 & \cdots & 0.2087 & \cdots \\
0.2218 & 0.2465 & \cdots & 0.3497 & \cdots \\
0.0897 & 0.0765 & \cdots & 0.0334 & \cdots \\
0.1789 & 0.0898 & \cdots & 0.2012 & \cdots \\
0.1275 & 0.0383 & \cdots & 0.1954 & \cdots \\
0.2565 & 0.1756 & \cdots & 0.2232 & \cdots \\
\vdots & \vdots & \ddots & \vdots & \vdots \\
1 & -1.1325 & \cdots & -0.9177 & \cdots \\
0.5355 & -0.9927 & \cdots & -0.5740 & \cdots \\
-0.2058 & -0.6619 & \cdots & -0.7495 & \cdots
\end{pmatrix}$$

128D HOG

9D Color Moments

query time for retrieving $1+\in$ near neighbors of u_i is bounded by $O\left(n^{1/1+\in}\right)$

Denote $\{u_i, i = 1, 2...,n\}$ as the region feature vectors composed of HOG and color moment, where n is the total number of regions for all training images. Firstly, we generate a b-bit hash key $H(u_i)=[h_1(u_i), h_2(u_i),...h_b(u_i)]$ for every feature vector u_i, here $h_k()$ denotes the k-th locality sensitive hash function. Assume the similarity between any sample pair u_i and u_j can be calculated by the function $\kappa\left(u_i, u_j\right)$. A well-known property of the LSH functions is that $\Pr\left[h_k\left(u_i\right) = h_k\left(u_j\right)\right] = \kappa\left(u_i, u_j\right)$ if $\kappa(\ ,\ )$ returns a scalar in [0, 1] which implies higher collision probability (i.e. being assigned with the same hash key) of more similar examples in the constructed hash table. In the retrieving phase, only the samples staying in the same bucket as the query are collected as the short-listed k-NN candidates, and the distances between original feature vectors are computed to determine the exact k nearest neighbors. In this way, the computation time is drastically reduced compared with exhaustive linear scan. Figure 5 illustrates the constructed hash table, while Figure 6 illus-trates the constructed region-level based k-NN graph.

As we mentioned before, the regions are seg-mented with different scales ranged from coarse to fine. Obviously, the small-size regions may associate to a single label, while the large-size regions usually present multiple labels. The high probability which exists of certain multiple labels can reveal the label co-occurrence. We can not only investigate the label locality through similar-ity among the small-size single-label regions, but also explore the label co-occurrence from the similarity of large-size regions.

Region-to-Image

In this subsection, a Region-to-Image (R2I) pro-cedure is provided to generate image approximate semantic similarity based on region-level based k-NN graph. For two images I_m and I_n, they have been respectively segmented into p^m and p^n regions in the first step. Denote the region set correspond-ing to image I_m as $\left\{r_1^m,...,r_{p^m}^m\right\}$, similarly the image I_n's region set is $\left\{r_1^n,...,r_{p^n}^n\right\}$. With the knowledge of region-level based k-NN graph, each region's k-nearest neighbors and the corresponding simi-

Figure 5. Hash table: shows the result of the hash table construction. First every region is encoded, then merged into different buckets according to Hamming distance. The result is gratifying that even the sky in orange color can be searched out in the first bucket.

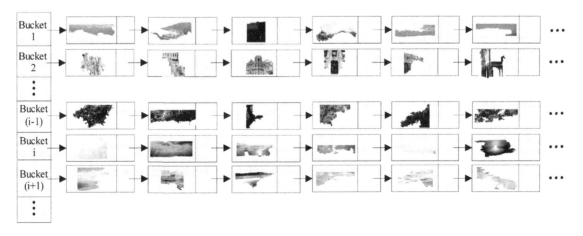

Figure 6. Region-level k-NN graph: illustrates the region level based k-NN graph. The regions k-nearest neighbors are obtained by the result of hash table construction, and the weight of the vertex edge is the Euclidean distance based on RBF kernel.

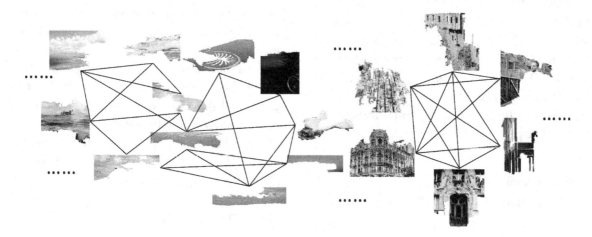

larity values are given. Obviously, the similarity between image I_m and I_n is only relative to the relationships between the pairwise regions from these two image respectively. Denote T as the number of pairwise regions which bear the nearest neighbor relatively (i.e. either region is among the k-nearest neighbor regions of another one in the pair) between two images. Let the pairwise nearest neighbor regions be $\left\{ \left(r_{k_1^m}^m, r_{k_1^n}^n \right), \left(r_{k_2^m}^m, r_{k_2^n}^n \right), ..., \left(r_{k_t^m}^m, r_{k_t^n}^n \right) \right\}$, here $k_1^m, k_2^m, ..., k_t^m \in \left\{ 1, ..., p^m \right\}$, and $k_1^n, k_2^n, ..., k_t^n \in \left\{ 1, ..., p_n \right\}$. Note that k_i^m and k_j^m, $i, j \in \left\{ 1, 2, ..., k \right\}$, may be referred to the same index. That is, $r_{k_i^m}^m$ and $r_{k_i^n}^n$, $i \in \left\{ 1, 2, ..., k \right\}$, are a pairwise nearest neighbor, here $r_{k_i^m}^m$, $r_{k_i^n}^n$ belong to image m and n respectively. Also, the similarity between $r_{k_i^m}^m$ and $r_{k_i^n}^n$ is denoted as κ_i^{mn}.

As shown in Figure 7, we can calculate the similarity between image I_m and I_n as follows:

$$S_{mn} = \frac{\sum_{i=1}^t \kappa_i^{mn}}{t} \quad (1)$$

From this formula, we can get the image approximate similarity matrix S. Since the calculation for image similarity relies on the region-level based k-NN graph and the value of "k" is significantly smaller than the total number of regions, the image similarity matrix will be quite sparse (Figure 8).

Semi-Supervised Learning

(Subramanya, 2009) proposed an entropic graph regularized semi-supervised learning algorithm, which can be easily extended to multi-label and large-scale applications, also easily handle label uncertainty and integrate priors. The algorithm is detailed as follows.

Let the number of labeled and unlabeled images be N_t and N_u respectively, and the symmetric k-nearest neighbor graph is associated with $S=[S_{ij}]$, which is already obtained by the R2I procedure. Obviously, the matrix S is sparse, let $N(i)$ be the set of neighbors of vertex i. We first construct an undirected weighted graph $G=(V,E)$, where the vertices (nodes) $V=\{1,2,...,m\}$, $N_m=N_t+N_u$, are the

Figure 7. Region to image: This figure shows the pairwise regions from every two images. Each pairwise region contributes a weight to the similarity of the corresponding two images. The calculation of image similarity is shown in Equation 1.

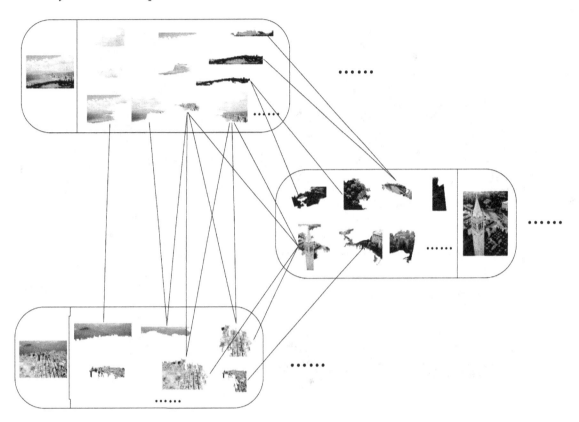

data points in D and edges $E \subseteq V \times V$. Let V_t and V_u be the set of labeled and unlabeled vertices respectively. G represented via the image similarity matrix S which is referred as weight matrix. For each $i \in V$ and $j \in V_l$, define probability measures p_i and r_j are multinomial distributions, $p_i(y)$ is the probability for the i-th image to belong to class y. $\{r_j(y)\}, j \in V_l$ is the probability that the j-th labeled image belongs to class y. The objective function to optimize is constructed as follows:

$$p^* = \min_p C_1(p) = \min_p$$
$$\left\{ \sum_{i=1}^{N_t} D_{KL}\left(r_i \| p_i\right) + \mu \sum_{i=1}^{N_m} \sum_{j \in N(i)} w_{ij} D_{KL}\left(p_i \| p_j\right) - v\sum_{i=1}^{N_m} H\left(p_i\right) \right\}$$

C_1 is not a menable to optimization using AM and a modified version is proposed:

$$\left(p^*, q^*\right) = \min_{p,q} C_2\left(p,q\right) = \min_{p,q}$$
$$\left\{ \begin{array}{l} \sum_{i=1}^{N_t} D_{KL}\left(r_i \| q_i\right) + \mu \sum_{i=1}^{N_m} \\ \sum_{j \in N(i)} w_{ij} D_{KL}\left(p_i \| p_j\right) - v\sum_{i=1}^{N_m} H\left(p_i\right) \end{array} \right\}$$

Here, the q_i plays a similar role as p_i. $W' = W + \alpha I_n$, $N' = \left\{\{i\} \cup N(i)\right\}$, and $\alpha \geq 0$. The update equations for solving $C_2(p,q)$ are given by

Figure 8. Image-level based k-NN graph: This figure illustrates the image-level based k-NN graph, the nearest neighbors are obtained by the R2I process, and weight of the vertex edge is the image similarity calculated by Equation 1.

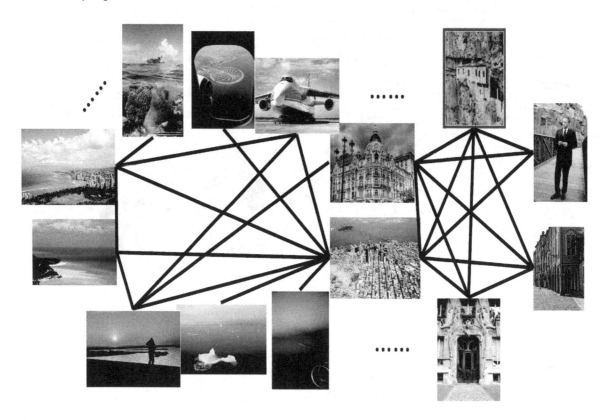

$$p_i^{(n)}(y) =$$

$$\frac{\exp\left\{\frac{\mu}{\gamma i}\sum_j w'_{ij}\log q_j^{(n-1)}(y)\right\}}{\sum_y \exp\left\{\frac{\mu}{\gamma i}\sum_j w'_{ij}\log q_j^{(n-1)}(y)\right\}}$$

and

$$q_i^{(n)}(y) =$$

$$\frac{r_i(y)\delta(i \leq l) + \mu\sum_j w'_{ji} p_j^{(n)}(y)}{\delta(i \leq l) + \mu\sum_j w'_{ji}}$$

where $\gamma_i = v + \mu\sum_i w'_{ij}$.

EXPERIMENTS

In this section, we systematically evaluate the effectiveness and efficiency of the region-aware and scalable multi-label propagation framework.

Data Sets

Since our framework focuses on large scale problem, the purposes of experiments are to test the annotation precision comparing with the non-segmentation approach and the computational complexity against the non-hash-coding approach on large scale dataset. Since it is impractical to test the non-hash-coding approach in the large scale dataset due to the high computational cost, we choose a smaller dataset to compare the computational complexity between the non-hash-coding one and ours, while we also select a large scale dataset to verify the advantage in annotation precision using our method against the non-segmentation one.

Two publicly available datasets, NUS-WIDE (Chua, 2009) and Corel 5k (Duygulu, 2002), satisfy our demands. The NUS-WIDE dataset, crawled from Flickr website, was recently collected by the National University of Singapore (NUS). It is the largest available real-world web image dataset, which contains 269,648 images with 81 labels and has about 2 labels per image. We utilize this dataset to test the annotation precision of our framework for the large scale case. We randomly split the whole dataset into a labeled set and an unlabeled set, and the number of unlabeled samples is two times of that of labeled ones.

The Corel 5k dataset, containing 5000 images associated with 374 labels, is the most broadly adopted dataset in the community of image retrieval. We leverage this dataset to test the computational cost of our framework comparing with the approach without exploiting LSH method. Since some labels are relatively rare, we select 149 labels which are tagged on more than 10 images. Ignoring 14 images which do not include any of these 149 labels, a dataset with 4986 images is finally obtained. We also randomly split it into two subsets for labeled set and unlabeled set respectively. The labeled set includes 1661 images, while the unlabeled set includes 3325 images.

Baseline and Evaluation Criteria

As we mentioned before, we choose NUS-WIDE dataset to test the annotation precision in large scale application, so we select the approach without segmentation as the baseline to evaluate the framework in scalability and accuracy. Meanwhile, for Corel 5k, we choose the approach without segmentation and hash coding as the baseline to test the running computational complexity.

The baseline of the experiment on NUS-WIDE is to construct the image k-NN graph without considering the similarity among regions, that is, without regard to segmenting the image into regions, referred as to NSA (Non-segmentation Algorithm). In implementation, we extract the image global features, composed of HOG and color moments, instead of region-based features. We divide every image into 8x8 blocks uniformly, and extract every block's HOG and color moments features, then concatenate these 64 sets of block features as an entire vector of 8768 (137x64) dimensions. Next, these image global features are coded into a 20-bit hash key to accelerate the query of 3000-nearest neighbors, then the image-level based k-NN graph is naturally constructed. Last, the same semi-supervised learning algorithm is utilized to propagate labels.

The baseline of the experiment on Corel 5k is to reveal image similarity without speeding up query rate by LSH method, referred as to NLA (Non-LSH Algorithm). To reduce the computational cost, we also represent the image global features instead of region-based feature as in the baseline of NUS-WIDE to decrease the dimensionality. In implementation, we also segment every image into 8x8 blocks uniformly, and extract HOG and color moments features, then concatenate these 64 sets of block feature as an entire vector as in the baseline of NUS-WIDE. We define the similarity of the every two images as follows:

$$S_{mn} = \exp\left(-\gamma \left\| x_m - x_n \right\|^2\right), \gamma > 0$$

With this similarity matrix, the preconditions for semi-supervised learning process are satisfied.

Many measurements can be used to evaluate multi-label image annotation performance, *e.g.*, ROC curve, precision recall curve, average precision, and so on. For the large scale of samples, it's highly computational to calculate the curve. Thus, we choose average precision, that is, the most widely accepted one, for our algorithmic performance evaluation.

Setting and Results

In this subsection, we will detail some settings for the experiments on these two datasets, and show some interesting results.

NUS-WIDE

In our framework, for each image, we do segmentation for 4 times with the scales at about 2000, 3500, 5000, 7500 pixels for each region, and obtain about 18 regions. There are 5362,754 regions together for the whole dataset. We choose 70 keys to construct hash tables, and the distance is selected as Euclidean distance. We choose k=700

in constructing region-level based k-NN graph, while choose k=3000 in image-level based k-NN graph. For the baseline, we set 30 keys to encode all images into hash tables, and choose k=3000 in constructing image-level based k-NN graph.

Figure 9 shows the annotation precision results of our framework and the baseline: NSA (Non-segmentation Algorithm). The second column indicates the average precision over all the labels, while the other columns from the third on indicate the label-specific precision's for 20 different labels, which are randomly chosen from the total 81 labels. The average precision of our approach RSMP (Region-aware and Scalable Multi-label Propagation) is 0.6506, while the baseline NSA is 0.5815. From the figure, we can see that for the specific single label, our approach outperforms baseline NSA greatly.

Figure 10 illustrates the results from k-nearest neighbors at region level in our approach. We

Figure 9. Performance comparison (AP) of different algorithms for semi-supervised label propagation to unlabeled data on the NUS-WIDE dataset. The dark bars show the results of the baseline NSA (Non-segmentation Algorithm), and the light bars show the ones of the approach RSMP (Region-aware and Scalable Multi-label Propagation). The first column indicates the average precision over all the labels, and other columns from the second on indicate the label-specific AP's for different labels.

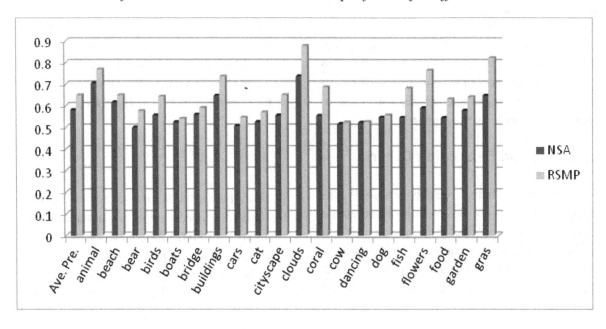

Figure 10. Results of region K-nearest neighbors: There are 12 rows in the table, and every 3 rows illustrate one query result. In these 3 rows, the second row illustrates the query region and the query result, that is, the authors query the region in the second column, and its nearest neighbors are the regions in the following 5 columns. In the third row, they also show the corresponding original image associated with the region, which is located in the same column of the second row.

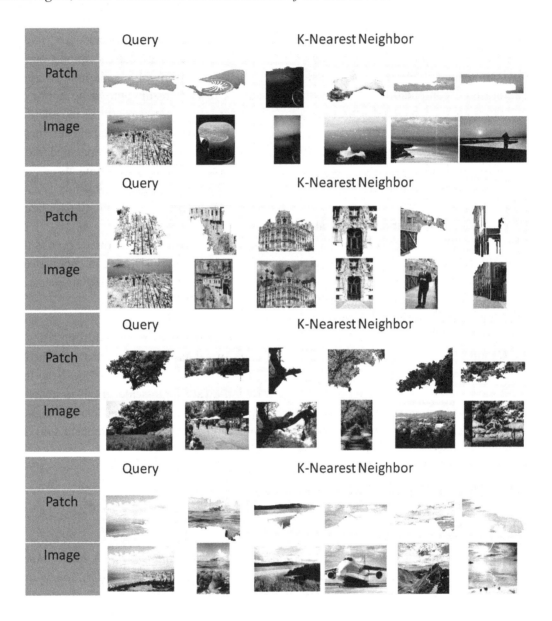

select four common regions as samples to show the nearest neighbor results. The first query region is on sky, and the nearest neighbor regions we got are mostly correct, especially the last region describing the sky in orange, which indicates that the HOG feature plays an important role in representation. The second query is the region of building, and similarity satisfying results can be observed. We pay attention to the last query region, which describes three correlative labels, sky, cloud and sea. It is acceptable that the cloud always appears with sky, and sky also goes along with sea. From the nearest neighbor result, we can see that, there are three regions including these three labels, while the second and the third region, in the query result, include sky and cloud.

Corel 5k

In this experiment, we choose a smaller dataset Corel 5k, which contains 5000 images and to evaluate the algorithmic computational complexity. The process in our approach includes three steps:

1. Segment every image at four scales of 1500, 2500, 4500, 6500 pixels respectively to get 2,7814 segmented regions for the whole dataset.
2. Choose 40 keys to construct 4 hash tables and construct 100-NN graph at region-level.
3. Calculate image similarity; and 4) label propagation. In order to compare the efficiency of our approach, we choose Non LSH Algorithm (NLA) as our baseline. The NLA includes two steps:
    a. Calculate image similarity.
    b. Label propagation.

Since the computational cost of the first step increases exponentially with the size of the dataset, it is too time-consuming to be computed as the size reaches 10,000 images, which is far from the large scale requirement. The details of computational cost in every step and average precision for two algorithms are listed in the Table 1.

CONCLUSION

In this chapter, we introduced a novel scalable label-locality driven image annotation framework, which possesses four characteristics, namely:

1. The inter-label co-occurrence is revealed with the relationships among super-size regions from the segmentation algorithm
2. The relationships among the atomic regions are investigated to explore the relationships between regions and labels and these relationships are further propagated into image level similarity measurements
3. The locality-sensitive hashing is exploited to accelerate the computation for large scale applications
4. To the best of our knowledge, it is the first time that multi-label semi-supervised learning algorithm is applied to large scale dataset up to 260k images.

Extensive experiment results on NUS-WIDE and Corel datasets demonstrate the effectiveness and efficiency of the framework. Note that this region-aware large-scale graph is general, and can benefit any graph-based learning algorithms, thus can be widely used to replace conventional global image based graphs.

Table 1. Computational cost and Accuracy comparison of two algorithms on the Corel5k dataset. T_s represents the time duration in the segmentation process, T_h represents the time duration in the hash table and patch-level k-NN graph construction, T_i represents the time duration in the image similarity calculation, T_p represents the time duration in the label propagation, T represents the total time in the whole process.

Algorithm	Computational Cost					Accuracy
	T_s	T_h	T_i	T_p	T	AP
NLA	N/A	N/A	6795s	12s	6807s	0.5849
RSMP	2298s	3s+494s	36s	13s	2884s	0.6163

REFERENCES

Bao, B.-K., Ni, B., Mu, Y., & Yan, S. (2011). Efficient region-aware large graph construction towards scalable multi-label propagation. *Pattern Recognition, 3*(44), 598–606. doi:10.1016/j.patcog.2010.10.001

Charikar, M. (2002). Similarity estimation techniques from rounding algorithms. In *Proceedings of the thiry-fourth annual ACM symposium on Theory of Computing,* (pp. 380 – 388).

Chen, G., Song, Y., Wang, F., & Zhang, C. (2008). Semi-supervised multi-label learning by solving a Sylvester equation. In *SIAM International Conference on Data Mining (SDM)*, Atlanta, Georgia, (pp. 410–419).

Chen, Y., Bi, J., & Wang, J. Z. (2006). Miles: Multiple-instance learning via embedded instance selection. *IEEE Transactions on Pattern Analysis and Machine Intelligence, 28*(12), 1931–1947. doi:10.1109/TPAMI.2006.248

Chua, T. S., Tang, J., Hong, R., Li, H., Luo, Z., & Zheng, Y. (2009). Nus-wide: A real-world web image database from national university of Singapore. In *Proceedings of ACM Conference on Image and Video Retrieval (CIVR)*.

Collobert, R., Sinz, F., Weston, J., & Bottou, L. (2006). Large scale transductive SVMS. *Journal of Machine Learning Research, 7*, 1687–1712.

Dalal, N., Triggs, B., Rhone-Alps, I., & Montbonnot, F. (2005). Histograms of oriented gradients for human detection. In *IEEE Computer Society Conference on Computer Vision and Pattern Recognition*, Vol. 1.

Delalleau, O., Bengio, Y., & Le Roux, N. (2005). Efficient non-parametric function induction in semi-supervised learning. In *Proceedings of the Tenth International Workshop on Artificial Intelligence and Statistics (AISTAT)*.

Duygulu, P., Barnard, K., De Freitas, J., & Forsyth, D. (2002). Object recognition as machine translation: Learning a lexicon for a fixed image vocabulary. In *Proceedings of the Seventh European Conference on Computer Vision (ECCV)*, (pp. 349–354).

Felzenszwalb, P. F., & Huttenlocher, D. P. (2004). Efficient graph-based image segmentation. *International Journal of Computer Vision, 59*(2), 167–181. doi:10.1023/B:VISI.0000022288.19776.77

Gionis, A., Indyk, P., & Motwani, R. (1999). Similarity search in high dimensions via hashing. In *Proceedings of International Conference on Very Large Data Bases*.

Gu, C., Lim, J. J., Arbelaez, P., & Malik, J. (2009). Recognition using regions. In *Proceedings of IEEE Conference on Computer Vision and Pattern Recognition (CVPR)*.

Indyk, P., & Motwani, R. (1998). Approximate nearest neighbors: towards removing the curse of dimensionality. In *Proceedings of Symposium on Theory of Computing,* (pp. 604–613). New York, NY: ACM.

Jain, P., Kulis, B., Dhillon, I., & Grauman, K. (2008). Online metric learning and fast similarity search. In *Advances in Neural Information Processing Systems*. NIPS.

Karlen, M., Weston, J., Erkan, A., & Collobert, R. (2008). *Large scale manifold transduction.* In International Conference on Machine Learning (ICML).

Liu, Y., Jin, R., & Yang, L. (2006). Semi-supervised multi-label learning by constrained non-negative matrix factorization. In *Proceedings of National Conference on Artificial Intelligence and Innovative Applications of Artificial Intelligence Conference (AAAI)*, (Vol. 21, pp. 666–671).

Moore, A. (1991). *An intoductory tutorial on kd-trees*. Ph.D. dissertation, Carnegie Mello University.

Qi, G. J., Hua, X. S., Rui, Y., Tang, J., Mei, T., & Zhang, H. J. (2007). Correlative multi-label video annotation. In *Proceedings of the 15th ACM International Conference on Multimedia (MM)*, (pp. 17–26).

Sindhwani, V., & Selvaraj, S. (2006). Large scale semi-supervised linear support vector machines. In *Proceedings of the 29th Annual International ACM SIGIR Conference on Research and Development in Information Retrieval*.

Subramanya, A., & Bilmes, J. (2009). *Entropic graph regularization in non-parametric semi-supervised classification. Neural Information Processing Society*. Vancouver, Canada: NIPS.

Xu, X., & Frank, E. (2004). Logistic regression and boosting for labeled bags of instances. In *Proceedings of the Pacific Asia Conference on Knowledge Discovery and Data Mining*, (pp. 272–281).

Yu, H., Li, M., Zhang, H., & Feng, J. (2002). Color texture moments for content-based image retrieval. In *International Conference on Image Processing*, (Vol. 3, pp. 929–932).

Yuan, J., Li, J., & Zhang, B. (2007). Exploiting spatial context constraints for automatic image region annotation. In *Proceedings of the 15th ACM International Conference on Multimedia*, (pp. 595–604).

Zhou, Z., & Zhang, M. (2007). Multi-instance multi-label learning with application to scene classification. *Advances in Neural Information Processing Systems*, *19*, 1609–1616.

Chapter 14
Copy Detection Using Graphical Model:
HMM for Frame Fusion

Wei Shikui
Beijing Jiaotong University, China

Zhao Yao
Beijing Jiaotong University, China

Zhu Zhenfeng
Beijing Jiaotong University, China

ABSTRACT

With the growing popularity of video sharing websites and editing tools, it is easy for people to involve the video content from different sources into their own work, which raises the copyright problem. Content-based video copy detection attempts to track the usage of the copyright-protected video content by using video analysis techniques, which deals with not only whether a copy occurs in a query video stream but also where the copy is located and where the copy is originated from. While a lot of work has addressed the problem with good performance, less effort has been made to consider the copy detection problem in the case of a continuous query stream, for which precise temporal localization and some complex video transformations like frame insertion and video editing need to be handled. In this chapter, the authors attack the problem by employing the graphical model to facilitate the frame fusion based video copy detection approach. The key idea is to convert frame fusion problem into graph model decoding problem with the temporal consistency constraint and three relaxed constraints. This work employs the HMM model to perform frame fusion and propose a Viterbi-like algorithm to speedup frame fusion process.

DOI: 10.4018/978-1-4666-1891-6.ch014

INTRODUCTION

By analyzing the video archives in large-scale network database, some researchers found that certain video content copied from the same source is frequently occurred in lots of different videos due to its popularity or importance, such as popular network video and important news shots. Generally, the usage of those popular video clips is not authorized by the original authors or organization, and tracking those clips is an important problem for digital copyright protection and law enforcement investigations. As an alternative to the watermarking technique, content-based video copy detection (CBCD) offers a quite different manner to media tracking and copyright protection. For watermarking techniques, they require some secret information to be embedded in the target video, and then perform copyright detection by retrieving the secret information. This means that some secret information must be embedded before the video archive is distributed. In practice, it may be difficult to fulfill the requirement since huge amounts of video data have earlier been distributed without such processing. In contrast, the CBCD does not pose any additional requirements (Kim, 2005), which directly detects copies by matching a query video with a reference database (Gengembre, 2008) (Joly, 2007) (Law-To, 2006).

Formally, CBCD refers to judging whether a query video contains any content originated from copyright protected video via some feature extraction and matching techniques (Yang, 2003). The key challenge in CBCD is how to precisely localize the pair of a copy and its original clip in both the query video stream and the reference database despite various video transformations on the copy. This challenge becomes more difficult and complicated as the size of reference database increases. To this end, a lot of work has been done in recent years. In the earlier work, the main effort focuses on frame feature extraction and video matching based on the aligned frames. For example, those reported in (Chen, 2008) (Hua,

2004) (Kim, 2005) (Lee, 2008) (Oostveen, 2002) treat a whole query video as a detection unit and attempt to match it with all possible subsequences of equal length within a long reference video, where a threshold is set to determine if there is a copy or not. However, those schemes fail if only a small segment in the query video is a copy in many practical applications Law-To, (2006). An example is a broadcast stream in which only some clips are potential copies. Therefore, more flexible detection methods need to be designed to address this issue. Recently, frame fusion based methods provide a possibility to detect copied segments (Douze, 2008) (Gengembre, 2008) (Hampapur, 2002) (Kim, 2008). These methods first search the reference database and return a list of similar reference frames for each query frame. Then the copies can be determined by fusing these returned reference frames according to a temporal consistency assumption. However, those methods generally process the query video in batch, that is, the query frames in one batch need to be parsed beforehand. This may limit or compromise the application or performance of those schemes for detecting copies in a continuous query video stream, such as the broadcast video stream.

To address the above problem, we consider a frame fusion based copy detection approach, which detects copies by similar frame search and frame fusion under a temporal consistency assumption. In this chapter, our work focuses mainly on the critical frame fusion stage that performs copy determination and temporal localization by employing a graphical model (here, HMM model). To improve fusion efficiency, the proposed scheme employs a Viterbi-like dynamic programming algorithm which comprises an on-line backtracking strategy with three relaxed constraints, namely, emission constraint, transition constraint, and gap constraint. In particular, when a new query frame is read and a list of similar reference frames is retrieved for it, the emission constraint and transition constraint are then used to build transition relationship between reference frames in the current list and reference frames in previous lists. Finally the gap constraint is employed to determine the starting and ending positions of complete paths. Using the on-line back-tracking, we can get a few complete paths at current time instant, which correspond to the original video clips. Note that the starting and ending positions indicate the boundaries of potential copies in the query video stream.

To facilitate the following discussions, we clarify some terms used in this paper. A copy refers to a video clip originated from a copyright protected video. "Original video" and "reference video" are interchangeable throughout the paper, which mean the copyright protected video.

BACKGROUND

Content-based video copy detection involves two key techniques: feature extraction and video matching. We will review the existing work from these two aspects.

Feature Extraction

A copy is usually a transformed version of the reference clip. That is, the video signal of a copy is distorted from its original version. Therefore, the features used for copy detection should not only be distinctive enough for identification but also be robust enough to tolerate signal distortions. According to the feature nature, we can classify them into global features and local features.

Many research studies (Chen, 2008) (Chiu, 2008) (Hua, 2004) (Kim, 2005) (Oostveen, 2002), especially in the earlier work, have paid much attention to the extraction of global features so as to deal with a variety of simple signal distortions. For example, Oostveen et al. (Oostveen, 2002) proposed a global binary feature for tolerating the changes in resolution and contrast. Ordinal measure based features (Chiu, 2008) (Hua, 2004) (Kim, 2005) are employed for dealing with color

degradation and change of display format. On the whole, however, global features are normally based on the statistics of the entire frame or the whole clip. Although those features are usually more compact and can be extracted more efficiently, they can only deal with some simple transformations. For some post-production transformations such as picture in picture, they are not workable since partial matching is needed in these cases. Compared with global features, the local features are automatically resistant to the transformations caused by some post-production operations (Joly, 2005) since a part of original content always remains in the copy. Most of local features used in CBCD are based on the interest points. Normally, all the interest points in a frame are detected first, and then a local descriptor is computed around each interest point. A lot of methods exist for both interest point detection and local descriptor calculation. Different combinations construct different extraction schemes (Douze, 2008) (Douze, 2010) (Gengembre, 2008) (Joly, 2005) (Joly, 2007) (Satoh, 2007) (Vaiapury, 2006) (Wu, 2009) (Zhou, 2009) (Zhu, 2008). In (Can, 2007) (Gengembre, 2008) (Jegou, 2008), for example, a fast Hessian detector is used to detect the interest points, and a SIFT local descriptor (Lowe, 2004) is computed around each interest point. To improve the matching efficiency of local features, some efforts have been made on dimensionality reduction (Ke, 2004) (Law-To, 2006) and local feature selection (Joly, 2005). Another alternative scheme for compacting features is the bag-of-features used frequently in the latest literature (Can, 2007) (Douze, 2008) (Douze, 2010). The key idea is to represent each frame as an orderless collection of local descriptors (Jiang, 2007). Usually, a visual word vocabulary is generated first by clustering a large training set of local features, and each cluster center is treated as a visual word. Afterwards, the local features in a frame are mapped to those visual words, and then a visual word histogram is built for representing the frame. A main advantage lies in that it can generate a more compact representation as well as keep the partial matching feature. Moreover, the bag-of-features scheme can facilitate building index construction for speeding up search process. In our video copy detection system, we adopt the bag-of-features scheme in (Nister, 2006).

Video Matching

As the other key aspect, video matching plays an important role in the content-based video copy detection. A lot of matching methods have been proposed in recent years. According to the difference of matching manner, these matching methods can roughly be classified into two groups: sequence matching and frame fusion based matching.

The key idea of sequence matching lies in that two video clips are matched directly by frame-to-frame matching. Given a short query sequence Q=(q1,q2,…,qN) and a long reference sequence R=(r1,r2,…,rM), those methods slide the Q in the matching with R and result in a series of scores between Q and total (M-N+1) subsequences of R. Then a judgment mechanism involving a threshold is employed to determine whether the

query Q is originated from a subsequence of R. Examples include the matching methods proposed in (Chen, 2008) (Hua, 2004) (Kim, 2005) (Lee, 2008) (Oostveen, 2002). Figure 1 illustrates the matching process. However, those matching methods cannot efficiently deal with the scenario where a copy is only a small segment of the query video. With the sequence matching, we need to match all the possible subsequences in both the query and reference videos, which results in high computational complexity. In addition, it is also difficult for sequence matching to cope with some post-production transformations, such as frame dropping, fast/slow motion, although some attempts (Chiu, 2008) have been made to alleviate it. Moreover, it is usually difficult to find an appropriate threshold beforehand due to various copy types.

Recently, frame fusion based matching methods (Douze, 2008) (Gengembre, 2008) (Hampapur, 2002) (Kim, 2008), which provide a more flexible manner for copy detection, attract increasing attention. Unlike the sequence matching, the frame fusion based matching avoids directly

Figure 1. An illustration of video sequence matching process, where V1 is the query video and V2 is a long reference video

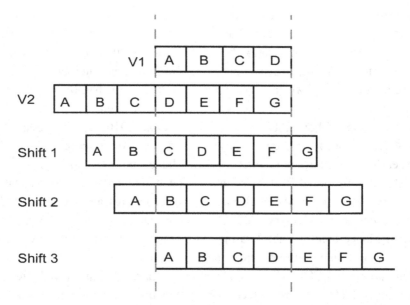

matching query video with all equal-length reference clips. Instead, it first searches the reference database and returns a list of similar reference frames for each query frame. Then the copies can be determined by fusing the reference frames in the returned lists. Previous methods are based mainly on the statistics of the whole returned reference matches. That is, the whole query video needs to be processed beforehand. For example, a 2D Hough histogram is employed for frame fusion by accumulating the votes on video identifier and time shift (Douze, 2008). However, since the matches of all the query frames need to be obtained beforehand, this kind of scheme is not suitable for coping with a continuous query streams. In addition, while previous schemes pay more attention to detection precision and similarity search efficiency, they normally skip the localization precision and frame fusion efficiency.

The proposed frame fusion can smartly overcome these limitations by combining a backtracking strategy and three relaxed constraints into a Viterbi-like algorithm. By dynamically determining the starting and ending time instants of potential copies, the proposed approach can detect video copies in an on-line manner. In fact, similar strategy is also used for detecting sequential gesture patterns in (Uchida, 2007), which employs a Logical DP matching for efficiently detecting similar subsequences.

Copy Detection

A complete detection process normally involves both feature extraction and video matching. Different combinations form different copy detection schemes. For example, an initial step for the sequence matching method is to calculate the distances between frames in two aligned video clips. Different feature schemes result in different similarity measurements. Likewise, similarity matching between query frames and reference frames is also required in the frame fusion based matching method.

However, for frame fusion based matching methods, there is another key difference among different schemes, that is, the frame fusion strategy. The performance of different schemes remains uncertain due to various fusion strategies. Our main effort just focuses on the critical problem of frame fusion.

OVERALL FRAMEWORK

Although our work focuses mainly on the frame fusion phase, we also need a complete video copy detection system to validate our scheme. The system architecture is illustrated in Figure 2. Each component will be detailed in the following sub-sections.

Keyframe Extraction

It is redundant and time-consuming to process all the frames within a video, thus the keyframe selection is a necessary step for improving the efficiency of copy detection. However, the selection of frame sampling rate will greatly influence the detection effectiveness. A high sampling rate means that the query and the reference video have higher probability to match perfectly, while a low sampling rate encounters the insufficient number of matching frame pairs. In addition, higher sampling rate also means more memory and computational cost. In our scheme, we combine the shot-based sampling scheme and the uniform sampling scheme (Douze, 2008) into a unified framework. First, we partition the reference video into shots using the method proposed in (Petersohn, 2004). Then we uniformly sample each shot at a fixed sampling rate. In our experiment, we sample three frames per second.

The main feature of this sampling strategy is that each uniformly sampled frame is associated with a shot boundary. As shown in Figure 3, each reference frame is represented by a triple, i.e, (2008shotVideoID, ShotID, time stamp of key

Figure 2. Framework of proposed video copy detection system

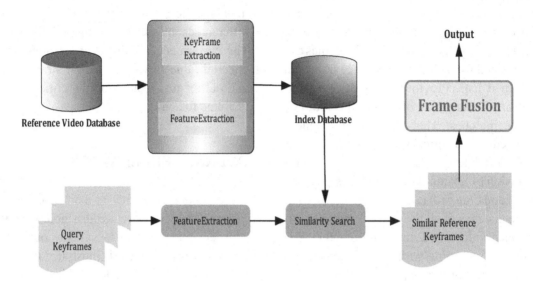

frame). This boundary information is very important for tolerating the matching offset caused by some signal distortions or the imperfection of low-level features.

In addition, the shot boundary information is also useful for localizing where the copy is derived from, which will be explained later. Note that, for the query video, we just uniformly sample three frames per second, while shot detection step is not performed in order to speed up the query process.

Figure 3. An illustration of frame sampling with shot boundary information

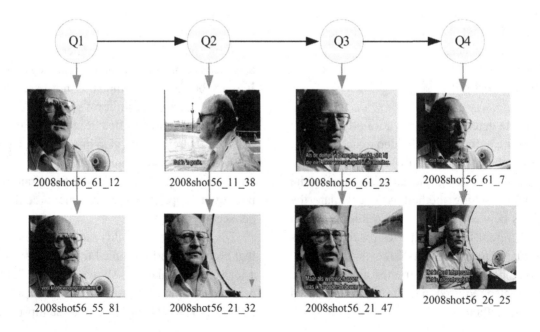

Feature Extraction

As mentioned above, local features are inherently resistant to the transformations caused by some post-production operations, such as cropping and shifting. Therefore, our copy detection system is also based on the local features. In particular, Hessian-Affine region extractor (Mikolajczyk, 2004) is employed to extract the affine-invariant key points for each frame, and then the SIFT descriptor (Lowe, 2004) is used to represent each key point by a 128-dimensional vector. In our experiments, the software of (Mikolajczyk) is used for both detecting Hessian-Affine regions and generating SIFT descriptors with default parameter settings. After that, the bag-of-features approach in (Nister, 2006) is further employed for compacting the feature representation. The key idea of this approach is to perform hierarchical k-means clustering on a training descriptor set to construct a visual vocabulary where each cluster centriod is treated as a visual word. Given a new local descriptor extracted from a frame, it is mapped to a visual word by searching the nearest centriod in the visual vocabulary. We implemented this procedure by using the VLFeat package available in (Vedaldi). In our experiments, a visual vocabulary with four levels and 100,000 leaf nodes is used for evaluating the proposed method, and another smaller vocabulary with four levels and 10,000 leaf nodes is employed for validating the effect of description on the overall detection performance.

To facilitate similarity search and indexing, we further map each visual word in the vocabulary into a unique pseudo-word. This means that each visual word is explicitly represented with a unique text string, and a frame containing lots of descriptors is transferred to a text document with pseudo-words. In this way, we can directly index and search visual contents using the existing tools in the text information retrieval field.

Similarity Search and Indexing

As discussed above, pseudo-word text documents are separately generated for frames in both the query and reference video. Therefore, some existing similarity matching models in the text retrieval area can be employed directly. In our scheme, we adopt the Okapi BM25 scoring function (Robertson, 1995) (Robertson, 1976), which represents state-of-the-art scoring function in the text information retrieval area. Given a query q containing pseudo-words $\{w_1, w_2, ..., w_m\}$, the Okapi BM25 score ranking a reference document d is

$$s(q,d) = \sum_{i=1}^{m} RSJ(w_i) \cdot \frac{f(w_i, d) \cdot (k+1)}{f(w_i, d) + k \cdot (1 - b + b \cdot \frac{|d|}{avgdl})} \tag{1}$$

where $f(w_i, d)$ is the w_i's term frequency of w_i in the document d, $|d|$ is the length of the document d in pseudo-words, $avgdl$ is the average length of the documents in the test database. k and b are free parameters, which are set to 2 and 0.75, respectively. $RSJ(w_i)$ is the Robertson-Sparck Jones weight (Kim, 2008) of the query term w_i which is computed as follows:

$$RSJ(w_i) = \log \frac{(r + 0.5)/(R - r + 0.5)}{(n - r + 0.5)/(N - n - R + r + 0.5)} \tag{2}$$

where N is the total number of documents in the reference database, n is the number of documents containing w_i, R and r are two parameters related to relevance feedback. Since no relevance feedback is used in our scheme, we set both R and r to zero.

Likewise, we also improve the scoring efficiency by building an inverted table, which stores a mapping from the pseudo-words to the reference frames. The inverted table is equivalent to the index database in Figure 1. In our experiment, we use the implementation in the Lemur toolkits (Lemur, 2011) for both similarity search and text document indexing.

Frame Fusion

For each query frame, a list of similar reference frames with their scores is returned according to the scoring Equation 1. Our purpose is to determine whether the query video contains a copy derived from the reference video by fusing the returned reference frames according to the temporal relationships among them. In this paper, we target at this critical frame fusion phase, which will be discussed in more detail in the next two sections.

FORMULATION OF FRAME FUSION

Problem Definition

$$Q = (q_1, q_2, \cdots, q_t, \cdots, q_T) \qquad (3)$$

$$L = (L_1, L_2, \cdots, L_t, \cdots, L_T) \qquad (4)$$

where q_t is the key frame at time instant t of the query sequence Q, and L_t is the list of similar reference frames returned for q_t. T is the length of the query stream, which may be a very large number even up to infinite. We assume that the top M most similar reference frames are returned for each query frame, hence the length of each list is fixed to M. Figure 4 shows an example with T=7, M=4.

The frame fusion is to detect possible copies from by fusing the reference frames in the returned lists. Since a copy is usually a small part of the query sequence, we further define subsequences for both the query sequence and the sequence of lists as follows:

Figure 4. Illustrates the process of similarity search with T=7 and M=4

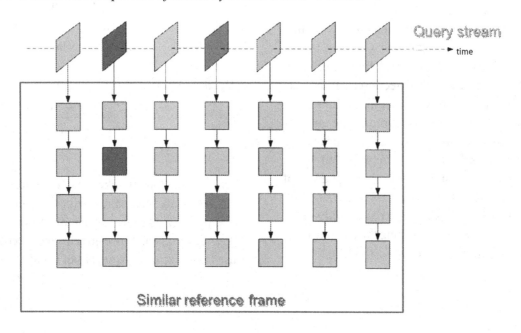

$$Q_{sub}(i,j) =$$
$$\left\{ \left(q_i, q_{i+1}, \cdots, q_t, \cdots, q_j \right) | 1 \le i \le T, i \le t \le j \le T \right\} \tag{5}$$

$$L_{sub}(i,j) =$$
$$\left\{ (L_i, L_{i+1}, \cdots, L_t, \cdots, L_j) | 1 \le i \le T, i \le t \le j \le T \right\} \tag{6}$$

where $Q_{sub}(i,j)$ is a temporally successive subsequence from time instant i to j in the query sequence Q; $L_{sub}(i,j)$ is the corresponding list subsequence of $Q_{sub}(i,j)$

Therefore, the problem is changed to determining whether $\mathbf{Q_{sub}(i,j)}$ is a copy by fusing the reference frames in $\mathbf{L_{sub}(i,j)}$. A key step of frame fusion is to reconstruct reference frame sequences from $L_{sub}(i,j)$ according to the temporal consistency information. According to the temporal consistency information, if two video clips are similar, their aligned frames should be successively similar. Figure 5 illustrates the constraint.

The key idea of frame fusion based copy detection method is to reconstruct reference video clip from similar reference frames of query frames according to the temporal consistent constraint. Figure 6 illustrates the process of reference clip reconstruction. In fact, $\mathbf{L_{sub}(i,j)}$ can be treated as a frame sequence hypothesis space $\mathbf{H_{sub}(i,j)}$ containing total $\mathbf{M}^{(j-i+1)}$ reference frame sequences with length $(j-i+1)$, which can be denoted as

$$H_{sub}(i,j) =$$
$$\{ (h_i, h_{i+1}, \cdots, h_t, \cdots, h_j) | \tag{7}$$
$$1 \le i \le T, \quad i \le t \le j \le T, h_t \in L_t$$

where $H_{sub}(i,j)$ is constructed by concatenating the reference frames selected from the aligned lists of similar reference frames; h_t is a frame selected from L_t at time instant t

Let h be a reference frame sequence in the hypothesis space $H_{sub}(i,j)$. Now, judging whether $Q_{sub}(i,j)$ is a copy is equivalent to checking whether there exists a reference frame sequence h that meets a certain temporal consistency assumption. Figure shows the idea of clip reconstruction, where the clip constructed by following the red arrows is the reference frame sequence h.

Figure 5. Illustrates the constraint of temporal consistency

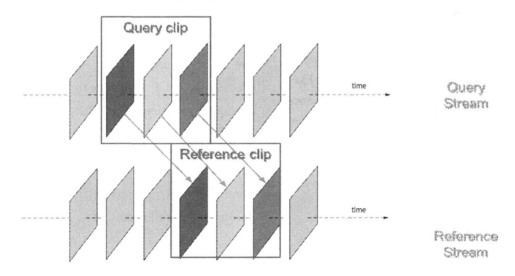

Figure 6. Illustrates the process of reference clip reconstruction

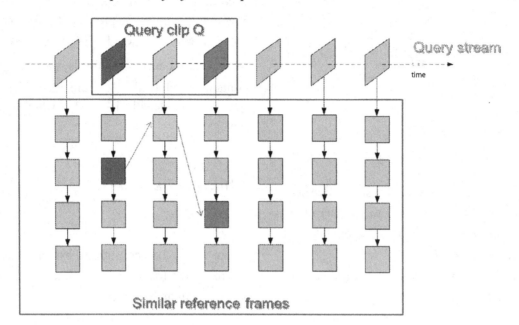

Problem Solution

In fact, the frame fusion problem can be further transformed to the decoding problem of Hidden Markov Model (HMM) (Rabiner, 1989). The following shows their high similarity in definition.

- **HMM Decoding Problem:** Given a particular emission sequence $E_{seq} = (e_1, e_2, \cdots, e_t, \cdots, e_T)$ and a model $\lambda = \{Tr, Em\}$, from state set $S = \{s_1, s_2, \cdots, s_n, \cdots, s_N\}$, how we can find a state sequence $h = (h_1, h_2, \cdots, h_t, \cdots, h_T)$ that is most likely to have generated the emission sequence E_{seq}. Here, Tr and Em are the state transition and emission probability matrices, respectively; h_t is a state selected from S at time instant t of the state sequence h

- **Frame Fusion Problem:** Given a query subsequence $Q_{sub}(i, j)$ and a list subsequence $L_{sub}(i, j)$, under some constraints, how we can find a reference subsequence $h = (h_i, h_{i+1}, \cdots, h_t, \cdots, h_j)$ that is most likely to have generated the query subsequence $Q_{sub}(i, j)$. Here, h_t is a frame selected from L_t at time instant t

We can easily convert the frame fusion problem into HMM decoding problem. In particular, the query subsequence can be directly treated as the emission sequence E_{seq} and the reference frame in $L_{sub}(i, j)$ constitute the state set S after Unique operation. Here, the *Unique* symbol denotes the duplicate-removal operation on $L_{sub}(i, j)$ by which the corresponding state set S can be constituted with the remained frames from $L_{sub}(i, j)$. The conversion model can be formulated as follows:

$$E_{seq} = \left(q_i, q_{i+1}, \cdots, q_t, \cdots, q_j\right)$$
$$\Leftarrow \left(e_i, e_{i+1}, \cdots, e_t, \cdots, e_j\right) \tag{8}$$

$$S = \left\{s_1, s_2 \cdots, s_n, \cdots, s_N\right\}$$
$$\Leftarrow Unique\left\{L_i, L_{i+1}, \cdots, L_t, \cdots, L_j\right\} \tag{9}$$

$$H(i,j) = \{(h_i, h_{i+1}, \cdots, h_t, \cdots, h_j) \mid$$
$$1 \leq i \leq T, \quad i \leq t \leq j \leq T, h_t \in S$$
$$\tag{10}$$

$$h^* = \underset{h \in H(i,j)}{argmax}\, P\left(E_{seq}, h\right)$$
$$= \underset{h \in H(i,j)}{argmax}\, P\left(h\right) \cdot P\left(E_{seq} \mid h\right)$$
$$= \underset{h \in H(i,j)}{argmax}\left\{P\left((h_i, h_{i+1}, \cdots, h_t, \cdots, h_j)\right) \cdot\right.$$
$$\left. P\left((e_i, e_{i+1}, \cdots, e_t, \cdots, e_j) \mid (h_i, h_{i+1}, \cdots, h_t, \cdots, h_j)\right)\right\} \tag{11}$$

where $H(i,j)$ is a superset of $H_{sub}(i,j)$ and h_t is a frame selected from S. Figure 7 illustrates the model conversion process.

In our context, $P\left((h_i, h_{i+1}, \cdots, h_t, \cdots, h_j)\right)$ reflects the transition relationship among the returned reference frames, whereas $P\left((e_i, e_{i+1}, \cdots, e_t, \cdots, e_j) \mid (h_i, h_{i+1}, \cdots, h_t, \cdots, h_j)\right)$ implies the similarity measurement between the query sequence $\left(q_i, q_{i+1}, \cdots, q_t, \cdots, q_j\right)$ and a reference frame sequence $(h_i, h_{i+1}, \cdots, h_t, \cdots, h_j)$. We employ the first-order Markov chain to model the transition relationship, which assumes that the present state is only dependent on the previous state. That is:

$$P\left(h_t \mid h_{t-1}, \cdots, h_i\right) =$$
$$P\left(h_t \mid h_{t-1}\right), t = i+1, \cdots, j.$$

Figure 7. An example of model conversion with i=1,j=4,N=6

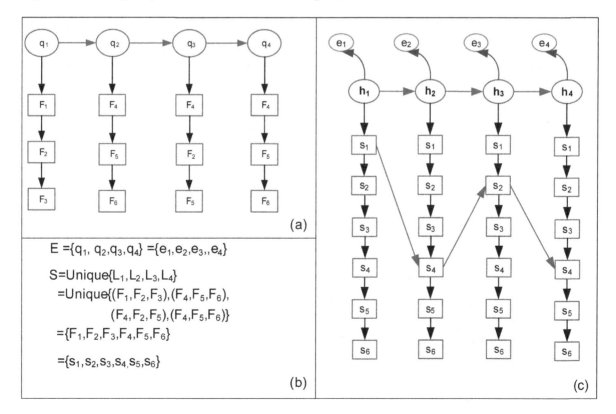

For similarity measurement, since we perform an independent similarity search for each query frame, $P(e_t|h_t), t = i, \cdots, j$, are independent of each other. Therefore, we can rewrite the objective Equation 11 as

$$
h^* = \underset{h \in H(i,j)}{argmax} \Big\{ P(h_i) \cdot P(e_i|h_i) \cdot \\
\prod_{t=i+1}^{j} P(h_t \mid h_{t-1}) P(e_t|h_t) \Big\}
\tag{12}
$$

In order to calculate the above objective function, we need to estimate both $P(h_t \mid h_{t-1})$ and $P(e_t|h_t)$, i.e., the state transition probability $Tr = \Big(P(s_y \mid s_x) | x \, and \, y \in \{1, 2, \ldots, N\} \Big)$ and the emission probability

$$
Em = \\
\Big(P(e_t \mid s_x) | x \in \{1, 2, \ldots, N\}, t \in \{i, i+1, \ldots, j\} \Big)
$$

where N is the total number of states. To this end, two relaxed constraints are given in the following. Note that we assume $P(s_x)$ follows the uniform distribution. Hence, $P(s_x)$ is set to $\frac{1}{N}$, that is, $P(h_i)$ is set to $\frac{1}{N}$

- **Transition Constraint:** According to the strict temporal consistency assumption, if a query frame subsequence $(q_i, q_{i+1}, \cdots, q_t, \cdots, q_j)$ is a copy of a reconstructed reference frame subsequence $(h_i, h_{i+1}, \cdots, h_t, \cdots, h_j)$, then the reconstructed reference frame sequence should be a temporally successive frame sequence in a reference video. That is, for any two

frames h_{t-1} and h_t, $t = i+1, \cdots, j$, h_{t-1} can transfer to h_t if and only if h_t is the next frame of h_{t-1} in the same reference clip. However, there may be some drawbacks with this assumption. First, a copy is usually a transformed version of its original video clip, thus it is difficult to get perfect matches along all the aligned key frames in two clips due to the limitation of feature representation. We even cannot align them if the copy is obtained by dropping some frames from or inserting some frames into its original video clip. In addition, adjacent frames in a video clip are usually perceptually similar with each other due to the high redundancy of video content. Therefore, even if all the frames in the sequence $(h_i, h_{i+1}, \cdots, h_t, \cdots, h_j)$ belong to the same reference clip and the clip indeed generates the query sequence $(q_i, q_{i+1}, \cdots, q_t, \cdots, q_j)$ it is also less possible to guarantee the reference sequence to be aligned with the query sequence in the completely correct temporal order. Hence, we constrain the transition relationship with a more relaxed assumption. Assume that, for any two reference frames (states) s_x and s_y, s_x can transfer to s_y if and only if s_x and s_y are in the same shot or in two adjacent shots. In this way, we can tolerate a certain matching offset. This constraint is described as follows:

$$
P(s_y \mid s_x) = \\
\begin{cases}
\partial_1, & s_x \in V_t \, and \, s_y \in V_t \\
\partial_2, & s_x \in V_t \, and \, s_y \in V_{t+1} \\
0, & otherwise
\end{cases}
\tag{13}
$$

where V_t and V_{t+1} are two temporally successive shots in the same reference video; ∂_1 and ∂_2 are two constants representing transition probabilities, which are set to 1 and 0.8 in our experiment, respectively.

- **Emission Constraint:** As discussed above, the state set S consists of all the unrepeated similar reference frames in the returned lists. For a specific emission e_t (i.e., the query frame q_t), since its corresponding list L_t containing similar reference frames is only a subset of state set S, not all the states will produce the emission. Therefore, we have

$$P\left(e_t | s_x\right) = P\left(q_t | s_x\right) = \begin{cases} score\left(q_t, s_x\right), & if\, s_x \in L_t \\ 0, & otherwise \end{cases}$$

(14)

where score(*,*) is the scoring function for similarity search. All similarity scores are normalized beforehand.

So far, given a query subsequence, we need to find the most likely state sequence that might have generated the query subsequence according to objective Equation 12. If we exhaustively evaluate all possible state sequences, it is computationally prohibitive. Therefore, the Viterbi algorithm, as a kind of dynamic programming algorithm, is employed. At any time instant, the Viterbi algorithm avoids tracking all possible paths by keeping only the most likely path (the partial best path) for each state. After arriving at the end of the query sequence, a whole best path can be obtained by a path back-tracking process.

FRAME FUSION USING VITERBI-LIKE ALGORITHM

In the above section, we formulate the problem of frame fusion and provide a feasible solution. However, it raises two problems if we directly follow it. First, high computational cost is inevitable. In order to detect copied clips, we need to separately check all possible and temporally successive query subsequences. If the query length is T then we need to check a total of $\dfrac{T \cdot (T+1)}{2}$ query subsequences. Given the average length T_{sub} of subsequences and the length M of each list, a computational complexity of $O(\dfrac{T \cdot (T+1)}{2} \cdot M^{T_{sub}})$ is required using the exhaustive search method. Even if we can reduce the complexity to $O(\dfrac{T * (T+1)}{2} \cdot T_{sub} \cdot M^2)$ using the Viterbi algorithm (Rabiner, 1989), it is still expensive. More importantly, this method is not convenient for dealing with unbounded query stream since it is impossible to obtain all possible query subsequences beforehand in this case.

To address these problems, we refine the scheme by modifying the conventional Viterbi algorithm and introducing an additional gap constraint.

Viterbi-Like Algorithm

Instead of separately checking all possible query subsequences, we attempt to detect copies from a continuous query video stream in an on-line manner. The core problem is how to precisely localize boundaries of copies in the continuous query stream. To this end, we introduce an additional gap constraint and redefine the partial best path. The gap constraint provides a mechanism for distinguishing copies from non-copy video clips as well as tolerating some video transformations like frame insertion operation. The redefined partial best path records a reference frame sequence that is most likely to generate its corresponding query subsequence. The starting and ending nodes of each path corresponding to a reconstructed reference video clip are determined by the gap constraint. The following describes them in details.

- **Gap Constraint:** Given the query subsequence $\left(q_{i-\Delta t}, \cdots, q_{i-1}, q_i, q_{i+1}, \cdots, q_t, \cdots, q_j, q_{j+1}, \cdots, q_{j+\Delta t}\right)$ and a reference frame sequence $\left(h_{i-\Delta t}, \cdots, h_{i-1}, h_i, h_{i+1}, \cdots, h_t, \cdots, h_j, h_{j+1}, \cdots, h_{j+\Delta t}\right)$, if there is not any transition from h_i to the previous Δt reference frames, the time instant i can serve as a possible starting point of a copy. The constraint means that we can determine the starting instant of a copy based on the transition relationship among similar reference frames at different time instants. Likewise, we can determine the ending instant in the same way. In addition, the gap constraint can also deal with video transformations caused by inserting some non-copy frames. The length of Δt limits the maximum number of non-copy keyframes allowed to be inserted in the copy clip. We describe this constraint as follows:

The query subsequence $\left(q_i, q_{i+1}, \cdots, q_t, \cdots, q_j\right)$ is possibly a copy of the reference sequence $\left(h_i, h_{i+1}, \cdots, h_t, \cdots, h_j\right)$ if and only if:

$$\begin{cases} P\left(h_i \mid h_{i-1}\right) = 0 \\ P\left(h_i \mid h_{i-2}\right) = 0 \\ \quad \cdots \\ P\left(h_i \mid h_{i-\Delta t}\right) = 0 \end{cases} \tag{15}$$

$$\text{and } \begin{cases} P\left(h_j \mid h_{j+1}\right) = 0 \\ P\left(h_j \mid h_{j+2}\right) = 0 \\ \quad \cdots \\ P\left(h_j \mid h_{j+\Delta t}\right) = 0 \end{cases} \tag{16}$$

Equations 15 and 16 can determine the starting instant i and the ending instant j, respectively.

- **Partial Best Path:** Let $\delta\left(t, x\right)$ be the best score of all possible state sequences starting at any states at any previous time instants and ending at state s_x at time instant t. The partial best path $Path\left(t, x\right)$ is the state sequence (or reference frame sequence) which achieves the best score. Note that the partial best path ending at state s_x at time t may start at any previous time instants, instead of starting at time $t = 1$ as Viterbi algorithm does.

At time $t = 1$ $\delta\left(t, x\right)$ is calculated as follows:

$$\delta\left(1, x\right) = Em\left(1, x\right) \tag{17}$$

where $Em\left(1, x\right)$ is the emission probability from state s_x to emission e_1, which can be calculated according to the emission constraint in Equation 14. At time $2 \leq t \leq \infty$ $\delta\left(t, x\right)$ is calculated as follows:

$$\delta\left(t, x\right) = \begin{cases} \mu\left(\overset{*}{t}, n^*\right) + Em\left(t, x\right), & if \ Em\left(t, x\right) > 0 \\ 0, & otherwise \end{cases} \tag{18}$$

$$\mu\left(\tilde{t}^*, n^*\right) = \delta\left(\tilde{t}^*, n^*\right) \cdot Tr\left(n^*, x\right) \qquad (19)$$

$$\left(\tilde{t}^*, n^*\right) =$$

$$\begin{cases} \underset{1 \leq \tilde{t} < t, 1 \leq n \leq N_t}{argmax} (\delta\left(\tilde{t}, n\right) \cdot Tr\left(n, x\right)), t \leq \Delta t \\ \underset{t-\Delta t+1 \leq \tilde{t} < t, 1 \leq n \leq N_t}{argmax} (\delta\left(\tilde{t}, n\right) \cdot Tr\left(n, x\right)), t > \Delta t \end{cases}$$

$$(20)$$

where N_t is the size of state set at time instant t; $(\tilde{t}^*, n^*)$ indicates the state s_{n^*} at time instant $\tilde{t}^*$, from which $\delta\left(t, x\right)$ achieves the best score; $\mu\left(\tilde{t}^*, n^*\right)$ indicates the maximum transition score from states at previous different time instants to state s_x at time instant t; $Tr\left(n, x\right)$ is the transition probability from state s_n to s_x which can be calculated according to the transition constraint (13). For Equation 18, the right side is $\mu\left(\tilde{t}^*, n^*\right) + Em\left(t, x\right)$ which is different from the original form $\mu\left(\tilde{t}^*, n^*\right) \cdot Em\left(t, x\right)$ in the conventional Viterbi algorithm. By this way, when the state s_x at time instant t has no any transition with states at previous different time instants (i.e., $\mu\left(\tilde{t}^*, n^*\right) = 0$), it can serve as a starting point of new partial best paths if $Em\left(t, x\right) > 0$. In addition, using this form can also void the problem of data overflow due to the product of a large number of values which are far lower than one.

Note that the Equation 19 implies the gap constraint (15). If $\mu\left(\tilde{t}^*, n^*\right) = 0$ then $\delta\left(t, x\right) = Em(t, x)$ which means that no transition exists between the state s_x at time t or any states in the past. That is, the state s_x at time instant t can serve as a starting node of new partial best paths. The back-tracking strategy is formulated in Equation 20. It means that, at any time instant t we search backward the best partial paths obtained at several time instants in the past. In this way, we can iteratively use the previous detection information and speed up the copy detection.

Using the Viterbi-Like algorithm, the problem of frame fusion becomes the back-tracking of the partial paths. Once certain partial best paths meet the gap constraint, we can then localize both the copies in the query video stream and their original clips in the reference video. For detailed description of the Viterbi-like algorithm, please refer to (Wei, 2011).

Note that both emission and transition matrices are updated dynamically since new emissions and states are generated when new query frames come. Still, the construction of the transition and emission matrices is based on the proposed transition and emission constraints (13, 14), respectively. Because the dynamic programming method used in the conventional Viterbi algorithm is remained, the efficiency of frame fusion is high. The main difference from the conventional Viterbi algorithm is that Viterbi-like algorithm back-tracks the partial best paths at each time instant, instead of back-tracking once after traveling forward all the time instants. It means that the back-tracking process will never stop until arriving at the end of the query stream. In this way, it can deal with a continuous query stream by making on-line decision. Another difference lies in that the Viterbi-like algorithm builds the partial best path for the current time instant by looking back several time instants in the past, instead of checking only the previous one time instant as the conventional Viterbi algorithm does. The Equation 20 implies this strategy. By this way, we can enlarge the match scope and then tolerate more complex transformations.

Pruning and Localization

Each partial best path is a reference frame sequence, which corresponds to a query subsequence. Because we make a decision when each new query frame comes, we need to determine whether the partial best paths (reference sequences) at current time instant indeed generate their corresponding query sequences. Intuitively, we still need a hard threshold to solve this problem. Here, the hard threshold means a fixed score value that is used for all queries to determine whether copies occur in queries. However, according to gap constraint, only the partial best paths which meet Equations 15 and 16 are retained. The corresponding query subsequences of the retained paths are treated as copies. Note that we need to check the following Δt query frames so as to determine whether the partial best paths at current time instant are ended. In order to further filter out false copies, we compute the Pearson's correlation coefficient between the aligned time

stamps of corresponding query sequence and partial best path. Figure 8 shows how to get two time stamp sequences for a pair of query sequence and partial best path with four frames. Given two time stamp sequences $X = \left(x_1, x_2, \cdots, x_n\right)$ and $Y = \left(y_1, y_2, \cdots, y_n\right)$ the Pearson's correlation coefficient is given by

$$\rho\left(X, Y\right) = \frac{n \cdot \left(\sum_{i=1}^{n} x_i \cdot y_i\right) - \left(\sum_{i=1}^{n} x_i\right) \cdot \left(\sum_{i=1}^{n} y_i\right)}{\sqrt{n \cdot \left(\sum_{i=1}^{n} x_i^2\right) - \left(\sum_{i=1}^{n} x_i\right)^2} \cdot \sqrt{n \cdot \left(\sum_{i=1}^{n} y_i^2\right) - \left(\sum_{i=1}^{n} y_i\right)^2}}$$

(21)

The correlation coefficient ranges from -1 to 1, and it is greater than 0 if two sequences are positive correlation. In our context, only the pairs with positive correlation are reserved. The resulting partial best paths are further filtered out by pruning those short paths. Here, we consider a path as short path if the number of its nodes is less than six.

After we have obtained a series of partial best paths and query subsequences, we need to consider how to localize them in the reference database and in the query stream, respectively. In fact, since the frames in the query sequence

Figure 8. An example illustrating how to get two time stamp sequences for a pair of query sequence and partial best path. Note that the subscripts of query frames and reference frames indicate the time instants relative to the first frame in query sequence and partial best path, respectively.

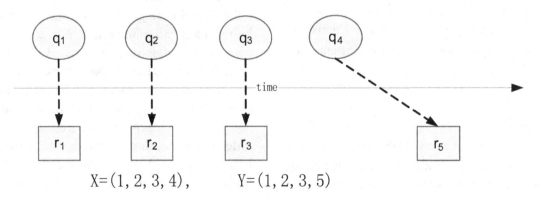

are ordered temporally, the starting and ending time instants of a path localize a possible copy in the query video stream. To find the location of a partial best path in the reference database, the boundary information of shots is used. According to the transition constraint, all the reference frames in a path may be out of order temporally, but they must be in the same shot or adjacent shots. Therefore, we can localize the reference clip in the database by searching lower and upper boundary of frames in the corresponding shots.

Since our localization of reference clips is based on the boundaries of shots, it is very likely to generate the same reference clip for different paths. In our scheme, for all the paths corresponding to the same reference clip, we only remain the one with the largest length.

FUTURE RESEARCH DIRECTIONS

A complete copy detection system comprises a few key components including the sampling rate of key frames, feature extraction, similarity search as well as frame fusion results. The overall performance of such a system depends on the aggregated result of all the components. For example, the overall performance may greatly vary with different frame sampling rates and feature schemes. Simply improving both the sampling rate and visual vocabulary size, we can remarkably improve the detection performance. Therefore, In the future, some methods to improve other components in copy detection system should be developed to achieve a better overall performance. The main effort should focus on the more discriminative description schemes and more efficiency indexing schemes.

CONCLUSION

In this chapter, we discuss a graph model based video copy detection scheme, which involves similar frame search and frame fusion. Our main effort focuses on how to convert reference frame fusion problem into the graph model problem. In our scheme, the HMM model is employed for frame fusion, where a Viterbi-like dynamic programming algorithm that comprises an on-line back-tracking strategy and three relaxed constraints is proposed for speeding up fusion efficiency. The major advantages of this scheme lie in the following three novel aspects: 1) propose a real-time frame fusion, which can apply to the copy detection problem in a continuous query video stream; 2) relax strict temporal consistency constraint to handle complex transformations and tolerate matching offset and misalignment; 3) avoid the difficult problem of threshold selection and provide precisely temporal localization. In addition, since the proposed frame fusion procedure is under a dynamic programming framework, the fusion efficiency is very high.

REFERENCES

Can, T., & Duygulu, P. (2007). Searching for repeated video sequences. In *Proceedings of the ACM International Workshop Multimedia Information Retrieval*, Augsburg, Bavaria, Germany.

Chen, L., & Stentiford, F. W. M. (2008). Video sequence matching based on temporal ordinal measurement. *Pattern Recognition Letters*, *29*(13), 1824–1831.

Chiu, C.-Y., Chen, C.-S., & Chien, L.-F. (2008). A framework for handling spatiotemporal variations in video copy detection. *IEEE Transactions on Circuits and Systems for Video Technology*, *18*(3), 412–417.

Douze, M., Gaidon, A., Jegou, H., Marszatek, M., & Schmid, C. (2008). Inria-Lear's video copy detection system. In *Proceedings of TRECVID*, Gaithersburg, USA.

Douze, M., Jégou, H., & Schmid, C. (2010). An image-based approach to video copy detection with spatio-temporal post-filtering. *IEEE Transactions on Multimedia, 12*(4). Retrieved from http://lear.inrialpes.fr/pubs/2010/DJS10/

Gengembre, N., & Berrani, S.-A. (2008). A probabilistic framework for fusing frame-based searches within a video copy detection system. In *Proceedings of the ACM International Conference on Content-based Image and Video Retrieval*, Niagara Falls, Canada.

Hampapur, A., & Bolle, R. M. (2002). *VideoGREP: Video copy detection using inverted file indices*. IBM research division, Tech. Rep.

Hua, X.-S., Chen, X., & Zhang, H.-J. (2004). Robust video signature based on ordinal measure. In *Proc. IEEE International Conference on Image Processing*, (Vol. 1, pp. 685-688).

Jegou, H., Douze, M., & Schmid, C. (2008). Hamming embedding and weak geometric consistency for large scale image search. In *Proceedings of the European Conference on Computer Vision*. Marseille, France: Springer.

Jiang, Y.-G., Ngo, C.-W., & Yang, J. (2007). Towards optimal bag-of-features for object categorization and semantic video retrieval. In *Proceedings of the ACM International Conference on Image and Video Retrieval*, Amsterdam, Netherlands.

Joly, A., & Buisson, O. (2005). Discriminant local features selection using efficient density estimation in a large database. In *Proceedings of the ACM SIGMM International Workshop Multimedia Information Retrieval*, Hilton, Singapore.

Joly, A., Buisson, O., & Frelicot, C. (2007). Content-based copy retrieval using distortion-based probabilistic similarity search. *IEEE Transactions on Multimedia, 9*(2), 293–306.

Joly, A., Law-to, J., & Boujemaa, N. (2008). "INRIA-IMEDIA TRECVID 2008: Video copy detection. In *Proceedings of TRECVID*, Gaithersburg, USA.

Ke, Y., Sukthankar, R., & Huston, L. (2004). An efficient parts-based near-duplicate and sub-image retrieval system. In *Proceedings of ACM International Conference Multimedia*, New York, NY, USA.

Kim, C., & Vasudev, B. (2005). Spatiotemporal sequence matching for efficient video copy detection. *IEEE Transactions on Circuits and Systems for Video Technology, 15*(1), 127–132.

Kim, H.-S., Lee, J., Liu, H., & Lee, D. (2008). Video linkage: Group based copied video detection. In *Proceedings of the ACM International Conference on Content-based Image and Video Retrieval*, Niagara Falls, Canada.

Law-To, J., Buisson, O., Gouet-Brunet, V., & Boujemaa, N. (2006). Robust voting algorithm based on labels of behavior for video copy detection. In *Proceedings of the ACM International Conference on Multimedia*, Santa Barbara, CA, USA.

Lee, S., & Yoo, C. D. (2008). Robust video fingerprinting for content-based video identification. *IEEE Transactions on Circuits and Systems for Video Technology, 18*(7), 983–988.

Lemur. (2011). *The Lemur toolkit for language modeling and information retrieval*. Retrieved from http://www.lemurproject.org/

Lowe, D. G. (2004). Distinctive image features from scale-invariant keypoints. *International Journal of Computer Vision, 60*(2), 91–110.

Mikolajczyk, K. (n.d.). *Binaries for affine covariant region descriptors*. Retrieved from http://www. robots.ox.ac.uk/_vgg/research/affine/

Mikolajczyk, K., & Schmid, C. (2004). Scale & affine invariant interest point detectors. *International Journal of Computer Vision, 60*(1), 63–86.

Nister, D., & Stewenius, H. (2006). Scalable recognition with a vocabulary tree. In *Proceedings of IEEE Conference on Computer Vision and Pattern Recognition*, (pp. 2161-2168).

Oostveen, J., Kalker, T., & Haitsma, J. (2002). *Feature extraction and a database strategy for video fingerprinting (Vol. 2314*, pp. 117–128). Visual Lecture Notes in Computer Science.

Petersohn, C. (2004). TRECVID 2004: Shot boundary detection system. In *Proceedings of TRECVID*, Gaithersburg, USA.

Rabiner, L. R. (1989). A tutorial on hidden Markov models and selected applications in speech recognition. *Proceedings of the IEEE, 77*(2), 257–286.

Robertson, S. E., & Sparck Jones, K. (1976). Relevance weighting of search terms. *Journal of the American Society for Information Science American Society for Information Science, 27*, 129–146.

Robertson, S. E., Walker, S., Jones, S., Hancock-Beaulieu, M. M., & Gatford, M. (1995). Okapi at TREC-3. In *Proceedings of, TREC-3*, 109–126.

Satoh, S. I., Takimoto, M., & Adachi, J. (2007). Scene duplicate detection from videos based on trajectories of feature points. In *Proceedings of the ACM International Workshop Multimedia Information Retrieval*, Augsburg, Bavaria, Germany.

TRECVID. (2008). *TREC video retrieval evaluation*. Retrieved from http://www-nlpir.nist.gov/projects/trecvid/

Uchida, S., Mori, A., Kurazume, R., Taniguchi, R.-I., & Hasegawa, T. (2007). Logical DP matching for detecting similar subsequence. *8th Asian Conference on Computer Vision, LNCS, Vol. 4843*, ACCV2007, Tokyo, Japan, (pp. 628-637).

Vaiapury, K., Atrey, P. K., Kankanhalli, M. S., & Ramakrishnan, K. (2006). Non-identical duplicate video detection using the SIFT method. In *IET International Conference on Visual Information Engineering*, (pp. 537-542).

Vedaldi, A., & Fulkerson, B. (2010). *VLFeat: An open and portable library of computer vision algorithms*. Retrieved from http://www.vlfeat.org/

Wei, S. K., Zhao, Y., Zhu, C., Xu, C. S., & Zhu, Z. F. (2011). Frame fusion for video copy detection. *IEEE Transactions on Circuits and Systems for Video Technology, 21*(1), 15–28.

Wu, X., Ngo, C.-H., Hauptmann, A. G., & Tan, H.-K. (2009). Real-time near-duplicate elimination for web video search with content and context. *IEEE Transactions on Multimedia, 11*(2), 196–207.

Yang, X. F., Sun, Q. B., & Tian, Q. (2003). Content-based video identification: A survey. In *Proceedings of the International Conference on Information Technology: Research and Education*, (pp. 50-54).

Zhou, X. M., Zhou, X. F., Chen, L., Bouguettaya, A., Xiao, N., & Taylor, J. A. (2009). An efficient near-duplicate video shot detection method using shot-based interest points. *IEEE Transactions on Multimedia, 11*(5), 879–891.

Zhu, J. K., Hoi, S. C. H., Lyu, M. R., & Yan, S. C. (2008). Near-duplicate keyframe retrieval by nonrigid image matching. In *Proceedings of the ACM International Conference on Multimedia*, Vancouver, British Columbia, Canada.

Section 4
Graph–Based Methods for Image Processing

Chapter 15
Multi-Scale Exemplary Based Image Super-Resolution with Graph Generalization

Wang Jinjun
Epson Research and Development, Inc. USA

ABSTRACT

Exemplary based image super-resolution (SR) approaches decompose low-resolution (LR) images into multiple overlapped local image patches, and find the best high-resolution (HR) pair for each LR patch to generate processed HR images. The super-resolving process models these multiple HR/LR patches in a Markov Network where there exists both confidence constraint between the LR patch and the selected HR patch from database, and the harmonic constraint between neighboring HR patches. Such a graphical structure, however, makes the optimization process extremely slow, and therefore extensive research efforts on improving the efficiency of exemplary based SR methods have been reported. In this chapter, the focus is on those methods that aim at generating high quality HR patches from the database, while ignoring the harmonic constraint to speed up processing, such as those that model the problem as an embedding process, or as a feature selection process. As shown in this chapter, these approaches can all be regarded as a coding system. The contributions of the paper are two-fold: First, the chapter introduces a coding system with resolution-invariance property, such that it is able to handle continues-scale image resizing as compared to traditional methods that only support single integer-scale upsizing; second, the author generalizes the graphical model where the typical non-linear coding process is approximated by an easier-to-compute function. In this way, the SR process can be highly parallelized by modern computer hardware. As demonstrated by the chapter, the proposed system gives very promising image SR results in various aspects.

DOI: 10.4018/978-1-4666-1891-6.ch015

INTRODUCTION

Visual data is usually represented in two digital formats, specifically the raster image or the vector image. Raster image is a rectangular grid of pixels, and the human perceptual clarity of a raster image is decided by its spatial resolution which measures how closely the grid can be resolved. Although higher pixel density are usually desirable in many applications, such as high resolution (HR) medical images for cancer diagnosis, high quality video conference, high definition television broadcasting, Blu-ray movies, etc, raster images are resolution dependent, and thus cannot scale to an arbitrary resolution without loss of apparent quality. The other format, the vector image, represents the visual data using geometrical primitives such as points, lines, curves, and shapes or polygon. For instance, the widely used "SVG" (Scalable Vector Graphics) format uses 14 primitives including paths, shape, text, and color (SVG). The vector image is totally scalable, which largely contrasts the deficiency of raster representation.

The idea of vectorizing raster image for resolution enhancement has long been studied. Recently, Ramanarayanan *et al.* (2004) added the vectorized region boundaries to the original raster images to improve sharpness in scaled results; Dai *et al.* (2007) represented the local image patches using the background/foreground descriptors and reconstructed the sharp discontinuity between the two; To allow efficient vector representation for multi-colored region with smooth

transitions, gradient mesh technique has also been attempted (Sun, 2003). In addition, commercial softwares such as (Vector-Magic) are already available. However, vector-based techniques are limited in the visual complexity and robustness. For real photographic images with fine texture or smooth shading, these approaches tend to produce over-segmented vector representations using a large number of irregular regions with flat colors. To illustrate, Figure 1(a) and (b) are vectorized and grown up to ×3 scale using methods in (Dai, 2007) and (Vector-Magic). The discontinuity artifacts in region boundaries can be easily observed, and the over-smoothed texture regions make the scaled image watercolor like.

Alternatively, researchers have proposed to vectorize raster image with the aids of a suitable bases set to realize higher modeling capacity than those simple geometrical primitives. For example, in image/video compression domain, pre-fixed bases, such as the DCT/DWT bases adopted in JPEG/JPEG-2000 standard, and the anisotropic bases such as countourlets (Do, 2006), have already been explicitly proposed to capture different 2-D edge/texture patterns, because they lead to sparse representation which is very preferable for compression (Hong, 2006). In addition to pre-fixed bases, to capture the significantly different geometric structures and/or statistical characteristics in natural images, adaptive mixture model representations were also reported. For example, the Bandelets model (Erwan, 2005) partitions an image into squared regions according to local geometric flows, and represents each

Figure1. Comparison of scaling vectorized image and the author's method

(a) method by (Dai, 2007) (b) method by (Vector-Magic) (c) ~ (e) our method using NN, LLE and SC models respectively

region by warped wavelet bases; the primal sketch model (Guo, 2003) detects the high entropy regions in the image through a sketching pursuit process, and encodes them with multiple Markov random fields. These adaptive representations capture the stochastic image generating process, therefore they are suited for image parsing, recognition and synthesis.

In the image resolution enhancement literature, similarly, both pre-fixed bases and local adaptive bases have been utilized. In simple scenario, the BiLinear/BiCubic basis functions are widely used in 2-D image interpolation. In the large body of example-based image resolution enhancement, or called "Single Frame Super-Resolution (SR in short)", researchers utilize the co-occurrence prior between LR and HR representations in an over-completed bases set to "infer" the HR image. For example, Freeman *et al.* (Freeman, 2000) represented each local region in the LR image using one example LR patch, and applied the co-occurrence prior and global smoothness dependence through a parametric Markov Network to estimate the HR image representation. Qiang *et al.* (2005) adopted Conditional Random Field to infer both the missing HR patches and the point-spread-function parameters. Chang *et al.* (2004) utilized Locally Linear Embedding (LLE) to learn the optimal combination weights of multiple LR bases elements to estimate the optimal HR representations. In our previous work (Wang, 2009) and (Yang, 2008), the sparse-coding model is applied to obtain the optimal reconstruction weight using the whole bases set. In addition to example patches, representing images in transferred domain, such as edge profile (Sun, 2008), wavelet coefficients (Jiji, 2004), image contourlet (Jiji, 2006), etc, has also been examined.

Using prefixed BiLinear/BiCubic basis for 2-D image interpolation is fast and capable of resizing the image to any continues scale. Although it has been widely implemented in commercial raster image viewing/editing systems today, the quality of interpolated images is limited because the missing high-frequency information cannot be recovered; On the other side, the example-based SR methods significantly improve image quality, the bases used by existing approaches have only single scale capacity, i.e., the base used for $\times 2$ up-sizing cannot be used for $\times 3$ up-sizing. Hence these existing methods are not capable for multi-scale image resizing. To cope with these limitations to achieve fast multi-scale image resizing, this paper presents a learning based method for analyzing the local image patterns for reconstruction. The contributions are threefold:

- The paper extends the Resolution-Invariant Image Representation (RIIR) framework (Wang, 2009) by showing that the resolution-invariant property is applicable to multiple coding schemes as illustrated in Figure 2. A comprehensive evaluation was conducted to evaluate the advantages of different coding scheme over different aspects, such that the user can select depending on their own application requirements.

- The paper proposes to further reduce the computational cost by generalizing the coding function using Multi-task learning. A two layer neural network is constructed to approximate the non-linear coding function. Since coding operates on each local image patch, the process to reconstruct the HR image can be highly parallel.

- The paper applies the technique to support Continuous Image Scaling. A new base for any arbitrary resolution level can be generated using existing RIIR set on the fly. In this way the input image can be enlarged to multiple scales and even continues floating-point scales using only matrix-vector multiplication, which can be implemented very efficiently by modern computers.

Figure 2. Comparison of scaling using different bases

(a) BiCubic interpolation

(b) ~ (d)author's method using NN, LLE and SC models respectively

BACKGROUND

Image Representation

Example-based SR approaches (Freeman, 2000) assume that, an HR image (Figure 3a) $\mathbf{I} = \mathbf{I}^h + \mathbf{I}^m + \mathbf{I}^l$ (Figure 3. a) consist of a high frequency layer (denoted as $\mathbf{I}^h$, Figure 3b), a middle frequency layer ($\mathbf{I}^m$, Figure 3c), and a low frequency layer ($\mathbf{I}^l$, Figure 3d). The downgraded LR image $\bar{\mathbf{I}} = \mathbf{I}^m + \mathbf{I}^l$ results from discarding the high frequency components from the original HR version. Hence the image super-resolving process strives to estimate the missing high frequency layer $\mathbf{I}^h$ by maximizing $Pr(\mathbf{I}^h \mid \mathbf{I}^m, \mathbf{I}^l)$ for any input LR image. In addition, since the high frequency layer $\mathbf{I}^h$ is independent of $\mathbf{I}^l$ (Freeman 2000), it is only required to maximize $Pr(\mathbf{I}^h \mid \mathbf{I}^m)$ which greatly reduces the variability to be stored in the example set.

A typical example-based SR resolving process works as follows: Given an HR image $\mathbf{I}$ and the corresponding LR image $\bar{\mathbf{I}}'$, $\bar{\mathbf{I}}'$ is interpolated to the same size as $\mathbf{I}$ and denoted as $\bar{\mathbf{I}}$ The missing high frequency layer $\mathbf{I}^h$ can be obtained by $\mathbf{I}^h = \mathbf{I} - \bar{\mathbf{I}}$. An arbitrarily defined Gaussian filter $\mathbf{G}^l$ is applied on $\bar{\mathbf{I}}$ so that the middle frequency layer $\mathbf{I}^m$ can be obtained by $\mathbf{I}^m = \bar{\mathbf{I}} - \bar{\mathbf{I}} \otimes \mathbf{G}^l$. Now from $\mathbf{I}^h$ and $\mathbf{I}^m$, an example patch pair set $S = \{S^m, S^h\}$ is extracted for future image representation. $S^m = \{\mathbf{p}_i^m\}_{i=1}^N$ and $S^h = \{\mathbf{p}_i^h\}_{i=1}^N$ represent the middle frequency and the high frequency bases respectively. Each element pair $\{\mathbf{p}_i^m, \mathbf{p}_i^h\}$ is the column expansion of a square image patch from the middle frequency layer $\mathbf{I}^m$ and the corresponding high frequency layer $\mathbf{I}^h$. The dimensions of $\mathbf{p}_i^m$ and $\mathbf{p}_i^h$ are $D^m \times 1$ and $D^h \times 1$ respectively, and often $D^m \neq D^h$. Now from a given LR input, the middle frequency patches can be extracted accordingly and denoted as $\{\mathbf{y}_j^m\}$. The missing high frequency components $\{\mathbf{y}_j^h\}$ are estimated based on the co-occurrence patterns stored in S. The following subsections review three different models for the estimation process.

Figure 3. Image frequency layers

 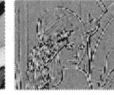  

(a) original   (b) $\mathbf{I}^h$ layer   (c) $\mathbf{I}^m$ layer   (d) $\mathbf{I}^l$ layer

Graphical Model

Assuming that image patches follow Gaussian distribution, i.e., $Pr(\mathbf{y}^m) \sim N(\mu^m, \Sigma^2)$ and $Pr(\mathbf{y}^h \mid \mathbf{y}^m) \sim N(\mu^h, \Sigma^2)$ it can be easily verified that, for any observed patch $\mathbf{y}^m_j$ from the LR input, the maximum likelihood (ML) estimation of μ^m_j minimizes the following objective function

$$\{\mu^{m*}_j\} = {}_{\{\mu^m_j\} \subset \{\mathbf{p}^m_i\}^N_{1=1}} \| \mathbf{y}^m_j - \mu^m_j \|^2 \qquad (1)$$

which yields a 1-Nearest Neighboring (1-NN) solution. With the co-occurrence prior, the corresponding μ^{h*}_j is the ML estimation of μ^h_j which is then used as the missing $\mathbf{y}^h_j$ for reconstruction.

The 1-NN estimation only considers the local observation. Freeman et al proposed a parametric Markov Network (MN) to incorporate neighboring smoothness constraint (Freeman, 2000). His method strives to find $\mu^m_j \in \{\mathbf{p}^m_i\}^N_{i=1}$ such that μ^m_j is similar to $\mathbf{y}^m_j$, and the corresponding μ^h_j follows certain smoothness constrain from the 4-connection neighborhood. This equals to minimizing the following objective function for the whole network

$$\{\mu^{m*}_j\} =$$
$${}_{\{\mu^m_j\} \subset \{\mathbf{p}^m_i\}^N_{i=1}} \sum_j (\| \mathbf{y}^m_j - \mu^m_j \|^2 + \lambda \| \mu^h_j - O(\mu^h_j) \|^2)$$

$$(2)$$

where $O(\mu^h_j)$ represents the overlapped region in μ^h_j by neighboring patches. Basically, the second term in Equation 2 penalizes the pixel difference ar overlapped regions. Comparing to Equation 1, Equation 2 obtains a maximum a posteriori (MAP) estimation of μ^m, hence the result is more stable and robust. The graphical model of the MN is presented in Figure 4.

However, due to cyclic dependencies of Markov Network, exact inference of Equation 2 is a #P-complete problem, and thus computationally intractable. One feasible solution is to break the inference process into two individual steps (Freeman 2000, Wang 2005, Mudenagudi 2006): First, for each input patch $\mathbf{y}^m_j$, K-NN $\{\mathbf{p}^m_k\}^K_{k=1}$ are selected from the training data. This minimizes the $\| \mathbf{y}^m_j - \mu^m_j \|^2$ term in Equation 2; Second, the K corresponding high frequency patch $\{\mathbf{p}^h_k\}^K_{k=1}$ are used as candidates to search for a winner that minimizes $\| \mu^h_j - O(\mu^h_j) \|^2$ using approximation techniques, such as Bayesian belief propagation (Freeman, 2000), Gibbs Sampling (Wang, 2005),

Figure 4. Markov network representation

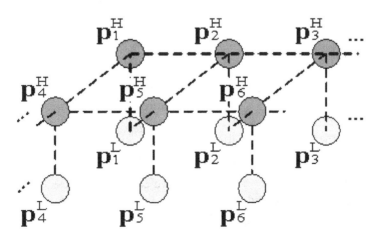

Graph-Cut (Mudenagudi, 2006), etc. The winner is the estimated μ_j^{h*} which is then used as the final $\mathbf{y}_j^h$ for reconstruction.

Coding Based Reconstruction

The two-step strategy in solving Equation 2 is computationally expensive. Besides, the improvement in SR image quality over the 1-NN is limited. Chang et al (Chang 2004) introduced an alternative approach where the problem of reconstruct the optimal $\mathbf{y}_j^h$ is regarded as discovering the Local Linear Embedding (LLE) in the original R^{D^m} space (The input middle frequency patch space) and reconstruct in another R^{D^h} space (The high frequency patch space). The LLE method works in the following manner. First, for each input patch $\mathbf{y}_j^m$, K nearest neighboring patches $\{\mathbf{p}_k^m\}_{k=1}^K$ are selected as that in the previous subsection. Next, an optimal embedding weights $\mathbf{x}_j^*$ is obtained by

$$\{\mathbf{x}_j^*\} = {}_{\{\mathbf{x}_j\}} || \mathbf{y}_j^m - \mathbf{P}_j^m \mathbf{x}_j ||^2 + \lambda || \mathbf{x}_j ||^2 \qquad (3)$$

where $\mathbf{P}_j^m$ is the $D^m \times K$ matrix representation of $\{\mathbf{p}_k^m\}_{k=1}^K$ and $\mathbf{x}_j = [x_1, ..., x_K]^\top$. The regularization term $\lambda || \mathbf{x}_j ||^2$ is added to improve the condition of the least square fitting problem.

Then $\mathbf{x}_j^*$ is used to estimate μ_j^{h*} by

$$\{\mu_j^{h*}\} = \{\mathbf{P}_j^h \mathbf{x}_j^*\} \qquad (4)$$

where $\mathbf{P}_j^h$ is the $D^h \times K$ matrix representation of $\{\mathbf{p}_k^h\}_{k=1}^K$ that corresponds to $\{\mathbf{p}_k^m\}_{k=1}^K$. μ_j^{h*} is used as the computed $\mathbf{y}_j^h$ for final reconstruction, and pixels in the neighboring overlapped regions simply take their average values.

The performance of the LLE method is limited by the quality of the K candidates $\{\mathbf{p}_k^m\}_{k=1}^K$,

hence the solution by LLE is sub-optimal. In fact, the searching and embedding steps in the LLE method can be addressed simultaneously, i.e., searching for a set of bases elements whose combination is a good estimation of the input. This equals to learning the optimal $\{\mathbf{x}_j^*\}$ that minimizes the following objective function,

$$\{\mathbf{x}_j^*\} = {}_{\{\mathbf{x}_j\}} || \mathbf{y}_j^m - \mathbf{P}^m \mathbf{x}_j ||^2 + \gamma \phi(\mathbf{x}_j) \qquad (5)$$

where $\mathbf{P}^m$ is an $D^m \times N$ matrix representing the middle frequency patch set $S^m = \{\mathbf{p}_i^m\}_{i=1}^N$ in the training data.

It can be easily found that, Equation 5 is very similar to Equation 3, except $\mathbf{P}^m$ is used instead of $\mathbf{P}_j^m$. Since S^m is usually over-complete, the regularization term $\phi(\mathbf{x}_j)$ is very important. In our previous work (Wang 2009) and (Yang 2008), an L1 regularization is suggested, where $\phi(\mathbf{x}_j) = | \mathbf{x}_j |_1$. In this way the optimization problems becomes as performing sparse-coding (SC) (Lee 2007) for each $\mathbf{y}_j^m$ individually. More details can be found in (Wang 2009).

The obtained $\{\mathbf{x}_j\}^*$ can be applied to estimate the high frequency layer to estimate $\{\mu_j^{h*}\}$ using Equation 4, and then $\{\mathbf{y}_j^h\}$ accordingly.

Invariant Property Between Different Frequency Layers

In the above subsections, each image patch $\mathbf{y}_j^m$ is converted into a local representation $\mathbf{x}_j^*$ using either the NN, LLE or SC model. Each representation $\mathbf{x}_j^*$ is a sparse $N \times 1$ vector with only 1 non-zero element (in the NN model), K-non-zero elements (in the LLE model), or around K non-zero elements (in the SC model). For simplicity, we call such process the coding process. When $\{\mathbf{x}_j^*\}$ is obtained, the reconstruction process calculates Equation 4 for all the three models. The difference among the three models is the objective function used during the coding process:

- In the NN model, $\mathbf{x}_j^*$ is obtained by writing Equation 1 as

$$\mathbf{x}_j^* = {}_{\mathbf{x}_j} || \mathbf{y}_j^m - \mathbf{P}^m \mathbf{x}_j ||^2 \qquad (6)$$

$$st.\mathbf{x}_j \in \{0,1\}^N \, \& \sum \mathbf{x}_j = 1$$

where $\mathbf{P}^m$ is the same as that used in Equation 5.

- In the LLE model, according to Equation 3, $\mathbf{x}_j^*$ is obtained by

$$\mathbf{x}_j^* = {}_{\mathbf{x}_j} || \mathbf{y}_j^m - (\mathbf{P}^m \cdot \mathbf{A}_j) \mathbf{x}_j ||^2 + \lambda || \mathbf{x}_j ||^2 \qquad (7)$$

where the term $\mathbf{P}^m \cdot \mathbf{A}_j$ denotes the neighboring relation using matrix manipulation. $\mathbf{A}_j$ is an $D^m \times N$ matrix and can be factorized by $\mathbf{A}_j = \mathbf{I}^m \mathbf{a}_j$. $\mathbf{I}^m$ is an $D^m \times 1$ unit vector. $\mathbf{a}_j \in \{0,1\}^N$, and for each element a_k in $\mathbf{a}_j$:

$$a_k = \begin{cases} 1 & if \, || \mathbf{y}_j^m - \mathbf{p}_k^m ||^2 \le d_{thr}, \mathbf{p}_k^m \in S^m \\ 0 & otherwise \end{cases} \qquad (8)$$

where d_{thr} is a pre-defined threshold that controls the number of NNs to be selected. It can be regarded as a constant variable.

- In the SC model, $\mathbf{x}_j^*$ is obtained by Equation 5 with $\phi(\mathbf{x}_j) = | \mathbf{x}_j |_1$

Our intension to discuss these different coding models is that, although $\mathbf{x}_j^*$ is learned from the middle frequency layer by Equation 1, Equation 3 or Equation 5, it can be directly applied to compute the missing components in the high frequency layer by Equation 4. Such invariant property can be generalized in Corrollary 1 below:

- **Corollary 1:** The optimal representation $\mathbf{x}^*$ is invariant across different frequency layers given respective bases representing corresponding frequency components.

Corrollary 1 is a direct result of the image co-occurrence prior, and has been validated by numerous example-based SR work. However, such invariant property depends on the example patch pair set S, i.e., the optimal representation $\mathbf{x}^*$ across the middle and the high frequency layer is invariant only under a defined up-scaling factors, such as $\times 2$, $\times 3$ etc. In this paper, the correlations between bases sets of different scales are further studied. The following section introduces another invariant property between different bases sets, with which the proposed continues image up-sizing is made possible. We call it Resolution-Invariant Image Representation (RIIR) (Wang 2009).

RESOLUTION-INVARIANT IMAGE REPRESENTATION

Generating Multi-Resolution Base Set

To examine the relation among different resolution versions of a same image, a multi-resolution image patch pair set S is generated: First, each image $\mathbf{I}$ in a given dataset is processed to obtain its LR version $\overline{\mathbf{I}}_u$ by first downsampling $\mathbf{I}$ to $1/u$ scale, then upsampling it back to the original size. As explained previously, in this way N image patch pairs can be extracted from the $\mathbf{I}^m$ and $\mathbf{I}^h$ layers respectively, and we denote the obtained set as $S_u = \{S_u^m, S_u^h\} = \{\mathbf{p}_{i,u}^m, \mathbf{p}_{i,u}^h\}_{i=1}^N$

Next, multiple $u = 1, ..., U$ is applied to obtain a multi-resolution bases set. In particular, the order of the elements in each set is specially arranged such that the ith pair in $\{S_u^m, S_u^h\}$ and the ith pair in $\{S_U^m, S_U^h\}$ are from patches at the same location as highlighted in Figure 5.

With the obtained $S = \{S_u\}$, $u = 1, ..., U$ the next subsection examines the relation among these multiple bases sets to reveal another invariance property.

Invariant Property between Different Frequency Layers

Ideally, obtaining $\bar{\mathbf{I}}_u$ requires first a downsampling process and then an upsampling process. The downsampling process consists of applying an anti-aliasing filter to reduce the bandwidth of the signal and then a decimator to reduce the sample rate; the upsampling process, on the other side, increases the sample rate and then applies an interpolation filter to remove the aliasing effects (Oppenheim 1999). Both the interpolation and the anti-aliasing filters are low-pass filters, and they can be combined into a single filter. Particularly, the filter with the smallest bandwidth is more restrictive and, thus, can be used in place of both filters.

Now assuming both the HR image $\mathbf{I}$ and several downgraded LR images $\bar{\mathbf{I}}_u$ are available

Figure 5. Sampling the base set

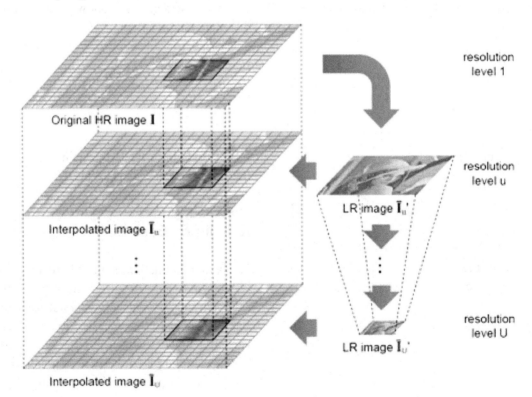

for training, and hereafter the notation $\mathbf{I}$ and $\mathbf{I}_1$ is interchangeable. Each $\bar{\mathbf{I}}_u$ can be modeled by

$$\bar{\mathbf{I}}_u = ((\mathbf{I}_1 \otimes \mathbf{G}_{\perp}) \downarrow_{\frac{\perp}{u}} \uparrow_{\frac{u}{1}}) \otimes \mathbf{G}_{\frac{u}{1}} = \mathbf{I}_1 \otimes \mathbf{G}_u^m \tag{9}$$

where $\mathbf{G}_{\frac{\perp}{u}}$ is the anti-aliasing filter, $\mathbf{G}_{\frac{u}{1}}$ is the interpolation filter, and $\downarrow_{\frac{\perp}{u}} / \uparrow_{\frac{u}{1}}$ is the downsampler/upsampler. The combined filter is the one with the smallest bandwidth between $\mathbf{G}_{\frac{\perp}{u}}$ and $\mathbf{G}_{\frac{u}{1}}$. For simplicity, we denote the true combined filter as $\mathbf{G}_u^m$ for later discussion.

The downsampling/upsampling steps are generally not reversible. The difference between the obtained $\bar{\mathbf{I}}_u$ and the original $\mathbf{I}_1$ is the missing high frequency layer $\mathbf{I}_u^h$ that needs to be estimated (Subsection 2.1). Similarly, the middle frequency $\mathbf{I}_u^m$ can be obtained by

$$\mathbf{I}_u^m = \bar{\mathbf{I}}_u - \bar{\mathbf{I}}_u \otimes \mathbf{G}_u^l =$$
$$\mathbf{I}_1 \otimes \mathbf{G}_u^m - \mathbf{I}_1 \otimes \mathbf{G}_u^m \otimes \mathbf{G}_u^l = \mathbf{I}_1 \otimes \mathbf{G}_u \tag{10}$$

where $\mathbf{G}_u = \mathbf{G}_u^m - \mathbf{G}_u^m \otimes \mathbf{G}_u^l$ and $\mathbf{G}_u^l$ denotes the combined filter to further discard the middle frequency layer from $\bar{\mathbf{I}}_u$

Let $\mathbf{P}_u^m$ be an $D_u^m \times N$ matrix to represent all the elements in S_u^m where D_u^m is the dimension of patch $\mathbf{p}_u^m$, $\mathbf{y}_u^m$ be the middle frequency component of an input patch $\mathbf{y}_u$ and $\mathbf{g}_u$ be the column expansion of $\mathbf{G}_u$. With Equation 10, we can have

$$\mathbf{P}_u^m = \mathbf{P}_1^m \otimes \mathbf{g}_u \tag{11}$$

where the convolution applies on each row of $\mathbf{P}$, and

$$\mathbf{y}_u^m = \mathbf{y}_1^m \otimes \mathbf{g}_u. \tag{12}$$

Now it can be proven that for certain $\mathbf{g}_u$ the representation learned from either NN, LLE or SC is independent of u. To elaborate, using the SC model for example (The proof for NN and LLE model is given in Appendix 1). Taking Equation 11 and Equation 12 into Equation 5, the optimal representation under resolution u is obtained by

$$\begin{aligned} \mathbf{x}_u^* &=_{\mathbf{x}_u} || \mathbf{y}_u^m - \mathbf{P}_u^m \mathbf{x}_u ||^2 + \gamma | \mathbf{x}_u | \\ &=_{\mathbf{x}_u} || \mathbf{y}_1^m \otimes \mathbf{g}_u - (\mathbf{P}_1^m \otimes \mathbf{g}_u) \mathbf{x}_u ||^2 + \gamma | \mathbf{x}_u | \\ &=_{\mathbf{x}_u} || \mathbf{C}_u (\mathbf{y}_1^m - \mathbf{P}_1^m \mathbf{x}_u) ||^2 + \gamma | \mathbf{x}_u | \end{aligned} \tag{13}$$

where $\mathbf{C}_u$ is the convolution matrix formed by $\mathbf{g}_u$

The solution is independent of u, i.e., $\mathbf{x}_u^* = \mathbf{x}_1^*$, when $\mathbf{C}_u^\top \mathbf{C}_u$ is an unit matrix. To satisfy this condition, $\mathbf{g}_u$ needs to be the Dirac Delta function. Although in realistic imaging process, $\mathbf{g}_u$ is a low-pass filter, the next subsection shows that, in real imaging process, $\mathbf{g}_u$ approximate a Dirac Delta function well, and hence $\mathbf{x}^*$ can be invariant across different resolution scales.

Validation for Realistic Imaging System

For $\mathbf{g}_u$ taking Dirac Delta function, the obtained $\mathbf{C}_u^\top \mathbf{C}_u$ is a unit matrix as shown in Figure 6 (a). According to subsection 3.1, in obtaining $\bar{\mathbf{I}}_u$ from $\mathbf{I}$ the information in each pixel is propagated to the neighboring u pixels. This equals to an $\mathbf{g}_u$ with $2 \times u + 1$ non-zero elements. The corresponding $\mathbf{C}_u^\top \mathbf{C}_u$ for $\times 2$, $\times 3$ and $\times 6$ are shown in Figure 6(b), (c) and (d) respectively. As can be seen from these figures, when the scale factor is relatively small (e.g., $\leq \times 3$), $\mathbf{C}_u^\top \mathbf{C}_u$ approximates unit matrix well, which implies that the optimal $\mathbf{x}^*$ can be resolution invariant.

Figure 6. Simulated image downgrading filters

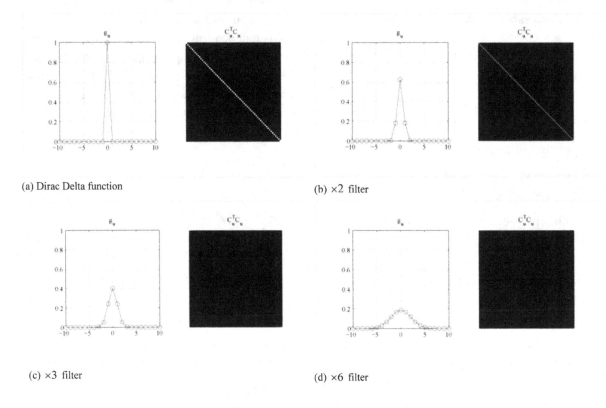

(a) Dirac Delta function

(b) ×2 filter

(c) ×3 filter

(d) ×6 filter

To examine how much the invariant property holds for real images, the following experiments examine the similarity of the optimal representation **x** learned from 5 different resolution versions of a same image (*i.e.* $U = 5$). First, from a training HR image, we generated a multi-resolution patch pair set S with around 8000 patch pairs in each resolution level. Next, for each testing image, we extracted around 2000 patches from every resolution version as well, and five versions were used as that in S . Then we solved Equation 2, Equation 3, and Equation 5 to get the optimal representations $\mathbf{x} = \{\mathbf{x}_{j,u}\}_{j=1}^{2000}$, $u = 1, ..., 5$ at each resolution level for the NN, LLe and SC model respectively. Next, if Corrollary 1 holds, $\mathbf{x}_{j,u}$ should be very similar to $\mathbf{x}_{j,v}$, $u \neq v$. Hence we computed the overall similarity between every two elements in $\mathbf{x}_j = \{\mathbf{x}_{j,1}, \mathbf{x}_{j,2}, \mathbf{x}_{j,3}, \mathbf{x}_{j,4}, \mathbf{x}_{j,5}\}$ by

$$sim(\mathbf{x}_j) = \frac{1}{C_5^2} \sum_{u=1}^{4} \sum_{v=u+1}^{5} cor_{u,v}^j \qquad (14)$$

where $cor_{u,v}^j$ is the correlation between $\mathbf{x}_{j,u}$ and $\mathbf{x}_{j,v}$. Finally, the overall similarity is averaged over the 2000 patched to get a score.

To make the experiment more comprehensive, we tested different redundancy level in the base set by either random removing or using K-Mean clustering methods to reduce the base cardinality from 8000 to until 50. The experiments were repeated 5 times with different training images, and the results are shown in Figure 7. As can be seen from Figure 6, the minimal similarity score is greater than 0.44, and the maximal score reaches almost 0.8. The results validate the high similarities between x_u and x_v from different resolutions. The reason why the scores are relatively lower when the cardinality is large is due to the nature of images, where there are very similar elements in the base, such that the coding process may not select exactly the same elements for reconstruction. When such redundancy is removed, the similarity between representations becomes significantly higher.

Based on both theoretical proof in Equation 15 and the experimental validation in Figure 7, we can generalize the second invariant property for a multi-resolution base set:

- **Corollary 2:** The optimal representation $\mathbf{x}^*$ is invariant across different resolution inputs given respective bases representing corresponding resolutions.

Corrollary 1 reveals that, if the different resolution versions of the same image are related by Equation 11, then the optimal representation learned from any resolution version can also be applied for another version. For simplicity, we call Corollary 2 the Resolution-Invariant Image Representation (RIIR) property, and the multi-resolution sets S an RIIR set. With RIIR property, it is able to saves the computational expensive coding process in the NN, LLE or SC model for multi-scale resolution enhancement tasks, hence it's very desirable in may important applications, such as Continues Image Scaling (CIS) discussed in the following section.

APPROXIMATE AND GENERALIZATION USING MULTI-TASK LEARNING

To the best of our knowledge, Equation 6, 7, and 8 can be base solved in between $O(n \log(n))$, $O(k \log(n) + n)$ and $O(n^2)$ with Equation 8, the slowest but with best quality. Since the coding process operates on each local image patch, this step is the most computational expensive step in the SR process. In this section, we apply a two-layer neural network to approximate the coding process.

Figure 7. Correlation between different resolution versions

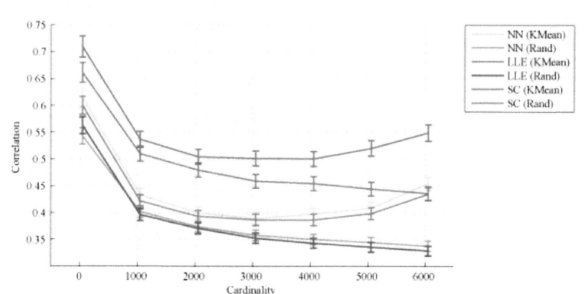

Simple One Scale Neural Network

Using the same notation as above, a two layer neural network $\overline{\mathbf{p}}^h = f_{nn}^k(\mathbf{p}^m) = f_{\theta_2}(f_{\theta_1}(\mathbf{p}^m))$ can be learned by minimizing the reconstruction error between $\overline{\mathbf{p}}^h$ and $\mathbf{p}^h$. k denotes the number of neuro I the middle layer. The first layer, $f_{\theta_1}(\mathbf{p}) = T(\mathbf{p}\mathbf{W}_1) - \mathbf{b}_1$ approximates the coding function. Hence we can apply a latent variable $\mathbf{z}$ to explicitly model output for the first layer by minimizing

$$\sum_i \| \mathbf{z}_i - T(\mathbf{p}_i\mathbf{W}_1) - \mathbf{b}_1 \|^2 + \lambda log(1 + \mathbf{z}_i^2) \tag{15}$$

where $T(\cdot)$ is the transfer function, and in our implementation we have $T(\mathbf{p}_i\mathbf{W}_1) = Tanh(\mathbf{p}_i\mathbf{W}_1)$. The second term in Equation 15 is to enforce sparsity for $\mathbf{z}$.

In ideal case, $\mathbf{z}$ should be identical to $\mathbf{x}$ as we could get from either Equation 6, Equation 7, or Equation 8. In that case, the parameter $\theta_2 = \{\mathbf{W}_2, \mathbf{b}_2\}$ for the second layer of the neural network should be identical to $\mathbf{P}^h$ such that $f_{\theta_2}(\mathbf{z}) = \mathbf{z}\mathbf{P}^h$ can be expected to be similar to Equation 4. To obtain a neural network with such property, the training process strives to minimize the following objective

$$\phi_{\theta,\mathbf{Z}}(\mathbf{P}^m, \mathbf{P}^h) = \sum_{i=1}^{L} (\alpha \| \mathbf{z}_i - T(\mathbf{p}_i^m\mathbf{W}_1) - \mathbf{b}_1 \|^2 \\ + \| \mathbf{p}_i^h - T(\mathbf{z}_i\mathbf{W}_2) - \mathbf{b}_2 \|^2 \\ + \lambda log(1 + \mathbf{z}_i^2)) \tag{16}$$

MULTI-TASK LEARNING FOR MULTI-SCALE IMAGE RESIZING

Equation 2 can be extended in the following way to support multi-scale image resizing. Since the latent variable, $\mathbf{z}$, is to approximate $\mathbf{x}$ in Equation 8, it is resolution-invariant. Hence we could add additional outputs into the second layer of the network. These outputs share the same $\mathbf{z}$, while each of these outputs should reconstruct the missing high frequency of one resolution scale. This makes the whole model a typical multi-task learning framework with the graphical representation in Figure 8. Hence the objective becomes

$$\phi_{\theta,\mathbf{Z}}(\mathbf{P}^m, \mathbf{P}^h) = \\ \sum_{i=1}^{L} (\alpha \| \mathbf{z}_i - T(\mathbf{p}_i^m\mathbf{W}_1) - \mathbf{b}_1 \|^2 + \\ \sum_{u=1}^{U} \| \mathbf{p}_{ui}^h - T(\mathbf{z}_i\mathbf{W}_{u,2}) - \mathbf{b}_{u,2} \|^2 \\ + \lambda log(1 + \mathbf{z}_i^2)) \tag{17}$$

When $\{\mathbf{W}_1, \mathbf{b}_1, \mathbf{W}_{u,2}, \mathbf{b}_{u,2}\}$, $u = 1, ..., U$ are trained, the missing high frequency component of scale u for an input $\mathbf{y}^m$ can be estimated as $\mathbf{y}^{h*} = (Tanh(\mathbf{y}^m\mathbf{W}_1) + \mathbf{b}_1)\mathbf{W}_{u,2} + \mathbf{b}_{u,2}$

EXPERIMENTAL RESULTS

Multi-Scale Image Magnification

There are many scenarios where users need different resolution image/video of a same object, *e.g.* viewing an image in a PDF/Word document at different zooming, streaming videos over wireless channels to users with different receiver resolutions, etc. All these applications require multi-scale image magnification capacity. An RIIR set $S = \{S_u\}u = 1, ..., U$ is born with the multi-scale resizing ability, because each S_u is

Figure 8. Graphical representation of the generalized multi-scale coding framework

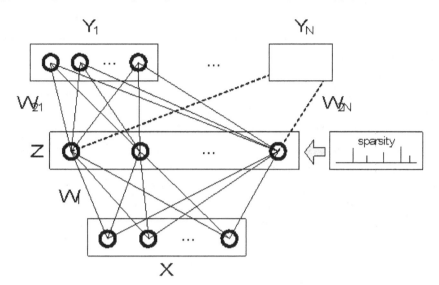

the same as what's been used for $\times u$ image magnification by many existing example-based SR method (Freeman, 2000). However, instead of solving the optimal representation $\{\mathbf{x}^*\}$ under each scale independently, under the RIIR framework, $\{\mathbf{x}^*\}$ only needs to be learned once. Then by applying different S_u, the same $\{\mathbf{x}^*\}$ can be used to reconstruct the image at multiple scales. Finer magnification scales can be achieved by simply increasing the level of resolutions used in creating S. The advantage of the method is that, the magnification process requires only matrix-vector multiplication by Equation 4, which can be implemented very efficiently. In addition, the RIIR set can be stored locally, and the computed RIIR can be transmitted together with the image/ video document.

To further extend multi-scale image magnification to CIS, in traditional example-based SR technique, the users have to store a continuous set of models, or at least at a very fine granularity, which requires huge storage space and computation power. With the RIIR method, the user only needs to store a limited scale of bases which can then be used to generate a new base at the

required scale on the fly. For instance, assume that the S generated in section 3.1 has 5 scales, i.e., $S = \{S_u\}_{u=1}^5$, we can generated a new base at $\times 2.4$ scale using S_2 and S_3. To elaborate, let v be the target scale factor which is between u and $u+1$, the ith element in S_v can be obtained by

$$\mathbf{p}_{i,v} = w_{u,v}\tilde{\mathbf{p}}_{i,u} + (1 - w_{u,v})\tilde{\mathbf{p}}_{i,u+1} \tag{18}$$

where $\tilde{\mathbf{p}}_{i,u}$ is the patch interpolated from scale u, and $\tilde{\mathbf{p}}_{i,u+1}$ is interpolated from scale $u + 1$. The weight

$$w_{u,v} = (1 + exp((v - u - 0.5) * \tau))^{-1}$$

where in our implementation, $\tau = 10$ empirically.

The first experiment compares the quality of magnified images by RIIR framework with existing SR methods. Since most of these benchmark methods do not support continues magnification, we compared the image quality under multiple fixed scales. To begin with, an RIIR set S was trained. Around 20000 patch pair examples were extracted from some widely used images, *e.g.* "peppers". First, 25 testing images were processed to compare with existing example-based SR methods, i.e., "KNN" (Freeman, 2000), "LLE" (Chang, 2004) and "SC" (Yang, 2008), that use the same coding model but without the RIIR technique. Multiple up-scale factor from $\times 2$ to $\times 6$ was specified, and the RIIR was solved at *times*3 scale. The processing time is logged from a Dell Precision 490 PC (3.2 GHz CPU, 2G RAM), and the results are listed in Table 1. As can be seen from Table 1, while the same amount of computation is required at calculating the coding at $\times 3$ scale, for the rest scales, the computation is significantly reduced.

Next, the quality of the generated SR images was evaluated. In addition to those benchmark methods used in Table 1, two functional interpolation SR methods, "Enhance" (Wang 2008) and "Soft edge " (Dai 2007), were also implemented for comparison. The PSNR score over BiCubic interpolation is presented in Figure 9. As can be seen from Figure 9, in most scales, the best image quality is achieved by the SC method, while the proposed RIIR method using SC model achieves the second best image quality, losing only a very small margin. This is a very promising result because according to Table 1, the RIIR method saves a considerable amount of computation while sacrifices only negligible amount of image quality. In fact, comparing the three coding models with/without the RIIR framework, the achieved

image quality are always comparable. In the NN coding model, the achieved image PSNR score is even higher than that without the RIIR framework. This is reasonable because the NN method tends to over-fit to the example patch pair set, which the computed representation by Equation 1 may not generalize well to the high-frequency layer well. On the other side, solving Equation 1 under the RIIR framework incorporates stronger regularization, such that the learned representation is more reliable in estimating the high-frequency components for reconstruction.

The second experiment demonstrated the CIS application under the RIIR framework (section 4). We first generated the RIIR base set S from $\times 1 \sim \times 6$ scales, with step size 0.5, *i.e.* a base is trained at every u and $u+0.5$ scales, $u = 1, ..., 6$. This would take up 15Mb storage space if the cardinality is selected to be 2000. For each testing image, the RIIR is learned at scale $\times 3$. Next we conducted continuous scaling between $\times 1 \sim \times 6$ with step size 0.05. A Dell Precision 490 PC (3.2 GHz CPU, 2G RAM) was used to conduct a subjective user study where 12 people were asked to compare the image quality with BiCubic interpolation. All of them rated significantly higher scores for our results, and most of them were not aware of the processing delay in generating the magnified images. These results validate the good performance of CIS using RIIR method as well as the low computational cost in generating the up-scaled images. Some example images can be

Table 1. Comparison of average SR processing time (seconds) with/without RIIR

Scale	NN	RIIR (NN)	LLE	RIIR (LLE)	SC	RIIR (SC)
$\times 2$	3.89	**0.11**	7.03	**0.13**	19.45	**0.16**
$\times 3$	**11.15**	11.15	**13.97**	13.97	**54.22**	54.22
$\times 4$	14.39	**0.19**	22.73	**0.23**	98.59	**0.28**
$\times 5$	14.69	**0.28**	26.86	**0.34**	159.92	**0.45**
$\times 6$	15.11	**0.42**	28.94	**0.52**	249.68	**0.66**

Figure 9. Average SR quality under different scales

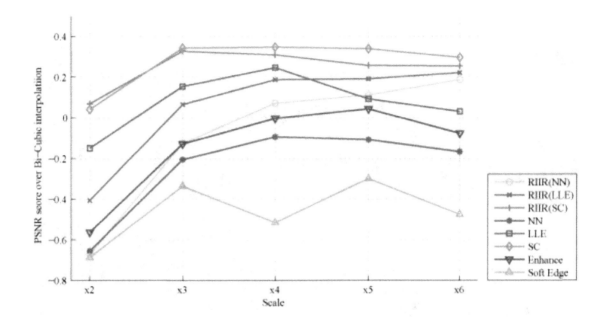

found in Figure 10 and Figure 11. A video demonstration of the real Continues Image Scaling process can be found at http://www.neclabs. com/~jjwang/demo/Continues_Image_Scaling. wmv

The third experiments tested the performance of the generalized reconstruction. We first tested the processing time of using the learned approximating function f_{nn}^k to reconstruct the high frequency components. We applied the following setting to compare with using the original coding criteria, i.e., RIIR (NN), RIIR (LLE) and RIIR (SC) from Table 1. As can be seen from Table 2, the generalized coding function reduces between 87.5% to 77.3% of the processing time if using the SC criteria.

Next we tested the quality of using generalized coding function to reconstruct the SR image. We compared the quality of multiple scale upsizing from ×2 to ×6, same as that used in the above experiment. The results are listed in Figure 12 below. As can be seen, the quality of using generalized coding function (128 neurons, kmean

initialization with $\lambda = 1$) decreases slightly from that using the RIIR with SC criteria, but gives better quality than other criteria such as RIIR with LLE or with NN criteria.

We also compared the SR quality under different parameters used for training the coding function (Equation 17) The following figures lists the results using random or k-mean initialization of $\mathbf{W}_2$, using the sparsity regularization or not $\left(\lambda = 0 \text{ or } \lambda = 1\right)$ and number of neurons for the middle layer (64, 128, 256, 512 and 1024).

In Figure 13, the setting with the best average quality is shown on top of each subfigure. As can be seen, the best results were obtained with 128 neurons, kmean initialization and $\lambda = 1$. Although using k-mean and the sparsity regularization improves the score, the most important parameter is the number of neurons. When more than 256 neurons were used, the quality actually decreased. One possible reason is the insufficient training data used to learn a more complex neural network.

Figure 10. Illustration of continuous image scaling (top-left: the original image; first row: BiCubic interpolation; second row: RIIR with NN model; third row: RIIR with LLE model; last row: RIIR with SC model)

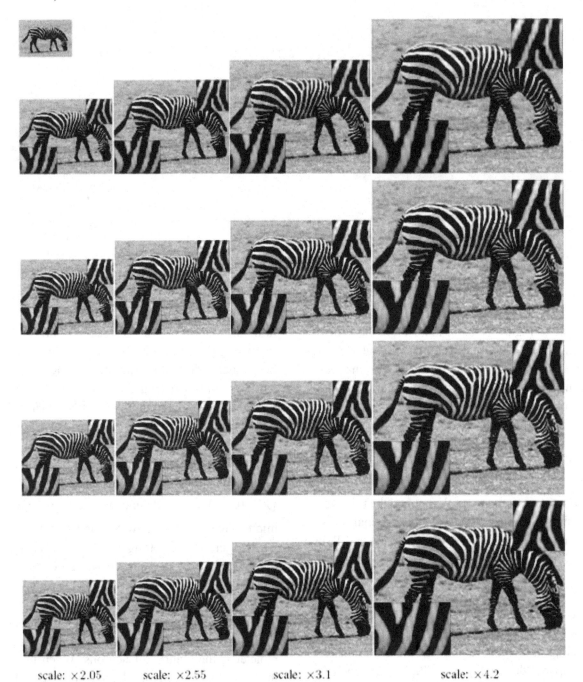

scale: ×2.05   scale: ×2.55   scale: ×3.1   scale: ×4.2

Figure 11. Illustration of continuous image scaling (top-left: the original image; first row: BiCubic interpolation; second row: RIIR with NN model; third row: RIIR with LLE model; last row: RIIR with SC model)

scale: ×2.65   scale: ×3.15   scale: ×3.85   scale: ×4.35

Table 2. Comparison of average SR processing time (seconds) with/without RIIR

Scale	RIIR (NN)	RIIR (LLE)	RIIR (SC)	f_{nn}^{64}	f_{nn}^{128}	f_{nn}^{256}	f_{nn}^{512}	f_{nn}^{1024}
×3	11.15	13.97	54.22	6.03	6.80	7.64	9.20	12.32

Figure 12. Comparison of SR quality under different RIIR implementation

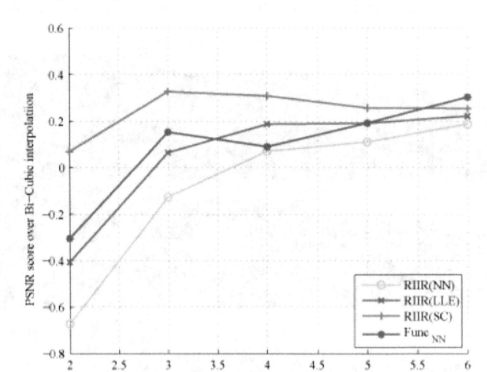

Figure 13. Comparison of parameters for the coding function

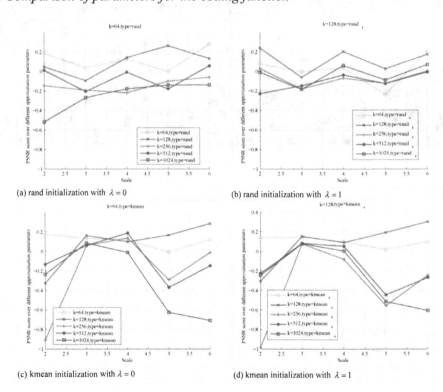

(a) rand initialization with $\lambda = 0$

(b) rand initialization with $\lambda = 1$

(c) kmean initialization with $\lambda = 0$

(d) kmean initialization with $\lambda = 1$

CONCLUSION

The paper presents the Resolution-Invariant Image Representation (RIIR) framework based on the idea that the same image should have identical representation at various resolution levels. In the framework, an RIIR bases set is constructed first. With the RIIR bases set, it is validated that three coding models, i.e., the Nearest-Neighbor, Local Linear Embedding and Sparse-Coding model, can all represent the image with resolution-invariant property. In this way the computational cost in multi-scale image magnification can be significantly reduced. More importantly, the method to extend RIIR to support continues image scaling is also discussed, such that the proposed RIIR framework can support additional applications that existing image SR approaches cannot handle. For instance, in (Wang 2009) the RIIR framework is applied for content-based zooming for mobile users. Experimental results show that our RIIR based method outperforms existing methods in various aspects. The future work of the research includes the following issues: first, in addition to image magnification, the possibility of applying the RIIR framework to improve image shrinking quality will be investigated; second, additional optimization strategies to improve the coding speed will be examine; third, the implementation of the coding and reconstructing process will be parallelized with modern CPU and/or GPU support; and fourth, other application domains in image compression, streaming, personalization, etc, will be explored.

REFERENCES

W3C. (2011). *Scalable vector graphics, 1.1* (2ⁿᵈ ed.). Retrieved from http://www.w3.org/tr/svg11/

Chang, H., Yeung, D., & Xiong, Y. (2004). Super-resolution through neighbor embedding. *Proceedings of CVPR, 04*, 275–282.

Dai, S., Han, M., Xu, W., Wu, Y., & Gong, Y. (2007). Soft edge smoothness prior for alpha channel super resolution. In *Proceedings of IEEE Conference on Computer Vision and Pattern Recognition*, (pp. 1–8).

Do, M. N., & Vetterli, M. M. (2005). The contourlet transform: An efficient directional multiresolution image representation. *IEEE Transactions on Image Processing, 14*(12), 2091–2106.

Erwan, L., & Stephane, M. (2005). Sparse geometric image representations with bandelets. *IEEE Transactions on Image Processing, 14*(4), 423–438.

Freeman, W., Pasztor, E., & Carmichael, O. (2000). Learning low-level vision. *International Journal of Computer Vision, 1*, 25–47.

Guo, C., Zhu, A., & Wu, Y. (2003). Towards a mathematical theory of primal sketch and sketchability. *Proceedings of ICCV'03*, (pp. 1228–1235).

Hong, W., Wright, J., Kun, H., & Yi, M. (2006). Multiscale hybrid linear models for lossy image representation. *IEEE Transactions on Image Processing, 15*(12), 3655–3671.

Jiji, C., Joshi, M., & Chaudhuri, S. (2004). Single-frame image super-resolution using learned wavelet coefficients. *International Journal of Imaging Systems and Technology, 3*, 105–112.

Jiji, C., & Subhasis, C. (2006). Single-frame image super-resolution through contourlet learning. *EURASIP Journal on Applied Signal Processing, 73767*(11).

Lee, H., Battle, A., Raina, R., & Ng, A. (2007). Efficient sparse coding algorithms. [MIT Press.]. *Advances in Neural Information Processing Systems, 801–808.

Mudenagudi, U., Singla, R., Kalra, P. K., & Banerjee, S. (2006). Super resolution using graph-cut. *Proceedings of ACCV'06*, (pp. 385–394).

Oppenheim, A. V., Schafer, R. W., & Buck, J. R. (1999). *Discrete-time signal processing* (2nd ed.). Prentice Hall.

Ramanarayanan, G., Bala, K., & Walter, B. (2004). Feature-based textures. *Proceedings of EGSR, 04*, 186–196.

Sun, J., Tao, H., & Shum, H. (2003). Image hallucination with primal sketch priors. *Proceedings of IEEE CVPR, 03*, 729–736.

Sun, J., Xu, Z., & Shum, H. (2008). Image super-resolution using gradient profile prior. *Proceedings of CVPR '08*.

Vector-Magic. (n.d.). Home. Retrieved from http://www.vectormagic.com

Wang, J., & Gong, Y. (2008). Fast image super-resolution using connected component enhancement. *Proceedings of ICME '08*.

Wang, J., Zhu, S., & Gong, Y. (2009a). Resolution-invariant image representation and its applications. *Proceedings of CVPR '09*.

Wang, J., Zhu, S., & Gong, Y. (2009b). Resolution-invariant image representation for content-based zooming. *Proceedings of ICME '09*.

Wang, J., Zhu, S., & Gong, Y. (2009). Resolution enhancement based on learning the sparse association of image patches. *Pattern Recognition Letters, 31*(1). doi:doi:10.1016/j.patrec.2009.09.004

Wang, Q., Tang, X., & Shum, H. (2005). Patch based blind image super resolution. *Proceedings of ICCV '05*, (Vol. 1, pp. 709–716).

Yang, J., Wright, J., Huang, T., & Yi, M. (2008). Image super-resolution as sparse representation of raw image patches. *Proceedings of CVPR '08*.

APPENDIX 1: RESOLUTION INVARIANCY IN NN MODEL

According to Equation 6, at level u, for each input patch   (the subscript j is omitted), the optimal representation   can be obtained by

$$x_u^* = \arg\min_{x_u} \| y_u^m - P_u^m x_u \|^2$$
$$st. \, x_u \in \{0,1\}^N \, \mathcal{E} \sum_u x_u = 1 \tag{19}$$

where   is an   matrix to represent all the elements in   Taking Equation 12 into Equation 19,

$$x_u^* = \arg\min_{x_u} \| (y_1^m \otimes g_u) - (P_1^m \otimes g_u)_u \|^2$$
$$st. \, x_u \in \{0,1\}^N \mathcal{E} \sum_d x_u = 1,$$
$$= \arg\min_{x_u} \| C_u (y_1^m - P_1^m x_u) \|^2$$
$$st. \, x_u \in \{0,1\}^N \mathcal{E} \sum_u x = 1,$$

which is identical to Equation 15. Hence the approximation shown in Figure 5 applies.

APPENDIX 2: RESOLUTION INVARIANCY IN LLE MODEL

According to Equation 8, for each input patch y_u the optimal representation weight x_u^* minimizes

$$x_u^* = \arg\min_{x_u} \| y_u^m - (P_u^m \cdot A_u) x_u \|^2 + \lambda \| x_u \|^2 . \tag{20}$$

Taking Equation 8 and Equation 12 into Equation 20, we can have

$$x_u^* = \arg\min_{x_u} \| y_1^m \otimes g_u - ((P_1^m \otimes g_u) \cdot (A_1 \otimes g_u)) x_u \|^2 + \lambda \| x_u \|^2$$
$$= \arg\min_{x_u} \| C_u (y_1^m - (P_1^m \cdot A_1) x_u) \|^2 + \lambda \| x_u \|^2,$$

which is identical to Equation 15. Hence the approximation shown in Figure 5 applies.

Chapter 16
Graph Heat Kernel Based Image Smoothing

Zhang Fan
University of York, UK

Edwin R. Hancock
University of York, UK

Liu Shang
Beihang University, China

ABSTRACT

This chapter presents a new method for smoothing both gray-scale and color images, which relies on the heat diffusion equation on a graph. The image pixel lattice using a weighted undirected graph is presented. The edge weights of the graph are determined by the Gaussian weighted distances between local neighboring windows. The associated Laplacian matrix (the degree matrix minus the adjacency matrix) is computed then. The authors capture anisotropic diffusion across this weighted graph-structure with time by the heat equation, and find the solution, i.e. the heat kernel, by exponentiating the Laplacian eigensystem with time. Image smoothing is accomplished by convolving the heat kernel with the image, and its numerical implementation is realized by using the Krylov subspace technique. The method has the effect of smoothing within regions, but does not blur region boundaries. The relationship is also demonstrated between the authors' method, standard diffusion-based PDEs, Fourier domain signal processing, and spectral clustering. The effectiveness of the method is illustrated by experiments and comparisons on standard images.

1. INTRODUCTION

Smoothing is one of the most fundamental and widely studied problems in low-level image processing. The main purpose of image smoothing is to reduce undesirable distortions and noise while preserving important features such as discontinuities, edges, corners and texture. During the last two decades diffusion-based filters have become a powerful and well-developed tool for image smoothing and multi-scale image analysis (Weickert, 1998) (Sapiro, 2001). Witkin (Witkin,

DOI: 10.4018/978-1-4666-1891-6.ch016

1983) and Koenderink (Koenderink, 1984) were the first to formalise the multi-scale description of images and signals in terms of scale-space filtering. Their basic idea is to use convolutions with the Gaussian filter to generate fine to coarse resolution image descriptions. This is equivalent to evolving the original image using the classical heat equation (Koenderink, 1984) (Babaud, 1986), and is known as isotropic diffusion. Since the diffusivity of the isotropic diffusion is constant in all directions, boundaries and other image features will be blurred while removing the noise. In the influential work of Perona and Malik (P-M) (Perona, 1990), an anisotropic diffusion scheme for scale-space description and image smoothing was developed. The method breaks the isotropy condition and outperforms Gaussian filtering. The basic idea of this nonlinear smoothing method was to smooth images with a direction selective diffusion that preserves edges. Catte et al. (Catte, 1992) and Alvarez et al. (Alvarez, 1992) identified the ill-posedness of the P-M diffusion process and proposed a regularised modification. This nonlinear diffusion technique has been subsequentially extensively analysed and developed (Saint-Marc, 1991) (You, 1996) (Witkin, 1983) (Weickert, 1999) (Black, 1998) (Bao, 2004) (Gilboa, 2004). More recently, diffusion-based PDEs has also been developed for smoothing multi-valued images (Chambolle, 1994) (Sapiro, 1996) (Sochen, 1998) (Blomgren, 1998) (Tschumperle, 2005).

Most diffusion-based PDEs for image smoothing assume that the image is a continuous two dimensional function on R2 and consider discretization for the purpose of numerical implementation. It is desirable that the implementation is fast, accurate, and numerically stable, but these requirements are sometimes difficult to achieve. Moreover, images, and especially noisy ones, may not be sufficiently smooth to give reliable derivatives. Thus, for filtering noisy images it is more natural to consider the image as a smooth function defined on a discrete sampling structure.

1.1 Contribution

In this paper, we present a discrete framework for anisotropic diffusion which relies on the diffusion process on graphs. We admit the discrete nature of images from the outset, and use graphs to represent the arrangement of image pixels. Here the vertices are pixels. Each edge is assigned a real-valued weight, computed using Gaussian weighted distances between local neighboring windows. This weight corresponds to the diffusivity of the edge. Instead of using diffusion-based PDEs in a continuous domain, our method is based on the heat equation on a graph (Chung, 1997) (Kondor, 2002). The advantage of formulating the problem on a graph is that it requires purely combinatorial operators and as a result no discretization is required. We therefore incur no discretization errors. We pose the problem of anisotropic diffusion in a graph-spectral setting using the heat kernel. We exploit the relationship between the graph heat-kernel and the Laplacian eigensystem to develop a new method for edge-preserving image smoothing. This is accomplished by convolving the heat kernel with the image. By varying the diffusion time we control the amount of smoothing resulting from heat diffusion. The resulting algorithm can be implemented in two ways. The exact solution of the algorithm can be efficiently computed without iterations by using the Krylov subspace projection technique (Hochbruck, 1997) (Sidje, 1998). An iteration-based scheme is also provided by discretising time. The method is a type of discrete anisotropic diffusion that can be applied to smooth both gray-scale and color images over the graph representing the pixel lattice.

Our smoothing process can hence be regarded as isotropic diffusion on a weighted graph. It is the variation in weights that introduce anisotropy. Anisotropic diffusion on the original image is achieved by using an isotropic diffusion on a weighted graph representation. This transfers the complexity of the image (a function on R2) to the topology of the underlying graph. Thus, we recast the problem of finding a detailed diffusion-based PDE for image smoothing to that of finding a good representation of the image using a weighted undirected graph. Here, the edge weight of the graph plays an important role, which characterises the similarity between pixels. There are several methods in the literature for edge weight calculation (Geman, 1984) (Smolka, 2001) (Black, 1998) (Coifman, 2006). The preciseness of the similarity (weight) determines how well the algorithm preserves the details of the image while eliminating noise.

Since, it is based on a graph-based representation and its implementation relies on the specification of edge-weights, the proposed algorithm is akin to the mesh smoothing or fairing methods already described in the literature (Taubin, 1995) (Desbrun, 1999). However, the algorithms underpinning these meshbased methods are very different to that described in this paper, not only in terms of their theoretical foundation and formulation, but also the application domain studied. In (Desbrun, 1999), Desbrun et al. present a new numerical method for smoothing 3D meshes based on anisotropic diffusion. This work represents a direct improvement of the method described in the seminal paper of Taubin (Taubin, 1995). It does so by providing a more efficient implementation based on implicit integration. Our algorithm, on the other hand, is formulated from the perspective of spectral graph theory. It therefore belongs to the family of graph-based image processing algorithms which include graph-based segmentation (Shi, 2000). The work of Desbrun et al (Desbrun, 1999) uses the conventional continuous diffusion equation for mesh smoothing. The continuous Laplace operator of the diffusion equation is approximated using second differences computed on the mesh. By contrast, in our algorithm the heat equation is controlled by the discretely defined Laplacian graph. Stated succinctly, our algorithm uses graph-spectral methods to solve the heat equation where flow is controlled by the discrete

Laplacian, and Desbrun et al use robust numerical difference methods to solve the continuous heat equation on a mesh.

Although the diffusion method developed in this paper is motivated in terms of a heat diffusion process on a graph, it can also be viewed as a low-pass filter acting in the frequency domain. As a result, when viewed from the perspective of signal processing, our approach represents an extension of Fourier analysis to images (signals) defined on graphs. This connection is based on the observation that the classical Fourier analysis of signals defined in certain continuous domains can be regarded as the decomposition of the signal into a linear combination of the eigenvectors of the graph Laplacian (Coifman, 2006). The eigenvalues correspond to the frequencies of the eigenfunctions. Thus, the heat kernel can be viewed as a low-pass filter that enhances the low frequencies and attenuates higher ones. This idea has alson been used for surface mesh smoothing in (Taubin, 1995). Moreover, the present algorithm also has a close relationship with spectral clustering methods (Shi, 2000) (Belkin, 2003). These methods embed a graph represention of proximity data in the low-dimensional space spanned by the first few eigenvectors of the graph Laplacian, and then partition the data in this low-dimensional space. Since the long time behavior of the heat kernel is also governed by the first few eigenvectors of the graph Laplacian, image segments will appear in the smoothed image with a long time diffusion of our algorithm. As a consequence, our diffusion algorithm can smooth images while preserving region structure.

A preliminary version of the work reported here first appeared in (Zhang, 2005) (Zhang, 2006). This paper develops our early work in a number of ways. First, we provide a deeper theoretical analysis of the heat kernel smoothing and its relationship to alternatives. Second, the experimental study and comparison with alternative methods is more extensive.

The paper is organized as follows. In Section 2, we cover the background material on diffusion-based approaches to image smoothing, and also review the applications of the graph Laplacian in image analysis. Section 3 presents our graph-spectral method for image smoothing and provides implementation details. In Section 4, we theoretically analyse the properties of the proposed algorithm by establishing relationships between our method and alternative algorithms. In Section 5, we experimentally illustrate the effectiveness of the method and compare it with several state of the art methods. Finally, we conclude the paper in Section 6.

2. PRIOR WORK

This section first discusses diffusion-based approaches to image smoothing which provide the prerequisitesfor our method. We then review the applications of the graph Laplacian for image analysis and its relationship with the Laplace-Beltrami operator for a continuous manifold.

2.1 Anisotropic Diffusion for Image Smoothing

For a given noisy image $I\left(x\right) : \copyright \subset R^2 \to R$, we consider the following general diffusion equation

$$\frac{\partial u}{\partial t} = \text{div}\left(D \cdot \nabla u\right) \qquad (1)$$

with the boundary condition u(x,0)=I(x). Here D is the diffusivity that describes the rate of diffusion in different directions. If the diffusion process is isotropic, then D is constant. Setting $D = 1$ for all directions of ∇u, the diffusion equation reduces to the well-known heat equation

$$\frac{\partial u}{\partial t} = \nabla u \qquad (2)$$

where ∇ is the Laplace operator. Equation 2 possesses the unique solution

$$u\left(x,t\right) = \begin{cases} I\left(x\right) & (x \in R^2, t = 0) \\ \dfrac{1}{4\pi t} \displaystyle\int_{R^2} e^{-\frac{|x-y|^2}{4t}} I(y)dy & (x, y \in R^2, t > 0) \end{cases}$$

$$(3)$$

At this point we note that if we smooth the image I(x) with a Gaussian filter

$$G\left(x, \tilde{A}\right) = \frac{1}{2\grave{A}\tilde{A}^2} e^{-\frac{|x|^2}{4\tilde{A}^2}}$$

with width or standard deviation σ, then

$$G\left(x, \tilde{A}\right) * I\left(x\right) = \int_{R^2} G(x - y, \tilde{A})I(y)dy, \quad x, y \in R^2.$$

Thus, a linear isotropic diffusion at time t is equivalent to Gaussian filtering with spatial width $\sqrt{2t}$ (Koenderink, 1984) (Babaud, 1986). Since Equation 2 sets D to be constant for all gradient directions, it is isotropic and has a uniform blurring effect at all image locations. Hence, while the region interiors are smoothed, their boundaries are blurred.

Based on these observations, Perona and Malik (Perona, 1990) suggested an alternative definition of diffusion. Their idea is to halt the heat-flow process at object boundaries. To do this they control the diffusivity D using the magnitude of the image gradient by letting $D = g\left(\nabla u\right)$. When the gradient is large, which indicates the existence of a likely edge, the value of D is small. When the gradient is small, on the other hand, the value of D is large. Substituting this definition of diffusivity into Equation 2 results in the anisotropic diffusion equation

$$\frac{\partial u}{\partial t} = \text{div}\Big(g\big(\nabla u\big)\nabla u\Big) \tag{4}$$

where

$$g = e^{-\frac{\nabla u^2}{k^2}}$$

or

$$g = \frac{1}{1 + \frac{\nabla u^2}{k^2}}$$

The method is demonstrated to outperform Gaussian blurring, preserving boundary sharpness and location. There has been a considerable body of work aimed at understanding the mathematical properties, numerical implementation and stability of the Perona- Malik method. For instance, You et al. (You, 1996) formulated the anisotropic diffusion equation as an optimization problem. Black et al. (Black, 1998) showed that anisotropic diffusion is equivalent to a robust estimation procedure. Gilboa et al. (Gilboa, 2004) generalised anisotropic diffusion to the complex domain. Unfortunately, the Perona-Malik model is ill-posed since it not only has forward diffusion for noise removal, but also involves backward diffusion in the proximity of intensity discontinuities (Catte, 1992) (Alvarez, 1992). To avoid these problems, Catte et al. (Catte, 1992) proposed a regularization method that is both robust to noise and has a unique smooth solution. Instead of evaluating the diffusivity D in Equation 1 using the exact intensity gradient, they use the gradient computed from

a pre-filtered image. Hence, they set $D = g\big(\nabla u_{\tilde{A}}\big)$ where $\nabla u_{\tilde{A}} = \nabla\big(G_{\tilde{A}}*u\big)$ is the well-known Canny edge operator (Canny, 1986).

Based on the idea of the P-M method, a more general formulation of anisotropic diffusion was proposed by Weickert (Weickert, 1998), who considers D in Equation (1) as a diffusion tensor (a 2×2 positive symmetric definite matrix), instead of a scalar-valued diffusivity. This model not only takes into account the modulus of the edge detector $\nabla u_{\tilde{A}}$, but also its direction. To do this, they construct an orthonormal system of eigenvectors $\frac{3}{4}_1$, $\frac{3}{4}_2$ for the diffusion tensor D according to the estimated edge structure: $\frac{3}{4}_1 \parallel \nabla u_{\tilde{A}}$, $\frac{3}{4}_1 \perp \nabla u_{\tilde{A}}$. Several schemes have been introduced to select the eigenvalues of D for specific tasks (Cottet, 1993) (Weickert, 1998) (Weickert, 1999). For instance, in order to encourage smoothing along the edge over smoothing across it, Weickert (Weickert, 1998) choose the corresponding eigenvalues to be $^3{}_1 = g\big(\big\|\nabla u_{\tilde{A}}\big\|^2\big)$, $^3{}_2 = 1$.

2.2 The Graph Laplacian

The diffusion process on a graph is captured by the heat equation, which is determined by the graph Laplacian (the degree matrix minus the adjacency matrix). Thus, the graph Laplacian plays the most important role in our diffusion algorithm. It has been widely studied by spectral graph theory (Chung, 1997) (Cvetkovic, 1995) which is a branch of mathematics that is concerned with characterising the structural properties of graphs using the eigenvalues and eigenvectors of the adjacency or Laplacian matrices. Recently, one of the most important applications of spectral graph theory in image analysis and pattern recognition has been to use the Fiedler vector (the eigenvector associated with the second smallest eigenvalue of the graph

Laplacian) for the purposes of data-clustering (Sarkar, 1996) (Shi, 2000) (Belkin, 2003). Perhaps the best known example is Shi andMalik's normalised cut method for image segmentation (Shi, 2000). Here, the idea is to characterise the similarity of image pixels using a weight matrix, from which the Laplacian matrix of the associated weighted graph is computed. The bi-partition of the graph that minimises the normalised cut is located using the Fiedler eigenvector of the Laplacian matrix. Belkin and Niyogi (Belkin, 2003) partition data by embedding high-dimensional data into a low dimensional space using the first few eigenvectors of the graph Laplacian. However, the Laplacian spectrum is a rich source of information and also lends itself to a diverse set of problems including routing analysis (Atkins, 1998) and information retrieval (Azary, 2001). In our algorithm, the heat kernel describes heat flow with time across the edges of a graph, so it is a compact representation of the distribution of path lengths on a graph. It can be used to describe the continuous time random walk on a graph, and determines both the hitting and commute times of the discrete time random walk (Kondor, 2002).

There is a close relationship between the discrete graph Laplacian and the continuous manifold Laplace-Beltrami operator. It has been well known for some time that as the number of sample points or nodes increases, then the discrete operator converges towards the continuous one (Zucker, 1978). Belkin and Niyogi (Belkin, 2003) consider the conditions under which the graph Laplacian of a point cloud approaches the Laplace-Beltrami operator. Hein et al. (Hein, 2005) present a more recent analysis of convergence which draws on the concept of pointwise consistency. Their analysis considers both the variance and bias of the estimate of continuous Laplace-Beltrami operator provided by the discrete Laplacian when particular choices of the adjacency weight matrix are made. In fact, an image is a two-dimensional manifold embedded in three-dimensional (five-dimensional) space for gray-scale images (color images) (Sochen,

1998). Thus, the graph representation of the image can be considered as the discrete mesh of the manifold, and the graph Laplacian converges to the continuous Laplace- Beltrami operator of the manifold. As a result, our discrete diffusion has a close connection with the continuous anisotropic diffusion.

3. A GRAPH SPECTRAL APPROACH TO ANISOTROPIC DIFFUSION

This section describes the algorithm in three stages. These are:

1. Representing an image as a weighted undirected graph
2. Establishing and solving the diffusion equation
3. Practical details of implementation

3.1 Graph Representation

To commence, we represent a gray-scale or color image using a weighted undirected graph $G = (V,E)$ with node (vertex) set V and edge set $E \subseteq V \times V$. The nodes V of the graph are the pixels of the image. An edge, denoted by $e_{ij} \in E$, exists if the corresponding pair of pixel sites satisfies the connectivity requirement on the pixel lattice. The weight of an edge, e_{ij}, is denoted by $w(i, j)$. The edge weights play an important role in our graph-based diffusion method, since they control the flow of heat across the graph. If the edge weight $w(i, j)$ is large, then heat can flow easily between nodes v_i and v_j. By contrast, if $w(i, j)$ is small, it is difficult for heat to flow from v_i to v_j, i.e., a weight of zero means that heat may not flow along the edge.

In order to represent the image structure by a graph without losing information, we must define a function that maps changes in the image data to edge weights. This is a common feature of all graph-based algorithms for image analysis (Shi,

2000) (Grady, 2005). Here, for simplicity we choose the Gaussian weighting function which is the most popular one used to characterize the relationship between different pixels. More detailed discussion concerning the edge weights and a more sophisticated method for computing them will be given in Section 3.3. If we encode the intensities of the image as a column vector $\bar{I}$ via sequential row or column raster ordering of the image pixels, then we compute the edge weight by

$$
w\left(i,j\right) =
\begin{cases}
\exp\left(-\dfrac{d^{2}\left(i,j\right)}{k^{2}}\right) & \textit{if}\, X\left(i\right) - X(j)_{2} \leq r, \\
0 & \textit{otherwise,}
\end{cases}
$$

$$(5)$$

where X(i) is the location of pixel i, r is the distance threshold between two neighbouring pixels which controls the local connectivity of the graph, and $d\left(i,j\right) = \left|\bar{I}\left(i\right) - \bar{I}(j)\right|$ is the difference between the intensities $\bar{I}\left(i\right)$ and $\bar{I}\left(i\right)$ of the two adjacent pixels indexed i and j. To adapt the parameter κ to images of different contrast, we normalize the distances d to span the interval [0, 1] before application of Equation 5. In other words, we set the minimum distance to be 0 and the maximum distance to be 1, and rescale the intermediate values accordingly. In the case of color images or general vector-valued data, then

$$
d\left(i,j\right) = \sqrt{\left[\bar{I}\left(i\right) - \bar{I}\left(j\right)\right]^{T}\left[\bar{I}\left(i\right) - \bar{I}\left(j\right)\right]}
$$

For images with low levels of noise, we believe that Equation 5 can efficiently characterise the intensity changes in the image data. That is to say, w(i, j) is large when pixels i and j belong to the same region, and w(i, j) is small if they are from different regions. However, in the case of images corrupted by high levels of noise, it introduces very large oscillations of brightness values for pixels from the same region. Thus, in this case most of the small weights w(i, j) are due to the noise rather than the feature differences. As in the P-M model, this will also prevent our method from efficiently removing noise. In the literature (Catte, 1992) (Alvarez, 1992) (Weickert, 1999), the Gaussian filter is widely used as a regularization operator to improve the performance of nonlinear diffusion-based smoothing methods. In order to do so, they convolve the image with a Gaussian filter before the gradient is calculated, i.e., the gradient $\left|\nabla u\right|$ is replaced by its smoothed estimate $\left|\nabla u_{\tilde{A}}\right|$. Following (Catte, 1992) (Alvarez, 1992) (Weickert, 1999), we compute the intensity difference of noise contaminated images using

$$
d_{\tilde{A}}\left(i,j\right) = \left|\bar{I}_{\tilde{A}}\left(i\right) - \bar{I}_{\tilde{A}}\left(i\right)\right|
$$

$$(6)$$

where $\bar{I}_{\tilde{A}} = G_{\tilde{A}} * \bar{I}$

3.2 Graph Smoothing

Since we wish to adopt a graph-spectral approach, we make use of the weighted adjacency matrix W for the graph G where the elements are W(i, j) = w(i, j). We also construct the diagonal degree matrix T with entries $T\left(i,i\right) = \deg\left(i\right) = \sum_{j \in V} w(i,j)$.

From the degree matrix and the weighted adjacency matrix we construct the combinatorial Laplacian matrix L = T − W, whose elements are

$$
L\left(i,j\right) =
\begin{cases}
T\left(i,i\right) - w\left(i,i\right) & \textit{if}\, i = j, \\
-w\left(i,j\right) & \textit{if}\, e_{ij} \in E, \\
0 & \textit{otherwise.}
\end{cases}
$$

$$(7)$$

The spectral decomposition of the Laplacian is $L = \mid \rangle \mid^{T}$, where $\rangle = \mathrm{diag}(»_{1}, »_{2}, \cdots, »_{|V|})$ is the diagonal matrix with the eigenvalues ordered according to increasing magnitude ($0 = \lambda 1 < \lambda 2 \leq \lambda 3 \ldots$) as diagonal elements and $\mid = (\phi_{1} \mid \phi_{2} \cdots \mid \phi_{|V|})$ is the matrix with the correspondingly ordered eigenvectors as columns. Since L is symmetric and positive semi-definite, the eigenvalues of the Laplacian are all non-negative. The eigenvector $\varphi 2$ associated with the smallest non-zero eigenvalue $\lambda 2$ is referred to as the Fiedler-vector.

As noted by Chung (Chung, 1997), we can view the graph Laplacian L as an operator L over the set of real-valued functions $f : V \mapsto R$ such that, for a pair of nodes, i and $j \in V$, we have

$$Lf(i) = \sum_{e_{ij \in E}} \left(f(i) - f(j) \right) W(i, j) \qquad (8)$$

In matrix form the heat equation on a graph associated with the Laplacian L is (Chung, 1997) (Chung, 2000) (Kondor, 2002)

$$\frac{\partial H_{t}}{\partial t} = -LH_{t} \qquad (9)$$

where the $|v| \times |V|$ matrix Ht is the heat kernel and t is time. The heat kernel encapsulates information concerning the path length distribution on the graph. The definition of the heat kernel for graphs is exactly the parallel of the heat kernel for Riemannianmanifolds (Chavel, 1984). Recently, the heat kernel has been widely used in machine learning for dimensionality reduction, semi-supervised learning and data clustering (Kondor, 2002) (Belkin, 2003) (Lafon, 2004) (Coifman, 2006). The heat kernel can hence be viewed as describing the flow of heat across the edges of the graph with time, where the rate of flow is determined by the Laplacian of the graph.

The heat kernel satisfies the initial condition H0 = I|V| where I|V| is the $|V| \times |V|$ identity matrix. The solution to the heat equation is found by exponentiating the Laplacian matrix with time t, i.e.

$$H_{t} = e^{-tL} = I - tL + \frac{t^{2}}{2!}L^{2} - \frac{t^{3}}{3!}L^{3} + \cdots \qquad (10)$$

If we express the Laplacian using its eigenspectrum, i.e $L = \mid \rangle \mid^{T}$, and substitute it into the second equality of Equation 10, we have

$$H_{t} = \mid e^{-t\rangle} \mid^{T} \qquad (11)$$

The heat kernel is a $|V| \times |V|$ symmetric matrix. For the nodes i and j of the graph G the resulting element is

$$H_{t}(i, j) = \sum_{k=1}^{|V|} e^{-»_{k}t} \phi_{k}(i) \phi_{k}(j) \qquad (12)$$

When t tends to zero, then Ht ; I − Lt, i.e. the heat kernel depends on the local connectivity structure or topology of the graph. Since the Laplacian L encodes the local structure of a graph, it dominates the heat-kernel at small time. If, on the other hand, t is large, then $H_{t} = e^{-»_{2}t} \phi_{2} \phi_{2}^{T}$ where $\lambda 2$ is the smallest non-zero eigenvalue and $\varphi 2$ is the associated eigenvector, i.e. the Fiedler vector. Hence, the large time behavior is governed by the global structure of the graph, which emerges in Ht as time t increases.

The value of Ht(i, j) decays exponentially with the weight w(i, j) of the edge eij. It is useful to consider the following picture of the heat diffusion process on graphs. Suppose we inject a unit amount of heat at a node l of a graph, and allow the heat to diffuse through the edges of the graph. The rate of diffusion along the edge eij is determined by its edge weight w(i, j). At time t, the sum of the column j of the heat kernel, i.e. $\sum_{k=1}^{|v|} H_t(k, j)$ can be interpreted as the amount of heat accumulated at node j. This process is illustrated by Figure 1.

In order to use the diffusion process to smooth a gray-scale image, we inject at each node an amount of heat energy equal to the intensity of the associated pixel. The heat initially injected at

Figure 1. Illustration of the heat diffusion on a graph. There are two synthetic segments in the graph which are separated by the dashed line. The weight of the edge within each segment is large, and the weight is small for the edges across two segments. (a) show the weight of each edge and the initial heat on each node. One of nodes has a unit amount of heat and the others are zero. (b), (c) and (d) show the heat accumulated at each node (conveyed by the heat kernel) at time t = 0.1, t = 0.5 and t = 3 respectively. Heat can easily diffuse within each segment, but it is difficult for heat to flow from one segment to the other.

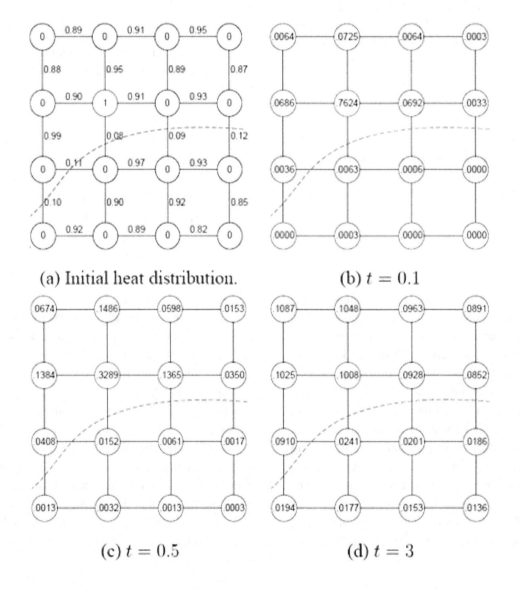

(a) Initial heat distribution.

(b) $t = 0.1$

(c) $t = 0.5$

(d) $t = 3$

each node diffuses through the graph edges as time t progresses. The edge weight plays the role of thermal conductivity. According to the edge weights determined from Equation 5, if two pixels belong to the same region, then the associated edge weight is large. As a result heat can flow easily between them. On the other hand, if two pixels belong to different regions, then the associated edge weight is very small, and hence it is difficult for heat to flow from one region to another, as shown in Figure 1. This heat diffusion process is again governed by the differential equation in Equation 9, however, the initial conditions are different. Now the initial heat residing at each vertex is determined by the corresponding pixel intensity. Thus, the evolution of the column vector $\bar{I}$ of pixel intensities for the image follows the equation

$$\begin{cases} \dfrac{\partial \bar{u}_t}{\partial t} = -L\, \bar{u}_t \\ \bar{u}_0 = \bar{I}, \end{cases} \qquad (13)$$

where $\bar{u}_t$ is a real-valued function, i.e. $\bar{u}(x,t) : V \times R \mapsto [0, 255]$, which means the intensity of the pixel x at time t. The solution of Equation 13 is

$$\bar{u}_t = e^{-tL}\, \bar{I} = H_t\, \bar{I} \qquad (14)$$

As a result the smoothed image intensity of pixel j at time t is

$$\bar{u}_t(j) = \sum_{i=1}^{|V|} \bar{I}(i) \times H_t(i, j) \qquad (15)$$

This is a measure of the total intensity to flow from the remaining nodes to node j during the elapsed time t. When t is small, we have $\bar{u}_t \cong (I - (D - W)t)\bar{I}$. Since each row i of the heat kernel Ht satisfies the conditions $0 \le Ht(i, j) \le 1$ for $\forall j$ and $\sum_{j=1}^{|V|} H_t(i, j) = 1$ the total integrated intensity over the set of pixels in the image is identical at all times.

In the case of color, or general vector-valued images, we let each component of the image diffuse separately on the graph constructed from the weighting function in Equation 5 using the Euclidean distances between color values. We thus apply Equation 13 to each of the three independent components (RGB in our case) of the color images, and this forms a system of three coupled heat equations. The coupling results from the fact that the edge weight or diffusivity of the graph depends on all the image channels. Most of the literature on diffusion-like PDEs for image denoising concerns gray-scale images. Extension of these regularisation PDEs to multivalued images also leads to a system of coupled equations for all the image channels (Sapiro, 1996) (Weickert, 1999) (Tschumperle, 2005). Most of the coupling schemes are formulated using the local geometry of the image via Di Zenzo's structure tensor (Di Zenzo, 1986). For instance, Sapiro et al. (Sapiro, 1996) used Di Zenzo's structure tensor (Di Zenzo, 1986) to compute image gradients and set up a system of coupled PDEs for all the image channels using the scalar diffusion technique in (Alvarez, 1992). Here the coupling is a result of the fact that the image gradient depends on all the components of the image. By contrast, in our graph smoothing method the coupling of the equations is realized by computing the graph edge weight using information conveyed by all the image channels.

3.3 Edge Weight

For the present algorithm, the choice of edge weights can significantly affect the extent to which discontinuities are preserved while eliminating noise. In (You, 1996), a detailed analysis of this behavior is given. There are several weighting methods used in the literature (Geman, 1984) (Smolka, 2001) (You, 1996) (Black, 1998) (Buades, 2005) (Coifman, 2006). For instance, Smolka et al. (Smolka, 2001) compute the weights using Gibbs distribution of the intensities for the adjacent pixels. A treatment based on robust statistics is described in (Black, 1998).

Although Section 3.1 provides a method to calculate the weight using intensity differences, this method is not robust to image noise. The reason for this is that it calculates the weight between two adjacent pixels using only the potential noisy intensities associated with them. We aim to use the noisy weight to restore the true intensity values. Hence, there is a chicken-and-egg problem here. A more reliable approach is to represent each pixel not only using the intensity of the pixel itself, but also using the intensities of the neighbouring pixels. Briefly, we characterise each pixel by a window of neighbors instead of using a single pixel alone. Thus, we can measure the similarity between two pixels using the windows surrounding them. This method of similarity measurement was first used for image denoising by Buades et al. (Buades, 2005), who proposed a non-local mean denoising algorithm that was demonstrated to produce results that compare favorably with state-of-the-art methods. The same measurement has recently also been used in the graph-based setting for multiscale image analysis and denoising using diffusion wavelets (Coifman, 2006). The window representation of pixels takes advantage of the high degree of redundancy in natural images. The basic idea is that pixel windows in neighbouring image region may be statistically very similar. Here, we simply use square windows of fixed size n. Figure 2 illustrates the square window representation of pixels and the similarities between them. Let Ni denote the window of pixel i, and the intensities within window Ni are encoded as a vector $\vec{N}_i$. Hence, we can measure the similarity between two pixels i and j using the Gaussian weighted Euclidean distance between the windows $\vec{N}_i$ and $\vec{N}_j$, i.e.,

$$d_{\tilde{A}}(i,j) = \left\|\vec{N}_i - \vec{N}_j\right\|_{2,\tilde{A}} = \left\|G_{\tilde{A}} * \vec{N}_i - \vec{N}_j\right\|_2 \qquad (16)$$

The Gaussian filter is used here to improve the stability of the distances to noise. Efros and Leung (Efros, 1999) showed that this distance is a reliable measure for the comparison of image windows in a texture patch. In fact, the regularized intensity difference in Equation 6 is a special case of Equation 16 with window size equal to 1, i.e. n = 1. The measurement in Equation 16 is well suited for removing additive white noise, and this type of noise alters the distance between windows in a uniform way (Buades, 2005), i.e.

$$E\left(\left\|\vec{N}_i - \vec{N}_j\right\|_{2,\tilde{A}}\right) = \left\|\underline{\vec{N}_i} - \vec{N}_j\right\|_{2,\tilde{A}} + 2\epsilon^2 \text{ where } E(\cdot)$$

is the expectation; $\underline{\vec{N}_i}$ is the window at i in the ground truth image; and ϵ^2 is the variance of the noise. This shows that the Gaussian weighted Euclidean distance preserves the order of similarity between pixels. So the most similar windows to Ni in the ground truth image are also expected to be the most similar windows to Ni in the noisy one. We thus choose to compute the edge weight using

Figure 2. Illustration of the window representation of pixels. w(i,j) is large because their neighbouring windows are similar to each other, although the intensity at pixel i may be different from that at pixel j due to the noise. On the other side w(i,l) is much smaller because their neighbouring windows are very different.

preserve fine detail and image structure, such as the hair and eyes.

3.4 Numerical Implementation

$$
w\left(i,j\right) =
\begin{cases}
\exp\left(-\dfrac{\left\|\bar{N}_i - \bar{N}_{j2,\tilde{A}}\right\|^2}{k^2}\right) & if\ \left\|X\left(i\right) - X(j)\right\|_2 \leq r,\ \dots \\
\quad 0 & otherwise.
\end{cases}
$$

$$(17)$$

Figure 3 shows a comparison of the performance of weighting function in Equation 5 and in Equation 17. The figure shows that our graph smoothing method with a large neighbourhood window for edge weight computation can better

A direct method to compute smoothed images from Equation 14 is to first compute the heat kernel and then perform matrix multiplication with the vectorised image $\bar{I}$. In practice the number of image pixels is large, e.g. 256 × 256 = 65536 pixels, so it is not tractable to calculate the heat kernel through computing the complete eigen-spectrum of the Laplacian matrix needed for matrix exponentiation (Golub, 1996) (Moler, 2003).

313

Figure 3. Illustration of the effectiveness of the weights calculated from neighbouring windows. (a): noisy image (b): graph smoothing using weights from Equation 5. (c): graph smoothing using neighbouring windows to compute weights from Equation 17 with window size n = 7. All other parameters are the same as in (b). The smoothed result in (c) better preserves the fine details than that in (b).

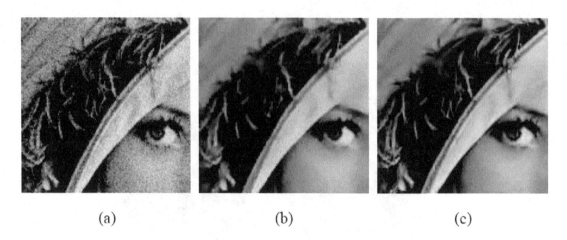

(a)   (b)   (c)

To overcome this problem, here we make use of the Krylov subspace projection technique (Saad, 1992) (Sidje, 1998) (v2003) (Hochbruck, 1997), which is an iterative method for sparse matrix problems. This allows us to compute the action of a matrix exponential operator on an operand vector, i.e. $e^{-tL}\,\vec{I}$, without having to compute explicitly the matrix exponential e^{-tL} in isolation. The underlying principal of the Krylov subspace technique is to approximate $\vec{u}_t = e^{tA}\,\vec{I} = e^{-tL}\,\vec{I}$ by an element of the Krylov subspace

$$K_m \equiv \mathrm{span}\left\{\vec{I}, (tA)\vec{I}, \cdots, (tA)^{m-1}\vec{I}\right\} \qquad (18)$$

where m is typically small compared to the order of L (usually $m \leq 50$, while the order of the principal matrix L can exceed many thousands). The approximation being used is

$$\vec{u}_t \approx {}^2 V_m e^{tH_m} \ddot{A}_1 \qquad (19)$$

where $\ddot{A}_1$ is the first column of identity matrix Im; Vm and Hm are, respectively, the orthonormal basis of the Krylov subspace Km and the upper Hessenberg matrix resulting from the well-known Arnoldi process (Saad, 1992) (Golub, 1996). Thus, the initial large but sparse e^{tA} problem in Equation 14 is reduced to a much smaller but dense e^{tH_m} problem in Equation 19 which is computationally more desirable. For our local connected graphs, the Laplacian matrix L is symmetric, positive-definite and very sparse with few circulant nonzero elements in each row. As a result, the above Arnoldi process can be replaced by the Lanczos process which decreases the computational complexity and saves CPU time (Saad, 1992) (Sidje, 1998). Moreover, Krylov subspace methods may be efficiently parallelized (Saad, 1989).

Obviously, solving Equation 14 is the main computational bottleneck for the algorithm and requires the greatest time. The implementation of the Krylov subspace method for solving Equation 14 in this paper relies on the MATLAB subroutines from the Expokit package (Sidje, 1998). Tests on a PC with an Intel P4 2.8GHZ CPU and 1.5GB of memory show that it requires approximately 3: 6 seconds to solve Equation 14 for the Laplacian matrix of a 4-connected or 8-connected graph with 256×256 nodes.

3.4.1 Continuous vs. Discrete Scale

Although we have presented the exact solution of our diffusion Equation 13, there also exists a discrete approximation of the diffusion equation, as is the case with all diffusion-based PDE methods. If we discretise the time (or scale) t of Equation 13, we obtain the following discrete version of our continuous diffusion process

$$\overset{k+1}{\vec{u}} = \left(I - \varphi L \right) \overset{k}{\vec{u}} \qquad (20)$$

where $\varphi > 0$ is the time step size. The discrete version in Equation 20 converges to the continuous diffusion process in Equation 13 for small φ. It is sometimes difficult to set the step size φ and construct the graph efficiently enough to update graph Laplacian over many time steps. Hence, we choose the exact solution for continuous time in our implementation.

3.5 Algorithm Summary

To summarise, the steps of the algorithm are:

1. Use Equation 17 to generate edge weights of the graph for a gray-scale or color image and encode the image intensities (or each channel of a color image) as a long-vector $\vec{I}$

2. Compute $\vec{u}_t$ from Equation 14 at time t for a gray-scale image (or each channel of a color image) using the Krylov subspace technique.

3. Unpack the resulting vector $\vec{u}_t$ to recover the smoothed image.

4. ANALYSIS OF THE ALGORITHM

In this section, we analyse different the properties of our algorithm. We commence by theoretically discussing the relationship of our graph smoothing algorithm to classical Gaussian filtering in detail. We then establish relationships with the standard methods of anisotropic diffusion, Fourier domain signal processing and spectral clustering.

4.1 Relationship to Gaussian Filtering

We commence by demonstrating that the proposed graph-spectral smoothing method has a close relationship with Gaussian smoothing. The idea here is based on the work in (Belkin, 2003) which connects the Laplace-Beltrami operator on a manifold with the corresponding graph Laplacian through the heat kernel on a manifold.

Let an image I(x), $x \in \Omega \subset R2$ evolve under Equation 2 with the initial condition u(x, 0) = I(x). At time t the solution is $u(x, t) = \int_{\odot} \ddot{} (x - y, t) I(y) dy$ where $\ddot{} (x, t) = \frac{1}{4 \varphi t} e^{-\frac{|x|^2}{4t}}$ is the Green's function of Equation 2. For time t = 0, we have

$$
\begin{aligned}
\Delta u(x, 0) &= \Delta I(x) = \left(\frac{\partial u}{\partial t} \right) t = 0 \\
&= \left\{ \frac{\partial}{\partial t} \left[\int_{\odot} \ddot{} (x - y, t) I(y) dy \right] \right\}_{t=0}
\end{aligned}
\qquad (21)
$$

From the above equation, we have

$$\Delta I\left(x\right) \approx$$

$$\frac{1}{t}\left[\int_\mathbb{C}^{\cdot\cdot}\left(x-y,t\right)I\left(y\right)dy - \lim_{t\to 0}\int_\mathbb{C}^{\cdot\cdot}\left(x-y,t\right)I\left(y\right)dy\right] \qquad (22)$$

Since $\lim_{t\to 0}\int_{|x|<r}^{\cdot\cdot}\left(x,t\right)dx = 1$ for any $r > 0$ (Grigor'yan, 2005), $\lim_{t\to 0}^{\cdot\cdot}\left(x,t\right)$ is an approximation of the identity (or Dirac function). Hence,

$$\lim_{t\to 0}\int_\mathbb{C}^{\cdot\cdot}\left(x-y,t\right)I\left(y\right)dy = I\left(x\right) \qquad (23)$$

Let $x1, x2,..., xk$ be points in the image domain Ω. If we combine Equations 23 and 22, we have

$$\Delta I\left(x\right) \approx \frac{1}{t}\left\{\int_\mathbb{C}^{\cdot\cdot}\left(x-y,t\right)I\left(y\right)dy - I(x)\right\} \qquad (24)$$

As a result, Equation 24 can be discretised in the following

$$^{\cdot\cdot}\left(x,t\right) = \frac{1}{4\grave{A}t}e^{-\frac{|x|^2}{4t}}$$

$$\Delta I\left(x_i\right) \approx \frac{1}{t}\left\{\frac{1}{4\grave{A}tk}\sum_{\substack{x_j \\ |x_i-x_j|\le r}}e^{-\frac{|x_i-x_j|^2}{4t}}I\left(x_j\right) - I\left(x_i\right)\right\} \qquad (25)$$

The above equation is defined for any function $I(x)$. If we let $I(x)$ be a constant, that is $\Delta I(x) = 0$, then from Equation 25 we have

$$4\grave{A}tk = \sum_{\substack{x_j \\ |x_i-x_j|\le r}}e^{-\frac{|x_i-x_j|^2}{4t}} \qquad (26)$$

Substituting Equation 26 into Equation 25, we have

$$\Delta I\left(x_i\right) \approx \frac{1}{4\grave{A}t^2 k}\left\{\sum_{\substack{x_j \\ |x_i-x_j|\le r}}e^{-\frac{|x_i-x_j|^2}{4t}}(I\left(x_j\right)-I(x_i))\right\} \qquad (27)$$

Since t is an infinitesimal and k is very large, it is reasonable to set $t = \frac{1}{\sqrt{4\grave{A}k}}$, that is $\frac{1}{4\grave{A}t^2 k} = 1$. Hence, if we let the graph edge weight function w be

$$w\left(i,j\right) = \begin{cases} e^{-\frac{x_i-x_j^2}{4t}} & if\, x_i - x_{j2} \le r, \\ 0 & otherwise, \end{cases}$$

then from Equation 27, $L\bar{L}\bar{I}\left(x\right) \approx \Delta I\left(x\right)$. In other words, the graph Laplacian L on a function defined on G is an efficient approximation of the continuous Laplace operator Δ on the corresponding function defined on $\Omega \subset R2$ (Here, G is a mesh of the continuous domain Ω.). Thus, the heat diffusion on graphs with edge weight given by Equation 28 is equivalent to isotropic diffusion (Gaussian smoothing) on images.

Figure 4. Illustration of the surface representation of images. An image (left) can be considered as a 2D surface (right) embedded in 3D space.

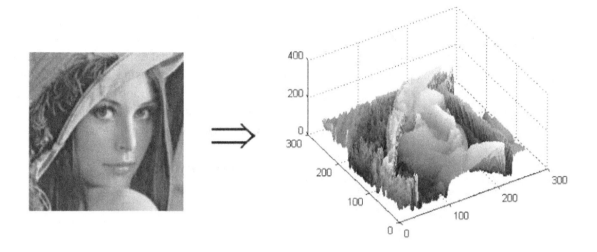

4.2 Relationship to Anisotropic Diffusion

We now turn our attention to the relationship between the continuous nonlinear PDE methods and our framework of graph-spectral smoothing. Because isotropic diffusion does not consider the geometry of an image, it blurs features while smoothing out noise. In our method, the geometry of the image is captured by the weight and connectivity structure of the graph representation. A gray-scale image I can be regarded as a two-dimensional manifold M embedded in R3 (Sochen, 1998), i.e.

$$X : \left(x^1, x^2\right) \in \mathbb{C} \subset R^2 \rightarrow \\ \left(x^1, x^2, I\left(x^1, x^2\right)\right) \in M \subset R^3 \qquad (29)$$

This is demonstrated in Figure 4. The 2×2 metric tensor J of the manifold M is given by

$$J = \begin{pmatrix} 1 + I_{x^1}^2 & I_{x^1} I_{x^2} \\ I_{x^1} I_{x^2} & 1 + I_{x^2}^2 \end{pmatrix} \qquad (30)$$

where $I_{x^1} = \dfrac{\partial I}{\partial x^1}$

We can thus regard the graph representation of the image as a discrete mesh of the manifold. Based on the idea in Section 4.1, if we set the edge weight between two nodes i and j (corresponding to two points $x_i = \left(x_i^1, x_i^2, I\left(x_i^1, x_i^2\right)\right)$ and $x_j = \left(x_j^1, x_j^2, I\left(x_j^1, x_j^2\right)\right)$ on M) as

$$w\left(i, j\right) = \\ \begin{cases} e^{-\frac{\|x_i - x_j\|^2}{4t}} = e^{\left(x_i^1 - x_j^1\right)^2 + \left(x_i^2 - x_j^2\right)^2 + \left(I\left(x_i^1, x_i^2\right) - I\left(x_j^1, x_j^2\right)\right)^2} \\ 0 \qquad\qquad\qquad\qquad\qquad\qquad\text{otherwise,} \end{cases} \\ \text{if } \|x_i - x_j\|_2 \le r \qquad (31)$$

then the graph Laplacian converges to the continuous Laplace-Beltrami operator $\triangle M$ of the manifold M. Thus, our graph-based diffusion process in Equation 13 converges to the following continuous heat equation on the manifold M

$$\frac{\partial f}{\partial t} = -\Delta_M f \qquad (32)$$

where f is a function defined on M, i.e. f(x, t): M × R → R, with initial condition f(x, 0) = I(x). The Laplace-Beltrami operator for M is defined as (Rosenberg, 1997)

$$\Delta_M f = -\sum_{k=1}^{2}\sum_{l=1}^{2} \frac{1}{\sqrt{|J|}} \partial_k \left(\sqrt{|J|} J^{kl} \partial_l f\right) \qquad (33)$$

where |J| is the determinant of J; J_{ij} are the components of the inverse of the metric tensor J and $\partial_k = \frac{\partial}{\partial x^k}$. If we substitute Equation 30 and Equation 33 into Equation 32, we have the following diffusion equation

$$\frac{\partial f}{\partial t} = \frac{1}{\sqrt{1 + |\Delta I|^2}} \operatorname{div}\left(D \Delta f\right) \qquad (34)$$

where ∇ and div are the gradient and divergence operators defined on R2, and the diffusion tensor D is given by

$$D = \sqrt{|J| J^{-1}} = \frac{1}{\sqrt{1 + |\Delta I|^2}} \begin{pmatrix} 1 + I_{x^1}^2 & -I_{x^1} I_{x^2} \\ -I_{x^1} I_{x^2} & 1 + I_{x^2}^2 \end{pmatrix} \qquad (35)$$

Thus, for the choice of weights in Equation 31, our algorithm has a similar formulation to continuous PDE methods in the literature (Weickert, 1998). However, for a different choice of graph representation, e.g. using the weighting method in Equation 17, it is difficult to formulate our graph diffusion explicitly using a continuous PDE in terms of a diffusion tensor. This is because it may not be easy to analyse the geometry of the underlying graph in this case. Although our method evolves a linear equation on a graph representation of an image, it is a highly non-linear analysis of the image in the original spatial coordinates in R2. Thus, we recast the problem of finding a sophisticated diffusion-based nonlinear PDE for image smoothing to that of finding a faithful representation of the image using a weighted graph. It is often easier to find a graph representation that preserves image structures than to find a diffusion tensor for an equivalent continuous PDE.

4.3 A Signal Processing View of the Algorithm

The present algorithm can also be understood in terms of Fourier analysis, which is a natural tool for image smoothing. An image (a function defined on R^2) normally contains a mixture of different frequency components. The low frequency components are regarded as the image content, and the high frequency components as the noise content. From the signal processing viewpoint, our approach is an extension of the Fourier analysis to images (signals) defined on graphs. This is based on the observation that the classical Fourier analysis of signals defined in a continuous domain can be seen as the decomposition of the signal into a linear combination of the eigenvectors of the graph Laplacian. The eigenvalues of the Laplacian represent the frequencies of the eigenfunctions. As the frequency (eigenvalue) increases, then so the corresponding eigenvector changes more rapidly from vertex to vertex. This idea has been used for surface mesh smoothing in (Taubin, 1995).

The image $\vec{I}$ defined on the graph G can be decomposed into a linear combination of the eigenvectors of the graph Laplacian L, i.e.

$$\vec{I} = \sum_{k=1}^{|v|} a_k \Phi_k \qquad (36)$$

To smooth the image using Fourier analysis, the terms associated with the high frequency eigenvectors should be discarded. However, because the Laplacian L is very large even for a small image, it is too computationally expensive to calculate all the terms and the associated eigenvectors in Equation 36. An alternative is to estimate the projection of the image onto the subspace spanned by the low frequency eigenvectors, as is the case with most of the low-pass filters. We wish to pass low frequencies, but attenuate the high frequencies. According to the heat kernel picture in Figure 5, the function e^{-tx} acts as a transfer function of the filter such that $e^{-tx} \approx 1$ for low frequencies, and $e^{-tx} \approx 0$ for high frequencies. This is illustrated in Figure 5. As the value of t increases, then the transfer function becomes steeper. Thus, the graph heat kernel can be regarded as a low-pass filter kernel.

4.4 Relationship to Spectral Clustering

Spectral clustering has proved to be a powerful tool for image segmentation (Shi, 2000), and, data analysis and clustering (Weiss, 1999) (Belkin, 2003). In its simplest form it uses the second eigenvector (Fidler eigenvector) of the graph Laplacian matrix constructed from the weighted affinity graph for the sample points to obtain a bi-partition of the samples into two groups (Shi, 2000). Often, instead of considering only the second eigenvector, one uses the first k eigenvectors (for some small number k) simultaneously to obtain a multi-partition into several sets (Weiss, 1999) (Belkin, 2003).

In the present algorithm, the heat kernel reduces the effect of the large eigenvalues to zero as time t increases (see Figure 5). As mentioned in Section 3.2, if t is large the behavior of the heat

Figure 5. Graph of the transfer function e^{-tx} with different values of t

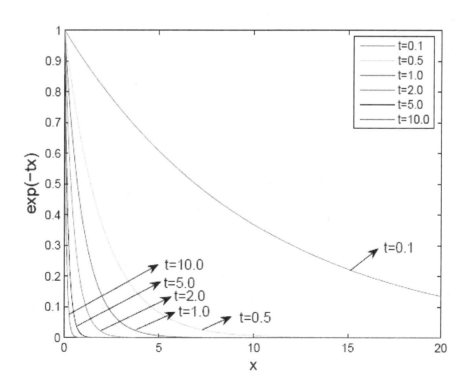

kernel is governed by the second eigenvector of the graph Laplacian, i.e. $H_t \cong I - e^{-t\lambda_2}\varnothing_2\varnothing_2^T$. To smooth an image, the algorithm then projects the noisy image onto the space spanned by the first few eigenvectors. This process has a similar effect to spectral clustering algorithms (Weiss, 1999) (Shi, 2000) (Belkin, 2003). Thus, our smoothing method is structure preserving due to the fact that the first few eigenvectors of the Laplacian encode the region-structure of the image.

5. EXPERIMENTS

In this section, we provide experimental results of applying the graph-spectral smoothing method to a variety of image data. We also give qualitative and quantitative comparisons with several state of the art methods. In our experiments (implemented using MATLAB), we simply use 8-connected graphs to represent all images (except Figure 10). We choose neighbouring windows with fixed size 5×5 to compute the edge weights from Equation 17. Although graphs with larger connectivity and windows with larger size (Buades, 2005) may improve the performance of the algorithm, they require more CPU time.

There are three free parameters that depends on different images. These are σ of Equation 16, κ of Equation 17 and the optimal diffusion stopping time t_s. Here, we consider how to regulate these three parameters. First, the choice of σ depends on the level of noise in the image to be smoothed. In our examples, we contaminate the images using independent and identically distributed (IID) additive zero-mean Gaussian noise. We find that setting σ equal to half the standard deviation of the zero-mean additive noise works well. Second, the method for choosing the value of κ for computing edge weights is similar to that used in (Perona, 1990) (Shi, 2000). Since the exponential function decreases rapidly, it makes significant differences in the weights (diffusivity)

between intra-region edges and inter-region edges. The parameter κ has the effect of controlling the degree of anisotropy and the velocity of the diffusion process. Since we normalize the value of $d_\sigma(i, j)$ before applying Equation 17, the value of κ is usually set in the interval 0.05: 0.15. Third, the optimal stopping time t_s is chosen manually in our experiments. Empirically, the optimal smoothed result is achieved with a small diffusion time (< 10). We have investigated the effect of the parameters on the smoothing process. To do this we have added noise to the standard Lenna and Barbara images. We have then computed the RMS error as a function of κ and t. The results of doing this are shown in Figure 6; the left-hand plot is for the Lenna image and the right-hand plot is for the Barbara image. The main feature to note from these plots is that the lowest RMS values are obtained with a large value of κ and a small value of t. As κ is decreased, then so t must be increased to compensate. For a particular choice of κ, there is an optimal value of t that must be chosen to give the lowest RMS error.

5.1 Gray-Scale Case

The top row of Figure 7 shows the result of applying graph smoothing on the standard House image. The algorithm preserves fine structures while removing noise. Because the image has periodic patterns, the performance of the algorithm can hence be improved with a larger connectivity graph (large value of r in Equation 17). The reason is as follows. For images with repeated texture, the neighbourhoods are very similar (Buades, 2005). Thus, each pixel not only acquires support from its neighbouring pixels, but also from non-local pixels. The middle row of Figure 7 gives the result of processing an MRI slice of a head with complex structures. This example demonstrates that the graph smoothing can work well on images with low intensity contrast. The image in the bottom row of Figure 7 is a portion of the standard Baboon with complicated skin textures.

Figure 6. RMS errors at different values of t and κ. Case (a): smoothing the standard Lenna image with additive noise. Case (b): smoothing the standard Barbara image with additive noise.

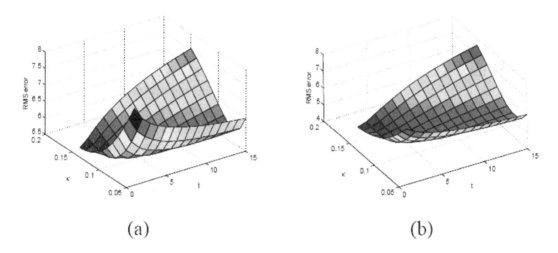

(a)   (b)

Figure 7. Column (a): noisy images- standard house (top), MRI image of a head (middle) and a part of the standard baboon (bottom); (b): smoothed results- The parameters for the top image is t = 3, κ = 0.15, σ = 0.7, middle image t = 3, κ = 0.09, σ = 0, and bottom image t = 3, κ = 0.12, σ = 0.7. All three examples are filtered using window size 5×5 and 8-connected graphs. (c): zoomed portions of the noisy images (d): corresponding zoomed portions of the smoothed images.

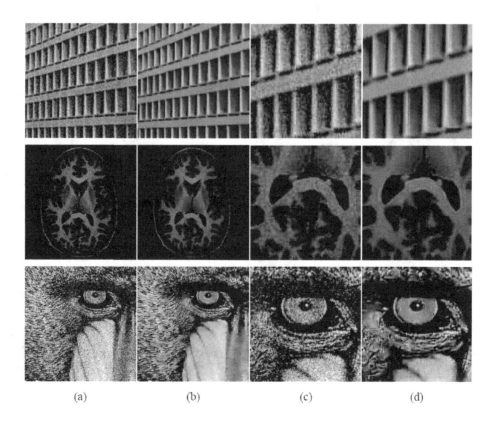

(a)   (b)   (c)   (d)

The algorithm restores well the eyes and nose regions, and does fairly well for the fine details of the textured skin regions.

In Figure 8 and Figure 9, we have qualitatively compared the behavior of our method with state of the art denoisers. Figure 8 shows the comparison on the standard Barbara image contaminated by mild IID noise. Figure 9 shows results on the standard Lenna image with a large amount of additive zero-mean noise. Both figures shows the results of applying our graph smoothing algorithm (GRAPH), the regularised Perona-Malik (RPM) method (Catte, 1992), non-linear complex ramp-preserving diffusion (NCRD) (Gilboa, 2004), coherence-enhancing diffusion (CED) (Weickert, 1999), total-variation (TV) denoising (Rudin, 1992) and wavelet filtering (WAVELET) (Portilla, 2003) to restore the noisy images. In both cases, our method gives notice-ably better results than the alternative PDE-based methods for both noise elimination and feature preservation. Wavelet denoising may better restore the fine details of the image than the PDE-based filters. This is the case in the region of hair in the Lenna image. However, it also introduces some ring-like artifacts in the smooth regions. This effect has been noted previously in the literature (Awate, 2006).

The fingerprint image in Figure 10 contains complicated line structure that is dense and has intersections. Both our graph smoothing and the aforementioned methods are used to restore the noisy image in panel (a). Because of the complicated line patterns of the fingerprint images, in this example, we use a larger neighbouring window with r = 4. The reason of this is as follows. For our smoothing method, each pixel is characterised by a neighbouring window surrounding

Figure 8. Noisy Barbara (b) zoomed portion (c) graph smoothing with t = 3, κ = 0.09, σ = 0, window size n = 5, and 8-connected graph. (d) regularised Perona-Malik (Catte, 1992) (e) complex ramp-preserving diffusion (Gilboa, 2004) (f) coherence-enhancing diffusion (Weickert, 1999) (g) total-variation denoising (Rudin, 1992) (h) wavelet filtering (Portilla, 2003)

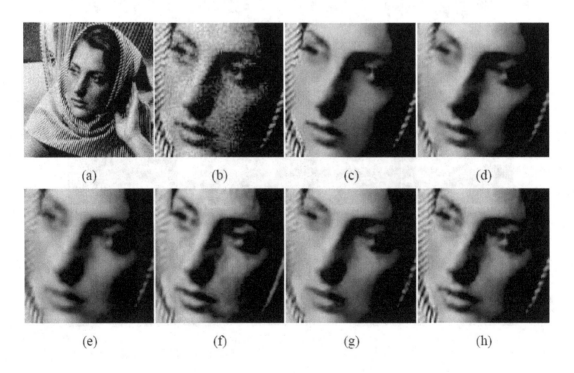

Figure 9. (a) noisy Lenna (b) zoomed portion (c) graph smoothing with t = 5, κ = 0.1, σ = 1.0, window size n = 5, and 8-connected graph. (d) regularised Perona-Malik (Catte, 1992) (e) complex ramp-preserving diffusion (Gilboa, 2004) (f) coherence-enhancing diffusion (Weickert, 1999) (g) total-variation denoising (Rudin, 1992) (h) wavelet filtering (Portilla, 2003)

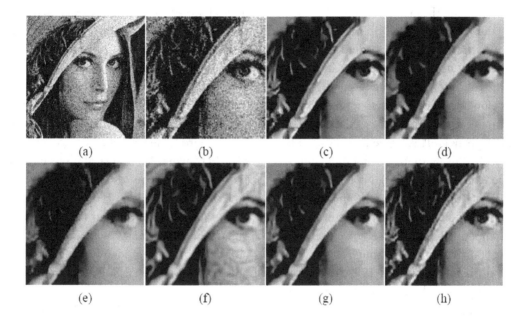

Figure 10. (a): Noisy fingerprint image (b1): our graph smoothing with t = 3, κ = 0.12, σ = 0, window size n = 7, graph connectivity r = 4. (b2): our graph smoothing with t = 10 and all other parameters are the same as in (b1). (c): regularised Perona-Malik (Catte, 1992) (d): complex ramp-preserving diffusion (Gilboa, 2004) (e): coherence-enhancing diffusion (Weickert, 1999) (f): total-variation denoising (Rudin, 1992) (g): wavelet filtering (Portilla, 2003)

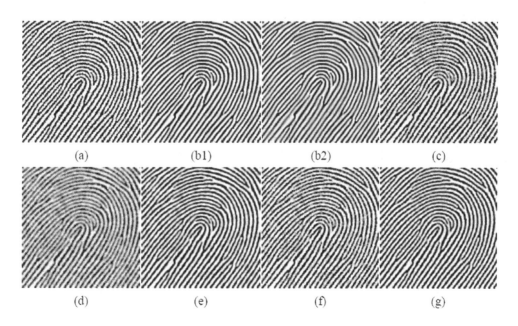

it. The larger the size of the window used, the more precisely it adapts to the features of the image. As a result, the edge weight can more accurately capture the similarity between two pixels. The panels (b1) and (b2) give the smoothed images using our method at two different times, t = 3 and t = 10 respectively. Our algorithm preserves well the line structure of the fingerprints, and even enhances the contrast with the background. Moreover, the elongated curves of the fingerprints become smoother after graph-based smoothing. The remaining panels of the figure show the results obtained with the alternative smoothing algorithms. The RPM (Catte, 1992), NCRD (Gilboa, 2004) and TV (Rudin, 1992) algorithms perform poorly on this kind of image. They are effective neither at smoothing away noise nor preserving the details of the fingerprint. Although coherence-enhancing diffusion (Weickert, 1999) does preserve the elongated structures, it also blurs the image and decreases the contrast between features and the background. The wavelet filter (Portilla, 2003) over smoothes the image and introduces smudge-like artifacts into the spaces between neighbouring lines when the spacing small.

In order to better analyse the performance of the graph-based smoothing method, we also compare quantitatively the performance of the proposed algorithm with the aforementioned alternative filters. We test each of these filters with the five images mentioned above, i.e. four standard images widely used in the image processing literature and one MRI image. Table 1 shows the root mean- square (RMS) error of the filtered images. The table shows that our method gives smaller RMS error than the alternative PDE-based methods referred to above. The wavelet filtering (Portilla, 2003) gives better results than our method on the standard Barbara image and the house image. However, our algorithm gives a smaller RMS error than that of wavelet filtering on the standard Lenna image, the Baboon image and the MRI image. Moreover, the wavelet filtering (Portilla, 2003) requires significantly more CPU time than our method.

We have also evaluated the performance of our method on images with different levels of noise. The most degraded image has a signal-to-noise ratio (SNR) of 3.8dB. Here, SNR is evaluated using the definition of $SNR = 20 \log\left(\frac{\sigma_I}{\sigma_n}\right)$, where σ_I and σ_n are the standard deviations of the ground truth image and noise respectively. Specifically, we make noisy images as follows. We take the standard 256×256 gray-scale Lenna image as the ground truth. To create noise corrupted images, we scale the intensities of the ground truth image to the range 0: 1.0 and corrupt it using IID additive zero-mean noise with increasing standard deviation. We then rescale the noisy

Table 1. RMS errors for graph smoothing and state-of-the-art filters

Example	Initial RMS Error	Graph Dmoothing	RPM (Catte, 1992)	NCRD (Gilboa, 2004)	CED (Weickert, 1999)	TV (Rudin, 1992)	WAVELET (Portilla,2003)
Standard Barbara	7.3240	5.4425	6.6167	6.8175	6.1597	6.4073	5.0114
Standard Lenna	9.3648	5.4189	5.9209	7.0591	6.3288	6.0856	5.5158
Standard Baboon	9.3519	8.3403	8.7419	9.0323	8.7531	8.5902	8.4752
House	7.3230	3.8535	4.6618	7.0557	3.6956	5.1284	3.4976
MRI Brain	5.6200	3.0128	4.1019	4.4023	3.9665	3.8667	3.5866

intensities to the range 0: 255 to create a sequence of noisy images. Both our method and the afore-mentioned filters, i.e., RPM (Catte, 1992), NCRD (Gilboa, 2004), CED (Weickert, 1999), TV (Rudin, 1992) and WAVELET (Portilla, 2003), were applied to the sequence of noisy images. For each noisy image, we manually choose the parameters of each method to obtain the best result. To compare these methods, we again computed the RMS error of the reconstructed images as a function of the noise standard deviation for each method. The results are plotted in Figure 11. The plot shows that our method gives results that are comparable to those of wavelet filtering (Portilla, 2003) and also shows that our method outperforms the alternative PDE-based approaches (Catte, 1992) (Gilboa, 2004) (Weickert, 1999) (Rudin, 1992).

5.2 Color Case

Figure 12 shows the results of applying our graph smoothing on three color images. Each channel of the color images is corrupted by IID zero-mean noise. The standard Peppers image in the top row comprises large segments that are corrupted by heavy noise. The algorithm well preserves the boundaries and smoothes out the noise. The image in the second row comprises segments with only small color contrast. The method almost perfectly recovers the fine details while efficiently removing noise. The neighboring window at each pixel for color images can more accurately characterise the pixel than the window with the same size for gray-scale images. The bottom row of Figure 12 demonstrates the effectiveness of the algorithm for processing an image with complex structure, as shown in the zoomed portion.

Figure 11. RMS error comparison of graph smoothing with RPM (Catte, 1992), NCRD (Gilboa, 2004), CED (Weickert, 1999), TV (Rudin, 1992) and WAVELET Portilla, (2003) on standard Lenna image corrupted by additive zero-mean noise with increasing standard deviation.

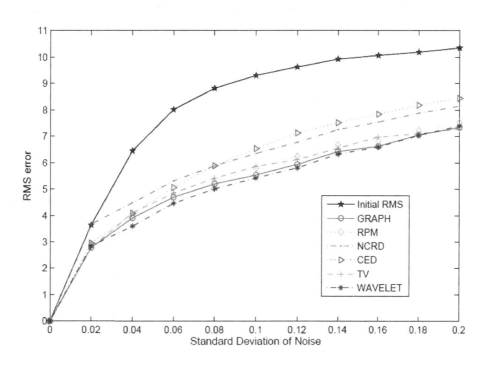

Figure 12. Column (a): noisy images. Column (b): smoothed results. The parameters for the top image is t = 3, κ = 0.11, σ = 1.1, middle image t = 3, κ = 0.1, σ = 1, and bottom image t = 3, κ = 0.08, σ = 0.8. All three examples are filtered using window size 5×5 and 8-connected graphs. Column (c): zoomed portions of the noisy images. Column (d): corresponding zoomed portions of the smoothed images.

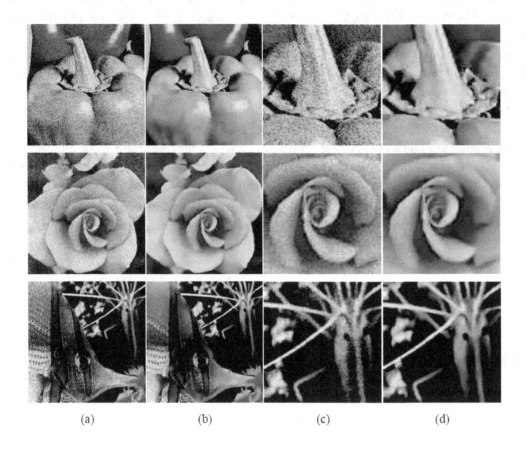

(a)   (b)   (c)   (d)

We also compared the performance of our method on color images with that of the curvature-preserving PDE regularisation (Tschumperle, 2006). Figure 13 gives the results of applying the two methods on the standard Lenna image and the standard Airplane image. Both images are corrupted by a large amount of additive noise. As the figure shows, our method not only preserves the object boundaries and features, such as the eyes and hair of the face of Lenna and the numbers on the Airplane, but it is also not sensitive to noise. Although the curvature-preserving PDE (Tschumperle, 2006) works fairly well and is able to eliminate severe noise, but it has a tendency to over smooth and blur the fine details of the objects.

6. CONCLUSION

In this paper, we have proposed a novel algorithm for gray-scale and color image smoothing. Unlike most continuous PDE-based methods for image smoothing, we formulate the problem using a graph-spectral approach. We represent image pixel lattices using weighted undirected graphs, and the edge weights are computed using the Gaussian weighted Euclidean distances between neighbouring windows of pixels. Heat diffusion on these graphs is captured by the heat equation, which is governed by the Laplacian matrix. The solution to the heat equation, i.e. the heat-kernel, is found by exponentiating the Laplacian eigensystem with

Figure 13. Column (a): noisy images. Column (b): zoomed portions of the noisy images. Column (c): graph smoothed results. The parameters for the top image is t = 3, κ = 0.15, σ = 0.7, middle image t = 3, κ = 0.09, σ = 0, and bottom image t = 3, κ = 0.12, σ = 0.7. Both examples are filtered using window size 5 × 5 and 8-connected graphs. Column (d): corresponding zoomed portions of the smoothed images using curvature-preserving PDE method.

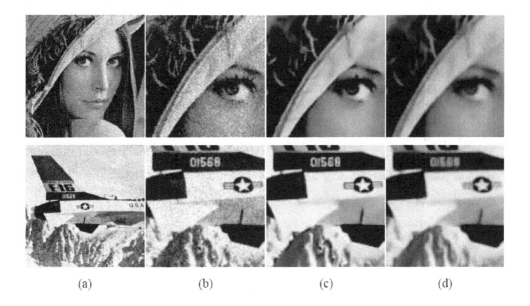

(a)   (b)   (c)   (d)

time. We smooth images by allowing the image intensities to diffuse across the graph structure. The solution of this image evolution process is found by simply convolving the heat kernel with the original image. The numerical implementation of the algorithm can be accomplished using the Krylov subspace projection technique, which performs efficiently. Unlike the mesh smoothing method in (Desbrun, 1999), which presents an efficient numerical method for implementing the continuous diffusion equation for surface fairing, our algorithm is based on spectral graph theory and formulated using the discrete heat equation on a graph. We have theoretically demonstrated the relationships between our graph smoothing method and a number of alternatives including the standard diffusion-based PDE, signal processing and spectral clustering. We have presented the results of applying the algorithm to a diverse collection of images. We also demonstrated the effectiveness of the method by qualitatively and

quantitatively comparing it with several state of the art filters.

There are a number of ways in which the method can be further improved. First, we are investigating how to automatically select the optimal stoping time for the graph-based diffusion process. There are several methods in the literature (Mrazek, 2003) for selecting the optimal stopping time for nonlinear diffusion filtering. However, they are all for iteration-based implementations of continuous diffusion-based PDEs and are inappropriate for our algorithm. Second, the edge weight computation scheme may be improved. We are studying how to calculate the edge weights from the statistics of local pixel neighborhood. Third, although the algorithm is able to deal with both scalar and vector image data, we are currently investigating how to extend the method to the processing of directional fields and diffusion tensor MRI, whose features reside on non-Euclidean manifolds.

REFERENCES

Alvarez, L., Lions, P., & Morel, J. (1992). Image selective smoothing and edge detection by nonlinear diffusion. *SIAM Journal on Numerical Analysis, 29*, 845–866.

Atkins, J., Bowman, E., & Hendrickson, B. (1998). A spectral algorithm for seriation and the consecutive ones problem. *SIAM Journal on Computing, 28*(1), 297–310.

Awate, S., & Whitaker, R. (2006). Unsupervised, information-theoretic, adaptive image filtering for image restoration. *IEEE Transactions on Pattern Analysis and Machine Intelligence, 28*(3), 364–376.

Azary, Y., Fiaty, A., Karlinz, A., McSherryz, F., & Saia, J. (2001). Spectral analysis of data. In *Proceedings of the ACM Symposium on Theory of Computing*, (pp. 619–626).

Babaud, J., Witkin, A., Baudin, M., & Duda, R. (1986). Uniqueness of the Gaussian kernel for scale-space filtering. *IEEE Transactions on Pattern Analysis and Machine Intelligence, 8*(1), 26–33.

Bao, Y., & Krim, H. (2004). Smart nonlinear diffusion: A probabilistic approach. *IEEE Transactions on Pattern Analysis and Machine Intelligence, 26*(1), 63–72.

Belkin, M., & Niyogi, P. (2003). Laplacian eigenmaps for dimensionality reduction and data representation. *Neural Computation, 15*(6), 1373–1396.

Black, M., Sapiro, G., Marimont, D., & Heeger, D. (1998). Robust anisotropic diffusion. *IEEE Transactions on Image Processing, 7*(3), 421–432.

Blomgren, P., & Chan, T. (1998). Color TV: Total variation methods for restoration of vector-valued images. *IEEE Transactions on Image Processing, 7*(3), 304–309.

Buades, A., Coll, B., & Morel, J. (2005). A review of image denoising algorithms, with a new one. *Multiscale Modeling and Simulation, 4*(2), 490–530.

Canny, J. (1986). A computational approach to edge detection. *IEEE Transactions on Pattern Analysis and Machine Intelligence, 8*(6), 679–698.

Catte, F., Lions, P., Morel, J., & Coll, T. (1992). Image selective smoothing and edge detection by nonlinear diffusion. *SIAM Journal on Numerical Analysis, 29*, 182–193.

Chambolle, A. (1994). Partial differential equations and image processing. In *Proceedings of IEEE International Conference on Image Processing*, (pp. 16–20).

Chavel, I. (1984). *Eigenvalues in Riemannian geometry*. Academic Press.

Chung, F., & Yau, S.-T. (2000). Discrete Green's FUNCTIONS. *Journal of Combinatorial Theory, 91*, 191–214.

Chung, F. R. K. (1997). *Spectral graph theory*. American Mathematical Society.

Coifman, R., & Maggioni, M. (2006). Diffusion wavelets. *Applied and Computational Harmonic Analysis, 21*, 53–94.

Cottet, G., & Germain, L. (1993). Image processing through reaction combined with nonlinear diffusion. *Mathematics of Computation, 61*, 659–673.

Cvetkovic, D., Doob, M., & Sachs, H. (1995). *Spectra of graphs: Theory and applications*. Johann Ambrosius Barth.

Desbrun, M., Meyer, M., Schroder, P., & Barr, A. (1999). Implicit fairing of irregular meshes using diffusion and curvature flow. In *Proceedings of SIGGRAPH*, (pp. 317–324).

Di Zenzo, S. (1986). A note on the gradient of a multi-image. *Computer Vision Graphics and Image Processing, 33*, 116–125.

Efros, A., & Leung, T. (1999). Texture synthesis by non parametric sampling. In *Proceedings of IEEE International Conference on Computer Vision*, (pp. 1033–1038).

Geman, S., & Geman, D. (1984). Stochastic relaxation, Gibbs distributions, and the Bayesian restoration of images. *IEEE Transactions on Pattern Analysis and Machine Intelligence, 6*(6), 721–741.

Gilboa, G., Sochen, N., & Zeevi, Y. (2004). Image enhancement and denoising by complex diffusion processes. *IEEE Transactions on Pattern Analysis and Machine Intelligence, 26*(8), 1020–1036.

Golub, G., & Van Loan, C. (1996). *Matrix computations* (3rd ed.). The Johns Hopkins University Press.

Grady, L. (2005). Multilabel random walker image segmentation using prior models. In *Proceedings of IEEE Conference on Computer Vision and Pattern Recognition*, (pp. 763–770).

Grigoryan, A. (2005). *Analysis on manifolds and heat kernel*. Personal lecture notes.

Hein, M., Audibert, J., & von Luxburg, U. (2005). From graphs to manifolds̵weak and strong pointwise consistency of graph Laplacians. In *Proceedings of the 18th Conference on Learning Theory*, (pp. 470–485).

Hochbruck, M., & Lubich, C. (1997). On Krylov subspace approximations to the matrix exponential operator. *SIAM Journal on Numerical Analysis, 34*, 1911–1925.

Koenderink, J. (1984). The structure of images. *Biological Cybernetics, 50*, 363–370.

Kondor, R., & Lafferty, J. (2002). Diffusion kernels on graphs and other discrete structures. In *Proceedings of the 19th International Conference on Machine Learning*, (pp. 315–322).

Lafon, S. (2004). *Diffusion maps and geometric harmonics*. PhD dissertation, Yale University.

Moler, C., & Van Loan, C. (2003). Nineteen dubious ways to compute the exponential of a matrix, twenty-five years later. *SIAM Review, 45*(1), 3–49.

Mrazek, P., & Navara, M. (2003). Selection of optimal stopping time for nonlinear diffusion filtering. *International Journal of Computer Vision, 52*, 189–203.

Perona, P., & Malik, J. (1990). Scale-space and edge detection using anisotropic diffusion. *IEEE Transactions on Pattern Analysis and Machine Intelligence, 12*(7), 629–639.

Portilla, J., Strela, V., Wainwright, M., & Simoncelli, E. (2003). Image denoising using scale mixtures of Gaussians in the wavelet domain. *IEEE Transactions on Image Processing, 12*(11), 1338–1351.

Rosenberg, S. (1997). *The Laplacian on a Riemannian manifold*. Cambridge University Press.

Rudin, L., Osher, S., & Fatemi, E. (1992). Nonlinear total variation based noise removal algorithms. *Physica D. Nonlinear Phenomena, 60*, 259–268.

Saad, Y. (1989). Krylov subspace methods on supercomputers. *SIAM Journal on Scientific and Statistical Computing, 10*, 1200–1232.

Saad, Y. (1992). Analysis of some Krylov subspace approximations to the matrix exponential operator. *SIAM Journal on Numerical Analysis, 29*, 209–228.

Saint-Marc, P., Chen, J., & Medioni, G. (1991). Adaptive smoothing: A general tool for early vision. *IEEE Transactions on Pattern Analysis and Machine Intelligence, 13*(6), 514–529.

Sapiro, G. (2001). *Geometric partial differential equations and image analysis*. Cambridge University Press.

Sapiro, G., & Ringach, D. (1996). Anisotropic diffusion of multivalued images with application to color filtering. *IEEE Transactions on Image Processing, 5*(11), 1582–1586.

Sarkar, S., & Boyer, K. (1996). Quantitative measures of change based on feature organization: Eigenvalues and eigenvectors. In *Proceedings of the IEEE Conference on Computer Vision and Pattern Recognition*, (p. 478).

Shi, J., & Malik, J. (2000). Normalized cuts and image segmentation. *IEEE Transactions on Pattern Analysis and Machine Intelligence, 22*(8), 888–905.

Sidje, R. (1998). Expokit: A software package for computing matrix exponentials. *ACM Transactions on Mathematical Software, 24*(1), 130–156.

Smolka, B., & Wojciechowski, K. (2001). Random walk approach to image enhancement. *Signal Processing, 81*, 465–482.

Sochen, N., Kimmel, R., & Malladi, R. (1998). A general framework for low level vision. *IEEE Transactions on Image Processing, 7*(3), 310–318.

Taubin, G. (1995). A signal processing approach to fair surface design. In *Proceedings of SIGGRAPH*, (pp. 351–358).

Tschumperle, D. (2006). Fast anisotropic smoothing of multi-valued images using curvature- preserving PDE's. *International Journal of Computer Vision, 68*(1), 65–82.

Tschumperle, D., & Deriche, R. (2005). Vector-valued image regularization with PDEs: A common framework for different applications. *IEEE Transactions on Pattern Analysis and Machine Intelligence, 27*(4), 506–517.

Weickert, J. (1998). *Anisotropic diffusion in image processing*. Stuttgart, Germany: Teubner-Verlag.

Weickert, J. (1999). Coherence-enhancing diffusion filtering. *International Journal of Computer Vision, 31*, 111–127.

Weiss, Y. (1999). Segmentation using eigenvectors: A unifying view. In *Proceedings of IEEE International Conference on Computer Vision*, (pp. 975–982).

Witkin, A. (1983). Scale-space filtering. In *Proceedings of the International Joint Conference on Artificial Intelligence*, (pp. 1019–1021).

You, Y., Xu, W., Tannenbaum, A., & Kaveh, M. (1996). Behavioral analysis of anisotropic diffusion in image processing. *IEEE Transactions on Image Processing, 5*(11), 1539–1553.

Zhang, F., & Hancock, E. R. (2005). Image scale-space from the heat kernel. In *Proceedings of the Iberoamerican Congress on Pattern Recognition, Springer LNCS 3773*, (pp. 181–192).

Zhang, F., & Hancock, E. R. (2006). Heat kernel smoothing of scalar and vector image data. In *Proceedings of the IEEE International Conference on Image Processing*, (pp. 1549–1552).

Zucker, S. (1978). Estimates for the classical parametrix for the Laplacian. *Manuscripta Mathematica, 24*, 1432–1785.

Compilation of References

Adiv, G. (1985). Determining three-dimensional motion and structure from optical flow generated by several moving objects. *IEEE Transactions on Pattern Analysis and Machine Intelligence*, 7(4), 384–401. doi:10.1109/TPAMI.1985.4767678

Agarwal, S., Branson, K., & Belongie, S. (2005). Higher order learning with graphs. In the *Proceedings of the 22nd International Conference on Machine Learning*.

Agarwal, S., Lim, J., Zelnik-Manor, L., Perona, P., Kriegman, D., & Belongie, S. (2005). Beyond pairwise clustering. In *Proceedings of the 2005 IEEE Computer Society Conference on Computer Vision and Pattern Recognition (CVPR '05) - Vol. 2*, (pp. 838–845). Washington, DC, USA, 2005.

Agathos, A., Pratikakis, I., Papadakis, P., Perantonis, S., Azariadis, P., & Sapidis, N. (2009). *Retrieval of 3D articulated objects using a graph-based representation*. In Eurographics Workshop on 3D Object Retrieval.

Aho, A. V., Hopcroft, J. E., & Ullman, J. D. (1974). *The design and analysis of computer algorithms*. Addison Wesley.

Allen, R., Cinque, L., Tanimoto, S., Shapiro, L. G., & Yasuda, D. (1997). A parallel algorithm for graph matching and its MasPar implementation. *IEEE Transactions on Parallel and Distributed Systems*, 8(5), 490–501. doi:10.1109/71.598276

Almohamad, H. A. (1991). Polynomial transform for matching pairs of weighted graphs. *Applied Mathematical Modelling*, 15, 216–222. doi:10.1016/0307-904X(91)90011-D

Almohamad, H. A., & Duffuaa, S. O. (1993). A linear programming approach for the weighted graph matching problem. *IEEE Transactions on Pattern Analysis and Machine Intelligence*, 15(5), 522–525. doi:10.1109/34.211474

Alon, N., & Milman, V. (1985). $\lambda 1$, isoperimetric inequalities for graphs, and superconcentrators. *Journal of Combinatorial Theory Series B*, 38, 73–88. doi:10.1016/0095-8956(85)90092-9

Alpaydinm, E., & Alimoglu, F. (1998). *Pen-based recognition of handwritten digits*. Dept. of Computer Engineering, Bogazici University.

Alpert, C. J., & Kahng, A. B. (1995). Recent directions in netlist partitioning: A survey. *Integration: The VLSI Journal*, 19, 1–81. doi:10.1016/0167-9260(95)00008-4

Alvarez, L., Lions, P., & Morel, J. (1992). Image selective smoothing and edge detection by nonlinear diffusion. *SIAM Journal on Numerical Analysis*, 29, 845–866.

Ambauen, R., Fischer, S., & Bunke, H. (2003). Graph edit distance with node splitting and merging and its application to diatom identification. In E. Hancock & M. Vento (Eds.), *Proceedings of the 4th International Workshop on Graph Based Representations in Pattern Recognition, LNCS 2726*, (pp. 95-106). Springer.

Ambauen, R., Fischer, S., & Bunke, H. (2003). Graph edit distance with node splitting and merging, and its application to diatom identification. *Lecture Notes in Computer Science*, 2726. doi:10.1007/3-540-45028-9_9

Ambler, A. P., Barrow, H. G., Brown, C. M., Burstall, R. M., & Popplestone, R. J. (1973). A versatile computer-controlled assembly system. *Proceedings of the 3rd International Joint Conference on Artificial Intelligence*, (pp. 298-307).

Andrews, S., Hamarneh, G., & Saad, A. (2010). Fast random walker with priors using precomputation for interactive medical image segmentation. *Lecture Notes in Computer Science, 6363,* 9–16. doi:10.1007/978-3-642-15711-0_2

Antiqueira, L., Nunes, M. G. V., Oliveira, O. N., et al. (2005). *Strong correlations between text quality and complex networks features.* Retrieved from http://arxiv.org/abs/physics/0504033

Antonio, R. K., & Hancock, E. R. (2003). Edit distance from graph spectra. In *IEEE International Conference on Computer Vision, Vol. 1,* (pp. 234-241).

Antonio, R. K., & Hancock, E. R. (2005). Graph edit distance from spectral seriation. *IEEE Transactions on Pattern Analysis and Machine Intelligence, 27*(3), 365–377. doi:10.1109/TPAMI.2005.56

Apostoloff, N., & Fitzgibbon, A. (2004). Bayesian video matting using learnt image priors. *Proceedings of the IEEE Conference on Computer Vision and Pattern Recognition.*

Aslan, C., & Tari, S. (2005). An axis based representation for recognition. *ICCV: IEEE International Conference on Computer Vision,* (pp. 1339-1346).

Atkins, J., Bowman, E., & Hendrickson, B. (1998). A spectral algorithm for seriation and the consecutive ones problem. *SIAM Journal on Computing, 28*(1), 297–310.

August, J., Siddiqi, K., & Zucker, S. (1999). Ligature instabilities and the perceptual organization of shape. *Computer Vision and Image Understanding, 76*(3), 231–243. doi:10.1006/cviu.1999.0802

Awate, S., & Whitaker, R. (2006). Unsupervised, information-theoretic, adaptive image filtering for image restoration. *IEEE Transactions on Pattern Analysis and Machine Intelligence, 28*(3), 364–376.

Ayer, S., & Sawhney, H. (1995). *Layered representation of motion video using robust maximum-likelihood estimation of mixture models and MDL encoding.* International Conference on Computer Vision.

Azary, Y., Fiaty, A., Karlinz, A., McSherryz, F., & Saia, J. (2001). Spectral analysis of data. In *Proceedings of the ACM Symposium on Theory of Computing,* (pp. 619–626).

Babaud, J., Witkin, A., Baudin, M., & Duda, R. (1986). Uniqueness of the Gaussian kernel for scale-space filtering. *IEEE Transactions on Pattern Analysis and Machine Intelligence, 8*(1), 26–33.

Backes, A. R., & Bruno, O. M. (2010). Shape classification using complex network and multi-scale fractal dimension. *Pattern Recognition Letters, 31*(1), 44–51. doi:10.1016/j.patrec.2009.08.007

Backes, A. R., Casanova, D., & Bruno, O. M. (2009). A complex network-based approach for boundary shape analysis. *Pattern Recognition, 42*(1), 54–67. doi:10.1016/j.patcog.2008.07.006

Baeza-Yates, R., & Valiente, G. (2000). An image similarity measure based on graph matching. *Proceeding of the Seventh International Symposium on String Processing and Information Retrieval,* (pp. 28 – 38).

Bagdanov, A. D., & Worring, M. (2003). First order Gaussian graphs for efficient structure classification. *Pattern Recognition, 36*(6), 1311–1324. doi:10.1016/S0031-3203(02)00227-3

Bai, X., & Hancock, E. R. (2004). Graph matching using spectral embedding and alignment. *Proceedings of the 17th International Conference on Pattern Recognition,* (pp. 398–401).

Bai, X., Latecki, L. J., & Liu, W.-Y. (2006). Skeleton pruning by contour partitioning. In *International Conference on Discrete Geometry for Computer Imagery,* (pp. 567-579).

Bai, X., Yu, H., & Hancock, E. R. (2004). Graph matching using spectral embedding and alignment. In *International Conference on Pattern Recognition, Vol. 3,* (pp. 23-26).

Bai, X., Hancock, E. R., & Wilson, R. C. (2009). Graph characteristics from the heat kernel trace. *Pattern Recognition, 42*(11), 2589–2606. doi:10.1016/j.patcog.2008.12.029

Bai, X., & Latecki, L. J. (2008). Path similarity skeleton graph matching. *IEEE Transactions on Pattern Analysis and Machine Intelligence, 30*(7), 1282–1292. doi:10.1109/TPAMI.2007.70769

Bai, X., Latecki, L. J., & Liu, W.-Y. (2007). Skeleton pruning by contour partitioning with discrete curve evolution. *IEEE Transactions on Pattern Analysis and Machine Intelligence, 29*(3), 449–462. doi:10.1109/TPAMI.2007.59

Bai, X., & Sapiro, G. (2007). *A geodesic framework for fast interactive image and video segmentation and matting* (pp. 1–8). IEEE Computer Society.

Bai, X., Wilson, R., & Hancock, E. (2009). A generative model for graph matching and embedding. *Computer Vision and Image Understanding, 113*, 778–789.

Bai, X., Yang, X., & Latecki, L. J. (2008). Skeleton-based shape classification using path similarity. *International Journal of Pattern Recognition and Artificial Intelligence, 22*(4), 733–746. doi:10.1142/S0218001408006405

Balas, E., & Yu, C. S. (1986). Finding a maximum clique in an arbitrary graph. *SIAM Journal on Computing, 15*(4), 1054–1068. doi:10.1137/0215075

Bao, B.-K., Ni, B., Mu, Y., & Yan, S. (2011). Efficient region-aware large graph construction towards scalable multi-label propagation. *Pattern Recognition, 3*(44), 598–606. doi:10.1016/j.patcog.2010.10.001

Bao, Y., & Krim, H. (2004). Smart nonlinear diffusion: A probabilistic approach. *IEEE Transactions on Pattern Analysis and Machine Intelligence, 26*(1), 63–72.

Barnard, S. T., & Simon, H. D. (1994). A fast multilevel implementation of recursive spectral bisection for partitioning unstructured problems. *Concurrency (Chichester, England), 6*, 101–107. doi:10.1002/cpe.4330060203

Basri, R., Costa, L., Geiger, D., & Jacobs, D. (1998). Determining the similarity of deformable shapes. *Vision Research, 38*, 2365–2385. doi:10.1016/S0042-6989(98)00043-1

Bauckhage, C., Wachsmuth, S., & Sagerer, G. (2001). 3D assembly recognition by matching functional subparts. *Proceedings of the 3rd IAPR-TC15 Workshop on Graph-based Representations in Pattern Recognition,* (pp. 95 – 104).

Bay, H., Ess, A., Tuytelaars, T., & Gool, L. J. V. (2008). Speeded-up robust features (surf). *Computer Vision and Image Understanding, 110*(3), 346–359. doi:10.1016/j.cviu.2007.09.014

Beer, E., Fill, J. A., Janson, S., & Scheinerman, E. R. (2010). *On vertex, edge, and vertex-edge random graphs.* Retrieved from http://arxiv.org/abs/0812.1410v2

Belkin, M., & Niyogi, P. (2003). Laplacian eigenmaps for dimensionality reduction and data representation. *Neural Computation, 15*(6), 1373–1396. doi:10.1162/089976603321780317

Belongie, S., & Malik, J. (2000). Matching with shape contexts. *Proceedings of IEEE Workshop on Content-based Access of Image and Video Libraries,* (pp. 20 – 26).

Belongie, S., Puzhicha, J., & Malik, J. (2002). Shape matching and object recognition using shape contexts. *IEEE Transactions on Pattern Analysis and Machine Intelligence, 24*(4), 509–522. doi:10.1109/34.993558

Berretti, S., Del Bimbo, A., & Vicario, E. (2000a). A look-ahead strategy for graph matching in retrieval by spatial arrangement. *International Conference on Multimedia and Expo,* (pp. 1721 – 1724).

Berretti, S., Del Bimbo, A., & Vicario, E. (2000b). The computational aspect of retrieval by spatial arrangement. *Proceedings of 15th International Conference on Pattern Recognition,* pp. 1047 - 1051.

Berretti, S., Del Bimbo, A., & Vicario, E. (2001). Efficient matching and indexing of graph models in content-based retrieval. *IEEE Transactions on Pattern Analysis and Machine Intelligence, 23*(10), 1089–1105. doi:10.1109/34.954600

Bertrand, G. (1994). Simple points, topological numbers and geodesic neighborhoods in cubic grids. *Pattern Recognition Letters, 15*(10), 1003–1011. doi:10.1016/0167-8655(94)90032-9

Bichot, C.-E., & Siarry, P. (Éds.). (2011). *Graph partitioning.* ISTE - Wiley.

Bichot, C.-E. (2009). Co-clustering documents and words by minimizing the normalized cut objective function. *Journal of Mathematical Modelling and Algorithms, 9*, 131–147. doi:10.1007/s10852-010-9126-0

Birchfield, S., & Tomasi, C. (1999). *Multiway cut for stereo and motion with slanted surfaces.* International Conference on Computer Vision.

Black, M., Sapiro, G., Marimont, D., & Heeger, D. (1998). Robust anisotropic diffusion. *IEEE Transactions on Image Processing, 7*(3), 421–432.

Blake, A., Rother, C., Brown, M., Perez, P., & Torr, P. (2004). Interactive image segmentation using an adaptive GMMRF model. In T. Pajdla, & J. Matas (Eds.), *Proceedings of the European Conference on Computer Vision (ECCV)* (Vol. 3021, pp. 428-441). Berlin, Germany Springer.

Blomgren, P., & Chan, T. (1998). Color TV: Total variation methods for restoration of vector-valued images. *IEEE Transactions on Image Processing, 7*(3), 304–309.

Blum, H. (1973). Biological shape and visual science. *Journal of Theoretical Biology, 38,* 205–287. doi:10.1016/0022-5193(73)90175-6

Boeres, M. C., Ribeiro, C. C., & Bloch, I. (2004). A randomized heuristic for scene recognition by graph matching. In C. C. Ribeiro & S. L. Martins (Eds.), *Lecture Notes in Computer Science, Vol. 3059, Experimental and Efficient Algorithms: Third International Workshop,* (WEA 2004), (pp. 100 – 113).

Bolla, M. (1993). Spectra, Euclidean representations and clusterings of hypergraphs. *Discrete Mathematics, 117*(1-3), 19–39. doi:10.1016/0012-365X(93)90322-K

Bomze, I. M. (1997). Evolution towards the maximum clique. *Journal of Global Optimization, 10,* 143–164. doi:10.1023/A:1008230200610

Borg, I., & Groenen, P. (2005). *Modern multidimensional scaling: Theory and applications.* Springer.

Borgwardt, K., & Kriegel, H.-P. (2005a). Shortest-path kernels on graphs. In *Proceedings of the 5th International Conference on Data Mining,* (pp. 74-81).

Borgwardt, K., Ong, C., Schönauer, S., Vishwanathan, S., Smola, A., & Kriegel, H.-P. (2005b). Protein function prediction via graph kernels. *Bioinformatics (Oxford, England), 21*(1), 47–56. doi:10.1093/bioinformatics/bti1007

Boykov, Y. Y., & Jolly, M.-P. (2001). Interactive graph cuts for optimal boundary & region segmentation of objects in N-D images. *Proceedings of the Eighth IEEE International Conference on Computer Vision,* Vol. 1, (pp. 105-112).

Boykov, Y., & Kolmogorov, V. (2003). Computing geodesics and minimal surfaces via graph cuts. *Proceedings of the Ninth IEEE International Conference on Computer Vision,* Vol. 2, (pp. 26-33). IEEE Computer Society.

Boykov, Y., & Kolmogorov, V. (2004). An experimental comparison of min-cut/max-flow algorithms for energy minimization in vision. *IEEE Transactions on Pattern Analysis and Machine Intelligence, 26*(9), 1124–1137. doi:10.1109/TPAMI.2004.60

Boykov, Y., Veksler, O., & Zabih, R. (2001). Fast approximate energy minimization via graph cuts. *IEEE Transactions on Pattern Analysis and Machine Intelligence, 23*(11), 1222–1239. doi:10.1109/34.969114

Branca, A., Stella, E., & Distante, A. (1999). Feature matching by searching maximum clique on high order association graph. *Proceedings of the 10th International Conference on Image Analysis and Processing,* (pp. 642 – 658).

Breiman, L. (1992). *Probability.* Society for Industrial Mathematics. doi:10.1137/1.9781611971286

Bron, C., & Kerbosch, J. (1973). Finding all cliques of an undirected graph. *Communications of the ACM, 16*(9), 575–577. doi:10.1145/362342.362367

Buades, A., Coll, B., & Morel, J. (2005). A review of image denoising algorithms, with a new one. *Multiscale Modeling and Simulation, 4*(2), 490–530.

Bunke, H., & Vento, M. (1999). Benchmarking of graph matching algorithms. *Proceedings of the 2nd IAPR TC-15 GbR Workshop,* Haindorf, (pp. 109-114).

Bunke, H., Dickinson, P. J., Kraetzl, M., & Wallis, W. D. (2007). A graph-theoretic approach to enterprise network dynamics. *Progress in Computer Science and Applied Logic, 24.*

Bunke, H., Foggia, P., Vento, M., Sansone, C., & Guidobaldi, C. (2002). A comparison of algorithms for maximum common subgraph on randomly connected graphs. *Proceeding of the Joint IAPR International Workshops SSPR and SPR,* (pp. 123 – 132).

Bunke, H. (1997). On a relation between graph edit distance and maximum common subgraph. *Pattern Recognition Letters, 18*(8), 689–694. doi:10.1016/S0167-8655(97)00060-3

Bunke, H. (1999). Error correcting graph matching: On the influence of the underlying cost function. *IEEE Transactions on PAMI, 21*(9), 917–922. doi:10.1109/34.790431

Bunke, H., & Allermann, G. (1983). Inexact graph matching for structural pattern recognition. *Pattern Recognition Letters, 1*, 245–253. doi:10.1016/0167-8655(83)90033-8

Bunke, H., Foggia, P., Guidobaldi, C., & Vento, M. (2003). Graph clustering using the weighted minimum common supergraph. In Hancock, E., & Vento, M. (Eds.), *Graph Based Representations in Pattern Recognition (Vol. 2726*, pp. 235–246). Lecture Notes in Computer Science Berlin, Germany: Springer. doi:10.1007/3-540-45028-9_21

Bunke, H., & Messmer, B. T. (1997). Recent advances in graph matching. *International Journal of Pattern Recognition and Artificial Intelligence, 11*(1), 169–203. doi:10.1142/S0218001497000081

Bunke, H., & Sanfeliu, A. (Eds.). (1990). *Syntactic and structural pattern recognition*. World Scientific.

Bunke, H., & Shearer, K. (1998). A graph distance metric based on the maximal common subgraph. *Pattern Recognition Letters, 19*(3), 255–259. doi:10.1016/S0167-8655(97)00179-7

Burge, M., & Burger, W. (2000). Ear biometrics in computer vision. *Proceedings of 15th International Conference on Pattern Recognition*, (pp. 822 – 826).

Caelli, T., & Kosinov, S. (2004). An Eigenspace projection clustering method for inexact graph matching. *IEEE Transactions on Pattern Analysis and Machine Intelligence, 26*(4), 515–519. doi:10.1109/TPAMI.2004.1265866

Caelli, T., & Kosinov, S. (2004). Inexact graph matching using eigen-subspace projection clustering. *International Journal of Pattern Recognition and Artificial Intelligence, 18*(3), 329–355. doi:10.1142/S0218001404003186

Can, T., & Duygulu, P. (2007). Searching for repeated video sequences. In *Proceedings of the ACM International Workshop Multimedia Information Retrieval*, Augsburg, Bavaria, Germany.

Candemir, S., & Akgul, Y. S. (2010). Adaptive regularization parameter for graph cut segmentation. *Lecture Notes in Computer Science, 6111*, 117–126. doi:10.1007/978-3-642-13772-3_13

Canny, J. (1986). A computational approach to edge detection. *IEEE Transactions on Pattern Analysis and Machine Intelligence, 8*(6), 679–698.

Carcassoni, M., & Hancock, E. R. (2001). Weighted graph-matching using modal clusters. *Proceedings of the 3rd IAPR-TC15 Workshop on Graph-based Representations in Pattern Recognition*, (pp. 260 – 269).

Cardoso, J. S., & Real, L. C. (2005). Toward a generic evaluation of image segmentation. *IEEE Transactions on Image Processing, 14*(11), 1773–1782. doi:10.1109/TIP.2005.854491

Carroll, J., & Chang, J. (1970). Analysis of individual differences in multidimensional scaling via an n-way generalization of Eckart-Young decomposition. *Psychometrika, 35*(3), 283–319. doi:10.1007/BF02310791

Caselles, V., Kimmel, R., & Sapiro, G. (1997). Geodesic active contours. *International Journal of Computer Vision, 22*(1), 61–79. doi:10.1023/A:1007979827043

Catte, F., Lions, P., Morel, J., & Coll, T. (1992). Image selective smoothing and edge detection by nonlinear diffusion. *SIAM Journal on Numerical Analysis, 29*, 182–193.

Chalumeau, T. da F. Costa, L., & Laligant, O., et al. (2006). Meriaudeau, texture discrimination using hierarchical complex networks. In *International Conference on Signal–Image Technology and Internet-Based Systems*, (pp. 543–550)

Chambolle, A. (1994). Partial differential equations and image processing. In *Proceedings of IEEE International Conference on Image Processing*, (pp. 16–20).

Chan, P. K., Schlag, M. D. F., & Zien, J. Y. (1993). Spectral k-way ratio-cut partitioning and clustering. In *DAC '93: Proceedings of the 30th International Design Automation Conference*, (pp. 749–754). New York, NY: ACM.

Chang, H., Yeung, D., & Xiong, Y. (2004). Super-resolution through neighbor embedding. *Proceedings of CVPR, 04*, 275–282.

Changhua, L., Bing, Y., & Weixin, X. (2000). Online hand-sketched graphics recognition based on attributed relational graph matching. *Proceedings of the 3rd World Congress on Intelligent Control and Automation*, (pp. 2549 – 2553).

Chan, K. P. (1996). Learning templates from fuzzy examples in structural pattern recognition. *IEEE Transactions on Systems, Man and Cybernetics. Part B, 26*(1), 118–123.

Charikar, M. (2002). Similarity estimation techniques from rounding algorithms. In *Proceedings of the thiry-fourth annual ACM symposium on Theory of Computing*, (pp. 380 – 388).

Charnoz, A., Agnus, V., Malandain, G., Soler, L., & Tajine, M. (2005). Tree matching applied to vascular system. In L. Brun & M. Vento (Eds.), *Proceedings of 5th IAPR-TC-15 Workshop on Graph-based Representations in Pattern Recognition (GbRPR 2005), Lecture Notes in Computer Science, Vol. 3434*, (pp. 183-192).

Chavel, I. (1984). *Eigenvalues in Riemannian geometry*. Academic Press.

Chen, G., Song, Y., Wang, F., & Zhang, C. (2008). Semi-supervised multi-label learning by solving a Sylvester equation. In *SIAM International Conference on Data Mining (SDM)*, Atlanta, Georgia, (pp. 410–419).

Chen, H. T., Lin, H., & Liu, T. L. (2001). Multi-object tracking using dynamical graph matching. *Proceedings of the 2001 IEEE Computer Society Conference on Computer Vision and Pattern Recognition*, (pp. 210 – 217).

Chen, D., Tian, X., Shen, Y., & Ouhyoung, M. (2003). On visual similarity based 3D model retrieval. *Computer Graphics Forum, 22*(3), 223–232. doi:10.1111/1467-8659.00669

Chen, J., & Saad, Y. (2009). *Co-clustering of high order relational data using spectral hypergraph partitioning. Technical Report UMSI 2009/xx*. University of Minnesota Supercomputing Institute.

Chen, L. H., & Lieh, J. R. (1990). Handwritten character recognition using a 2-layer random graph model by relaxation matching. *Pattern Recognition, 23*, 1189–1205. doi:10.1016/0031-3203(90)90115-2

Chen, L., & Stentiford, F. W. M. (2008). Video sequence matching based on temporal ordinal measurement. *Pattern Recognition Letters, 29*(13), 1824–1831.

Chen, Y., Bi, J., & Wang, J. Z. (2006). Miles: Multiple-instance learning via embedded instance selection. *IEEE Transactions on Pattern Analysis and Machine Intelligence, 28*(12), 1931–1947. doi:10.1109/TPAMI.2006.248

Chiu, C.-Y., Chen, C.-S., & Chien, L.-F. (2008). A framework for handling spatiotemporal variations in video copy detection. *IEEE Transactions on Circuits and Systems for Video Technology, 18*(3), 412–417.

Cho, S. J., & Yoo, S. I. (1998). Image retrieval using topological structure of user sketch. *IEEE International Conference on Systems, Man, and Cybernetics*, (pp. 4584 – 4588).

Choi, W.-P., Lam, K.-M., & Siu, W.-C. (2003). Extraction of the Euclidean skeleton based on a connectivity criterion. *Pattern Recognition, 36*(3), 721–729. doi:10.1016/S0031-3203(02)00098-5

Christmas, W. J., Kittler, J., & Petrou, M. (1995). Structural matching in computer vision using probabilistic relaxation. *IEEE Transactions on Pattern Analysis and Machine Intelligence, 17*(8), 749–764. doi:10.1109/34.400565

Chua, T. S., Tang, J., Hong, R., Li, H., Luo, Z., & Zheng, Y. (2009). Nus-wide: A real-world web image database from national university of Singapore. In *Proceedings of ACM Conference on Image and Video Retrieval (CIVR)*.

Chuang, Y., Agarwala, A., Curless, B., Salesin, D., & Szeliski, R. (2002). Video matting of complex scenes. *Proceedings of Association of Computing Machinery's Special Interest Group on Computer Graphics and Interactive Techniques*.

Chum, O., & Zisserman, A. (2007). *An exemplar model for learning object classes*. In IEEE Conference on Computer Vision and Pattern Recognition.

Chung, D., MacLean, W. J., & Dickinson, S. (2004). Integrating region and boundary information for improved spatial coherence in object tracking. In *CVPRW '04: Proceedings of the 2004 Conference on Computer Vision and Pattern Recognition Workshop (CVPRW '04)*, Vol. 1.

Chung, F. R. K. (1997). *Spectral graph theory*. American Mathematical Society.

Chung, F., & Yau, S.-T. (2000). Discrete Green's FUNCTIONS. *Journal of Combinatorial Theory, 91*, 191–214.

Çigla, C., & Alatan, A. A. (2010). Efficient graph-based image segmentation via speeded-up turbo pixels. *17th IEEE International Conference on Image Processing* (pp. 3013-3016).

Coifman, R., & Maggioni, M. (2006). Diffusion wavelets. *Applied and Computational Harmonic Analysis, 21*, 53–94.

Collobert, R., Sinz, F., Weston, J., & Bottou, L. (2006). Large scale transductive SVMS. *Journal of Machine Learning Research, 7*, 1687–1712.

Conte, D., Foggia, P., Guidobaldi, C., Limongiello, A., & Vento, M. (2004). An object tracking algorithm combining different cost functions. In Campilho, A., & Kamel, M. (Eds.), *ICIAR 2004* (*Vol. 3212*, pp. 614–622). Lecture Notes in Computer Science Berlin, Germany: Springer. doi:10.1007/978-3-540-30126-4_75

Conte, D., Foggia, P., Jolion, J. M., & Vento, M. (2006). A graph-based, multi-resolution algorithm for tracking objects in presence of occlusions. *Pattern Recognition, 39*(4), 562–572. doi:10.1016/j.patcog.2005.10.012

Conte, D., Foggia, P., Sansone, C., & Vento, M. (2004). Thirty years of graph matching in pattern recognition. *International Journal of Pattern Recognition and Artificial Intelligence, 18*(3), 265–298. doi:10.1142/S0218001404003228

Conte, D., Guidobaldi, C., & Sansone, C. (2003). A comparison of three maximum common subgraph algorithms on a large database of labeled graphs. In Hancock, E., & Vento, M. (Eds.), *Graph Based Representations in Pattern Recognition* (*Vol. 2726*, pp. 130–141). Lecture Notes in Computer Science Berlin, Germany: Springer. doi:10.1007/3-540-45028-9_12

Cook, D., & Holder, L. (Eds.). (2007). *Mining graph data*. Wiley-Interscience.

Cordella, L. P., Foggia, P., Sansone, C., & Vento, M. (1996). An efficient algorithm for the inexact matching of ARG graphs using a contextual transformational model. *Proceedings of the 13th International Conference on Pattern Recognition*, (pp. 180 – 184).

Cordella, L. P., Foggia, P., Sansone, C., & Vento, M. (1999). Performance evaluation of the VF graph matching algorithm. *Proceedings of the International Conference on Image Analysis and Processing*, (pp. 1172 – 1177).

Cordella, L. P., Foggia, P., Sansone, C., & Vento, M. (2000). Fast graph matching for detecting CAD image components. *Proceedings of 15th International Conference on Pattern Recognition*, (pp. 1034 – 1037).

Cordella, L. P., Foggia, P., Sansone, C., & Vento, M. (2001). An improved algorithm for matching large graphs. *Proceedings of the 3rd IAPR-TC15 Workshop on Graph-based Representations in Pattern Recognition*, (pp. 149 – 159).

Cordella, L. P., Foggia, P., Sansone, C., Tortorella, F., & Vento, M. (1998). Graph matching: A fast algorithm and its evaluation. *Proceedings of 14th International Conference on Pattern Recognition*, (pp. 1582 - 1584).

Cordella, L. P., Foggia, P., Sansone, C., & Vento, M. (1997). Subgraph transformations for inexact matching of attributed relational graphs. *Computing, 12*, 43–52.

Cordella, L. P., Foggia, P., Sansone, C., & Vento, M. (2002). Learning structural shape descriptions from examples. *Pattern Recognition Letters, 23*(12), 1427–1437. doi:10.1016/S0167-8655(02)00103-4

Cordella, L. P., Foggia, P., Sansone, C., & Vento, M. (2004). A (sub)graph isomorphism algorithm for matching large graphs. *IEEE Transactions on Pattern Analysis and Machine Intelligence, 26*(10), 1367–1372. doi:10.1109/TPAMI.2004.75

Cornea, N. D., Silver, D., Yuan, X., & Balasubramanian, R. (2005). Computing hierarchical curve-skeletons of 3D objects. *The Visual Computer, 21*, 945–955. doi:10.1007/s00371-005-0308-0

Correia, P. L., & Pereira, F. (2003). Objective evaluation of video segmentation quality. *IEEE Transactions on Image Processing, 12*(2), 186–200. doi:10.1109/TIP.2002.807355

Costa, L. da F. (2004). *Complex networks, simple vision*. Retrieved from http://arxiv.org/abs/condmat/0403346

Costa, L. D. F., Rodrigues, F. A., Travieso, G., & Villas Boas, P. R. (2005). Characterization of complex networks: A survey of measurements. *Advances in Physics, 56*(1), 167–242. doi:10.1080/00018730601170527

Cottet, G., & Germain, L. (1993). Image processing through reaction combined with nonlinear diffusion. *Mathematics of Computation, 61*, 659–673.

Couprie, C., Grady, L., Najman, L., & Talbot, H. (2009). Power watersheds: A new image segmentation framework extending graph cuts, random walker and optimal spanning forest, (pp. 731-738).

Cour, T., Benezit, F., & Shi, J. (2005). Spectral segmentation with multiscale graph decomposition. In *CVPR '05: Proceedings of the 2005 IEEE Computer Society Conference on Computer Vision and Pattern Recognition (CVPR'05)*, (pp. 1124–1131).

Cousty, J., Bertrand, G., Najman, L., & Couprie, M. (2009). Watershed cuts: Minimum spanning forests and the drop of water principle. *IEEE Transactions on Pattern Analysis and Machine Intelligence, 31*(8), 1362–1374. doi:10.1109/TPAMI.2008.173

Cox, I. J., Miller, M. L., Minka, T. P., Papathomas, T. V., & Yianilos, P. N. (2000). The Bayesian image retrieval system – Pichunter: Theory, implementation and psychophysical experiments. *IEEE Transactions on Image Processing, 9*, 20–37. doi:10.1109/83.817596

Cox, T., Cox, M., & Branco, J. (1991). Multidimensional scaling for n-tuples. *The British Journal of Mathematical and Statistical Psychology, 44*.

Cvetkovic, D., Doob, M., & Sachs, H. (1995). *Spectra of graphs: Theory and applications*. Johann Ambrosius Barth.

Dahlhaus, E., Johnson, D., Papadimitriou, C., Seymour, P., & Yannakakis, M. (1992). *The complexity of multiway cuts. ACM Symposium on Theory of Computing*, (pp. 241-251).

Dai, S., Han, M., Xu, W., Wu, Y., & Gong, Y. (2007). Soft edge smoothness prior for alpha channel super resolution. In *Proceedings of IEEE Conference on Computer Vision and Pattern Recognition*, (pp. 1–8).

Dalal, N., Triggs, B., Rhone-Alps, I., & Montbonnot, F. (2005). Histograms of oriented gradients for human detection. In *IEEE Computer Society Conference on Computer Vision and Pattern Recognition*, Vol. 1.

Dantzig, G. B. (1951). Application of the simplex method to a transportation problem. In Koopmans, T. C. (Ed.), *Activity analysis of production and allocation* (pp. 359–373).

David, J. M., & Carey, E. P. (2008). Predicting unobserved links in incompletely observed networks. *Computational Statistics & Data Analysis, 52*(3), 1373–1386. doi:10.1016/j.csda.2007.03.016

De Mauro, C., Diligenti, M., Gori, M., & Maggini, M. (2003). Similarity learning for graph-based image representations. *Pattern Recognition Letters, 24*(8), 1115–1122. doi:10.1016/S0167-8655(02)00258-1

De Santo, M., Foggia, P., Sansone, C., & Vento, M. (2003). A large database of graphs and its use for benchmarking graph isomorphism algorithms. *Pattern Recognition Letters, 24*(8), 1067–1079. doi:10.1016/S0167-8655(02)00253-2

Delalleau, O., Bengio, Y., & Le Roux, N. (2005). Efficient non-parametric function induction in semi-supervised learning. In *Proceedings of the Tenth International Workshop on Artificial Intelligence and Statistics (AISTAT)*.

DeMenthon, D., & Megret, R. (2002). Spatio-temporal segmentation of video by hierarchical mean shift analysis. In *CVPR '02: Proceedings of the 2002 IEEE Computer Society Conference on Computer Vision and Pattern Recognition (CVPR'02)*.

Demirci, F., Shokoufandeh, A., Dickinson, S., Keselman, Y., & Bretzner, L. (2004). Many-to-many feature matching using spherical coding of directed graphs. In *ECCV: European Conference on Computer Vision*, (pp. 322-335).

Demirci, F., Shokoufandeh, A., Keselman, Y., Bretzner, L., & Dickinson, S. (2006). Object recognition as many-to-many feature matching. *International Journal of Computer Vision, 69*(2), 203–222. doi:10.1007/s11263-006-6993-y

Demko, C. (1997). Generalization of two hypergraphs: Algorithm of calculation of the greatest sub-hypergraph common to two hypergraphs annotated by semantic information. *Computing, 12*, 1–9.

Dempster, A. P., Laird, N. M., & Rubin, D. B. (1977). Maximum-likelihood from incomplete data via the EM algorithm. *Journal of the Royal Statistical Society. Series B. Methodological, 39*, 1–38.

Deng, J., Dong, W., Socher, R., Li, L., Li, K., & Li, F. (2009). ImageNet: A large scale hierarchical image database. In *IEEE Conference on Computer Vision and Pattern Recognition*, (pp. 248–255).

Depiero, F., Trivedi, M., & Serbin, S. (1996). Graph matching using a direct classification of node attendance. *Pattern Recognition, 29*(6), 1031–1048. doi:10.1016/0031-3203(95)00140-9

Desbrun, M., Meyer, M., Schroder, P., & Barr, A. (1999). Implicit fairing of irregular meshes using diffusion and curvature flow. In *Proceedings of SIGGRAPH*, (pp. 317–324).

Deza, M. M., & Rosenberg, I. (2000). n-Semimetrics. *European Journal of Combinatorics, 21*, 797–806. doi:10.1006/eujc.1999.0384

Dhillon, I. S., Guan, Y., & Kulis, B. (2007). Weighted graph cuts without Eigenvectors: A multilevel approach. *IEEE Transactions on Pattern Analysis and Machine Intelligence, 29*, 1944–1957. doi:10.1109/TPAMI.2007.1115

di Di Ruberto, C. (2004). Recognition of shapes by attributed skeletal graphs. *Pattern Recognition, 37*(1), 21–31. doi:10.1016/j.patcog.2003.07.004

Di Zenzo, S. (1986). A note on the gradient of a multi-image. *Computer Vision Graphics and Image Processing, 33*, 116–125.

Ding, C., & He, X. (2004). *K-means clustering via principal component analysis*. International Conference in Machine Learning (ICML).

Do, M. N., & Vetterli, M. M. (2005). The contourlet transform: An efficient directional multiresolution image representation. *IEEE Transactions on Image Processing, 14*(12), 2091–2106.

Donath, W., & Hoffman, A. (1972). Algorithms for partitioning graphs and computer logic based on eigenvectors of connection matrices. *IBM Technical Disclosure Bulletin, 15*, 938–944.

Donath, W., & Hoffman, A. (1973). Lower bounds for the partitioning of graphs. *IBM Journal of Research and Development*, 420–425. doi:10.1147/rd.175.0420

Dorko, G., & Schmid, C. (2003). Selection of scale-invariant parts for object class recognition. In *International Conference on Computer Vision*, (pp. 634–640).

Dosch, P., & Valveny, E. (2007). Report on the second symbol recognition contest. In W. Liu & J. Llados (Eds.), *Graphics Recognition: Ten Years Review and Future Perspectives– Proceedings of the 6th International Workshop on Graphics Recognition, LNCS 3926,* (pp. 381-397). Springer.

Doulamis, N., Doulamis, A., & Kollias, S. (1999). Efficient content-based retrieval of humans from video databases. *Proceedings of the International Workshop on Recognition, Analysis, and Tracking of Faces and Gestures in Real-Time Systems*, (pp. 89 – 95).

Douze, M., Gaidon, A., Jegou, H., Marszatek, M., & Schmid, C. (2008). Inria-Lear's video copy detection system. In *Proceedings of TRECVID*, Gaithersburg, USA.

Douze, M., Jégou, H., & Schmid, C. (2010). An image-based approach to video copy detection with spatio-temporal post-filtering. *IEEE Transactions on Multimedia, 12*(4). Retrieved from http://lear.inrialpes.fr/pubs/2010/DJS10/

Duc, B., Fischer, S., & Bigun, J. (1999). Face authentication with Gabor information on deformable graphs. *IEEE Transactions on Image Processing, 8*(4), 504–516. doi:10.1109/83.753738

Duda, O. R., Hart, E. P., & Stork, G. D. (2001). *Pattern classification* (2nd ed.). New York, NY: Wiley Interscience.

Duda, R. O., Hart, P. E., & Stork, D. G. (2000). *Pattern classification*. Prentice Hall.

Duda, R., Hart, P., & Stork, D. (2000). *Pattern classification* (2nd ed.). Wiley-Interscience.

Dumay, A. C. M., van der Geest, R. J., Gerbrands, J. J., Jansen, E., & Reiber, J. H. C. (1992). Consistent inexact graph matching applied to labelling coronary segments in arteriograms. *Proceedings of the International Conference on Pattern Recognition, Conference C*, (pp. 439 – 442).

Dupé, F. X., & Brun, L. (2009). Tree covering within a graph kernel framework for shape classification. In *Proceedings of the Fifteenth Int. Conference on Image Analysis and Processing.*

Durand, P. J., Pasari, R., Baker, J. W., & Tsai, C.-C. (1999). An efficient algorithm for similarity analysis of molecules. *Internet Journal of Chemistry, 2*.

Duygulu, P., Barnard, K., De Freitas, J., & Forsyth, D. (2002). Object recognition as machine translation: Learning a lexicon for a fixed image vocabulary. In *Proceedings of the Seventh European Conference on Computer Vision (ECCV)*, (pp. 349–354).

Efros, A., & Leung, T. (1999). Texture synthesis by non parametric sampling. In *Proceedings of IEEE International Conference on Computer Vision*, (pp. 1033–1038).

Elagin, E., Steffens, J., & Neven, H. (1998). Automatic pose estimation system for human faces based on bunch graph matching technology. *Proceedings of the Third IEEE International Conference on Automatic Face and Gesture Recognition*, (pp. 136 – 141).

Elsässer, R., Lücking, T., & Monien, B. (2003). On spectral bounds for the k-partitioning of graphs. *Theory of Computing Systems*, *36*, 461–478. doi:10.1007/s00224-003-1083-9

El-Sonbaty, Y., & Ismail, M. A. (1998). A new algorithm for subgraph optimal isomorphism. *Pattern Recognition*, *31*(2), 205–218. doi:10.1016/S0031-3203(97)00041-1

Emms, D., Wilson, R., & Hancock, E. R. (2007). Graph embedding using quantum commute times. In *Graph-Based Representations in Pattern Recognition (Vol. 4538*, pp. 371–382). LNCS. doi:10.1007/978-3-540-72903-7_34

Englert, R., Cremers, A. B., & Seelmann-Eggebert, J. (1997). Recognition of polymorphic pattern in parameterized graphs for 3D building reconstruction. *Computing*, *12*, 11–20.

Erdös, P., & Rényi, A. (1960). On the evolution of random graphs. *Publication of the Mathematical Institute of the Hungarian Academy of Sciences*, *5*(1), 17–61.

Erdös, P., & Rényi, A. (1961). On the strength of connectedness of a random graph. *Acta Mathematica Academiae Scientiarum Hungaricae*, *12*(1-2), 261–267. doi:10.1007/BF02066689

Erwan, L., & Stephane, M. (2005). Sparse geometric image representations with bandelets. *IEEE Transactions on Image Processing*, *14*(4), 423–438.

Eshera, M. A., & Fu, K. S. (1984a). A similarity measure between attributed relational graphs for image analysis. *Proceedings of the 7th International Conference on Pattern Recognition*, (pp. 75 – 77).

Eshera, M. A., & Fu, K. S. (1984b). A graph distance measure for image analysis. *IEEE Transactions on Systems, Man, and Cybernetics*, *14*(3), 398–408.

Eshera, M. A., & Fu, K. S. (1986). An image understanding system using attributed symbolic representation and inexact graph-matching. *IEEE Transactions on Pattern Analysis and Machine Intelligence*, *8*(5), 604–618. doi:10.1109/TPAMI.1986.4767835

Fan, K. C., Liu, C. W., & Wang, Y. K. (1998). A fuzzy bipartite weighted graph matching approach to fingerprint verification. *Proceedings of the IEEE International Conference on Systems, Man, and Cybernetics*, (pp. 4363 – 4368).

Fan, J., Zeng, G., Body, M., & Hacid, M. S. (2005). Seeded region growing: An extensive and comparative study. *Pattern Recognition Letters*, *26*(8), 1139–1156. doi:10.1016/j.patrec.2004.10.010

Fatih Demirci, M., Shokoufandeh, A., Keselman, Y., Bretzner, L., & Dickinson, S. (2006). Object recognition as many-to-many feature matching. *International Journal of Computer Vision*, *69*(2), 203–222. doi:10.1007/s11263-006-6993-y

Feder, J. (1971). Plex languages. *Information Sciences*, *3*, 225–241. doi:10.1016/S0020-0255(71)80008-7

Felzenszwalb, P. F., & Huttenlocher, D. P. (2004). Efficient graph-based image segmentation. *International Journal of Computer Vision*, *59*(2), 167–181. doi:10.1023/B:VISI.0000022288.19776.77

Fergus, R., Perona, P., & Zisserman, A. (2003). *Object class recognition by unsupervised scale-invariant learning.* In IEEE Conference on Computer Vision and Pattern Recognition.

Fergus, R., Perona, P., & Zisserman, A. (2006). A sparse object category model for efficient learning and complete recognition. In *Toward Category-Level Object Recognition*, (pp. 443–461).

Fernàndez, M. L., & Valiente, G. (2001). A graph distance metric combining maximum common subgraph and minimum common supergraph. *Pattern Recognition Letters*, *22*(6), 753–758. doi:10.1016/S0167-8655(01)00017-4

Fiduccia, C. M., & Mattheyses, R. M. (1982). A linear-time heuristic for improving network partitions. In *DAC '82: Proceedings of the 19th Design Automation Conference*, (pp. 175–181). Piscataway, NJ: IEEE Press.

Fieldler, M. (1973). Algebraic connectivity of graphs. *Czechoslovak Mathematical Journal, 23*(98), 298–305.

Figueiredo, M. A. F., & Jain, A. K. (2002). Unsupervised learning of finite mixture models. *IEEE Transactions on Pattern Analysis and Machine Intelligence, 24*(3), 381–396. doi:10.1109/34.990138

Filatov, A., Gitis, A., & Kil, I. (1995). Graph-based handwritten digit string recognition. *Proceedings of the 3rd International Conference on Document Analysis and Recognition*, (pp. 845 – 848).

Fischer, S., Gilomen, K., & Bunke, H. (2002). Identification of diatoms by grid graph matching. *Proceeding of the Joint IAPR International Workshops SSPR and SPR*, (pp. 94 – 103).

Fischler, M. A., & Bolles, R. C. (1987). Random sample consensus: a paradigm for model fitting with applications to image analysis and automated cartography. In *Readings in computer vision: Issues, problems, principles, and paradigms* (pp. 726–740). San Francisco, CA: Morgan Kaufmann Publishers Inc.doi:10.1145/358669.358692

Fischler, M., & Elschlager, R. (1973). The representation and matching of pictorial structures. *IEEE Transactions on Computers, 22*, 67–92. doi:10.1109/T-C.1973.223602

Foggia, P., Sansone, C., & Vento, M. (2001). A database of graphs for isomorphism and sub-graph isomorphism benchmarking. *Proceedings of the 3rd IAPR TC-15 Workshop on Graph-based Representations in Pattern Recognition*, Ischia, May 23-25, (pp. 176-187).

Foggia, P., Sansone, C., & Vento, M. (2001). A performance comparison of five algorithms for graph isomorphism. *Proceedings of the 3rd IAPR-TC15 Workshop on Graph-based Representations in Pattern Recognition*, (pp. 188 – 199).

Foggia, P., Genna, R., & Vento, M. (2001). Symbolic vs. connectionist learning: an experimental comparison in a structured domain. *IEEE Transactions on Knowledge and Data Engineering, 13*(2), 176–195. doi:10.1109/69.917559

Foggia, P., Sansone, C., Tortorella, F., & Vento, M. (1999). Definition and validation of a distance measure between structural primitives. *Pattern Analysis & Applications, 2*, 215–227. doi:10.1007/s100440050030

Folkers, A., Samet, H., & Soffer, A. (2000). Processing pictorial queries with multiple instances using isomorphic subgraphs. *Proceedings of the 15th International Conference on Pattern Recognition*, (pp. 51 – 54).

Freedman, D., & Drineas, P. (2005). Energy minimization via graph cuts: Settling what is possible. *Proceedings of the 2005 IEEE Computer Society Conference on Computer Vision and Pattern Recognition*, (pp. 939-946).

Freeman, W., Pasztor, E., & Carmichael, O. (2000). Learning low-level vision. *International Journal of Computer Vision, 1*, 25–47.

Frey, B. J. J., & Dueck, D. (2007). Clustering by passing messages between data points. *Science, 315*.

Fu, Y., Cheng, J., Li, Z., & Lu, H. (2008). Saliency cuts: An automatic approach to object segmentation. *19th International Conference on Pattern Recognition* (pp. 1-4).

Fuchs, F., & Le Men, H. (1999). Building reconstruction on aerial images through multi-primitive graph matching. *Proceedings of the 2nd IAPR-TC15 Workshop on Graph-based Representations in Pattern Recognition*, (pp. 21 – 30).

Fuchs, F., & Le Men, H. (2000). Efficient subgraph isomorphism with 'a priori' knowledge. *Proceeding of the Joint IAPR International Workshops SSPR and SPR*, (pp. 427 – 436).

Gao, X. B., Xiao, B., & Tao, D. C. (2008). Image categorization: Graph edit distance + edge direction histogram. *Pattern Recognition, 41*(10), 3179–3191. doi:10.1016/j.patcog.2008.03.025

Gao, X. B., Xiao, B., & Tao, D. C. (2010). A survey of graph edit distance. *Pattern Analysis & Applications, 13*(1), 113–129. doi:10.1007/s10044-008-0141-y

Garey, M. R., & Johnson, D. S. (1990). *Computers and intractability; A guide to the theory of NP-completeness*. New York, NY: W. H. Freeman & Co.

Gärtner, T., Flach, P., & Wrobel, S. (2003b). On graph kernels: Hardness results and efficient alternatives. In B. Schökopf & M. Warmuth (Eds.), *Proceedings of the 16th Annual Conference on Learning Theory*, (pp. 129-143).

Gärtner, T. (2003a). A survey of kernels for structured data. *SIGKDD Explorations*, 5(1), 49–58. doi:10.1145/959242.959248

Gärtner, T. (2008). *Kernels for structured data*. World Scientific.

Ge, F., Wang, S., & Liu, T. (2006). Image-segmentation evaluation from the perspective of salient object extraction. *IEEE Conference on Computer Vision and Pattern Recognition* (pp. 1146-1153).

Gehler, P. V., & Nowozin, S. (2009). Let the kernel figure it out; principled learning of pre-processing for kernel classifiers. In *IEEE Conference on Computer Vision and Pattern Recognition*, (pp. 2836–2843).

Geiger, D., Liu, T., & Kohn, R. V. (2003). Representation and self-similarity of shapes. *IEEE Transactions on Pattern Analysis and Machine Intelligence*, 25(1), 86–99. doi:10.1109/TPAMI.2003.1159948

Geman, S., & Geman, D. (1984). Stochastic relaxation, Gibbs distributions, and the Bayesian restoration of images. *IEEE Transactions on Pattern Analysis and Machine Intelligence*, 6(6), 721–741.

Gendreau, M., Salvail, L., & Soriano, P. (1993). Solving the maximum clique problem using a Tabu search approach. *Annals of Operations Research*, 41, 385–403. doi:10.1007/BF02023002

Gengembre, N., & Berrani, S.-A. (2008). A probabilistic framework for fusing frame-based searches within a video copy detection system. In *Proceedings of the ACM International Conference on Content-based Image and Video Retrieval*, Niagara Falls, Canada.

Genton, G. M., Cristianini, N., Taylor, S. J., & Williamson, R. (2001). Classes of kernels for machine learning: a statistics perspective. *Journal of Machine Learning Research*, 2, 299–312.

Ghahraman, D. E., Wong, A. K. C., & Au, T. (1980). Graph optimal monomorphism algorithms. *IEEE Transactions on Systems, Man, and Cybernetics*, 10(4), 181–188. doi:10.1109/TSMC.1980.4308468

Gilboa, G., Sochen, N., & Zeevi, Y. (2004). Image enhancement and denoising by complex diffusion processes. *IEEE Transactions on Pattern Analysis and Machine Intelligence*, 26(8), 1020–1036.

Gionis, A., Indyk, P., & Motwani, R. (1999). Similarity search in high dimensions via hashing. In *Proceedings of International Conference on Very Large Data Bases*.

Gold, S., & Rangarajan, A. (1996). A graduated assignment algorithm for graph matching. *IEEE Transactions on Pattern Analysis and Machine Intelligence*, 18(4), 377–388. doi:10.1109/34.491619

Golub, G., & Loan, C. V. (1996). *Matrix computations* (3rd ed.). Baltimore, MD: Johns Hopkins University Press.

Gomila, C., & Meyer, F. (2001). Tracking objects by graph matching of image partition sequences. *Proceedings of the 3rd IAPR-TC15 Workshop on Graph-based Representations in Pattern Recognition*, (pp. 1 – 11).

Grady, L. (2005). Multilabel random walker image segmentation using prior models. *IEEE Conference on Computer Vision and Pattern Recognition* (Vol. 1, pp. 763-770).

Grady, L., & Funka-Lea, G. (2004). Multi-label image segmentation for medical applications based on graph-theoretic electrical potentials. *Proceedings of the 8th ECCV Workshop on Computer Vision Approaches to Medical Image Analysis and Mathematical Methods in Biomedical Image Analysis* (pp. 230-245).

Grady, L., & Sinop, A. K. (2008). Fast approximate random walker segmentation using eigenvector precomputation. *IEEE Conference on Computer Vision and Pattern Recognition* (pp. 1-8).

Grady, L. (2006). Random walks for image segmentation. *IEEE Transactions on Pattern Analysis and Machine Intelligence*, 28(11), 1768–1783. doi:10.1109/TPAMI.2006.233

Grady, L., & Schwartz, E. L. (2006). Isoperimetric graph partitioning for image segmentation. *IEEE Transactions on Pattern Analysis and Machine Intelligence*, 28(3), 469–475. doi:10.1109/TPAMI.2006.57

Granger, C. (1969). Investigating causal relations by econometric models and cross-spectral methods. *Econometrica: Journal of the Econometric Society, 37*(3), 424–438. doi:10.2307/1912791

Grau, V., Mewes, A. U. J., Alcaniz, M., Kikinis, R., & Warfield, S. K. (2004). Improved watershed transform for medical image segmentation using prior information. *IEEE Transactions on Medical Imaging, 23*(4), 447–458. doi:10.1109/TMI.2004.824224

Gregory, L., & Kittler, J. (2002). Using graph search techniques for contextual colour retrieval. *Proceeding of the Joint IAPR International Workshops SSPR and SPR*, (pp. 186 – 194).

Grigoryan, A. (2005). *Analysis on manifolds and heat kernel*. Personal lecture notes.

Grimson, W. E. (1991). *Object recognition by computer: The role of geometric constraints*. MIT Press.

Gu, C., Lim, J. J., Arbelaez, P., & Malik, J. (2009). Recognition using regions. In *Proceedings of IEEE Conference on Computer Vision and Pattern Recognition (CVPR)*.

Guattery, S., & Miller, G. L. (1998). On the quality of spectral separators. *SIAM Journal on Matrix Analysis and Applications, 19*, 701–719. doi:10.1137/S0895479896312262

Guo, C., Zhu, A., & Wu, Y. (2003). Towards a mathematical theory of primal sketch and sketchability. *Proceedings of ICCV'03*, (pp. 1228–1235).

Haasdonk, B. (2005). Feature space interpretation of SVMs with indefinite kernels. *IEEE Transactions on Pattern Analysis and Machine Intelligence, 27*(4), 482–492. doi:10.1109/TPAMI.2005.78

Hadley, S. W. (1995). Approximation techniques for hypergraph partitioning problems. *Discrete Applied Mathematics, 59*(2), 115–127. doi:10.1016/0166-218X(93)E0166-V

Hagenbuchner, M., Gori, M., Bunke, H., Tsoi, A. C., & Irniger, C. (2003). Using attributed plex grammars for the generation of image and graph databases. *Pattern Recognition Letters, 24*(8), 1081–1087. doi:10.1016/S0167-8655(02)00254-4

Hall, M. K. (1971). R-dimensional quadratic placement algorithm. *Management Science, 17*, 219–229. doi:10.1287/mnsc.17.3.219

Hampapur, A., & Bolle, R. M. (2002). *VideoGREP: Video copy detection using inverted file indices*. IBM research division, Tech. Rep.

Han, X., Xu, C., & Prince, J. L. (2003). A topology preserving level set method for geometric deformable model. *IEEE Transactions on Pattern Analysis and Machine Intelligence, 25*(6), 755–768. doi:10.1109/TPAMI.2003.1201824

Haralick, R. M., & Shapiro, L. G. (1985). Image segmentation techniques. *Computer Vision Graphics and Image Processing, 29*, 100–132. doi:10.1016/S0734-189X(85)90153-7

Haralick, R., & Shapiro, L. (1985). Survey: image segmentation techniques. *Computer Vision Graphics and Image Processing, 29*(1), 100–132. doi:10.1016/S0734-189X(85)90153-7

Haris, K., Efstradiatis, S. N., Maglaveras, N., Pappas, C., Gourassas, J., & Louridas, G. (1999). Model-based morphological segmentation and labeling of coronary angiograms. *IEEE Transactions on Medical Imaging, 18*(10), 1003–1015. doi:10.1109/42.811312

Hasinoff, S., Kang, S., & Szeliski, R. (2004). *Boundary matting for view synthesis*. IEEE Workshop on Image and Video Registration.

Haussler, D. (1999). *Convolution kernels on discrete structures*. Technical Report UCSC-CRL-99-10, University of California, Santa Cruz.

Hayashi, C. (1972). Two dimensional quantification based on the measure of dissimilarity among three elements. *Annals of the Institute of Statistical Mathematics, 24*(1), 251–257. doi:10.1007/BF02479755

He, J., Li, M., Zhang, H.-J., Tong, H., & Zhang, C. (2004). *Manifold-ranking based image retrieval*. In ACM MULTIMEDIA '04.

He, X., & Niyogi, P. (2003). *Locality preserving projections*. Seventeenth Annual Conference on Neural Information Processing Systems (NIPS).

He, X., Ma, W.-Y., King, O., Li, M., & Zhang, H. (2002). *Learning and inferring a semantic space from user's relevance feedback for image retrieval.* In ACM MUL-TIMEDIA '02.

Hein, M., Audibert, J., & von Luxburg, U. (2005). From graphs to manifoldsłweak and strong pointwise consistency of graph Laplacians. In *Proceedings of the 18th Conference on Learning Theory*, (pp. 470–485).

Heiser, W. J., & Bennani, M. (1997). Triadic distance models: Axiomatization and least squares representation. *Journal of Mathematical Psychology*, *41*(2), 189–206. doi:10.1006/jmps.1997.1166

He, J., Li, M., Zhang, H., Tong, H., & Zhang, C. (2006). Generalized manifold ranking-based image retrieval. *IEEE Transactions on Image Processing*, *15*(10), 3170–3177. doi:10.1109/TIP.2006.877491

Hendrickson, B., & Leland, R. W. (1995). A multilevel algorithm for partitioning graphs. *Proceedings of Supercomputing.*

Hilaga, M., Shinagawa, Y., Kohmura, T., & Kunii, T. L. (2001). Topology matching for fully automatic similarity estimation of 3D shapes. In *ACM SIGGRAPH*, (pp. 203-212).

Hlaoui, A., & Wang, S. (2002). A new algorithm for graph matching with application to content-based image retrieval. *Proceeding of the Joint IAPR International Workshops SSPR and SPR*, (pp. 291 – 300).

Hochbaum, D. S. (2010). Polynomial time algorithms for ratio regions and a variant of normalized cut. *IEEE Transactions on Pattern Analysis and Machine Intelligence*, *32*(5), 889–898. doi:10.1109/TPAMI.2009.80

Hochbruck, M., & Lubich, C. (1997). On Krylov subspace approximations to the matrix exponential operator. *SIAM Journal on Numerical Analysis*, *34*, 1911–1925.

Hofmann, T. (1998). Probabilistic latent semantic indexing. *In ACM SIGIR International Conference* (pp. 50–57).

Hofmann, T. (1999). Probabilistic latent semantic indexing. *Proceedings of the Twenty-Second Annual International SIGIR Conference on Research and Development in Information Retrieval* (SIGIR-99).

Hong, P., Wang, R., & Huang, T. (2000). Learning patterns from images by combining soft decisions and hard decisions. *Proceedings of the 2000 IEEE Computer Society Conference on Computer Vision and Pattern Recognition*, (pp. 79 – 83).

Hong, W., Wright, J., Kun, H., & Yi, M. (2006). Multiscale hybrid linear models for lossy image representation. *IEEE Transactions on Image Processing*, *15*(12), 3655–3671.

Hopcroft, J. E., & Wong, J. (1974). Linear time algorithm for isomorphism of planar graphs. *Proceedings of the 6th Annual ACM Symposium on Theory of Computing*, (pp. 172-184).

Hsieh, A. J., Fan, K. C., & Fan, T. I. (1995). Bipartite weighted matching for on-line handwritten Chinese character recognition. *Pattern Recognition*, *28*, 143–151. doi:10.1016/0031-3203(94)00090-9

Hua, X.-S., Chen, X., & Zhang, H.-J. (2004). Robust video signature based on ordinal measure. In *Proc. IEEE International Conference on Image Processing*, (Vol. 1, pp. 685-688).

Huang, Y., Liu, Q., & Metaxas, D. (2009). Video object segmentation by hypergraph cut. *IEEE Computer Society Conference on Computer Vision and Pattern Recognition*, (pp. 1738–1745).

Huang, Y., Liu, Q., Zhang, S., & Metaxas, D. N. (2010). *Image retrieval via probabilistic hypergraph ranking.* IEEE Computer Society Conference on Computer Vision and Pattern Recognition.

Huet, B., & Hancock, E. R. (1998). Fuzzy relational distance for large-scale object recognition. *Proceedings of IEEE Conference on Computer Vision and Pattern Recognition*, (pp. 138-143).

Huet, B., Kern, N. J., Guarascio, G., & Merialdo, B. (2001). Relational skeletons for retrieval in patent drawings. *Proceedings of the International Conference on Image Processing*, (pp. 737 – 740).

Huet, B., & Hancock, E. R. (1999). Shape recognition from large image libraries by inexact graph matching. *Pattern Recognition Letters*, *20*(11-13), 1259–1269. doi:10.1016/S0167-8655(99)00093-8

Hu, T., & Moerder, K. (1985). Multiterimnal flows in hypergraphs. In Hu, T. C., & Kuh, E. S. (Eds.), *VLSI circuit layout* (pp. 81–86). IEEE Press.

Huttenlocher, D. P., Klanderman, G. A., & Rucklidge, W. J. (1993). Comparing images using the Hausdorff distance. *IEEE Transactions on Pattern Analysis and Machine Intelligence, 15*(9), 850–863. doi:10.1109/34.232073

Ihler, E., Wagner, D., & Wagner, F. (1993). Modeling hypergraphs by graphs with the same mincut properties. *Information Processing Letters, 45*(4), 171–175. doi:10.1016/0020-0190(93)90115-P

Indyk, P., & Motwani, R. (1998). Approximate nearest neighbors: towards removing the curse of dimensionality. In *Proceedings of Symposium on Theory of Computing,* (pp. 604–613). New York, NY: ACM.

Irniger, C., & Bunke, H. (2001). Graph matching: Filtering large databases of graphs using decision trees. *Proceedings of the 3rd IAPR-TC15 Workshop on Graph-based Representations in Pattern Recognition,* (pp. 239 – 249).

Irniger, C., & Bunke, H. (2003). Theoretical analysis and experimental comparison of graph matching algorithms for database filtering. In Hancock, E., & Vento, M. (Eds.), *Graph Based Representations in Pattern Recognition* (*Vol. 2726*, pp. 118–129). Lecture Notes in Computer Science Berlin, Germany: Springer. doi:10.1007/3-540-45028-9_11

Isard, M., & Blake, A. (1998). Condensation - Conditional density propagation for visual tracking. *International Journal of Computer Vision, 29*(1), 5–28. doi:10.1023/A:1008078328650

Jagota, A., Pelillo, M., & Rangarajan, A. (2000). A new deterministic annealing algorithm for maximum clique. *Proceedings of the International Joint Conference on Neural Networks,* (Vol. 6, pp. 505 – 508).

Jain, P., Kulis, B., Dhillon, I., & Grauman, K. (2008). Online metric learning and fast similarity search. In *Advances in Neural Information Processing Systems*. NIPS.

Jegou, H., Douze, M., & Schmid, C. (2008). Hamming embedding and weak geometric consistency for large scale image search. In *Proceedings of the European Conference on Computer Vision*. Marseille, France: Springer.

Jia, J., & Abe, K. (1998). Automatic generation of prototypes in 3D structural object recognition. *Proceedings of the Fourteenth International Conference on Pattern Recognition,* (pp. 697 – 700).

Jiang, X., & Bunke, H. (1998). Marked subgraph isomorphism of ordered graphs. *Proceeding of the Joint IAPR International Workshops SSPR and SPR,* (pp. 122 – 131).

Jiang, X., Munger, A., & Bunke, H. (1999). Synthesis of representative symbols by computing generalized median graphs. *Proceedings of the International Workshop on Graphics Recognition GREC ' 99,* (pp. 187 – 194).

Jiang, Y.-G., Ngo, C.-W., & Yang, J. (2007). Towards optimal bag-of-features for object categorization and semantic video retrieval. In *Proceedings of the ACM International Conference on Image and Video Retrieval*, Amsterdam, Netherlands.

Jiang, X. Y., & Bunke, H. (1999). Optimal vertex ordering of graphs. *Information Processing Letters, 72*(5-6), 149–154. doi:10.1016/S0020-0190(99)00148-9

Jiang, X., Münger, A., & Bunke, H. (2001). On median graphs: Properties, algorithms, and applications. *IEEE Transactions on Pattern Analysis and Machine Intelligence, 23*(10), 1144–1151. doi:10.1109/34.954604

Jiji, C., Joshi, M., & Chaudhuri, S. (2004). Single-frame image super-resolution using learned wavelet coefficients. *International Journal of Imaging Systems and Technology, 3*, 105–112.

Joly, A., & Buisson, O. (2005). Discriminant local features selection using efficient density estimation in a large database. In *Proceedings of the ACM SIGMM International Workshop Multimedia Information Retrieval*, Hilton, Singapore.

Joly, A., Law-to, J., & Boujemaa, N. (2008). "INRIA-IMEDIA TRECVID 2008: Video copy detection. In *Proceedings of TRECVID*, Gaithersburg, USA.

Joly, A., Buisson, O., & Frelicot, C. (2007). Content-based copy retrieval using distortion-based probabilistic similarity search. *IEEE Transactions on Multimedia, 9*(2), 293–306.

Joly, S., & Calv, G. (1995). Three-way distances. *Journal of Classification, 12*(2), 191–205. doi:10.1007/BF03040855

Jung, C., Kim, B., & Kim, C. (2010). Automatic segmentation of salient objects using iterative reversible graph cut. *International Conference on Multimedia and Expo* (pp. 590-595).

Jury, E. (1958). *Sampled-data control systems*. John Wiley & Sons.

Justice, D., & Hero, A. (2006). A binary linear programming formulation of the graph edit distance. *IEEE Transactions on Pattern Analysis and Machine Intelligence, 28*(8), 1200–1214. doi:10.1109/TPAMI.2006.152

Kälviäinen, H., & Oja, E. (1990). Comparisons of attributed graph matching algorithms for computer vision. In *Proceedings of STEP-90, Finnish Artificial Intelligence Symposium,* (pp. 354-368). Oulu, Finland, June.

Kandola, J., Shawe-Taylor, J., & Cristianini, N. (2002). Learning semantic similarity. *Neural Information Processing Systems, 15,* 657–664.

Karlen, M., Weston, J., Erkan, A., & Collobert, R. (2008). *Large scale manifold transduction*. In International Conference on Machine Learning (ICML).

Karypis, G., & Kumar, V. (1995). Analysis of multilevel graph partitioning. *Proceedings of Supercomputing.*

Karypis, G., & Kumar, V. (1999). Multilevel k-way hypergraph partitioning. In *DAC '99: Proceedings of the 36th Annual ACM/IEEE Design Automation Conference,* (pp. 343–348). New York, NY: ACM.

Karypis, G., & Kumar, V. (1998a). A fast and high quality multilevel scheme for partitioning irregular graphs. *SIAM Journal on Scientific Computing, 20,* 359–392. doi:10.1137/S1064827595287997

Karypis, G., & Kumar, V. (1998b). Multilevel k-way partitioning scheme for irregular graphs. *Journal of Parallel and Distributed Computing, 48,* 96–129. doi:10.1006/jpdc.1997.1404

Kashima, H., & Inokuchi, A. (2002). Kernels for graph classification. In *Proceedings of the ICDM Workshop on Active Mining,* (pp. 31-36).

Kashima, H., Tsuda, K., & Inokuchi, A. (2003). Marginalized kernel between labeled graphs. In *Proceedings of the Twentieth International Conference on Machine Learning.*

Kazius, J., McGuire, R., & Bursi, R. (2005). Derivation and validation of toxicophores for mutagenicity prediction. *Journal of Medicinal Chemistry, 48*(1), 312–320. doi:10.1021/jm040835a

Ke, Q., & Kanade, T. (2001). *A subspace approach to layer extraction*. IEEE Conference on Computer Vision and Pattern Recognition.

Ke, Q., & Kanade, T. (2002). *A robust subspace approach to layer extraction*. IEEE Workshop on Motion and Video Computing.

Ke, Q., & Kanade, T. (2004). *Robust subspace clustering by combined use of kNND metric and SVD algorithm*. IEEE Conference on Computer Vision and Pattern Recognition.

Ke, Y., & Sukthankar, R. (2004). PCA-SIFT: A more distinctive representation for local image descriptors. In *IEEE Conference on Computer Vision and Pattern Recognition,* (pp. 506–513).

Ke, Y., Sukthankar, R., & Huston, L. (2004). An efficient parts-based near-duplicate and sub-image retrieval system. In *Proceedings of ACM International Conference Multimedia,* New York, NY, USA.

Kernighan, B. W., & Lin, S. (1970). An efficient heuristic procedure for partitioning graphs. *The Bell System Technical Journal, 49*(1), 291–307.

Khan, S., & Shah, M. (2001). *Object based segmentation of video using color, motion and spatial information*. IEEE Conference on Computer Vision and Pattern Recognition.

Khoo, K. G., & Suganthan, P. N. (2001). Multiple relational graphs mapping using genetic algorithms. *Proceedings of the 2001 Congress on Evolutionary Computation,* (pp. 727 – 733).

Kim, H.-S., Lee, J., Liu, H., & Lee, D. (2008). Video linkage: Group based copied video detection. In *Proceedings of the ACM International Conference on Content-based Image and Video Retrieval,* Niagara Falls, Canada.

Kim, C., & Vasudev, B. (2005). Spatiotemporal sequence matching for efficient video copy detection. *IEEE Transactions on Circuits and Systems for Video Technology, 15*(1), 127–132.

Kim, W. Y., & Kak, A. C. (1991). 3-D object recognition using bipartite matching embedded in discrete relaxation. *IEEE Transactions on Pattern Analysis and Machine Intelligence, 13*(3), 224–251. doi:10.1109/34.75511

Kitchen, L., & Rosenfeld, A. (1979). Discrete relaxation for matching relational structures. *IEEE Transactions on Systems, Man, and Cybernetics, 9*, 869–874. doi:10.1109/TSMC.1979.4310140

Kittler, J., & Hancock, E. R. (1989). Combining evidence in probabilistic relaxation. *International Journal of Pattern Recognition and Artificial Intelligence, 3*, 29–51. doi:10.1142/S021800148900005X

Kleinberg, J. M. (1999). Authoritative sources in a hyperlinked environment. *Journal of the ACM, 46*, 604–632. doi:10.1145/324133.324140

Koch, I. (2001). Enumerating all connected maximal common subgraphs in two graphs. *Theoretical Computer Science, 250*(1), 1–30. doi:10.1016/S0304-3975(00)00286-3

Koenderink, J. (1984). The structure of images. *Biological Cybernetics, 50*, 363–370.

Kolmogorov, V., & Zabih, R. (2001). *Visual correspondence with occlusions using graph cuts.* International Conference on Computer Vision.

Kolmogorov, V., & Zabih, R. (2002). *Multi-camera scene reconstruction via graph cut.* European Conference on Computer Vision.

Kondor, R., & Lafferty, J. (2002). Diffusion kernels on graphs and other discrete input spaces. In *Proceedings of the 19th International Conference on Machine Learning,* (pp. 315-322).

Koo, H. I., & Cho, N. I. (2009). Graph cuts using a riemannian metric induced by tensor voting. *IEEE 12th International Conference on Computer Vision* (pp. 514-520).

Koo, J. H., & Yoo, S. I. (1998). A structural matching for two-dimensional visual pattern inspection. *Proceedings of the IEEE International Conference on Systems, Man, and Cybernetics,* (pp. 4429 – 4434).

Kosinov, S., & Caelli, T. (2002). Inexact multisubgraph matching using graph Eigenspace and clustering models. *Proceeding of the Joint IAPR International Workshops SSPR and SPR,* (pp. 133 – 142).

Kotropoulos, C., Tefas, A., & Pitas, I. (2000). Frontal face authentication using morphological elastic graph matching. *IEEE Transactions on Image Processing, 9*(4), 555–560. doi:10.1109/83.841933

Kropatsch, W. (2001). Benchmarking graph matching algorithms – A complementary view. *Proceedings of the 3rd IAPR – TC15 Workshop on Graph-based Representations,* Italy, (pp. 170-175).

Lades, M., Vorbruggen, J. C., Buhmann, J., Lange, J., von der Malsburg, C., Wurz, R. P., & Konen, W. (1993). Distortion invariant object recognition in the dynamic link architecture. *IEEE Transactions on Computers, 42*(2-3), 300–311. doi:10.1109/12.210173

Lafferty, J., & Lebanon, G. (2003). Information diffusion kernels. *Advances in Neural Information Processing Systems, 15*, 375–382. MIT Press.

Lafferty, J., & Lebanon, G. (2005). Diffusion kernels on statistical manifolds. *Journal of Machine Learning Research, 6*, 129–163.

Lafon, S. (2004). *Diffusion maps and geometric harmonics.* PhD dissertation, Yale University.

Laptev, I., & Lindeberg, T. (2003). Space-time interest points. In *IEEE International Conference on Computer Vision* (pp. 432–439).

Larrosa, J., & Valiente, G. (2002). Constraint satisfaction algorithms for graph pattern matching. *Mathematical Structures in Computer Science, 12*, 403–422. doi:10.1017/S0960129501003577

Latecki, L. J., Lakamper, R., & Eckhardt, U. (2000). Shape descriptors for non-rigid shapes with a single closed contour. In *CVPR: IEEE International Conference on Computer Vision and Pattern Recognition,* (pp. 424-429).

Latecki, L. J., Megalooikonomou, V., Wang, Q., Lakamper, R., Ratanamahatana, C. A., & Keogh, E. (2005). Partial elastic matching of time series. In *ICDM: IEEE International Conference on Data Mining,* (pp. 701-704).

Latecki, L. J., & Lakamper, R. (1999). Convexity rule for shape decomposition based on discrete contour evolution. *Computer Vision and Image Understanding, 73*(3), 441–454. doi:10.1006/cviu.1998.0738

Latecki, L. J., & Lakamper, R. (2000). Shape similarity measure based on correspondence of visual parts. *IEEE Transactions on Pattern Analysis and Machine Intelligence*, *22*(10), 1185–1190. doi:10.1109/34.879802

Lawler, E. S. (2001). *Combinatorial optimization: Networks and matroids* (p. 374). Dover Books.

Law-To, J., Buisson, O., Gouet-Brunet, V., & Boujemaa, N. (2006). Robust voting algorithm based on labels of behavior for video copy detection. In *Proceedings of the ACM International Conference on Multimedia*, Santa Barbara, CA, USA.

Lazarescu, M., Bunke, H., & Venkatesh, S. (2000). Graph matching: Fast candidate elimination using machine learning techniques. *Proceeding of the Joint IAPR International Workshops SSPR and SPR*, (pp. 236 – 245).

Lee, R. S. T. Liu, & J. N. K. (1999). An oscillatory elastic graph matching model for recognition of offline handwritten Chinese characters. *Third International Conference on Knowledge-Based Intelligent Information Engineering Systems*, (pp. 284 – 287).

Lee, W. J., & Duin, R. (2009). A labelled graph based multiple classifier system. In J. A. Benediktsson, J. Kittler, & F. Roli (Eds.), *Proceedings of the 8th International Workshop on Multiple Classifier Systems, LNCS 5519*, (pp. 201-210).

Lee, H., Battle, A., Raina, R., & Ng, A. (2007). Efficient sparse coding algorithms. [MIT Press.]. *Advances in Neural Information Processing Systems*, 801–808.

Lee, S., & Yoo, C. D. (2008). Robust video fingerprinting for content-based video identification. *IEEE Transactions on Circuits and Systems for Video Technology*, *18*(7), 983–988.

Lee, Y. J., & Grauman, K. (2009). Foreground focus: Unsupervised learning from partially matching images. *International Journal of Computer Vision*, *85*(2), 143–166. doi:10.1007/s11263-009-0252-y

Leibe, B., Leonardis, A., & Schiele, A. (2004). *Combined object categorization and segmentation with an implicit shape model*. In Workshop on Statistical Learning in Learning in Computer Vision, European Conference on Computer Vision.

Lemur. (2011). *The Lemur toolkit for language modeling and information retrieval*. Retrieved from http://www.lemurproject.org/

Leordeanu, M., & Hebert, M. (2009). A spectral technique for correspondence problem using pairwise constraints. In *IEEE International Conference on Computer Vision, Vol.2* (pp. 1482-1489)

Li, C., & Hamza, B. A. (2011). Skeleton path based approach for nonrigid 3D shape analysis and retrieval. In *Combinatorial Image Analysis – 14th International Workshop (IWCIA), LNCS 6636/2011*, (pp. 84-95).

Li, F., & Perona, P. (2005). Bayesian hierarchical model for learning natural scene categories. In *IEEE Conference on Computer Vision and Pattern Recognition*, (pp. 524–531).

Li, W. J., & Lee, T. (2000). Object recognition by subscene graph matching. *IEEE International Conference on Robotics and Automation*, (pp. 1459 – 1464).

Li, F., Fergus, R., & Perona, P. (2006). One-shot learning of object categories. *IEEE Transactions on Pattern Analysis and Machine Intelligence*, *28*(4), 594–611. doi:10.1109/TPAMI.2006.79

Lim, R., & Reinders, M. J. T. (2001). Facial landmarks localization based on fuzzy and gabor wavelet graph matching. *The 10th IEEE International Conference on Fuzzy Systems*, (pp. 683 – 686).

Ling, H., & Jacobs, D. W. (2007). Shape classification using inner-distance. *IEEE Transactions on Pattern Analysis and Machine Intelligence*, *29*(2), 286–299. doi:10.1109/TPAMI.2007.41

Liu, C. W., Fan, K. C., Horng, J. T., & Wang, Y. K. (1995). Solving weighted graph matching problem by modified microgenetic algorithm. *IEEE International Conference on Systems, Man and Cybernetics*, (pp. 638 – 643).

Liu, J., Luo, J., & Shah, M. (2009). Recognizing realistic actions from videos in the wild. In *IEEE International Conference on Computer Vision and Pattern Recognition* (pp. 1996–2003).

Liu, T., & Geiger, D. (1999). Approximate tree matching and shape similarity. In *ICCV: IEEE International Conference on Computer Vision*, (pp. 456-462).

Liu, Y., Jin, R., & Yang, L. (2006). Semi-supervised multi-label learning by constrained non-negative matrix factorization. In *Proceedings of National Conference on Artificial Intelligence and Innovative Applications of Artificial Intelligence Conference (AAAI)*, (Vol. 21, pp. 666–671).

Liu, Z., & Sarkar, S. (2004). *Simplest representation yet for gait recognition: Averaged silhouette*. In IEEE International Conference on Pattern Recognition.

Liu, J. Z., Ma, K., Cham, W. K., & Chang, M. M. Y. (2000). Two-layer assignment method for online Chinese character recognition. *IEEE Proceedings Vision. Image and Signal Processing*, *147*(1), 47–54. doi:10.1049/ip-vis:20000103

Llados, J., Lopez-Krahe, J., & Marti, E. (1996). Hand drawn document understanding using the straight line Hough transform and graph matching. *Proceedings of the 13th International Conference on Pattern Recognition*, (pp. 497 – 501).

Llados, J., Marti, E., & Villanueva, J. J. (2001). Symbol recognition by error-tolerant subgraph matching between region adjacency graphs. *IEEE Transactions on Pattern Analysis and Machine Intelligence*, *23*(10), 1137–1143. doi:10.1109/34.954603

Lowe, D. (2004). Distinctive image features from scale-invariant keypoints. *International Journal of Computer Vision*, *60*(2), 91–110. doi:10.1023/B:VISI.0000029664.99615.94

Lowe, D. G. (2004). Distinctive image features from scale-invariant keypoints. *International Journal of Computer Vision*, *60*(2), 91–110.

Lucas, B. D., & Kanade, T. (1981). An iterative image registration technique with an application to stereo vision. In *Proceedings of the 7th International Joint Conference on Artificial Intelligence (IJCAI '81)*, (pp. 674–679).

Luks, E. M. (1982). Isomorphism of graphs of bounded valence can be tested in polynomial time. *Journal of Computer and System Sciences*, *25*, 42–65. doi:10.1016/0022-0000(82)90009-5

Luo, B., Robles-Kelly, A., Torsello, A., Wilson, R. C., & Hancock, E. R. (2001). Clustering shock trees. *Proceedings of the 3rd IAPR-TC15 Workshop on Graph-based Representations in Pattern Recognition*, (pp. 217 – 228).

Luo, D., Ding, C., Huang, H., & Li, T. (2009). Non-negative Laplacian embedding. *International Conference in Data Mining (ICDM)*, (pp. 337–346).

Luo, B., & Hancock, E. R. (2001). Structural graph matching using the EM algorithm and singular value decomposition. *IEEE Transactions on Pattern Analysis and Machine Intelligence*, *23*(10), 1120–1136. doi:10.1109/34.954602

Luo, B., Wilson, R. C., & Hancock, E. R. (2003). Spectral embedding of graphs. *Pattern Recognition*, *36*(10), 2213–2230. doi:10.1016/S0031-3203(03)00084-0

Luo, B., Wilson, R., & Hancock, E. (2003). Spectral embedding of graphs. *Pattern Recognition*, *36*(10), 2213–2223. doi:10.1016/S0031-3203(03)00084-0

Lu, S. W., Ren, Y., & Suen, C. Y. (1991). Hierarchical attributed graph representation and recognition of handwritten Chinese characters. *Pattern Recognition*, *24*, 617–632. doi:10.1016/0031-3203(91)90029-5

Lyons, M. J., Budynek, J., & Akamatsu, S. (1999). Automatic classification of single facial images. *IEEE Transactions on Pattern Analysis and Machine Intelligence*, *21*(12), 1357–1362. doi:10.1109/34.817413

MacArthur, S., Brodley, C., & Shyu, C. (2000). Relevance feedback decision trees in content-based image retrieval. In *CBAIVL '00: Proceedings of the IEEE Workshop on Content-based Access of Image and Video Libraries*, (p. 68).

Macqueen, J. B. (1967). Some methods of classification and analysis of multivariate observations. In *Proceedings of the Fifth Berkeley Symposium on Mathematical Statistics and Probability*, (pp. 281–297).

Mahe, P., Ueda, N., & Akutsu, T. (2005). Graph kernels for molecular structures -- Activity relationship analysis with support vector machines. *Journal of Chemical Information and Modeling*, *45*(4), 939–951. doi:10.1021/ci050039t

Mah, P., & Vert, J. P. (2008). Graph kernels based on tree patterns for molecules. *Machine Learning*, *75*(1), 3–35. doi:10.1007/s10994-008-5086-2

Maio, D., & Maltoni, D. (1996). A structural approach to fingerprint classification. *Proceedings of the 13th International Conference on Pattern Recognition*, (pp. 578 – 585).

Marszalek, M., Laptev, I., & Schmid, C. (2009). Actions in context. In *IEEE International Conference on Computer Vision and Pattern Recognition* (pp. 2929–2936).

Martin, D., Fowlkes, C., Tal, D., & Malik, J. (2001). *IEEE 8th International Conference on Computer Vision* (Vol. 2, pp. 416-423).

Martin, D. R., Fowlkes, C., Tal, D., & Malik, J. (2001). *A database of human segmented natural images and its application to evaluating segmentation algorithms and measuring ecological statistics. Technical report* (pp. 416–425). University of Caloifornia at Berkeley.

McAllester, D., Felzenszwalb, P., & Girshick, R. (2010). *Cascade object detection with deformable part models.* In The IEEE Conference on Computer Vision and Pattern Recognition.

McGregor, J. J. (1982). Backtrack search algorithm and the maximal common subgraph problem. *Software, Practice & Experience, 12*(1), 23–34. doi:10.1002/spe.4380120103

McKay, B. D. (1981). Practical graph isomorphism. *Congressus Numerantium, 30*, 45–87.

Medasani, S., & Krishnapuram, R. (1999). A fuzzy approach to content-based image retrieval. *Proceedings of the IEEE International Conference on Fuzzy Systems,* (pp. 1251 – 1260).

Medasani, S., Krishnapuram, R., & Choi, Y. S. (2001). Graph matching by relaxation of fuzzy assignments. *IEEE Transactions on Fuzzy Systems, 9*(1), 173–182. doi:10.1109/91.917123

Messmer, B. (1995). *Efficient graph matching algorithm for preprocessed model graphs.* PhD Thesis, Institut fur Informatik und Angewandte Mathematik, Univ. of Bern.

Messmer, B. T., & Bunke, H. (1998). A new algorithm for error-tolerant subgraph isomorphism detection. *IEEE Transactions on Pattern Analysis and Machine Intelligence, 20*(5), 493–504. doi:10.1109/34.682179

Messmer, B. T., & Bunke, H. (1999). A decision tree approach to graph and subgraph isomorphism detection. *Pattern Recognition, 32*(12), 1979–1998. doi:10.1016/S0031-3203(98)90142-X

Messmer, B. T., & Bunke, H. (2000). Efficient subgraph isomorphism detection: A decomposition approach. *IEEE Transactions on Knowledge and Data Engineering, 12*(2), 307–323. doi:10.1109/69.842269

Meth, R., & Chellappa, R. (1996). Target indexing in synthetic aperture radar imagery using topographic features. *Proceedings of the IEEE International Conference on Acoustics, Speech, and Signal Processing,* (pp. 2152 – 2155).

Mignotte, M. (2008). Segmentation by fusion of histogram-based K-means clusters in different color spaces. *IEEE Transactions on Image Processing, 17*(5), 780–787. doi:10.1109/TIP.2008.920761

Mikolajczyk, K. (n.d.). *Binaries for affine covariant region descriptors.* Retrieved from http://www.robots.ox.ac.uk/_vgg/research/affine/

Mikolajczyk, K., & Schmid, C. (2004). Scale & affine invariant interest point detectors. *International Journal of Computer Vision, 60*(1), 63–86.

Mikolajczyk, K., Tuytelaars, T., Schmid, C., Zisserman, A., Matas, J., & Schaffalitzky, F. (2005). A comparison of affine region detectors. *International Journal of Computer Vision, 65*(1-2), 43–72. doi:10.1007/s11263-005-3848-x

Miyazaki, T. (1997). The complexity of McKay's canonical labeling algorithm. *Groups and Computation II. DIMACS Series Discrete Mathematics Theoretical Computer Science, 28*, 239–256.

Moler, C., & Van Loan, C. (2003). Nineteen dubious ways to compute the exponential of a matrix, twenty-five years later. *SIAM Review, 45*(1), 3–49.

Moore, A. (1991). *An intoductory tutorial on kd-trees.* Ph.D. dissertation, Carnegie Mello University.

Mortensen, E., Deng, H., & Shapiro, L. (2005). A SIFT descriptor with global context. In *IEEE International Conference on Computer Vision and Pattern Recognition* (pp. 184–190).

Mrazek, P., & Navara, M. (2003). Selection of optimal stopping time for nonlinear diffusion filtering. *International Journal of Computer Vision, 52*, 189–203.

Mudenagudi, U., Singla, R., Kalra, P. K., & Banerjee, S. (2006). Super resolution using graph-cut. *Proceedings of ACCV'06*, (pp. 385–394).

Myers, R., Wilson, R. C., & Hancock, E. R. (2000). Bayesian graph edit distance. *IEEE Transactions on Pattern Analysis and Machine Intelligence, 22*(6), 628–635. doi:10.1109/34.862201

Neuhaus, M., & Bunke, H. (2007). *Bridging the gap between graph edit distance and kernel machines.* River Edge, NJ: World Scientific Publishing.

Neuhaus, M., Riesen, K., & Bunke, H. (2006). Fast suboptimal algorithms for the computation of graph edit distance. In D.-Y. Yeung, J. T. Kwok, A. Fred, F. Roli, & D. de Ridder (Eds.), *Proceedings of the 11th International Workshop on Structural and Syntactic Pattern Recognition, LNCS 4109*, (pp. 163-172). Springer.

Neuhaus, M., & Bunke, H. (2003). An error-tolerant approximate matching algorithm for attributed planar graphs and its application to fingerprint classification. In Fred, A., Caelli, T., & Camphilho, A. (Eds.), *SSPR 2004 (Vol. 3138*, p. 180). Lecture Notes in Computer Science. doi:10.1007/978-3-540-27868-9_18

Ng, A., Jordan, M., & Weiss, Y. (2001). On spectral clustering: Analysis and an algorithm. In *Advances in Neural Information Processing Systems*. NIPS.

Ni, B., Yan, S., & Kassim, A. (2009). Recognizing human group activities with localized causalities. In *IEEE International Conference on Computer Vision and Pattern Recognition* (pp. 1470–1477).

Niebles, J., Wang, H., & Li, F. (2008). Unsupervised learning of human action categories using spatial-temporal words. *International Journal of Computer Vision, 79*, 299–318. doi:10.1007/s11263-007-0122-4

Nister, D., & Stewenius, H. (2006). Scalable recognition with a vocabulary tree. In *Proceedings of IEEE Conference on Computer Vision and Pattern Recognition*, (pp. 2161-2168).

Nowak, E., & Jurie, F. (2007). *Learning visual similarity measures for comparing neverseen never seen objects.* In IEEE Conference on Computer Vision and Pattern Recognition.

Oflazer, K. (1997). Error-tolerant retrieval of trees. *IEEE Transactions on Pattern Analysis and Machine Intelligence, 19*(12), 1376–1380. doi:10.1109/34.643897

Ogniewicz, R. L., & Kubler, O. (1995). Hierarchic Voronoi skeletons. *Pattern Recognition, 28*(3), 343–359. doi:10.1016/0031-3203(94)00105-U

Olatunbosun, S., Dowling, G. R., & Ellis, T. J. (1996). Topological representation for matching coloured surfaces. *Proceedings of the International Conference on Image Processing*, (pp. 1019 – 1022).

Oostveen, J., Kalker, T., & Haitsma, J. (2002). *Feature extraction and a database strategy for video fingerprinting (Vol. 2314*, pp. 117–128). Visual Lecture Notes in Computer Science.

Oppenheim, A. V., Schafer, R. W., & Buck, J. R. (1999). *Discrete-time signal processing* (2nd ed.). Prentice Hall.

Otsu, N. (1979). A threshold selection method from gray-level histograms. *IEEE Transactions on Systems, Man, and Cybernetics, 9*(1), 62–66. doi:10.1109/TSMC.1979.4310076

Ozer, B., Wolf, W., & Akansu, A. N. (1999). A graph based object description for information retrieval in digital image and video libraries. *Proceedings of the IEEE Workshop on Content-Based Access of Image and Video Libraries*, (pp. 79 – 83).

Pardalos, P., Rappe, J., & Resende, M. G. C. (1998). *An exact parallel algorithm for the maximum clique problem: High performance algorithms and software in nonlinear optimization.* Kluwer Academic Publishers.

Park, I. K., Yun, I. D., & Lee, S. U. (1997). Models and algorithms for efficient color image indexing. *Proceedings of the IEEE Workshop on Content-Based Access of Image and Video Libraries*, (pp. 36 – 41).

Patras, I., Hendirks, E., & Lagendijk, R. (2001). Video segmentation by MAP labeling of watershed segments. *IEEE Transactions on Pattern Analysis and Machine Intelligence, 23*(3), 326–332. doi:10.1109/34.910886

Pavlidis, T., Sakoda, W. J., & Shi, H. (1995). Matching graph embeddings for shape analysis. *Proceedings of the Third International Conference on Document Analysis and Recognition*, (pp. 729 – 733).

Pekalska, E., & Duin, R. (2005). *The dissimilarity representation for pattern recognition: Foundations and applications.* World Scientific, 2005.

Pelillo, M. (1998). A unifying framework for relational structure matching. *Proceedings of Fourteenth International Conference on Pattern Recognition,* (pp. 1316–1319).

Pelillo, M. (1995a). Relaxation labeling networks for the maximum clique problem. *Journal of Artificial Neural Networks, 2,* 313–328.

Pelillo, M. (1999). Replicator equations, maximal cliques, and graph isomorphism. *Neural Computation, 11*(8), 1933–1955. doi:10.1162/089976699300016034

Pelillo, M. (2002). Matching free trees, maximal cliques and monotone game dynamics. *IEEE Transactions on Pattern Analysis and Machine Intelligence, 24*(11), 1535–1541. doi:10.1109/TPAMI.2002.1046176

Pelillo, M., & Jagota, A. (1995b). Feasible and infeasible maxima in a quadratic program for maximum clique. *Journal of Artificial Neural Networks, 2,* 411–420.

Pelillo, M., Siddiqi, K., & Zucker, S. W. (1999). Matching hierarchical structures using association graphs. *IEEE Transactions on Pattern Analysis and Machine Intelligence, 21*(11), 1105–1120. doi:10.1109/34.809105

Peng, B., & Veksler, O. (2008). *Parameter selection for graph cut based image segmentation.* British Machine Vision Conference.

Peng, B., Zhang, L., & Yang, J. (2009). *Iterated graph cuts for image segmentation.* 9th Asian Conference on Computer Vision.

Penrose, M. (Ed.). (2003). *Random geometric graphs.* Oxford, UK: Oxford University Press. doi:10.1093/acprof:oso/9780198506263.001.0001

Perchant, A., Boeres, C., Bloch, I., Roux, M., & Ribeiro, C. (1999). Model-based scene recognition using graph fuzzy homomorphism solved by genetic algorithm. *Proceedings of the 2nd IAPR-TC15 Workshop on Graph-based Representations in Pattern Recognition,* (pp. 61–70).

Perez, P., Gangnet, M., & Blake, A. (2003). Poisson image editing. *Proceedings of Association of Computing Machinery's Special Interest Group on Computer Graphics and Interactive Techniques.*

Perona, P., & Malik, J. (1990). Scale-space and edge detection using anisotropic diffusion. *IEEE Transactions on Pattern Analysis and Machine Intelligence, 12*(7), 629–639.

Petersohn, C. (2004). TRECVID 2004: Shot boundary detection system. In *Proceedings of TRECVID,* Gaithersburg, USA.

Petrakis, G. M., & Faloutsos, C. (1997). Similarity searching in medical image databases. *IEEE Transactions on Knowledge and Data Engineering, 9*(3), 435–447. doi:10.1109/69.599932

Portilla, J., Strela, V., Wainwright, M., & Simoncelli, E. (2003). Image denoising using scale mixtures of Gaussians in the wavelet domain. *IEEE Transactions on Image Processing, 12*(11), 1338–1351.

Price, B. L., Morse, B., & Cohen, S. (2010). Geodesic graph cut for interactive image segmentation. *IEEE Conference on Computer Vision and Pattern Recognition* (pp. 3161-3168).

Qi, G. J., Hua, X. S., Rui, Y., Tang, J., Mei, T., & Zhang, H. J. (2007). Correlative multi-label video annotation. In *Proceedings of the 15th ACM International Conference on Multimedia (MM),* (pp. 17–26).

Quack, T., Ferrari, V., Leibe, B., & Gool, L. J. V. (2007). Efficient mining of frequent and distinctive feature configurations. In *International Conference on Computer Vision,* (pp. 1–8).

Rabiner, L. R. (1989). A tutorial on hidden Markov models and selected applications in speech recognition. *Proceedings of the IEEE, 77*(2), 257–286.

Ralaivola, L., Swamidass, S. J., Saigo, H., & Baldi, P. (2005). Graph kernels for chemical informatics. *Neural Networks, 18*(8), 1093–1110. doi:10.1016/j.neunet.2005.07.009

Ramanarayanan, G., Bala, K., & Walter, B. (2004). Feature-based textures. *Proceedings of EGSR, 04,* 186–196.

Rangarajan, A., & Mjolsness, E. D. (1996). A Lagrangian relaxation network for graph matching. *IEEE Transactions on Neural Networks, 7*(6), 1365–1381. doi:10.1109/72.548165

Rao, S. R., Mobahi, H., Yang, A. Y., Sastry, S. S., & Ma, Y. (2009). *Natural image segmentation with adaptive texture and boundary encoding.* 9th Asian Conference on Computer Vision.

Riesen, K., & Bunke, H. (2008a). IAM graph database repository for graph based pattern recognition and machine learning. In N. da Vitoria Lobo, et al., (Eds.), *Proceedings of the International Workshops on Structural, Syntactic, and Statistical Pattern Recognition, LNCS 5342,* (pp. 287-297).

Riesen, K., & Bunke, H. (2009b). Dissimilarity based vector space embedding of graphs using prototype reduction schemes. In P. Perner (Ed.), *Proceedings of the 6th International Conference on Machine Learning and Data Mining in Pattern, LNCS 5632,* (pp. 617-631).

Riesen, K., & Bunke, H. (2008b). Non-linear transformations of vector space embedded graphs. In Juan-Ciscar, A., & Sanchez-Albaladejo, G. (Eds.), *Pattern recognition in information systems* (pp. 173–186).

Riesen, K., & Bunke, H. (2008c). Reducing the dimensionality of dissimilarity space embedding graph kernels. *Engineering Applications of Artificial Intelligence, 22*(1), 48–56. doi:10.1016/j.engappai.2008.04.006

Riesen, K., & Bunke, H. (2009a). Approximate graph edit distance computation by means of bipartite graph matching. *Image and Vision Computing, 27*(4), 950–959. doi:10.1016/j.imavis.2008.04.004

Riesen, K., & Bunke, H. (2009c). Graph classification based on vector space embedding. *International Journal of Pattern Recognition and Artificial Intelligence, 23*(6), 1053–1081. doi:10.1142/S021800140900748X

Riesen, K., & Bunke, H. (2010). *Classification and clustering of vector space embedded graphs.* World Scientific.

Riesen, K., Neuhaus, M., & Bunke, H. (2007). Graph embedding in vector spaces by means of prototype selection. *Graph-Based Representations in Pattern Recognition, LNCS, 4538,* 383–39. doi:10.1007/978-3-540-72903-7_35

Robertson, S. E., & Sparck Jones, K. (1976). Relevance weighting of search terms. *Journal of the American Society for Information Science American Society for Information Science, 27,* 129–146.

Robertson, S. E., Walker, S., Jones, S., Hancock-Beaulieu, M. M., & Gatford, M. (1995). Okapi at TREC-3. In. *Proceedings of, TREC-3,* 109–126.

Robles-Kelly, A., & Hancock, E. (2007). A Riemannian approach to graph embedding. *Pattern Recognition, 40,* 1024–1056. doi:10.1016/j.patcog.2006.05.031

Robles-Kelly, A., & Hancock, E. R. (2005). Graph edit distance from spectral seriation. *IEEE Transactions on Pattern Analysis and Machine Intelligence, 27*(3), 365–378. doi:10.1109/TPAMI.2005.56

Rocha, J., & Pavlidis, T. (1994). A shape analysis model with applications to a character recognition system. *IEEE Transactions on Pattern Analysis and Machine Intelligence, 16*(4), 393–404. doi:10.1109/34.277592

Rodriquez, J. (2003). On the Laplacian spectrum and walk-regular hypergraphs. In *Linear and Multilinear Algebra, 51*(3), 285-297.

Rosenberg, S. (1997). *The Laplacian on a Riemannian manifold.* Cambridge University Press.

Rosenfeld, A., Hummel, R. A., & Zucker, S. W. (1976). Scene labelling by relaxation operations. *IEEE Transactions on Systems, Man, and Cybernetics, 6*(6), 420–433. doi:10.1109/TSMC.1976.4309519

Rother, C., Kolmogorov, V., & Blake, A. (2004). GrabCut? Interactive foreground extraction using iterated graph cuts. *Proceedings of the Association of Computing Machinery's Special Interest Group on Computer Graphics and Interactive Techniques.*

Rother, C., Minka, T. P., Blake, A., & Kolmogorov, V. (2006). Cosegmentation of image pairs by histogram matching - Incorporating a global constraint into MRFS. In *IEEE Conference on Computer Vision and Pattern Recognition,* (pp. 993–1000).

Rother, C., Kolmogorov, V., & Blake, A. (2004). "GrabCut": Interactive foreground extraction using iterated graph cuts. *ACM Transactions on Graphics, 23*(3), 309–314. doi:10.1145/1015706.1015720

Roweis, S. T., & Saul, K. L. (2000). Nonlinear dimensionality reduction by locally linear embedding. *Science, 290*(22), 2323–2326. doi:10.1126/science.290.5500.2323

Rubner, Y., Tomasi, C., & Guibas, L. J. (2000). The earth mover's distance as a metric for image retrieval. *International Journal of Computer Vision, 40*(2), 99–121. doi:10.1023/A:1026543900054

Rudin, L., Osher, S., & Fatemi, E. (1992). Nonlinear total variation based noise removal algorithms. *Physica D. Nonlinear Phenomena, 60*, 259–268.

Rui, Y., Huang, T. S., & Chang, S.-F. (1999). Image retrieval: Current techniques, promising directions, and open issues. *Journal of Visual Communication and Image Representation, 10*(1), 39–62. doi:10.1006/jvci.1999.0413

Russel, S. J., & Norvig, P. (1995). *Artificial intelligence: A modern approach*. Prentice Hall Series in Artificial Intelligence.

Ruzon, M., & Tomasi, C. (2000). *Alpha estimation in natural images*. IEEE Conference on Computer Vision and Pattern Recognition.

Ryoo, M., & Aggarwal, J. (2007). Hierarchical recognition of human activities interacting with objects. In *IEEE International Conference on Computer Vision and Pattern Recognition* (pp. 1–8).

Saad, Y. (1989). Krylov subspace methods on supercomputers. *SIAM Journal on Scientific and Statistical Computing, 10*, 1200–1232.

Saad, Y. (1992). Analysis of some Krylov subspace approximations to the matrix exponential operator. *SIAM Journal on Numerical Analysis, 29*, 209–228.

Sahbi, H., Audibert, J., & Keriven, R. (2007). *Graph-cut transducers for relevance feedback in content based image retrieval*. In ICCV'07: IEEE International Conference on Computer Vision.

Saint-Marc, P., Chen, J., & Medioni, G. (1991). Adaptive smoothing: A general tool for early vision. *IEEE Transactions on Pattern Analysis and Machine Intelligence, 13*(6), 514–529.

Salotti, M., & Laachfoubi, N. (2001). Topographic graph matching for shift estimation. *Proceedings of the 3rd IAPR-TC15 Workshop on Graph-based Representations in Pattern Recognition*, (pp. 54 – 63).

Sanfeliu, A., & Fu, K. S. (1983). A distance measure between attributed relational graphs for pattern recognition. *IEEE Transactions on Systems, Man, and Cybernetics (Part B), 13*(3), 353–363.

Sanfeliu, A., Serratosa, F., & Alquezar, R. (2004). Second-order random graphs for modeling sets of attributed graphs and their application to object learning and recognition. *International Journal of Pattern Recognition and Artificial Intelligence, 18*(3), 375–396. doi:10.1142/S0218001404003253

Sapiro, G. (2001). *Geometric partial differential equations and image analysis*. Cambridge University Press.

Sapiro, G., & Ringach, D. (1996). Anisotropic diffusion of multivalued images with application to color filtering. *IEEE Transactions on Image Processing, 5*(11), 1582–1586.

Sarkar, S., & Boyer, K. (1996). Quantitative measures of change based on feature organization: Eigenvalues and eigenvectors. In *Proceedings of the IEEE Conference on Computer Vision and Pattern Recognition*, (p. 478).

Satoh, S. I., Takimoto, M., & Adachi, J. (2007). Scene duplicate detection from videos based on trajectories of feature points. In *Proceedings of the ACM International Workshop Multimedia Information Retrieval*, Augsburg, Bavaria, Germany.

Scheinerman, E. R., & Kimberly, T. (2010). Modeling graphs using dot product representations. *Computational Statistics, 25*(1), 1–16. doi:10.1007/s00180-009-0158-8

Schenker, A., Bunke, H., Last, M., & Kandel, A. (2005). *Graph-theoretic techniques for Web content mining*. World Scientific.

Schmidt, D. C., & Druffel, L. E. (1976). A fast backtracking algorithm to test directed graphs for isomorphism using distance matrices. *Journal of the ACM, 23*, 433–445. doi:10.1145/321958.321963

Schölkopf, B., & Smola, A. (2002). *Learning with kernels*. MIT Press.

Schölkopf, B., Smola, A., & Müller, K.-R. (1998). Nonlinear component analysis as a kernel eigenvalue problem. *Neural Computation, 10*, 1299–1319. doi:10.1162/089976698300017467

Schuldt, C., Laptev, I., & Caputo, B. (2004). Recognizing human actions: A local SVM approach. In *IEEE International Conference on Pattern Recognition* (pp. 32–36).

Scott, G. L., & Longuett-Higgins, H. C. (1991). An algorithm for associating the features of two images. *Proceedings. Biological Sciences, 244*, 21–26. doi:10.1098/rspb.1991.0045

Sebastian, T. B., Klein, P. N., & Kimia, B. B. (2001). Recognition of shapes by editing shock graphs. In *ICCV: IEEE International Conference on Computer Vision*, (pp. 755-762).

Sebastian, T. B., & Kimia, B. B. (2005). Curves vs skeletons in object recognition. *Signal Processing, 85*(2), 247–263. doi:10.1016/j.sigpro.2004.10.016

Sebastian, T. B., Klein, P. N., & Kimia, B. B. (2003). On aligning curves. *IEEE Transactions on Pattern Analysis and Machine Intelligence, 25*(1), 116–125. doi:10.1109/TPAMI.2003.1159951

Sebastian, T. B., Klein, P. N., & Kimia, B. B. (2004). Recognition of shapes by editing their shock graphs. *IEEE Transactions on Pattern Analysis and Machine Intelligence, 26*(5), 550–571. doi:10.1109/TPAMI.2004.1273924

Senthilkumaran, N., & Rajesh, R. (2009). Edge detection techniques for image segmentation-a survey of soft computing approaches. *International Journal of Recent Trends in Engineering, 1*(2), 250–254.

Seong, D., Kim, H. S., & Park, K. H. (1993). Incremental clustering of attributed graphs. *IEEE Transactions on Systems, Man, and Cybernetics, 23*(5), 1399–1411. doi:10.1109/21.260671

Serratosa, F., Alquezar, R., & Sanfeliu, A. (1999). Function-described graphs: A fast algorithm to compute a sub-optimal matching measure. *Proceedings of the 2nd IAPR-TC15 Workshop on Graph-based Representations in Pattern Recognition*, (pp. 71 – 77).

Serratosa, F., Alquezar, R., & Sanfeliu, A. (2000). Efficient algorithms for matching attributed graphs and function-described graphs. *Proceedings of 15th International Conference on Pattern Recognition*, (pp. 867 – 872).

Shaked, D., & Bruckstein, A. M. (1998). Pruning medial axes. *Computer Vision and Image Understanding, 69*(2), 156–169. doi:10.1006/cviu.1997.0598

Shapiro, L. G., & Haralick, R. M. (1981). Structural descriptions and inexact matching. *IEEE Transactions on Pattern Analysis and Machine Intelligence, 3*(5), 504–519. doi:10.1109/TPAMI.1981.4767144

Shapiro, L. G., & Haralick, R. M. (1985). A metric for comparing relational descriptions. *IEEE Transactions on Pattern Analysis and Machine Intelligence, 7*(1), 90–94. doi:10.1109/TPAMI.1985.4767621

Shapiro, L. S., & Brady, J. M. (1992). Feature-based correspondence: an eigenvector approach. *Image and Vision Computing, 10*(5), 283–288. doi:10.1016/0262-8856(92)90043-3

Sharvit, D., Chan, J., Tek, H., & Kimia, B. B. (1998). Symmetry-based indexing of image databases. *Proceedings of the IEEE Workshop on Content-Based Access of Image and Video Libraries*, (pp. 56 – 62).

Shasha, D., Wang, J. T. L., Zhang, K., & Shih, F. Y. (1994). Exact and approximate algorithms for unordered tree matching. *IEEE Transactions on Systems, Man, and Cybernetics, 24*(4), 668–678. doi:10.1109/21.286387

Shawe-Taylor, J., & Cristianini, N. (2004). *Kernel methods for pattern analysis*. Cambridge University Press. doi:10.1017/CBO9780511809682

Shearer, K., Bunke, H., & Venkatesh, S. (2001a). Video indexing and similarity retrieval by largest common subgraph detection using decision trees. *Pattern Recognition, 34*(5), 1075–1091. doi:10.1016/S0031-3203(00)00048-0

Shearer, K., Bunke, H., Venkatesh, S., & Kieronska, S. (1997). Efficient graph matching for video indexing. *Computing, 12*, 53–62.

Shearer, K., Venkatesh, S., & Bunke, H. (2001b). Video sequence matching via decision tree path following. *Pattern Recognition Letters, 22*(5), 479–492. doi:10.1016/S0167-8655(00)00121-5

Shechtman, E., & Irani, M. (2007). *Matching local self-similarities across images and videos*. In IEEE Conference on Computer Vision and Pattern Recognition, June.

Shervashidze, N., Vishwanathan, S. V., Petri, T. H., Mehlhorn, K., & Borgwardt, K. M. (2009). *Efficient graphlet kernels for large graph comparison*. In Twelfth International Conference on Artificial Intelligence and Statistics.

Shervashidze, N., & Borgwardt, K. M. (2009). Fast subtree kernels on graphs. *Advances in Neural Information Processing Systems*, 22.

Shi, J., & Malik, J. (1998). Motion segmentation and tracking using normalized cuts. In *IEEE International Conference on Computer Vision (ICCV)*, (pp. 1154–1160).

Shi, J., & Tomasi, C. (1994). *Good features to track*. IEEE Conference on Computer Vision and Pattern Recognition.

Shi, J., & Malik, J. (1998). *Motion segmentation and tracking using normalized cuts*. International Confeerence on Computer Vision.

Shi, J., & Malik, J. (2000). Normalized cuts and image segmentation. *IEEE Transactions on Pattern Analysis and Machine Intelligence*, 22(8), 888–905. doi:10.1109/34.868688

Shilane, P., Min, P., Kazhdan, M., & Funkhouser, T. (2004). The Princeton shape benchmark. In *Proceedings of Shape Modeling International*, (pp. 167-178).

Shinano, Y., Fujie, T., Ikebe, Y., & Hirabayashi, R. (1998). Solving the maximum clique problem using PUBB. *Proceedings of the First Merged International Parallel Processing Symposium*, (pp. 326 – 332).

Shokoufandeh, A., & Dickinson, S. (2001). A unified framework for indexing and matching hierarchical shape structures. In C. Arcelli, L. P. Cordella, & G. Sanniti di Baja (Eds.), *Workshop on Visual Form, Lecture Notes in Computer Science, Vol. 2059*, (pp. 67-84).

Shokoufandeh, A., Macrini, D., Dickinson, S., Siddiqi, K., & Zucker, S. W. (2005). Indexing hierarchical structures using graph spectra. *IEEE Transactions on Pattern Analysis and Machine Intelligence*, 27(7), 1125–1140. doi:10.1109/TPAMI.2005.142

Shoukry, A., & Aboutabl, M. (1996). Neural network approach for solving the maximal common subgraph problem. *IEEE Transactions on Systems, Man and Cybernetics. Part B*, 26(5), 785–790.

Siddiqi, K., Shkoufandeh, A., Dickinson, S., & Zucker, S. (1998). Shock graphs and shape matching. In *ICCV: IEEE International Conference on Computer Vision*, (pp. 222-229).

Siddiqi, K., & Kimia, B. B. (1995). Parts of visual form: Computational aspects. *IEEE Transactions on Pattern Analysis and Machine Intelligence*, 17(3), 239–251. doi:10.1109/34.368189

Siddiqi, K., Kimia, B. B., Tannenbaum, A., & Zucker, S. (1999). Shocks, shapes, and wiggles. *Image and Vision Computing*, 17(5-6), 365–373. doi:10.1016/S0262-8856(98)00130-9

Siddiqi, K., Shokoufandeh, A., Dickinson, S., & Zucker, S. (1999). Shock graphs and shape matching. *International Journal of Computer Vision*, 35(1), 13–32. doi:10.1023/A:1008102926703

Siddiqi, K., Zhang, J., Macrini, D., Shokoufandeh, A., Bouix, S., & Dickinson, S. (2008). Retrieving articulated 3D models using medial surfaces. *Machine Vision and Applications*, 19(4), 261–274. doi:10.1007/s00138-007-0097-8

Sidje, R. (1998). Expokit: A software package for computing matrix exponentials. *ACM Transactions on Mathematical Software*, 24(1), 130–156.

Sindhwani, V., & Selvaraj, S. (2006). Large scale semi-supervised linear support vector machines. In *Proceedings of the 29th Annual International ACM SIGIR Conference on Research and Development in Information Retrieval*.

Sinop, A. K., & Grady, L. (2007). A seeded image segmentation framework unifying graph cuts and random walker which yields a new algorithm. *Proceedings of International Conference on Computer Vision* (pp. 1-8).

Smola, A., & Kondor, R. (2003). Kernels and regularization on graphs. In *Proceedings of the 16th International Conference on Comptuational Learning Theory*, (pp. 144-158).

Smolka, B., & Wojciechowski, K. (2001). Random walk approach to image enhancement. *Signal Processing, 81,* 465–482.

Sochen, N., Kimmel, R., & Malladi, R. (1998). A general framework for low level vision. *IEEE Transactions on Image Processing, 7*(3), 310–318.

Sorlin, S., & Solnon, C. (2005). Reactive tabu search for measuring graph similarity. In L. Brun & M. Vento (Eds.), *Proceedings of the 5th International Workshop on Graph-based Representations in Pattern Recognition, LNCS 3434,* (pp. 172-182). Springer.

Spillmann, B., Neuhaus, M., Bunke, H., Pekalska, E., & Duin, R. (2006). Transforming strings to vector spaces using prototype selection. In D.-Y. Yeung, J. T. Kwok, A. Fred, F. Roli, & D. de Ridder (Eds.), *Proceedings of the 11th International Workshop on Structural and Syntactic Pattern Recognition, LNCS 4109,* (pp. 287-296). Springer.

Stein, A., Hoiem, D., & Hebert, M. (2007). *Learning to find object boundaries using motion cues.* In IEEE International Conference on Computer Vision (ICCV), October 2007.

Subramanya, A., & Bilmes, J. (2009). *Entropic graph regularization in non-parametric semi-supervised classification. Neural Information Processing Society.* Vancouver, Canada: NIPS.

Suganthan, P. N. (2000) Attributed relational graph matching by neural-gas networks. *Proceedings of the 2000 IEEE Signal Processing Society Workshop on Neural Networks for Signal Processing X,* 2000, (pp. 366 – 374).

Suganthan, P. N., Teoh, E. K., & Mital, D. (1995). A self organizing Hopfield network for attributed relational graph matching. *Image and Vision Computing, 13*(1), 61–73. doi:10.1016/0262-8856(95)91468-S

Suganthan, P. N., Teoh, E. K., & Mital, D. (1995). Pattern recognition by graph matching using the potts MFT neural networks. *Pattern Recognition, 28*(7), 997–1009. doi:10.1016/0031-3203(94)00166-J

Suganthan, P. N., & Yan, H. (1998). Recognition of handprinted Chinese characters by constrained graph matching. *Image and Vision Computing, 16*(3), 191–201. doi:10.1016/S0262-8856(97)00066-8

Sun, D., Ding, C., Luo, B., & Tang, J. (2011). *Angular decomposition.* Twenty-second International Joint Conference on Artificial Intelligence (IJCAI).

Sun, J., Jia, J., Tang, C., & Shum, H. (2004). *Poisson matting.* ACM SIGGRAPH, 2004.

Sun, J., Wu, X., Yan, S., Cheong, L., Chua, T., & Li, J. (2009). Hierarchical spatiotemporal context modeling for action recognition. In *IEEE International Conference on Computer Vision and Pattern Recognition* (pp. 2004–2011).

Sun, J., Xu, Z., & Shum, H. (2008). Image super-resolution using gradient profile prior. *Proceedings of CVPR '08.*

Sun, K. B., & Super, B. J. (2005). Classification of contour shapes using class segment sets. In *CVPR: IEEE International Conference on Computer Vision and Pattern Recognition,* (pp. 727-733).

Sun, J., Tao, H., & Shum, H. (2003). Image hallucination with primal sketch priors. *Proceedings of IEEE CVPR, 03,* 729–736.

Tang, J., Jiang, B., & Luo, B. (2011). Graph matching based on dot product representation of graphs. In *Graph-Based Representations in Pattern Recognition* (*Vol. 6658,* pp. 175–184). LNCS. doi:10.1007/978-3-642-20844-7_18

Tao, H., Sawhney, H., & Kumar, R. (2002). Object tracking with Bayesian estimation of dynamic layer representations. *IEEE Transactions on Pattern Analysis and Machine Intelligence, 24*(1), 75–89. doi:10.1109/34.982885

Taubin, G. (1995). A signal processing approach to fair surface design. In *Proceedings of SIGGRAPH,* (pp. 351–358).

Tefas, A., Kotropoulos, C., & Pitas, I. (2001). Using support vector machines to enhance the performance of elastic graph matching for frontal face authentication. *IEEE Transactions on Pattern Analysis and Machine Intelligence, 23*(7), 735–746. doi:10.1109/34.935847

Tenenbaum, J. B., de Silva, V., & Langford, C. J. (2000). A global geometric framework for nonlinear dimensionality. *Science, 290*(22), 2319–2323. doi:10.1126/science.290.5500.2319

Thillou, C. M., & Gosselin, B. (2006). Spatial and color spaces combination for natural scene text extraction. *International Conference on Image Processing* (pp. 985-988).

Thillou, C., & Gosselin, B. (2007). Color text extraction with selective metric-based clustering. *Computer Vision and Image Understanding, 107*(1-2), 97–107. doi:10.1016/j.cviu.2006.11.010

Tieu, K., & Viola, P. (2000). Boosting image retrieval. *International Journal of Computer Vision, 56*(1-2), 228–235.

Tong, S., & Chang, E. (2001). *Support vector machine active learning for image retrieval.* In ACM MULTI-MEDIA '01. Gemert, J. van, Geusebroek, J., Veenman, C., & Smeulders, A. (2008). *Kernel codebooks for scene categorization.* In ECCV'08: European Conference on Computer Vision 2008.

Torralba, A., Murphy, K., Freeman, W., & Rubin, M. (2003). Context-based vision system for place and object recognition. In *IEEE International Conference on Computer Vision* (pp. 273–280).

Torr, P. H. S., & Zisserman, A. (2000). Mlesac: A new robust estimator with application to estimating image geometry. *Computer Vision and Image Understanding, 78*(1), 138–156. doi:10.1006/cviu.1999.0832

Torsello, A., & Hancock, E. R. (2001). Computing approximate tree edit-distance using relaxation labeling. *Proceedings of the 3rd IAPR-TC15 Workshop on Graph-based Representations in Pattern Recognition,* (pp. 125 – 136).

Torsello, A., & Hancock, E. R. (2002). Learning structural variations in shock trees. *Proceeding of the Joint IAPR International Workshops SSPR and SPR,* (pp. 113 – 122).

Torsello, A., & Hancock, E. R. (2004). A skeletal measure of 2D shape similarity. *Computer Vision and Image Understanding, 95*(1), 1–29. doi:10.1016/j.cviu.2004.03.006

Torsello, A., & Hancock, E. R. (2007). Graph embedding using tree edit-union. *Pattern Recognition, 40,* 1393–1405. doi:10.1016/j.patcog.2006.09.006

Torsello, A., Hidovic-Rowe, D., & Pelillo, M. (2005). Polynomial-time metrics for attributed trees. *IEEE Transactions on Pattern Analysis and Machine Intelligence, 27*(7), 1087–1099. doi:10.1109/TPAMI.2005.146

TRECVID. (2008). *TREC video retrieval evaluation.* Retrieved from http://www-nlpir.nist.gov/projects/trecvid/

Triesch, J., & von der Malsburg, C. (2001). A system for person-independent hand posture recognition against complex backgrounds. *IEEE Transactions on Pattern Analysis and Machine Intelligence, 23*(12), 1449–1453. doi:10.1109/34.977568

Tsai, W. H., & Fu, K. S. (1979). Error-correcting isomorphisms of attributed relational graphs for pattern analysis. *IEEE Transactions on Systems, Man, and Cybernetics, 9*(12), 757–768. doi:10.1109/TSMC.1979.4310127

Tsai, W. H., & Fu, K. S. (1983). Subgraph error-correcting isomorphisms for syntactic pattern recognition. *IEEE Transactions on Systems, Man, and Cybernetics, 13*(1), 48–61.

Tschumperle, D. (2006). Fast anisotropic smoothing of multi-valued images using curvature- preserving PDE's. *International Journal of Computer Vision, 68*(1), 65–82.

Tschumperle, D., & Deriche, R. (2005). Vector-valued image regularization with PDEs: A common framework for different applications. *IEEE Transactions on Pattern Analysis and Machine Intelligence, 27*(4), 506–517.

Tsuda, K. (1999). Support vector classification with asymmetric kernel function. In M. Verleysen (Ed.), *Proceedings 7th European Symposium on Artificial Neural Networks,* (pp. 183-188).

Tu, Z., & Yuille, A. L. (2004). Shape matching and recognition: using generative models and informative features. In *ECCV: European Conference on Computer Vision,* (Vol. 3, pp. 195-209).

Turaga, P., Chellappa, R., Subrahmanian, V., & Udrea, O. (2008). Machine recognition of human activities: A survey. *IEEE Transactions on Circuits and Systems for Video Technology, 18*(11), 1473–1488. doi:10.1109/TCSVT.2008.2005594

Uchida, S., Mori, A., Kurazume, R., Taniguchi, R.-I., & Hasegawa, T. (2007). Logical DP matching for detecting similar subsequence. *8th Asian Conference on Computer Vision, LNCS, Vol. 4843,* ACCV2007, Tokyo, Japan, (pp. 628-637).

Ullman, J. R. (1976). An algorithm for subgraph isomorphism. *Journal of the Association for Computer Machinery, 23*, 31–42. doi:10.1145/321921.321925

Umeyama, S. (1987). Weighted graph matching algorithms using Eigen-decomposition Approach. *Transactions of the Institute of Electronics, Information and Communication Engineers, Section E., 70*, 809–816.

Umeyama, S. (1988). An Eigendecomposition approach to weighted graph matching problems. *IEEE Transactions on Pattern Analysis and Machine Intelligence, 10*(5), 695–703. doi:10.1109/34.6778

Unnikrishnan, R., & Hebert, M. (2005). Measures of similarity. *IEEE Workshop on Applications of Computer Vision* (pp. 394-400).

Unnikrishnan, R., Pantofaru, C., & Hebert, M. (2007)... *IEEE Transactions on Pattern Analysis and Machine Intelligence, 29*(6), 929–944. doi:10.1109/TPAMI.2007.1046

Vaiapury, K., Atrey, P. K., Kankanhalli, M. S., & Ramakrishnan, K. (2006). Non-identical duplicate video detection using the SIFT method. In *IET International Conference on Visual Information Engineering*, (pp. 537-542).

Valiente, G. (2001). An efficient bottom-up distance between trees. *Proceedings of the Eighth International Symposium on String Processing and Information Retrieval*, (pp. 212 – 219).

van Wyk, B. J., & van Wyk, M. A. (2002a). Non-Bayesian graph matching without explicit compatibility calculations. *Proceeding of the Joint IAPR International Workshops SSPR and SPR*, (pp. 74 – 82).

van Wyk, B. J., van Wyk, M. A., & Hanrahan, H. E. (2002b). Successive projection graph matching. *Proceeding of the Joint IAPR International Workshops SSPR and SPR*, (pp. 263 – 271).

van Wyk, B. J., & van Wyk, M. A. (2003). Kronecker product graph matching. *Pattern Recognition, 36*, 2019–2030. doi:10.1016/S0031-3203(03)00009-8

van Wyk, M. A., Durrani, T. S., & van Wyk, B. J. (2002). A RKHS interpolator-based graph matching algorithm. *IEEE Transactions on Pattern Analysis and Machine Intelligence, 24*(7), 988–995. doi:10.1109/TPAMI.2002.1017624

Vapnik, V. (1998). *Statistical learning theory*. John Wiley.

Vector-Magic. (n.d.). Home. Retrieved from http://www.vectormagic.com

Vedaldi, A., & Fulkerson, B. (2010). *VLFeat: An open and portable library of computer vision algorithms*. Retrieved from http://www.vlfeat.org/

Vidal, R., & Ma, Y. (2004). *A unified algebraic approach to 2-D and 3-D motion segmentation*. European Conference on Computer Vision.

von Luxburg, U. (2007). A tutorial on spectral clustering. *Statistics and Computing, 17*(4), 395–416. doi:10.1007/s11222-007-9033-z

W3C. (2011). *Scalable vector graphics, 1.1* (2nd ed.). Retrieved from http://www.w3.org/tr/svg11/

Wallis, W. D., Shoubridge, P., Kraetz, M., & Ray, D. (2001). Graph distances using graph union. *Pattern Recognition Letters, 22*(6), 701–704. doi:10.1016/S0167-8655(01)00022-8

Walshaw, C., & Cross, M. (2000). Mesh partitioning: A multilevel balancing and refinement algorithm. *SIAM Journal on Scientific Computing, 22*, 63–80. doi:10.1137/S1064827598337373

Wang, C., & Abe, K. (1995). Region correspondence by inexact attributed planar graph matching. *Proceedings of the Fifth International Conference on Computer Vision*, (pp. 440 – 447).

Wang, H., Ding, C., & Huang, H. (2010). Multilabel linear discriminant analysis. *11th European Conference on Computer Vision*, (pp. 126–139).

Wang, J. T. L., Zhang, K., & Chirn, G. W. (1994). The approximate graph matching problem. *Proceedings of the 12th IAPR International Conference on Pattern Recognition - Conference B*, (pp. 284 – 288).

Wang, J., & Gong, Y. (2008). Fast image super-resolution using connected component enhancement. *Proceedings of ICME'08*.

Wang, J., Zhu, S., & Gong, Y. (2009a). Resolution-invariant image representation and its applications. *Proceedings of CVPR'09*.

Wang, J., Zhu, S., & Gong, Y. (2009b). Resolution-invariant image representation for content-based zooming. *Proceedings of ICME'09*.

Wang, M., Iwai, Y., & Yachida, M. (1998). Expression recognition from time-sequential facial images by use of expression change model. *Proceedings of the Third IEEE International Conference on Automatic Face and Gesture Recognition*, (pp. 354 – 359).

Wang, Q., Tang, X., & Shum, H. (2005). Patch based blind image super resolution. *Proceedings of ICCV'05*, (Vol. 1, pp. 709–716).

Wang, J., & Adelson, E. (1994). Representing moving images with layers. *IEEE Transactions on Image Processing, 3*(5), 625–638. doi:10.1109/83.334981

Wang, J., Zhu, S., & Gong, Y. (2009). Resolution enhancement based on learning the sparse association of image patches. *Pattern Recognition Letters, 31*(1). doi:doi:10.1016/j.patrec.2009.09.004

Wang, Y. K., Fan, K. C., & Horng, J. T. (1997). Genetic-based search for error-correcting graph isomorphism. *IEEE Transactions on Systems, Man and Cybernetics. Part B, 27*(4), 589–597.

Wang, Y., & Mori, G. (2009). Human action recognition by semi-latent topic models. *IEEE Transactions on Pattern Analysis and Machine Intelligence, 31*(10), 1762–1774. doi:10.1109/TPAMI.2009.43

Watkins, C. (1999). *Kernels from matching operations.* Technical Report CSD-TR-98-07, Royal Holloway College.

Watkins, C. (2000). Dynamic alignment kernels. In Smola, A., Bartlett, P. L., Schölkopf, B., & Schuurmans, D. (Eds.), *Advances in large margin classifiers* (pp. 39–50). MIT Press.

Watts, D. J., & Strogatz, S. H. (1998). Collective dynamics of 'small-world' networks. *Nature, 393*, 440–442. doi:10.1038/30918

Weber, M., Welling, M., & Perona, P. (2000). Unsupervised learning of models for recognition. In *European Conference on Computer Vision,* (Vol. 1, pp. 18–32).

Weickert, J. (1998). *Anisotropic diffusion in image processing*. Stuttgart, Germany: Teubner-Verlag.

Weickert, J. (1999). Coherence-enhancing diffusion filtering. *International Journal of Computer Vision, 31*, 111–127.

Wei, S. K., Zhao, Y., Zhu, C., Xu, C. S., & Zhu, Z. F. (2011). Frame fusion for video copy detection. *IEEE Transactions on Circuits and Systems for Video Technology, 21*(1), 15–28.

Weiss, Y. (1999). Segmentation using eigenvectors: A unifying view. In *Proceedings of IEEE International Conference on Computer Vision,* (pp. 975–982).

Wexler, Y., Fitzgibbon, A., & Zisserman, A. (2002). *Bayesian estimation of layers from multiple images*. European Conference on Computer Vision.

Williams, M. L., Wilson, R. C., & Hancock, E. R. (1999). Deterministic search for relational graph matching. *Pattern Recognition, 32*(7), 1255–1271. doi:10.1016/S0031-3203(98)00152-6

Wills, J., Agarwal, S., & Belongie, S. (2003). What went where. In *CVPR '03: Proceedings of the 2003 IEEE Computer Society Conference on Computer Vision and Pattern Recognition (CVPR'03)*, (pp. 37–44).

Wilson, R. C., & Hancock, E. R. (1997). Structural matching by discrete relaxation. *IEEE Transactions on Pattern Analysis and Machine Intelligence, 19*(6), 634–648. doi:10.1109/34.601251

Wilson, R. C., & Hancock, E. R. (1999). Graph matching with hierarchical discrete relaxation. *Pattern Recognition Letters, 20*(10), 1041–1052. doi:10.1016/S0167-8655(99)00071-9

Wilson, R. C., Hancock, E., & Luo, B. (2005). Pattern vectors from algebraic graph theory. *IEEE Transactions on Pattern Analysis and Machine Intelligence, 27*(7), 1112–1124. doi:10.1109/TPAMI.2005.145

Wiskott, L. (1997b). Phantom faces for face analysis. *Proceedings of the International Conference on Image Processing,* (pp. 308 – 311).

Wiskott, L., Fellous, J. M., Kruger, N., & von der Malsburg, C. (1997a). Face recognition by elastic bunch graph matching. *IEEE Transactions on Pattern Analysis and Machine Intelligence, 19*(7), 775–779. doi:10.1109/34.598235

Witkin, A. (1983). Scale-space filtering. In *Proceedings of the International Joint Conference on Artificial Intelligence*, (pp. 1019–1021).

Wong, A. K. C., & You, M. (1985). Entropy and distance of random graphs with application to structure pattern recognition. *IEEE Transactions on Pattern Analysis and Machine Intelligence*, *7*(5), 599–609. doi:10.1109/TPAMI.1985.4767707

Wong, A. K. C., You, M., & Chan, S. C. (1990). An algorithm for graph optimal monomorphism. *IEEE Transactions on Systems, Man, and Cybernetics*, *20*(3), 628–638. doi:10.1109/21.57275

Wu, X., Ngo, C.-H., Hauptmann, A. G., & Tan, H.-K. (2009). Real-time near-duplicate elimination for web video search with content and context. *IEEE Transactions on Multimedia*, *11*(2), 196–207.

Wu, Z., & Leahy, R. (1993). An optimal graph theoretic approach to data clustering: Theory and its application to image segmentation. *IEEE Transactions on Pattern Analysis and Machine Intelligence*, *15*(11), 1101–1113. doi:10.1109/34.244673

Xia, X., & Hancock, E. R. (2009). Graph-based object class discovery. In *International Conference on Computer Analysis of Images and Patterns*, (pp. 385–393).

Xiao, J., & Shah, M. (2003). *Two-frame wide baseline matching.* International Conference on Computer Vision.

Xiao, J., & Shah, M. (2004). *Motion layer extraction in the presence of occlusion using graph cut.* IEEE Conference on Computer Vision and Pattern Recognition.

Xu, L., Li, W., & Schuurmans, D. (2009). Fast normalized cut with linear constraints. *IEEE Conference on Computer Vision and Pattern Recognition* (pp. 2866-2873).

Xu, X., & Frank, E. (2004). Logistic regression and boosting for labeled bags of instances. In *Proceedings of the Pacific Asia Conference on Knowledge Discovery and Data Mining*, (pp. 272–281).

Xu, L., & King, I. (2001). A PCA approach for fast retrieval of structural patterns in attributed graphs. *IEEE Transactions on Systems, Man and Cybernetics. Part B*, *31*(5), 812–817.

Yang, J., Wright, J., Huang, T., & Yi, M. (2008). Image super-resolution as sparse representation of raw image patches. *Proceedings of CVPR '08.*

Yang, X. F., Sun, Q. B., & Tian, Q. (2003). Content-based video identification: A survey. In *Proceedings of the International Conference on Information Technology: Research and Education*, (pp. 50-54).

Yang, W., Cai, J., Zheng, J., & Luo, J. (2010). User-friendly interactive image segmentation through unified combinatorial user inputs. *IEEE Transactions on Image Processing*, *19*(9), 2470–2479. doi:10.1109/TIP.2010.2048611

Yan, S., Xu, D., Zhang, B., Zhang, H., Yang, Q., & Lin, S. (2007). Graph embedding and extensions: A general framework for dimensionality reduction. *IEEE Transactions on Pattern Analysis and Machine Intelligence*, *29*(1), 40–51. doi:10.1109/TPAMI.2007.250598

Yokobayashi, M., & Wakahara, T. (2005). Segmentation and recognition of characters in scene images using selective binarization in color space and GAT correlation. *8th International Conference on Document Analysis and Recognition* (Vol. 1, pp. 167-171).

Yokobayashi, M., & Wakahara, T. (2006). Binarization and recognition of degraded characters using a maximum separability axis in color space and GAT correlation. *18th International Conference on Pattern Recognition* (Vol. 2, pp. 885-888).

Young, S. J., & Scheinerman, E. R. (2007). Random dot product graph models for social networks. In Milios, E. (Ed.), *Algorithms and Models for the Web-Graph (Vol. 4936*, pp. 138–149). LNCS. doi:10.1007/978-3-540-77004-6_11

You, Y., Xu, W., Tannenbaum, A., & Kaveh, M. (1996). Behavioral analysis of anisotropic diffusion in image processing. *IEEE Transactions on Image Processing*, *5*(11), 1539–1553.

Yu, H., Li, M., Zhang, H., & Feng, J. (2002). Color texture moments for content-based image retrieval. In *International Conference on Image Processing*, (Vol. 3, pp. 929–932).

Yuan, J., Bae, E., & Tai, X. C. (2010). A study on continuous max-flow and min-cut approaches. *IEEE Conference on Computer Vision and Pattern Recognition* (pp. 2217-2224).

Yuan, J., Li, J., & Zhang, B. (2007). Exploiting spatial context constraints for automatic image region annotation. In *Proceedings of the 15th ACM International Conference on Multimedia*, (pp. 595–604).

Zager, L. A., & Verghese, G. C. (2008). Graph similarity scoring and matching. *Applied Mathematics Letters, 21,* 86–94. doi:10.1016/j.aml.2007.01.006

Zelnik-Manor, L., & Irani, M. (1999). *Multi view subspace constraints on homographies*. International Conference on Computer Vision.

Zeng, Y., Samaras, D., Chen, W., & Peng, Q. (2008). Topology cuts: a novel min-cut/max-flow algorithm for topology preserving segmentation in N-D images. *Computer Vision and Image Understanding, 112*(1), 81–90. doi:10.1016/j.cviu.2008.07.008

Zhang, F., & Hancock, E. R. (2005). Image scale-space from the heat kernel. In *Proceedings of the Iberoamerican Congress on Pattern Recognition, Springer LNCS 3773,* (pp. 181–192).

Zhang, F., & Hancock, E. R. (2006). Heat kernel smoothing of scalar and vector image data. In *Proceedings of the IEEE International Conference on Image Processing,* (pp. 1549–1552).

Zhang, H., & Yan, H. (1999). Graphic matching based on constrained Voronoi diagrams. *Proceedings of the Fifth International Symposium on Signal Processing and its Applications,* (pp. 431 – 434).

Zhang, J., Zheng, J., & Cai, J. (2010). A diffusion approach to seeded image segmentation. *IEEE Conference on Computer Vision and Pattern Recognition* (pp. 2125-2132).

Zhang, D. M., Sun, D. D., Fu, M. S., & Luo, B. (2010). Extended dot product representations of graphs with application to radar image segmentation. *Optical Engineering (Redondo Beach, Calif.), 49*(11), 17201. doi:10.1117/1.3505865

Zhang, H., Fritts, J. E., & Goldman, S. A. (2008). Image segmentation evaluation: A survey of unsupervised methods. *Computer Vision and Image Understanding, 110*(2), 260–280. doi:10.1016/j.cviu.2007.08.003

Zhang, J., Marszalek, M., Lazebnik, S., & Schmid, C. (2007). Local features and kernels for classification of texture and object categories: A comprehensive study. *International Journal of Computer Vision, 73*(2), 213–238. doi:10.1007/s11263-006-9794-4

Zhao, G., et al. (2007). Using eigen-decomposition method for weighted graph matching. In *3rd International Conference on Intelligent Computing, ICIC 2007,* (pp. 1283-1294).

Zhou, D., Bousquet, O., Lal, T. N., Weston, J., & Schokopf, B. (2003). *Learning with local and global consistency.* In NIPS'03: Advances in Neural Information Processing Systems (NIPS) 2003.

Zhou, D., Huang, J., & Schokopf, B. (2006). *Learning with hypergraphs: Clustering, classification, and embedding.* In Advances in Neural Information Processing Systems, 2006.

Zhou, Y., & Tao, H. (2003). *A background layer model for object tracking through occlusion.* International Conference on Computer Vision.

Zhou, Y., Yan, S., & Huang, T. (2008). Pair-activity classification by bi-trajectory analysis. In *IEEE International Conference on Computer Vision and Pattern Recognition* (pp. 1–8).

Zhou, X. M., Zhou, X. F., Chen, L., Bouguettaya, A., Xiao, N., & Taylor, J. A. (2009). An efficient near-duplicate video shot detection method using shot-based interest points. *IEEE Transactions on Multimedia, 11*(5), 879–891.

Zhou, Z., & Zhang, M. (2007). Multi-instance multi-label learning with application to scene classification. *Advances in Neural Information Processing Systems, 19,* 1609–1616.

Zhu, J. K., Hoi, S. C. H., Lyu, M. R., & Yan, S. C. (2008). Near-duplicate keyframe retrieval by nonrigid image matching. In *Proceedings of the ACM International Conference on Multimedia,* Vancouver, British Columbia, Canada.

Zhu, X. (2005). *Semi-supervised learning with graphs.* Unpublished PhD Thesis.

Zhu, S. C., & Yuille, A. L. (1996). FORMS: A flexible object recognition and modeling system. *International Journal of Computer Vision, 20*(3), 187–212.

Zien, J. Y., Schlag, M. D. F., & Chan, P. K. (1996). Multilevel spectral hypergraph partitioning with arbitrary vertex sizes. In *Proceedings of the International Conference on Computer-Aided Design*, (pp. 201–204). IEEE Press.

Zucker, S. (1978). Estimates for the classical parametrix for the Laplacian. *Manuscripta Mathematica, 24*, 1432–1785.

About the Contributors

Bai Xiao received the B.Eng. degree in Computer Science from Beihang University (BUAA) of China in 2001. From 2002 to 2006, he was a Ph.D. student at Computer Science Department, University of York, U.K. under the supervision of Professor Edwin R. Hancock. From September 2006 to December 2008, he was a Research Officer (Fellow, Scientist) at Computer Science Department, University of Bath. He is now an Associate Professor at Computer Science School, Beihang University (BUAA). He has published more than 30 papers in journals and refereed conferences. His current research interests include computer vision, image processing, and pattern recognition.

Jian Cheng is currently an Associate Professor of Institute of Automation, Chinese Academy of Sciences. He received the B.S. and M.S. degrees in Mathematics from Wuhan University in 1998 and in 2001, respectively. In 2004, he got his PhD degree in Pattern Recognition and Intelligent Systems from Institute of Automation, Chinese Academy of Sciences. From 2004 to 2006, he has been working as postdoctoral researcher in Nokia Research Center. Then he joined National Laboratory of Pattern Recognition, Institute of Automation. His current research interests include image and video search, machine learning, et cetera. He has authored or co-authored more than 40 academic papers in these areas. He was the recipient of Lu Jia Xi Young Talent award in 2010. Dr. Cheng served as Technical Program Committee member for some international conferences, such as ACM Multimedia 2009 (content), IEEE Conference on Computer Vision and Pattern Recognition (CVPR'08), IEEE International Conference on Multimedia and Expo (ICME'08), Pacific-Rim Conference on Multimedia (PCM'08), IEEE International Conference on Computer Vision (ICCV'07), et cetera. He has also co-organized one special issue on *Pattern Recognition Journal*, and several special sessions on PCM 2008, ICME 2009, and PCM 2010.

Edwin R. Hancock studied Physics as an undergraduate at the University of Durham and graduated with honors in 1977. He remained at Durham to complete the PhD degree in the area of High-Energy Physics in 1981. Following this, he worked for 10 years as a researcher in the fields of high-energy nuclear physics and pattern recognition at the Rutherford-Appleton Laboratory (now the Central Research Laboratory of the Research Councils). In 1991, he moved to the University of York as a Lecturer in the Department of Computer Science. He was promoted to Senior Lecturer in 1997 and to reader in 1998. In 1998, he was appointed to a Chair in Computer Vision. Professor Hancock now leads a group of some 15 faculty, research staff, and PhD students working in the areas of computer vision and pattern recognition. His main research interests are in the use of optimization and probabilistic methods for high and intermediate level vision. He is also interested in the methodology of structural and statistical pattern recognition. He is currently working on graph-matching, shape-from-X, image databases, and statistical learning theory. He has published more than 90 journal papers and 350 refereed conference publications. He was awarded the Pattern Recognition Society medal in 1991 and an outstanding paper award in 1997 by the journal *Pattern Recognition*. In 1998, he became a fellow of the International Association for Pattern Recognition. He has been a member of the editorial boards of the journals *IEEE Transactions on Pattern Analysis* and *Machine Intelligence and Pattern Recognition.* He has also been a guest editor for special editions of the journals *Image and Vision Computing* and *Pattern Recognition*.

* * *

Xiang Bai received the BS and MS degrees in Electronics and Information Engineering from Huazhong University of Science and Technology (HUST), Wuhan, China, in 2003 and 2005, respectively. He is currently working toward the PhD degree at HUST. From January 2006 to May 2007, he was with the Department of Computer Science and Information, Temple University. From October 2007 to October 2008, he was with the University of California, Los Angeles, as a joint PhD student. He is now an Associate Professor of EI Dept. at Huazhong University of Science and Technology.

Bing-Kun Bao received the Ph.D. degree in Control Theory and Control Application, Department of Automation, University of Science and Technology of China (USTC), China, in 2009; and the B.E. degree from the School of Computing, Hefei University of Technology, China, in 2004. She is currently a Research Engineer in Electrical and Computer Engineering at the National University of Singapore (NUS). Her research interests are in the areas of multimedia and computer vision.

Charels-Edmond Bichot is now an Assistant Professor at Ecole Centrale de Lyon, France. He received his PhD degree at 2004 in Computer Science in the Laboratoire d'Optimisation Globale (Global Optimization Laboratory) of the Ecole Nationale de l'Aviation Civile (French Civil Aviation University), and the Direction des Services de la Navigation A´erienne, Toulouse, France. His research subjects are graph partitioning, data mining and image segmentation.

Jiang Bo received the Bachelor of Science degree in Mathematical Science from Anhui University of China in 2009. He is currently a Master student in Computer Science at University of Anhui. His current research interests include image and graph matching, image feature extraction, and statistical pattern recognition.

Horst Bunke received his M.S. and Ph.D. degrees in Computer Science from the University of Erlangen, Germany. In 1984, he joined the University of Bern, Switzerland, where he is a Professor in the Computer Science Department. He was Department Chairman from 1992 to 1996, Dean of the Faculty of Science from 1997 to 1998, and a member of the Executive Committee of the Faculty of Science from 2001 to 2003. From 1998 to 2000 Horst Bunke served as 1st Vice-President of the International Association for Pattern Recognition (IAPR). In 2000 he also was Acting President of this organization. Horst Bunke is a Fellow of the IAPR, former Editor-in-Charge of the *International Journal of Pattern Recognition and Artificial Intelligence*, Editor-in-Chief of the journal *Electronic Letters of Computer Vision and Image Analysis,* Editor-in-Chief of the book series on Machine Perception and Artificial Intelligence by WorldScientific Publ.Co., Advisory Editor of Pattern Recognition, Associate Editor of

Acta Cybernetica and *Frontiers of Computer Science* in China, and Former Associate Editor of the *International Journal of Document Analysis and Recognition*, and *Pattern Analysis and Applications*. Horst Bunke received an honorary doctor degree from the University of Szeged, Hungary, and held visiting positions at the IBM Los Angeles Scientific Center (1989), the University of Szeged, Hungary (1991), the University of South Florida at Tampa (1991, 1996, 1998–2006), the University of Nevada at Las Vegas (1994), Kagawa University, Takamatsu, Japan (1995), Curtin University, Perth, Australia(1999), and Australian National University, Canberra(2005). He served as a co-chair of the 4th International Conference on Document Analysis and Recognition held in Ulm, Germany, 1997 and as a Track Co-Chair of the 16th and 17th International Conference on Pattern Recognition held in Quebec City, Canada and Cambridge, UK in 2002 and 2004, respectively. Also he was chairman of the IAPRTC2 Workshop on Syntactic and Structural Pattern Recognition held in Bern 1992, a co-chair of the 7th IAPR Workshop on Document Analysis Systems held in Nelson, NZ, 2006, and a co-chair of the 10th International Workshop on Frontiers in Handwriting Recognition, held in La Baule, France, 2006. Horst Bunke was on the program and organization committee of many other conferences and served as a referee for numerous journals and scientific organizations. He is on the Scientific Advisory Board of the German Research Center for Artificial Intelligence (DFKI). Horst Bunke has more than 550 publications, including 36 authored, co-authored, edited, or co-edited books and special editions of journals.

Chris Ding received the PhD degree from Columbia University. He did research at the California Institute of Technology, the Jet Propulsion Laboratory, and Lawrence Berkeley National Laboratory before joining the University of Texas at Arlington in 2007 as a Professor of Computer Science. His main research areas are machine learning and bioinformatics. He serves on many program committees of international conferences and gave tutorials on spectral clustering and matrix models. He is an associate editor of the journal *Data Mining and Bioinformatics* and is writing a book on spectral clustering to be published by Springer. He is a member of the IEEE.

Pasquale Foggia received in 1995 a Laurea degree (cum laude) in Computer Engineering, and in 1999 a Ph.D. in Electronic and Computer Engineering from the "Federico II" University of Naples, Italy. Since December 2004, he is Associate Professor of Computer Science at the Department of Computer Science and Systems at the same university, where he is a member of the Artificial Vision Research Group. He is the author of several research papers on these subjects. Prof. Foggia has also served as a referee for many journals and conferences in the field of pattern recognition. He is a member of the IAPR, and has been involved in the activities of the IAPR Technical Committee 15 (Graph-based Representations in Pattern Recognition) since 1997. His research interests include graph-based techniques such as graph matching, structural learning and graph-based clustering, and their applications in the fields of computer vision and pattern recognition.

Tony Han is presently an Assistant Professor of Electrical & Computer Engineering at the University of Missouri (MU). He received his Ph.D. degree in Electrical and Computer Engineering from the University of Illinois at Urban-Champaign in 2007. Dr. Han's specialties lie in computer vision and machine learning, with emphasis on human/object detection, large scale image retrieval, object tracking, action recognition, video analysis, and biometrics. He is a recipient of the CSE fellowship and is an IEEE member.

Xiangjian He graduated with a Bachelor of Science (BSc) degree in Mathematics from Xiamen University. Then, he became a postgraduate (Master by Research) student in Fuzhou University. After he graduated from Fuzhou University with a Master of Science (MSc) degree in Mathematics, he went to Australia for further study. He received a PhD degree in Computer Science and a Graduate Certificate in Higher Education from the University of Technology, Sydney in 1999. Professor Xiangjian He has taught and/or worked in various universities or research institutes in different countries. Since 1999, he has been working in and permanently employed by the University of Technology, Sydney (Australia) as a Lecturer, a Senior Lecturer, an Associate Professor, a Reader and a Full Professor. He has also been a full-time academic, a visiting Professor, an adjunct Professor, a postdoctoral researcher, and a senior researcher in various universities/institutions including Xiamen University, China, University of New England, Australia, University of Georgia, USA, Electronic and Telecommunication Research Institute (ETRI) of Korea, University of Aizu, Japan, and Hongkong Polytechnic University.

Yuchi Huang is now a Research Scientist at General Electronic. He was a Ph.D. student in the Department of Computer Sciences of Rutgers, the State University of New Jersey since September 2004. Prior to this he received his M.Sc. in Pattern Recognition from Chinese Academy of Sciences in 2001, and B.E. in Automatic Control from Beijing University of Aeronautics and Astronautics. Areas of his research interest include computer vision, machine learning, image categorization, object recognition and segmentation, image retrieval, shape alignment and tracking, and video analysis.

Wenjing Jia is now a PhD student at the University of Technology, Sydney (UTS), majored in Computing Sciences. She is currently doing research on Pattern Recognition within Spiral Architecture.

Longin Jan Latecki received the PhD degree in Computer Science from Hamburg University, Germany, in 1992. He is a Professor of Computer Science at Temple University, Philadelphia. His main research interests include shape representation and similarity, object detection and recognition in images, robot perception, machine learning, and digital geometry. He has published over 190 research papers and books. He is an editorial board member of Pattern Recognition and *International Journal of Mathematical Imaging*. He received the annual Pattern Recognition Society Award together with Azriel Rosenfeld for the best article published in the journal *Pattern Recognition* in 1998. He is the recipient of the 2000 Olympus Prize, the main annual award, from the German Society for Pattern Recognition (DAGM).

Chunyuan Li received the B.S. degree in Electronics and Information Engineering from Huazhong University of Science and Technology (HUST), Wuhan, China, in 2011. He is going to pursue the M.Sc. degree in Concordia University, Montreal, Canada. His research interests include computer vision and pattern recognition.

Bin Luo received his BEng degree in Electronics and MEng degree in Computer Science from Anhui University of China in 1984 and 1991, respectively. In 2002, he was awarded the Ph.D. degree in Computer Science from the University of York, the United Kingdom. He has published some 200 papers in journals, edited books, and refereed conferences. He is at present a Professor at Anhui University of China. His current research interests include random graph theory and applications, graph spectral analysis, image and graph matching, and statistical pattern recognition.

Jixin Ma is a Reader at School of Mathematics and Computing, University of Greenwich, UK. He received Doctoral degree in Computer Science from University of Greenwich. He is a member of the American Association of Artificial Intelligence Committee, member of China-Britain Technology and Trade Association, member of World Scientific and Engineering Society, and a member of UK Temporal Reasoning, Artificial Intelligence and Logic Group. His main research interests include: artificial intelligence, software engineering, and mathematical logic. Special research interests are in: temporal logic, temporal databases, reasoning about action and change, case-based reasoning, pattern recognition, and graph matching.

Kaspar Riesen received his M.S. and Ph.D. degrees in Computer Science from the University of Bern, Switzerland, in 2006 and 2009, respectively. Currently he is a Researcher and Lecture Assistant in the research group of Computer Vision and Artificial Intelligence at the University of Bern, Switzerland. His research interests include structural pattern recognition and in particular graph embeddings in real vector spaces. He has more than 30 publications, including six journal papers.

Liu Shang received the B.S. degree in Computer Science from Beihang University (BUAA) of China in 2009. She is now perusing her Master degree at School of Computer Science and Engineering, Beihang University. Her research interests include Image processing, image classification, and pattern recognition application.

Dengdi Sun received his B.Sc and M.Sc degree from the School of Mathematics and Computation Science of Anhui University in 2005 and 2008, respectively. He is a PhD student in the School of Computer Science and Technology of Anhui University. His research interests include computer vision, statistical pattern recognition, and machine learning.

Jin Tang received the B.Eng. degree in Automation in 1998, and the Ph.D. degree in Computer Science in 2007 from Anhui University, Hefei, China. Since 2009, he has been an Associate Professor at the School of Computer Science and Technology at the Anhui University. His research interests include image processing, pattern recognition, machine learning, and computer vision.

Mario Vento is a fellow member of International Association Pattern Recognition (IAPR). Currently he is Full Professor of Computer Science and Artificial Intelligence in the University of Salerno, where he is the coordinator of Artificial Vision Lab. From 2002 to 2006, he was chairman of Technical Committee TC15 of IAPR "Graph Based Representation in Pattern Recognition," and from 2003, Associate Editor of the *Electronic Letters on Computer Vision and Image Analysis*. He is Scientific Coordinator of several research projects funded by the Italian Ministry of University and by the European Community. He is especially focused on real time video analysis and interpretation for traffic monitoring and video surveillance applications, classification techniques (either statistical, syntactic, or structural), exact and inexact graph matching, multi-expert classification and learning methodologies for structural descriptions. He has authored over 170 research papers in international journals and conference proceedings and serves as referee for many relevant journals in the field of pattern recognition. His research interests include artificial intelligence, image analysis, pattern recognition, machine learning, and artificial vision.

Jinjun Wang received the B.E. and M.E. degree from Huazhong University of Science and Technology, China, in 2000 and 2003. He received the PhD degree from Nanyang Technological University, Singapore, in 2006. From 2006 to 2009, Dr. Wang was with NEC Laboratories America, Inc. as a post-doctoral research scientist, and in 2010, he joined Epson Research and Development, Inc. as a senior research scientist. His research interests include pattern classification, image/video enhancement and editing, content-based image/video annotation and retrieval, semantic event detection, et cetera.

Shikui Wei received the B.E. degree in Electrical Engineering from Hebei University, Hebei, China, in 2003, the M.E. degree in Signal and Information Processing from Beijing Jiaotong University (BJTU), Beijing, China, in 2005, and the Ph.D. degree from the Institute of Information Science, BJTU, in 2010. Currently, he is a Research Fellow with the School of Computer Engineering, Nanyang Technological University, Singapore. His current research interests include computer vision, image/video analysis and retrieval, and copy detection.

Jiangjian Xiao is a professor in Ningbo Industrial Technology Research Institute (NITRI), CAS. Before joining NITRI in October 2010, he worked as a Senior Member Technique Staff in computer vision division at Sarnoff Corporation since 2005. He earned his PhD degree at the Computer Science Department at University of Central Florida (UCF) in 2004. Dr. Xiao's areas of expertise are computer vision, image and video processing, computer graphics, 3D visualization, and pattern recognition. His current research work is focused on wide area airborne surveillance, object detection and tracking, 3D reconstruction, video segmentation and scene understanding, optical flow estimation, and object recognition. Dr. Xiao also received both B.S. degree and M.S. degree from Beijing University of Aeronautics and Astronautics, Beijing, P.R. China, in 1994 and 1997, respectively. He is an Associate Editor of *Machine Vision and Application Journal*. He has served as a session chair in IEEE Conference on Computer Vision and Pattern Recognition 2008, program chair for IEEE CVPR workshop WVAP2011, and program chair for DEA2011.

Changsheng Xu is a Professor of National Lab of Pattern Recognition, Institute of Automation, Chinese Academy of Sciences. He is also the Executive Director of China-Singapore Institute of Digital Media. His research interests include multimedia content analysis, image processing, pattern recognition, and computer vision. He has published over 180 refereed book chapters, journal and conference papers in these areas. He is an Associate Editor of *ACM/Springer Multimedia System Journal* and is on the Editorial Board of *International Journal of Multimedia Intelligence and Security*. He served as Program Co-Chair of ACM Multimedia 2009, Program Co-Chair of 2009 International Conference on Internet Multimedia Computing and Services, General Co-Chair of Pacific-Rim Conference on Multimedia (PCM) 2008, Short Paper Co-Chair of ACM Multimedia 2008, General Co-Chair of 2007 Asia-Pacific Workshop on Visual Information Processing, Program Co-Chair of Asia-Pacific Workshop on Visual Information Processing, and Industry Track Chair and Area Chair of 2007 International Conference on Multimedia Modeling. He is on organizing committees and program committees in many prestigious multimedia conferences including ACM Multimedia, ICME, PCM, CIVR, MMM, among others. He is Director of Programs of ACM SIG Multimedia Beijing Chapter. Dr. Xu is a Senior Member of IEEE and Member of ACM.

Min Xu received Ph.D degree of IT from University of Newcastle, Australia, Master degree of Science (Computing) from National University of Singapore, and Bachelor degree of Engineering from University of Science and Technology of China in 2010, 2004, and 2000, respectively. Dr. Xu's expertise is in multimedia and IT. She introduced audio keywords to assist video content analysis in 2003. Her proposed method outperformed most traditional visual based methods and attached a lot of followed research on joined audio and video content analysis. She further proposed a multimodality mid-level representation framework to bridge the gap between low-level audio and video features and high-level video content. In 2006, she developed a video adaptation system based on MPEG-21 Digital Item Adaptation framework. The proposed system, one of the earliest such systems, considered user preference of video content as well as normal bandwidth constraints and provided a personalised video access. Another of her recent achievements is affective content analysis using multiple modality features. Dr. Xu has published over 40 research papers in high quality international journals and conferences. Over 400 citations of her research papers show her reputation in her research field.

Shuicheng Yan is currently an Assistant Professor in the Department of Electrical and Computer Engineering at National University of Singapore, and the founding lead of the Learning and Vision Research Group (http://www.lv-nus.org). Dr. Yan's research areas include computer vision, multimedia and machine learning, and he has authored or co-authored over 200 technical papers over a wide range of research topics. He is an associate editor of *IEEE Transactions on Circuits and Systems for Video Technology*, and has been serving as the guest editor of the special issues for TMM and CVIU. He received the Best Paper Awards from ACM MM'10, ICME'10 and ICIMCS'09, the winner prize of the classification task in PASCAL VOC'10, the honorable mention prize of the detection task in PASCAL VOC'10, 2010 TCSVT Best Associate Editor (BAE) Award, 2010 Young Faculty Research Award, and the co-author of the best student paper awards of PREMIA'09 and PREMIA'11.

Xingwei Yang received the BE degree in Electronics and Information Engineering from Huazhong University of Science and Technology (HUST), Wuhan, China, in 2006. In 2011, he obtained PhD degree in the Department of Computer and Information Science at Temple University, Philadelphia, USA. He is now a research scientist at GE Global Research Center in United States.

Chao Zeng is now a PhD student at the University of Technology, Sydney (UTS), majored in Computing Sciences. His supervisor is Prof. Xiangjian He.

Guoxing Zhao is now a Lecturer at Beijing Normal University. He received PhD of temporal logic, at University of Greenwich, UK. His research interests are mathematical logic and application, graph matching, and GPU computing.

Guangyu Zhu received the B.S., M.S. and Ph.D. degrees in Computer Science from the Harbin Institute of Technology in 2001, 2003, and 2008, respectively. He worked as a research scientist in NEC Laboratories America. He is now a senior research faculty with the Department of Electrical and Computer Engineering of National University of Singapore. His research interests include the image processing, computer vision, machine learning and multimedia analysis. He has published more than 20 papers in journals and refereed conferences. He also published 2 academics books and held 1 industry patent. He was the technical program committee member of ACM MMM'07, ACM CIVR'10, IEEE ICIP'10, and ACM ICIMCS'10. He was the special session chair of ACM ICIMCS'09.

Fan Zhang received the BSc degree in Computer Science and BEng degree in Civil Engineering from Zhejiang University, China, in 2003 and the PhD degree in Computer Vision from the Department of Computer Science at the University of York in 2008 under the supervision of Professor E.R. Hancock. In 2006, as a graduate student he visited the University of North Carolina at Chapel Hill, USA, as part of the Gibbs/Plessey Award for the best research proposal to visit an overseas research laboratory. He received the Piero Zamperoni Best Student Paper Award from ICPR 2006. His research interests are in the use of geometrical and Bayesian methods for vision and medical image analysis. He now works for IBM.

Yao Zhao received the B.E. degree from Fuzhou University, Fuzhou, China, in 1989, and the M.E. degree from Southeast University, Nanjing, China, in 1992, both from the Radio Engineering Department, and the Ph.D. degree from the Institute of Information Science, Beijing Jiaotong University (BJTU), Beijing, China, in 1996. He was an Associate Professor with BJTU in 1998 and a Professor in 2001. From 2001 to 2002, he was a Senior Research Fellow with the Information and Communication Theory Group, Faculty of Information Technology and Systems, Delft University of Technology, Delft, The Netherlands. He is currently the Director of the Institute of Information Science, BJTU. Currently, he is leading several national research projects from the 973 Program, the 863 Program, the National Science Foundation of China, and the Fok Ying Tong Education Foundation. His current research interests include image/video coding, fractals, digital watermarking, and content-based image retrieval.

Index

A

activity recognition 182
adjacency matrix 76
adjacent vertices 73
angular decomposition 232
association graph (AG) 50-51
Attributed Relational Graph (ARG) 6
Attributed Skeleton Graph (ASG) 195
augmenting path 143
automatic annotation 23
average precision (AP) 185

B

bag-of-patterns 11
bag-of-regions (BOR) 246
bag-of-words method 178, 185, 217
Bayesian classification 209
Bipartite Graph Matching (BGM) 9
boundary term 143
broadcast stream 262
brute-force angular embedding (BAE) 235

C

classindependent selection 164
classwise selection 164
clustering 240
coherence-enhancing diffusion (CED) 322
Color Region Adjacency Graph (CRAG) 13
Complete Relational Graph (CRG) 16
complex network 43
compound jet 19
Computer Aided Tomography (CAT) 27
Constraint Satisfaction Problem (CSP) 4
content-based image retrieval (CBIR) 130, 226

content-based video copy detection (CBCD) 262
Continues Image Scaling (CIS) 291
continuous image scaling 283
convolution kernels 159
copy 263
copy detection 265
co-segmentation 218

D

database indexing 23
database retrieval 23
degree of a vertex 73
dense layer segmentation 95
diffusion kernels 159
digital matting 96
dimensionality reduction 232
Dirac Delta function 289
Directed Acyclic Graph 9
directed edge 141
Directed Ordered Acyclic Graph (DOAG) 25
Discounted Cumulative Gain (DCG) 208
discrete curve evolution (DCE) 192
dissimilarity 161

E

earth mover distance (EMD) 219
edge weight 74, 141
edit distance 162
Eigen-Decomposition-Based Graph Matching (EDGM) 59
Elastic Graph Matching (EGM) 10
Expectation-Maximization (EM) 7, 97
Expectation-Maximization (EM) algorithm 7

F

fast Hessian detector 263
feature extraction 249, 263
Fiedler vectors 79, 306
fingerprint recognition 20
Fourier analysis 319
frame fusion 262
Function Described Graphs (FDG) 6
Fuzzy Graph Matching (FGM) 8

G

Gaussian Mixture Model (GMM) 217
Generalized Edge (GE) random graph 45
general occlusion constraint 105
geodesic active contours 89
geodesic skeleton paths 190
Gradient-Based Kronecker Product Graph Matching (GBKPGM) 59
Graduated Assignment Graph Matching (GAGM) 8
Granger causality test (GCT) 180
graph conversion 73
graph edit distance 6
graph embedding 10, 37, 49, 156-157, 160
graph kernel 11, 158
graph matching 1-2, 156, 162
    exact 2
    graph isomorphism 2
    inexact 5
    node-to-node 58
    subgraph isomorphism 3
Greedy Graph Growing Partitioning (GGGP) 83

H

Hamming space 250
hand posture recognition 19
hard threshold 276
heat kernel 304
Heavy Edge Matching (HEM) 82
Hidden Markov Model (HMM) 270
high-resolution (HR) 281
Histogram of Oriented Gradient (HOG) 247
Hubs and Authorities Graph Matching (HAGM) 59
Hungarian method 8
hyperedge 119
hypergraph 118

I

image segmentation 72
image smoothing 302
incident vertices 73
independent and identically distributed (IID) 320
infinite impulse response (IIR) 181
interaction amount discovery 184
interactions 176
Interpolator-Based Kronecker Product Graph Matching (IBKPGM) 59
isoperimetric graph partitioning 150
isotropic diffusion 303

J

jets 17

K

kernel machines 158
kernel trick 158
keyframe extraction 265
Krylov subspace 314

L

label propagation 247
Laplacian Embedding (LE) 232
Laplacian graph 306
layer clustering 95
Least Squares Kronecker Product Graph (LSKPGM) 59
Light Field Distribution (LFD) 207
linear discriminant analysis (LDA) 165
Locality Sensitive Hashing (LSH) 244, 246
Locally Linear Embedding (LLE) 232, 283
Local Tangent Space Alignment (LTSA) 232
loop structure 195
low-resolution (LR) 281

M

Markov stationary distribution 178
Maximum A-Posteriori (MAP) 97
Maximum Common Subgraph (MCS) 3
Maximum-Likelihood Estimation (MLE) 97
maximum likelihood (ML) 285
McGill Articulated Shape Database 206

minimum spanning tree 148
missing value graph model 50
Model-Based Segmentation 27
Modified Color Adjacency Graph (MCAG) 25
monomorphism 3
motion estimation 21
Multidimensional Scaling (MDS) 121
multi-level method 80
multi-way cuts 103

N

Nearest Neighbor (NN) 208
netgraph 4
node 141
node attribute function 63
node similarity 58
noncentral chi-square distribution 46
non-linear complex ramp-preserving diffusion (NCRD) 322
non-LSH algorithm (NLA) 255
non-segmentation algorithm (NSA) 256
normalized cut 149
normalized partition cut 77

O

object classification 1
object recognition 1, 12
object tracking 1, 21
Okapi BM25 scoring function 267
optical flow 125
optimal subsequence bijection (OSB) 198
Orthonormal Kernel Kronecker Product Graph Matching (OKKPGM) 59

P

pairwise matching 218
partition ratio cut 77
pattern exploration 184
Pearson's correlation coefficient 276
pixel adjacency graph 74
Principal Component Analysis (PCA) 109, 165, 232
printed circuit board images 14
probabilistic Latent Semantic Analysis (pLSA) 174
probability density function (PDF) 109
prototypes 156, 158
pruning 276
Pyramid Match Kernel (PKM) 218

Q

quaternion descriptor 176

R

Random Dot Product Graph (RDPG) 47
Random Geometric Graph (RGG) 44
random walk 146, 160
raster image 282
recursive neural network 25
refinement algorithms 84
Region Adjacency Graphs (RAG) 17
regional term 143
Region-aware and Scalable Multi-label Propagation (RSMP) 256
region of interest (ROI) 141
Region-to-Image (R2I) 246-247, 251
regular graph 74
regularized Perona-Malik method 322
relaxation labeling 7
relaxation networks 8
relevance feedback (RF) 132
Reproducing Kernel Hilbert Spaces (RHKS) 8
Resolution-Invariant Image Representation (RIIR) 283, 287, 291, 299
Robertson-Sparck Jones weight 267
robot navigation 20
root mean square (RMS) 324
Rutgers Tools Database 202

S

saliency cut 146
Scalable Vector Graphics (SVG) 282
seed images 245
segmentation evaluation 151
semi-supervised graph partitioning 226, 244, 252
shape context 12
shape recognition 12
Shock graph 195
SIFT feature 178
signal-to-noise ratio (SNR) 324
similarity kernel (sim) 164
similarity matrix 245
sink 143
skeleton 191
skeleton branch 196
source 143
sparse-coding (SC) 286
spatial domain image modeling 42

spatial-temporal neighbors 127
spectral clustering 120
spectral graph partitioning 78
spectral methods 8
statistical approach 157
stereo reconstruction 20
string 157
super-resolution (SR) 281
supervised graph partitioning 88, 92, 142
support vector machine (SVM) 132, 165

T

tensor voting 145
Topographical Primal Sketch (TPS) 12
Topological Signature Vector (TSV) 9
tottering 160
trajectory atoms 176
tree 157
tree edit distance 14
tree search 6, 143

U

unsupervised graph partitioning 77-78, 148

V

vector image 282
Vertex Random Graph (VRG) 45
vertices 73
VF algorithm 4
video matching 262
video object segmentation 124
visual inspection 12
visual words 217

W

watershed cut 89
Weighted Bipartite Graph Matching problem
    (WBGM) 9
Weighted Graph Matching (WGM) 3